MW00378017

THE BATSFORD

CHESS

ENCYCLOPEDIA

THE BATSFORD CHESS ENCYCLOPEDIA

Nathan Divinsky

B. T. Batsford Ltd, *London*

First published 1990
© Nathan Divinsky 1990

ISBN 0 7134 6214 0
A CIP catalogue record for this book is available from
the British Library

All rights reserved. No part of this book may be
reproduced, by any means, without prior permission
of the publisher

Typeset by Latimer Trend Co, Plymouth, Devon
and printed in Great Britain by
The Bath Press, Bath

for the publishers,
B. T. Batsford Ltd, 4 Fitzhardinge Street,
London W1H 0AH

A BATSFORD CHESS BOOK
Adviser: R. D. Keene GM, OBE

'Tis all a Chequer-board of Nights and Days
Where Destiny with Men for Pieces plays;
Hither and thither moves, and mates, and slays
And one by one back in the Closet lays.

Rubaiyat of Omar Khayyam (1123)
Translation by Fitzgerald

To Marilyn for her cheerful support
and encouragement

Introduction

A number of terms and abbreviations are used throughout this book which some readers may not recognize. This brief introduction explains them.

Many entries make use of the standard Algebraic Notation for writing down moves. This is explained in the entry on Notation and it is recommended that if you are not familiar with this you read this item first. Experienced players who are more used to Descriptive Notation may also find this helpful.

The organizational structure of international chess is quite complex, based on its rating system and the awarding of titles. The rest of the introduction should give you a feel for how the system works and will help to place the entries in the encyclopedia in their context.

Chess players are carefully rated by a mathematical system devised in the early 1960s by Dr Arpad Elo. Roughly speaking the rating numbers are:

2300 and up = International Master = IM

2500 and up = International Grandmaster = GM

2600 and up = candidate for World Championship challenger = Candidate

2700 and up = World Champion

For example, as of January 1, 1990, there were 2 players above 2700: World Champion Kasparov (2800) and ex-World Champion Karpov (2730). There were 27 players in the 2600s from Timman (2680) down to Nunn (2600). Kasparov's 2800 is the highest rating ever achieved.

GM and IM titles have been awarded since 1950 by FIDE, the world chess federation. Great players who died before 1950 were not awarded any official titles. Capablanca and Alekhine for example, were World Champions and reached Elo ratings of about 2700. Though they are not officially GMs, it is clear that they were of GM strength.

Tournaments are rated by the strength of the participating players. A set of categories has been established:

XVII average strength 2651 and higher
XVI average strength 2626 to 2650
XV average strength 2601 to 2625
XIV average strength 2576 to 2600
XIII average strength 2551 to 2575
XII average strength 2526 to 2550
XI average strength 2501 to 2525
X average strength 2476 to 2500
IX average strength 2451 to 2475
VIII average strength 2426 to 2450
VII average strength 2401 to 2425
VI average strength 2376 to 2400
V average strength 2351 to 2375
IV average strength 2326 to 2350
III average strength 2301 to 2325
II average strength 2276 to 2300
I average strength 2251 to 2275

There have only just been four Category XVII tournaments: AVRO 1938 and The Hague/Moscow 1948 tournaments in Amsterdam 1988.

A player's strength varies with age and it often happens that a GM who peaked at say 2600, declines in old age to a rating of say 2300. Once a player achieves a GM title, he or she never loses it. Tournament categories are computed by using the ratings of the players at the time they played in that tournament.

A careful system of zonal tournaments, interzonal tournaments and Candidates tournaments or Candidates matches was established in 1950.

We shall use the following terms:

IM	International Master as officially awarded by FIDE.
GM	International Grandmaster as officially awarded by FIDE.
of GM strength	A player who died before 1950 who achieved a rating of 2500 or higher.
Honorary GM	A player, usually an IM, who in old age is made a GM by FIDE for his contribution to chess in general.
Candidate	A player who reached the Candidates tournament or match level, or one who actually played a match for the World Championship.
Tournament category	From I to XVII and defined in the chart above.

Acknowledgements

All illustrations are from the archives of B. T. Batsford, except for the following: Adams, Andersson, Bronstein, Miles, Polgar, Seirawan, Short, Speelman and Timman: Mark Huba; Capablanca–Lasker, Gaprindashvili and Reshevsky: Hulton–Deutsch; Staunton: Mansell; Spassky: Camera Press.

The photograph of the author on the dust jacket is by D. Bidner.

The author wishes to thank Mei Ling Fong and her team for their hard work in typing the text.

Ā

Abrahams, Gerald

[*April 15 1907–March 15 1980*] English author, barrister and strong amateur, whose name is associated with the variation: 1 d4 d5 2 c4 c6 3 ♘c3 e6 4 ♘f3 dc 5 a4 ♗b4 6 e3 b5 7 ♗d2 a5 (Holmes–Abrahams 1925) 8 ab ♗xc3 9 ♗xc3 cb 10 b3 ♗b7 11 bc b4 with chances for both sides. This is also called the Noteboom Variation. Abrahams beat GM Ragozin $1\frac{1}{2}$–$\frac{1}{2}$ in the 1946 Anglo–Soviet radio match. He was a witty author, his main chess work being *The Chess Mind*, London 1951.

Abramovic, Bosko [*February 14 1951– *]

Yugoslav GM (1984) who won at Belgrade 1984 and was second at Montpellier 1986.

Abu 'L-Fath Ahmad [*11th century*]

Chess author whose texts were only recently discovered (1950s).

Accumulation of Advantages

One of the foundations of Steinitz's theories: avoid permanent weaknesses, especially in one's pawn structure; induce one's opponent to create permanent weaknesses in his position. Then the sum of these small advantages may grow into a decisive force.

Adams, Michael [*November 17 1971– *]

Young talented English GM (1989) who was equal 1st at Bayswater 1988(X) and may, in the future, surpass Short and Speelman. He was 1st at the Park Hall International 1989(X) and is the world's youngest GM. In 1989 he became the youngest ever winner of the British Championship.

English Grandmaster Michael Adams became the third youngest holder of the title in history in 1989, the year in which he also became the youngest-ever winner of the British Championship.

Adianto, Utut [*March 16 1965– *]

Indonesian GM (1986) who was equal 3rd at Jakarta 1986 and equal first at San Francisco 1987.

Adjournment

In tournament and match play, a game unfinished at the conclusion of the playing session is adjourned and resumed later. Hours or days may elapse before the continuation and both players are free to analyse in depth during this interval. To avoid giving one player the advantage of considering a position in which it is his turn to move, the universal practice (first introduced at Paris 1878) is to 'seal' the last move before adjournment: the player on move decides upon his next move, but instead of playing it on the board, he writes it on a sheet of paper and encloses it in an envelope, which is then entrusted to the care of the tournament arbiter. Upon resumption the envelope is opened, the move is played on the board, clocks are started and play continues as usual. If an ambiguous or illegal move has been sealed, the offender loses the game.

To minimize the number of adjourned games, many tournaments play 40 moves in 2 hours, then 20 moves per hour, and have 6 hour sessions. This forces 60 moves to be played before any adjournment and in practice it almost eliminates adjourned games. Older players were brought up on 40 moves in $2\frac{1}{2}$ hours, then 16 moves per hour, with 5 hour sessions. Since many games go beyond 40 moves, there were many adjourned games. At the 1989 FIDE Congress, Botvinnik urged a return to 40 moves in $2\frac{1}{2}$ hours, in order to preserve the quality and beauty of GM games.

Adjudication

When time is limited (usually in team matches) and a game is unfinished, an impartial expert is often called upon to adjudicate the position and decide whether it is a draw or a win. This can lead to abuses (but life is not always fair).

Adjust (J'Adoube)

When a piece is not properly in its square and a player wishes to centre it, it is customary to say 'I adjust' or 'J'adoube', to distinguish such an adjustment from the beginning of an actual move and to be free of the law that says you must move a piece if you touch it. This should of course be said *before* the piece is touched.

It is not proper for a player to touch a piece, intending to move it, to realize it would be a blunder, to leave the piece where it is, and *then* to say 'J'adoube'. In fact GM Matulovic did this in 1967 (against Bilek at the Suisse interzonal) and has since been nicknamed J'adoubovic.

Adorjan, Andras   [March 31 1950–]

Hungarian GM (1973) who started out with great promise. He was second behind Karpov in the World Junior Championship (Stockholm 1969) and became a world title Candidate in Riga 1979. He lost his match to Hubner $+1=7-2$ in 1980. He won or tied for first at Budapest (1982), Gjovik (1983), Esbjerg (1985) and the New York Open (1987). However, he has not made it into the world top ten. He played in junior tournaments under the name Jocha.

Advantage

A player has the advantage when his position in an overall sense is better than his opponent's position. Evaluating the overall balance, however, can be quite difficult.

There are three basic factors which determine a position's strength: material, space and time. Having more material or controlling more space, especially in the centre, or having more pieces developed, can lead to an advantage. In real life, one side often has an edge in some area but a deficiency in another area.

There are also other kinds of strengths: two bishops versus a bishop and knight or versus two knights; a queenside pawn majority; control of an open file or an important square; control of the centre. And there are weaknesses: doubled pawns, isolated pawns, backward pawns, weak squares.

It takes a keen sense of judgement and experience to take all of these factors into account, to decide whether a weakness is vulnerable and to come to an accurate assessment of the overall evaluation of a position.

Often a player achieves an overall advantage, loses it, through inaccurate play, but is not aware that he has lost it. He then continues to play as if he had an advantage and thereby loses the game. Had he realized that his edge was gone, he might have played more circumspectly and held the draw.

One sign of a great player is his ability to transform one kind of advantage into another kind, thus preserving his edge or even augmenting it.

Agdestein, Simen   [May 15 1967–]

Norwegian GM (1985) who placed second behind Salov in the European Junior Championship (1983/4) and was equal 1st with Arencibia in the World Junior Championship 1986. He won the London Open in 1986, was equal 1st at Jerusalem 1986 and equal 2nd at Marseille 1987. He has also played soccer for Norway.

Age

Most GMs reach their peak in their early 30s and begin to decline in strength in their late 40s. There are exceptions. Korchnoi for example did not reach his peak until his mid 40s and achieved excellent results even in his late 50s. Lasker and Smyslov achieved wonderful results in their 60s.

Ager Chessmen

Chess set made of rock-crystal, preserved in the parish church of Ager, a village near Urgel, in Catalonia. It was made in the 13th or perhaps the 12th century. A similar but smaller set is in the Dom treasury at Osnabruck. The popular tradition that this set belonged to Charlemagne is charming but untrue—Charlemagne lived long before this set was made.

Agzamov, Georgy Tadzhiyevich

[September 6 1954–August 27 1986] USSR GM (1984) who had several fine victories: Belgrade 1982, Sochi 1984, and a tie for first at Tashkent 1984. He won at Calcutta in February 1986, but was killed accidentally just before his 32nd birthday. It happened in Sevastopol, where he took a short cut to go swimming and fell down between two rocks. People heard his cries for help, but he was too deep down, and by the time firemen got to him, it was too late.

He was a great fighter at the chess board and often played very long games. He was one of the hardest workers among Soviet players and loved the struggle, even in equal positions.

AIPE

Organization of chess journalist (Association Internationale de la Presse Echiquéenne) founded in 1968 by Jordi Puig, which awards the so-called chess Oscars to the outstanding male and female players of the year.

Ajeeb

The second famous automaton, made in 1868 by Charles Alfred Hooper, an English cabinet maker. It was similar in appearance to The Turk. It was first exhibited at the Royal Polytechnical Institute, then at the Crystal Palace, and in 1886 it went to the US. At the Eden Musée in New York, Pillsbury was its hidden operator, and after his death, Ajeeb stopped playing chess and played only draughts (checkers). It disappeared during WWII.

See Automatons; Mephisto; The Turk.

See also The Oriental Wonder by K. Whyld in the *British Chess Magazine*, January 1978.

Akhmilovskaya, Elena Bronisklavovna

[*March 11 1957– *]
USSR Woman GM (1977) who was the 1986 challenger but lost $+1=9-4$ to Chiburdanidze. She was equal 1st in the 1988 challengers, but lost the playoff $+0=4-1$ to Ioseliani.

At the 1988 Olympiad in Greece, Akhmilovskaya caused a stir by eloping with John Donaldson, the captain of the US Ladies' team. She will now play for the US.

Ala'Addin, As Tabrizi (Ali Shatranji)

[*14th/15th century*]
Lawyer from Samarkand, known as Aladdin, who was at the court of Timur (Tamerlane). A 15th century manuscript in the library of the Royal Asiatic Society in London gives some of his life story, where he claims to have travelled extensively and beaten all comers at chess. He also says he could play 4 games blindfolded while conversing with friends, and win—through the Divine favour.

Al-Adli

[*9th Century*]
The first great Arabic chess champion and author who lived during the reign of Caliph Mutawakkil. His book (now since lost) contained problems, endgames and openings, some of which have come down to us.

Alapin, Semyon Zinovievich

[*November 7 1856–July 15 1923*]
Russian of GM strength who never made it into the world top ten, but was a solid tournament competitor at the turn of the century (equal 6th at Berlin 1897, 10th in the great Jubilee tournament at Vienna 1898, and 5th at Monte Carlo 1901). He won a few minor events (Berlin 1897/8, Munich 1911), drew a match $+1=4-1$ with Schlechter in 1899 and has several obscure variations named after him (1 e4 e5 2 ♘e2 and 3 ... ♗b4 as a defence to the Ruy Lopez). He was an opening analyst of some repute and he livened his writings with fictitious games between Defendarov and Attakinsky.

Alatortsev, Vladimir Alexeyevich

[*May 14 1909–January 1987*]
USSR Honorary GM (1983) who played in nine USSR Championships (during 1931–50), coming second to Botvinnik in the 1933 event. He tied for 11th in the powerful Moscow 1935 tournament and drew a match with Lilienthal ($+4=4-4$) in 1935. He became a chess teacher and organizer and was head of the Soviet chess organization (1954–61). His major work is *Problems in Modern Chess Theory* (1960).

Albin Counter-Gambit

1 d4 d5 2 c4 e5.
This overly aggressive response to the Queen's Gambit was played in 1881 (by Cavalotti against Salvioli), but became well known when Albin played it against Lasker at New York 1893.

The main line is 1 d4 d5 2 c4 e5 3 de d4 4 ♘f3 ♘c6 5 ♘bd2.

Alburt, Lev Osipovich

[*August 21 1945– *]
USSR GM (1977) who defected to the USA in 1979. In 1974 he won the Ukranian Championship and tied for fifth in the USSR Championship. He led the US team at the Malta Olympiad 1980, and won the US Championship in both 1984 and 1985. In 1986 he drew an 8-game match with British Champion Speelman and tied for second in the US Championship.

Alekhine, Alexander Alexandrovich

[*November 1 1892–March 24 1946*]
Chess Champion of the World 1927–35 and 1937–46, who is considered by many to rank as one of the greatest players of all time. He was born in Moscow to a noble father and a wealthy mother—she taught him chess when he was seven. He had a normal chess development—neither a child prodigy, nor a latecomer to the game.

The well known master Duz-Khotimirsky was hired to give young Alekhine lessons at home (about 1900, for fifteen roubles) and jokingly said that it was these lessons that explained those shortcomings in Alekhine's play which appeared later. By 1904 Alekhine was completely in love with chess and this profound commitment lasted until the moment of his death.

From 1908 on, he grew in strength and in 1913/14 he was equal 1st with Nimzowitsch in the Russian Championship. This allowed both of them to play in the great St Petersburg tournament of 1914. Alekhine succeeded in being one of the five finalists, leaving behind such stars as Rubinstein, Bernstein, Janowski and of course Nimzowitsch. The main drama was the colossal struggle between Lasker and Capablanca and this overshadowed Alekhine's remarkable 3rd prize, ahead of Tarrasch and Marshall. Though $3\frac{1}{2}$ points behind Lasker, Alekhine's achievement combined with the beauty of his games—bold, original,

Alexander Alekhine, the first deposed World Champion to regain his title.

full of fantasy and sparkling combinations—made the chess world take notice of this new star from the East—a worthy successor to Chigorin.

In the summer of 1914, Alekhine was leading in the Mannheim tournament when war broke out. The tournament was never finished, Alekhine was interned, then released and ended up serving in the Russian medical corps. Shell-shock put him in hospital and he was in Odessa and then Moscow when the Russian revolution overturned his country and his world.

He toyed with becoming a movie actor, worked for the Moscow Criminal Investigation Department and then was an interpreter for the Communist International. He won the first USSR Championship (1920) and married a Russian baroness. In 1921 he married a Swiss journalist (Anna Roog) and they were legally able to leave the Soviet Union. Alekhine never set foot on Russian soil again.

He settled in France and scored several victories in 1921, though he was only able to draw a six-game match versus the ageing Teichmann. In 1922 he was equal 2nd behind Bogoljubow (Pistyan), 2nd behind the newly crowned World Champion Capablanca (London), 1st at Hastings and a distant equal 4th at Vienna. In 1923 he was equal 2nd at (Margate) and equal 1st with Maroczy and Bogoljubow (Carlsbad). In 1924 at New York he was outclassed by the two giants: Lasker and Capablanca.

At this point, Alekhine spent a year writing the New York 1924 tournament book and produced magnificent annotations. The book is a treasure-house of analytic insights—profound, deep and accurate. Only Bronstein's Zurich 1953 rivals it. Alekhine then wrote *My Best Games 1908–1923* and these two books established him as the leading chess annotator (supplanting Tarrasch and Marco).

About this time Alekhine married Nadezda Vasiliev—his third wife. Having done some pre-law in Russia, Alekhine now enrolled at the Sorbonne and said he earned a doctorate in law. He was considered the genius of chess combination and apart from Lasker and Capablanca, was the third darling of the chess world. Capablanca described him as '... over six feet in height, fair-haired, with blue eyes. He always makes a striking impression ... fluent in six languages ... the most outstanding chess memory ... can remember by heart all the games played between masters ... during the last 15–20 years'.

It is interesting that behind this brilliant facade, things were not quite what they should have been.

First of all, it is doubtful whether he ever actually graduated from the Sorbonne. Many talented people have difficulty with the thin line between 'I could have' and 'I did' (see for example Zukertort). Even if Alekhine's doctorate has a touch of fantasy, it harmed no one since he never attempted to practise law.

Secondly, he seems to have ruthlessly abandoned wife number two, having used her status to get out of the USSR.

Thirdly, as Kotov points out: 'He ... did all he could to maintain this reputation, portraying certain games with ostentatious commentaries, trying to present ... the exceptional chess talent of Alekhine'. Euwe says: '... at the chess board he was mighty, away from chess ... he was like a little boy who would get up to mischief and naively think that no one was watching him'. Finally, Golombek writes '... Alekhine the supreme amoralist ... he had two great passions, Alekhine and chess'.

The next few years were not entirely successful. He had a good win at Baden Baden (1925) but in 1926 he came 2nd to Spielmann at Semmering, 2nd to Nimzowitsch at Dresden and could barely beat (+3 = 5 − 2) the inexperienced Dr Euwe. In the great New York 1927 tournament he came a distant 2nd to Capablanca and though he edged out Nimzowitsch and Vidmar, it was clear that Capablanca (and probably Lasker) were in a class by themselves.

Nevertheless, the brilliant facade allowed Alekhine to raise the high stake ($15 000) Capablanca demanded and in 1927 they met in their celebrated match in Buenos Aires. Alekhine had never won a game from the Cuban genius and Capablanca took the match lightly. Both Capablanca and the chess world were stunned when Alekhine won the first game and after a mighty struggle, Alekhine wrenched the title (+6 = 25 − 3) from the surprised Cuban's grip.

As World Champion, Alekhine is often said to have made it clear that he never wanted to face Capablanca again.

He would not play in a tournament if Capablanca was to be there and he busied himself with matches against Bogoljubow (1929 and 1934). He won these easily and scored famous tournament victories at San Remo (1930) and Bled (1931) far ahead of the field. However, a rematch was fixed for May 1 1930, for which Capablanca was unable to raise the necessary funding.

During 1932–5 Alekhine kept winning, but his play weakened and became stale. In 1934 he married Grace Wishart—his fourth wife.

Alekhine had an alcohol problem and he lost control of it during his 1935 title match with Euwe. To everyone's surprise Euwe won the title +9=13−8. Alekhine stumbled further when he came 6th at the strong Nottingham tournament in 1936 and lost his individual game to Capablanca—their first encounter since 1927. However, he conquered his alcohol problem and won his return match with Euwe +10=11−4 in 1937.

By now a new generation of stars had appeared and in the super AVRO tournament of 1938, Alekhine could only manage equal 4th, behind Keres, Fine, and Botvinnik. In 1939 he published *My Best Games 1924–1937*, another wonderful collection.

Alekhine was at the Olympiad in Buenos Aires when the war broke out. He returned to France and joined the army as an interpreter. When France fell he went south to Marseille and Lisbon and made efforts to go to the Americas.

In 1941 several shockingly anti-Jewish articles appeared in the Nazi press over Alekhine's signature. He later denied writing them, but after his death, the original manuscripts in his handwriting, were found among his wife's papers. He was unable to obtain a visa and ended up under German control. During 1942 and '43 he won tournaments at Salzburg, Munich and Prague. From 1943 on, he lived in Spain and

Portugal, and was negotiating a title match with Botvinnik when the end came. He was ill and penniless—a sad conclusion for a great chess creator.

The Soviets were anxious to have him buried in Moscow, but his widow refused and he is buried next to her in the Montparnasse cemetary in Paris.

A recent mathematical study of the greatest masters (by Keene and Divinsky) places Alekhine 18th in the all time list. Most people would place him in the top five or at least the top ten, and this mathematical surprise deserves some attention. In terms of life scores, he crushed Tarrasch (+9=2−1), Maroczy (+6=5−0), Marshall (+6=7−0), Bernstein (+6=4−1), Flohr (+5=7−0) and Keres (+5=8−1). He lost to Lasker (+1=4−3), Capablanca (+7=33−9), Teichmann (+2=3−3), Fine (+2=4−3), and Botvinnik (+0=2−1).

Against his most frequent opponents, Bogoljubow (+35=37−13) and Euwe (+27=36−20), he won, but not so overwhelmingly.

He was a great player, a great annotator, a great opening theorist and a great publicity market manager who, like Ely Culbertson, in bridge, made his game popular throughout the world, but slightly overemphasized his own importance. Nevertheless, he has left us a large number of wonderful games. Alexander writes: '... in playing through an Alekhine game one suddenly meets a move which simply takes one's breath away. His games have a beauty and fascination entirely of their own'.

His major works are *New York 1924*, *My Best Games 1908–23*, *My Best Games 1924–37*.

Major books about him:
Alekhine's Best Games 1938–45 by C. H. O'D. Alexander (1949), *Alekhine's Greatest Games of Chess*, by Alexander and Alekhine (1989), *Alexander Alekhine*, by A. Kotov (1975).

Bogoljubow–Alekhine
Hastings 1922

1 d4 f5 2 c4 ♘f6 3 g3 e6 4 ♗g2 ♗b4+ 5 ♗d2 ♗xd2+ 6 ♘xd2 ♘c6 7 ♘gf3 0-0 8 0-0 d6 9 ♕b3 ♔h8 10 ♕c3 e5 11 e3 a5 12 b3 ♕e8 13 a3 ♕h5 14 h4 ♘g4 15 ♘g5 ♗d7 16 f3 ♘f6 17 f4 e4 18 ♖fd1 h6 19 ♘h3 d5 20 ♘f1 ♘e7 21 a4 ♘c6 22 ♖d2 ♘b4 23 ♗h1 ♕e8 24 ♖g2 dc 25 bc ♗xa4 26 ♘f2 ♗d7 27 ♘d2 b5 28 ♘d1 ♘d3 29 ♖xa5 b4 30 ♖xa8 bxc3 31 ♖xe8

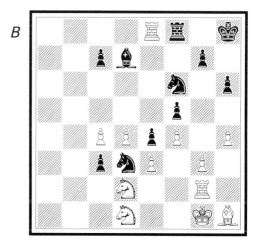

31 ... c2! 32 ♖xf8+ ♔h7 33 ♘f2 c1(♕)+ 34 ♘f1 ♘e1 35 ♖h2 ♕xc4 36 ♖b8 ♗b5 37 ♖xb5 ♕xb5 39 g4 ♘f3+ 39 ♗xf3 exf3 40 gf ♕e2 41 d5 ♔g8 42 h5 ♔h7 43 e4 ♘xe4 44 ♘xe4 ♕xe4 45 d6 cd 46 f6 gf 47 ♖d2 ♕e2 48 ♖xe2 fe 49 ♔f2 exf1(♕)+ 50 ♔xf1 ♔g7 51 ♔f2 ♔f7 52 ♔e3 ♔e6 53 ♔e4 d5+ 54 Resigns

Réti–Alekhine
Baden-Baden 1925

1 g3 e5 2 ♘f3 e4 3 ♘d4 d5 4 d3 ed 5 ♕xd3 ♘f6 6 ♗g2 ♗b4+ 7 ♗d2 ♗xd2+ 8 ♘xd2 0-0 9 c4 ♘a6 10 cd ♘b4 11 ♕c4 ♘bxd5 12 ♘2b3 c6 13 0-0 ♖e8 14 ♖fd1 ♗g4 15 ♖d2 ♕c8 16 ♘c5 ♗h3 17 ♗f3 ♗g4 18 ♗g2 ♗h3 19 ♗f3 ♗g4 20 ♗h1 h5 21 b4 a6 22 ♖c1 h4 23 a4 hg 24 hg ♕c7 25 b5 ab 26 ab

26 ... ♖e3 27 ♘f3 cb 28 ♕xb5 ♘c3 29
♕xb7 ♕xb7 30 ♘xb7 ♘xe2+ 31
♔h2 ♘e4 32 ♖c4 ♘xf2 33 ♗g2 ♗e6
34 ♖cc2 ♘g4+ 35 ♔h3 ♘e5+ 36
♔h2 ♖xf3 37 ♖xe2 ♘g4+ 38 ♔h3
♘e3+ 39 ♔h2 ♘xc2 40 ♗xf3 ♘d4
41 Resigns (after 41 ♖f2 ♘xf3+ 42
♖xf3 ♗d5)

Alekhine's Defence

1 e4 ♘f6.

This attempt to lure White's centre pawns on, in the hope that they will become weak, was discussed in Allgaier's *Lehrbuch* in the early 1800s, and introduced into modern practice by Alekhine at Budapest 1921.

At first, the main line was 1 e4 ♘f6 2 e5 ♘d5 3 c4 ♘b6 4 d4 d6 5 f4 (the Four Pawns Attack), but today the quieter 1 e4 ♘f6 2 e5 ♘d5 3 d4 d6 4 ♘f3 is used in the attempt to maintain white's opening advantage.

Alexander, Conel Hugh O'Donel

[*April 19 1909–February 15 1974*]
British IM (1950) who was a mathematically talented chess amateur. He broke codes during WWII and later worked for the Foreign Office. His best result was equal 2nd at Hastings 1937/8 where he tied with Keres, behind Reshevsky, but ahead of Fine and Flohr. He also tied for first with Bronstein at Hastings 1953/4. He won the British title in 1938 and 1946, played on six English Olympiad teams (1933–58) and tied Botvinnik +1−1 in the 1946 Anglo–Soviet radio match.

He wrote for several English newspapers and wrote several books: *Alekhine's Best Games of Chess 1938–1945* (1949), *Fischer–Spassky* (1972), *A Book of Chess* (1973), *Chess* (1974).

There is a book of his best games by Golombek and Hartston (1976).

Alexandre, Aaron [1766–1850]

Jewish rabbi who was born in Bavaria, moved to Paris (1793) and worked inside the famous automaton, the Turk. He wrote an opening encyclopedia (1837) and *The Beauties of Chess* (1846) which contains about 2000 problems and endgames.

Alexandria, Nana Georgievna

[*October 13 1949– *]
USSR Woman GM (1976) who was the challenger twice: in 1975 she lost +3=1−8 to Gaprindashvili and in 1981 she drew +4=8−4 with Chiburdanidze. Alexandria was 2nd in the 1986 Candidates but only 5th in 1988. She was USSR Woman Champion in 1966, 68 and 69.

Alfonso the Wise (El Sabio)

[*1221–1284*]
King of Castile (1251–84) who had the monks of the monastery of St. Lorenzo del Escorial (near Madrid) create a beautiful illustrated parchment manuscript dealing with chess, dice and other board games. It was completed in 1283 and is known as the Alfonso MS. It is an important historical document (of 98 pages).

Algebraic Notation

See Notation.

Aliqlidisi, B. [10th century ?]

Arabic champion who wrote *A Collection of Chess Problems.*

Al-Lajlaj (the stutterer) [10th century]

Arabic champion who wrote a book on chess problems.

Allgaier, Johann Baptist

[*June 19 1763–January 2 1823*]
German player and author who intended to enter the church but ended up as the leading chess master and theoretician in Vienna. His major work was *Neue theoretisch-praktische Anweisung zum Schachspiel*, Vienna 1795. It went through seven editions, up to 1843. In it he analysed the King's Gambit (1819) and the variation 1 e4 e5 2 f4 ef 3 ♘f3 g5 4 ♗c4 g4 5 ♘g5 now bears his name. He also analysed what is now called Alekhine's Defence (1 e4 ♘f6). Curiously, he recommended a kingside pawn majority—of course by the 1840s it became established that in fact it is just the other way around! Nevertheless this book was the best textbook of its time.

He made a living playing for money, giving lessons and operating the famous automaton, the Turk. He also served as quartermaster accountant in the Austrian army.

Amaurosis scachistica

One of Dr Tarrasch's little jokes, giving a serious medical-sounding name to chess blindness or blundering—a universal ailment that affects even GMs.

American Chess Bulletin

A bi-monthly magazine founded by Hermann Helms (New York) in 1904. Helms edited it until 1956, when Edgar Holladay took over. It ceased publication in February 1963, shortly after Helms' death.

American Chess Magazine

This name was used in 1846, 1872–4 and 1875 but none of the magazines lasted very long. The best and longest run was from 1897–9 when William Borsodi published a high quality magazine, out of Philadelphia and then New York. It had full reports, excellent photographs and fine annotations but unfortunately folded after some 30 issues.

Amsterdam

The financial and cultural centre of Dutch life and one of the most civilized cities in the world. It staged two games of the 1929 Alekhine–Bogoljubow title match, much of the Alekhine–Euwe matches of 1935 and 1937, a few games of AVRO 1938, and a fine Olympiad in 1954, but its first world class tournament was the 3rd Candidates in 1956. Most of it was played in Amsterdam with rounds 10 and 11 held in Leeuwarden.

Geller led at the halfway mark but with 3 rounds to go, it was Smyslov (9), Keres (9), Geller (8½) and Bronstein (8½). Smyslov then beat Bronstein, drew with Spassky and beat Pilnik, while Keres could only draw with Panno, lose to Filip and draw with Petrosian.

Time Limit: 40 moves in 2½ hours and then 16 moves per hour.

Prizes: (Swiss Francs) 5000, 3500, 2500, 2000, 1750, 1500, 1250.

Tournament book by B. H. Wood as a supplement in *Chess*.

One of the best games was this, played on March 28, 1956 (Round 2).

Geller–Smyslov
Amsterdam 1956

1 d4 ♘f6 2 c4 e6 3 ♘c3 ♗b4 4 a3 ♗xc3+ 5 bc c5 6 e3 b6 7 ♘e2 ♘c6 8 ♘g3 0-0 9 ♗d3 ♗a6 10 e4 ♘e8 11 ♗e3 ♘a5 12 ♕e2 ♖c8 13 d5 ♕h4 14 0-0 ♘d6 15 ♖ad1 f5 16 de de 17 ef ef 18 ♕f3 ♗b7 19 ♕f4 ♕f6 20 ♗b1 ♘e4 21 ♖d7 ♕c6 22 ♖xb7 ♕xb7 23 ♘xf5 ♖ce8 24 ♕g4 ♔h8 25 ♘g3 ♘xg3 26 hg ♕f7 27 ♕h4 h6 28 ♗d3 ♕f6 29 ♕h5 ♖d8 30 ♗e2 ♕f5 31 ♕h4 ♕f6 32 ♕h5 ♘c6 33 g4 ♕f7 34 ♕h4 ♘e7 35 ♕h3 ♘g6 36 ♕h2 ♘f4 37 ♗f3 ♕xc4 38 g5 ♖d6 39 ♖c1 ♖g6 40 gh ♖xh6 41 ♕g3

B

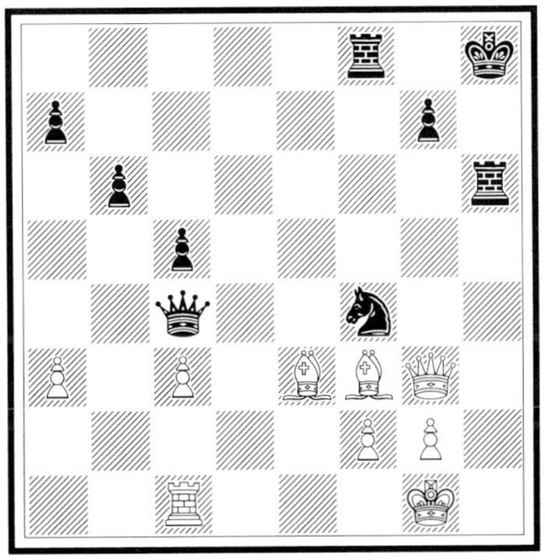

41 ... ♕e4! 42 ♕xf4 ♕xf4 43 ♗xf4 ♖xf4 44 ♖e1 ♖a4 45 ♖e8+ ♔h7 46 ♗e4+ g6 47 g4 ♖xa3 48 ♖e6 ♖xc3 49 ♔g2 b5 50 f3 b4 51 g5 ♖h4 52 ♗xg6+ ♔g7 53 ♔g3 ♖d4 54 ♗e8 b3 55 g6 ♖d8 56 ♖e7+ and White lost on time. He is lost in any case after 56 ... ♔f6 57 g7 ♖xe8 58 ♖xe8 ♔xg7.

Amsterdam has staged many other tournaments including the strong 1964 Interzonal, but recently it has had 3 extremely strong four-man affairs. In 1987 Karpov (4) and Timman (4) beat out Korchnoi (2½) and van der Wiel (1½) in a double round category XVI event. In March 1988 Short (4) won ahead of Karpov (3½) Ljubojevic (3½) and Timman (1) in a double round category XVII (average Elo 2658) event. In May 1988 Amsterdam obtained both super Ks to go with Timman and van der Wiel and thus had the world top three. Had they used Belyavsky (2645) instead of van der Wiel the average Elo would have been 2696.

Kasparov outdid himself and crushed the opposition in his aim for a 2800 Elo rating. Van der Wiel learnt much but was a little out of his class against the world top three.

One of the most exciting games was this, played in Round 5.

Kasparov – Karpov

1 e4 c6 2 d4 d5 3 ♘d2 de 4 ♘xe4 ♘d7 5 ♘f3 ♘gf6 6 ♘g3 e6 7 ♗d3 ♗e7 8

Amsterdam 1956 — Candidates Tournament

		1		2		3		4		5		6		7		8		9		10		
1	Smyslov	–	–	½	½	½	½	0	½	½	½	½	1	1	1	½	1	1	½	½	1	11½
2	Keres	½	½	–	–	½	½	½	½	½	½	½	1	½	½	½	0	1	½	1	½	10
3	Szabo	½	½	½	½	–	–	1	½	½	½	½	½	½	1	0	½	½	½	0	1	9½
	Spassky	1	½	½	½	0	½	–	–	½	½	½	1	0	½	½	½	½	½	½	1	9½
	Petrosian	½	½	½	½	½	½	½	½	–	–	0	½	0	1	1	½	½	½	1	½	9½
	Bronstein	½	0	½	0	½	½	½	0	1	½	–	–	½	1	1	½	½	½	½	1	9½
	Geller	0	0	½	½	½	0	1	½	1	0	½	0	–	–	1	1	½	1	1	½	9½
8	Filip	½	0	½	1	1	½	½	½	0	½	0	½	0	0	–	–	1	0	½	1	8
	Panno	0	½	0	½	½	½	½	½	½	½	½	½	½	0	0	1	–	–	1	½	8
10	Pilnik	½	0	0	½	1	0	½	0	0	½	½	0	0	½	½	0	0	½	–	–	5

	1				2				3				4				
1 Kasparov	—	—	—	—	½	1	½	1	½	½	1	½	1	½	1	1	9
2 Karpov	½	0	½	0	—	—	—	—	½	½	½	½	1	1	½	1	6½
3 Timman	½	½	0	½	½	½	½	½	—	—	—	—	1	0	½	½	5½
4 van der Wiel	0	½	0	0	0	0	½	½	0	1	½	½	—	—	—	—	3

0-0 c5 9 ♕e2 0-0 10 ♖d1 ♕c7 11 c4
cd 12 ♘xd4 a6 13 b3 ♖e8 14 ♗b2 b6
15 ♘h5 ♗b7 16 ♘xe6?! fe 17 ♕xe6+
♔f8 18 ♗xh7 ♘c5 19 ♕h3 ♘xh7 20
♗xg7+ (better is 20 b4) 20 ... ♔g8 21
♗b2 ♕c6 22 ♖d4 ♘e4 23 ♖e1
♘eg5 24 ♕g4 ♗a3 25 ♗c3

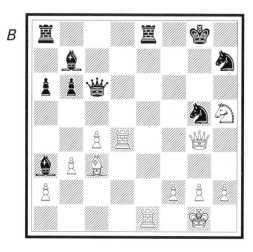

25 ... ♖xe1+? (25 ... ♗b2 wins); 26
♗xe1 ♖e8 27 ♗d2 ♗c1 28 h4 ♗xd2
29 ♖xd2 ♖e1+ 30 ♔h2 ♖e4 (better
is 30 ... ♕c7+) 31 f4 ♕e6 32 ♖d8+
♔f7 33 ♖d7+ ♔f8 34 ♕xe6 ♖xe6
35 hg ♖e7 36 ♖xe7 ♔xe7 37 g4 ♗e4
38 ♔g3 ♗b1 39 a3 Black lost on time.
After 39 ... ♗a2 40 b4 ♗xc4 White has
winning chances. A fantastic struggle.
[Time limit 40 moves in 2 hours].

Numerically, this tournament was the
highest rated tournament of all time.
However the Hague/Moscow 1948 (Elo
2665) and AVRO 1938 (Elo 2658) were
distinguished not only by their high
rating but by having all of the top 5 or
top 8 players in the world. To be a super
tournament an event should not only
have the best players, but almost no one
of comparable strength should be absent. Both Hague/Moscow and AVRO
were super tournaments, whereas
Amsterdam March 1988 did not have
Kasparov, Belyavsky, Korchnoi or Tal
while May 1988 did not have
Belyavsky, Korchnoi or Tal.

The reason the ratings seem out of
line is that there are many more GMs
with ratings above 2599 in the 1980s
(29 of them as of January 1 1990) than
there were in the 1940s or 1930s. Besides, it is accepted wisdom that Elo
ratings from one era should not be
compared too precisely to those of
another era.

Anand, Viswanathan

[*December 11 1969– *]
Indian GM (1988) who won the World
Junior title in 1987 and was equal 2nd
behind Csom, at Delhi 1987.

Anderssen, Adolf

[*July 6 1818–March 13 1879*]
German mathematics teacher who won
the first major international tournament
(London 1851) and thus became the
world's leading player. This tournament
was a knock-out event (like tennis is
today) and on his road to victory,
Anderssen beat the previous world
number one, Staunton, by 4 to 1.
Though Anderssen lost matches to
Morphy (1858) and Steinitz (1866) he
continued to dominate the tournament
world with fine victories at London
(1862) and Baden Baden (1870). Even in
1877, he was equal 2nd at Leipzig. His
match play was not up to his tournament performances, but he was always

*Adolf Anderssen, winner of the first major
international tournament (London 1851).*

in the world top 3 from 1851 until his
death.

Anderssen and von der Lasa (who
never played in a tournament, but beat
both Staunton and Anderssen in series
of games) were the first two players to
achieve a 2600 ELO rating (around
1850).

Anderssen was tall, bald, shy,
pleasant, honest and honorable. He
never married and led a quiet academic
life in Breslau (then in Germany, now in
Poland and called Wroclaw). He lived
with his mother and sister and taught at
the Gymnasium. He took an almost
childlike pleasure in chess and gave his
love, devotion and untiring zeal to the
game. On vacations he went to Berlin or
Leipzig for chess 'orgies'. All the fine
players came to test themselves against
this perennial champion of Germany.

Before Anderssen, even the leading
players produced games that were un-
focused, long-winded and filled with
blunders. Anderssen's lively, fresh play
was full of ideas, surprises and happy
inspirations. Sacrifices were his stock in
trade and he showed enormous
ingenuity both in conception and ex-

ecution. His play was absolutely brilliant and in stark contrast to his quiet and modest life-style.

After his loss to Morphy, when his admirers asked him why he didn't play brilliantly, he replied: 'Morphy wouldn't let me'. In fact, Morphy understood the importance of the centre and knew that attacks succeeded against top opposition only when an advantage had first been established and/or the centre was controlled. Against these insights, Anderssen's relatively haphazard inspiration was simply not enough.

In 1865 Breslau University conferred an honorary doctorate on Anderssen.

Some of his life scores were: +11=0−11 (Steinitz), +25=10−27 (Zukertort) +6=1−3 (Blackburne) +3=2−12 (Morphy).

His major work was a book on problems (1842): *Aufgaben für Schachspieler*.

Books about him are *Adolf Anderssen* (1912) by H. von Gottschall and *World History of Chess—Anderssen I* (1968) by G. Pollak.

His two most famous games are:

Anderssen–Kieseritzky

London 1851
'The Immortal Game'

1 e4 e5 2 f4 ef 3 ♗c4 ♕h4+ 4 ♔f1 b5 5 ♗xb5 ♘f6 6 ♘f3 ♕h6 7 d3 ♘h5 8 ♘h4 ♕g5 9 ♘f5 c6 10 g4 ♘f6 11 ♖g1 cxb5 12 h4 ♕g6 13 h5 ♕g5 14 ♕f3 ♘g8 15 ♗xf4 ♕f6 16 ♘c3 ♗c5 17 ♘d5 ♕xb2

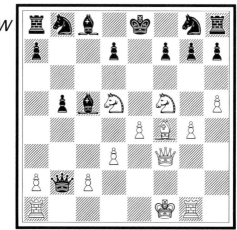

18 ♗d6! ♗xg1 19 e5 ♕xa1+ 20 ♔e2 ♘a6 21 ♘xg7+ ♔d8 22 ♕f6+ ♘xf6 23 ♗e7 mate

Anderssen–Dufresne

Berlin 1852
'The Evergreen Game'

1 e4 e5 2 ♘f3 ♘c6 3 ♗c4 ♗c5 4 b4 ♗xb4 5 c3 ♗a5 6 d4 ed 7 0-0 d3 8 ♕b3 ♕f6 9 e5 ♕g6 10 ♖e1 ♘ge7 11 ♗a3 b5 12 ♕xb5 ♖b8 13 ♕a4 ♗b6 14 ♘bd2 ♗b7 15 ♘e4 ♕f5 16 ♗xd3 ♕h5 17 ♘f6+ gf 18 ef ♖g8

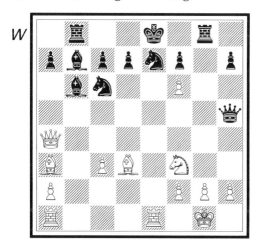

19 ♖ad1! ♕xf3 20 ♖xe7+ ♘xe7? 21 ♕xd7+ ♔xd7 22 ♗f5+ ♔e8 23 ♗d7+ ♔d8 24 ♗xe7 mate

Anderssen's Opening

1 a3

First played by Anderssen in his 1858 match with Morphy. It may turn out to be useful in certain lines, but it does nothing to develop White's pieces and thus gives up White's first-move initiative. It does avoid well-known opening lines and forces an opponent to rely on his own inner resources rather than on memorized opening variations.

Andersson, Ulf [*June 27 1951– *]

Swedish GM (1972) who is the all-time drawing master among top GMs. In over 400 games against top-level opposition, he drew some 74% of these games (while winning 10% and losing

Ulf Andersson of Sweden. His extremely solid approach makes him one of the hardest players in the world to beat.

16%). During 1972–82, he was in the top ten of the world with victories or equal 1sts at Dortmund 1973, Capablanca Memorial (Cienfuegos 1974 and 1975), Belgrade 1977, Buenos Aires 1978, Hastings 1978/9, London 1980, Johannesburg 1981, London 1982, Turin 1982, Wijk aan Zee 1983, Rio 1985, Reggio Emilia 1985 and Rome 1985 and 1986.

He drew a six-game match with Tal in 1983, but lost 2–4 to Kasparov in 1985.

He led the Swedish Olympiad team during the 1970s and 80s. He is hard to beat and he often wins by encouraging his opponents to overreach themselves.

Andersson–Stein

Reykjavik 1972

1 e4 c5 2 ♘f3 ♘c6 3 d4 cd 4 ♘xd4 ♘f6 5 ♘c3 d6 6 ♗c4 ♕b6 7 ♘b3 e6 8 0-0 a6 9 ♗e3 ♕c7 10 ♗d3 ♗e7 11 f4 b5 12 a4 b4 13 ♘b1 a5 14 ♘1d2 0-0 15 ♕e2 e5 16 f5 d5 17 g4 de 18 ♘xe4 ♘d5 19 f6 gf 20 ♗h6 ♖d8 21 ♖f3 ♘f4

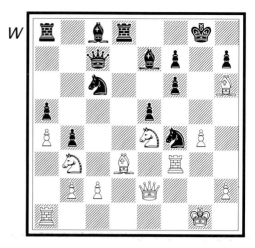

22 ♖xf4 ♖xd3 23 cd ♗e6 24 ♘xf6+
♗xf6 25 ♖xf6 ♗xb3 26 ♖c1 ♗d5 27
♕f2 ♖e8 28 ♖c5 ♗e6 29 ♕h4 ♔h8
30 ♖f2 Resigns

Annotation

A commentary on the moves of a game, an attempt to explain what went on in the minds of the players, why certain moves were played and why others were rejected. A good annotator will pinpoint the errors and the excellent moves, keep track of the balance of the position, point out who has the advantage and how and when it shifts from one side to another.

Steinitz established that winning was not just a matter of ingenuity and luck, but dependent on one's opponent making one or more errors. His annotations were then a significant improvement over those of his predecessors. Great annotators who followed Steinitz were Tarrasch, Marco, Alekhine, Botvinnik, Bronstein, Fischer and Kasparov.

Antoshin, Vladimir Sergeyevich

[May 14 1929–] USSR GM (1963) and technical designer who was a second level participant in USSR Championships (1955–70).

Aphorisms

Chess, like love, like music, has the power to make men happy (Tarrasch)

Chess is a lake in which a gnat may bathe and an elephant may drown (Indian proverb)

You cannot play at chess if you are kindhearted (French proverb)

There are tough players and nice guys, and I'm a tough player (Fischer)

The game has three phases: the first when one hopes one has an advantage; the second when one believes one has an advantage; and the third when one knows one is going to lose (Tartakower)

Castling is the first step towards a well-ordered life (Tartakower)

The blunders are all there on the board waiting to be made (Tartakower)

The great master places a knight at e5; checkmate follows by itself (Tartakower)

Tempi are not meant to be counted but weighed (Tartakower)

In a gambit you give up a pawn for the sake of getting a lost game (Boden)

From Anderssen I learnt how to make combinations; from Tarrasch I learned how to avoid making them (Spielmann)

Pawn endings are to chess what putting is to golf (Purdy)

Never miss a check, it might be mate (proverbial)

Whereas the tactician knows what to do when there is something to do, it requires the strategist to know what to do when there is nothing to do (Abrahams)

He is a player who can be relied upon to snatch defeat from the jaws of victory (Walsh)

Place the contents of the chessbox in your hat, shake them up vigorously, pour them on to the board at a height of two feet, and you get the style of Steinitz (Bird)

Never move a pawn and you will never lose a game (Tarrasch)

Every pawn move loosens the position (Tarrasch)

Rubinstein is not one of those players who try to cash in on the cunningly subtle difference between variations A16 and C117(a) and, while firing blanks from toy pistols, are under the impression they are discharging heavy artillery (Brinkmann)

He who sees much can endure much (Lasker)

On the chessboard lies and hypocrisy do not survive long. The creative combination lays bare the presumption of a lie; the merciless fact, culminating in a checkmate, contradicts the hypocrite (Lasker)

Only a strong player knows how weakly he plays (Tartakower)

The player who wins is the one who makes the mistake before the last (Tartakower)

It is not enough to be a strong player, one must also play well (Tarrasch)

Mistrust is the most necessary characteristic of the chess-player (Tarrasch)

Arbiter

The director of a tournament or match who knows the laws of chess and is able to enforce them in an impartial manner.

FIDE has, since 1951, awarded the title of International Arbiter (or Judge) to those who know the rules of play and all FIDE regulations, who have had experience, who are impartial and who have a working knowledge of two official FIDE languages (English, French, German, Spanish and Russian).

Ardiansyah, H. [December 5 1951–]
Indonesian GM (1986) who tied for first at Jakarta 1986.

Arnason, John L.

[November 13, 1960–] Icelandic GM (1986) who won at Husavik 1985 and Plovdiv 1986 and tied for first at Helsinki 1986.

Ar-Razi [9th century]
Arabic champion and author of *Elegance in Chess*. He competed against Al-Aldi.

Art and Advertising

Chess has been frequently used in the

visual arts (see Duchamp) and has even penetrated the world of advertising. A chess master is considered to be intelligent, alert and to have an artistic dimension. Such an atmosphere lends itself to selling exclusive items like clothes, cars or watches.

See *Chess in Art*, by Roseler (1973)

Asperling, B. [*17th century*]
Swiss author of *Traitte du Jeu Royal des Echets* (around 1690). The entire text of this rare volume is in the *Deutsche Schachzeitung* for 1872.

As-Sarakhsi [*9th century*]
Arabic author of *Book of Higher Chess*.

As-Suli [*880–946*]
Arabic champion and author who improved on Al-Aldi. He was a scholar and historian, wrote two chess books and was famous for over 600 years.

Asztalos, Lajos
[*July 29 1889–October 31 1956*]
Hungarian IM (1950) and International Arbiter (1961). After the First World War he moved to Yugoslavia as a professor of philosophy and played on the Yugoslav Olympiad team (1927, 1931 and 1936). His best result was fourth at Kecskemet 1927. He returned to Hungary in 1942 and practised journalism. He became vice president of the Hungarian Chess Federation and secretary to FIDE's Qualification Committee. He was a cultured and kindly gentleman and during several difficult years he served as a useful chess diplomat between the communist East and the noncommunist West.

Atkins, Henry Ernest
[*August 20 1872–January 31 1955*]
British IM (1950) who was a schoolmaster who devoted relatively little time to chess. Nevertheless, he became one of the strongest amateurs ever known to the royal game, and was called 'the little

Steinitz'. Out of eleven appearances in the British Championship, he won nine times (during 1905–25)—only Penrose has won it more often (ten times!). It should be noted that in his first try (1904) Atkins actually tied for first and lost the play-off to Napier, while in his last try (1937) he tied for 3rd at age 65.

He only played in six international events. He was equal 2nd behind Maroczy at the Hastings Minor Tournament 1895 and in 1899 he swept the field at Amsterdam with a four point edge. At Hanover 1902 he came third behind Janowski and Pillsbury, but ahead of Chigorin and Marshall, among others. In London 1922 he came only tenth out of sixteen, but he had wins over Rubinstein and Tartakower. He played in a dozen Anglo-American cable matches and on two English Olympiad teams (1927, 1935). R. N. Coles has written (1952): *H. E. Atkins, Doyen of British Chess Champions.*

Automatons
Machines that gave the illusion of playing chess. Early ones had human beings hidden inside. After 1878 humans could operate the machine from a distance, using electricity. The cabinet construction that hid the operator even when the insides were revealed is part of the history of magic. The mechanism that allowed the hidden operator to see the board and manipulate the pieces, is more of a straight engineering problem.

The first automaton was Kempelen's The Turk (1769). Then came Hooper's Ajeeb (1868) and finally Gumpel's Mephisto (1878). In 1890 the Spanish scientist Torres y Quevedo (1852–1936) built a machine that actually played the ending of king and rook versus king. This very first chess playing machine is in the Polytechnic Museum in Madrid. After 1949, real computer programs for playing chess came into existence.

See Ajeeb; Mephisto; The Turk

See also *Chess and Computers* by David Levy (1976); *Chess: Man vs Machine* by Bradley Ewart (1980)

Averbakh, Yuri Lvovich
[February 8, 1922–]
USSR GM (1952) whose playing career reached a peak when he qualified for the 1953 Candidates tournament in Zurich (where he placed tenth out of fifteen) and won the USSR Championship in 1954. He played in fifteen USSR Championships during 1948–70 and in addition to his 1954 win, he tied for first in 1956, but lost the play-off. He almost made it into the world top ten, but was always just a touch behind players like Geller, Keres, Bronstein and Boleslavsky. In over 200 games against the cream of the world's Grandmasters he won 13%, lost 18% and drew 69% of the games.

He is a complete all-round chess talent. He wrote a major multi-volumed endgame treatise during the late 1950s, was president of the Soviet Chess Federation (1972–7), is an International Arbiter (1969), an International Judge of Chess Compositions, is editor of the principal USSR magazine *Shakhmaty* and takes an active role in several important FIDE committees. Even his daughter is married to a GM (Taimanov).

He is a charming, modest man, with an inquiring mind and, even in his 60s, a youthful interest in new ideas.

AVRO
In November 1938, the Dutch radio company Omroep, called AVRO, sponsored the strongest tournament (Category XVII) of all time for more than 5 players (see The Hague/Moscow 1948). The World Champion (Alekhine) and every one of his major challengers was there. As Keres said, it would be an honour not to come last.

The players were based in Amsterdam, but each round was played in a different Dutch city: Amsterdam, The Hague, Rotterdam, Groningen, Zwolle, Haarlem, Amsterdam, Utrecht, Arnhem, Breda, Rotterdam, The Hague, Leiden, Amsterdam, with the players returning to Amsterdam every night. This made the playing conditions appalling because on playing days the competitors were often forced to miss dinner and did not get to bed till after 2:00 a.m. These circumstances naturally favoured the younger challengers at the expense of the veterans Alekhine and Capablanca. In addition, Capablanca may have had a mild stroke during the second round robin, and that is when he suffered his only ever loss to Euwe as well as his only tournament loss to Alekhine. Furthermore, Czechoslovakia had fallen to the Nazis and poor Flohr suddenly had nowhere to call home.

Fine started off with 5½/6; however with 2 rounds to go it was Keres who led (7½), from Fine (7), Alekhine (6½), Botvinnik (6½), Reshevsky (6), Capablanca (5½), Euwe (5½), and Flohr (3½). Keres drew with Capablanca but Fine beat Alekhine. Before the last round it was Keres (8), Fine (8) and Botvinnik (7); Botvinnik then drew with Alekhine while Keres and Fine had a short draw, thus tying for 1st. Keres was declared the winner since he had the better tie-breaking Sonnenborn–Berger.

Some of the best games were Botvinnik–Capablanca (see Botvinnik) and Fine–Keres (see Keres).

Time Limit: 40 moves in 2½ hrs and then 16 moves per hr.

Tournament book: by Euwe (in Dutch) with good annotations.

Azmaiparashvili, Zurab

[March 16, 1960–]
USSR GM (1988) who was 1st at Pavlodar 1982 (VI), equal 1st at Moscow 1986 (VII), 1st at Albena 1986 (VII), 1st at Tbilisi 1986 (X) and 1st at London (Lloyds Bank) Open 1989.

AVRO 1938

		1		2		3		4		5		6		7		8		
1	Keres	—	—	1	½	½	½	½	½	½	½	1	½	1	½	½	½	8½
	Fine	0	½	—	—	1	½	1	1	1	0	1	0	½	½	1	½	8½
3	Botvinnik	½	½	0	½	—	—	1	½	½	0	1	½	½	1	½	½	7½
4	Alekhine	½	½	0	0	0	½	—	—	1	½	½	½	½	1	½	1	7
	Euwe	½	½	0	1	½	1	0	½	—	—	0	½	0	1	1	½	7
	Reshevsky	0	½	0	1	0	½	½	½	1	½	—	—	½	½	1	½	7
7	Capablanca	0	½	½	½	½	0	½	0	1	0	½	½	—	—	½	1	6
8	Flohr	½	½	0	½	½	½	½	0	0	½	0	½	½	0	—	—	4½

B

Bachmann, Ludwig

[August 11 1856–June 22 1937] German biographer of Steinitz (4 volumes), Anderssen, Charousek and Pillsbury. Not as painstakingly accurate as Gaige or Whyld, but an important chess historian of his time.

Major Works: *Chess Annuals* (1897 to 1930), *Aus Vergangenen Zeiten* (2 Volumes) (1920), *Das Schachspiel und seine historische Entwicklung* (1920).

Backward pawn

See Pawn Structure.

Back Rank Mate

A castled king with his unmoved pawns in front of him, is vulnerable to a mate when his own rook leaves to do service elsewhere and an enemy rook or queen checks him on the back rank. This theme occurs frequently, for example:

1 ♕g4 ♕b5 (if 1 ... ♕xg4; 2 ♖xe8 + ♖xe8 3 ♖xe8 mate) 2 ♕c4 ♕d7 3 ♕c7 ♕b5 4 a4 ♕xa4 5 ♖e4 ♕b5 6 ♕xb7 and Black resigns because he can no longer stop the back rank mate without heavy material loss.

This allegedly occurred in E. Adams–C. Torre (1920), but the game may have been 'invented'. In any case it is a good illustration of a back rank mate.

Bacon, Francis *[1561–1626]*

English essayist, philosopher and statesman who played chess but felt it was 'too wise a game'.

Bad Bishop

A bishop hemmed in by its own pawns. In the diagram, White has a bad bishop and is quite lost even though material is equal.

When heading for an endgame where you will have one bishop, it is wise to try to keep your pawns on squares of the opposite colour to your bishop. Though the bishop will not then be able to protect them, it will have mobility and be able to attack the enemy pawns.

If you are heading for an endgame where you will end up with a bad bishop, it is wise to try to exchange it before such an ending is reached.

Baden–Baden

A charming gingerbread-like city in Germany which held a strong tournament in 1925, won by Alekhine (16) ahead of Rubinstein (14½), Sämisch (13½) and Bogoljubow (13). However Baden Baden's major chess achievement took place in 1870 when it held the first international tournament in Germany. All the greatest players were there except for Mackenzie. Anderssen again proved that he was the greatest tournament player, even though he had lost a match to Steinitz four years earlier.

There was a tenth player, Adolf Stern, but the Franco–Prussian war broke out during the tournament and Stern was called to the colours. He withdrew after playing 4 games (a draw and a loss to Steinitz, a win and a loss with Minckwitz) and all his results were cancelled. Rosenthal also forfeited two games.

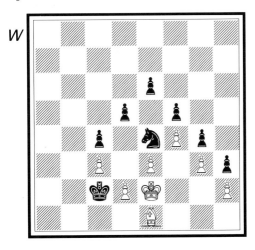

Time Limit: 20 moves per hour.
Prizes: Francs 3000, 600, 400.

There were 58 wins and only 14 draws. The games were extremely hard fought (*see* Neumann).

Steinitz–Anderssen

1 e4 e5 2 ♘c3 ♗c5 3 f4 d6 4 ♘f3 ♘f6 5 ♗c4 c6 6 fe de 7 ♕e2 ♘bd7 8 d3 b5 9 ♗b3 a5 10 a3 ♕b6 11 ♘d1 a4 12 ♗a2 0-0 13 ♘e3 ♗a6 14 ♘f5 b4 15 ab ♕xb4+ 16 c3 ♕a5 17 ♘g5 ♖ad8 18 ♕f3 ♕b6 19 ♗b1 a3 20 b4 ♗xb4 21 cb ♕xb4+ 22 ♔e2 a2 23 ♗d2 ♕b5 24 ♖xa2 ♘c5 25 ♖xa6 ♕xa6 26 ♗b4 ♖b8 27 ♗xc5 ♖b2+ 28 ♔e3 ♕a5

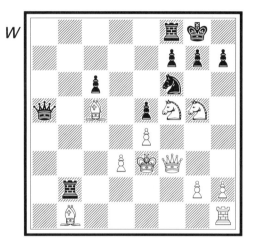

29 ♖d1 ♕xc5+ 30 d4 ed+ 31 ♔f4 h6 32 ♘h3 ♖e8 33 ♕d3 g5+ 34 ♔f3 g4+ 35 ♔g3 ♖xe4 36 ♕f1 ♕e5+ 37 ♔h4 gh+ 38 ♔xh3 ♖b3+ 39 g3 ♖f4 40 ♘xh6+ ♔f8 41 ♕c4 ♖h4+ 42 ♔g2 ♖xh2+ 43 ♔xh2 ♕xg3+ 44 ♔h1 ♕h3+ 45 ♔g1 ♖g3+ 46 Resigns—it is mate in 3.

Bagirov, Vladimir Konstantinovich

[*August 16 1936–*]
USSR GM (1978) who played in nine USSR Championships between 1960 and 1978. His best results were 4th in 1960 and equal 5th with Tal and Geller in 1977. His modest achievements extended to other events: equal 1st with Gufeld at Tbilisis 1971, equal 2nd at Erevan 1982 (IX) and 1st at Cascais 1986 (VII). He helped train Kasparov.

Balashov, Yuri Sergeyevich

[*March 12 1949–*]
USSR GM (1973) who played in some 14 USSR Championships between 1969 and 1986, with over 55% in about 150 games. He never won the title but he placed second to Karpov in 1976, was equal 3rd with Kasparov in 79, was 5th in the powerful 1983 (XIV) event and equal 2nd in 1986 (X).

In other events he has an impressive list of successes: 1st Moscow Championship 1970, 2nd behind Tal, Wijk aan Zee 1973, equal 1st Vilnius 1975, 1st Halle 1976, 1st Lvov 1978 (XIII), equal 1st Munich 1979, 1st Karlova 1979, equal 1st Wijk aan Zee 1982 (XIII), 1st Helsinki 1984, equal 1st Minsk 1985, 1st Minsk 1986, equal 1st Voronezh 1987, 1st Dortmund 1987 (XII). Nevertheless he has never made it into the Candidates or the exclusive circle of the world top ten.

Balinas, Rosendo Carrean

[*September 10 1941–*]
Philippine lawyer and GM (1976) who tied for 6th at Manila 1975 and won at Odessa 1976. He played on several Philippine Olympiad teams.

Ballet

Chess lends itself naturally to the ballet because the board, the personages and the moves of the pieces lead to interesting costumes, intricate dance steps and drama.

A Ballet des Échecs was performed before Louis XIV of France. Somewhat later, at the Paris World Exhibition of 1937, the ballet Checkmate had its world premiere—choreography by Ninette de Valois, book and music by Arthur Bliss. More recently (1986) the musical Chess, by Tim Rice, played to critical acclaim in London.

Bana

See Harschacharita.

Barbero, Gerardo F.

[*August 21 1961–*]
Argentine GM (1987) who won at Montpellier 1986 (VIII) and at Pro-

Baden–Baden 1870

		1		2		3		4		5		6		7		8		9		
1	Anderssen	–	–	1	1	1	½	0	0	1	1	1	0	½	1	1	1	0	1	11
2	Steinitz	0	0	–	–	0	½	1	1	1	1	1	1	1	1	0	½	1	½	10½
3	Blackburne	0	½	1	½	–	–	½	0	0	1	1	½	1	1	1	1	½	½	10
	Neumann	1	1	0	0	½	1	–	–	0	1	1	1	0	1	1	1	½	0	10
5	Paulsen	0	0	0	0	1	0	1	0	–	–	½	1	1	0	1*	½	1	½	7½
6	Winawer	0	1	0	0	0	½	0	0	½	0	–	–	0	1	1	1	1	½	6½
	de Vere	½	0	0	0	0	0	1	0	0	1	1	0	–	–	0	1	1	1*	6½
8	Minckwitz	0	0	1	½	0	0	0	0*	0	½	0	0	1	0	–	–	1	1*	5
	Rosenthal	1	0	0	½	½	½	½	1	0	½	0	½	0	0*	0	0*	–	–	5

*by default

kuplje 1987 (VII). He also won the Kecskemet Open in 1987.

Barcelona
Major Spanish city which staged World Cup IV in April 1989. Ljubojevic led throughout and was just caught by Kasparov who had to beat Spassky in the last round.

Barcza, Gideon
[*August 21 1911–February 27 1986*] Hungarian GM (1954) who was a mathematics instructor and later a director of studies in Budapest. Though slightly overshadowed by Szabo, he played a significant role in Hungarian chess. During the 1940s and 50s he won the Hungarian Championship eight times and from 1936–68 he played on seven Hungarian Olympiad teams. In the 1956 event he scored 11½–4½ on second board, and this included a fine win over Smyslov.

In international tourneys, first prizes eluded him, but he had seconds at three tournaments in 1948 and thirds at Moscow 1962, Havana 1963 and Leningrad 1967.

His major book (written jointly) was *The World Chess Champions* (1959).

The opening 1 ♘f3 d5 2 g3 is now called the Barcza System.

Barczay, Laszlo [*February 21 1936–*]
Hungarian GM (1967) who scored +10=2 on bottom board at the 1966 Olympiad in Havana—his only Olympiad appearance. He was equal 1st at the 1967 Asztalos Memorial, 1st at Polanica Zdroj 1969 and 1st at Astor 1982 (VII). He was a major Hungarian force but one with rather variable results.

Bardeleben, Kurt von
[*March 4 1861–January 31 1924*] German lawyer of GM strength who won the minor tournament at London 1883 and was equal 1st at Leipzig 1888, Kiel 1893 and Coburg 1904. In matches he drew with Blackburne 1895, lost 1½–2½ to Lasker (1889), beat Teichmann in 1895, then lost to him in 1910 and lost 1½–4½ to the young Alekhine in 1908.

He is most famous for a wonderful loss to Steinitz in the first Hastings tournament. It was round 10, played on August 17 1895. Chigorin was leading with 8 points followed by Pillsbury and Bardeleben at 7½ and Lasker at 7. The ageing Steinitz was far back at 4½ having lost his last four games. Steinitz played Bardeleben and produced a masterpiece which won the first brilliancy prize. Poor Bardeleben was crushed—in fact he left the hall and lost on time. He only scored 1 point out of his next 7 games and ended up equal 7th (while Steinitz finished 5th). The Hastings book describes Bardeleben as

> '... a carefully dressed, delicate looking man, with a straw hat generally poised on his head, and with a modest and gentlemanly demeanour, though of a somewhat retiring disposition.'

He wrote a good deal, primarily about openings.

He suffered a great deal after 1918 and was plagued with poverty, hunger and illness. Sadly, he committed suicide by jumping out of an upper window of his boarding house.

Barcelona 1989 — World Cup IV Category XV

		1	2	3	4	5	6	7	8	9	10	11	12	13	14	15	16	17	
1	Kasparov	–	½	1	1	½	1	½	1	½	1	½	0	1	½	½	1	½	11
	Ljubojevic	½	–	½	½	½	½	½	1	½	½	1	½	1	1	1	½	1	11
3	Salov	0	½	–	½	1	1	½	½	½	½	0	1	1	0	1	1	1	10
4	Korchnoi	0	½	½	–	0	½	1	1	1	½	½	½	1	1	1	0	½	9½
5	Hübner	½	½	0	1	–	½	1	½	½	½	½	½	½	1	½	½	½	9
	Short	0	½	0	½	½	–	½	½	1	½	1	1	0	0	1	1	1	9
7	Nikolic	½	½	½	0	0	½	–	½	½	½	½	½	½	½	½	1	1	8
8	Belyavsky	0	0	½	0	½	½	½	–	0	1	½	½	1	1	1	½	0	7½
	Ribli	½	½	½	0	½	0	½	1	–	½	½	½	½	½	½	½	½	7½
	Spassky	0	½	½	½	½	½	½	0	½	–	½	½	½	½	½	1	½	7½
	Vaganian	½	0	1	½	½	0	½	½	½	½	–	1	½	0	½	0	1	7½
	Yusupov	1	½	0	½	½	0	½	½	½	½	0	–	½	½	½	1	½	7½
13	Speelman	0	0	0	0	½	1	½	0	½	½	½	½	–	½	½	1	1	7
14	Hjartarson	½	0	1	0	0	1	½	0	½	½	1	½	½	–	0	½	0	6½
	Seirawan	½	0	0	0	½	0	½	0	½	½	½	½	½	1	–	½	1	6½
16	Illescas	0	½	0	1	½	0	0	½	½	0	1	0	0	½	½	–	½	5½
	Nogueiras	½	0	0	½	½	0	0	1	½	½	0	½	0	1	0	½	–	5½

Steinitz–von Bardeleben

1 e4 e5 2 ♘f3 ♘c6 3 ♗c4 ♗c5 4 c3
♘f6 5 d4 ed 6 cd ♗b4+ 7 ♘c3 d5 8 ed
♘xd5 9 0-0 ♗e6 10 ♗g5 ♗e7 11
♗xd5 ♗xd5 12 ♘xd5 ♕xd5 13 ♗xe7
♘xe7 14 ♖e1 f6 15 ♕e2 ♕d7 16
♖ac1 c6 17 d5 cd 18 ♘d4 ♔f7 19 ♘e6
♖hc8 20 ♕g4 g6 21 ♘g5+ ♔e8

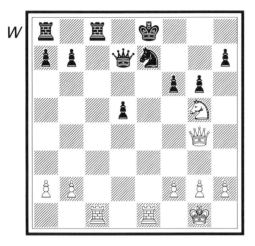

22 ♖xe7+ ♔f8 23 ♖f7+ ♔g8 24
♖g7+ ♔h8 25 ♖xh7+, at which
point Black left and lost on time. Steinitz
then pointed out: 25 ... ♔g8 26 ♖g7+
♔h8 27 ♕h4+ ♔xg7 28 ♕h7+ ♔f8
29 ♕h8+ ♔e7 30 ♕g7+ ♔e8 31
♕g8+ ♔e7 32 ♕f7+ ♔d8 33
♕f8+ ♔e8 34 ♘f7+ ♔d7 35 ♕d6
mate

Barden, Leonard William

[*August 20 1929–*]
English player who was joint British
Champion (1954) and played on four
English Olympiad teams during 1952–
62. He became a fine author and journalist and has edited the *Guardian* chess
column since 1956. He takes a special
interest in junior chess.

Major works: *The Ruy Lopez* (1963),
The King's Indian Defence (1968).

Bareev, Evgeny [*November 21 1966–*]
USSR GM (1989) who was equal 4th at
Sochi 1988 (XII).

Barlov, Dragan [*January 30 1957–*]
Yugoslav GM (1986) who placed 2nd at
Sochi 1985 (XI) and won the Yugoslav
Championship in 1986 (IX).

Batsford Chess Openings

A single-volume openings manual, first
published in 1982, and written by
GMs Kasparov and Keene. Similar in
intent to *Modern Chess Openings, BCO*
differs in that it uses figurine algebraic
notation (rather than *MCO*'s English
descriptive) and contains many more
variations.

See *Modern Chess Openings*.

Becker, Albert

[*September 5 1896–May 7 1984*]
Austrian IM (1953) whose best result
was equal 5th with Euwe and Vidmar at
the strong 1929 Carlsbad tournament.
He played on two Olympiad teams:
1931 for Austria and 1939 for Germany.
He was games editor of the *Wiener
Schachzeitung* (1926–35) and joint
author with Grünfeld of the excellent
tournament book of Teplitz–Schonau
1922. After 1939 he settled in Argentina and continued to write opening
essays.

See *Albert Becker: Praxis eines Theore-
tikers* by M. A. Lachaga (1975).

Belfort

A small fortress city in Eastern France,
near the Swiss border at Basel, which
staged World Cup II in June/July 1988.
After 9 rounds it was Ehlvest (7) ahead

Belfort 1988		World Cup II Category XV															
		1	2	3	4	5	6	7	8	9	10	11	12	13	14	15	16
1	Kasparov	–	0	1	½	½	1	½	1	½	1	1	1	1	½	1	1	11½
2	Karpov	1	–	1	½	½	0	1	½	½	½	½	1	1	1	½	1	10½
3	Ehlvest	0	0	–	½	½	½	½	½	1	½	1	½	1	1	½	1	9
4	Ribli	½	½	½	–	½	½	½	½	1	½	½	½	½	½	½	½	8
	Hübner	½	½	½	½		½	½	½	½	0	½	1	½	½	½	1	8
	Sokolov	0	1	½	½	½	–	½	½	½	1	½	0	½	½	½	1	8
	Spassky	½	0	½	½	½	½	–	½	½	½	½	½	½	1	1	½	8
8	Short	0	½	½	½	½	½	½	–	½	1	½	½	½	0	1	½	7½
9	Speelman	½	½	0	0	½	½	½	½	–	½	½	½	½	½	½	1	7
10	Ljubojevic	0	½	½	½	1	0	½	0	½	–	½	½	½	½	½	½	6½
	Andersson	0	½	0	½	½	½	½	½	½	½	–	½	½	0	½	1	6½
	Nogueiras	0	0	½	½	0	1	½	½	½	½	½	–	½	1	½	0	6½
	Belyavsky	0	0	0	½	½	½	½	½	½	½	½	½	–	1	1	0	6½
14	Hjartarson	½	0	0	½	½	½	0	1	½	½	1	0	0	–	½	0	5½
	Yusupov	0	½	½	½	½	½	0	0	½	½	½	½	0	½	–	½	5½
	Timman	0	0	0	½	0	0	½	½	0	½	0	1	1	1	½	–	5½

of Kasparov (6½), Karpov (5½) and Spassky (5½). Ehlvest lost to Karpov (round 10) and Kasparov (round 12) and with 2 rounds to go it was Kasparov (10½) ahead of Karpov (8½) and Ehlvest (8). The mighty Ks met in the second last round and Kasparov needed a win to reach or break Fischer's all time Elo rating of 2785. However Karpov produced one of the greatest artistic achievements of his career, playing his queen like a Stradivarius. This closed the gap but Kasparov beat Sokolov in the last round to take first prize and settle for a mere 2775 Elo rating.

Time Limit: 40 moves in 2 hours and then 20 moves per hour.

Tournament Book by DeSanto, Gravend and Touze has magnificent photos and 13 well annotated games. This one is from Round 14:

Karpov–Kasparov

1 d4 ♘f6 2 c4 g6 3 ♘c3 d5 4 cd ♘xd5 5 e4 ♘xc3 6 bc ♗g7 7 ♗c4 c5 8 ♘e2 ♘c6 9 ♗e3 0-0 10 0-0 ♗g4 11 f3 ♘a5 12 ♗xf7+ ♖xf7 13 fg ♖xf1+ 14 ♔xf1 ♕d6 15 e5 ♕d5 16 ♗f2 ♖d8 17 ♕a4! b6 18 ♕c2 ♖f8 19 ♔g1 ♕c4 20 ♕d2 ♕e6 21 h3 ♘c4 22 ♕g5 h6 23 ♕c1 ♕f7 24 ♗g3 g5 25 ♕c2 ♕d5 26 ♗f2 b5 27 ♘g3 ♖f7 28 ♖e1 b4 29 ♕g6 ♔f8 30 ♘e4 ♖xf2 31 ♔xf2 bc 32 ♕f5+ ♔g8 33 ♕c8+ ♔h7 34 ♕xc5 ♕f7+ 35 ♔g1 c2 36 ♘g3 ♗f8 37 ♘f5 ♔g8 38 ♖c1 resigns

The white Queen moves (17, 18, 20, 22, 23, 25, 29) are remarkably subtle and deserve deep study.

Belgrade

Capital of chess-loving Yugoslavia, but much of the international activity occurs in smaller Yugoslav centres. Olympiads for example, were held in Dubrovnik (1950), Skopje (1972) and Novi Sad (1990).

Belgrade did have the last quarter of 1959 Candidates (see Bled) and held a strong (XIV) tournament in 1987, which

Belgrade 1970 — USSR vs Rest of the World

				USSR	Rest of World				
½	1	0		Spassky	Larsen	½	0	1	1
			0	Stein					
0	0	½	½	Petrosian	Fischer	1	1	½	½
½	½	0	½	Korchnoi	Portisch	½	½	1	½
0	½	½	½	Polugayevsky	Hort	1	½	½	½
1	½	½	½	Geller	Gligoric	0	½	½	½
½	1	0	1	Smyslov	Reshevsky	½	0	1	
					Olafsson				0
1	1	½	0	Taimanov	Uhlmann	0	0	½	1
1	½	½	½	Botvinnik	Matulovic	0	½	½	½
½	0	1	½	Tal	Najdorf	½	1	0	½
½	1	½	1	Keres	Ivkov	½	0	½	0
5½	6	4	5 = 20½			4½	4	6	5 = 19½

Herzeg Novi 1970 — Blitz Tournament

		1	2	3	4	5	6	7	8	9	10	11	12	
1	Fischer	–	2	1	2	1½	1½	2	2	1½	1½	2	2	19
2	Tal	0	–	2	1	0	2	1½	½	2	1½	2	2	14½
3	Korchnoi	1	0	–	½	0	2	2	2	1	1½	2	2	14
4	Petrosian	0	1	1½	–	1	1	1½	1	1	1½	2	2	13½
5	Bronstein	½	2	2	1	–	½	½	1	½	1½	1½	2	13
6	Hort	½	0	0	1	1½	–	1	2	2	1	1	2	12
7	Matulovic	0	½	0	½	1½	1	–	½	2	2	1½	1	10½
8	Smyslov	0	1½	0	1	1	0	1½	–	½	1	1	2	9½
9	Reshevsky	½	0	1	1	1½	0	0	1½	–	½	1½	1	8½
10	Uhlmann	½	½	½	½	½	1	0	1	1½	–	0	2	8
11	Ivkov	0	0	0	0	½	1	½	1	½	2	–	2	7½
12	Ostojic	0	0	0	0	0	0	1	0	1	0	0	–	2

was won by Ljubojevic (8) ahead of Timman (7½) and Belyavsky (7). But probably the most dramatic event held in Belgrade was the first USSR versus the Rest of the World match (see photograph p. 224). The USSR fielded 5 World Champions but lost badly on the top 4 boards. Keres was their highest scorer while Fischer led the way for the Rest of the World. The whole idea of such a match is quite dramatic, but it was not repeated until 1984 (see: London).

After this exciting match, a 5 minute blitz tournament was held in nearby Herzeg Novi. Fischer scored a stunning victory and won the $400 first prize.

At Belgrade 1989, Kasparov won to take his Elo rating to a new record of 2800, surpassing Fischer's old record.

Bellon Lopez, Juan Manuel

[May 8 1950–]
Spanish GM (1978) who won at Torremolinos 1978 (V) and was equal 2nd at Montilla 1978 (VIII). He has had a few wins in modest open tournaments.

Belyavsky, Alexander Gennrikhovich *[December 17 1953–]*

USSR GM (1975) who in the 1980s

Alexander Belyavsky of the Soviet Union. His career has been overshadowed by the dominance of Karpov and Kasparov, but for whom he might have become World Champion himself.

belongs to the world top ten and who might well have been World Champion if the two superstars Karpov and Kasparov did not exist. He has a most impressive record. In 11 USSR Championships during 1973 to 1987, he has three equal 1sts. He won the World Junior in 1973, about a dozen first prizes in Category X–XII tournaments and two outstanding wins at the Category XV tournaments in Tilburg 1981 and 1986. In the 1984 USSR–Rest of World match he scored $3\frac{1}{2}$–$\frac{1}{2}$ against Seirawan and Larsen.

He became a Candidate in 1982, but was crushed by Kasparov $+1=4-4$ (1983). At Montpellier 1985 he just missed becoming a quarter-finalist when he was equal 6th with Spassky.

Benedict, Clare   [*1871–1961*]
US chess patroness who moved to Switzerland and sponsored a series of European team tournaments.

Benjamin, Joel   [*March 11 1964– *]
US GM (1986) who was equal 3rd in the 1982 World Junior Championship, beat Short decisively $+4=3-0$ in December 1983 and was equal 2nd at Hastings 1984/85 (X). In US Championships he was 2nd in 1985 (X), equal 2nd

in 1986 (X) and finally equal 1st in 1987 (XII).

Benko Gambit

1 d4 ♘f6 2 c4 c5 3 d5 b5!? 4 cb a6 5 ba ♗xa6.

A modern counter-gambit popularized by Pal Benko in the 1960s and 70s. Black intends to undermine white's advanced pawn centre and create open files on the queenside for his major pieces. The absence of immediate tactical threats allows White a certain latitude, but there is no known refutation, and the gambit is probably sound enough to secure Black equality. A typical continuation is 6 ♘c3 g6 7 e4 ♗xf1 8 ♔xf1 d6 9 g3 ♗g7 10 ♔g2 0-0 when black has considerable pressure on the queenside to compensate for the sacrificed pawn.

Black can vary with an early ... e6 (e.g. on move 5 or 6) to produce the Volga Gambit, an inferior system closely related to the Blumenfeld Counter-gambit.

See *The Benko Gambit* by Benko (1974).

Benko, Pal   [*July 15 1928– *]
US GM (1958) who was born in France, raised in Hungary and emigrated to the US in 1956. He won the 1948 Hungarian Championship and played on their 1956 Olympiad team.

He was a Candidate for the world title in 1959 when he placed 8th and in 1962 when he came 6th. In 1970 he yielded his interzonal place to Fischer, who went on to win the world title.

He played on 6 US Olympiad teams (1962–72) and won or was equal 1st in 8 US Open Championships (1961–75). In round-robin tournaments he could only manage an equal 1st with Quinteros at Torremolinos 1973 and in US closed championships his best was an equal 2nd in 1974.

He never made it into the world top ten but he was a pugnacious competitor. He wrote *The Benko Gambit* (1974).

US Grandmaster Pal Benko (left) takes on Mikhail Tal. The dark glasses were an attempt to minimize the apparent effects of Tal's hypnotic stare.

Benoni Defence

1 d4 ♘f6 2 c4 c5.

First analysed in 1825 by Aaron Reinganum, who called it Beni-Oni (son of sadness, in Hebrew) because he did his analysis as a refuge from melancholy. It was little used in the 19th century—two games won by Staunton as white against Saint-Amant are among the few recorded instances—and it was not until the 1930s that it became respectable, largely through the efforts of Alekhine, Spielmann and Tartakower. In its modern form the Benoni is considered a sharp counter-attacking weapon which offers good practical chances.

After White's natural 3 d5 Black has a choice between 3 ... e5 (Old Benoni—variation A) and 3. ... e6 (Modern Benoni—variation B):

A 3 ... e5 4 ♘c3 d6 5 e4 ♗e7 6 ♘f3 0-0 7 ♗e2 ♘e8 8 0-0 ♘d7

B 3 ... e6 4 ♘c3 ed 5 cd d6. White now has several alternatives, including:

   (a) 6 g3 g6 7 ♗g2 ♗g7 8 ♘f3 0-0 9 0-0 ♕e7;

   (b) 6 e4 g6 7 f4 ♗g7 8 e5 ♘fd7;

   (c) 6 e4 g6 7 f4 ♗g7 8 ♗e2 0-0 9 0-0 ♖e8.

The Modern Benoni abounds in combinative traps and tactical chances and is ideal for those who enjoy complications.

Berger, Johann Nepomuk

[April 11 1845–October 17 1933] Austrian polyhistorian interested in problems and endgames, who was an author, problemist, endgame composer and polemicist. He was co-editor of the *Deutsche Schachzeitung* (1898–1907) and sole editor until 1911. Here he fought pitched literary battles with Kohtz.

He suggested a new scoring system, similar to one proposed by Sonneborn, and this became a useful method to break ties.

Major works: *Das Schachproblem und dessen kunstgerechte Darstellung* (1884), *Theorie und Praxis der Endspiele* (1890, revised 1922, and an appendix to it appeared in 1933), *Katechismus des Schachspiels* (1891).

Berlin

Germany's capital city whose first major tournament was held in 1881. Blackburne (14) won, far ahead of Zukertort (11), Chigorin (10½) and Winawer (10½). Steinitz and Mackenzie were absent.

The next major event, 1897, was Charousek's (14½) great victory, ahead of Walbordt (14), Blackburne (13) and Janowski (12½).

In April 1918, with the great war still raging, a four-man double-round tournament saw Vidmar (4½) beat Schlechter (3½), Mieses (3) and Rubinstein (1).

As the war came near to ending, an even stronger four-man tournament was held, from September 28–October 11 1918.

Schlechter was to die 2½ months later.

In 1928 an eight-man double-round tournament saw Capablanca (8½) win easily over Nimzowitsch (7) and Spielmann (6½). Tarrasch withdrew after 3 rounds and his score (3 losses) was cancelled.

Berlin 1918

		1		2		3		4		
1	Lasker	–	–	½	½	½	1	1	1	4½
2	Rubinstein	½	½	–	–	1	½	½	1	4
3	Schlechter	½	0	0	½	–	–	½	½	2
4	Tarrasch	0	0	½	0	½	½	–	–	1½

Berlin also had its share of world Championship matches: Lasker–Janowski 1910, half of Lasker–Schlechter 1910 and 6 games of Alekhine–Bogoljubow 1929.

Berlin Defence

See Ruy Lopez.

Berlin Pleiades

The group of young chess enthusiasts who gathered around Bledow in Berlin 1836–45 (*See* Bledow).

Bernstein, Ossip Samoilovich

[*October 2 1882–November 30 1962*] Russian GM (1950) who was in the world top ten from 1903 to the early 1930s. He was second to Chigorin in the third Russian Championship (1903) and equal 4th in both Coburg 1904 and Barmen 1905. In 1906 he earned his Doctorate (law) at Heidelberg and became a successful financial lawyer and amateur chess player. He was equal 1st with Rubinstein at Ostende 1907, 5th at St Petersburg 1909, equal 8th at San Sebastian 1911, 2nd to Rubinstein at Vilna 1912 and equal 5th with Rubinstein at St Petersburg 1914.

San Sebastian 1911 was limited to players who had won at least two 3rd prizes in previous first-class international tournaments. Capablanca, who won the tournament, did not really qualify and he wrote: 'An exception was made with respect to me, because of my victory over Marshall. Some of the masters objected to my entry.... One of them was Dr Bernstein. I had the good fortune to play him in the first round, and beat him in such fashion as to obtain the Rothschild prize for the most brilliant game ... a profound feeling of respect for my ability remained throughout the rest of the contest'.

Bernstein lost his first fortune in the 1917 revolution, and after many life-threatening vicissitudes, settled in Paris in 1920 and amassed a second fortune which disappeared in the 1930 depression.

He was equal 5th at Berne 1932, equal 6th at Zurich 1934 and in 1933 played a drawn training match ($+1=2-1$) with Alekhine. He amassed a third fortune which evaporated in 1940 when France fell. As late as 1954 he was equal 2nd with Najdorf at Montevideo and scored 50% on top board for France at the Amsterdam Olympiad.

In terms of life scores he had plusses against Teichmann, Maroczy, Janowski, Schlechter, Duras and Kotov, and he had equal scores against Lasker ($+2=1-2$) Rubinstein ($+1=7-1$) Nimzowitsch ($+1=4-1$) Chigorin ($+1=0-1$) and Flohr ($=3$).

Bernstein was the world's strongest amateur (and probably the best fortune amasser among chess masters). He was a *bon vivant* and raconteur and was happily married to one wife for 54 years.

Best early score
See Tie-Breaking Systems.

Beverwijk
See Hoogoven.

Bilek, Istvan   [*August 11 1932– *]
Hungarian GM (1962) who won three Hungarian Championships (1963, 1965 and 1970) and during 1958–74 played on 9 Hungarian Olympiad teams. He made it into the interzonals of 1962 and 1964. His best results were equal 1st at Balatonfured 1960, Salgotarjan 1967 and Debrecen 1970.

Bilguer, Paul Rudolf Von
See Handbuch

Bird, Henry Edward
          [*July 14 1830–April 11 1908*]
English accountant of only IM strength whose life somehow spanned the growth of chess in the 19th century. He played many tournaments and matches

and has an opening (1 f4) named after him.

He played in the great London tournaments of 1851, 1883 and 1899, and at Hastings 1895. His best result was equal 5th at Vienna 1873. He lost matches to Steinitz ($+5=5-6$) in 1866, to Blackburne ($+2=0-5$) in 1879 and to Lasker ($+2=3-7$) in 1890 and ($+0=0-5$) in 1892. He did draw a match with Burn ($+9=0-9$) in 1886.

He was a regular at Simpson's Divan from 1846 until it closed in 1903. He wrote a book on railway finance as well as numerous chess items, including *Chess Masterpieces* (1875), *Chess Openings Practically Considered* (1877), *Chess History and Reminiscences* (1893) and *Chess Novelties* (1895).

Bird's Defence
See Ruy Lopez.

Bird's Opening
1 f4.
Popularized by Bird in the second half of the 19th century. Its main point is the control of e5 and other central dark squares, but it does have drawbacks. After 1 f4 d5 2 e3 ♘f6 3 ♘f3 ♗g4 4 ♗e2 ♗xf3 5 ♗xf3 ♘bd7 6 c4 e6 7 cd ed 8 ♘c3 c6 9 0-0 ♗e7 the position is even.

Black can also try the From Gambit 1 f4 e5 2 fe d6 3 ed ♗xd6 with a dangerous initiative for the sacrificed pawn.

Bisguier, Arthur Bernard
          [*October 8 1929– *]
US GM (1957) who won the US closed championship in 1954 and the US Open Swiss in 1950, 1956 and 1959. He was 2nd to Fischer in the US closed in 1962/63, equal 2nd at San Juan 1969 and 1st at Lone Pine 1973. He made it into the interzonals in 1955 and 1962 and was on 5 US Olympiad teams during 1952–72.

He is co-author of *American Chess Masters from Morphy to Fischer* (1974). He is one of the few chess GMs who plays bridge at a master level (others are Ståhlberg and Rossetto).

Bishop
A so-called minor piece which moves on the diagonals. The ones that start out on f1 and c8 remain on the light-coloured squares throughout the game while the ones that start out on c1 and f8 remain on the dark squares. It is only together that the bishops can control the entire board and thus a pair of bishops is worth more than twice the value of one bishop alone.

Originally this piece was an elephant (fil or al-fil in Persian) and could only move diagonally and jump over one square). In Europe, it remained alfil in Spain, became alfiere (standard bearer) in Italy, aufin and then fou (jester) in France. In Germany it became läufer (runner) and in the Nordic countries it became a bishop, probably because it stood to the right of the king.

At the end of the 15th century it finally became our present-day bishop, being able to move to the end of any vacant diagonal, but losing its power to leap over a square.

Bishop's Gambit
See King's Gambit.

Bishops of Opposite Colours
When one side has only one bishop and it is on the dark squares, and the other side has only a light-coloured bishop, then these bishops of opposite colours are unable to fight directly with each other. Pawn endings with bishops of opposite colours are usually drawn, even when one side has one or two pawns more.

Bishop's Opening
1 e4 e5 2 ♗c4.
Favoured by Philidor and Staunton, but

seldom used today. It was advocated by Weaver Adams in the 1930s and Larsen used it in the 1960s. One main line is 1 e4 e5 2 ♗c4 ♘f6 3 d3 c6.

Bismarck, Otto von [1815–1898]
The 'Iron' chancellor of the German Empire (1871–90) enjoyed chess.

Biyiasis, Peter [November 19 1950–]
US GM (1978) who studied mathematics and developed his chess in Canada and then moved south. He won the Canadian Championship in 1972 and 1975, and made it into the interzonals of 1973 and 1976. He played on several Canadian Olympiad teams in the late 1970s before moving to the US. His best results are equal 4th at Wijk aan Zee (XI) and equal 2nd at Zrenjanin (VII) both in 1980.

For a time in the early 1980s he was one of the few players on friendly terms with Fischer.

Blackburne, Joseph Henry
[December 10 1841–September 1 1924]
English player of GM strength who was a highly successful tournament player and one of the top 5 or 6 players in the world during the 1870s and 80s. He did not learn to play chess until the age of 19 when he was inspired by Morphy's

Joseph Blackburne, known in his heyday as 'The Black Death'.

achievements. Soon he was the top British player and in 1868 he abandoned his business interests and adopted chess as a profession.

His international tournament career spans an impressive 52 years, from London 1862 to St Petersburg 1914. He played in 33 top class events and though he seldom won, he generally finished in the top half. His fierce competitive spirit and great combinative ability earned him the pleasant nickname of the 'Black Death'. His most notable successes were equal 1st with Steinitz at Vienna 1873 (Blackburne lost the play-off match), 1st at Berlin 1881 (three points ahead of Zukertort, who was 2nd), 3rd at London 1883, and 2nd behind Tarrasch at Manchester 1890.

He won the British Championship in 1868 and for many years was ranked as Britain's foremost player. Even in 1914—at the age of 72—Blackburne was equal 1st at the British congress in Chester.

He was less successful in matches. Though he beat Bird in 1888 and won one match with Gunsberg in 1881, he lost heavily to Lasker in 1892 and to Steinitz in 1862/3 and again in 1876.

He played in 11 Anglo-American cable matches. His special expertise was blindfold play and a major portion of his income came from simultaneous exhibitions and blindfold performances. He toured Britain regularly and popularized the game througout the country with happy and friendly displays of his brilliant talent.

See *Mr. Blackburne's Games at Chess* by P. A. Graham (1899).

Blackburne–Schwarz
Berlin 1881
1 e4 e6 2 d4 d5 3 ♘c3 ♘f6 4 ed ed 5 ♘f3 ♗d6 6 ♗d3 c6 7 0-0 0-0 8 ♘e2 ♗g4 9 ♘g3 ♕c7 10 ♗e3 ♘bd7 11 ♕d2 ♖fe8 12 ♖ae1 ♘e4 13 ♕c1 ♗xf3 14 gf ♘xg3 15 hg ♗xg3 16 ♔g2 ♗d6 17 ♖h1 ♘f8 18 ♖h3 g6 19 ♖eh1 ♖ad8 20 ♗g5 ♖d7 21 c4 dc 22 ♗xc4 h5 23 ♖h4 b5 24 ♗b3 ♘e6 25 ♗f6 ♘f4+ 26 ♕xf4 ♗xf4

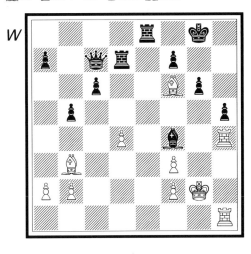

27 ♖xh5 gh 28 ♖xh5 Resigns

Blackmar Gambit
1 d4 ♘f6 2 f3 d5 3 e4 de 4 ♘c3. Interesting but unsound gambit. Black gets a fine game with either 4 ... ef or 4 ... ♗f5.

Bled
A Slovene holiday resort in Yugoslavia near the Austrian border which staged a double-round 14-player international tournament in 1931. Alekhine $(20\frac{1}{2})$ was far ahead of Bogoljubow (15) and Nimzowitsch (14) but several top contenders were not there: Capablanca, Euwe, Lasker, Marshall and Bernstein.

The great tournament held in Yugoslavia was the 4th Candidates—1959. The first half (14 rounds) was played in Bled, the second half in Zagreb (rounds 15–21) and Belgrade (rounds 22–28). Four of the 8 players were or became World Champions, including 16-year-old Fischer and 22-year-old Tal. The sentimental favourite was Keres—he played well, beat Tal 3 to 1 and scored 66% but he could not match Tal's 4–0 sweep of Fischer. Here is the stirring decisive game (*see also* Tal).

Fischer–Tal
1 e4 c5 2 ♘f3 d6 3 d4 cd 4 ♘xd4 ♘f6

5 ♘c3 a6 6 ♗c4 e6 7 ♗b3 b5 8 f4 b4 9 ♘a4 ♘xe4 10 0-0 g6 11 f5 gf 12 ♘xf5 ♖g8 (not ... ef 13 ♕d5 ♖a7 14 ♕d4 wins) 13 ♗d5 ♖a7 14 ♗xe4 ef 15 ♗xf5 ♖e7 16 ♗xc8 ♕xc8 17 ♗f4 ♕c6 18 ♕f3 ♕xa4 19 ♗xd6 ♕c6 20 ♗xb8 ♕b6+ 21 ♔h1 ♕xb8

W

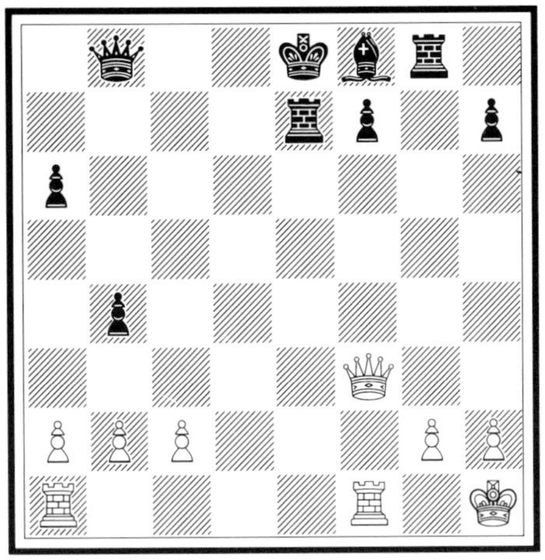

22 ♕c6+? (correct is 22 ♖ae1 ♔d8 23 ♖xe7 ♗xe7 24 ♕xf7 ♖g6 25 ♕xh7 with a slight edge) 22 ... ♖d7 23 ♖ae1+ ♗e7 24 ♖xf7 ♔xf7 25 ♕e6+ ♔f8 26 ♕xd7 ♕d6 27 ♕b7 ♖g6 28 c3 a5 29 ♕c8+ ♔g7 30 ♕c4 ♗d8 31 cb ab 32 g3 ♕c6+ 33 ♖e4 ♕xc4 34 ♖xc4 ♖b6 35 ♔g2 ♔f6 36 ♔f3 ♔e5 37 ♔e3 ♗g5+ 38 ♔e2 ♔d5 39 ♔d3 ♗f6 40 ♖c2 ♗e5 41 ♖e2 ♖f6 42 ♖c2 ♖f3+ 43 ♔e2 ♖f7 44 ♔d3 ♗d4 45 a3 b3 46 ♖c8 ♗xb2 47 ♖d8+ ♔c6 48 ♖b8 ♖f3+ 49 ♔c4 ♖c3+ 50 ♔b4 ♔c7 51 ♖b5 ♗a1 52 a4 b2 53 Resigns

In 1961 Bled held another powerful tournament (only Botvinnik, Smyslov and Reshevsky were absent) with ex-World Champion Tal facing Fischer, Keres and Petrosian. Fischer ($7\frac{1}{2}$) led after 10 rounds but by round 15, he (11) and Tal (11) were tied. Then Tal forged ahead with $3\frac{1}{2}$ out of 4 while Fischer could only manage $2\frac{1}{2}$ out of 4.

Time Limit: 40 moves in $2\frac{1}{2}$ hours and then 16 moves per hour.

Prizes: $1000 + 500 000 dinars, $800 + 400 000, $600 + 300 000, $450 + 200 000, $350 + 150 000 Dinars.

The critical game was Fischer's first win over Tal:

Fischer–Tal

1 e4 c5 2 ♘f3 ♘c6 3 d4 cd 4 ♘xd4 e6 5 ♘c3 ♕c7 6 g3 ♘f6 7 ♘db5 ♕b8 8 ♗f4 ♘e5 9 ♗e2 ♗c5 10 ♗xe5 ♕xe5 11 f4 ♕b8 12 e5 a6 13 ef ab 14 fg ♖g8 15 ♘e4 ♗e7 16 ♕d4 ♖a4 17 ♘f6+ ♗xf6 18 ♕xf6 ♕c7

W

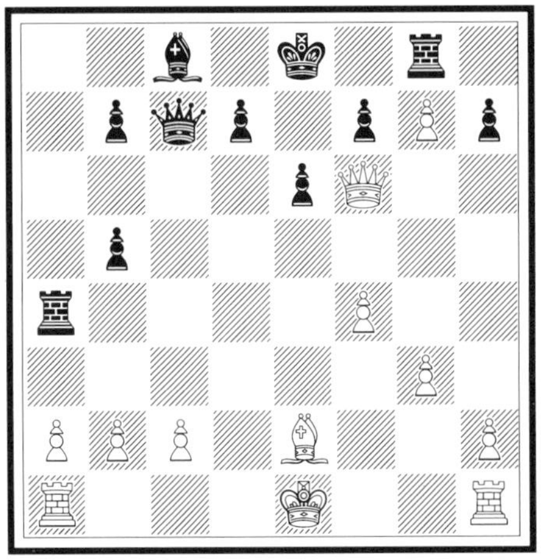

19 0-0-0 ♖xa2 20 ♔b1 ♖a6 21 ♗xb5 ♖b6 22 ♗d3 e5 23 fe ♖xf6 24 ef ♕c5 25 ♗xh7 ♕g5 26 ♗xg8 ♕xf6 27 ♖hf1 ♕xg7 28 ♗xf7+ ♔d8 29 ♗e6 ♕h6 30 ♗xd7 ♗xd7 31 ♖f7 ♕xh2 32 ♖dxd7+ ♔e8 33 ♖de7+ ♔d8 34 ♖d7+ ♔c8 35 ♖c7+ ♔d8 36 ♖fd7+ ♔e8 37 ♖d1 b5 38 ♖b7 ♕h5 39 g4 ♕h3 40 g5 ♕f3 41 ♖e1+ ♔f8 42 ♖xb5 ♔g7 43 ♖b6 ♕g3 44 ♖d1 ♕c7 45 ♖1d6 ♕c8 46 b3 ♔h7 47 ♖a6 Resigns

Bledow, Ludwig Erdman

[*July 27 1795–August 6 1846*]

German mathematics schoolmaster who was the strongest player in Berlin about 1840 and who was the leading light in organizing and developing chess in Berlin. He collected around him a group with talent and enthusiasm—this group was called the Berlin Pleiades and included von der Lasa, Bilguer, Horwitz and Hanstein.

Bledow won small matches against several leading players, founded the *Deutsche Schachzeitung* and helped inspire Bilguer and Lasa to produce their famous *Handbuch.*

Blindfold chess

Chess played without looking at the board or pieces. Originally players were *actually* blindfolded, but now they simply sit with their backs to the boards.

The great Arab masters of the 10th and 11th centuries could play 3 or 4

Bled/Zagreb/Belgrade 1959 Candidates Tournament

		1				2				3				4				5				6				7				8				
1	Tal	–	–	–	–	0	0	1	0	½	½	½	½	0	1	½	1	1	1	1	1	1	½	1	1	1	1	1	½	1	1	1	½	20
2	Keres	1	1	0	1	–	–	–	–	0	½	½	½	1	½	½	0	0	1	0	1	½	½	1	1	1	1	1	0	1	1	1	1	18½
3	Petrosian	½	½	½	½	1	½	½	½	–	–	–	–	½	½	0	½	1	1	½	½	0	½	½	1	1	0	0	½	½	1	1	½	15½
4	Smyslov	1	0	½	0	0	½	½	1	½	½	1	½	–	–	–	–	½	½	1	0	0	½	1	0	½	1	½	1	½	0	1	1	15
5	Fischer	0	0	0	0	1	0	1	0	0	0	½	½	½	½	0	1	–	–	–	–	1	0	½	½	0	1	½	1	½	1	½	1	12½
6	Gligoric	0	½	0	0	½	½	0	0	1	½	½	0	1	½	0	1	0	1	½	½	–	–	–	–	½	½	1	0	½	1	½	½	12½
7	Olafsson	0	0	0	½	0	0	0	1	0	1	1	½	½	0	½	0	1	0	½	0	½	½	0	1	–	–	–	–	0	0	½	1	10
8	Benko	0	0	0	½	0	0	0	0	½	0	0	½	½	1	0	0	½	0	½	0	½	0	½	½	1	1	½	0	–	–	–	–	8

Bled 1961

		1	2	3	4	5	6	7	8	9	10	11	12	13	14	15	16	17	18	19	20	
1	Tal	–	0	½	½	½	½	½	1	1	1	½	1	1	1	1	½	1	1	1	1	14½
2	Fischer	1	–	½	½	1	1	1	½	1	½	½	½	½	1	½	1	½	1	½	½	13½
3	Gligoric	½	½	–	½	0	½	½	1	1	½	½	½	½	1	½	1	1	1	1	1	12½
	Keres	½	½	½	–	½	½	½	½	0	½	½	1	½	1	1	1	1	½	1	1	12½
	Petrosian	½	0	1	½	–	½	½	1	½	½	½	½	1	1	½	0	1	1	1	1	12½
6	Geller	½	0	½	½	½	–	½	1	0	½	½	½	½	0	1	1	½	1	1	½	10½
	Trifunovic	½	0	½	½	½	½	–	½	½	½	½	½	½	½	½	½	½	½	1	1	10½
8	Parma	0	½	½	½	0	0	½	–	½	½	½	½	½	1	1	½	½	½	1	1	10
9	Bisguier	0	0	0	1	½	1	½	½	–	0	½	0	1	0	1	½	½	½	1	1	9½
	Matanovic	0	½	0	½	½	½	½	½	1	–	½	½	0	1	½	½	0	1	1	½	9½
11	Darga	½	½	½	½	½	½	½	½	½	½	–	½	½	0	0	½	½	1	0	1	9
	Donner	0	½	½	0	½	½	½	½	1	½	½	–	1	0	1	½	½	0	0	1	9
	Najdorf	0	½	½	½	0	½	½	½	0	1	½	0	–	1	0	½	½	1	1	½	9
14	Olafsson	0	0	½	0	0	1	½	0	1	0	1	1	0	–	½	1	½	½	½	½	8½
15	Ivkov	0	½	0	0	½	0	½	0	0	½	1	0	1	½	–	1	1	½	½	½	8
	Portisch	½	0	½	0	1	0	½	½	½	½	½	½	½	0	0	–	½	½	½	½	8
17	Pachman	0	½	0	0	0	½	0	½	½	1	½	½	½	½	0	½	–	½	½	½	7
18	Bertok	0	0	0	½	0	0	½	½	½	0	0	1	0	½	½	½	½	–	½	1	6½
19	Germek	0	½	0	0	0	0	0	0	0	0	1	1	0	½	½	½	½	½	–	½	5½
20	Udovcic	0	½	0	0	0	½	0	0	0	½	0	0	½	½	½	0	½	0	½	–	4

games blindfold simultaneously. This practice fell into disuse until Philidor revived it in 1744 when he played 2 blindfold games simultaneously. Later he regularly played 3.

Alekhine played 26 at New York in 1924. Koltanowski played 34 at Edinburgh in 1937, scoring + 24 = 10. Najdorf played 40 in 1943 and 45 at Sao Paulo in 1947. Janos Flesch played 52 at Budapest in 1960, scoring + 31 = 18 − 3. But perhaps the most impressive such display was done by Pillsbury at Hanover 1902. On his free day he played 21 opponents, all of whom were playing in the Hauptturnier and therefore almost masters. They included Bernstein, Kagan, Exner, Englund and Fahrni. Pillsbury scored + 3 = 11 − 7, a remarkable achievement.

Blitz

Chess played at an extremely rapid pace. Each player is allowed 5 minutes (sometimes 7) for the entire game. It is surprising how many moves can be squeezed in, in a matter of seconds.

Blitz is a favourite pastime of tournament players during their free time. It seems to relieve some tension as well as giving practice and pleasure.

Blockade

A position where one side is permanently prevented from bringing his pieces into play without loss. In Feigin–Monticelli, Munich 1936, the position opposite was reached after 16 ♗d6:

White threatens to win the knight with a4 and a5 and Black's position is in a blockade. The game continued 16 ... a5 17 ♗c7 ♖a6 18 c5 ♘d5 19 ♗xa6 ♘xc7 20 ♗c4 b6 21 cb ♘a8 22 0-0-0 ♘xb6 23 ♖d6 Resigns

Blocked pawn

See Pawn Structure

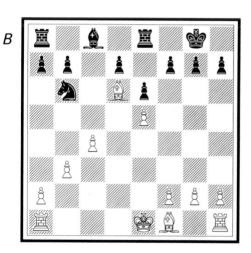

B

Blumenfeld counter-gambit

1 d4 ♘f6 2 c4 e6 3 ♘f3 c5 4 d5 b5

The intention is to destroy White's centre at the cost of a pawn. It enjoyed a considerable reputation in the 1920s after its celebrated international debut, Tarrasch–Alekhine, Pistyan 1922. However, modern theory considers the line

23

dubious if White declines the offer with 5 ♗g5.

Blunder

A bad move that overlooks a piece or a mate and either loses the game or at least puts it in jeopardy.

Board games

Present day chess goes back about 500 years and earlier versions of chess (chaturanga) go back about 1400 years and it is possible that the earliest versions go back 5000 years (*see* History of Chess).

See *History of Board Games other than Chess* by Murray (1952), *The Board Game Book* by R. C. Bell (1979).

Bobotsov, Milko Georgiev

[*October 30 1931– *]
First Bulgarian GM (1961) whose best result by far was equal 2nd in the strong (XIII) Alekhine Memorial, Moscow 1967. He played on 8 Bulgarian Olympiad teams, but in 1972 he suffered a stroke, since when he has played infrequently.

Boden, Samuel Standidge

[*April 4 1826–January 13 1882*]
British player, considered by Morphy to have been his strongest English opponent (Staunton having retired). Boden's record against Morphy in casual games was (+ 1 = 4 − 6).

Boden won the London Provincial tournament 1851, was 2nd at both Manchester 1857 and Bristol 1861 and beat Owen in a match (1858) + 7 = 2 − 2.

He was chess editor of *The Field* (1858–73) and his name is linked with the Boden–Kieseritzky Gambit: 1 e4 e5 2 ♗c4 ♘f6 3 ♘f3 ♘xe4 4 ♘c3 ♘xc3 5 dc f6.

Bönsch, Uwe [*October 15 1958– *]

East German GM (1986) who won or was equal 1st at Leipzig 86 (VIII), Budapest 1986 Open, Leipzig 1986 (IX), Portoroz 1987 (IX) and Polanica Zdroj 1987 (IX).

Bogart, Humphrey [*1900–1957*]

Actor and chess enthusiast whose scene in the famous movie Casablanca (1943) where he studies a chess position while talking to Peter Lorre, was probably filmed that way because of Bogart's passion for the royal game.

Bogo-Indian Defence

1 d4 ♘f6 2 c4 e6 3 ♘f3 ♗b4 + .

A solid alternative to the Queen's Indian Defence, first played by Bogoljubow in 1920. It is technically not an Indian Defence but it often transposes into a Nimzo–Indian or a Queen's Indian.

Bogoljubow, Efim Dmitrievich

[*April 14 1889–June 18 1952*]
Russian (Ukranian) student of theology and GM (1951) who belonged to the world top ten during the 1920s. He had only modest results up to 1914, but when he was interned following the Mannheim tournament he gained experience and success in the eight tournaments played among the interned masters (1915).

He was 1st at Pistyan (1922), equal 1st at Carlsbad (1923) and he peaked with a fine win at Moscow 1925 (XI) ahead of Lasker and Capablanca. He also won the USSR Championships of 1924 and 1925. There was also a 1st at Bad Kissingen 1928, but in between these highs were several indifferent results.

He played two World Championship matches against Alekhine. In 1929 he lost + 5 = 9 − 11 and in 1934 he lost + 3 = 15 − 8.

His play was marked by boundless energy, supreme optimism and an ability to combine manoeuvres on both sides of the board. Such talents worked well against average masters, but his life scores against the elite were not impressive. He scored + 1 = 1 − 4 against Lasker, + 0 = 2 − 5 against Capablanca, + 1 = 5 − 5 against Vidmar. Against Alekhine he scored + 13 = 37 − 35 and this is quite respectable compared to the other results. He also lost + 10 = 22 − 11 against Euwe and + 12 = 10 − 13 against Rubinstein.

He became a German citizen in 1927, won the German championship in 1925, 1931, 1933 and 1949, and continued an active chess career until his death. Part of his name has become attached to the Bogo-Indian Defence: 1 d4 ♘f6 2 c4 e6 3 ♘f3 ♗b4 + .

His writings are meagre and unfortunately uninspired. Books about him: *Grossmeister Bogoljubow* by A. Brinckmann (1953); *The Chess Career of Bogoljubow*, 2 vols., by J. Spence (1971–5).

Bogoljubow–Mieses

Baden–Baden 1925
1 d4 f5 2 g3 ♘f6 3 ♗g2 e6 4 ♘f3 d5 5 0-0 ♗d6 6 c4 c6 7 ♘c3 ♘bd7 8 ♕c2 ♘e4 9 ♔h1 ♕f6 10 ♗f4 ♗xf4 11 gf ♕h6 12 e3 ♘df6 13 ♘e5 ♘d7 14 ♖g1 ♘xe5 15 de ♘xc3 16 bc ♗d7 17 ♖ad1 b5 18 ♕b2 0-0 19 ♕a3 ♖fd8 20 cb cb 21 ♕a6 ♕h5

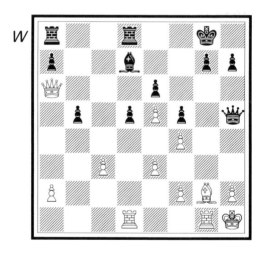

22 ♗xd5 ed 23 ♖xg7+ ♔xg7 24 ♕f6+ ♔g8 25 ♖g1+ ♕g4 26 ♖xg4+ fg 27 f5 ♖dc8 28 e6 ♗c6 29 ♕f7+ ♔h8 30 f6 ♖g8 31 ♕c7 ♖ac8 32 ♕e5 d4+ 33 ♔g1 ♗d5 34 f7+ ♖g7 35 ♕xd5 Resigns

Bohatirchuk, Feodor Parfenovich

[*November 26 1892–September 4 1984*] Russian of GM strength who was a professor of radiological anatomy and who had a successful chess career in the USSR. He won the Kiev title in 1910 ahead of Bogoljubow, was equal 3rd in the USSR Championships of 1912, 1923, 1924, 1931 and 1934 and was equal 1st with Romanovsky in the 1927 Championship. He played in Moscow 1925 and 1935 and overall had a plus score against Botvinnik (his former pupil).

He had difficulties with the authorities because they wanted him to play more often than he wanted to play and in 1945 he left the USSR with the retreating Germans. After playing for a short time in Germany, he settled in Canada (1948) as a professor in Ottawa. He was 3rd in the 1951 Canadian championship and played on Canada's 1954 Olympiad team. He was made an IM (1954). He was an imposing figure with a large head and penetrating eyes.

Boi, Paolo   [1528–98]

Sixteenth-century Sicilian master, born in Syracuse and hence sometimes known as 'il Siracusano'.

He was a dashing combinative player, known for his quick sight of the board and for his ability to play three blindfold games simultaneously, which astonished his contemporaries.

Itinerant throughout his life, he prospered on the patronage of the nobility. Pope Pius V is said to have offered him a rich benefice if he would consent to taking holy orders. In 1575 Boi visited Spain and defeated the two leading Spanish players, Ruy Lopez and Ceron, as had his countryman Leonardo da Cutri a few months earlier. For this success King Philip II rewarded Boi with official appointments in Sicily producing an annual income of 500 crowns and gave him a letter of introduction to his brother, Don John of Austria.

While returning to Italy, Boi was allegedly captured by Algerian pirates, sold as a slave, and earned his freedom by making (for his master) a fortune at chess. His subsequent travels took him to Genoa, Milan, Venice and even as far as Hungary, where he played games against Turks while mounted on horseback. He died in Naples under suspicious circumstances, possibly as a result of poison.

Bolbochan, Julio   [*March 20 1920– *]

Argentine GM (1977) who played on 7 Argentine Olympiad teams during 1950–70 and won the Argentine Championship in 1946 and 1948. His best results were at Mar del Plata where he was equal 1st in 1951, 1952 and 1956. He made it into three interzonals but ill health interfered with his participation (1952 and 1967) and dampened his achievement (1962). He surpassed his brother Jacobo (1906–84) who was an IM (1965).

Boleslavsky, Isaak Yefremovich

[*June 9 1919–February 15 1977*] USSR GM (1950) who was one of the all time greats of the chess world, just a step behind giants like Keres, Tal and Alekhine. He played in 11 USSR Championships from 1940–61 and came 2nd to Botvinnik in 1945 and 2nd to Keres in 1947. In some 200 games in these championships, he scored over 58%. His best result was equal 1st with Bronstein in the 1950 Candidates (XVI). He did lose the play-off match to Bronstein but he ranked third in the world at that time. He played on the 1952 USSR Olympiad team and was again a Candidate in 1953.

He was a round teddy bear of a man, with a gentle and sweet disposition. He lacked the killer instinct and as his gentleness matured, his results (after 1952) fell off—although he had a good 2nd at Moscow 1966. He became a teacher and trainer, and much of Petro-

Isaak Boleslavsky enjoying a relaxed moment away from the chessboard.

sian's success in becoming World Champion in 1963 was due to Boleslavsky.

He developed the King's Indian Defence and proved that it was a viable system and he established that ... e5 in the Sicilian Defence was playable. His insights and judgements were of the highest class. In the Curacao Candidates of 1962, when Mrs Petrosian or Mrs Geller really wanted to know how their husbands' games were going, they ignored the opinions of Tal and Keres and went to 'Isaak' to find out the truth. Isaak was in fact, always right.

His life score against Botvinnik ($+0=5-6$) was bad but he did well against Smyslov ($+5=13-3$), Korchnoi ($+4=5-1$) and Flohr ($+3=6-0$). And he scored $+1=8-1$ against Petrosian and $+3=4-3$ against Geller.

Major work: *Izbrannye Partii* (1957)

See *Grossmeister Boleslavsky* by A. S. Suetin, 1981.

Boleslavsky–Dzhindzhihashvili
USSR 1967

1 d4 d5 2 c4 dc 3 ♘f3 ♘f6 4 e3 e6 5 ♗xc4 c5 6 0-0 a6 7 ♘c3 b5 8 ♗b3 ♗b7 9 ♕e2 ♘bd7 10 ♖d1 ♕b8 11 d5

ed 12 ♘xd5 ♘xd5 13 ♗xd5 ♗xd5 14 ♖xd5 ♕b7 15 e4 ♗e7 16 ♗g5 ♘b6 17 ♖ad1 h6 18 ♗xe7 ♘xd5 19 ♗xc5 ♘e7 20 ♘e5 ♖c8 21 ♖d7 ♖c7

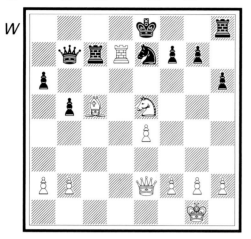

22 ♖d8＋! ♔xd8 23 ♘xf7＋ ♔d7 24 ♕g4＋ ♔c6 25 ♕e6＋ Resigns

Bondarevsky, Igor Zakharovich

[*May 12 1913–June 14 1979*] USSR GM (1950) who played in 9 USSR Championships during 1937–63, and came equal 1st with Lilienthal in 1940, ahead of Smyslov, Keres and Botvinnik. He qualified for the 1950 Candidates, but illness prevented him from playing.

He was an economist and a refined intellectual, and he switched from playing to teaching and training. He worked with Spassky and acted as Spassky's second during his 1966 and 1969 world title matches against Petrosian.

Bondarevsky contributed to opening theory, especially in the French Defence and the Queen's Gambit Declined.

Major work: *Combinations in the Middle Game* (1960).

Böök, Eero Einar [*February 9 1910–*]

Finnish engineer and IM (1950) who became an honourary GM in 1984. He won the Finnish Championship five times during 1930–63, and played on six Finnish Olympiad teams from 1935–60. He qualified for the 1948 interzonal.

Botvinnik, Mikhail Moiseyevich

[*August 17 1911–*] Chess champion of the world 1948–57, 1958–60, 1961–63, and one of the 5 or 6 greatest players that ever lived. Keene and Divinsky rank him as the fourth greatest player of all time.

Botvinnik was born near St Petersburg, learnt chess at the age of 12 and became the first Soviet (as distinct from Russian) master to achieve world pre-eminence. In 1931 he graduated in electrical engineering from the Leningrad Polytechnic and in the same year won the 7th USSR Championship. He played in 11 USSR Championships from 1927–55 and won the title 6 times (1931, 1933, 1939, 1944, 1945 and 1952). In 180 games in these championships he scored over 70%. Only Alekhine (1920) and Bogoljubow (1924 and 1925) achieved a higher percentage and only Tal equalled his 6 victories. Botvinnik also won the so-called Absolute Championship in 1941.

He began to play internationally in the 1930s. He drew (+2=6−2) a match with Flohr in 1933 and in 1934 won at Leningrad ahead of Euwe. After a relative failure on his first venture abroad—Hastings 1934/5, where he finished only equal 5th—a string of successes soon established him as a Grandmaster of world class: equal 1st with Flohr ahead of Lasker and Capablanca at Moscow 1935, 2nd behind Capablanca at Moscow 1936 and equal 1st with Capablanca at Nottingham 1936.

In the important AVRO 1938 tournament Botvinnik was only 3rd behind Keres and Fine. Nevertheless, by his victories in individual games over Alekhine and Capablanca, he strengthened his claim to be a world title candidate.

During the 1940s Botvinnik was in a class by himself. He won 7 strong tournaments in a row: the Absolute Championship of the USSR in 1941 ahead of Keres, Smyslov and Boleslavsky, Sver-dlovsk 1943, 13th USSR Championship 1944, 14th USSR Championship 1945, the first major post-war tournament—Groningen 1946, ahead of Euwe and Smyslov, the Chigorin Memorial at Moscow 1947 and the World Championship at Moscow/The Hague 1948—the strongest tournament ever held.

This last tournament was organized by FIDE when the World Championship was left vacant by Alekhine's death in 1946. The contenders were Botvinnik, Smyslov, Keres, Reshevsky and Euwe (Fine declined his invitation). Botvinnik finished as a clear winner, 3 points ahead of Smyslov, his nearest rival.

Winning the World Championship seemed, temporarily, to sate Botvinnik's chess ambitions. He returned to his engineering studies and obtained a doctorate in 1951. And now began a 12-year period when Botvinnik was, as he put it, a first among equals, rather than a clear dominant force. He fought to keep his world crown against the challenges of Bronstein, Smyslov, Tal and Petrosian.

In 1951 he retained his crown by drawing (+5=15−5) the title match with Bronstein. In 1954 he did the same, drawing (+7=10−7) with Smyslov. He had a good equal 1st with Smyslov at the 1956 Alekhine Memorial in Moscow. Finally in 1957 he was dethroned, losing +3=13−6 to Smyslov. His play may then have been affected by his wife's illness for in the following year he won the return match +7=11−5.

This drama was repeated three years later when he lost +2=13−6 to Tal in 1960 and regained the title in 1961 by winning +10=6−5. Finally in 1963 he lost +2=15−5 to Petrosian. This time the loss was permanent, for by a new FIDE ruling Botvinnik was no longer entitled to a return encounter and he felt disinclined to attempt to qualify through the 1965 Candidates matches.

Mikhail Botvinnik, the only man to win the World Championship three times.

After 1963 Botvinnik continued to obtain good results in Soviet team events and tournaments. Young rising stars always cherished the dream of winning a game from the grand old man. He won at Hastings 1966/7, was equal 2nd at Palma 1967, 2nd at Monte Carlo 1968 and equal 1st at Hoogoven 1969. In 1970 he announced his retirement from active play.

In life scores he edged out Lasker ($+1=3-0$), Alekhine ($+1=2-0$), Smyslov ($+26=48-21$), Bronstein ($+7=16-6$), and Spassky ($+1=6-0$). He equalled Capablanca ($+1=5-1$), Euwe ($+2=8-2$), Tal ($+12=20-12$), Korchnoi ($+1=2-1$) and Fischer ($=1$). Against his own generation he beat Keres ($+8=9-3$), Reshevsky ($+5=7-2$), Flohr ($+5=22-2$) and Boleslavsky ($+6=5-0$). He did lose to Petrosian ($+3=18-6$), Geller, ($+1=5-4$) and Fine ($+0=2-1$). He played on 6 USSR Olympiad teams from 1954–64, and scored $+39=31-3$ for almost 75%.

During 1934–70 he played many matches and 31 hard tournaments where he faced the cream of the Grandmasters: Lasker, Capablanca and Alekhine in his youth, Tal, Spassky and Fischer in his late period. His opposition in general was much stronger than that faced by Lasker, Capablanca or Alekhine.

Part of the secret of Botvinnik's genius was his immense capacity for hard work. Every game he played was subjected afterwards to intensive analysis and he proved to be his own most severe critic, without a trace of self-deception. He was the first to suggest that tournament preparation should include physical as well as mental exercises. He disliked tobacco and, feeling that he was sometimes distracted by opponents who smoked, acquired immunity by requesting his trainer, Ragozin, to smoke constantly during training games. But the other part of his secret was a great talent which saw deeply and quickly into the heart of a position. Even as late as 1970 (in Leiden), when analysing with Euwe and Spassky, he astonished them with his profundity.

Being the top chess star of the USSR during the 1930s, 40s and 50s was no easy matter, because so much depended on the political masters of Soviet chess. To accommodate himself to this non-chess dimension, Botvinnik developed a toughness that was not always appreciated by his chess colleagues and he has always had more than his share of enemies. After his equal 1st at Nottingham 1936, he sent a curious victory telegram printed in Pravda two days after the event ended. Botvinnik cabled his thanks to the whole nation, the party and to Stalin, the 'beloved teacher and leader', for their support. (Some of this was written for Botvinnik by Krylenko!).

His relationship with Paul Keres is a mystery—some say he helped get Keres out of jail in 1940 or '41, and others say

27

he helped put Keres into jail. Certainly Keres was his chief rival and it is curious that after 1940, Keres played so weakly whenever he faced Botvinnik.

Botvinnik took his engineering work seriously and during the war years worked at power plants in the Urals and in the Molotov High Tension Lab. Since he retired he has worked on computer chess programs and developed chess schools for young talent like Karpov and Kasparov.

He played the endgame very well and specialized in a few openings, like the Winawer French and the Rubinstein Nimzo-Indian. But his real forte was the middlegame, and the more complicated the better.

Euwe wrote (1940):
Botvinnik almost makes you feel that difficulty attracts him and stimulates him to the full unfolding of his powers. Most players feel uncomfortable in difficult positions, but Botvinnik seems to enjoy them.

Where dangers threaten from every side and the smallest slackening of attention might be fatal; in a position which requires a nerve of steel and intense concentration—Botvinnik is in his element. His style is anything but defensive; it is a mistake to assume that he accepts difficult positions so as to hold on to some small advantage as did Steinitz so often. On the contrary, his thoughts are always of attack.

Botvinnik was an excellent annotator and his books are highly thought of.

Major works: *Championship Chess* (1947), *One Hundred Selected Games* (1951), *Selected Games 1967–1970* (1981), *Half a Century of Chess* (1984).

See *Botvinnik the Invincible* by F. Reinfeld (1946), *Botvinnik's Best Games 1947–1970* by B. Cafferty (1972), *Shakhmatnoye Tvorchestvo Botvinnika* (3 vols.) by V. D. Baturinsky (1965–8).

Botvinnik–Capablanca

Avro 1938

1 d4 ♘f6 2 c4 e6 3 ♘c3 ♗b4 4 e3 d5 5 a3 ♗xc3+ 6 bc c5 7 cd ed 8 ♗d3 0-0 9 ♘e2 b6 10 0-0 ♗a6 11 ♗xa6 ♘xa6 12 ♗b2 ♕d7 13 a4 ♖fe8 14 ♕d3 c4 15 ♕c2 ♘b8 16 ♖ae1 ♘c6 17 ♘g3 ♘a5 18 f3 ♘b3 19 e4 ♕xa4 20 e5 ♘d7 21 ♕f2 g6 22 f4 f5 23 exf6 ♘xf6 24 f5 ♖xe1 25 ♖xe1 ♖e8 26 ♖e6 ♖xe6 27 fe ♔g7 28 ♕f4 ♕e8 29 ♕e5 ♕e7

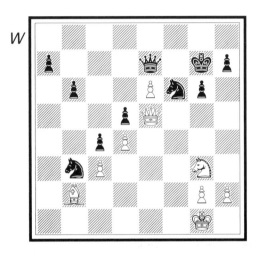

30 ♗a3! ♕xa3 31 ♘h5+ gh 32 ♕g5+ ♔f8 33 ♕xf6+ ♔g8 34 e7 ♕c1+ 35 ♔f2 ♕c2+ 36 ♔g3 ♕d3+ 37 ♔h4 ♕e4+ 38 ♔xh5 ♕e2+ 39 ♔h4 ♕e4+ 40 g4 ♕e1+ 41 ♔h5 Resigns

Bouwmeester, Hans

[September 16 1929–]
Dutch IM (1954), author, mathematics teacher and pianist who plays an important part in Dutch chess life. He was appointed the first official coach of the Royal Dutch Chess Federation. He was editor of *Losbladige Schaakberichten* from 1956–68, played on 7 Dutch Olympiad teams from 1956–70 and was non-playing captain in 1972. His publications include a took on Tal, a book on efficient chess training and several written from the pedagogic point of view.

Breakthrough

A combination usually involving a sacrifice of material, which leads to the penetration of an apparently well defended position. This is often the culmination of superior strategy.

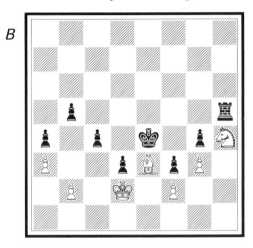

In Lund–Nimzowitsch, Kristiania 1921, Black made a breakthrough with 1 ... b4 2 ab ♖xh4 3 gh g3 4 fg c3+ 5 bc a3 6 Resigns

Brentano's Chess Monthly

An opulently produced magazine published in New York for only 16 months during 1881–2. Its predecessor was a column in *Brentano's Monthly*, a literary magazine, the style of which was retained in its chess counterpart.

Brevity [miniature]

A short (not more than 20 or so moves) but interesting (not usually drawn) game. The most celebrated example is Morphy–Duke of Brunswick and Count Isouard, played in 1858 in a box at the Paris Opera during a performance of the Barber of Seville: 1 e4 e5 2 ♘f3 d6 3 d4 ♗g4 4 de ♗xf3 5 ♕xf3 de 6 ♗c4 ♘f6 7 ♕b3 ♕e7 8 ♘c3 c6 9 ♗g5 b5 10 ♘xb5 cb 11 ♗xb5+ ♘bd7 12 0-0-0 ♖d8 13 ♖xd7 ♖xd7 14 ♖d1 ♕e6 15 ♗xd7+ ♘xd7 16 ♕b8+ ♘xb8 17 ♖d8 mate.

See *200 Miniature Games of Chess* by

J. DuMont (1941) *1000 Best Short Games of Chess* by I. Chernev (1955)

Breyer, Gyula (Julius)

[*April 3 1894–November 10 1921*] Hungarian of GM strength who was a pioneering leader of the hypermoderns. He won the Hungarian championship in 1912 and became a major force by winning the strong tournament in Berlin 1920, ahead of Bogoljubow, Tartakower, Réti, Maroczy, Mieses, Tarrasch, Sämisch, Leonhardt and Spielmann. The fruits of his success were never to materialize, for Breyer died one year later, without being able to participate in another event of a similar calibre; truly a lost talent.

For most of his brief life Breyer was fascinated by intellectual problems of all kinds, which possibly explains his interest in chess. It was indeed in the sphere of ideas that Breyer left his greatest mark and he was considered a leading member of the 'Hypermodern School' (which included Nimzowitsch and Breyer's close friend Réti) which challenged the fixed notions of chess strategy advocated by classical masters such as Tarrasch, Teichman and Rubinstein. It was Breyer who said: 'after the first move 1 e4 white's game is in the last throes'.

Much of Breyer's games leave a mysterious, paradoxical impression—masterpieces imbued with rich and strange hues which make one wonder what he could have achieved had he survived his twenty-seventh year.

He did set a new blindfold record in 1921 when he played 25 games simultaneously.

Breyer also made important contributions to opening theory. The most popular closed variation of the modern Ruy Lopez is named after him, although nobody is very sure when (1911?) or where he advocated Black's paradoxical ninth move: 1 e4 e5 2 ♘f3 ♘c6 3 ♗b5 a6 4 ♗a4 ♘f6 5 0-0 b5 6 ♗b3 ♗b7 7 ♖e1 d6 8 c3 0-0 9 h3 ♘b8. The idea of Black's knight retreat is to redeploy this knight to d7, bolstering his pawn on e5. For detailed analysis of the line, see *Ruy Lopez: Breyer System* by L. S. Blackstock (1976).

Brilliancy Prize

A prize given in addition to the regular prize fund, to the winner of the game that contains the most brilliant combination in the tournament or match. This is not quite the same as a best game prize for best overall strategy. Such prizes are often given by a private chess enthusiast, like Baron Rothschild, Prince Dadien of Mingrelia or Isaac Turover, who is not connected with the organizers of the match or tournament.

Such prizes began in New York 1876 (Bird 1 Mason 0) and Steinitz won the first such match prize for his 8th game win over Chigorin in 1889.

Players have not always been pleased with the judges' decisions. Tarrasch (St Petersburg 1914) was so angry, he simply named the judges (Burn, Pollner and Znosko-Borovsky) and assumed the public would judge them. Nimzowitsch (New York 1927) wrote: 'This move contains an original point which the prize judges probably failed to appreciate; otherwise they would have awarded this game (Nimsowitsch's second win over Marshall, move 23) the first beauty prize rather than the third'.

See *Les Prix de Beauté aux Echecs* by F. Le Lionnaires (1951).

Brinckmann, Alfred

[*January 3 1891–May 30 1967*] German IM (1953) who won at Berlin 1927, ahead of Bogoljubow and Nimzowitsch, but who is best known as an author. He was a brilliant stylist and he introduced important literary and philosophical subjects into his books. He wrote the tournament books of Bad Niendorf 1927, Rogaska Slatina 1929 and Aachen 1934. His major works are *Schachmeister, wie sie Kampfen und Siegen* (1932), *Der Angriff in der Schachpartie* 1935, *Grossmeister Bogoljubow* (1953), *S. Tarrasch Lehrmeister der Schachwelt* (1963), *Streifzuge und Irrtumer auf 64 Feldern* (1967).

British Chess Magazine

Monthly magazine which began as the *Huddersfield College Magazine* in October 1872. In 1881 it became the *British Chess Magazine* and has been the magazine of record in British chess for 110 years. It has had only 8 editors: Watkinson, Green, Brown, Griffith, Golombek, Du Mont, Reilly and Cafferty.

Bronstein, David Ionovich

[*February 19 1924–*] USSR GM (1950) who is one of the all-time greats of the chess world, just a step behind giants like Keres and Tal. He played in 20 USSR Championships

David Bronstein, one of the great artists of the chessboard, who shares with Schlechter the distinction of tying his only World Championship match and thus missing the title by the narrowest possible margin.

during 1944–75 and was equal 1st in both 1948 and 1949. In some 375 games in these championships, he scored over 56%. He reached his peak when he was equal 1st in the 1950 Candidates, won the play-off (+ 3 = 9 − 2) with Boleslavsky and went on to draw the 1951 world title match with Botvinnik (+ 5 = 14 − 5).Bronstein thus shares with Schlechter the unenviable distinction of having come as close as possible to the World Championship without actually winning it.

He was equal 2nd in the 1953 Candidates and equal 3rd in the 1956 Candidates. Then his star waned and though he won many tournaments, he never got near the world title again. He was equal 1st at Hastings 1975/76, 1st at Budapest 1977 and did well even in 1987 with an equal 2nd at Pancevo.

He is sociable, friendly and interested in a wide range of topics from cybernetics to the history of the cinema. He is an intellectual eccentric. This manifests itself in his games, where he produces weird but wonderful moves. And it also reveals itself in his private life where 'he is extremely vulnerable. A breaking of ethics puts him in a state of shock and he cannot bear rudeness'. (Vainstein). Botvinnik describes Bronstein as: '... colourful ... A brilliant master of attack and capable of taking the most original decisions'.

In life scores he did well against Reshevsky (+ 3 = 1 − 0), Keres (+ 5 = 18 − 4), Boleslavsky (+ 5 = 21 − 3) and Korchnoi (+ 6 = 8 − 5). He did less well with Botvinnik (+ 6 = 16 − 7), Smyslov (+ 4 = 22 − 7), Petrosian (+ 1 = 19 − 3), Tal (+ 4 = 17 − 7) and Spassky (+ 0 = 19 − 4). He had 2 draws with Fischer.

Bronstein played on 4 USSR Olympiad teams during 1952–8 and scored + 30 = 18 and only 1 loss. He played a large role with Boleslavsky in establishing the soundness of the King Indian Defence.

Bronstein's book of the Zurich 1953 Candidates is quite different from Alekhine's New York 1924 book, but they stand out together as the best tournament books written. Most of us believe that authors annotate the moves of the games. Bronstein writes that 'the moves played in each game serve to annotate the author's ideas.'

Major works: *Zurich 1953* (1954), *200 Open Games* (1970).

See *David Bronstein* by Roman Toran (1962), *David Bronstein—Chess Improviser* By B. S. Vainstein (1976).

Bronstein–Ljubojevic
Petropolis Interzonal 1973

1 e4 ♘f6 2 e5 ♘d5 3 d4 d6 4 c4 ♘b6 5 f4 de 6 fe c5 7 d5 e6 8 ♘c3 ed 9 cd c4 10 ♘f3 ♗g4 11 ♕d4 ♗xf3 12 gf ♗b4 13 ♗xc4 0-0 14 ♖g1 g6 15 ♗g5 ♕c7 16 ♗b3 ♗c5 17 ♕f4 ♗xg1

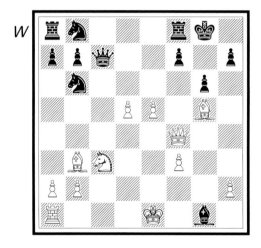

18 d6 ♕c8 19 ♔e2 ♗c5 20 ♘e4 ♘8d7 21 ♖c1 ♕c6 22 ♖xc5 ♘xc5 23 ♘f6+ ♔h8 24 ♕h4 ♕b5+ 25 ♔e3 h5 26 ♘xh5 ♕xb3+ 27 ab ♘d5+ 28 ♔d4 ♘e6+ 29 ♔xd5 ♘xg5 30 ♘f6+ ♔g7 31 ♕xg5 ♖fd8 32 e6 fe+ 33 ♔xe6 ♖f8 34 d7 a5 35 ♘g4 ♖a6+ 36 ♔e5 ♖f5+ 37 ♕xf5 gf 38 d8 (♕) fg 39 ♕d7+ ♔h6 40 ♕xb7 ♖g6 41 f4 Resigns

Tal–Bronstein
32nd USSR Championship 1964

1 e4 e6 2 d4 d5 3 ♘c3 ♗b4 4 e5 ♘e7 5 a3 ♗xc3+ 6 bc c5 7 ♕g4 cd 8 ♗d3 ♕a5 9 ♘e2 ♘g6 10 h4 ♘c6 11 h5 ♘cxe5 12 ♕xd4 ♘xd3+ 13 cd e5 14 ♕e3 d4 15 ♕g3 ♘e7 16 ♕xg7 ♖g8 17 ♕f6 dc 18 0-0 ♕c7 19 d4 ♗g4 20 f3 ♘d5 21 ♕h4 ♗e6 22 de ♕xe5 23 ♖e1 ♖c8 24 ♖b1 b6 25 ♖b5 a6 26 ♖b3 ♕g7 27 ♕f2 ♖c4 28 h6 ♕f6

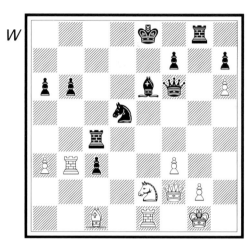

29 ♘xc3 ♘xc3 30 ♖xb6 ♕d8 31 ♖xa6 ♖g6 32 ♕b2 ♔e7 33 ♖a7+ ♔f6 34 ♖e4 ♕d1+ 35 ♔h2 ♖xe4 36 ♕xc3+ ♖e5 37 ♗f4 ♕e2 38 ♗xe5+ ♕xe5+ 39 ♕xe5+ ♔xe5 40 ♖a5+ ♔d4 41 ♖h5 ♗d5 42 ♔h3 f5 43 Resigns

Browne, Walter Shawn
[January 10 1949]
US GM (1970) who was born in Australia, came to the US as a child, spent 1968–73 back in Australia and then settled in the US. He won or was equal 1st in 6 US Championships during 1974–83. He threatened to be a major force by winning at Venice 1971, Wijk aan Zee 1974 and Reykjavik 1978, and coming equal 1st at Wijk aan Zee 1980, Buenos Aires 1980, Surakarta 1982, Gjovik 1983 and Naestved 1985 (XIII), but he never made it to the Candidates level.

He won the Australian Championship (1968), the German title (1975), played on 2 Australian Olympiad teams (1970 and 1972) and 4 US Olympiad teams during 1974–84.

He is accomplished at both poker and backgammon. During his youth he had problems with tournament etiquette and behaviour but these began to disappear in the late 1970s.

Brussels

The beautiful capital of Belgium that began having strong tournaments in April 1986, sponsored by SWIFT (Society for Worldwide Interbank Financial Telecommunication). Karpov (9) won this Category XIII event ahead of Korchnoi (7). Belgium had not had such a fine tournament since Ostend 1907, but even better things were to come.

The OHRA firm staged a Category XVI event in December 1986 where Kasparov was in awesome form and played some wonderful games, though he was lucky against Korchnoi. Short and Portisch both had disastrous second halves.

Kasparov–Short

1 d4 e6 2 ♘f3 ♘f6 3 c4 d5 4 ♘c3 ♗e7 5 ♗g5 h6 6 ♗xf6 ♗xf6 7 e3 0-0 8 ♖c1 c6 9 ♗d3 ♘d7 10 0-0 dc 11 ♗xc4 e5 12 h3 ed 13 ed ♘b6 14 ♗b3 ♗f5 15 ♖e1 ♗g5 16 ♖a1 ♘d7 17 d5 ♖c8 18 ♘d4 ♗g6 19 ♘e6! fe 20 de ♔h7 21 ♕xd7 ♕b6 22 e7 ♖fe8

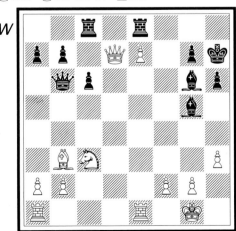

23 ♕g4! ♕c5 24 ♘e4 ♕xe7 25 ♗c2 ♖f8 26 g3 ♕d8 27 ♖ad1 ♕a5 28 h4 ♗e7 29 ♘c3 ♗xc2 30 ♖xe7 ♗g8 31 ♖dd7 ♗f5 32 ♖xg7+ ♔h8 33 ♕d4 Resigns

Kasparov–Korchnoi

1 d4 ♘f6 2 c4 e6 3 ♘f3 ♗b4+ 4 ♗d2 c5 5 g3 ♕b6 6 ♗g2 ♘c6 7 d5 ed 8 cd ♘xd5 9 0-0 ♘de7 10 e4 d6 11 ♗e3 ♕c7 12 a3 ♗a5 13 ♗f4 ♘e5 14 b4 cb 15 ab ♗xb4 16 ♕a4+ ♘7c6 17 ♘d4 a5 18 ♘c3 ♗d7 19 ♘d5 ♕d8 20 ♘f5 0-0 21 ♕d1 ♗c5 22 ♖c1 a4 23 g4 a3 24 g5 a2 25 ♕h5 ♗xf5 26 ef ♗d4 27 ♗xe5 ♘xe5 28 ♗e4 ♖e8 29 ♖c7 a1♕ 30 ♖xa1 ♖xa1+ 31 ♔g2

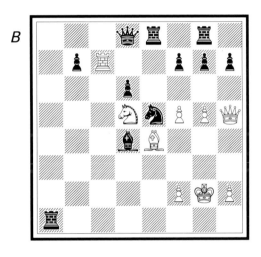

31 ... ♖a2 32 ♖e7 ♖xf2+ 33 ♔g3 ♖xe7? 34 f6 ♘g6 35 ♘xe7+ ♔f8 36 ♕xh7 ♗xf6 37 ♘xg6+ fg 38 ♔xf2 ♕b6+ 39 ♔g2 ♕b2+ 40 ♔h3 ♗xg5 41 ♕xg6 ♕f6 42 ♕xf6+ Drawn

Belyavsky–Tal

1 d4 d6 2 e4 ♘f6 3 ♘c3 g6 4 f4 ♗g7 5 ♘f3 c5 6 ♗b5+ ♗d7 7 e5 ♘g4 8 e6 ♗xb5 9 ef+ ♔xd7 10 ♘xb5 ♕a5+ 11 ♘c3 cd 12 ♘xd4 h5 13 h3 ♘c6 14 ♘de2 ♘h6 15 ♗e3 ♖af8 16 ♕d3

SWIFT staged its second major tournament (XIV) in April 1987. Kasparov (8½) and Ljubojevic (8½) were equal 1st ahead of Karpov (7) Korchnoi (6½) and Timman (6½). Hübner started with a draw (vs Ljubojevic) but withdrew with a bad flu and was replaced by Tal. At the end of the tournament, a double round robin speed tournament was held. Kasparov won +1=1−0 in a play-off against Timman (they had finished first and second).

In April 1988 SWIFT staged its third major tourament, but this one became the first World Cup tournament, organized by the new Grandmasters Association (see GMA). Vaganian withdrew after 4 rounds when his brother died unexpectedly. Winants represented the host country but did not count in the World Cup calculations.

At first Speelman led (5–2), then Belyavsky (5½−2½) and by round 11 it was Belyavsky and Karpov (7½−3½). Karpov then surged ahead and won convincingly. Salov gave notice of future greatness while Korchnoi began to show his 57 years. Time limit 40 moves in 2 hours.

One of the best games was this, played in Round 9.

Brussels 1986	OHRA				Category XVI					
	1	2		3	4		5		6	
1 Kasparov	–	–	½	½	1	1	1	1	0	1	1	½	7½
2 Korchnoi	½	½	–	–	1	0	½	½	½	1	0	1	5½
3 Hüebner	0	0	0	1	–	–	1	½	0	1	½	1	5
Nunn	0	0	½	½	0	½	–	–	1	1	½	1	5
5 Short	1	0	½	0	1	0	0	0	–	–	½	1	4
6 Portisch	0	½	1	0	½	0	½	0	½	0			3

Nf5 17 Bf2 Rxf7 18 0-0-0 h4 19 Kb1 Rc8 20 Qe4 b6 21 a3 Nd8 22 Rhe1 Qa6 23 Nd4 Qc4 24 Nd5 Bxd4 25 Bxd4

B

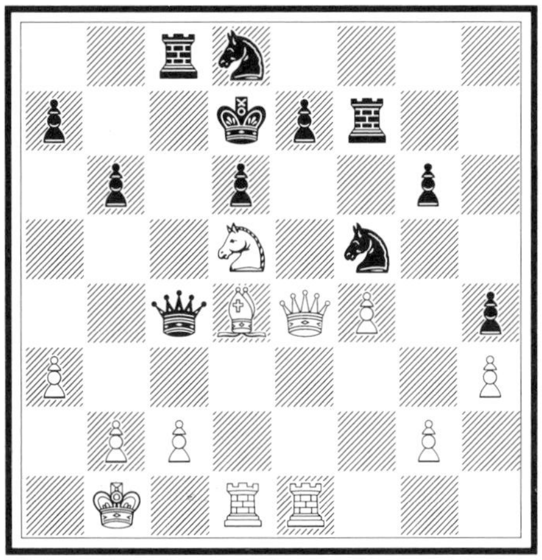

25 ... e6 [Not 25 ... Ng3 26 Qxe7+! Rxe7 27 Rxe7+ Kc6 28 Nb4+ Kb5 29 b3 Qg8 30 Bb2 Rc5 31 c4+ Rxc4 32 bc+ Kxc4 33 Rd4+ Kb5 34 Rd5+] 26 Ne3 Nxe3 27 Rxe3 Rxf4 28 Qxg6 Rf1 29 Ree1 Rxe1 30 Qg7+ Ke8 31 Qh8+ Kd7 32 Qg7+ Ke8 33 Rxe1 Qxc2+ 34 Ka1 Qd2 35 Bc3 Qf2 36 Rd1 Qf7 37 Qh8+ Kd7 38 Qxh4 Nc6 39 g4 e5 40 g5 Rg8 41 Qg3 Qh5 42 Qd3 Rg6 43 h4 Re6 44 Rh1 e4 45 Qa6 d5 46 Rc1 Kd6 47 Be1 Qe8 48 h5 Ke5 49 Qf1 e3 50 Bg3+ Ke4 51 Qf4+ Resigns. After 51 ... Kd3 52 Rd1+ Kc2 53 Qa4 is mate.

Buchholz Score

See Tie-Breaking Systems

Buckle, Henry Thomas

[*November 11 1821–May 29 1862*] Eminent historian and leading mid-nineteenth-century British amateur. Hampered from childhood by persistent ill-health, he nevertheless became a distinguished scholar who spoke seven and read twelve languages. Buckle won what was perhaps the first of all chess tournaments—the Divan tourney of 1849. In match play he defeated Kieseritsky in 1848 (+3=3−2) and Löwenthal in 1851 (+4=1−3). He also won a match against Staunton in 1843 (6 to 1) receiving odds of pawn and move. Steinitz regarded Buckle as a better player than Staunton, and Anderssen said he was the strongest player he had ever met (they had met in 1851 in a series of friendly games—with about equal results).

After 1851 Buckle rarely played in serious competitions, complaining that the game overtaxed his stamina, but remained a devotee of the Divan where he enjoyed casual games at odds. He began his great historical work: *A History of Civilization*, in the 1850s, caught typhoid fever in Damascus and died prematurely. The major part of his work was published posthumously.

Budapest

Beautiful capital of Hungary which held its first major tournament in October 1896. Chigorin (8½) and Charousek (8½) tied for 1st but Chigorin won the play-off. Then came Pillsbury (7½), Janowski (7) and Schlechter (7). Tarrasch (6) was 8th and Maroczy (5) was equal 9th. Lasker, Steinitz and Blackburne were not there.

Brussels 1988 SWIFT World Cup I Category XV

		1	2	3	4	5	6	7	8	9	10	11	12	13	14	15	16	17	
1	Karpov	–	½	1	½	0	½	½	1	1	½	½	1	½	1	1	½	1	11
2	Salov	½	–	1	½	1	½	½	½	½	½	½	½	1	½	½	½	1	10
3	Ljubojevic	0	0	–	1	½	½	1	½	1	½	½	1	1	½	½	½	½	9½
	Nunn	½	½	0	–	1	½	½	½	½	1	½	½	½	½	½	1	1	9½
	Belyavsky	1	0	½	0	–	½	½	½	½	1	½	½	1	1	½	½	1	9½
6	Andersson	½	½	½	½	½	–	½	½	½	½	½	½	1	½	1	½	½	9
	Portisch	½	½	0	½	½	½	–	½	0	½	1	1	½	½	½	1	1	9
8	Speelman	0	½	½	½	½	½	½	–	1	½	½	½	½	½	1	0	1	8½
9	Sokolov	0	½	0	½	½	½	1	0	–	0	1	½	½	½	½	1	1	8
10	Tal	½	½	½	0	0	½	½	½	1	–	½	0	0	1	½	1	½	7½
	Nikolic	½	½	½	½	½	½	0	½	0	½	–	½	½	0	1	½	1	7½
	Timman	0	½	0	½	½	½	0	½	½	1	½	–	½	½	0	1	1	7½
	Seirawan	½	0	0	½	0	0	½	½	½	1	½	½	–	½	1	½	1	7½
14	Negueiras	0	½	½	½	0	½	½	½	½	0	1	½	½	–	0	½	1	7
15	Kerchnoi	0	½	½	½	½	0	½	0	½	½	0	1	0	1	–	0	1	6½
16	Sax	½	½	½	0	½	½	0	1	0	0	½	0	½	½	1	–	0	6
17	Winants	0	0	½	0	0	½	0	0	0	½	0	0	0	0	0	1	–	2½
18	Vaganian	–	–	–	–	–	½	½	–	–	½	–	½	–	–	–	–	–	–

The next strong event was in June 1912—a six-man tournament where the Queen's Gambit Declined was obligatory! Marshall (3) and Schlechter (3) edged out Duras (2½), Maroczy (2½), Vidmar (2) and Teichmann (2).

In 1950 Budapest held the first FIDE Candidates tournament. Fine, Euwe and Bondarevsky declined to come, while Reshevsky could not get a visa from the US State Department. But even without these 4 and of course without the World Champion, Botvinnik, it was a Category XVI event. Boleslavsky seemed a clear winner, because with 2 rounds to go he led Bronstein by a full point. He took short draws with Kotov and Ståhlberg and now Bronstein had to beat Ståhlberg and Keres to tie for 1st. Bronstein was equal to the task. He won his last two games, tied for 1st, beat Boleslavsky in a hard fought play-off match and became the official challenger for Botvinnik's crown.

Perhaps the most exciting game of the tournament was this, from Round 3.

Bronstein–Kotov

1 d4 d5 2 c4 e6 3 ♘c3 c6 4 e4 de 5 ♘xe4 ♗b4+ 6 ♗d2 ♕xd4 7 ♗xb4 ♕xe4+ 8 ♗e2 ♘a6 9 ♗c3 ♘e7 10 ♗xg7 ♖g8 11 ♗c3 ♕xg2? (correct is ... ♘d5 12 cd ♕xg2) 12 ♕d2 ♕xh1 13 0-0-0 ♘d5 14 ♘f3 ♕xd1+ 15 ♗xd1 ♘xc3 16 ♕xc3 ♔e7 17 ♘e5 ♗d7

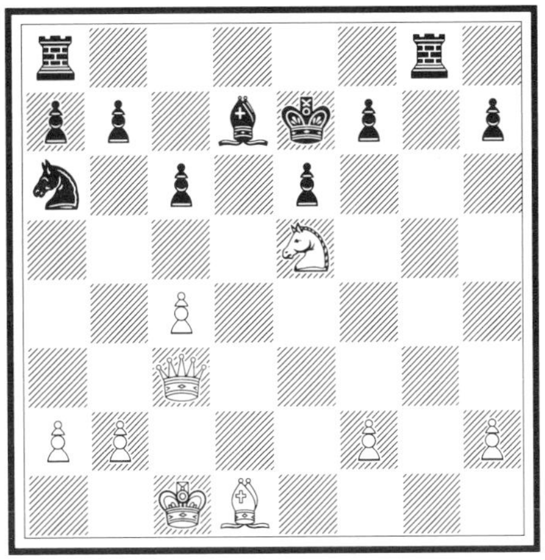

18 ♕a3+ c5 19 ♕f3 ♖ad8 20 ♕xf7+ ♔d6 21 ♕f4 ♖df8 22 ♘f7+ ♔e7 23 ♗h5 ♗c6 24 ♕d6+ ♔f6 25 ♘h6 ♖g1+ 26 ♔d2 ♔g7 27 ♘g4 ♖xg4 28 ♕e7+ ♔h6 29 ♗xg4 ♖xf2+ 30 ♔e3 ♖f1 31 h4 ♔g6 32 ♗h5+ Resigns. There is no defence to 33 ♕g5 mate.

In 1952 (March 3–April 3) Budapest staged a strong Maroczy Memorial Tournament which Keres (12½) won ahead of Geller (12), Botvinnik (11), Smyslov (11) and Ståhlberg (11).

Budapest Counter-Gambit

1 d4 ♘f6 2 c4 e5 3 de ♘g4 (or3 ... ♘e4, the Fajarowicz Variation).

Exciting but unsound gambit because Black must expend several tempi to regain his gambit pawn. It was generally supposed to have been introduced into master chess in Rubinstein–Vidmar, Berlin 1918, but it was Breyer who first played it against Esser at Budapest 1916.

Bugojno

Small town in central Yugoslavia which staged 5 strong tournaments between 1978 and 1986. The winners were Karpov and Spassky (1978), Karpov (1980), Kasparov (1982), Timman (1984) and Karpov (1986). The strongest of them was the 1986 tournament, though it missed having Kasparov, Korchnoi and Hübner.

Bukic, Enver [*December 2 1937–*]

Yugoslav GM (1976) who often plays in the Yugoslav Championship, and places well without actually coming first. He was equal 1st at the Kostic Memorial in Vrsac 1975.

Burn, Amos

[*December 31 1848–November 25 1925*] British player of GM strength who was second only to Blackburne in late 19th century British chess. He had a successful commercial career and though he was equal 1st in the 1871 British Cham-

Budapest 1950 — Candidates Tournament

		1		2		3		4		5		6		7		8		9		10		
1	Bronstein	–	–	½	½	0	1	½	1	1	1	1	½	0	1	½	1	½	½	1	½	12
	Boleslavsky	½	½	–	–	1	½	½	½	½	½	1	½	½	½	1	1	½	1	½	1	12
3	Smyslov	1	0	0	½	–	–	½	½	1	½	½	1	0	1	½	½	½	1	½	½	10
4	Keres	½	0	½	½	½	½	–	–	½	½	1	0	1	½	½	½	½	½	½	1	9½
5	Najdorf	0	0	½	½	0	½	½	½	–	–	½	½	½	½	½	½	1	1	½	1	9
6	Kotov	0	½	0	½	½	0	0	1	½	½	–	–	½	1	1	½	1	0	1	0	8½
7	Ståhlberg	1	0	½	½	1	0	0	½	½	½	½	0	–	–	½	½	½	½	½	½	8
8	Flohr	½	0	0	0	½	½	½	½	½	½	0	½	½	½	–	–	½	½	0	1	7
	Lilienthal	½	½	½	0	½	0	½	½	0	0	0	1	½	½	½	½	–	–	1	0	7
	Szabo	0	½	½	0	½	½	½	0	½	0	0	1	½	½	1	0	0	1	–	–	7

pionship (losing the play-off to Wisker)he did not devote himself seriously to chess until 1886. In that year he was equal 1st at London, losing the play-off to Blackburne, clear 1st at Nottingham and he drew matches with Bird (+9=0−9) and with Captain Mackenzie (+4=2−4). He was equal 1st with Gunsberg at London 1887 and he gained an international reputation by winning at Amsterdam 1889, ahead of the young Lasker, and finishing 2nd to Tarrasch at Breslau 1889. His best result was first at Cologne 1898 ahead of Charousek, Steinitz, Chigorin and Schlechter.

He specialized in solid defence and seldom combined unless forced to do so. He was chess editor of *The Field* from 1913 until his death.

Burr, Aaron [*1756–1836*]

The vice President of the USA (1801–05) and slayer of Alexander Hamilton was a keen chess player.

Bykova, Elizaveta Ivanovna

[*November 4 1911–March 8 1989*]

Women's World Champion 1953–6 and 1958–62. USSR Woman GM (1976) who beat Rudenko +7=2−5 in 1953 to win the world title. She was 2nd to Rubtsova in 1956 but beat Rubtsova +7=3−4 in 1958. She beat Zvorikina +6=5−2 in 1959, but in 1962 she lost +0=4−7 to Gaprindashvili. She was USSR Woman Champion in 1947, 1948 and 1950.

Byrne, Robert Eugene

[*April 20 1928–*]

US GM (1964) who won the 1960 US Open and came 2nd in the US Championships of 1959/60 and 1961/2, but who concentrated on his college teaching career until he turned chess professional in the late 1960s.

He won the 1972 US Championship and reached a peak when he placed 3rd in the 1973 Leningrad interzonal (XII) and became a Candidate. However, he lost his quarter-final match to Spassky (+0=3−3) in 1974. After that he did win at Torremolinos 1976, but then his top results were equal 4th at Baden bei Wien 1980 (XII) and equal 3rd at New York 1983 (X).

Since 1973 Byrne has edited the *New York Times* chess column with distinction. He has, since 1952, played on many US Olympiad teams. His younger brother Donald (1930–76) was also a talented player, IM (1962).

He wrote *Both Sides of the Chess Board* (with Ivo Nei) (1974).

Bugojno 1986 Category XVI

		1		2		3		4		5		6		7		8		
1	Karpov	–	–	0	½	1	½	½	½	1	½	½	1	½	½	½	1	8½
2	Sokolov	1	½	–	–	½	½	½	½	½	½	½	½	½	½	½	½	7½
	Ljubojevic	0	½	½	½	–	–	½	½	1	½	½	½	0	1	1	½	7½
4	Portisch	½	½	½	½	½	½	–	–	0	½	½	½	½	½	½	1	7
	Yusupov	0	½	½	½	0	½	1	½	–	–	½	½	1	1	½	0	7
	Spassky	½	0	½	½	½	½	½	½	½	½	–	–	½	½	1	½	7
7	Miles	½	½	½	½	1	0	½	½	0	0	½	½	–	–	1	0	6
8	Timman	½	0	½	½	0	½	½	0	½	1	0	½	0	1	–	–	5½

C

Cable and Radio Matches
Between 1896 and 1911 England and the USA played 13 cable matches, usually on 10 boards. The overall result was 6 wins each with 1 tie, and the total points were 64 to 64. Blackburne often led the English team while Pillsbury led the USA, and Blackburne won $3\frac{1}{2}$–$2\frac{1}{2}$ in their 6 encounters. In 1897 there was a cable match between the British House of Commons ($2\frac{1}{2}$) and the US House of Representatives ($2\frac{1}{2}$). Between 1926 and 1931 London played 5 cable matches against 4 US cities.

In 1945 there was a double-round radio match on 10 boards between the USA and the USSR. The USSR crushed the US $15\frac{1}{2}$–$4\frac{1}{2}$ and thus gave notice that they had become the great power in world chess. In 1946 the USSR decisively beat England 14–6.

Café de la Régence
The heart of Parisian chess from the 1740s to the 1850s, which was frequented by Legall, Philidor, Stamma, Labourdonnais, Deschappelles, Saint Amant, Kieseritsky and Harrwitz, as well as by the Duc de Richelieu, Voltaire, Jean Jacques Rousseau, Grimm, Benjamin Franklin, Robespierre and Napoleon (as a young officer). Morphy played there on his visit to Paris.

George Walker described it in 1840: 'Stove-heated to oppression, gas-heated, mirrors in abundance and slabs of marble to top its tables. On Sunday, all keep their hats on, to save space, and an empty chair is worth a ransom.'

The story goes that a girl disguised as a man, came there to play a game with Robespierre. She won, then revealed her identity to plead for the life of her condemned lover. She allegedly left the board with a written order for his immediate release.

It was originally located in the Place du Palais-Royal. It was relocated and the present Café is not far from the original site.

Caissa
The goddess of chess, from a 1763 poem by Sir William Jones. The story, dating back to Vida (1490–1566) tells of Mars falling in love with a nymph called Caissa (Scacchis in the original). His love is not returned and he convinces the god of sport to invent a game to soften her heart. This thoughtful game is called Caissa.

This is not how chess got its name nor how it came into being, but poetry need only be beautiful, not necessarily truthful.

Cambridge Springs Defence
1 d4 d5 2 c4 e6 3 ♘c3 ♘f6 4 ♗g5 ♘bd7 5 e3 c6 ♘f3 ♕a5.

A line in the Queen's Gambit, used often at Cambridge Springs 1904 and by Alekhine in his 1927 match with Capablanca. It tries to profit from the location of White's queen bishop at g5 and its inability to influence the dark squares on the queenside. To avoid this defence, White often plays the Exchange Variation 5 cd ed 6 e3.

Campomanes, Florencio [1927–]
Controversial president of FIDE since 1982, who unprecedentedly stopped the marathon Karpov–Kasparov match in February 1985, when Karpov seemed on

Florencio Campomanes, President of FIDE since 1982. His termination of the 1984/5 World Championship match caused great controversy.

35

the brink of collapse. This did not please Kasparov, nor did it sit well with many chess enthusiasts. Now that Kasparov is World Champion, the feud between him and 'Campo' is a threat to harmony in the chess world. It has, for example, led to the emergence of the GMA (Grandmasters Association).

Campomanes played on the Philippine Olympiad team in 1960.

Campora, Daniel Hugo

[*June 30 1957– *]
Argentine GM (1986) who led the Argentine team at the 1986 Olympiad. He has won several swiss tournaments and several Category VII and VIII tournaments. His best result was third at Biel 1987 (XIII).

Canadian Chess Chat   [*1947–1988*]
Monthly magazine founded in 1947 by D. A. MacAdam. After him, the editors were Yanofsky, then Divinsky and Macskasy, and finally Szarka.

Canal, Esteban

[*April 19 1896–February 14 1981*]
Peruvian honorary GM (1977) and IM (1950) who lived in Italy from 1923 onwards. He was equal 2nd at Meran (1926), 1st at Budapest (1933) and led the Peruvian team at the 1950 Olympiad.

Candidate
A player who succeeds at the interzonal level and makes it into the Candidates tournament or into the Candidates matches to select a challenger for the World Championship.

For Candidates tournaments *see* Amsterdam, Bled, Budapest, Curaçao and Zurich.

Capablanca, José Raoul

[*November 19 1888–March 8 1942*]
World Champion 1921–7. Capablanca was one of the 5 or 6 greatest players that ever lived and certainly the most

José Capablanca, World Champion 1921–7. He once went eight years without a single defeat in competitive chess.

pure, natural chess talent that ever existed. Keene and Divinsky place him fifth on the all-time list of great players. Many experts put him at the very top of their lists. For over 20 years his name was synonymous with chess perfection and people all over the world, people who had no idea of how the chess pieces moved, knew that Capablanca was the greatest player and a genius.

He was the hardest player to beat. In 248 games against the elite of the world's GMs, he lost only 19 games (7.7%) and 3 of those occurred in 1938 just after he had probably suffered a mild stroke. Only Karpov (9%) and Kasparov (10%) have come close to his invincibility standard. For example, Alekhine and Botvinnik lost 18%, Keres and Tal 17%, Lasker and Smyslov 16%, Petrosian 14% and Spassky 13%.

José Raoul Capablanca y Graupera was born in Havana of a distinguished family. He learned to play chess at the age of 4 by watching his father play with a friend.

By the age of 12 he was able to beat ($+4=6-2$) the champion of the Havana chess club, Juan Corzo. In 1904 Capablanca was sent to school in the US and in 1906 entered New York's Columbia University to study chemical engineering. During these years he frequented the Manhattan chess club, met many strong players including the mighty Lasker and proved his superb form in lightning games (10 seconds per move) by winning a rapid transit tournament in December 1906. He did this by beating Lasker in the final play-off.

Capablanca spent two years at the University and then, as he put it: 'I left the University and dedicated most of my time to chess'. In 1909 he made his first major mark by beating Marshall $+8=14-1$. This produced an invitation to San Sebastian (1911) and there he scored a sensational victory ahead of all the great players except Lasker.

In 1913 Capablanca was given a position in the Cuban Foreign Office and became an unofficial ambassador at large. He was 5'8" with blue eyes and black hair, an accomplished linguist, handsome, charming—a veritable prince of the world, a Cuban Hamlet.

He played many exhibition games (with great success) throughout Europe and at last, in 1914, he met Lasker in serious play at St Petersburg. After a Herculean struggle, Capablanca lost to Lasker and ended up 2nd, a mere $\frac{1}{2}$ point behind the World Champion. The two of them were far ahead of the field and it was clear that they were in a class by themselves.

During the war Capablanca won at New York 1915, 1916 and 1918. Then he won at Hastings 1919, crushed Kostic $+5=0-0$ and finally in 1921 he convincingly beat Lasker $+4=10-0$, to capture the world title.

Capablanca won at London 1922, was 2nd to a revived Lasker at New York 1924 and was a surprising 3rd (behind Bogoljubow and Lasker) at Moscow 1925. He re-established his supremacy with a resounding win at New York 1927 (XV) $2\frac{1}{2}$ points ahead of the field.

Capablanca seemed invincible. Although he paid little attention to the openings (just like Lasker), he played the endgame like a god, had an almost mystic talent for avoiding complications and knew exactly how to keep his pieces in harmony when the position was equal. He had an instant and profound sight of the board that was phenomenal. What others could not discover in a month's study, he saw at a glance. When Capablanca obtained a slight advantage, he displayed a faultless technique in holding on to it as the game progressed and in converting it to other forms, until the victory became clear. Combinative players could make

no impression on his clear classical game structure. He was an awesome opponent. Botvinnik wrote:

> (Capablanca's) phenomenal move-searching algorithm in those early years, when he possessed a wonderful ability for calculating variations very rapidly, made him invincible. Capablanca's pieces always worked harmoniously and even in simple positions this imparted a particular elegance to his play.

And yet Capablanca was human and, like Hamlet, had flaws. He had reached the top of the chess world without great effort and he found he could win even when he did not play flawlessly. He loved tennis and the ladies and was not inclined to work or study hard. He paid little attention to his psychological or physical endurance condition. What he didn't see immediately on the board, he never saw. He became overconfident.

Alekhine was a great talent, but had

never won a game from Capablanca (while losing five). He saw the small flaws in Capablanca's structure and threw his entire personality and soul into preparing for an assault on the great Cuban. Alekhine studied the openings assiduously, gave up any thoughts of a combinative attack, never looked at a chorus girl's legs and challenged Capablanca to a world title match in 1927.

The chess world was stunned when Capablanca lost the first game. Capablanca fought back and after 10 games, he actually led $5\frac{1}{2}-4\frac{1}{2}$. The struggle was ferocious. After 28 games Alekhine led 4 to 2 with 22 draws. Six wins were needed to win the title. Capablanca won game 29 and at 4–3 the match was arithmetically a cliff-hanger. But after 3 months of unexpected struggle, the Cuban's will was drained and Alekhine produced two superhuman efforts to win games 32, 34 and the world title by $+6=25-3$. Capablanca, like Hamlet, paid a terrible price for his slight flaws

Capablanca faces Lasker in 1925.

37

and, sad to say, was unable to raise funds for a return match.

Capablanca had a successful post-World Championship career. He won at Berlin 1928, was 2nd to Bogoljubow at Bad Kissingen 1928, and 2nd to Nimzowitsch at Carlsbad 1929. He won at Ramsgate and Budapest in 1929, was 2nd to Euwe at Hastings 1930/31 and then beat Euwe +2=8−0 in 1931.

After a few years absence he returned to tournament play but the quickness was gone and he had to learn how to deal with time trouble. He was equal 4th at Hastings 1934/35 and 4th at Moscow 1935 (behind Botvinnik, Flohr and the ageless Lasker). In 1936 Capablanca seemed to revive. His first marriage (1921) had unravelled and he was courting his new ladyfriend whom he married in 1938. He had a fine win at Moscow 1936 (XII) where he finally came ahead of Lasker. Then he had an excellent equal 1st with Botvinnik at Nottingham 1936 (XIV) where he met Alekhine for the first time since their 1927 match and had the deep satisfaction of winning their individual game. He was equal 3rd at Semmering 1937 and his last tournament was the super-strong AVRO 1938. Here he probably suffered a mild stroke and did not do well.

In life scores he beat Bogoljubow (+5=2−0), Nimzowitsch (+5=6−0), Vidmar (+3=6−0), Bernstein (+3=0−0), Maroczy (+3=5−0), Euwe (+4=13−1), Janowski (+9=1−1), Marshall (+20=28−2), Lasker (+6=16−2) and Alekhine (+9=33−7). He was on level terms with Botvinnik (+1=5−1) and Rubinstein (+1=7−1). The only top player Capablanca had a negative score against was Keres (28 years his junior), +0=5−1. Very few masters ever beat him twice!

Major works: *My Chess Career* (1920), *Chess Fundamentals* (1921).

See *The Immortal Games of Capablanca* by Reinfeld (1942), *Capablanca's 100 Best Games* by Golombek (1947), *Capab-*

lanca the Chess Phenomenon by Euwe and Prins (1949), *Chess History 14: Capablanca* by Hooper and Gilchrist (1963), *The Unknown Capablanca* by Brandreth and Hooper (1975),

Capablanca–Spielmann

New York 1927
First Brilliancy Prize
1 d4 d5 2 ♘f3 e6 3 c4 ♘d7 4 ♘c3 ♘gf6 5 ♗g5 ♗b4 6 cd ed 7 ♕a4 ♗xc3+ 8 bc 0-0 9 e3 c5 10 ♗d3 c4 11 ♗c2 ♕e7 12 0-0 a6 13 ♖fe1 ♕e6 14 ♘d2 b5 15 ♕a5 ♘e4 16 ♘xe4 de 17 a4 ♕d5

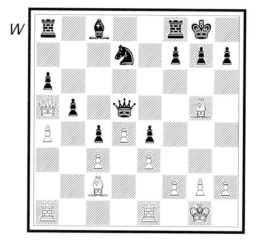

18 ab ♕xg5 19 ♗xe4 ♖b8 20 ba ♖b5 21 ♕c7 ♘b6 22 a7 ♗h3 23 ♖eb1 ♖xb1+ 24 ♖xb1 f5 25 ♗f3 f4 26 ef Resigns

Carlsbad

A famous central-European spa and resort which was called a Mecca for the sick and a paradise for the healthy. It was part of the Austro–Hungarian empire until 1918—now it is in Czechoslovakia and is called Karlovy Vary. It is some 80 miles west of Prague, near the German–Czech border.

There were 4 famous Carlsbad tournaments, under the excellent supervision of Victor Tietz, president of the Carlsbad chess organization. The first one, in 1907 (August 20–September 17) did not have Lasker or Tarrasch, but the younger generation

(Rubinstein, Nimzowitsch, Vidmar) did establish itself and the middle-aged (Maroczy, Schlechter, Teichmann, Marshall, Janowski) had to make room for them. Rubinstein (15) won ahead of Maroczy (14½), Leonhardt (13½), Nimzowitsch (12½), Schlechter (12½) and Vidmar (12). The tournament book, by Marco and Schlechter, is a treasure house of insights, ideas and annotations.

There were 26 competitors in 1911 (August 21–September 24) but Lasker, Tarrasch, Janowski, Maroczy and Capablanca were not there. Teichmann (18) won his greatest victory ahead of Rubinstein (17), Schlechter (17), Rotlevi (16), Nimzowitsch (15½), Marshall (15½), Vidmar (15) and young Alekhine (13½). The 2 volume tournament book by Vidmar is disappointingly thin in satisfactory annotations.

In 1923 (April 27–May 22), Lasker, Capablanca and Vidmar did not play but the 18 competitors were of top quality. Alekhine (11½), Boguljubow (11½) and the veteran Maroczy (11½) tied for first.

The 1929 (July 31–August 26) Carlsbad tournament was the strongest, even though Alekhine and the supposedly retired Lasker were not there. With 3 rounds to go, Capablanca (13) and Spielmann (13) led Nimzowitsch (12½) and Rubinstein (11½). Rubinstein beat Menchik, Capablanca only drew with Vidmar while Nimzowitsch won a crucial game from Spielmann. Thus with 2 rounds to go it was Capablanca (13½), Nimzowitsch (13½), Spielmann (13) and Rubinstein (12½). Spielmann had led through most of the tournament and could not bear to see the first prize slip away at the end. He concentrated all his remaining energy and beat Capablanca. Nimzowitsch only drew with Maroczy and Rubinstein drew with Becker. With 1 round to go it was Spielmann (14), Nimzowitsch (14), Capablanca (13½) and Rubinstein (13). Spielmann now had the best chance because he faced Mattison while Nimzowitsch had to play the more dangerous Tartakower. Rubinstein drew with Euwe, Capablanca crushed Maroczy while both Spielmann and Nimzowitsch obtained winning positions. Tartakower began to fight hard and it was unclear whether he could hold the draw. Spielmann was quite nervous and started exchanging pieces prematurely instead of simply winning a pawn. Spielmann only drew, falling back into a tie with Capablanca. Nimzowitsch struggled on and finally won his game and the tournament.

Time limit: 30 moves in 2 hours and then 15 moves per hour.

Prizes (Kronen): 20 000, 14 000, 10 000, 8000, 6000, 5000, 4000, 3000.

Brilliancy prizes: 1000, 800, 600, 500, 400, 300, 200, 100. In fact 14 prizes were awarded, including 1st: Sämisch for his win over Grünfeld; 2nd/3rd: Vidmar for his win over Euwe, and Maroczy for his win over Canal.

The Tournament Book by the *Wiener Schachzeitung* (Spielmann, Tartakower, Nimzowitsch, Becker and Kmoch) is quite outstanding with wonderful round by round reports by Kmoch. There is also a curious booklet by Nimzowitsch the eccentric, on Carlsbad 1929, with 30 of the 231 games.

The prize for best played game was shared by Nimzowitsch (for his game with Bogoljubow) and Euwe (for his game with Thomas).

Sämisch–Grünfeld

1 d4 ♘f6 2 c4 e6 3 ♘c3 ♗b4 4 a3 ♗xc3+ 5 bc d6 6 f3 0-0 7 e4 e5 8 ♗d3 ♘c6 9 ♘e2 ♘d7 10 0-0 b6 11 ♗e3 ♗a6 12 ♘g3 ♘a5 13 ♕e2 ♕e8 14 f4 f6 15 ♖f3 ♔h8 16 ♖af1 ♕f7 17 fe de 18 d5 ♘b7 19 ♘f5 ♘d6 20 ♖h3 g6 21 ♘h6 ♕g7 22 g4 g5 23 ♖h5 ♘c5 24 ♗xc5 bc 25 ♖f3 ♕e7 26 ♖fh3 ♗c8 27 ♕f2 ♘e8 28 ♖f3 ♘g7 29 ♖5h3 ♗d7 (better is 29 ... ♘e8) 30 ♖hg3 ♗e8 31 h4 gh 32 ♖g2 h3 33 ♖xh3 ♗g6 34 ♖f3 ♖ab8 35 ♕h4 ♖b3 36 ♖gf2 ♖xc3 37 g5 ♘e8 38 gf

B

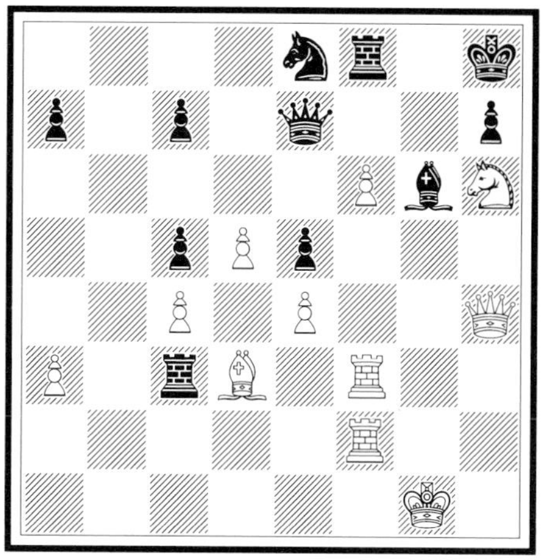

38 ... ♕d8 [if 38 ... ♘xf6 39 ♖xf6 ♖xf6 40 ♖xf6 ♖xd3 41 ♖xg6] 39 ♘g4 ♖xd3 40 ♖xd3 ♗xe4 41 ♖e3 ♘d6 42 ♘xe5 ♗f5 43 ♖xf5! ♘xf5 44 ♘g6+ ♔g8 45 ♖e7! ♖f7 46 ♖xf7

Carlsbad 1929

		1	2	3	4	5	6	7	8	9	10	11	12	13	14	15	16	17	18	19	20	21	22	
1	Nimzowitsch	–	½	1	½	½	1	1	1	½	½	1	½	½	1	½	1	0	1	½	1	½	1	15
2	Capablanca	½	–	0	½	1	½	½	½	½	½	1	1	1	½	1	0	1	1	1	1	½	1	14½
	Spielmann	0	1	–	0	½	½	½	½	1	0	½	1	1	½	1	1	½	1	1	1	1	1	14½
4	Rubinstein	½	½	1	–	½	½	½	½	1	1	1	½	½	½	1	½	½	1	½	0	½	1	13½
5	Becker	½	0	½	½	–	1	1	1	0	0	1	½	½	½	½	½	1	½	1	1	½	0	12
	Euwe	0	½	½	½	0	–	0	½	½	1	½	1	½	½	1	½	½	1	½	½	1	1	12
	Vidmar	0	½	½	½	0	1	–	½	½	½	½	1	½	1	0	½	½	0	1	1	1	1	12
8	Bogoljubow	0	½	½	½	0	½	½	–	½	½	½	1	0	0	1	1	1	0	½	1	1	1	11½
9	Grünfeld	½	½	0	0	1	½	½	½	–	½	½	0	1	½	½	0	1	½	1	½	1	½	11
10	Canal	½	½	1	0	1	0	½	½	½	–	1	0	0	½	½	½	0	1	0	½	1	1	10½
	Mattison	0	0	½	0	0	½	½	½	½	0	–	1	1	1	0	1	1	1	½	0	½	1	10½
12	Colle	½	0	0	½	½	0	0	0	1	1	0	–	1	½	1	½	1	0	½	0	1	1	10
	Maroczy	½	0	0	½	½	½	½	1	0	1	0	0	–	½	0	0	1	½	1	1	½	1	10
	Tartakower	0	½	½	½	½	½	0	1	½	½	0	½	½	–	½	½	½	½	½	½	½	1	10
	Treybal	½	0	0	0	½	0	1	0	½	½	1	0	1	½	–	½	½	0	1	1	½	1	10
16	Sämisch	0	1	0	½	½	½	½	0	1	½	0	½	1	½	½	–	½	0	½	½	1	0	9½
	Yates	1	0	½	½	0	½	½	0	0	1	0	0	0	½	½	½	–	1	½	½	1	1	9½
18	Johner	0	0	0	0	½	0	1	1	½	0	0	1	½	½	1	1	0	–	½	0	½	1	9
	Marshall	½	0	0	½	0	½	0	½	0	1	½	½	0	½	0	½	½	½	–	1	1	1	9
20	Gilg	0	0	0	1	0	½	0	0	½	½	1	1	0	½	0	½	½	1	0	–	½	½	8
21	Thomas	½	½	0	½	½	0	0	0	0	0	½	0	½	½	½	0	0	½	0	½	–	1	6
22	Menchik	0	0	0	0	1	0	0	0	½	0	0	0	0	0	0	1	0	0	0	½	0	–	3

♔xf7 47 ♘e5+ ♚f8 48 ♕xh7
Resigns

Caro–Kann
1 e4 c6.

Black intends to move into the centre with 2 ... d5, without hemming in his own queen bishop (as in the French Defence). White obtains greater mobility but Black's position is solid and safe, and tends to be drawish.

This defence was mentioned by Polerio (1590), used by Weiss (1883) and advocated (1886) by the English player Horatio Caro who lived in Berlin and by Marcus Kann of Vienna. It became popular when Capablanca used it in London 1922. The Panov–Botvinnik attack almost demolished it in the 1930s but Botvinnik himself used it in his championship matches (1958 and 1961).

After the usual 2 d4 d5 there are several main lines:

A (Panov–Botvinnik) 3 ed cd 4 c4 when White will control more space and aim for a kingside attack or a later c5. Black must defend carefully.

B (Classical–Capablanca) 3 ♘c3 de 4 ♘xe4 ♗f4 with a safe but at best drawish position, e.g. 5 ♘g3 ♗g6 6 h4 h6 7 ♘f3 ♘d7 8 ♗d3 ♗xd3 9 ♕xd3 ♕c7 10 ♗d2 ♘gf6 11 0-0-0. Black may also try 4 ... ♘d7 or even 4 ... ♘f6.

C (Advance–Tal) 3 e5 ♗f5 4 g4 when Black has some chances in the future but he must fend off the initial attack.

White can also try 2 ♘c3 d5 3 ♘f3 (the two knights line).

Castle
A colloquial word for rook.

Castling
A move of the king and a rook, counted as a single move. It must be done by touching the king first and moving it from its original square e1 to either g1 or c1 for White (from e8 to either g8 or c8 for Black). Then the rook towards which the king has moved is transferred over the king to the square the king has just crossed (f1 or d1 for White, f8 or d8 for Black).

Castling is permanently impossible if:
(1) the king has moved previously, or if:
(2) the rook involved has moved previously.

Castling is temporarily prevented if:
(3) the king is in check, or if
(4) the king must cross over or land on a square attacked by an enemy piece, or if
(5) there is any piece of either side, between the king and the rook involved.

Castling is allowed and legal if:
(6) the king was in check, but is no longer in check, or if
(7) the involved rook is attacked by an enemy piece, or if
(8) the involved rook crosses a square (b1 or b8) that is attacked by an enemy piece.

In early versions of chess, castling was somewhat up in the air. Our present version was established when Ruy Lopez gave it his approval (1561) and by the 17th century it was almost universally accepted. For some reason Italy continued to use various sorts of castling (free castling) until the 20th century.

See *Die historische Entwicklung der Rochade* by H. Suiwe, in *Schachwissenschaftliche Forschungen*, December 1975.

Catalan Opening
A Queen's Gambit combined with a fianchetto of white's king bishop. The name was selected by Tartakower at Barcelona 1929.

Catherine de Medici   [1518–89]
She was a keen chessplayer whose ambition was to meet Paolo Boi.

Catherine the Great of Russia
[1729–96]
Empress of Russia (1762–96) and an active correspondence chess player.

Caxton, William   [1422–91]
English businessman and printer who translated Cessolis' *Chess Morality* into English (from the French version by Vignay), called it *Game and Playe of the Chesse*, and dated 1474 (although actually published later, probably in 1476). It is one of the very first printed books in English. The second edition (1480) had 24 highly praised woodcuts added. There was an 1883 edition which was subsequently made available as a *British Chess Magazine* classic reprint.

Cebalo, Miso   [February 6 1945–]
Yugoslav GM(1985) who was equal 1st in the Yugoslav Championship 1985 and lost the play-off to Marjanovic. He was 1st at Kavala 1985 (VII) and his best result was equal 3rd at Biel 1986 (XII).

Centralization
Bringing one's important pieces to the centre, from where they can exert maximum influence over the entire board. In the late middlegame, just centralizing one's queen, without any clear-cut threats, can often lead to an advantage. In the endgame, centralizing one's king can be a crucial factor in winning or in holding the draw. Even when capturing with a lowly pawn, it is often advisable to take toward the centre.

Centre
The four squares d4, e4, d5 and e5 form the heart of the central area. From a strategic point of view they are the most important squares on the board because from them, every part of the board is readily accessible. The opening is a struggle for the centre and if one side can gain control of the centre, either by occupying it with pawns or with pieces, or even from further away,

then one has a strategic advantage. Even in the endgame, getting one's king to the centre can be crucial.

Centre Counter Defence

1 e4 d5.

First mentioned by Lucena and rarely played today. After the usual 2 ed Black has two main possibilities:

A 2 ... ♕xd5 3 ♘c3 ♕a5 (or ... ♕d8) 4 d4, when White maintains a slight opening advantage, and

B 2 ... ♘f6 3 c4 c6 4 d4 cd which is the Panov–Botvinnik line of The Caro–Kann. White can also accept the gambit with 4 dc ♘xc6 5 ♘f3.

Centre Game

1 e4 e5 2 d4.

One of the oldest openings, but after 2 ... ed 3 ♕xd4 ♘c6 Black achieves full equality. The difficulty is that the white queen comes out too early and Black gains tempi by attacking her. Better plans are 2 ♘f3 ♘c6 3 d4 (Scotch Game) or even 2 d4 ed 3 c3 (Danish Gambit).

Cessolis, Jacobus de

[13th century–14th century]

Dominican friar from north-west Italy who wrote the most famous and successful, 'chess morality': Liber de moribus Hominum et officiis Nobilium, sometime between 1275 and 1300. It consisted of 24 chapters in 4 books and was translated by Caxton into English (via a French edition) and published in the 1470s as the Game and Playe of the Chesse—one of the first printed books in English.

'Moralities' were popular at the time. For example one writer gave each piece of feminine attire the representation of a virtue, one that a good woman ought to have. Chess moralities gave pieces and their moves human characteristics, e.g. pawns are poor men, their move is straight except when they take anything! or: the knight's move is a combination of a straight move and an oblique one. The straight part is his legal power to collect rents etc. The oblique part is his extortion and wrong-doing.

Chess 'moralities' often gave wrong ideas about chess, but they spread knowledge of the game's existence all over Europe and they broke down ecclesiastic prejudice against chess.

Chandler, Murray Graham

[April 4 1960–]

New Zealand GM (1983) who settled in England in 1975. He was New Zealand Champion (1975), joint Commonwealth Champion (1984) and joint British Champion (1986). His best results were equal 2nds at London 1984 (XIV), London 1986 (XIII) and Amsterdam 1987 (XIII). He has won many open events and has played on three English Olympiad teams during 1982–6.

He has edited Tournament Chess since 1981.

Murray Chandler, the former New Zealander who now represents England. Chandler manages to combine top-level chess with a variety of business interests.

Charlemagne

[742–814]

King of the Franks (768–814) and King of the Holy Roman Empire (800–814) who has had many chess fables told about him. Some chess pieces and sets have been associated with him (see e.g. The Eight by Katherine Neville). However, the current historical view is that he was not a chessplayer.

Charles I of England

[1600–1649]

King of England (1625–49). From a contemporary letter describing Charles I, we learn: 'when he is neither in the field nor at the council, he passes most of his time at chess with the Marquis of Winchester'.

Charles the Bold, Duke of Burgundy

[1433–1477]

He was said to be the best chess player of his time.

Charles XII of Sweden

[1682–1718]

King of Sweden (1697–1718) who Voltaire described as a chess player who lost many games because he moved his king more than any other piece. In a letter of 1740, Frederick the Great wrote: 'I am like the chess king of Charles XII, always on the go'.

Chess was popular in Scandinavia. It was, for example, common for Norse parents to test the character of suitors for their daughters by playing chess with them and observing their conduct during the game.

Charousek, Rudolf

[September 19 1873–April 18 1900]

Hungarian of GM strength who was actually born in Prague and taken to Hungary as a child. He learned to play chess as an impoverished law student at the Hungarian College at Kashau (Kassa)—it is said that he copied out by hand Bilguer's Handbuch since he could not afford to buy it—and soon displayed immense ability. Charousek made his international debut at the strong Nuremberg 1896 tournament, finishing only 12th out of 19, but defeating the winner, World Champion Dr Lasker, in their individual game. A few months later he came equal 1st with Chigorin at Budapest 1896, but lost the play-off match. He lost a match to Maroczy (+ 2 = 2 − 6) in 1896 but went on to first prizes at Berlin 1897 and Budapest 1898. He was equal 2nd. at Cologne 1898 and was widely hailed as a brilliant player and potential World Championship contender. Ill health had always dogged him and he died tragically at 26, of tuberculosis.

See Charousek's Games of Chess by P. W. Sargeant (1919), *Rudolf Charousek* by L. Bachman.

Chatrang
See Early Versions of Chess.

Chaturanga
See Early Versions of Chess.

Chaucer   [? 1340–1400]
He was quite aware of chess—see the *Book of the Duchess* (1369).

Check
A move that attacks the king. The check must be met immediately, either by moving the king out of the way of the check, by interposing a piece or a pawn, or by capturing the enemy piece that is giving check. A player may not castle when his king is in check.

It used to be customary to say 'check' when one's piece gave a check to the enemy king. It was even polite to say 'check to the queen' when one's piece threatened the enemy queen, but such alerts are no longer used—at least they are not required by law or by custom.

Checkmate or Mate
When a player cannot get his king out of check, the king is checkmated or mated, and the game is over.

Chekhov, Valery Alexandrovich
[*November 27 1955– *]
USSR GM (1984) who was World Junior Champion (1975) and was 1st or equal 1st at Lvov 1983 (IX), Irkutsk 1983 (IX), Barcelona 1984 (VII), Dresden 1985 (IX) and at the 1986 Berlin Open.

Chernin, Alexander Mikhailovich
[*March 6 1960– *]
USSR GM (1985) who was equal 1st at Irkutsk 1983 (IX), 1st at Copenhagen 1984 (VIII), and equal 1st in the 1985 USSR Championship (XI). By beating Gavrikov $3\frac{1}{2}$–$2\frac{1}{2}$ he reached the 1985 Candidates tournament at Montpellier. He did not make it into the play-off matches. His best result was equal 2nd at Reggio Emilia 1986/87 (XIV).

He has played in three USSR Championships from 1984–7, scoring overall 29 to 24. He has the potential to be one of the future stars of the USSR.

Cheron, Andre
[*September 25 1895–1980*]
French born player, problem composer and author who lived in Switzerland. He was French Champion in 1926, 1927 and 1929, and played on the French Olympiad team in 1927. His major work ws the 4 volume *Lehr und Handbuch der Endspiele* (1952–8); second edition (1969–71).

Chess   [1935–]
Monthly magazine founded in 1935 by B. H. Wood and owned and edited by him for some 53 years. It gave the English chess world a lively alternative to the staid *British Chess Magazine*. Paul Lamford became editor in 1988, following the sale of the business.

Chess Amateur   [1906–1930]
Magazine published in England. It had an excellent problem section and Fairhurst contributed much to the clarification of Tarrasch's principles.

A magazine with the same title appeared in Malta in 1890 but lasted less than a year.

Chess and the Arts
See Art and Chess; Ballet; Cinema; Literature; Music; Poetry; and Theatre.

Chess Express   [1968–1975]
Swiss magazine in an English and a German edition, published between 18 and 40 times per year. It contained the very latest tournament results and games. Edited by W. Kuhnle-Woods and Heinz Schaufelberger and then by Michael Kuhnle.

Chess Informant   [1966–]
A serious record of all important tournament games and match games. It appears twice a year and was first called *Informator* (a name which has stuck). It began in 1966 as a Yugoslav enterprise but is now published under FIDE auspices. It contains compact notes, tournament tables, match results and Elo ratings of all the top players. Matanovic is the editor.

Chess Life   [1946–1969]
US chess federation official monthly publication. In 1969 it was amalgamated with *Chess Review* (becoming *Chess Life and Review*). Its editors were Hochberg, then Major and finally Reinhardt. The title has since contracted to *Chess Life*.

Chess in our time
What are the differences between chess today (1990) and chess in the past, and how large are these differences? Let us begin with some numbers. Today there are over 300 master and Grandmaster tournaments registered with FIDE, every year. In the 1950s there were not more than 20 or 30. In 1971, the first FIDE ranking list had a little over 500 names. In 1988 there were over 5000. Membership in FIDE has increased fourfold since the 1950s. As a result of this

phenomenal increase in chess activity, there is a kind of inflation in FIDE titles. Many players are 'hunting' for titles and eventually they get them, but not necessarily because they play better.

Masters today often play 100 difficult games per year—the majority of active Grandmasters play 70 to 80. In the 1950s we seldom played more than 40. Capablanca played only 600 in his entire life—about the same as Lasker. By the early 1960s Botvinnik said the expectation then was that a master would play about 1000 games in his lifetime. Today Karpov has already played more than 1000 and he will probably increase this number significantly before he hangs up his rooks. Gligoric, who is just finishing his playing career, believes he has played about 4000 games. And that is not the upper limit. Wandering 'stars' now travel continuously from one tournament to another, and will leave Gligoric's 4000 far behind.

Chess has become a true sport and at high levels of performance this means a heavy timetable and constant stress. This puts serious pressure on a player's health, both mental and physical. He must have a sound and solid nervous system, an ability to concentrate in short but intense time periods, the physical and mental endurance of a marathon runner, the ability to fight fatigue, and must learn how to ration his strength so as to be able to focus it on the most important tournaments.

Let us consider Botvinnik. He played all his tournaments with maximum strength. This was possible for 10 or 12 games. After that there was a falling off, but by then he had assured himself of a high prize. Such tactics would probably not bring him success under today's heavy schedule. Kasparov also puts out maximum effort, but he rations himself, depending on the importance of the tournament. Karpov has won many tournaments but he puts out just

enough energy in each one to gain victory.

Now that chess is a serious sport, young players dominate it, because it is easier for them to endure excessive playing, and equally important, to recover quickly. Winners therefore are becoming younger. Olympiads are now filled with young stars. There are exceptions of course, like Smyslov and Korchnoi, but chess is now a very young person's game.

Tournament preparation has also been transformed. Today there is so much information, one cannot absorb it all unless one does it systematically. A chess master today must examine some 5000 games and dozen of articles per year to keep up with opening novelties. Thus two or three players must form a 'creative' union and thus one needs friends or coaches or seconds. To aim for the World Championship one needs a large staff which includes opening specialists, physicians and psychologists, not to mention the masseurs and yoga experts used by some. Botvinnik used to say a potential World Champion had to be an investigator of new opening ideas in the silence of his study. Today such a person must be part of one's team.

At the beginning of the century, neither Lasker nor Capablanca paid much attention to openings. Their play was based on intuition, experience and creativity at the board, combined with powerful defence. Today it would be impossible to succeed with these methods.

Botvinnik was one of the first who analysed openings deeply and who introduced the scientific approach to his preparations. He investigated middlegame positions to study their tactical details. When playing Black, the plan was to construct a pawn bulwark, a 'hedgehog', to avoid an early confrontation and to prepare a counter-attack. Kotov called this the method of the

'coiled spring'. Today, these ideas are universally accepted by all top players, even ones of different styles.

Chess has also changed in a creative way—fighting has become more dynamic, more concrete. Instead of relying on fundamental rules, top players seek out the exceptions to the rules. And this method is promoted by the move to faster time controls and 6 hour sessions.

The chess world has been changing dramatically. We now have precise electronic clocks, electronic display boards, computers filled with the latest voluminous information about openings and about one's opponents. There are VCRs making it possible to learn all about chess by yourself. Now computer chess programs are commonplace. They are getting stronger and approaching true master levels. They can even, occasionally, beat a Grandmaster (e.g. Larsen). It is possible that by the end of the century a computer will occasionally be able to beat the World Champion. FIDE recently considered allowing a team of computers to play in the chess Olympiad. They rejected the idea partly because human teams that lost to computer teams might feel devastated.

Another exciting change is the growing playing level of the female sex. In the 1930s only Vera Menchik played in men's tournaments, but achieved only average results. Today Chiburdanidze, Gaprindashvili, Cramling and the three Polgar sisters compete in men's events, with fine results.

The study of chess has accelerated and we are much deeper into the game than previous generations were. We have used scientific and technological advances to try to discover the deep laws underlying the game and we are determined to pursue its mysteries. However, with all our advances, even our World Champions continue to make mistakes, and this may be the human condition. Our creative and psychological potentialities are unfortunately limited. Chess is a creative self-expression of many, where masterpieces must be produced in the midst of struggle—struggle against one's opponents and against oneself.

Grandmaster Yuri Averbakh

Chess Life and Review   *[1969–]*

US Chess Federation official monthly magazine which is the union of *Chess Life* and *Chess Review*. Like the old *Chess Review* it makes an effort to use many pictures. The name is now *Chess Life*.

Chess Monthly (Great Britain)
[1879–1896]

A magazine which was one of the first to give properly annotated games. The principal editor, Hoffer, was helped enormously by having Zukertort as co-editor (until 1888). There were four regular sections: news, annotated games, problems and endgames. In addition, Hoffer carried on a profoundly bitter feud with his one-time benefactor, Steinitz.

Chess Monthly (USA)   *[1857–1861]*

This short-lived magazine had the distinguished bibliophile D. W. Fiske as editor and Paul Morphy as games editor (1858–61). Morphy's notes are somewhat disappointing because they are so few.

Chess 'moralities'
See Cessolis

Chess Pieces and Sets

Serious chessplayers prefer pieces that are uncluttered in design and that clearly symbolize the piece they represent. There is however another world of chess sets, a world of decoration, beauty and artistry; a world peopled by collectors and by lovers of shapes and forms.

Individual pieces have survived and come down to us from the 8th century, but the oldest known complete set is the Lewis Set (11th or 12th century). Since

Just a few of the many unusual and beautiful chessmen that have been produced. Readers interested in exotic sets should consult Chessmen for Collectors, *by Victor Keats.*

then, chess sets have gone through many transformations, from the Ager chessmen of rock crystal (12th century) through gothic, renaissance (see Henry VIII), baroque, rococo, Indian and Chinese ivory (18th and 19th century), Wedgwood, Saint George, to today's Staunton pattern.

The decorative sets were sometimes made with two distinctive rival armies e.g. French with Napoleon versus English with Wellington. Perhaps the most beautiful are the ivory sets from India and China. There are wonderful collections in private hands and to visit a roomful of stunning chess sets can be a thrilling experience.

The standard playing set in the 18th and first half of the 19th century had the French Saint George pattern. The common design used today, the Staunton pattern, was designed by Nathaniel Cook in the mid 1830s, registered in 1849 to the firm of Jaques, and chosen by Staunton in 1850. A well-made Staunton set of good wood, weighted and felted on the bottom, is a pleasure to own and use.

In recent years new materials (like plastic) and new designs are being used.

Perhaps the best collections of chess sets are owned by: David Hafler (Philadelphia, USA), Herr Buhlen (Switzerland), Thomas Thomsen (Frankfurt, West Germany), Victor Keats (London, UK) and George Dean (Birmingham, Michigan, USA).

There are interesting pieces to be seen in the Germanisches chess National Museum, Nuremberg (8th century Arabic bone), Musée de Cluny, Paris (9th century ivory knight, 15th century rock crystal, topaz and silver), and the British Museum, London (10th century whalebone bishop and the Lewis chessmen).

See also Ager chessmen, Lewis chessmen.

See Book of Chessmen by Alex Hammond (1950), *Chess, the story of chesspieces from Antiquity to Modern Times*, by H. and S. Wichmann (1964), *Chessmen* by A. Mackett-Beeson (1968), *Chess Sets* by F. Lanier Graham (1968).

Chess Player, The [1971–1976]
Magazine founded by Tony Gillam, Nottingham, which was similar in style to *Chess Informant*. It gave for example, complete tournaments. After 1976 it changed from a magazine to 3 bound volumes per year.

Chess Player's Chronicle, The
[1841– ... 1902]
The first successful English-language magazine devoted exclusively to chess; George Walker's short-lived *Philidorian* had met little response in 1837–8. The proprietor and editor from 1841 to 1854 was Staunton. He had always had a wish to earn his living from his (at times vitriolic) pen and the magazine was a successful basis for this.

R. B. Brien took over in 1854, but was unable to continue its success and it ceased in 1856. It reappeared in 1859, edited by Kolisch, Zytogorski and Kling, but survived only until 1862. Thereafter magazines bearing the same or slightly modified name appeared from 1863 to 1867, 1868 to 1875 and 1877 to 1902. However, the quality never again compared with that achieved by Staunton, and competition from the excellent *British Chess Magazine* put an end to the title.

Chess Prodigies
Chess, like music and mathematics, has the ability to produce prodigies— youngsters full of talent and knowledge beyond their years. The greatest chess examples are Reshevsky and Capablanca. Others are Fischer, Morphy, Mecking and Judit Polgar.

Chess Review [1933–1969]
Monthly US magazine founded by Kashdan. Horowitz took it over in 1934 and finally sold it to the US Chess Federation in 1969. It made an effort to use many pictures.

See also Chess Life, Chess Life and Review.

Chess World (Australia) [1946–1967]
Australian magazine that followed on from the *Australian Chess Review* (1929–44) and *Check!* (1944–5). It was edited by Purdy and set a high standard of readability.

Chess World (Belgium)
Koltanowski edited this magazine during 1932–3. It was the first English-language chess magazine published in a non-English-speaking country.

Chessworld (USA) [1964]
A most wonderful magazine published by Frank Brady. It had excellent articles, pictures and artwork. For example, the second isue contained the full short story *The Royal Game* by S. Zweig. The first issue had Fischer's selection of the 10 greatest players of all time. Unfortunately there were only three issues— then the enterprise went bankrupt.

Chiburdanidze, Maia Grigoryevna
[January 17 1961–]

Maia Chiburdanidze, holder of the Women's World Championship since 1978, and one of only two women to hold the full Grandmaster title.

Woman World Champion 1978– .
USSR GM (1984) who won the woman's world title by beating Gaprindashvili +4=9−2 in 1978. She has successfully defended her title: +4=8−4 with Alexandria 1981, +5=7−2 over Levitina 1984, +4=9−1 over Akhmilovskaya 1986 and +3=11−2 over Ioseliani 1988.

She began very young and by age 12 was a force in women's chess. She was USSR Woman Champion in 1977.

Chiburdanidze competes successfully in men's events, coming equal 3rd at Bilbao 1987 (XII) and 2nd Brussels 1987 (X1). She and Gaprindashvili are the only two women who hold the full GM title.

Chigorin [Tchigorin], Mikhail Ivanovich

[*October 31 1850–January 25 1908*] Russian player of GM strength who was in the world top 5 during 1888–98. He

Mikhail Chigorin, the unsuccessful challenger for the World Championship in 1889 and 1892.

was the founder of the Russian school of chess and a great theoretician. He took a serious interest in the game relatively late in life and his first major tournament was Berlin 1881 where he came equal 3rd. He was 4th at London 1883 and equal 1st at New York 1889.

He made a respectable showing in his World Championship match with Steinitz in 1889, losing +6=1−10. In 1890 he held Gunsberg +9=5−9 and in 1890/91 he won 2 celebrated cable telegraph games with Steinitz (who was in New York). This led to a return match in 1892. Steinitz was 56 while Chigorin was at the peak of his powers. After 21 games the score was level at +8=5−8. Steinitz's enormous will to win gave him the energy to win the next game and in game 23 Chigorin overlooked a simple mate in 2, and lost +8=5−10.

In 1893 Tarrasch travelled to St Petersburg to play Chigorin in one of the great matches of all time. After 17 games Chigorin trailed +5=4−8 but he won the next 3 games (Tarrasch claimed he relaxed and did much sight-seeing) and the match ended +9=4−9. What made these matches so exciting was the clash of styles. Both Steinitz and Tarrasch were dogmatic about their theories. Chigorin was a rebel, who did not believe bishops were better than knights, or that it was necessary to control the centre with pawns. Chigorin loved to play the Evans Gambit, always opened 1 e4, always answered 1 e4 with 1 ... e5, defended the Queen's Gambit with 1 d4 d5 2 c4 ♘c6, played 1 e4 e6 2 ♕e2 against the French, and was rather pig-headed about his ideas.

In spite of his alcohol problem and his tendency to blunder, Chigorin did well during the next few years. He was an excellent 2nd at Hastings 1895 ahead of Lasker, Tarrasch and Steinitz. He did not do well at St Petersburg 1895/6 but he was equal 1st at Budapest 1896 and beat

Charousek +3=0−1 in the play-off. Chigorin had diabetes and, combined with his heavy drinking, this caused his results to deteriorate (as well as his liver). He did come equal 2nd at Cologne 1898 and won the first three All Russian Championships (1899, 1901, 1903). He was 1st at the Vienna 1903 King's Gambit tournament and beat Lasker +2=3−1 defending the Rice Gambit in 1903. He began in the 4th All Russian Championship in 1905/6 but withdrew after the 4th round. He beat the winner, Salwe, +7=3−5 later in 1906.

In life scores he beat Tarrasch (+14=8−13), Pillsbury (+8=6−7), Teichmann (+8=1−3) and Charousek (+4=1−3). He was level with Blackburne (+6=4−6) and lost to Steinitz (+24=8−27), Lasker (+1=4−8), Zukertort (+1=0−4), Rubinstein (+2=0−3), Schlechter (+6=10−9), Maroczy (+4=7−6) and Janowski (+4=4−17).

Marshall wrote (1903): '... (Chigorin) was a bundle of nervous energy and he constantly swung his crossed foot back and forth. Speaking only his native Russian, he was handicapped in getting along with the other masters'.

Chigorin popularized chess in Russia. He founded a chess club in St Petersburg, encouraged Russian magazines and wrote wonderful analysis.

See *Chigorin*, by Grekov (1949), *Chigorin*, by Romanov (1960), *Mikhail Chigorin: Selected Games*, by Bogoljubow (1987), *Weltgeschichte des Schachs, 9, Chigorin* by Lew Abramow (1960).

Tarrasch–Chigorin

Match 1893

1 e4 e5 2 ♘f3 ♘c6 3 ♗b5 a6 4 ♗a4 ♘f6 5 ♘c3 ♗b4 6 ♘d5 ♗a5 7 0-0 d6 8 d3 ♗g4 9 c3 ♘d7 10 ♘e3 ♗h5 11 ♗xc6 bc 12 ♕a4 ♗b6 13 ♕xc6 0-0 14 ♘f5 ♘c5 15 d4 ♘e6 16 de ♗xf3 17 gf de 18 ♔h1 ♕d3 19 ♗e3 ♕e2 20 ♘h4 ♗xe3 21 fe ♕xe3 22 ♕c4 ♖fd8 23

♘f5 ♕d2 24 ♖g1 g6 25 ♖g2 ♕f4 26 ♘e7+ ♔g7 27 ♘d5 ♕h6 28 ♖ag1 ♖d7 29 ♕c6 ♖ad8 30 ♕xa6 ♖d6 31 ♕e2 ♔h8 32 ♕e3 g5 33 ♕e1 f6 34 ♖f2 c6 35 ♘e3 ♕h5 36 ♘g2 ♖d3 37 ♖gf1

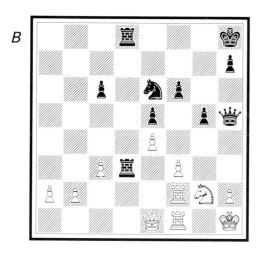

B

37 ... ♕f7 38 b4 ♕a7 39 ♕c1 ♕a6 40 ♕c2 ♕c4 41 ♖c1 ♖xc3 42 ♕xc3 ♕xc3 43 Resigns

After 43 ♖xc3 ♖d1+ 44 ♘e1 ♖xe1+ 45 ♔g2 ♘f4+ 46 ♔g3 ♖g1+ and mates.

Chinese Chess (Siang K'i)

Chess came to China from India about 750 AD and is mentioned in the *Book of Marvels* (written about 800, but only made public in 1088). The Chinese made significant changes to the game and their present version has only a general resemblance to chess. It is played on a board of 9 by 10 lines. The pieces (round discs with characters on the upper surface) are placed on the intersection points instead of the squares. There is a river added in the middle.

Each side has a general (G), two mandarins (M), two elephants (E), two horses (H), two chariots (Ch), two cannon (C) and five soldiers (S) and are set out as:

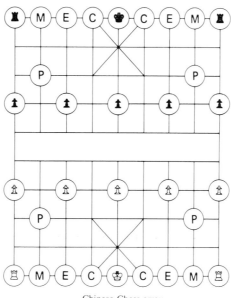

Chinese Chess array

The idea is to immobilize the opposing general (the generals are restricted to the fortress—the diagonal line areas in front of the generals).

Robert Hübner is a world class player of Chinese chess.
See *The Board Game Book* by R. C. Bell (1979), *Hsiang Ch'i, The Chinese Games of Chess* by Terence Donnelly (1974).

Christiansen, Larry Mark

[*June 27 1956–*]
US GM(1977) who was runner-up at the 1975 World Junior Championship, 1st at Torremolinos 1977 (VIII), 1st at Linares 1979 (IX), equal 1st at the 1980 US Championship and equal 1st with Karpov at Linares 1981 (XIII). Then there seemed to be a levelling off with a touch of decline. He was equal 1st at the 1983 US Championship and he beat Reshevsky +2=5−1 in 1984, but he could only manage an equal 10th at Linares 1985 (XIV) and equal 3rds at two Category X tournaments—US Championship 1985 and San Francisco 1987.

He has played on the US Olympiad teams from 1980 to 1986.

Churchill, Lord Randolph

[*February 13 1849–January 24 1895*]

Winston Churchill's father was an ardent chess player. He took lessons from both Steinitz and Zukertort, was a vice president of the British Chess Association and a frequent spectator at the great London tournament of 1883.

Steinitz played 6 blindfold simultaneous games at Oxford on May 17, 1870, and one of his wins was against Randolph Churchill. In August 1870 Steinitz drew against a group of allies that included Churchill (*see* Bachmann's *Steinitz*).

Cinema

Chess is often used in cinema to create an intellectual atmosphere, with the added benefit that exotic chess pieces are visually beautiful. For example chess was used in Casablanca (1943), A Matter of Life and Death or Stairway to Heaven (1946), The Wooden Horse (1950), From Russia with Love (1963) and The Thomas Crown Affair (1968).

Occasionally chess forms a vital part of the story, e.g. in L'Atlantide (1950 and earlier, in the 1930s), The Seventh Seal (1956), Die Schachnouvelle or The Royal Game (1960), The Bishop Murder Case (1930) and The Chess Player (about the automaton The Turk, 1938 and earlier in 1926). More recently Dangerous Moves (1984) deals with a world title match.

There are also some non-commercial chess movies like Chess Fever starring Capablanca (made during 1925 when Lasker and Capablanca played in Moscow), The White Snows of Russia (about Alekhine), Black and White Like Day is Knight, The Great Chess Movies (1983), and Three Moves to Freedom.

Ciocaltea, Victor

[*January 16 1932–September 10 1983*]
Romanian GM (1978) who was Romanian Champion 8 times during 1952–79. Internationally, he won at Reggio Emilia 1966/7 and 1968/9, Dortmund 1974 and Bucharest 1975. His last tournament

was at Thessalonika 1983, where he placed 3rd.

Ciric, Dragoljub Miladin

[*November 12 1935– *]
Yugoslav GM(1965) who rose almost to the top of Yugoslav chess. His best results are equal 1st with Tal at Sarajevo 1966, equal 1st with Lein at Sarajevo 1968, and equal 1st at Saint Felin de Guixols 1975.

He was on two Yugoslav Olympiad teams (1966 and 1968). Since then his health has given way and his results have declined.

Clarke, Peter Hugh

[*March 18 1933– *]
English player and author who placed 2nd in five British Championships and played on 8 English Olympiad teams during 1954–68.

Major works: *Tal's Best Games* (1961) *Petrosian's Best Games* (1965).

Clocks

Time limits were first enforced with sandglasses—an hour glass for each player. While White thought, his glass stood upright and sand trickled out, whereas Black's glass was put on its side. When White made his move, he stopped his sand by putting his glass on its side and putting Black's glass upright. In this way each player's thinking time was measured. Sandglasses were used in London 1862 to enforce the time limit of 20 moves in 2 hours.

Mechanical clocks replaced sandglasses about 1880 and were used at London 1883. Improvements were added over the years. Pendulum action (to start one clock and stop the other) was replaced by pushbuttons between 1895 and 1900. A small flag was introduced which was lifted by the minute hand and fell at the hour. And by the 1970s, electronic digital clocks made their appearance.

See Time Limit.

Closed Game

A game where the movement of pieces is restricted and there is much manoeuvring behind the lines in anticipation of the position opening up.

Closed Sicilian

See Sicilian Defence

Cochrane, John

[*February 4 1798–January 2 1878*]
A Scottish barrister of the Middle Temple and a leading London player of the early 19th century. His sacrificial style did not serve him well when he visited France in 1821. He lost a match to La Bourdonnais and at odds of pawn and two moves, he lost a match to Deschapelles. He left England in 1824 to join the Indian Bar and remained in India until his retirement in 1869. During 1841–3 he returned to London on leave. During this period he played over 600 casual games with Staunton (losing the majority) and he played a match with Saint-Amant, winning $+6=1-4$. His brilliant style was frequently unsound.

Major work: *A Treatise on the Game of Chess*(1822).

Colle System

1 d4 d5 2 ♘f3 ♘f6 3 e3.

The favourite opening of the Belgium master Edgar Colle. It looks modest and unassuming, but it can develop real force if Black is not careful. White plans the eventual central thrust e4. One main line is 3 ... c5 4 ♘bd2 ♘bd7 5 c3 e6 6 ♗d3 ♗e7 7 0-0 0-0 8 e4 de 9 ♘xe4 ♘xe4 10 ♗xe4 ♘f6 11 ♗c2 b6 with equality.

Collijn, Ludwig

[*November 20 1878–October 4 1939*]
Swedish author and organizer who is best known for his famous *Larobok*, a treatise on openings and endings written in collaboration with his brother Gustaf (1880–1968). They also wrote several tournament books together.

Ludwig organized and directed the 1937 Stockholm Olympiad and was president of the Swedish Chess Association (1917–39).

Major works: *Larobok i Schack* (1898), *Adolf Anderssen* (1918).

Combination

An unexpected sequence of forcing moves that usually involves a sacrifice and leads to some desirable goal for the player who initiates the combination.

Computers

The first genuine chess playing machine was designed and built in 1890 by the Spanish inventor Torres y Quevedo and is currently housed in the museum of Madrid Polytechnic. This electromechanical device was one of the earliest rule-based 'Expert Systems'. The machine could only play the ending of king and rook against king, but was always able to force a win, though not in the optimal number of moves. It worked by assigning each position to one of six categories, then using a rule for the appropriate category in order to generate its move.

The foundations of all modern chess programming lie in the seminal paper 'Programming a Computer for Playing Chess' by the American mathematician Claude Shannon. Based on a lecture given in April 1949, Shannon's paper was published in 1950 and suggested two fundamentally different programming strategies. Shannon's 'A' strategy was based on the concept of looking ahead to a fixed depth along all variations and evaluating all the positions at the resulting depth. This has the disadvantage that a program would be highly prone to error as a result of making assessments in a 'turbulent' position, for example in the middle of a sequence of captures. Recognizing this problem Shannon proposed the 'B' strategy in which the program would not always terminate its look-ahead at the same depth, but would sometimes continue searching until a 'quiescent' position was reached. The profundity of Shannons ideas can be gauged from the fact that 40 years later virtually every chess program employs the Shannon 'B' strategy in one form or another.

The period from 1950 to the late 1960s saw very little progress in computer chess because few people had access to computers. Research into the subject by Alan Turing (at Manchester University), Alex Bernstein (at IBM) and Alen Newell, Cliff Shaw and Herb Simon (at Carnegie Institute of Technology—now Carnegie Mellon University), failed to produce a program capable of giving a club player a good game. But in 1967 Richard Greenblatt, an undergraduate at MIT, wrote a program called MACHACK VI which gained a measure of success. The Greenblatt program was made an honorary member of the Massachusetts Chess Association and of the United States Chess Federation, and competed in a few local tournaments, achieving a performance rating on the USCF scale of 1640.

The relative success of MACHACK VI and the publicity it generated during the late 1960s acted as a catalyst. By 1970 interest in computer chess and the greater availability of computer time, particularly at universities, spawned enough programs to create a tournament in which all the participants were computers. This milestone event took place in the New York Hilton, from August 31st to September 2nd 1970, as part of the annual conference of the Association for Computing Machinery (ACM). It was won by a program called CHESS 3.0, written at Northwestern University by David Slate, Larry Atkin and Keith Gorlen. Various generations of this program won eight of the first ten annual ACM tournaments, as well as the 1977 World Computer Chess Championship which took place in Toronto.

In August 1968 the Scottish Chess Champion, David Levy, who subsequently gained the International Master title, started a bet that no computer program would be able to win a match against him within 10 years. In August 1978 Levy successfully defended the bet, which stood at £1250, in a match in Toronto against the World Champion program CHESS 4.7, scoring 3 wins, 1 draw and 1 loss. Levy won a subsequent bet of $1000 placed for a 5-year period, when he beat the reigning World Champion CRAY BLITZ in London, 1984, by a score of 4–0, but after that he stopped betting on himself!

The availability of microprocessors in the late 1970s brought chess programming within the range of computer hobbyists and created a market for dedicated chess computers. Programs such as MICROCHESS, written by Peter Jennings, and SARGON, by Kathe and Dan Spacklen, became instant successes in the market place for home computer software. The first commercially available chess computer was the 'Chess Challenger', launched by Fidelity Electronics of Chicago in January 1977. Fidelity built up a substantial international market demand with their 'Chess Challenger' range, and remain one of the major forces in the field. The chess computer business quickly grew into a multi-million dollar industry. Programmers such as the Spracklens, and later Richard Lang, who between them have won every World Microcomputer Chess Championship from 1980 to 1989, became highly marketable commodities. Powerful 32-bit chips and a wealth of clever programming ideas (often closely guarded secrets) have brought the strength of the best microprocessor-based programs close to that of programs running on multi-million dollar mainframes.

One of the biggest technical advances in computer chess was pioneered by Ken Thompson at Bell Telephone Labs in Murray Hill, New Jersey. Thompson created BELLE, which consisted largely of electronic hardware able to perform, at great speeds, tasks which are conventionally performed by software, such as generating a list of all the legal moves in a position. This speed-up made possible the evaluation of hundreds of thousands of chess positions per second and enabled BELLE to win the 1980 World Computer Chess Championship in Linz, Austria. Subsequently Thompson used BELLE to perform complete analyses of endgames involving only 4 or 5 pieces. His work corrected a number of errors in the chess endgame literature, and included a proof that king and two bishops v king and knight is nearly always a win (this ending had previously been considered to be drawn).

Thompson's work on special purpose hardware was taken one step further by Feng Hsiung-Hsu, a graduate student at Carnegie Mellon University. Hsu designed a single silicon chip to perform all the functions of BELLE, but at speeds allowing one million or more position evaluations per second. In 1988 Hsu's program DEEP THOUGHT tied for first place with Grandmaster Tony Miles at a tournament in Long Beach, California. Amongst the Grandmasters who finished behind DEEP THOUGHT in that event were Bent Larsen, who was defeated by the program in their individual game, and ex-World Champion Mikhail Tal. Hsu and two of his colleagues were subsequently hired by IBM, with the aim of producing a chess machine of Kasparov's calibre by 1994 or thereabouts. Most of the participants and expert spectators at the 1989 World Computer Chess Championship conjectured that it would take rather longer. In late 1989, DEEP THOUGHT was defeated 2–0 by Kasparov, but surpassed the previous benchmark of computer chess by beating Levy 4–0.

See Computer Chess Compendium,

David Levy (Editor) (1989), *How to Beat Your Chess Computer*, by Levy and Keene (1991).

See also International Computer Chess Association.

David Levy

Cook

A solution of a chess problem in fewer moves than the composer thought possible or an alternative solution that the composer was not aware of.

Coons score

See Tie breaking Systems

Correspondence Chess

Chess played at a distance or by mail has come a long way since, allegedly, Henry I of England played against Louis VI of France in about 1119. The first authenticated postal game began in 1804 (between F. W. de Mauvillon of Breda and an officer in The Hague). In 1824–8 Edinburgh beat London + 2 = 2 − 1; in 1834-6 Paris beat the Westminster Club + 2; and in 1842–6 Pest beat Paris + 2.

The International Correspondence Chess Association (ICCA) was founded in 1946 and became a Federation (ICCF) in 1949. *Fernschach*, a monthly magazine for correspondence chess, ran from 1929–39 and from 1951 onwards. It is the organ of the ICCF.

World correspondence chess championships began in 1950:

1. 1950–3 1 Purdy (Australia) 2/3 Malmgren (Sweden), Napolitano (Italy)

   Dyckhoff Memorial 1954–6 1 Schmid (West Germany) 2 O'Kelly (Belgium)
2. 1956–9 1 Ragozin (USSR) 2/3 Endzelins (Australia), Schmid (West Germany)
3. 1959–62 1 O'Kelly (Belgium) 2 Dubinin (USSR)
4. 1962–5 1 Zagorovsky (USSR) 2 Borisenko (USSR)
5. 1965–8 1 Berliner (USA) 2/3 Hybl (Czechoslovakia), Husak (Czechoslovakia)
6. 1968–71 1 Rittner (East Germany) 2 Zagorovsky (USSR)
7. 1972–5 1 Estrin (USSR) 2/3 Boey (Belgium), Zagorovsky (USSR)
8. 1975–80 1/2 Sloth (Denmark), Zagorovsky (USSR)
9. 1977–83 1 Yim (USSR) 2/3 Baumbach (East Germany), Michailov (USSR)
10. 1978–84 1 Palciauskas (US) 2 Morgado (Argentina)
11. 1982–8 1 Baumbach (East Germany) 2/3 Nesis (USSR) Mikhailov (USSR)
12. 1988– Now in Progress
13. Begun in November 1989

World Team Correspondence Championships

1952	Hungary	1972	USSR
1955	Czech and Sweden	1977	USSR
1961	USSR	1982	USSR
1964	USSR	1987	Great Britain
1968	USSR Czech		

International Correspondence GMs
Argentina: J. S. Morgado (1983); *Australia:* R. Arlauskas (1965); *Belgium:* J. Boey (1975), W. Maes (1988); *Bulgaria:* G. Popow (1976); *Canada:* D. Suttles (1982), J. Hebert (1984), B. Kivisho (1984), J. Berry (1985); *Czechoslovakia:* K. Husak (1968, J. Hybl (1968), Dr J. Franzen (1984), J. Jezek (1985); *Denmark:* J. Sloth (1978), E. Bang (1979), O. Ekebjaerg (1987); *East Germany:* H. Rittner (1960), Dr F. Baumbach (1973), V. M. Anton (1987), H. Handel (1987); *Finland:* R. Kauranen (1977), P. Palmo (1980), O. Koskinen (1982), J. Sorri (1982), P. Lehikoinen (1985); *Great Britain:* K. B. Richardson (1975), A. S. Hollis (1976), P. H. Clarke (1980), Dr J. Penrose (1983), S. Webb (1983), P. R. Markland (1984), D. M. Bryson (GB/S) (1986), N. E. Povah (1989); *Holland:* H. B. Sarink (1979), D. Smit (1979), A. den Ouden (1980), H. Bouwmeester (1981), H. Kramer (1984), G. C. van Perlo (1985), T. Wiersma (1985), G. J. Timmerman (1986); *Hungary:* L. Barczay (1979), S. Brilla-Banfalvi (1979); *Italy:* Dr M. Napolitano (1953); *Poland:* S. Brzozka (1985); *Romania:* G. Rotariu (1981), P. Diaconescu (1982), M. Breazu (1985); *Sweden:* A. Lundquist (1962), E. Arnlind (1968); *Switzerland:* J. Steiner (1973); *USA:* H. Berliner (1968), V. Palciauskas (1983); *USSR:* G. Borissenko (1965), W. Zagorowsky (1965), A. I. Chassin (1972), I. Morosow (1973), O. L. Moissejew (1977), D. I. Lapienis (1979), W. T. Kosenkow (1979), T. O. Yim (1981), A. I. Mikhailov (1983), D. Godes (1984), G. K. Sanakoew (1984), G. Nesis (1985), L. E. Omeltschenko (1986); *West Germany:* L. Schmid (1959), Dr H. W. Dünhaupt (1973), Dr K. Engel (1983), P. Heilemann (1984), G. Stertenbrink (1984), D. Stern (1985), H. Heemsoth (1987), R. Mallée (1989); *Yugoslavia:* M. Berta (1978), P. Keglevic (1978), F. Brglez (1979), B. Vukcevic (1982), R. Tomasevic (1984), M. Jovcic (1985), J. Kondali (1986).

Counter-Gambit

Originally this meant a gambit played in response to a gambit, like the Falkbeer or Albin Counter-Gambits. It usually was a line played by Black. Now, however, it seems to mean any gambit played by Black, e.g. the Budapest Counter-Gambit.

Cozio, Count Carlo Francesco

[*18th century*]
Italian author of a 2 volume chess book *Il Giuoco degli Scacchi*. Lothar Schmid owns the original 1740 manuscript (410 pages). The Ruy Lopez variation 1 e4 e5 2 ♘f3 ♘c6 3 ♗b5 ♘ge7 is called Cozio's Defence.

Csom, Istvan

[*June 2 1940–*]
Hungarian GM (1973) who won the

Hungarian Championship in 1972 and was equal 1st in 1973. He was 1st or equal 1st at Olot (1973), Hamburg (1974), Cleveland, Olot and Pulain (1975), Berlin (1979), Copenhagen (1983), Jarvenpaa (1985) and Delhi (1987).

He has played on several Hungarian Olympiad teams. He has never made it to the Candidates but he is a good solid GM.

Cunningham, Alexander [1654–1737]

Scottish historian and diplomat; British Minister in Venice 1715–20. He popularized the defence 1 e4 e5 2 f4 ef 3 ♘f3 ♗e7 to the King's Gambit and this line is called the Cunningham Gambit.

Curaçao

A Dutch island of the Netherlands Antilles in the Caribbean off the NW coast of Venezuela, which staged the 5th Candidates tournament in 1962.

Keres, Geller and Petrosian agreed to draw with each other thus giving themselves 8 easy rounds, and letting their play against the others determine the winner. This probably harmed Keres because he may have been a little stronger than Geller and Petrosian, and might well have achieved a plus against them. Fischer complained about Russian collusion though he lost 7 games and was unlikely to win the tournament in any case.

Korchnoi led (5–2) after the first round robin but seemed to burn out. At age 30 he should have been at his peak, but it turned out that he was at his best 15 years later, at age 45. Tal had kidney problems and went into hospital after the third round robin. He eventually lost one kidney.

With 3 rounds to go Keres (16) and Petrosian (16) led. Petrosian then drew with Benko, Fischer and Filip. Keres drew with Geller, lost to Benko and drew with Fischer.

Cvitan, Ognjen   [October 10 1961–]

Yugoslav GM (1987) who was the World Junior Champion (1981). He has won several open events, was equal 2nd at Vrsac 1985 (X) and was first at Prague 1987 (VII). Perhaps his best result was equal 4th at Vrsac 1987 (XII).

Czerniak, Moshe

[February 3 1910–August 31 1984] Player (IM 1952) and author who was born in Poland, emigrated to Palestine in the mid 1930s, lived in Argentina 1939–52 and finally settled in Israel. He was champion of Palestine (1936) and Israel (1955) and played on many Israeli Olympiad teams during 1952–68.

He was famous for his tenacity, having played a 191 move game (a record at the time) and having been the last player to finish at the Olympiads of 1952 and 1962.

Major works: *La Partida Francesa* (1950), *El Final* (1951).

Curaçao 1962 Candidates Tournament

		1		2		3		4		5		6		7		8		
1	Petrosian	—	—	½	½	½	½	½	1	½	½	½	½	½	1	1	1	17½
		—	—	½	½	½	½	½	½	1	1	1	½	1	½	½	—	
2	Geller	½	½	—	—	½	½	1	1	½	½	½	½	½	1	½	1	17
		½	½	—	—	½	½	½	0	1	½	½	1	1	½	1	—	
	Keres	½	½	½	½	—	—	0	½	½	½	1	1	½	1	1	½	17
		½	½	½	½	—	—	1	½	1	½	1	0	1	½	1	—	
4	Fischer	½	0	0	0	1	½	—	—	0	1	0	1	1	½	½	1	14
		½	½	½	1	0	½	—	—	0	½	½	1	1	½	½	—	
5	Korchnoi	½	½	½	½	½	½	1	0	—	—	½	½	1	1	1	0	13½
		0	0	0	½	0	½	1	½	—	—	½	0	1	1	½	—	
6	Benko	½	½	½	½	0	0	1	0	½	½	—	—	0	1	1	0	12
		0	½	½	0	0	1	½	0	½	1	—	—	1	½	½	—	
7	Filip	½	0	½	0	½	0	0	½	0	0	1	0	—	—	0	1	7
		0	½	0	½	0	½	0	½	0	0	0	½	—	—	½	—	
	Tal	0	0	½	0	0	½	½	0	0	1	0	1	1	0	—	—	7
		½	—	0	—	0	—	½	—	½	—	½	—	½	—	—	—	

D

Dake, Arthur William

[*April 8 1910– *]
US IM (1954) and honorary GM (1986) who played on three winning US Olympiad teams in the 1930s. He scored +13 = 5 − 0 on board four for the highest percentage in the Warsaw 1935 Olympiad. He was equal 3rd at Pasadena 1932 where he won a fine game from Alekhine. He did not do well in US Championships, but in the 1946 match with the USSR he drew his two games with Lilienthal.

Damiano [*15th–16th century*]
He was the author of *Questo libro e da imparare giocare a scachi et de li partiti*, the earliest Italian printed work on chess, published in Rome in 1512. Almost nothing is known of Damiano's life except that he was Portuguese by birth, from the town of Odemira, and an apothecary by profession.

His book is a mixture of problems, studies, aphorisms ('when you find a good move, look for a better') and opening analysis. It enjoyed considerable popularity (Ruy Lopez did not appear until 50 years later) running through eight Italian editions in the 16th century, and was translated into French, English and German. In it, he analysed what has come to be known as Damiano's Defence (1 e4 e5 2 ♘f3 f6), and he condemned it (3 ♘xe5 virtually refutes it).

Damjanovic, Mato

[*March 23 1927– *]
Yugoslav GM (1964) who was equal 2nd at Sochi 1964, 1st at Zagreb 1969 and equal 1st at Bad Pyrmont 1970. He played on the 1960 Yugoslav Olympiad team.

Damljanovic, Branko

[*June 17 1961– *]
Yugoslav GM (1989) who was 1st at the Graz Open (1987), equal 1st at the Belgrade Open (1987) and equal 2nd at the Saint John Swiss (1988).

Danish Gambit
1 e4 e5 2 d4 ed 3 c3.

This wild offshoot of the Centre Game is rarely seen nowadays because after 3 ... dc 4 ♗c4 cb 5 ♗xb2 d5 6 ♗xd5 ♘f6 7 ♗xf7+ ♔xf7 8 ♕xd8 ♗b4+ 9 ♕d2 ♗xd2+ 10 ♘xd2 c5 few White players are happy to be two pawns down, even if the resulting position is about equal, objectively speaking.

Dante (Alighieri) [*1265–1321*]
Italian poet, author of *The Divine Comedy*, and chess player.

Darga, Klaus Viktor

[*February 24 1934– *]
German GM (1964) who won the West German Championship in 1955 and 1961, and played on ten West German Olympiad teams from 1954–78. He was equal 1st with Panno in the 1953 World Junior Championship and had quite a successful chess career with wins at Madrid 1957, Bognor Regis 1960, equal 1st at Palma de Mallorca 1965 and an excellent equal 1st with Larsen at Winnipeg 1967. Darga never made it to the Candidates but he was a strong and solid GM. In the last 15 years he has devoted more time to his career as a computer programmer.

Dark Bishop
A bishop that moves on the dark squares, that is, one that starts out at c1 (white) or f8 (black). Also referred to as the dark-squared bishop.

Dawson, Thomas Rayner
[*November 28 1889–December 16 1951*]
British problemist who composed over 6000 problems. He pioneered and specialized in 'fairy chess' or non-orthodox problems. These involved helpmates, selfmates, retrograde analysis as well as new kinds of boards and new kinds of pieces. He invented, for example, the grasshopper—it moves like a queen but it must hop over another piece (of either colour) and land on the next square beyond. If that square has an enemy piece, the grasshopper can capture it. If

that square has a piece of the same colour as the grasshopper, then the move is not playable. Such new pieces add enormous variety to ordinary problems. The grasshopper is often represented as a queen upside-down.

Dawson edited *The Problemist* (1922–31), the problem section of the *British Chess Magazine* (1931-51) and the *Fairy Chess Review* (1930–51). He was president of the British Chess Problem Society (1931–43).

Major Works: *Retrograde Analysis* (1915), *Caissa's Wild Roses* (1935), *Caissa's Fairy Tales* (1947).

See *Chess Unlimited* by Fabel and Kemp (1969), *A Guide to Fairy Chess* by A. S. M. Dickens (1971).

De Firmian, Nicholas Ernest
[*July 26 1957– *]
US GM (1985) who was equal 4th at Oslo 1984 (XIII) and 2nd at the 1984 US Championship (XI). After a bad patch in 1985 and 1986, he was equal 1st at the 1987 US Championship (XII). He played on the 1984 and 86 US Olympiad teams.

De Groot, Adriaan
[*October 21 1914– *]
Dutch player and psychology professor who played on the Dutch Olympiad team in 1936, 1937 and 1939. He wrote *Thought and Choice in Chess* (1965), where he analysed chess masters' mental processes, based partly on his association and experiments with such prominent players as Alekhine and Fine.

Decoy Sacrifice
A sacrifice that lures a hostile piece to a disadvantageous square, or at least away from an important location.

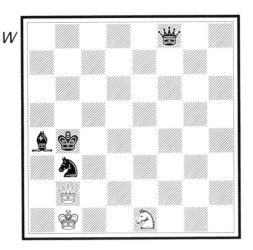

After the elegant 1 ♕a3+ Black must accept this decoy sacrifice otherwise he loses his queen. Then comes 1 ... ♚xa3 2 ♘c2 mate, proving that the a3 square is deadly dangerous for the black king.

Defence, The
Excellent novel by Vladimir Nabokov, about a chess master who becomes obsessed with the game and loses his mind. Originally written in Russian (1930) as *Luzhin's Defence*, under the pseudonym V. Sirin, it appeared in English in 1964.

Demonstration board
A large wall-board showing the position of a chess game, used either for a lecture or in a tournament. There are flat representative pieces and attendants move these pieces shortly after the moves are actually played. This allows spectators to see clearly what is happening on the actual playing board. Some demonstration boards also have clocks showing the two thinking times used.

There are now electronic wall-board and TV monitors that react instantly via a connection with the actual board and make it easy for an audience to be completely involved in the action.

Denker, Arnold Sheldon
[*February 21 1914– *]
US IM (1950) and Honorary GM (1981) who won the US Championship in 1944.

Deschapelles, Alexandre Louis Honore Lebreton
[*March 7 1780–October 27 1847*]
French player who was probably the strongest player in the world from 1800 to 1820. He was vain, boastful and colourful, but he did have a great natural talent for games in general and chess in particular.

He disdained opening knowledge and gave everyone odds, either pawn and move or pawn and two moves. When his star pupil (LaBourdonnais) surpassed him, he retired from chess (in the early 1820s) and took up whist. Here he made a great success and even today the Deschapelles coup in whist reminds us of his genius.

As late as 1836 he held his own (+1=1−1) conceding pawn and two moves to Saint-Amant.

Deschapelles, the son of a French marshal, served with distinction in Napoleon's army, and lost his right arm in the fighting.

Descriptive notation
See Notation

Desperado
When a piece is trapped or doomed to capture, or when it obstructs its own pieces from powerful action, it becomes a 'desperado'. It runs amok and impales itself, kamikaze like, inflicting maximum damage on the enemy.

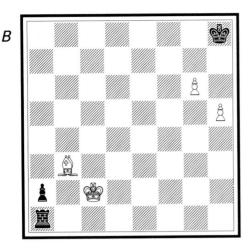

The black a-pawn is anxious to become a queen but it is obstructed by its own rook. The rook then is a desperado and after 1 ... ♖c1+, 2 ♔xc1 a1(♛)+ and wins.

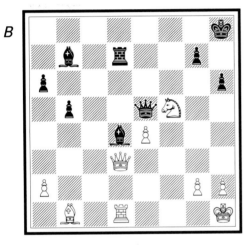

In this position from Popiel–Marco, the black bishop at d4 is doomed because it is attacked 3 times and cannot be defended, and because it cannot simply move away else White captures the black rook. Marco actually resigned here, but the bishop is a desperado and after 1 ... ♗g1! threatening mate at h2, White can only play 2 ♔xg1 ♖xd3 and Black would have won.

Deutsche Schachzeitung

The oldest chess magazine still in existence. Founded in 1846 by Bledow and called *Schachzeitung*, it took its current name in 1872. Its best period was 1900–

20. It stopped publishing in 1945 but started up again in October 1950.

Development

A measure of how many pieces have been brought into the action, or at least have moved off their starting squares. One can be ahead in development (have more pieces in play) or one can be better developed (have pieces more effectively placed). Either one usually confers an advantage. However, there are positions where, say, White is ahead in development while Black is better developed. For example:

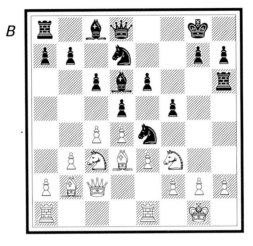

Here 6 of White's pieces are developed but only 4 of Black's. However, Black's pieces are more effectively placed and in fact Black can win a pawn with 1 ... ♗xh2+ 2 ♘xh2 ♛h4. The white knight at h2 dare not move because of 3 ... ♛h1 mate and thus White must give up this knight.

De Vere, Cecil

[February 14 1845–February 9 1875] Englishman (real name, Valentine Brown) who won the first official British Championship (1866) and was equal 1st in 1868 and 1872 (he lost the play-offs). He was handsome, charming and chivalrous and his chess career seemed full of promise. Steinitz was unable to give him odds of pawn and move in 1865/6, Steinitz losing +3=2−7 under these odds.

De Vere worked at Lloyds Bank. When he discovered he had tuberculosis, he gave up his employment and devoted himself to chess. He was 5th at Paris 1867, equal 6th at Baden Baden 1870 and equal 3rd at London 1872, but he could not make it into the top 5 or 6.

He did edit the chess column in *The Field* during 1872, but indolence, alcohol and depression, combined with his major illness, destroyed him.

Diagram

A pictorial representation of the chess board. Usually White plays up the page and Black down the page.

Diderot, Denis   *[1713–1784]*

French philosopher, critic and encyclopedist, who enjoyed chess.

Diez del Corral, Jesus

[April 6 1933–] Spanish GM (1974) who won the Spanish Championship in 1955 and 1965. He was the second Spanish player to become a GM (Pomar was the first). He is a genuine amateur (an accountant by profession) whose undoubted talents have been handicapped by his inability to give full time to chess. His best results are 2nd at Amsterdam 1969, 2nd at Olot 1972 and equal 3rd at Montilla 1973. He has played on several Spanish Olympiad teams.

Discovered check

A check given by a piece, itself stationary, when another piece is moved out of the way.

Distant opposition

See Opposition

Divinsky, Nathan Joseph

[October 29 1925–] Canadian mathematician, chessplayer and author. He played on the Canadian Olympiad team (1954 and 1966), edited

Canada's chess magazine (1959–74) and has been Canada's FIDE representative since 1987. He was on the BBC chess TV show during the London half of the Kasparov–Karpov match of 1986.

Major work: *Warriors of the Mind* (with R. Keene) (1989).

Dizdarevic, Emir   [*April 2 1958–*]
Yugoslav GM (1988) who was equal 1st at Pleven 1987 (VIII) and at Sarajevo 1988 (X).

Djuric, Stefan   [*July 26 1955–*]
Yugoslav GM (1982) who won at Vrnjacka Banja 1979 (VII) and Ljubljana 1981 (VII).

Dlugy, Maxim   [*January 29 1966–*]
US GM (1986) who was born in the USSR, but emigrated to the US as a young boy. He was equal 3rd in the 1984 US Championship (XI) and followed this up by winning the World Junior Championship in 1985. After an equal 2nd in New York 1985 (X) and an equal 2nd in Clichy 1986/87 (X) he was again equal 3rd in the 1987 US Championship (XII). He played on the 1986 US Olympiad team.

He is a bright, talented and charming young man with great potential. He does enjoy life and thus may find it difficult to work hard enough in order to climb up to the Candidates level.

Dodgson, Charles Lutwidge
      [*1832–1898*]
English mathematician and writer of books for children, better known as Lewis Carroll. His *Through the Looking Glass* is filled with chess pieces and a full chess game.

Dokhoian, Yuri   [*1964–*]
USSR GM (1988) who was 3rd at Erevan 1988 (XI) and did well at Plovdiv 1988 (IX).

Dolmatov, Sergei Viktorovich
      [*February 20 1959–*]
USSR GM (1982) who won the World Junior Championship in 1978. He has had wins at Amsterdam 1979, Bucharest 1981, Frunze 1983, Barcelona 1983 and a fine win at Tallinn 1985 (IX). Perhaps his best results were 2nd at Minsk 1982 (XI), equal 3rd at Moscow 1987 (XII), but above all 1st at Hastings 1989/90 (XIV).

He has played in 5 USSR Championships during 1979–87 and has achieved exactly 50% in the 85 games played.

Donner, Johannes Hendrikus (Jan Hein)
      [*July 26 1927–November 27 1988*]
Dutch GM (1959) who won the Dutch Championship in 1954, 1957 and 1958. In winning the 1954 event, he headed Euwe—the first time Euwe was unsuccessful in these championships since 1920. However, Donner lost a match to Euwe +0 =6 −4, in 1956.

Donner's best results were equal 1st at Beverwijk 1958, 1st at Beverwijk 1963, 1st at Amsterdam 1965, 1st at Venice 1967 and 2nd in the strong four-man event at Leiden 1970 (Botvinnik's last tournament). He played on 12 Dutch Olympiad teams from 1950–78 and had a win over Fischer at the 1962 Olympiad. He was never a Candidate, but he played interesting and strong chess.

He learned the moves on August 22 1941, a day he remembers well. He had learned the moves at school and upon returning home, he discovered that his father (a distinguished judge) had been arrested by the Nazis.

He stopped playing when he fell ill in 1983.

Dorfman, Iosif Davidovich
      [*May 1 1953–*]
USSR GM (1978) whose best result was an equal 1st with Gulko in the 1977 USSR Championship (XII). The play-off match was drawn +1 =4 −1. Dorfman played in 6 USSR Championships during 1975–84. He had a win at Warsaw 1983 (IX) and was equal 1st at Lvov 1984 (XI). After that things did not go well though he did win at Moscow 1985 (VIII). In December 1986 he could only manage an equal 5th at Minsk (IX) and he did not play during 1987.

Dorfman was Kasparov's second in his first four World Championship matches.

D'Orville, Peter August [*1804–1864*]
Russian born French problemist who wrote *Problems d'échecs*—some 250 of his problems.

Dory's Defence
1 d4 ♘f6 2 c4 e6 3 ♘f3 ♘e4.
Occasionally used by Keres in the 1930s, but rarely played today. Its originator, Baron Ladislaux Dory, was a strong Viennese amateur in the 1930s.

Double bishop sacrifice
Since the Lasker–Bauer game at Amsterdam 1889, the sacrifice of both bishops to smash open the enemy king position, has become a standard attacking procedure. A later example is Koltanowski–Defosse, Ghent 1936:

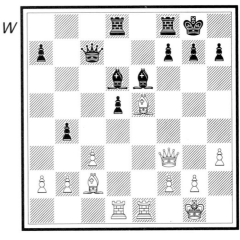

1 ♗xh7+ ♚xh7 2 ♕h5+ ♚g8 3 ♗xg7 ♚xg7 4 ♕g5+ ♚h8 5 ♖d4 ♗h2+ 6 ♔h1 ♕f4 7 ♖xf4 ♗xf4 8 ♕xf4 ♖g8 9 ♖e5 Resigns

Double Check

A discovered check in which both pieces check the enemy king. This is often a powerful weapon because the enemy king must move out of the way.

Double Fianchetto

Both bishops fianchettoed by one player.

Doubled Pawns

See Pawn Structure

Double Rook Sacrifice

The sacrifice of two rooks, as in the Immortal Game (*See* Anderssen). The rooks are passively allowed to be captured while exciting events are happening elsewhere. This is quite different from the double bishop sacrifice where the bishops are thrown at the enemy king position.

Dragon *See* Sicilian

Drama

See Theatre

Draw

A game where neither side wins. This can be achieved by repetition of moves, by stalemate, by the so-called 50 move rule (no exchanges and no pawn moves for 50 moves; see Fifty Move Rule for some modifications to this) or by mutual consent of the players. When using clocks, the proper way to offer a draw is to make one's move, then offer the draw and only then punch one's clock.

Drawing Master

Some top players draw many games and they are sometimes disparagingly called drawing masters. The top drawing master is Ulf Andersson who, against other top players, draws about 74% of his games (winning 10% and losing 16%). Other great drawers are Hort (70% =, 11% +, 19% −), Averbakh (69% =, 13% +, 18% −), Petrosian (69% =,

17% +, 14% −) and Flohr (67% =, 14% +, 19% −). More normal (although world title matches usually increase the number of draws) are Kasparov (62% =, 28% +, 10% −), Karpov (66% =, 25% +, 9% −), Fischer (45% =, 37% +, 18% −), Capablanca (61% =, 31% +, 8% −) and Lasker (35% =, 49% +, 16% −).

Dreyev, Alexei   [*January 30 1969–*]

USSR GM (1989) who was equal 1st at Protvino 1988(VIII) and equal 4th at Simferopol 1988(X). He won the European Junior Championship in December 1988.

Dubois, Serafino

[*October 10 1817–January 15 1899*] Italy's leading player in the mid 19th century who specialized in opening theory. He played infrequently but well. In 1845 he beat Wyvill in a series of games. In 1855 he beat Riviere + 22 = 3 − 8. In 1862 he placed 5th in London and lost a match (+ 3 = 1 − 5) to the young Steinitz.

He edited the first chess column (1847) in Italy and wrote up the 1875 Rome tournament (the first tournament in Italy), but his main effort was the three volume work on openings (1868–73): *Le principali apertura del gioco degli scacchi secondo i due diversi sistemi, italiano e francese.*

All of Europe except Italy used today's version of castling as established by Ruy Lopez in 1561. Italian players used different ways of castling, called free castling, and Dubois' writings dealt with both sets of rules. Italy did finally fall into line with the rest of Europe, shortly after Dubois' death.

Duchamp, Marcel

[*July 28 1887–October 1 1968*] Renowned French painter and chess player who was the father of Dadaism and a pioneer of Surrealism. He painted 'Portrait of Chess Players' 1911. In the

mid 1920s he devoted himself to chess and played in the French Championships and on French Olympiad teams (1928–33).

Dufresne, Jean

[*February 14 1829–April 13 1893*] German player who studied law and business administration but had to drop out to earn a living when his parents lost their money. He became a journalist and ended up as a newspaper editor in Berlin (1874).

He played many games with Anderssen and is well known for his sensational loss (the Evergreen game). In fact Anderssen felt that his success in London 1851 was partly due to the hard practice he had with Dufresne. Dufresne had a fine win over Harrwitz in 1848 with an Evans Gambit. He was 1st at the Berlin chess society tournament in 1853 and in that same year he beat Mayet 7 to 5.

He was involved with Anderssen in editing the *Berlin Schachzeitung* in 1857. He wrote *Theoretical and Practical Handbook* in 1863 and with Zukertort the *Great Chess Handbook* in 1871. He wrote books on Morphy, on problems and his popular *Kleine Lehrbuch des Schachspiels* in 1881. His writings were quite successful because of clever arrangement, careful selection and diligent labour.

He went totally deaf and had to abandon his newspaper career. He then turned completely to chess and in his last years he eked out a bare living writing columns and books. He wrote novels under the pseudonym E.S. Freund, an anagram of his real name. He died in penury, but he did teach many Germans the joy of chess.

Duras, Oldrich

[*October 30 1882–January 5 1957*] Czechoslovakian GM (1950) who won the Czech Championship in 1905, 1907 and 1909. He was very active from 1904 to 1914, and had equal 1sts at

Vienna 1908, Prague 1908 and Breslau 1912. He was second at Nuremberg 1906, Vienna 1907, Hamburg 1910, Abazzia 1911 and New York 1912. He was a fine positional player, good at both defence and attack, and stood just outside the top ten players of his time. He also composed deep studies and difficult problems.

In life scores he beat Teichmann (+6=6−2), Janowski (+3=0−1), Schlechter (+2=11−1) and Nimzowitsch (+3=2−2). He held his own against Tarrasch (+2=3−2) and Maroczy (+2=3−2) but was outclassed by Rubinstein (+2=1−10), Bernstein (+0=0−3), Vidmar (+3=2−8, Alekhine (+1=0−3), Marshall (+7 =5−8), Capablanca (+0=1−1) and Lasker (+0=0−1).

He stopped playing after Mannheim 1914—one of the very few European masters who stopped in mid-career. He was a civil servant and may have devoted himself to his career, but rumour has it that he married a wealthy lady and devoted himself to looking after her fortune.

See *O. Duras* by J. Louma *et al.* (1954).

Duras–Spielmann
Pistyan 1912

1 e4 e6 2 d4 d5 3 ♘c3 ♘f6 4 e5 ♘fd7 5 ♘ce2 c5 6 f4 ♘c6 7 c3 ♕b6 8 ♘f3 ♗e7 9 g3 f6 10 ♗h3 f5 11 0-0 0-0 12 g4 g6 13 gf gf 14 ♔h1 ♔h8 15 ♖g1 ♖f7 16 ♘g5 ♗xg5 17 ♖xg5 cd 18 ♕g1 ♘e7 19 ♘xd4 ♘f8 20 ♗f1 ♗d7 21 ♗e2 ♘fg6 22 ♕g3 ♖g8 23 b3 ♘c6 24 ♗e3 ♘xd4 25 ♗xd4 ♕a5 26 a4 a6 27 ♖g1 ♕d8 28 h4 ♕f8 29 h5

♕h6 30 ♗f3 ♖fg7 31 ♕h2 ♘e7 32 ♗c5 ♘c6 33 ♕h4 ♖g6 34 ♖1g2 ♗e8 35 b4 b5 36 ab ab 37 ♔h2 ♖xg5 38 fg ♕g7 39 ♕f4 ♘xe5 40 ♗d4 ♘xf3+ 41 ♕xf3 e5 42 h6 ♕e7 43 ♖e2 ♖xg5 44 ♖xe5 ♕d6

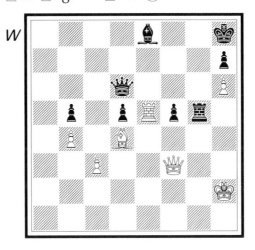

45 ♕g3! ♕xh6+ 46 ♕h3 ♕d6 47 ♔h1 ♔g8 48 ♖xe8+ ♔f7 49 ♖h8 Resigns.

Duz-Khotimirsky, Fyodor Ivanovich
[*September 26 1879–November 6 1965*] Russian IM (1950) who played in 5 USSR Championships during 1923 to 1933, scoring 46–41. He gave private lessons to Alekhine about 1900. He is best remembered for beating both prize-winners (Lasker and Rubinstein) at St Petersburg 1909. In 1910 he drew a 6 game match with Marshall.

In later life he played an organizational role in Soviet chess.

Dutch Defence
1 d4 f5.

This aggressive defence was favoured by Morphy, but only achieved

popularity when adopted by Botvinnik and Alekhine in the 1930s. Black weakens his position but hopes for compensating attacking prospects on the kingside. Chief variations are:

Staunton Gambit: 2 e4 fe 3 ♘c3. Introduced by Staunton in a match game vs Horwitz, London 1846. White sacrifices a pawn for long-term initiative.

Leningrad System: Black fianchettoes his king bishop.

Stonewall: 2 ♘f3 e6 3 g3 d5 when Black controls e4, but the weakness of his dark coloured squares is a serious handicap.

Fluid (Main Line): 2 ♘f3 e6 3 g3 ♘f6 4 ♗g2 ♗e7 5 0-0 0-0 6 c4 d6, when the success or otherwise of Black's strategy depends on White's ability to force through the advance e4 under favourable circumstances.

Dzindzihashvili, Roman Yakovlevich
[*May 5 1944– *] US GM (1977) who was born in the USSR, lived in Israel from 1976 to 1979 and then settled in the US. He played in two USSR Championships (1971 and 1972), won the Israeli Championship in 1977, won at Natanya 1977 and at Hastings 1977/78. His best result may have been his equal 3rd at Tilburg 1978 (XIV). He went on to win the Lone Pine Open 1980 and the 1983 US Championship (X). He led the US Olympiad team in 1984 scoring 8 to 3 on top board. After that his results declined, though he won several open tournaments during 1984 and 1985.

E

Early Versions of Chess

Chaturanga

One of the early versions of chess, invented in north-west India in the late 6th or early 7th century AD. The word *chaturanga* is Sanskrit for four-membered and represented the 4 parts of an Indian army infantry (*podati*)—our pawns; cavalry (*ashwa*)—our knights; chariots (*rat-ha*)—our rooks, and elephants (*hasti* or *gaja*)—our bishops. There was a king and a minister or advisor (*mantri*)—our queen.

The movements of the pieces were more restricted than they are today and thus the game was slower and more positional. The king, rook and knight moved as they do today but the *mantri* (queen) could only move to one adjacent diagonal square. The *hasti* (bishop) moved diagonally, leaping over the adjacent square to the next square. The *podati* (*pawn*) could not move 2 squares initially and when it reached the eighth rank, it had to become a *mantri*, which was no great improvement. There was no such thing as castling. However, the pieces were initially arranged as today and the aim of the game was the same.

See History of Chess

Chatrang

When *chaturanga* came to Persia in the 7th century, the Persians modified the name to *Chatrang* and their nomenclat-ure led to some of our names today. Our word 'checkmate' comes from *shah-mat*: the king is helpless or defeated. Our word 'pawn' comes from *pai*, the Persian word for foot (as in foot soldier).

Shatranj

When *Chantrang* came to the Arab world in the 7th century, the Arabs modified the name to *Shatranj*. There was also some option about the initial placing of the king and queen.

From 800 to 1000 AD, Islam led the world in *Shatranj* and produced a series of great masters, such as Al Adli, Ar Razi, As Suli and Al Lajlaj.

Edmondson, Edmund Broadley Jr., Lt. Colonel

[*August 13 1920–October 21 1982*] US chess organizer who played an essential role in Fischer's rise to the World Championship. He was president (1963) and executive director (1967–77) of the US Chess Federation, and US FIDE representative (1968–77). In 1969 he arranged the merger of *Chess Review* and *Chess Life*, the two major US chess publications.

Education and Acceptance of Chess

Chess had a difficult time being accepted as an honourable pastime. The Muslim religious lawyers debated for years before it was finally decided that though most games were forbidden, including chess played for money, the game of chess with no stake involved was not forbidden. It was officially disliked, but there was no penalty for playing. This allowed chess to flourish and Arabian players to become great masters.

The Christian church was at first quite hostile to chess but in time this intolerance eased, partially because of the moralities. The Jewish leadership absolutely forbade chess when played for money. Maimonides even said that professional chess players were unworthy witnesses in law courts. However, by the 16th century chess was accepted and recognized as a legitimate pastime even on the Sabbath. For example, after the plague of Cremona in 1575, the rabbis declared as a penance that all games, with the single exception of chess when not played for money, were prohibited for a year. Reshevsky, a religious Jew, was instructed in the 1940s that, since he was a chess professional, he could not play chess on the Sabbath—the day of rest.

Outside of religious restrictions, chess was popular. In 1100 'it formed a considerable part of the somewhat narrow education of a noble's children'. And 'chess was one of the knightly accomplishments'.

Chess certainly sharpens the brain and brings much pleasure to the players. However, it can become an obsession. It is desirable to have it available in schools as an option for those who are drawn to it. However, in the few cases where it has been made compulsory, it did not turn out to be a great success.

L'Echiquier   [1927–1939]
Belgian magazine of consistently high quality, edited by Edmond Lancel. It introduced figurine algebraic notation (*see* Notation).

Echo
A problem theme in which two or more defences are met with similar or corresponding attacking moves.

Edward I (Longshanks) [1239–1307]
King of England (1272–1307) who as a young man had a narrow escape from death while playing chess (*see Trivet's annales*, 1845). His wardrobe accounts for 1299/1300 lists a chess set made of crystal and jasper.

Edward III   [1312–1377]
King of England (1327–77) who, according to the *Froissart Chronicle* 1374, played chess with the Countess of Salisbury.

EG
An English quarterly magazine devoted to the endgame, founded by A. J. Roycroft.

Ehlvest, Jaan   [October 14 1962–]
USSR GM (1987) who was 2nd in the 1981 World Junior Championship and won the European Junior Championship in 1982/3. In 1987 he had good results in three Category XII tournaments: equal 3rd in the 54th USSR Championship, equal 2nd at Zagreb and equal 1st at Vrsac, and in 1990 he was 1st at Reggio Emilia (XVI), ahead of Ivanchuk and Karpov.

He played in 2 USSR Championships during 1984–7 and scored over 54%.

He was a Candidate in 1988, but lost his first match to Yusupov $+0=3-2$.

Eight Queens puzzle
See Puzzles

Eight Rooks puzzle
See Puzzles

Eingorn, Vereslav Semyenovich
                    [November 23 1956–]
USSR GM (1986) who played in 4 USSR Championships during 1984–7 and scored almost 58%. His best was equal 2nd in the 53rd Championship (1986).

His best results are equal 1st at Minsk 1983 (IX), equal 1st at Bor 1985 (X), equal 1st at Bor 1986 (XII), equal 1st at Moscow 1986 (XI) and equal 3rd in the 54th USSR Championship 1987 (XII).

Einstein, Albert
                    [March 14 1879–April 18 1955]
Famous physicist and developer of the theory of relativity, who was a friend and admirer of Lasker, but not a chess fan. He said: 'I have always disliked the fierce competitive spirit embodied in that highly intellectual game'.

Eliskases, Erich Gottlieb
                    [February 15 1913–]
Austrian GM (1952) who was stranded in Buenos Aires 1939 when war broke out and ended up an Argentinian. He was equal 1st in the 1929 Austrian Championship, beat Spielmann $+3=5-2$ in 1932 and won the Hungarian Championship in 1934, all at an early age. Things slowed down a little at this point. Though he beat Spielmann again ($+2=7-1$ in 1936 and $+2=8-0$ in 1937) he did not place at the strong Moscow 1936 tournament or at Semmering 1937. The field at Semmering was super-strong (Keres, Fine, Capablanca, Reshevsky, Flohr etc.) and Eliskases scored only $1\frac{1}{2}-5\frac{1}{2}$ in the first round robin, but he actually won the

second round robin $4\frac{1}{2}-2\frac{1}{2}$ with wins over Keres and Capablanca. He acted as Alekhine's second in the 1937 return match with Euwe. He had an excellent win at Noordvyik 1938 (XII) ahead of Keres and Euwe, won the German Championship in both 1938 and 1939, and in 1939 he beat Bogoljubow $+6=11-3$. He played in the Olympiad for Austria in 1930, 1933 and 1935, and for Germany in 1939.

He was a most difficult man to beat and his career seemed aimed for the very top. The war not only stranded him but dealt a cruel blow to his career by taking away 7 of his very best years. He continued to play and made a chess life for himself in South America but he never became a Candidate.

He was 1st at Sao Paulo 1941 and 1947, at Mar del Plata 1948 ahead of Najdorf and Stahlberg, and equal 2nd at Mar del Plata 1949. He was 1st at Punta del Este 1951, equal 1st at the 1951 South American zonal and equal 1st at Cordoba 1959. He played on Argentine Olympiad teams in 1952, 1958, 1960 and 1964.

Elizabeth I, Queen of England
                    [September 7 1533–March 24 1603]
She was a keen chess player, having been taught by her tutor Roger Ascham. She is supposed to have said: 'Darnley (the husband of Mary Queen of Scots) is only a pawn, but it may be checkmate if I am not careful'.

Ellerman, Arnoldo
                    [January 12 1893–November 21 1969]
Argentinian problemist who composed several thousand 'mate in two moves' problems. He wrote *1001 Problems* (1945).

Elo, Arpad Emrick
                    [August 25 1903–]
Hungarian-born US physicist and statistician who, in the early 1960s,

developed a mathematically sound and universally accepted (1970) rating system for chess players.

The Elo rating numbers range from about 2800 down. World Champions are about 2700, Grandmasters range between 2500 and 2700 and international masters range between 2300 and 2500.

A player's rating varies with performance and therefore with age. The highest rating ever achieved was Kasparov's 2800 in January 1990, ahead of Fischer's 2785 in 1972.

Elo was professor of physics at Marquette University in Milwaukee and was many times Wisconsin State chess champion.

See Age Changes in Master Chess Performance, in *Journal of Gerontology* (1965), *The Rating of Chess Players, Past and Present* (1978).

Encyclopaedia of Chess Openings

A 5-volume set of opening variations, edited by Matanovic. The original set came out in the late 1970s and revised versions keep it current.

Endgame

The final phase of a game, when most of the pieces have been removed from the board. Rules and theorems that hold for the opening and the middlegame often no longer hold in the endgame. For example the king, sheltered during the opening and middlegame, becomes an important and active piece in the endgame. A pawn, worth only about one third of a knight in the opening may be worth more than a ♕ + ♖ + ♘ in the endgame:

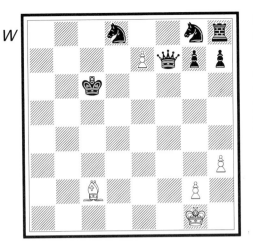

With 1 ed(♘)+ ♚d7 2 ♘xf7 and 3 ♘xh8, the pawn overwhelms the black army.

The practical player should know how to give mate in the basic endings where his opponent has only his king and he has either a queen or a rook or two bishops or a bishop and knight. It is curious that with king and two knights one cannot force a mate on a bare king, but there are some exceptional circumstances where the same pieces can force a mate against a king and pawn.

It is also useful to know that a rook pawn and a bishop of opposite colour to the queening square may not be enough to force a win, as in the diagram below.

Draw

The practical player should also know some basic facts about king and pawn endings, especially king and pawn ver-

sus king, because they come up often; and about rook and pawn endings.

Endings were not stressed by the Arabian masters in the 12th or 13th century because the queen was a weak piece in those days and queening a pawn did not have the same decisive impact as it does today (some examples do exist, however). It wasn't until Carrera (1617), Salvio (1634), Lolli (1763) and Cozio (1766) that the endgame was seriously studied. Kling and Horwitz (1851), Durand and Preti (1871), Salvioli (1877) and Berger (1891) made deep inroads. Today the major references are Fine (1941), Cheron (1952) and Averbakh (1956). For rook and pawn endings, Levenfish and Smyslov (1957, 1989) is useful.

See A Pocket Guide to Chess Endgames by D. V. Hooper (1970).

Endgame Studies

Composed endgame problems which have unique and (hopefully) artistic solutions. As André Cheron put it: '... have little in common with the banality of the every-day game. The endgame must have charm and give a sensation of beauty wherein are compounded surprise and astonishment, and admiration for the genius of the composer'. Two good examples are:

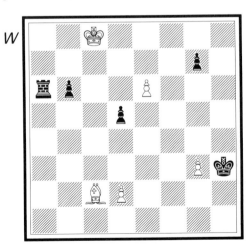

White to play and win, by Bergkvist 1916.

1 ♚b8 (not 1 ♚b7 ♖a1 2 ♗e4 ♖f1 3 e7 ♖f7) 1 … ♖a1 2 ♗e4 ♖e1 3 d3 de 4 d4 wins.

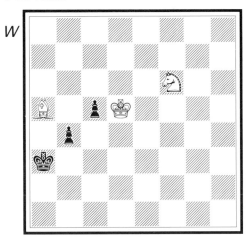

White to play and win, by Reti 1922.
1 ♚e4 (not 1 ♚c4 b3 2 ♘e4 b2 3 ♘c3 b1(=♛) 4 ♘xb1+ ♚a4 5. If the bishop moves away, it is stalemate and if the bishop stays, then 5 … ♚xa5 is a draw.) 1 … b3 2 ♘d5 b2 3 ♘c3 ♚b3 4 ♚d3 wins.

See *1000 Endgames* by C. E. C. Tattersall (1911), *1234 Modern Endgame Studies* by Sutherland and Lommer (1938), *The Chess Endgame Study* by A. J. Roycroft (1981).

Endzelins, Lucius   [1909–1981]
Estonian-born Australian who was equal 2nd (with Lothar Schmid) behind Ragozin in the 2nd World Correspondence Championship 1956–59. He was Australian Champion in 1961.

Englisch, Berthold
          [July 9 1851–October 19 1897]
Austrian player of GM strength who was active during the 1880s. He won the German Championship at Leipzig 1879, was equal 1st at Wiesbaden 1880, equal 5th at London 1883 and equal 2nd at Hamburg 1885.

He lost a match to Lasker (+0 =3 −2 in 1890) but held Pillsbury to +0 =5 −0 in 1896. His best result was a win at the Vienna quadrangular of 1896, ahead of Schlechter, Marco and Weiss.

He took ill while playing in Berlin, September 1897, withdrew and died shortly after.

English Opening
1 c4.

This opening is mentioned by Lucena and by Ruy Lopez—the latter adding the comment that the move is so bad that no player of any skill would use it. The modern history of the opening (and its name) derives from its adoption by Staunton in his 1843 match with Saint-Amant. Leading 20th century practitioners include Smyslov and Botvinnik, and the opening is considered one of White's strongest ways of opening. There are numerous transposition possibilities into the Réti, Queen's Gambit and various Indian systems. If Black replies with 1 … e5, White is effectively playing a Sicilian Defence with colours reversed and an extra move.

En passant
A pawn (on its 5th rank) attacking a square crossed by an enemy pawn which has just been advanced two squares, can capture the enemy pawn as though the latter had only been moved one square. This is called the *en passant* capture and must be done immediately or not at all. To illustrate:

If White plays 1 e4 then Black may capture this pawn as if it had only moved to e3. Black then plays 1 … de and the black pawn ends up at e3. Black's capture is sometimes denoted as 1 … de e.p.

En prise
A piece or pawn unintentionally left or placed where it can be captured is said to have been left *en prise*.

Eon de Beaumont, Charles D'
          [1728–1810]
French male transvestite and diplomat who was Louis XV's representative at London. He lived a flamboyant life and played chess—he won a game from Philidor in one of Philidor's blindfold exhibitions. His name has become a psychiatric term (eonism) for males who adopt feminine mannerism and clothing.

Equalize
To overcome and neutralize one's opponent's initiative. This is usually used to describe the result of an opening, when Black strives to equalize White's opening initiative.

Erasmus, Desiderius   [1466?–1536]
Dutch humanist, theologian and author who played chess but did not take it seriously. It is reported that while playing, he would stand and carry on a conversation full of wit and wisdom.

Ercole del Rio, Domenico
          [approximately 1718–1802]
Italian lawyer who wrote (1750) *Sopra il giuoco degli scacchi osservazioni pratiche d'anonimo autore Modenese* (Practical observations on the game of chess by an anonymous author of Modena). This slim volume, aimed at advanced players, was a significant improvement over previous books because it was well arranged and accurate. It contained important new items like the Scotch Game (1 e4 e5 2 ♘f3 ♘c6 3 d4) and the 3 … a6 defence to the Ruy Lopez.

The book did not give many details and in 1763, Lolli, another Modenese, expanded and filled it out.

Ercole del Rio and Lolli, together with Ponziani, were the leading lights of the so-called Modenese school.

Ermenkov, Evgenij Petkov

[*September 29 1949– *] Bulgarian GM (1977) who won the Bulgarian Championship in 1973, 1975, 1976 and 1979. He was equal 1st in 1984 and equal 2nd in 1987.

His best international result was 4th at Prague 1985 (X). He led the Bulgarian team at the Chess Olympiad in 1978 and 1980.

Escape Square

A square to which a king can go when he is checked. The typical case occurs with back-rank mate threats.

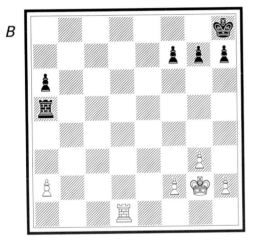

White threatens ♖d8 mate. Black has no time to capture the a-pawn. He must create an escape square by 1 ... h6 (or 1 ... g6). Then 2 ♖d8+ ♔h7 is harmless for Black.

Espig, Lutz [*January 5 1949– *]

East German GM (1983) who won the East German Championship in 1969 and 1971. He was 1st at Lublin 1970, 1st at Varna 1976, 2nd at Halle 1982 (VII), 1st at Varna 1983 (VII), equal 3rd at Leipzig 1983 (IX) and was 2nd at the Eger Open in 1987.

Estrin, Yakov Borisovich

[*April 21 1923–February 2 1987*] USSR IM (1975) who was a lawyer, a paratrooper and a chess professional. He excelled in postal games, coming third in the 6th World Correspondence Championship (1968–71) and winning the title in the 7th Championship (1972–5).

He wrote extensively on opening theory, in particular *Kurs Debyutov* (course on openings) with Panov and the 1985 *Small Openings Encyclopedia*.

Europe-Échecs [*1959– *]

French monthly chess magazine founded by Raoul Bertolo. It maintains a high literary standard.

European Team Championship

A Championship for teams of 8 players, instituted in 1957 and played every 4 years until 1983 for the Europa Cup trophy. It was reinstituted as a Swiss system event at Haifa in 1989.

Euwe, Machgielis (Max)

[*May 20 1901–November 26 1981*]

Max Euwe, World Champion in 1935–7 and President of FIDE from 1970 to 1978.

World Champion 1935–7. Dutch GM (1950) who never devoted himself completely to chess and became the only real amateur since Morphy's day to win the World Championship. He earned a doctorate in mathematics (1926) and throughout his peak years as a player, he continued to lecture in mathematics, mechanics and astronomy at an Amsterdam lyceum.

Euwe was taught chess at the age of four by his mother and entered his first tournament when he was ten. He became Dutch national champion in 1921 while still at university. His early successes included equal 2nd at Goteborg 1920 (ahead of Grünfeld and Sämisch) and a drawn match (+2=8−2) with Maroczy in 1921. After he took up his teaching post in 1924, his tournament appearances were largely confined to school holidays, although he continued to achieve creditable results, including notably 3rd at Bad Kissingen 1928 and 1st at Hastings 1930/31 (ahead of Capablanca). In match play he defeated Colle (+5 =0−3 in 1924 and +5=1−0 in 1928), Landau (+3=2−1 in 1931) and Noteboom (+3=3−0 in 1931), while losing matches narrowly to Alekhine (+2=5−3 in 1926/27), Bogoljubow (+2=5−3 and +1=7−2, both in 1928) and Capablanca (+0=8−2 in 1931).

The period 1932–5 saw the emergence of Euwe as a serious challenger for the world title. Tournament successes included 2nd at Berne 1932, 2nd at Zurich 1934 and equal 1st at Hastings 1934/35—all tournaments of high quality whose participants included Alekhine, Botvinnik, Capablanca, Bogoljubow, Flohr, Nimzowitsch and Lasker. In matches he defeated Spielmann twice (+2=2−0 in 1932 and +4=2−2 in 1935) and drew with Flohr (+3=10−3 in 1932). These results led to a match with Alekhine for the World Championship which was played in the

Netherlands in 1935. Although Alekhine started as heavy favourite in the eyes of the chess world, the contest developed into a closely fought marathon where Euwe's stamina and sobriety yielded him the victory ($+9=13-8$) and the world title.

While World Champion, Euwe was 2nd at Zandvoort 1936, equal 3rd at Nottingham 1936, equal 1st at Amsterdam 1936 and 1st at Bad Nauheim 1937. In 1937, Euwe lost the return match to Alekhine $+4=11-10$. After this second match, a further five exhibition games were played ending in a score of $+2=2-1$ for Euwe. In the powerful 1938 AVRO tournament, Euwe scored only 50% and at the end of 1939 he lost a close match ($+5=3-6$) to Keres, the winner of AVRO. Euwe's chess activities were curtailed by the German occupation of the Netherlands, since he would not participate in Nazi sponsored competitions, but he did play one important match in 1941, defeating Bogoljubow by $+5=3-2$.

After the war Euwe's greatest succes was 2nd (behind Botvinnik) at Groningen 1946. After that, perhaps due to the war as well as to age, his chess strength diminished.

In subsequent years Euwe established himself as a leading expert in the computer-based information sciences. From 1958–64 he was director of the Netherlands Research Centre for Information Sciences, and professor of that subject 1964–71 at the Universities of Tilburg and Rotterdam. From 1970–8 he was president of FIDE and he travelled throughout the world promoting chess. He was in charge of FIDE during the difficult Fischer years and the awkward Korchnoi–Karpov controversies.

He wrote voluminously. He produced a series of opening monographs: *Theorie der Schaakopeningen*, and he edited the monthly *Chess Archives*. His books include: *Judgement and Planning in Chess* (1937), *From My Games* (1938), *Meet the Masters* (1940), *Het Schaakphenomeen Capablanca* (1949) with Prins, *The Middle Game* (1964) with Kramer, *Road to Chess Mastery* (1968) with Meiden, *Development of Chess Style* (1968) and *Bobby Fischer and his Predecessors* (1976).

Euwe did not dominate the chess world the way previous World Champions did, and in fact his life scores against the world's best were not impressive: $+0=0-3$ vs Lasker, $+3=15-4$ vs Maroczy, $+1=13-4$ vs Capablanca, $+11=22-10$ vs Bogoljubow, $+20=36-27$ vs Alekhine, $+2=8-2$ vs Botvinnik, $+2=6-6$ vs Reshevsky, $+7=9-11$ vs Keres and $+1=0-7$ vs Smyslov.

Fine calls Euwe 'one of the greatest theoreticians of the age'. Kmoch wrote 'he is logic personified, a genius of law and order'. And Alekhine described Euwe as not an outstanding strategist, but a fine tactician who rarely made an unsound combination.

Euwe was married in 1926 and had 3 daughters. One evening after dinner your editor asked him who (and in what year) would he choose to play for him against the Devil for Euwe's soul. At first he considered selecting the 1930 Alekhine, but finally he sheepishly suggested that he would play himself.

Euwe–Alekhine
Match 1935
The Pearl of Zandvoort
1 d4 e6 2 c4 f5 3 g3 ♗b4+ 4 ♗d2 ♗e7 5 ♗g2 ♘f6 6 ♘c3 0-0 7 ♘f3 ♘e4 8 0-0 b6 9 ♕c2 ♗b7 10 ♘e5 ♘xc3 11 ♗xc3 ♗xg2 12 ♔xg2 ♕c8 13 d5 d6 14 ♘d3 e5 15 ♔h1 c6 16 ♕b3 ♔h8 17 f4 e4 18 ♘b4 c5 19 ♘c2 ♘d7 20 ♘e3 ♗f6 21 ♘xf5 ♗xc3 22 ♘xd6 ♕b8 23 ♘xe4 ♗f6 24 ♘d2 g5 25 e4 gf 26 gf ♗d4 27 e5 ♕e8 28 e6 ♖g8 29 ♘f3 ♕g6

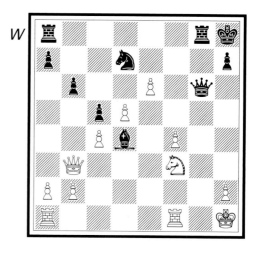

30 ♖g1 ♗xg1 31 ♖xg1 ♕f6 32 ♘g5 ♖g7 33 ed ♖xd7 34 ♕e3 ♖e7 35 ♘e6 ♖f8 36 ♕e5 ♕xe5 37 fe ♖f5 38 ♖e1 h6 39 ♘d8 ♖f2 40 e6 ♖d2 41 ♘c6 ♖e8 42 e7 b5 43 ♘d8 ♔g7 44 ♘b7 ♔f6 45 ♖e6+ ♔g5 46 ♘d6 ♖xe7 47 ♘e4+ Resigns.

Evans Gambit
See Evans, William Davies, Captain

Evans, Larry Melvyn
[*March 23 1932–*]
US GM (1957) who was a leading American player in the 1950s and 60s. He won the US Championship in 1951, 1961/2 and 1968; was equal 1st in 1980; was 2nd (to Fischer) in 1963/4 and 1966. He won the US open in 1951, 1952 and 1954, and was equal 1st in 1955. He played on 8 US Olympiad teams between 1950 and 1976, scoring 90% on board 5 in 1950.

He beat Taimanov $2\frac{1}{2}$–$1\frac{1}{2}$ in the 1954 USA–USSR radio match; reached the 1956 interzonal; beat Lombardy $5\frac{1}{2}$–$4\frac{1}{2}$ in 1962 and was equal 2nd in Venice 1967. He never made it to the Candidates level.

He was equally successful as an author, with his *New Ideas in Chess* 1958, the 10th edition of *MCO* (*Modern Chess Openings*) in 1965 and his helping Fischer with *My 60 Memorable Games* in 1969.

Today he is a widely read and syndicated chess columnist.

Evans, William Davies, Captain

[*January 27 1790–August 3 1872*] Welshman who invented the famous and popular Evans Gambit (in 1824)— once described as 'a gift of the gods to a languishing chess world'. He first played his gambit (in the delayed form) in 1826 or '27, in William Lewis' chess rooms, St Martin's Lane, London, and won a smart 20 move game against Alexander McDonnell. In 1838 he played many offhand games with Staunton, at the Westminster chess club.

Evans went to sea at age 14, worked on steam packets for the General Post Department and became a captain. He wrote: 'About the year 1824, being then in command of a Government Mail Steamer, the passages between Milford Haven and Waterford were favourable to the study of the game of chess . . .'. It must have been especially favourable, for that is when he invented his gambit.

He retired from the postal service in 1840, worked in the Mediterranean, settled in Ostend and continued to visit London to play chess.

He claimed that he invented a system of tri-coloured lights for ships to prevent collisions at night, and that the English government gave him £1500, while the Russian Tzar gave him a gold pocket chronometer and some cash. Here is the very first Evans Gambit:

Evans–McDonnell
1826 or 1827
1 e4 e5 2 ♘f3 ♘c6 3 ♗c4 ♗c5 4 0-0 d6 5 b4! ♗xb4 6 c3 ♗a5 7 d4 ♗g4 8 ♕b3 ♕d7 9 ♘g5 ♘d8 10 de de 11 ♗a3 ♘h6 12 f3 ♗b6+ 13 ♔h1 ♗h5 14 ♖d1 ♕c8

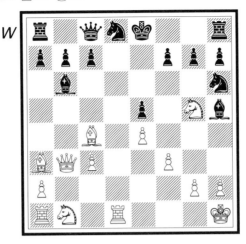

15 ♖xd8+ ♕xd8 16 ♘xf7 ♕h4 17 ♕b5+ c6 18 ♕xe5+ ♔d7 19 ♕e6+ ♔c7 20 ♗d6 mate

For more details see the 1928 *British Chess Magazine*, pages 6–18.

Evergreen Game
See Anderssen

Exchange

To capture an enemy piece or pawn and give up a piece or pawn of equal strength is called an exchange. Thus one exchanges queen for queen, for example, or knight for knight.

Since a rook is worth more than a knight or bishop, if one can exchange a knight or bishop for a rook one is said to have 'won the exchange'.

Most players believe that a bishop and knight are of equal strength (each worth about 3 pawns). Tarrasch, how-ever, preferred bishops and semi-jokingly labelled the exchange of knight for bishop as winning the minor exchange.

Exchange combination

A combination which involves a simple exchange but which produces a non-material gain in time, space or position. For example:

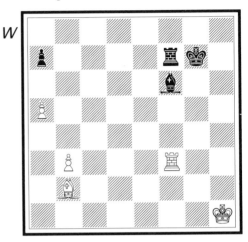

After the simple exchanges 1 ♗xf6+ ♖xf6 2 ♖xf6 ♔xf6 3 b4 ♔e6 4 b5 ♔d6 5 b6 ♔c6 6 ba ♔b7 black catches the white pawns. However, White can win one crucial tempo with the exchange combination 1 ♖xf6! ♖xf6 2 b4 ♔f7 3 ♗xf6 ♔xf6 4 b5 ♔e6 5 b6 ab 6 a6 ♔d7 7 a7 winning.

Ezra, Abraham ben
[*1088–1167?*] Spanish rabbi of Toledo who wrote the earliest Hebrew poem on chess. It is 76 lines long and gives the ancient Muslim rules for the moves of the pieces except that the queen (*fers*) is allowed to leap to a third square on its initial move.

F

Fabel, Karl
[*October 20 1905–March 3 1975*] German problemist who composed about 1200 problems, including mathematical problems and retrograde analysis.
See *Introduction to Retrograde Analysis* (1973)

Fairy Chess
See Dawson

Falkbeer, Ernst Karl
[*June 27 1819–December 14 1885*] Austrian player of IM strength who was 2nd at Birmingham 1858. He edited a chess column in the *Sunday Times* (1857–9) and in the *Neue Illustrierte Zeitung* (1877–85), but he is most famous for his counter-gambit 1 e4 e5 2 f4 d5 followed by 3 ed e4.

Family Check
A humorous way of describing a fork by a knight when it attacks the king and two other major pieces.

Farago, Ivan [*April 1 1946– *]
Hungarian GM (1976) who took a degree in economics but became a chess professional. He was equal 1st at Halle 1978, 1st at Kecskemet 1979, equal 1st (with Portisch) in the 1981 Hungarian Championship, 1st at Svendborg 1981, equal 1st at Bagneux 1983, 1st at Albena 1983 (IX), equal 1st at Wijk aan Zee 1987 (VIII) and 1st at Budapest 1987 (IX).

He is a good Hungarian GM but not in their front rank (Portisch, Ribli, Sax, Adorjan).

Fedorowicz, John P.
[*September 27, 1958– *] US GM (1986) who is growing in strength, but has not yet broken through to the very top of US chess. He was equal 3rd in the 1984 US Championship (XI), lost a short match $2\frac{1}{2}$–$3\frac{1}{2}$ to Dlugy in 1984, had a good equal 2nd at Hastings 1984/85 (IX) and another equal 2nd at Dortmund 1986 (X). In the 1986 Olympiad he scored 80% on board 4 for the US. In 1987 he was equal 1st at Cannes (X), 1st at Sesimbra (VII) and equal 3rd in the US Championship (XII). In 1990 he won the GM tournament at Wijk aan Zee (Category IX).

Fegatello (Fried Liver Attack)
See Two Knights Defence.

Fernandez Garcia, Jose L.
[*May 1954– *] Spanish GM (1986) who was equal 1st at Barcelona 1985 (VI), Torremolinos 1985 (VII) and Las Palmas 1987 (IX).

He played on three Spanish Olympiad teams (1982, 1984 and 1986) scoring 50% on board 1 in 1986.

Ferrer, Jose [*1909– *]
Movie actor who enjoys chess.

Fers
The mediaeval name for the queen, derived from the Persian vizier.

Fianchetto
The development of a bishop at b2 or g2 for White, b7 or g7 for Black. Such bishops, acting on the longest diagonals and bearing down on the centre, can be quite effective. However the b pawn or g pawn must be moved and this may create weak spots at a3, c3, f3 or h3 for White, or a6 c6 f6 or h6 for Black, especially if the fianchettoed bishop is exchanged.

Though used by Staunton and Paulsen, such development was considered eccentric until the 1920s. The word fianchetto comes from the Italian *financata*, meaning playing to the flank.

FIDE
The initials of the Fédération Internationale Des Échecs, representing the international chess federation. It has over 120 countries as members and deals with all aspects of chess: laws, correspondence chess, chess compositions, granting titles (FIDE Master, International Master, International Grandmaster for men and for women, arbiters etc),

interzonals, Candidates matches, world title matches and chess Olympiads. It is the accepted governing body for world chess.

It was founded in 1924 and after Alekhine's death in 1946 it took control of World Championship affairs. The Grandmasters Association (GMA) is at present challenging some of FIDE's control.

Presidents of FIDE have been: Alexander Reub (Holland) 1924–49; Folke Rogard (Sweden) 1949–70; Max Euwe (Holland) 1970–8; Fridrik Olafsson (Iceland) 1978–82 and Florencio Campomanes (Philippines) 1982– .

FIDE Master

A rank below International Master that corresponds to about a 2350 Elo rating.

Fifty Move Rule

The game is drawn when a player having the move claims a draw and demonstrates that at least the last 50 consecutive moves have been made by each side without the capture of any piece and without the movement of any pawn.

The number of 50 moves will be extended to 75 moves for the following positions:

(a) ♔ + ♖ + ♗ versus ♔ + ♖
(b) ♔ + ♘ + ♘ versus ♔ + ♙
(c) ♔ + ♕ + ♙ versus ♔ + ♕ when the ♙ is one square from promotion
(d) ♔ + ♕ versus ♔ + ♘ + ♘
(e) ♔ + ♕ versus ♔ + ♗ + ♗
(f) ♔ + ♗ + ♗ versus ♔ + ♘

See Draw

Figurine Algebraic Notation

See Notation

File

Any one of the 8 columns of the chess board. For example, the a-column, or the b-column, . . ., or the h-column.

See Notation

Filip, Miroslav   [*October 27 1928–*]

Czech GM (1955) who was a major force in Czech chess life. In his early years he was second to Pachman and later he was edged out by Hort, but during the 1950s and 60s he was always one of the top two or three Czech stars. He won the Czech Championship in 1952 and 1954 and was equal first in 1950.

He was a Candidate twice (1956 and 1962)—in fact, the first Czech to make the Candidates level. He did not succeed in these Candidates tournaments, but he did stand out from the general run of Grandmasters. He won the 1956 Steinitz Memorial in Prague. He played on 12 Czech Olympiad teams during 1952–74. Filip is a very tall, handsome man with a most gentle nature. He is a lawyer and can be called Dr Filip.

Fine, Reuben   [*October 11 1914–*]

US GM (1950) who was a dazzling star in the late 1930s, certainly among the top 4 or 5 players in the world. Then, like Morphy before him and Fischer after him, he virtually disappeared from the chess scene. Since this happens so rarely and since all three are Americans, it would seem that such a sudden stoppage may have something to do with being American. (It is true that the European GM Duras also stopped suddenly, but that may be the exception that proves the rule.)

Fine began to take chess seriously when he was 15, although he learnt the game much earlier. He won the 36th congress of the American Chess Federation in Milwaukee 1935. Then he went to Europe and won at Hastings 1935/36, Zandvoort 1936, Oslo 1936, Stockholm 1937, Moscow 1937, and Leningrad 1937. He was equal 1st at Amsterdam 1936, Margate 1937, and Ostend 1937. There were some failures

Reuben Fine of the USA. He turned down the invitation to compete for the World Championship in 1948.

mixed in: 9th at Kemeri 1937 and equal 4th at Hastings 1937/38. He was equal 2nd at Lodz 1935, equal 3rd at Nottingham 1936 and 2nd at Semmering 1937. In 1937 he beat Ståhlberg +4 = 2 − 2 and acted as Euwe's second in the 1937 return match with Alekhine. Fine also played on three (successful) US Olympiad teams in 1933, 1935 and 1937. He also played in several US Championships, but it is a curiosity that he never won a US title.

The climax to this excellent build up was the great AVRO tournament of 1938 (about Category XVII). In the first six rounds Fine beat Botvinnik, Reshevsky, Euwe, Flohr and Alekhine, and drew with Capablanca after missing a win. This was a sensational start for a 23 year old. Things got more difficult as the tournament progressed but Fine did end up equal 1st with Keres. It was clear that the days of Capablanca, Alekhine and perhaps Euwe were over, and that the world crown would soon belong to Keres, Fine or Botvinnik.

After this magnificent result, Fine returned to America to study mathematics. The war then put an end to international chess for six years and Fine lost some of his very best years. During these years he in fact studied psychology and took his PhD in 1948 (University of Southern California).

He was 2nd at Hollywood 1945 and 1st at New York 1948. He drew ($+2=4-2$) a match with Najdorf but declined to play in the World Championship 1948 Moscow/Hague. His last appearance was 4th at New York 1951.

In life scores, he had difficulty with Reshevsky ($+1=13-4$) and Keres ($+1=8-3$). He held his own with Capablanca ($=5$), Euwe ($+2=3-2$) and Najdorf ($+3=7-3$). He edged out Alekhine ($+3=4-2$), Flohr ($+2=8-0$) and Botvinnik ($+1=2$). He lost to Boleslavsky ($+0=1-1$).

Euwe's opinion (in *Meet the Masters* 1940) was that Fine liked sharp positions, was an excellent lightning player, was gifted in solving technical problems and liked to confront his opponents with tricky problems from the very first move. Euwe described Fine's play as crystal clear logic and thought; his main weakness was a none too cool temperament.

Fine is an excellent author. His 6th edition of *MCO* (*Modern Chess Openings*) (1939) was superb and his *Basic Chess Endings* (1941) became a classic. He wrote many other books, including: *Dr Lasker's Chess Career 1889–1914* (1935) (with Reinfeld), *The World's Great Chess Games* (1952), *The Psychology of Chess Players*, *Fischer's Conquest of the World Championship* (1973).

C. Torre–Fine
Match 1934
1 e4 c6 2 d4 d5 3 f3 e6 4 ♘c3 ♘f6 5 ♗e3 ♗e7 6 e5 ♘6d7 7 f4 c5 8 ♘f3 ♘c6 9 ♗b5 ♕b6 10 0-0 0-0 11 ♔h1 a6 12 ♗xc6 bc 13 ♘a4 ♕a5 14 c3 cd 15 cd c5 16 ♖c1 c4 17 g4 f6 18 ♖f2 fe 19 fe ♗b7 20 ♕c2 ♗c6 21 ♘c3

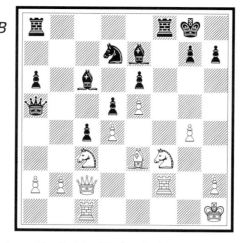

21 ... ♘c5 22 ♖cf1 ♘d3 23 ♖g2 ♘xe5 24 de d4 25 ♘e4 de 26 ♔g1 ♕d5 27 ♘c3 ♕d3 28 ♕xd3 cd 29 ♖g3 e2 30 Resigns

Fischer, Robert James (Bobby)
[*March 9 1943– *]
World Champion 1972–5. US GM (1958) who is one of the very greatest players of all time. He is in the class of Lasker, Capablanca and Botvinnik and many experts believe he is the best player that ever lived. In a recent mathematical study, Keene and Divinsky put him third on the all-time

Bobby Fischer caught in a lighter moment at the Manhattan Chess Club blitz tournament in 1971.

great list, behind Kasparov and Karpov.

Fischer began his top achievements by winning the US Championship. Between 1957/58 and 1966/67 he played in and won 8 US titles. He made it into the 1959 Candidates tournament at Bled and placed equal 5th. This ranked him as the 6th strongest player in the world, all at age 16. He was 2nd at Bled 1961 behind Tal and then had a drawn but unfinished match with Reshevsky $+2=7-2$. This was especially interesting because Reshevsky at age 50 was a top star on the way down while Fischer at 18 was on his way up.

Fischer was again a Candidate at Curaçao 1962 where he placed 4th. He did not play outside the USA during 1963 and 1964. In 1965 he was equal 2nd behind Smyslov at Havana and he was 2nd behind Spassky at Santa Monica 1966. By 1967 his playing strength had moved a notch higher and he won at Skopje 1967, Monaco 1967, Netanya 1968, and Vincovci 1968. By 1970 his power was awesome. In the 1970 USSR vs. Rest of World match he trounced Petrosian $+2=2-0$. He won at Buenos Aires 1970 and Zagreb 1970 and he won a super-strong blitz tournament at Herceg Novi 1970. At the 1970 Olympiad he scored 10 to 3, though he did lose his game against World Champion Spassky.

At the 1970 interzonal in Palma he was 1st, ending up $3\frac{1}{2}$ points ahead of the field. It was here that his strength reached full flower. He had had a draw with Uitumen on December 1, 1970 and then began a remarkable run of some 20 wins in a row! He beat Rubinetti, Uhlmann, Taimanov, Suttles, Mecking, and Gligoric. In the last round, December 12, Panno refused to play because of a protest and Fischer won by default. In the Candidates matches that followed, Fischer scored 6–0 against Taimanov (May 1971) and 6–0 against Larsen (July 1971). In the Candidates final against Petrosian, Fischer won the first

The 15 year-old Fischer engages in a practice game against Petrosian at the Moscow Central Chess Club in 1958.

game on September 30, 1971. The string was then broken when Petrosian won the next game, but from December 2 1970 until September 30 1971, Fischer won 20 consecutive games (19 real and 1 by default) against mostly GM opposition. This electrified the chess world.

He won the Candidates final +5=3−1 against Petrosian and in the summer of 1972 he beat Spassky +7=11−3 in their celebrated match. On August 31 1972 Fischer became World Champion and since that day he has not played one official competitive game of chess. Like Morphy and Fine before him, he simply stopped playing. It is sad that Fischer has never played the younger stars like Karpov, Kasparov, Yusupov, Timman, Belyavsky or Ljubojevic.

His life scores are impressive. He beat Najdorf (+4=4−1), Reshevsky (+9=13−4), Smyslov (+3=5−1), Petrosian (+8=15−4), Portisch (+4=5−0), Spassky (+7=13−5) and Larsen (+10=1−2). He was even with Keres (+3=4−3), and Korchnoi (+2=5−2) and he has negative results against Tal (+2=5−4) and Geller (+3=2−5).

Fischer's entire career was dogged with complaints, controversy and contumaciousness. His complete and utter devotion to chess made him rather one-dimensional. He found it difficult to trust anyone and he had permanent breakups with his mother, his chess guardian Edmondson, his long-time friend and colleague Larry Evans and his short-time friend and colleague Biyiasas. He wanted everything his own way, from lighting and money to spectators and TV. He blamed FIDE, the Russians and the US Chess Federation. He had 41 conditions to play in Zagreb 1970. Many times he got his way, but when he did not, he withdrew. That is why his 1961 match with Reshevsky was unfinished, why he did not play outside the USA in 1963 and 1964, why he with-

drew (while leading) from the 1967 interzonal at Sousse, why he did not play in 1969 and why he refused to defend his title in 1975 (against Karpov). His antics before the 1972 match with Spassky were almost straight out of a Marx Brothers movie.

His style of play is direct, sharp and super-aggressive. Since he is not interested in short draws, almost every one of his games is full of interest. He works extremely hard, especially on his opening repertoire. As Keene puts it: 'Fischer combines the scientific logic of Botvinnik with the fierce hunting instinct of Alekhine or Lasker and the lucid, effortless beauty achieved by Capablanca'.

Fischer's highest Elo rating, 2785, was not surpassed until Kasparov reached 2800 on the January 1 1990 rating list.

Fischer raised the financial expectation for all GMs and popularized the game throughout the world. He also liberated chess ambition in many countries by breaking the grip of Russian domination.

During the years of his retirement he has taken a serious interest in the World Church of God and has tried to disassociate himself from things Jewish, even though he is half-Jewish himself.

His *My 60 Memorable Games* (1969) is a wonderful book, full of superb analysis.

See The Games of Robert J. Fischer by Wade and O'Connell (1972), *Fischer's Chess Games*, by Levy and O'Connell (1980).

The following game has been labelled the 'Game of the Century':

D. Byrne–Fischer
New York 1956

1 ♘f3 ♘f6 2 c4 g6 3 ♘c3 ♗g7 4 d4 0-0 5 ♗f4 d5 6 ♕b3 dc 7 ♕xc4 c6 8 e4 ♘bd7 9 ♖d1 ♘b6 10 ♕c5 ♗g4 11 ♗g5 ♘a4 12 ♕a3 ♘xc3 13 bc ♘xe4 14 ♗xe7 ♕b6 15 ♗c4 ♘xc3 16 ♗c5 ♖fe8+ 17 ♔f1

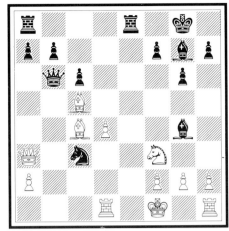

17 ... ♗e6 18 ♗xb6 ♗xc4+ 19 ♔g1
♘e2+ 20 ♔f1 ♘xd4+ 21 ♔g1
♘e2+ 22 ♔f1 ♘c3+ 23 ♔g1 ab 24
♕b4 ♖a4 25 ♕xb6 ♘xd1 26 h3
♖xa2 27 ♔h2 ♘xf2 28 ♖e1 ♖xe1 29
♕d8+ ♗f8 30 ♘xe1 ♗d5 31 ♘f3
♘e4 32 ♕b8 b5 33 h4 h5 34 ♘e5
♔g7 35 ♔g1 ♗c5+ 36 ♔f1 ♘g3+
37 ♔e1 ♗b4+ 38 ♔d1 ♗b3+ 29
♔c1 ♘e2+ 40 ♔b1 ♘c3+ 41 ♔c1
♖c2 mate

R. Byrne–Fischer

New York 1963

1 d4 ♘f6 2 c4 g6 3 g3 c6 4 ♗g2 d5 5
cd cd 6 ♘c3 ♗g7 7 e3 0-0 8 ♘ge2
♘c6 9 0-0 b6 10 b3 ♗a6 11 ♗a3 ♖e8
12 ♕d2 e5 13 de ♘xe5 14 ♖fd1 ♘d3

15 ♕c2 ♘xf2 6 ♔xf2 ♘g4+ 17 ♔g1
♘xe3 18 ♕d2 ♘xg2 19 ♔xg2 d4 20
♘xd4 ♗b7+ 21 ♔f1 ♕d7 22 Resigns
(after 22 ♕f2 ♕h3+ 23 ♔g1 ♖e1+
24 ♖xe1 ♗xd4)

Fiske, Daniel Willard

[*November 11 1831–September 17 1904*]
American polyglot and specialist on
Iceland who had a life-long interest in
chess. He co-edited (with Morphy) the
first American magazine, *Chess Monthly*,
and he organized the 1857 New York
tournament. He promoted chess in Iceland and founded the Reykjavik chess
club (1900). In 1868 he became professor of North European Languages at
Cornell University. His publications include *Chess in Iceland*, *Icelandic Literature*
(1905), and *Chess Tales and Chess Miscellanies*. The international tournament in
Reykjavik in 1968 was called the Fiske
Memorial in his honour. The Icelandic
National Library possesses a Fiske chess
collection, donated after his death.

Five Minute Chess

See Blitz

Flamberg, Alexander Davidovich

[*1880–January 24 1926*]
Polish player of almost GM strength
who won the Warsaw Championship in
1910 ahead of Rubinstein. In that same
year, he crushed the youthful Bogoljubow (+3 =0 −0) but lost to Rubinstein
(+0 =1 −4). He was 2nd at St Petersburg 1911, 5th at Vilna 1912 (ahead of
Alekhine), 1st at Warsaw 1913 and 3rd
at St Petersburg 1913/14 just half a
point behind Alekhine and Nimzowitsch. In the last round of this Russian
Championship he declined a draw (and
lost the game) which would have put
him equal 1st and perhaps have allowed
him into the great 1914 St Petersburg
tournament.

Internationally, he was at the ill-fated
Mannheim 1914 tournament where he
was interned when war broke out. He
was 1st at Baden-Baden 1914 and 3rd or
4th in four other tournaments for the
internees at Triberg 1914 and 1915.
After the war he was 2nd at Warsaw
1919, ahead of Rubinstein and in 1924
he led the Warsaw team to victory over
Lodz.

Flear, Glenn Curtis

[*February 12 1959– *]
English GM (1987) whose major victory
was his fine win at London 1986 (XIII).
He played on the 1986 English Olympiad team.

Fleischmann, Leo

[*October 5 1881–August 17 1930*]
Hungarian of GM strength who sometimes used his Hungarian surname Forgacs. He was quite active from 1905–13,
coming 1st at the minor Barmen 1905
tournament, equal 3rd at Nuremberg
1906, 1st at the 1907 Hungarian Championship, 5th at the strong 1907 Ostend
tournament and 3rd at San Remo 1911,
Budapest 1912 and Budapest 1913. He
did not return to competitive chess after
the 1914–18 war.

Flesch, Janos Laszlo

[*September 30 1933–Dec 9 1983*]
Hungarian IM (1963) and honorary GM
(1980) who was a specialist in simultaneous blindfold exhibitions. He claimed
a world record when he faced 52 opponents in Budapest 1960.

Flohr, Salomon Mikhailovich

[*November 21 1908–July 18 1983*]
Czech GM (1950) who was born in
Poland and became a leading contender
for the World Championship in the mid-
1930s. He seemed headed for the very
top when he led the Czech team in the
1930 Olympiad, scoring $14\frac{1}{2}$–$2\frac{1}{2}$ and
followed this up with an impressive
number of first prizes. In particular, he
was equal 1st with Botvinnik at Moscow 1935 ahead of Lasker and Capablanca. He drew matches with Euwe
(+3 =10 −3) in 1932 and Botvinnik
(+2 =8 −2) in 1933. He was Euwe's
second in the 1935 title match with
Alekhine and in 1937 FIDE named Flohr
as the official challenger. Alekhine accepted his challenge in 1938, but the

Salo Flohr. In 1937 he was named official challenger for the World Championship by FIDE, but the match never took place.

match never came to pass.

Flohr's style was quiet and positional. In the endgame 'he worked wonders ... he exploited small advantages in the virtuoso style' (Ståhlberg). His general approach was to beat the slightly inferior players and he did this regularly and superbly. On the other hand, he seldom beat the great masters. Euwe wrote: 'he is quite content to demonstrate not his superiority over but his equality with the other leading masters'. His life scores bear this out: Capablanca (+1=8−2), Alekhine (+0=7−5), Euwe (+3=12−7), Botvinnik (+2=22−5), Reshevsky (+0=8−1), Fine (+0=8−2), Keres (+1=17−2), Smyslov (+1=9−2), Boleslavsky (+0=6−3) and Bronstein (+1=8−1). He did edge out Petrosian (+1=5−0) and Korchnoi (+2=1−1). And he crushed old timers like Lasker (+2=3−0), Maroczy (+4=2-0) and Vidmar (+3=5−0).

Thus when a tournament had only a few top stars, Flohr did very well. When

there were many stars, his score suffered. He was a distant 3rd at Moscow 1936 and only equal 7th at Nottingham 1936. By 1936 Flohr's play seemed to lose some of its precision and he began to score too many draws. Ståhlberg attributes this to staleness from playing too much, but there were other reasons for a falling off in Flohr's results.

Flohr's Jewish parents were massacred in Poland and he moved to Czechoslovakia in 1916. In 1938 the Nazis were about to march into Czechoslovakia, overthrow his world, and threaten him directly. He was unable to raise the stake money for a match with Alekhine, and his mind may not have been fully focussed on chess. At the great AVRO tournament where the eight greatest masters gathered to cross swords in November 1938, as Czechoslovakia fell, Flohr came last. He escaped to Russia to find a new life.

He was 1st at Moscow/Leningrad 1939 and at Kemeri 1939, and after the war he was again a Candidate. He did not do well at the Candidates in Budapest 1950 and after that did not have any ambitions regarding the world title. He played in eight USSR Championships during 1944 to 1955, scoring 75−69. For the last 30 years of his life he became a respected journalist, an international arbiter (1963) and an author—*Soviet Chess 1917–1935*, with Kotov (1960).

Flohr–Botvinnik

Match 1933

1 d4 ♘f6 2 c4 e6 3 ♘c3 ♗b4 4 ♕c2 c5 5 dc ♘a6 6 a3 ♗xc3+ 7 ♕xc3 ♘xc5 8 f3 d6 9 e4 e5 10 ♗e3 ♕c7 11 ♘e2 ♗e6 12 ♕c2 0-0 13 ♘c3 ♖fc8 14 ♗e2 a6 15 ♖c1 ♘cd7 16 ♕d2 ♕b8 17 ♘d5 ♗xd5 18 cd ♖xc1+ 19 ♕xc1 ♕d8 20 0-0 ♖c8 21 ♕d2 ♕c7 22 ♖c1 ♕xc1+ 23 ♕xc1 ♖xc1+ 24 ♗xc1 ♔f8 25 ♔f2 ♔e7 26 ♗e3 ♔d8 27 ♔e1 ♔c7 28 ♔d2 ♘c5 (diagram) 29 b4 ♘cd7 30 g3 ♘b6 31 ♔c2 ♘bd7 32 a4 ♘b6 33 a5 ♘bd7 34 ♗c1 ♔d8 35 ♗b2 ♘e8

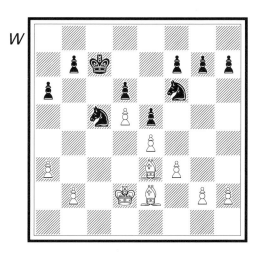

36 ♔d2 ♘c7 37 ♔e3 ♔e7 38 ♗f1 ♘b5 39 h4 ♘c7 40 ♗h3 ♘e8 41 f4 f6 42 ♗f5 g6 43 ♗h3 h6 44 ♗c1 ♘g7 45 fe de 46 ♔f3 h5 47 ♗e3 ♔d6 48 ♗h6 ♘e8 49 g4 hg+ 50 ♗xg4 ♘c7 51 ♗e3 ♘b5 52 ♔e2 ♘c7 53 ♔d3 f5 54 ef gf 55 ♗xf5 ♘xd5 56 ♗d2 ♘7f6 57 ♔c4 ♔c6 58 ♗g6 b5+ 59 ♔d3 ♘e7 60 ♗e4+ ♘ed5 61 ♗g5 ♘h5 62 ♗f3 ♘g3 63 ♗d2 ♔d6 64 ♗g4 ♘f6 65 ♗c8 ♔c6 66 ♗e1 e4+ 67 ♔d4 ♘gh5 68 ♗f5 ♔d6 69 ♗d2 Resigns.

Fool's Mate

1 g4 e6 (or e5) 2 f4 (or f3), ♕h4 mate. The shortest possible game of chess ending in checkmate.

Forbes, Duncan   [1798–1868]

Scottish author whose *History of Chess* (1860) was considered unreliable until recently (*see* History of Chess). Now it may in fact turn out that his intuitive guesses were correct.

Forgacs, Leo

See Fleischmann, Leo

Forintos, Gyozo Victor

[July 30 1935–]

Hungarian GM (1974) who is an economist. He won the 1969 Hungarian Championship and was 1st at Baja 1971. In 1974 at Reykjavik he was 2nd behind Smyslov. He played on six Hungarian Olympiad teams during 1958–74. In

1987 he was equal 1st at the Perpignan Open. His daughter is married to English GM Tony Kosten.

Fork

An attack on two enemy pieces at the same time. In the Vienna Game for example, after 1 e4 e5 2 ♘c3 ♘f6 3 ♗c4 ♘xe4 4 ♘xe4 d5 forks two pieces and wins one.

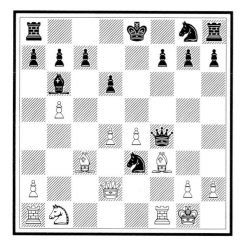

In the diagram, Black cannot play 1 ... ♞xf1 because the knight is pinned on the unprotected black queen. Black solves this dilemma with 1 ... ♛xh2 +; 2 ♔xh2 ♞xf1 + (a lovely fork) 3 ♔g1 ♞xd2 4. ♞xd2 and Black has won the exchange and a pawn.

Forsyth Notation
See Notation

Four Knights Game
1 e4 e5 2 ♘f3 ♘c6 3 ♘c3 ♘f6.

A solid and sound opening that was popular some 80 years ago but is too tame today. After 4 ♗b5 Black can play symmetrically or try Rubinstein's 4 ... ♘d4. White can try 4 d4 ed 5 ♘xd4 or even 5 ♘d5.

Four Pawns Attack
See King's Indian Defence

Franco-Indian (Keres) Defence
1 d4 e6 2 c4 ♗b4 + .

This combines features of the French and Nimzo-Indian Defences.

Franklin, Benjamin
[January 17 1706–April 17 1790] American scientist, inventor, statesman and chess player who believed that chess was a useful activity and that it taught valuable lessons that could be applied in real life. His *Morals of Chess* (1786) is the first American writing on chess.

Frederick II The Great *[1712–1786]*
King of Prussia (1740–86) who played correspondence chess.

French Defence
1 e4 e6.

First examined by Lucena (1497) but made popular in 1834 when Paris used it in a correspondence game to beat London. It was popular during Botvinnik's reign as World Champion because he played it with virtuosity.

Today the Sicilian Defence has overtaken it as Black's main line to avoid the Ruy Lopez and the gambit possibilities for White after 1 ... e5.

The idea in the French is to build a strong wall against White's attack and hope that in the endgame, the superior black pawn structure will tell. The negatives are the locking in of the queen's bishop, the ceding of the centre and the defensive outlook.

After the usual 2 d4 d5, the main lines are:

(a) 3 e5, the Advance Variation, favoured by Nimzowitsch but seldom used today;

(b) 3 ed ed the Exchange Variation, which is drawish;

(c) 3 ♘c3 ♘f6 4 ♗g5 the Classical Variation, leading to 4 ... ♗e7 5 e5 ♘fd7 6 h4 (the Chatard–Alekhine Attack), 4 ... de, Burn's line, or 4 ... ♗b4 (the MacCutcheon System);

(d) 3 ♘c3 ♘f6 4 e5, the Steinitz

Variation;

(e) 3 ♘d2, the Tarrasch Variation;

(f) 3 ♘c3 ♗b4, the Winawer Variation (known in continental Europe as the Nimzowitsch Variation).

From Gambit
1 f4 e5.

Named after the Danish player Martin From (1828–95) who played it against Mollerstrom in 1862.

Frydman, Paulino
[May 26 1905–1982] Polish IM (1955) of almost GM strength whose best result was 1st at Helsinki 1935 ahead of Keres and Ståhlberg. He was on seven Polish Olympiad teams during 1928–39 and settled in Argentina after being stranded there in 1939. In his last tournament, he placed 3rd at Buenos Aires 1941 behind Najdorf and Ståhlberg.

Ftacnik, Lubomir *[October 30 1957–]*
Czech GM (1980) who was European Junior Champion 1976/7 and Czech Champion in 1981, 1982, 1983, and 1985. He is now the leading Czech player (since Hort and Kavalek have emigrated) and has played on four Czech Olympiad teams (1980–6) scoring $9\frac{1}{2}$–$4\frac{1}{2}$ on second board in 1986. His major victories are equal 1st at Cienfuegos 1980, equal 1st at Dortmund 1981, 1st at Esbjerg 1982, 1st at Trnava 1983 (IX) 1st at Altensteig 1987 (IX) and 1st at Baden-Baden Open 1987. He played a $+0=4-0$ drawn match with Georgiev in 1987.

He has never been a Candidate, but is close to that strength and more can be expected of him.

Furman, Semyon Abramovich
[December 1 1920–March 17 1978] USSR GM (1966) who played in 13 USSR Championships between 1948 and 1975 and was 3rd in 1948 and equal

4th in 1965. He played primarily inside the USSR and was not too well known outside though he was 1st at Harrachov 1966, 3rd at Madrid 1973 and 3rd at Bad Lauterberg 1977. He was much stronger than his reputation, as his life scores show: $+3=3-1$ (Keres), $+2=3-0$ (Boleslavsky), $+1=3-0$ (Smyslov) $+2=10-2$ (Bronstein), $+4=11-4$ (Korchnoi), $+4=8-3$ (Taimanov), $=4$ (Karpov), $+2=4-3$ (Petrosian). He did less well against Spassky ($+1=2-5$), Tal ($+1=4-4$) Polugayevsky ($+0=3-5$) and Geller ($+2=4-6$).

He was a fine theoretician and the chief trainer of Karpov.

G

Gaige, Jeremy [*October 9 1927– *]
US journalist and archivist whose 4 volumes of *Chess Tournament Crosstables from 1851–1930*, published betwen 1969 and 1974, are remarkably accurate, painstakingly put together and indispensable for chess authors.

He has also published *A Catalog of Chessplayers and Problemists* (1969) and *A Catalog of USA Chess Personalia* (1980).

Gambit

In modern usage, any opening which involves the planned sacrifice of material, usually in the interests of some objective such as central control or rapid development. The word derives originally from the Italian *Gamba*, a leg. In the sixteenth century, Italian wrestlers coined the term *gambitare*, meaning roughly 'to set a trap', e.g. by offering the opponent a leg-hold. Ruy Lopez introduced the word into chess vocabulary to describe a variation of Damiano's Defence: 1 e4 e5 2 ♘f3 f6 3 ♘xe5 fe 4 ♕h5+ g6 5 ♕xe5+ ♕e7 6 ♕xh8 ♘f6 (White is winning).

Game of the Century
See Fischer.

Gaprindashvili, Nona Terentyevna
[*May 3 1941- *]
Women's World Champion 1962–78.

USSR GM (1978) who beat Bykova +7=4−0 in 1962 to win the world title. She defended it with wins over Kushnir: +7=3−3 in 1965, +6 =5−2 in 1969 and +5=7−4 in 1972. In 1975 she beat Alexandria +8=1−3 but in 1978 she lost +2=9−4 to Chiburdanidze. She was USSR Woman Champion 5 times during 1964–85.

Nona Gaprindashvili, Women's World Champion 1962–78. The only woman other than Chiburdanidze to hold the full Grandmaster title.

Gaprindashvili has competed successfully in men's tournaments, coming equal 1st at Lone Pine 1977, 2nd at Dortmund 1978 (VII), equal 1st at Wijk aan Zee 1987 (VIII) and 1st at Brussels 1987 (XI), and like Chiburdanidze has the full GM title.

Garcia Gonzales, Guillermo
[*December 9 1953– *]
Cuban GM (1976) who was Cuban Champion in 1974, 1976 and 1983. He won at Plovdiv 1975 and was equal 1st at Zurich 1975 and Orense 1976. Perhaps his best result was 1st at Portugalete 1986 (IX). He has played on several Cuban Olympiad teams.

Garcia Martinez, Silvino
[*July 4 1944– *]
The very first Cuban GM (1975) who was Cuban Champion in 1968, 1970, 1973 and 1979/80. He won the 1968 Pan American, was equal 3rd at the 1973 Capablanca Memorial (Cienfuegos) and was equal 2nd at Havana 1985, (IX). He is a regular member of the Cuban Olympiad team.

Garcia Palermo, Carlos
[*December 2 1953– *]
Argentine GM (1985) who won several Category VIII tournaments in 1983, 1984 and 1985. He was equal 1st at Havana 1986 and at Camaguey 1987,

both Category X. He played board 2 on the 1986 Argentine Olympiad team and scored 6½–4½.

Gavrikov, Viktor Nikolayevich

[*July 29 1957– *]

USSR GM (1984) who played in four USSR Championships between 1981 and 1987 and scored 37 to 33. He won several Category VIII and IX tournaments in 1983 and 1984, but his best results were equal 1st in the 1985 USSR Championship (XI) and equal 2nd in the 1986 USSR Championship (X).

He was 2nd in the Rapid (then 'Active') Chess World Championship in 1988 (30 minute games) after holding Karpov to a draw +2=6−2 in the play-off but losing on tie-break.

Gelbfuhs Score

See Tie-Breaking Systems

Gelfand, Boris [*June 24 1968– *]

USSR GM (1989) who was equal 1st in the World Junior Championship (under age 20) 1988, equal 1st at the Amsterdam Open 1988 and equal 1st at Klajpeda 1988 (IX).

Geller, Yefim Petrovich

[*March 8 1925– *]

USSR GM (1952) who was one of the most consistent top level performers that ever lived. He never achieved the high peaks of Tal, Fischer or Bronstein but for 25 years (1952–77) he was just one step away from World Championship levels. In terms of total life strength he ranked 13th in the all time list (Keene and Divinsky) ahead of Tal, Keres, Bronstein, Reshevsky and even Alekhine.

In terms of life scores he was a terror for World Champions. He scored against Smyslov (+11=31−7), Petrosian (+6=33−2), Botvinnik (+4 =5−1), Fischer (+5=2−3), Tal (+6 =22−6), Spassky (+6=22−9), Karpov (+1=5−2) and Kasparov (+0 =3−1). This is a total of (+39

= 123 − 31) against eight World Champions. He was not quite so successful against other contenders: Bronstein (+5=15−5), Reshevsky (+1=3−1), Keres (+6=22−7) and Korchnoi (+6=15−12).

Geller qualified for 23 USSR Championships between 1949 and 1985, and scored over 56%. No one has played *more* often—Taimanov equalled this record of 23. Geller won the title in 1955 and in 1979. He played on many USSR Olympiad teams during 1952 to 1980.

He was a Candidate 6 times. He was equal 6th with Najdorf at Zurich 1953 (XVI), equal 3rd at Amsterdam 1956 (XV) and equal 2nd with Keres at Curaçao 1962 (XVI). In the match format of the Candidates he lost to Spassky in 1965 and in 1968, and he lost to Korchnoi in 1971.

He won many tournaments and even as late as 1987 he was equal 2nd at Pancevo (IX). He was Spassky's second in the 1972 match with Fischer, and was chosen to assist Karpov in 1975.

Geller's strength lay in his profound

Yefim Geller, one of the elite throughout the third quarter of the century.

insights into openings and his attacking abilities. Kotov wrote: 'A master of swift attack and unusual combinations, Geller is weaker in positional battles and complicated endgames where iron logic and precise, methodical playing are the main factors of success'.

In the late 1960s Botvinnik said he considered Geller the best player in the world and his only drawback is his lack of Spassky's 'realistic approach'.

Geller is a stocky, round man with a degree in political science from Odessa University.

See *Grandmaster Geller at the chessboard* by B. Cafferty (1969).

Kotov–Geller

USSR championship 1949

1 d4 ♘f6 2 c4 g6 3 ♘c3 ♗g7 4 g3 0-0 5 ♗g2 d6 6 ♘f3 ♘bd7 7 0-0 e5 8 e4 ed 9 ♘xd4 ♘c5 10 f3 ♘fd7 11 ♗e3 c6 12 ♕d2 a5 13 ♖ad1 ♘e5 14 b3 a4 15 ♘de2

B

15 ... ab 16 ♗xc5 ♘xc4 17 ♕c1 ba 18 ♘xa2 ♕a5 19 ♕xc4 ♗e6 20 ♕c1 dc 21 ♘ac3 b5 22 ♘b1 b4 23 ♘f4 ♗b3 24 ♖d6 c4 25 ♖xc6 c3 26 ♘d5 ♗xd5 27 ed ♕xd5 28 f4 ♕d4+ 29 ♔h1 ♖a2 30 ♗f3 ♖b2 31 f5 ♗e5 32 ♕e1 ♖d8 33 ♗e4 ♔g7 34 f6+ ♔g8 35 ♖a6 h5 36 ♖a5 h4 37 ♗xg6 ♖xh2+ 38 ♔xh2 ♗xg3+ 39 ♕xg3 hg+ 40 ♔h3 fg 41 Resigns

Fischer–Geller
Monaco 1967
1 e4 c5 2 ♘f3 d6 3 d4 cd 4 ♘xd4 ♘f6 5 ♘c3 a6 6 ♗g5 e6 7 f4 ♕b6 8 ♕d2 ♕xb2 9 ♖b1 ♕a3 10 f5 ♘c6 11 fe fe 12 ♘xc6 bc 13 e5 ♘d5 14 ♘xd5 cd 15 ♗e2 de 16 0-0 ♗c5+ 17 ♔h1 ♖f8 18 c4 ♖xf1+ 19 ♖xf1 ♗b7 20 ♗g4 dc 21 ♗xe6 ♕d3 22 ♕e1

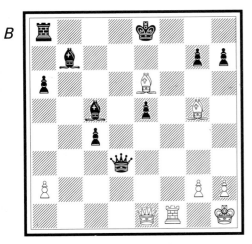

B

21 ... ♗e4 23 ♗g4 ♖b8 24 ♗d1 ♔d7 25 ♖f7+ ♔e6 26 Resigns. After 26

♖xg7 ♗xg2+ black mates 27 ♔xg2 ♖b2+ 28 ♔h1 ♕d5+

Georgadze, Tamas Vasilyevich
[*November 9 1947–*]
USSR GM (1977) who played in 3 USSR Championships (1978–80) and scored 50%. He has wins at Dortmund 1979 and Costa del Sol 1986 (VIII).

Georgiev, Kiril [*November 28 1965–*]
Bulgarian GM (1985) who was World Junior Champion in 1983. He was equal 1st in the 1984 Bulgarian Championship and won outright in 1986. He won several Category VII events in 1984. More recently he was 4th at Wijk aan Zee 1985 (XIII), 2nd at Plovdiv 1985 (X) and 3rd at Leningrad 1987 (XIV).

He led the Bulgarian Olympiad team in 1984 and 1986, scoring about 65%.

Georgiev, Krum [*May 24 1958–*]
Bulgarian GM (1988) who was equal 1st at Athens 1983 (VIII), equal 2nd at Albena 1985 (VIII), scored 7½–4½ on the 1986 Bulgarian Olympiad team on board 5 and was equal 3rd at Pleven 1987 (VIII).

Gheorghiu, Florin [*April 6 1944–*]
The very first Romanian GM (1965). He was World Junior Champion in 1963 and has won the Romanian Championship 10 times between 1960 and 1987. He has wins or equal 1sts at Hastings 1967/68, Reykjavik 1972, Orense 1973, Vratza 1975, Novi Sad 1979 and Timisoara 1987 (IX). He has played in many Swiss Opens, coming equal 1st at Griesbach 1983, Biel 1985 and Mendrisio 1987.

He is a tough competitor, with an even +1=2−1 score against Fischer. He narrowly missed out on becoming a Candidate in 1979.

He is a lecturer in languages at Bucharest University and has played on several Romanian Olympiad teams.

Ghitescu, Teodor
[*January 24 1934–*]
Romanian IM (1961) and honorary GM (1986) who was Romanian Champion in 1963. He was 1st at Bucharest 1976. He has played on many Romanian Olympiad teams, as recently as 1984.

Gianutio, Horatio (of Mantia)
[*16th century*]
Author of *Libro nel quale si tratta della Maniera di giocar' a Scacchi* (Turin 1597), the first chess pamphlet by a player from the Italian school. He discussed 6 openings (primarily the Two Knights Defence), odds-giving and 11 problems. As Murray says: 'there is very little of importance in any of his analysis'. The original 57 page pamphlet is quite rare, though it was translated into English in 1817 by J. H. Sarratt. Perhaps its principal chess interest is in its discussion of so-called free castling where the king goes to h1 as the rook goes to f1, or king to a1 while the rook goes to c1, or the king goes from e1 to g1 all by itself.

Gipslis, Aivar Petrovich
[*February 8 1937–*]
USSR (Latvian) GM (1967) who was Latvian Champion 8 times during 1955 to 1966. He played in 6 USSR Championships during 1958 to 1970, his best result being equal 3rd in 1966.

He was equal 1st at Bad Liebenstein 1963, Peco 1964, Vrnjacka Banja 1975, Hradec Kralove 1979/80 and Jurmala 1987 (X). His best result was equal 2nd at the Alekhine Memorial in Moscow 1967 (XIV).

He is an economist and was a longtime editor of Latvia's chess magazine *Sahs*.

Giuoco Piano
1 e4 e5 2 ♘f3 ♘c6 3 ♗c4 ♗c5

This quiet opening, also called the Italian Game, is one of the oldest on record, being mentioned in 1490 (Göttingen Manuscript). It can have a most peaceable nature with 4 d3 (pianissimo), but it can also flare up with 4 c3 or explode into an Evans Gambit with 4 b4.

Gligoric, Svetozar

[*February 2 1923– *]
Yugoslav GM (1951) and journalist who is Yugoslavia's most successful player of all time. His chess growth was interrupted by the Second World War, in which he fought actively for the Yugoslav cause. He has an impressive tournament record with wins or equal 1sts at Warsaw 1947, Mar del Plata 1950, Staunton Memorial 1951, Hastings 1951/2, 1956/7, 1959/60, 1960/1, 1962/3, Dallas 1957 (XII), Torremolinos 1961, Belgrade 1962, Sarajevo 1962, Reykjavik 1964, Tel Aviv 1967, Belgrade 1969, Berlin 1971, Montilla 1977 and Sochi 1986 (XII). He had a good 2nd at Zurich 1959 and a fine equal 3rd at Bled 1961 (XIII).

He was a Candidate in 1953, in 1959 (where he peaked with an equal 5th) and in 1968 when he lost his match to Tal. He beat Ståhlberg $+2=9-1$ in 1949 and lost to Reshevsky $+1=7-2$ in 1952.

He played in 18 Yugoslav Championships winning 11 times and was on 14 Yugoslav Olympiad teams.

His life scores against the very great are not impressive: Spassky ($+0 =15-5$), Tal ($+2=19-11$), Stein ($+1=0-6$), Korchnoi ($+1=13-6$), Keres ($+2=16-8$), Bronstein ($+0 =8-4$), Karpov ($+0=6$-4), Kasparov (-3). Nevertheless, he is an extremely tough competitor: Botvinnik ($+2 =5-2$), Smyslov ($+5=21-7$), Reshevsky ($+2=24-4$), Geller ($+1 =22-2$), Petrosian ($+7=19-10$) and Fischer ($+4=6-6$).

He is predominantly an attacking player, but he disciplined his temperament and evolved to a curious cross between Rubinstein and Capablanca. A man of many talents and interests including music and languages, he has always found time for chess and has emerged from any crisis more dedicated than before. He is also well known as a chess author and contributes to many magazines.

His major works are: *Spassky–Fischer Match* (1972), *Sicilian Defence* (with Sokolov) in Serbo Croat, *100 games of Gligoric* (1952) in Serbo Croat,

See *Svetozar Gligoric's Chess Career 1945–1970* by D. Levy (1972).

GMA

The Grandmasters Association, founded in Febuary 1987 under the leadership of Kasparov, Karpov, Timman, and Bessel Kok of Brussels, is dedicated to promote the interests of GMs, in terms of playing conditions, tournaments and fees. To this end it has organized the so-called World Cup during 1988/89, with 6 major tournaments: Brussels, Belfort (France), Reykjavik, Barcelona, Rotterdam and Skelleftea (Sweden).

See World Cup.

Godunov, Boris Fedorovich

[*1552–1605*]
Regent of Russia (1584–98) and Tsar (1598–1605) who was an avid chess player.

Goldin A.

USSR GM (1989) who was equal 1st at Polancia Zdroj 1988 (IX).

Golombek, Harry   [*March 1 1911– *]
English IM (1950), International Judge (1956) and honorary GM (1985) who won the British Championship in 1947, 1949 and 1955 and played on 9 English Olympiad teams during 1935–62. He edited the *British Chess Magazine* 1938–40 and has been chess editor of the London *Times* 1945–89.

He was the first British player to qualify for an Interzonal, though he was never a Candidate. He was awarded an OBE in 1966.

He played a major role in FIDE especially on the Rules Commission. He is a fine linguist and has supervised many important tournaments and matches.

He has written some 35 chess books including *Capablanca's Best Games* (1947), *Réti's Best Games* (1954) and a *History of Chess* (1976).

Golombek is one of the best dinner conversationalists in the chess world.

Göttingen Manuscript

A 33-page Latin tract containing a mixture of opening analysis and problems, probably written by Lucena, about 1500. It is in the University of Göttingen Library.

Gottschall, Hermann von

[*October 16 1862–March 7 1933*]
German author and player of IM strength whose best result was equal 2nd at Nuremberg 1888. He wrote *Adolf Anderssen* (1912), a book on problems (1926) and edited volumes 4 and 5 of Dufresne's *Sammlung von Schachaufgaben*.

Graf-Stevenson, Sonya

[*December 16 1914–March 6 1965*]
German-born US player of Woman GM strength who lost $+1=0-3$ to Menchik in 1934, and lost again $+2=5-9$ to Menchik in 1937. In 1939 she came 2nd to Menchik. Graf was the number 2 woman player in the world during the 1930s. She was US Woman Champion in 1957 and 1964.

Granda Zuniga, Julio E.

[*February 25 1967– *]
Peruvian GM (1986) whose best result was equal 1st at Havana 1986 (X). He scored $9\frac{1}{2}$-$4\frac{1}{2}$ at board 2 on Peru's 1986 Olympiad team.

Grandmaster

A loose term used in the early 1900s to describe the world top 5 or 10 players.

FIDE's International Grandmaster title (inaugurated in 1950) requires a player to satisfy carefully laid out achievement levels, as described in FIDE regulations (roughly equivalent to a 2500 Elo rating).

Grandmaster Draw

A derogatory term for a short drawn game where it is clear that neither side has made any real effort to fight. Such non-fights disappoint the spectators and go against the entire spirit of honourable competition but there are often reasonable explanations for them: both players are exhausted from a heavy schedule and need a rest, or one player has already won the tournament and is content with an easy draw, while his opponent (who may be near the bottom) is delighted to gain a half point from the tournament winner.

See Chess in our Time.

Grasshopper

See *Dawson*

Greco Counter Gambit

See Greco

Greco, Giaochino   [c. 1600–c. 1634]

The leading 17th century Italian master who travelled widely in Europe playing matches for high stakes. His influence did much to promote chess in those countries which he visited. In 1621 he earned 5000 crowns by defeating, among others, France's three leading players: Arnault le Carabin, Chaumont de la Salle and the Duc de Nemours. He came to England in 1622 where his fortune was stolen *en route* by brigands. In 1624 he returned to France, lived at the court of Philip IV in Madrid and died on a trip to the West Indies.

Greco published nothing directly but often sold analyses to wealthy patrons embellishing them with full games. Some of his manuscripts survive (see the Bodleian and British Libraries). The Greco Counter-Gambit 1 e4 e5 2 ♘f3 f5 was not his invention but he recommended it as sound.

Many people published various of his manuscripts. For a fine overview see *The Chess Games of Greco* by Prof. Louis Hoffman (1900).

Greek Gift

This describes a bishop sacrifice for the h-pawn, which leads to a forced win. For example:

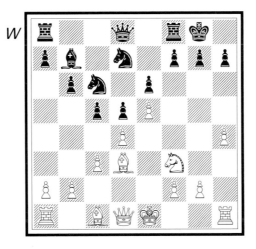

1 ♗xh7+ ♚xh7 (if ... ♚h8 2 ♘g5 g6 3 h5) 2 ♘g5+ ♚g8 (if ... ♚g6 3 h5+ ♚f5 4 ♛f3 mate) 3 ♛h5 ♜e8 4 ♛xf7+ 6 ♚h8 ♛h5+ ♚g8 ♛h7+ ♚f8 7 ♛h8+ ♚e7 8 ♛xg7 mate.

Greenfeld, Alon   [April 17 1964–]

Israeli GM (1989) who won a strong Open at Biel 1985, was 2nd at Beer-Sheva 1986 (VIII), equal 5th at Biel 1986 (XII), equal 4th at Beer-Sheva 1987 (XI) and equal 2nd at Polanica Zdroj 1987, (IX). He played board 2 for Israel at the 1984 Olympiad scoring 9–4, and he led the Israeli team at the 1988 Olympiad.

Grigoriev, Nikolai Dmitrijevich

[1895–1938]

Soviet player and endgame composer. He played in all 6 USSR Championships during 1920–9, coming equal 5th in 1920. He is especially famous for his pawn endings.

White to play and win (1930).

1 b3 (1 b4 ♚a6 draws. And not 1 ♚b8 b4 for if 2 c4 b3 and White would actually lose.) 1 ... ♚a5 (1 ... ♚a6 2 b4 ♚b6 3 ♚b8 wins. And not 1 ... b4 2 c4 wins) 2 ♚b8 (2 ♚b7 b4 3 c4 is stalemate. And not 2 b4+ ♚a6 draw) 2 ... b4 (if 2 ... ♚b6 3 b4 wins) 3 c4 ♚b6 4 ♚c8 ♚c6 5 ♚d8 ♚d6 6 ♚e8 ♚e6 7 ♚f8 ♚f6 8 ♚g8 ♚g6 9 ♚h8 ♚f6 10 ♚h7 ♚f7 11 ♚h6 ♚f6 12 ♚h5 ♚f5 13 ♚h4 ♚f4 14 ♚h3 ♚f5 15 ♚g3 ♚g5 16 ♚f3 ♚f5 17 ♚e3 ♚e5 18 ♚d3 and wins.

Books about him were written by Kan (1954) and Porreca (1965).

Grob's Attack

1 g4.

A highly irregular opening which is seldom played. It does little to further White's development and a lot to weaken his position. After 1 g4 d5 2 ♗g2 c6! Black's position is already preferable.

It is named after the Swiss IM Henry Grob (1904–74), who was equal 1st with Keres and Fine, at Ostend 1937 and its cause has frequently been championed in competition by the English IM Michael Basman.

Groszpeter, Attila   [June 9 1960–]

Hungarian GM (1986) who won at Prague and at Kecskemet 1986, both Category VII. Perhaps his best result was equal 2nd at the Hungarian Championship 1984 (X).

Grünfeld Defence

1 d4 ♘f6 2 c4 g6 3 ♘c3 d5.

Introduced by Ernst Grünfeld in 1922, this hypermodern defence allows White to occupy the centre with the idea that Black will have a clear target to attack. It has been used by Smyslov, Fischer and especially Kasparov. In his 1987 world title match against Karpov, Kasparov used the Grünfeld ten times.

White can play sharply with 4 cd ♘xd5 5 e4 ♘xc3 6 bc or more positionally with 4 ♘f3 ♗g7 5 ♕b3 dc 6 ♕xc4 0-0 7 e4 ♗g4 8 ♗e3 ♘6d7 (Smyslov).

Black can try a delayed or Neo-Grünfeld: 1 d4 ♘f6 2 c4 g6 3 g3 ♗g7 4 ♗g2 d5, when White fianchettoes his king's bishop.

Grünfeld, Ernst F.

[*November 23 1893–April 3 1962*]
Austrian GM (1950) who gave the world the Grünfeld Defence to the queen's pawn in 1922. He had some good results in the early and mid 1920s but he was inconsistent. He was equal 1st at Vienna 1920, 2nd at Budapest 1921, 3rd at Teplitz Schonau 1922, 4th at Pitsyan 1922, 1st at Margate 1923, equal 4th at Carlsbad 1923, 3rd at Mahrisch Ostrau 1923, 1st at Meran 1924, equal 1st at Budapest 1926, equal 1st at Vienna 1928 but only 9th at Carlsbad 1929. He was 1st at Mahrisch Ostrau 1933 and after a long absence he was 8th at Beverwijk 1961.

He was German Champion in 1923 and played on four Austrian Olympiad teams between 1927 and 1935. His speciality was opening theory and he shunned complications in the middle-game. In spite of being careful and avoiding risk, he lost more than his share of brilliant games—to Maroczy (Vienna 1920), Réti (Pistyan 1922), Alekhine (Carlsbad 1923), Sämisch (Carlsbad 1929) and Eliskases (Mahrisch Ostrau 1933).

He wrote *Queen's Pawn Openings* (1924) and a general opening book (1953).

He is supposed to have played 1 e4 only once (vs Capablanca, Carlsbad 1929). When asked why he avoided 1 e4, he said: 'I never make a mistake in the opening!'.

Grünfeld lost a leg in early childhood and was desperately poor all of his life. These defects had a major impact on his personality. He was uneducated, unsophisticated, superstitious and almost primitive. Chess gave him his only opportunity to taste life deeply.

Grünfeld, Yehuda

[*February 28 1956–*]
Polish born Israeli GM (1980) who was Israeli Champion in 1982. He won at Biel 1980, New York 1981, Dortmund 1984 (IX) and Munich 1987 (IX). He led the 1984 Israeli Olympiad team.

Gufeld, Eduard Yefimovich

[*March 19 1936–*]
USSR GM (1967) who played in 8 USSR Championships between 1959 and 1972. He was 1st at Gori 1971 and Tbilisi 1971, equal 1st at Tbilisi 1974 and clear 1st at Tbilisi 1980. More recently he was equal 1st at Havana 1985 (VIII). He is a well known and jolly figure at international events and a respected chess journalist.

Guimard, Carlos Enrique

[*April 6 1913–*]
Argentine GM (1960) who was Argentine Champion in 1937, 1938 and 1941, and played on four Argentine Olympiad teams during 1937–54.

Gulko, Boris Frantsevich

[*February 9 1947–*]
USSR GM (1976) and psychologist who was equal 1st with Timman at Sombor 1974, 1st at Kishniev 1975, equal 1st at Vilnius 1975, equal 2nd at the 1975 USSR Championship (XII), 1st at the Capablanca Memorial at Cienfuegos 1976, equal 1st with Dorfman at the 1977 USSR Championship and equal 1st with Timman at Niksic 1978 (XIII)—a most promising career.

Gulko and his family then decided they wanted to leave the USSR and move to Israel. The Soviets refused and the Gulko family became a *cause célebre*. They went on hunger strikes and public protests and their case was taken up by human rights activists in the western world. In May 1986 they were finally allowed to leave the USSR and later that year they moved to the USA.

During these difficult years Gulko's results were not good. He played in 7 USSR Championships during 1974–85 with an overall score of 57–58. Once released, his results improved: 1st at Marseilles 1986, Clichy 1987 and equal 1st at Cannes 1987, all Category X. Then 1st at Biel 1987 (XIII) and equal 2nd at Amsterdam 1987 (XIII). In his first US Championship (November 1987) Gulko could only manage equal 7th (XII). His fans expect him to do much better in the future.

Gumpel

See Mephisto

Gunsberg, Isidor Arthur

[*November 2 1854–May 2 1930*]
English player of GM strength who was one of Britain's strongest masters in the late 19th century. He was of Hungarian Jewish origin, born in Budapest and emigrated to England in 1863. He was the master who worked the famous automaton Mephisto and under his control it won the 1878 Counties Chess Association Handicap tournament in London and it edited a chess column in the London periodical *Knowledge*, from 1881 to 1890.

In 1881 Gunsberg lost a match to Blackburne + 4 = 2 − 7, but by 1885 his strength improved. He was 1st at London 1885, 1st at Hamburg 1885 and in 1886 he beat Bird +5=3−1 and Blackburne +5=6−2. He was equal 1st with Burn at London 1887 and their play-off match was drawn +1=3−1. He was 1st at Bradford 1888 and 3rd at the powerful tournament in New York 1889. There were also failures at Amsterdam and Breslau 1889 and at Manchester 1890.

Gunsberg's career peaked when he played a drawn match with Chigorin +9=5−9 in 1890 and lost narrowly to Steinitz +4=9−6 in a match for the World Championship 1890/91.

After that Gunsberg was troubled by chronic poor health and his results deteriorated (e.g. equal 15th at Hastings 1895) though he continued to compete until 1914.

He edited many chess columns and was involved with planning the five-stage 36-player Ostend tournament in 1906.

Gurevich, Dmitry

[*September 11 1956–*] US GM (1983) who won at New York 1983 (X) and was equal 1st at Jerusalem 1986 (XI). He has been equal 1st in several Opens but has not done well in US closed championships.

Gurevich, Mikhail N.

[*February 22 1959–*] USSR GM (1986) who was equal 1st in the 1985 USSR Championship. He won quite a few Category VII to XI events in 1985 and 1986. His results improved in 1987 when he was 1st at Moscow (XII) and 2nd at Leningrad (XIV) behind Vaganian.

Gurgenidze, Bukhuty Ivanovich

[*November 13 1933–*] USSR (Georgia) GM (1970) who played in 8 USSR Championships during 1957 to 1985. He was equal 1st with Tal at Tbilisi 1969/70 and was 1st at Olomoue 1976.

He is a geologist by profession.

Gutman, Lev

[*September 26 1945–*] Latvian-born Israeli GM (1986) who was Latvian champion in 1972. He won at Grindavik 1984 (VIII), Beer-Sheva 1985 (VII) and Wuppertal 1986 (VII). He has also won several Open events. He was board 3 on Israel's 1984 Olympiad teams.

The Hague
Dutch capital and home of the Koninklijke library which houses a wonderful chess collection (Niemeijer–Van der Linde). The Hague staged the second Olympiad in 1928 and the first two round robins of the 1948 World Championship tournament (*see* Moscow). The Hague also enjoyed a few games from AVRO 1938 as well as from the world title matches Alekhine–Bogoljubow 1929 and Alekhine–Euwe 1935 and 1937.

Halberstadt, Vitaly [*1903–1957*]
Russian-born French player and endgame study composer who wrote *Curiosities Tactiques* (1954).

Half-open file
A file on which only one player has pawns. It is then usually a good plan for the opponent to place a rook on this file and put pressure on the front pawn.

Hamilton-Russell, Frederick George
[*June 12 1867–September 3 1941*]
Patron of chess who donated a gold cup to FIDE in 1927, to be the trophy for the international team tournaments, now known as chess Olympiads. This Hamilton-Russell Cup is still in use (as of 1989).

He contributed financially to British chess and served as treasurer and later as president of the British Chess Federation.

Hammond, Alex [*1888–1962*]
British dealer in rare and beautiful chess sets who wrote *The Book of Chessmen* (1950).

Handbuch (*des Schachspiels*)
The bible of openings and endings for almost 90 years, this enormously influential book was conceived by Bilguer in 1840 and completed by von der Lasa in 1843. The first of the eight editions had 500 pages ($\frac{3}{4}$ devoted to openings, $\frac{1}{4}$ to endings). Lasa edited the editions of 1852, 1858, 1864 and 1874. Schwede (and van der Linde) edited the 1880 edition; Schallop (with Berger and Paulsen) edited the 1891 edition. The last edition (1916) was done by Schlechter (and Spielmann, Tarrasch, Teichmann, Kohtz (history), Koch (modern times), and Berger (endings)), and had some 1040 pages including 250 illustrative games.

Its influence faded in the 1920s when the hypermodern movement developed.

Handicap
A method of making the game interesting for two opponents of widely differing strengths. There are several ways of achieving this: the strong player takes on several weaker opponents simultaneously or even blindfold simultaneously; the stronger player counts a draw as a loss, or gives his opponent more time on the clock. But the most common arrangement is for the stronger player to give material odds:

(1) Pawn and move: the stronger player takes Black and removes one of his pawns, usually his f-pawn;

(2) Pawn and two moves: the stronger player takes Black, removes one of his pawns (again the f-pawn) and the weaker player is allowed to make two moves before Black responds;

(3) The stronger player removes one of his knights—usually the queen's knight;

(4) The stronger player removes one of his rooks—usually the queen's rook; and occasionally is then allowed to place his a-pawn at a3 (or a6 if he is playing Black);

(5) The stronger player removes his queen's rook and his f-pawn;

(6) The stronger player removes two of his minor pieces (knights and bishops);

(7) The stronger player removes his queen's rook and his queen's knight;

(8) The stronger player removes his queen;

(9) The stronger player removes

both of his rooks.

Perhaps the most severe handicap is a *'pion coiffé'*, i.e. one of the stronger player's pawns is crowned with a hat of paper. The strong player can only give mate with this pawn (and cannot promote it).

Another heavy handicap is mating only in a far corner with a bishop.

Hanging pawns

Steinitz used this term to describe a pair of pawns cut off from their brother pawns, who are on half-open files and are not passed pawns (d4 and e4 in the diagram). They are exposed to attack especially from enemy rooks. They are strongest when side by side (in phalanx) but under pressure may be forced to abandon this configuration, in which case the backward pawn can become quite weak. However, they control space, are mobile and can become a powerful attacking force. Current wisdom is that hanging pawns are weak if the rest of their army is behind in development, but strong if their side is ahead in development.

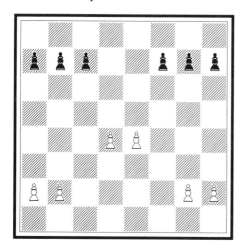

Hanham Variation (Philidor's Defence)

1 e4 e5 2 ♘f3 d6 3 d4 ♘d7.

A passive defence that correctly maintains the centre but blocks both bishops.

Hansen, Curt [*September 18 1964–*]

Danish GM (1985) who was European Junior Champion 1981/2 and World Junior Champion 1984. He was Nordic Champion 1983 and Danish Champion 1983, 1984 and 1985. He led the 1984 Danish Olympiad team, scoring 8–4. In matches he beat Knaak 2–0 in 1984 and Plachetka +5 = 1 in 1985. His best recent results were equal 2nd at Copenhagen 1985 and 3rd at Jerusalem 1986, both Category XI.

Hanstein, Wilhelm

[*August 3 1811–October 14 1850*] German player of IM strength who was one of the Berlin Pleiades and who helped found the *Berliner Schachzeitung*, later to become the *Deutsche Schachzeitung*.

Harkness score

See Tie-breaking systems

Harley, Brian

[*October 27 1883–May 18 1955*] British problemist who was chess correspondent for the *Observer* for over 20 years and president of the British Chess Problem Society 1947–9.

See *Mate in two Moves* (1931), *Mate in three Moves* (1943).

Harrwitz, Daniel

[*April 29 1823–January 9 1884*] German player of GM strength who was one of the top 3 or 4 players in the world during the 1850s. He was born in Breslau and he and Anderssen were the two superstars from that city. Harrwitz trained as a book dealer but soon devoted himself entirely to chess. In 1845 he went to seek his fortune in Paris and London.

He was no match for Staunton in 1846, losing +0 − 7, though he did better when Staunton spotted him pawn and 1 or 2 moves, scoring +9 − 5 = 1. His play then matured and for the next 12 years no player beat him in a match. He beat Horwitz +6 = 1 − 5 (1846), drew +5 − 5 with Anderssen (1848), beat Horwitz +7 = 12 − 6 (1849), beat Szen +3 = 1 − 1 (1852) and beat Löwenthal +11 = 12 − 8 (1853). Harrwitz defaulted 2 games in this latter match and technically, the final score reads +11 = 12 − 10. In fact Löwenthal led at one point +7 = 1 − 2 and Harrwitz let 2 more games go by default before he collected himself and returned to win the match.

Harrwitz had a high-strung nature and was not physically robust. When his health gave way he would withdraw from the chess scene until his vitality returned. In 1853 he founded the *British Chess Review*—quite a good magazine— to compete with Staunton's *Chess Chronicle*, and he also challenged Staunton to a match. The match never materialized and the *Review* lost its struggle and came to an end in the summer of 1854.

He played in just one tournament— Manchester 1857—a knockout affair. Unfortunately he was paired with Anderssen in the first round and lost. He did win several offhand games against Anderssen and one with both players blindfold. Harrwitz then left England for Paris where he dominated the chess scene and was known as the King of the Café de la Régence.

In the fall of 1858 Paul Morphy came to Paris to play the king. Harrwitz won an offhand game and the first two games of their match. Then things went Morphy's way and Harrwitz resigned the match when the score was +2 = 1 − 5. In fact this was quite a respectable result against the American genius, but it was Harrwitz's first match defeat since his loss to Staunton in 1846. In December 1858, inspired by Morphy's blindfold displays, Harrwitz played 8 simultaneous blindfold games scoring +6 = 1 − 1 in 8 hours. But his star was waning. He lost +1 = 2 − 3 to

Anderssen and could not hold his own against Kolisch in late 1859.

Harrwitz came into a modest family inheritance and retired to Bolzano in the Alps. In 1862 he published quite a good *Lehrbuch*.

Harrwitz had an elegant and technically polished style. He was extremely good in middlegames with minor pieces and in endgames. He energetically punished any small errors by his opponents. He was a great tactician, but lacked the deep strategical insights of Morphy.

Morphy–Harrwitz
Match 1858
1 e4 e5 2 ♘f3 d6 3 d4 ed 4 ♛xd4 ♘c6 5 ♗b5 ♗d7 6 ♗xc6 ♗xc6 7 ♗g5 ♘f6 8 ♘c3 ♗e7 9 0-0-0 0-0 10 ♖he1 h6 11 ♗h4 ♘e8 12 ♗xe7 ♛xe7 13 e5 ♗xf3 14 gf ♛g5+ 15 ♔b1 de 16 ♖xe5 ♛g2 17 ♘d5 ♛xh2 18 ♖ee1 ♛d6 19 ♖g1 ♔h7 20 ♛e3 f5 21 ♘f4 ♛b6 22 ♛e2 ♖f7 23 ♛c4 ♛f6

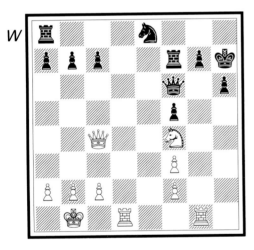

24 ♘h5 ♛e7 25 ♖de1 ♛d7 26 a3 ♘d6 27 ♛d4 ♖g8 28 ♖g2 ♘e8 29 ♛c3 f4 30 ♖h1 g6 31 ♖hg1 ♛d5 32 ♛e1 ♛xh5 33 ♖g5 ♛xf3 34 ♛e6 ♖f6 35 ♛e7+ ♖g7 36 ♛xe8 hg 37 ♛e1 ♛c6 38 Resigns

Harschacharita
An historical romance in Sanskrit by Bana, written in the early part of the 7th century. It is the third earliest (*see* Vasa-vadatta and Karnamak) reference to chess (*chaturanga*).

Hartston, William Roland
[*August 23 1947– *]
British IM (1973) who has a masters degree in mathematics from Cambridge, is an author and industrial psychologist and who won the British Championship in 1973 and 1975. He played on many English Olympiad teams during 1966 to 1980.

Hartston is a TV personality on BBC chess programmes and a lucid and lively author. His major works are: *The Benoni* (1969), *The Grünfeld* (1971), *The Best Games of C. H. O'D Alexander* (1976, with Golombek) and *The Kings of Chess* (1985).

Harun Ar-Rashid
[763–809]
Caliph of Islam who sponsored and supported chess masters at his court in Baghdad. It is written that he was 'the first of the Abbasid Caliphs to play chess and nard (backgammon). He favoured good players and granted them pensions'.

Hastings
A town on the south coast of England, whose chess club was founded in 1882. Since 1920, it has sponsored an annual chess congress, in late December, to which many great GMs have come, and young British players have had an opportunity to compete with non-British GMs.

In 1895 the club organized the strongest tournament ever held (up to that time) and all the leading players of the time were there. The favourites were: Lasker, the newly crowned World Champion who had recently recovered from a long and serious attack of typhoid fever; Steinitz, the recently dethroned World Champion; Tarrasch, the impressive winner of the last 4 major tournaments; and Chigorin, the Russian Champion who was Steinitz's great rival and who had recently drawn a brilliant match with Tarrasch. There were the veterans Bird and Blackburne, as well as a group of young tigers: Schlechter, Pillsbury, Walbrodt, Teichmann and Janowski.

With 3 rounds to go, Lasker ($14\frac{1}{2}$) led Chigorin (14) and Pillsbury ($13\frac{1}{2}$) with Tarrasch (11) and Steinitz (11) far back. With 2 rounds to go, Chigorin (15) led Lasker ($14\frac{1}{2}$) and Pillsbury ($14\frac{1}{2}$). Chigorin threw a somewhat premature victory party. With 1 round to go, the young American, Pillsbury ($15\frac{1}{2}$) led Chigorin (15) and Lasker ($14\frac{1}{2}$). After some excitement, all three leaders won their last round games and Pillsbury emerged the victor—the first time a relative unknown had won a major international event at his first attempt (Capablanca duplicated this feat at San Sebastian 1911).

Time Limit: 30 moves in 2 hours and then 15 moves per hour.

Prizes: £150, 115, 85, 60, 40, 30, 20.

Brilliancy prizes: £5: Steinitz 1, Bardeleben 0 (*see* Bardeleben), £3: Tarrasch 1, Walbrodt 0; Honourable Mention: Gunsberg 1, Mason 0; Albin 1, Janowski 0; Pillsbury 1, Janowski 0.

Tournament book: Edited by H. Cheshire. Notes by a dozen of the players. There were 173 wins and 58 draws.

Tarrasch–Walbrodt
Round 4, August 9 1895
2nd Brilliancy Prize
1 e4 e5 2 ♘f3 ♘c6 3 ♗b5 a6 4 ♗a4 ♘f6 5 ♘c3 d6 6 d4 ♗d7 7 ♗xc6 ♗xc6 8 ♛e2 ed 9 ♘xd4 ♗d7 10 0-0 ♗e7 11 b3 0-0 12 ♗b2 b5 13 a4 b4 14 ♘d1 c5 15 ♘f3 ♗c6 16 ♘d2 d5 17 e5 ♘e8 18 ♘e3 ♛d7 19 ♖ad1 d4 20 ♘(3)c4 ♛e6 21 f4 f5 22 ♘a5 ♗d5 23 ♛d3 ♔h8 24 ♛g3 ♖a7 25 ♘5c4 ♖g8 26 ♖de1 g5 27 ♖e2 ♗d8 28 ♛d3 ♖ag7 29 g3

B

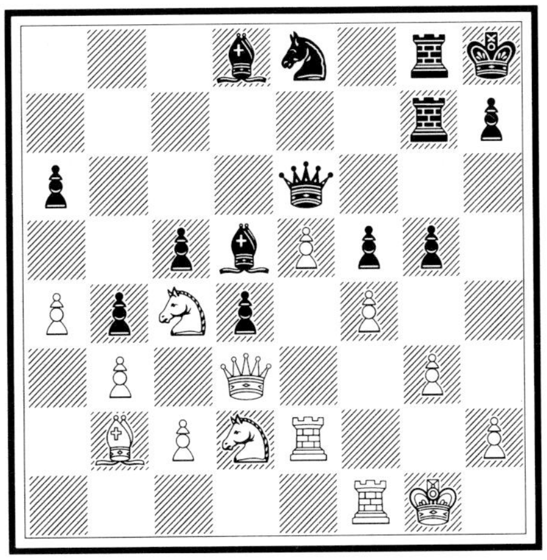

29 ... gf (better is 29... ♗c7) 30 ♖xf4 ♖g5 31 ♖ef2 ♘g7 32 ♘d6 ♕xe5 (correct is 32... ♗c7) 33 ♘xf5 ♘h5 34 ♖xd4 ♘xg3 35 ♘xg3 ♖xg3+ 36 hg ♖xg3+ 37 ♔f1 ♖xd3 38 ♖g4 Resigns.

Hastings 1988/9 and 1989/90 (both Category XIV) were the two strongest tournaments held in the UK. Short won the former, Dolmatov the latter.

Hauptturnier

A second level tournament (in Germany) for aspiring masters. Winners were allowed into a master tournament and if they scored at least 33% in the master tournament, they became masters themselves.

Havana

The capital of Cuba and the home of Capablanca, has had an active chess life for over 100 years and has staged many strong tournaments. It put on both the 1889 and the 1892 Steinitz–Chigorin world title matches as well as the 1921 Lasker–Capablanca title match.

Its most memorable event was the 17th Olympiad in 1966 when Fidel Castro and the entire island put on a magnificent chess spectacular the like of which may not be seen again.

Havel, Miroslav

[November 7 1881–July 8 1958]

Czech problemist whose real name was Miroslav Kostal.

W

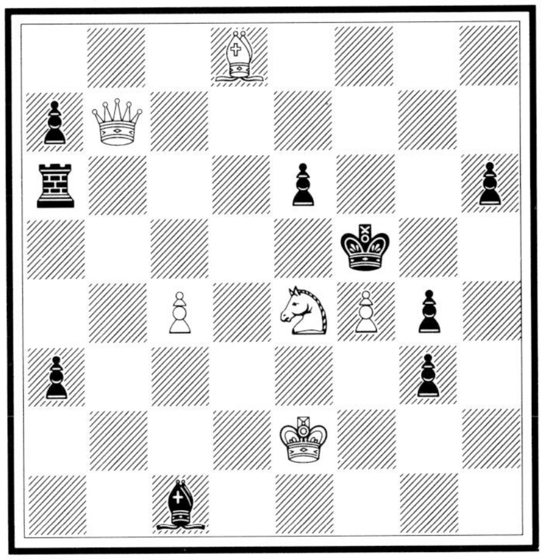

White to move and mate in 3 (1937)
Solution: 1 ♗h4 threatening 2 ♕h7+ ♔xf4 3 ♗xg3 mate.

Hastings 1895

		1	2	3	4	5	6	7	8	9	10	11	12	13	14	15	16	17	18	19	20	21	22	
1	Pillsbury	–	0	0	1	1	1	1	1	0	½	½	1	1	1	1	1	1	½	1	1	1	1	16½
2	Chigorin	1	–	1	1	0	0	1	1	1	1	½	1	0	1	½	1	½	1	1	1	½	1	16
3	Lasker	1	0	–	0	1	1	0	1	1	0	1	1	1	½	1	1	½	1	1	1	½	1	15½
4	Tarrasch	0	0	1	–	1	1	½	0	½	1	1	1	1	0	1	½	1	1	0	1	½	1	14
5	Steinitz	0	1	0	0	–	1	1	½	½	1	1	½	0	1	0	1	1	1	0	1	½	1	13
6	Schiffers	0	1	0	0	0	–	½	½	0	1	1	½	1	½	1	1	0	½	1	1	½	1	12
7	Bardeleben	0	0	1	½	0	½	–	½	½	0	0	1	½	1	½	1	½	1	1	0	1	1	11½
	Teichmann	0	0	0	1	½	½	½	–	½	0	0	1	½	1	1	0	½	1	½	1	1	1	11½
9	Schlechter	1	0	0	½	½	1	½	½	–	½	½	1	0	1	½	½	½	½	½	1	½	0	11
10	Blackburne	½	0	1	0	0	0	1	1	½	–	0	1	1	0	½	0	1	0	1	1	0	1	10½
11	Walbrodt	½	½	0	0	0	0	1	1	½	1	–	0	0	½	½	½	0	½	½	1	1	1	10
12	Burn	0	0	0	0	½	½	0	0	0	0	1	–	1	0	½	0	1	1	1	1	1	1	9½
	Janowski	0	1	0	0	1	0	½	½	1	0	1	0	–	½	½	0	0	1	½	0	1	1	9½
	Mason	0	0	½	1	0	½	0	0	0	1	½	1	½	–	1	0	½	0	1	0	1	1	9½
15	Bird	0	½	0	0	1	0	½	0	½	½	½	½	½	0	–	1	1	½	0	½	½	1	9
	Gunsberg	0	0	0	½	0	0	0	1	½	1	½	1	1	1	0	–	1	½	0	0	1	0	9
17	Albin	0	½	½	0	0	1	½	½	½	0	1	0	1	½	0	0	–	0	0	1	1	½	8½
	Marco	½	0	0	0	0	½	0	0	½	1	½	0	0	1	½	½	1	–	1	0	1	½	8½
19	Pollock	0	0	0	1	1	0	0	½	½	0	½	0	½	0	1	1	1	0	–	0	0	1	8
20	Tinsley	0	0	0	0	0	0	1	0	0	0	0	0	1	1	½	1	0	1	1	–	0	1	7½
	Mieses	0	½	½	½	½	½	0	0	½	1	0	0	0	0	½	0	0	0	1	1	–	1	7½
22	Vergani	0	0	0	0	0	0	0	0	1	0	0	0	0	0	0	1	½	½	0	0	0	–	3

If 1 ... ♗xf4 2 ♕h7+ ♚e5 3
♗f6++
1 ... ♚xf4 2 ♗xg3+ ♚f5 3
♕h7++
1 ... e5 2 ♘xg3+ ♚g6 3 f5++.

See *Havel Ceske Granaty* by I. Mikan
(1975).

Hecht, Hans Joachim

[*January 29 1939– *]
German GM (1973) who won the West
German Championship in 1970 and
1973. He was equal 1st at Bad Pyrmont
1970, 1st at Olot 1971, Malaga 1972,
Montilla-Moriles 1972 and equal 1st at
Dortmund 1973 (IX). He has played on
many West German Olympiad teams
between 1962 and 1986.

Heathcote, Godfrey

[*July 20 1870–July 8 1952*]
British problemist who was president of
the British Chess Problem Society
1951–2.

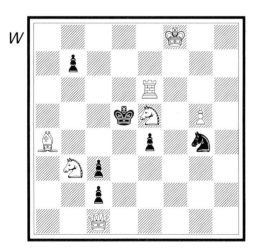

White to play and mate in three moves
(1925)
1 ♘c4
　If 1 ... ♚xc4 2 ♖d6 ♚b4 3
　♖d4++
　If 1 ... ♚xe6 2 ♕f4 ♚d5 3 ♕f7++
　If 1 ... e3 2 ♕h1+ ♚xe6 3
　♘d4++.

Heidenfeld, Wolfgang

[*May 29 1911–August 3 1981*]
German-born chess author and bridge
master who lived in South Africa and
then settled in Ireland. He was often
South African Champion (chess) in the
1950s and Irish Champion in the 1960s
and played on 5 Irish Olympiad teams.
His major works were *My Book of Fun
and Games* (1958), *Grosse Remis Partien*
(1968) and *Lacking the Master Touch*
(1970).

Hellers, Ferdinand

[*January 28 1969– *]
Swedish GM (1988) who was 1st at the
Amsterdam Open 1985 and had good
results at Berlin 1988 (VIII) and Buda-
pest 1988 (IX). He was European Junior
Champion in 1984–5.

Helms, Hermann

[*January 5 1870–January 6 1963*]
American chess journalist and editor
(with H. Cassel) of the *American Chess
Bulletin* from its inception in 1904 until
his death in 1963. He edited the superb
New York 1924 tournament book and
was named Dean of American chess in
1943.

Helpmate

A problem where both sides cooperate
to mate the black king. In such problems
it is Black that usually moves first.

Henley, Ronald Watson

[*December 5 1956– *]
US GM (1982) who was equal 1st at
Surakarta-Denpasar 1982.

Henry IV

[*1553–1610*]
King of France (1589–1610), first of the
Bourbon kings, who enjoyed playing
chess.

Henry VII

[*1457–1509*]
King of England (1485–1509), first of
the Tudor kings, who once lost almost
£3 playing at tables, chess, etc.

Henry VIII

[*1491–1547*]
King of England (1509–47) who must
have been a keen chess player because
his wardrobe accounts list more chess
sets than he had wives:

　One boxe blacke with chessemen
　　graven in bone
　One bagge of grene velvett with
　　chessemen and tablemen for the
　　same
　A case of black leather conteynynge
　　chestmen and table men
　A blake satin bag with chesmen
　A paire of tables of bone with table-
　　men and chestmen
　A paire of tables of bone clasped with
　　silver with tablemen and chestmen
　A paire of tables of bone clasped with
　　silver with tablemen and chessmen
　A boxe blacke with chessemen gra-
　　ven in bone
　A payre of tables of bone with chest-
　　men belonging to the same
　A set of chestmen of blacke and white
　　bone to them in a case of blacke
leather lined with greane clothe ...

Heraldry

A field where chess pieces, especially
knights and rooks, are often used.

Herbstman, Alexander Osipovich

[*1900–1982*]
USSR endgame study composer who
wrote *Izbrannye Shakhmatny Etyudi* (1964).

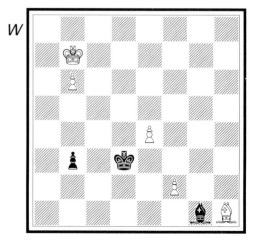

White to play and draw.

1 ♔a8 b2 2 b7 ♗h2 3 f4 ♗xf4 4 e5
♗xe5 5 b8(♕) ♗xb8 6 ♗d5 b1(♕ or
♖) 7 ♗e4+ Draw. If 6 ... ♗ moves 7
♗a2 and draws.

Hernandez, Roman

[*November 23 1949–*]
Cuban GM (1978) who was Cuban
Champion in 1981/2 and played on
several Cuban Olympiad teams
between 1970 and 1984.

Hickl, Joerg

[*April 16 1965–*]
West German GM (1988) who was 2nd
at Munich 1987(IX) and 1st at Tel Aviv
1988(VIII). He had a good equal 4th at
Munich 1988(XII).

History of Chess

Many myths exist about the history of
chess. Until recently, the best chess
historians (van der Linde, von der Lasa
and Murray) believed that it was
invented (or perhaps developed) in
North West India sometime during the
6th century AD, perhaps around 550.
Board games quite different from chess
go back to ancient Egypt and this led
some people to suggest that chess was
played in ancient Greece and Rome.
However, the oldest clear reference to
chess (*see* Karnamak, Vasavadatta and
Harschacharita) dates from around 600
AD. It seems unlikely that chess existed
long before 600 without any references
in articulate Greece or in businesslike
Rome. Chess probably developed from
earlier board games which used dice and
depended to some extent on luck.
At some critical point the dice were
discarded and chess, not quite as we
know it today, but clearly similar, came
into existence (*see* Early Versions of
Chess).

Nevertheless, recent excavations
(1955–62) of a 5000 year old town
(Harappa) on the river Indus have
revealed game pieces similar to chessmen. There seem to be recognizable
elephants and knights as well as chariots
and ships (in Indian four-handed chess,
our present-day rooks were represented
by chariots or warships). Furthermore,
clay boards sized 8 × 8 were found. *See*:
Lothal, a Halappan Port Town, by S. R.
Rao in *Archaeology Survey of India*, vol.
11, pp. 502–11 (1985); and an article by
Dr Joachim Petzold of Berlin (*Deutsche
Schachblätter*, May 1990, pp. 58–60)
where he concludes that:

Four to five thousand years ago, on
the banks of the Indus, games existed
that are at least the precursors of
chess. The pieces were models for
later chessmen.

This might rehabilitate Duncan
Forbes, the scholar on Indian matters,
who said that chess originated 5000
years ago.

Chess moved from India into Persia
in the late 500s and the Arabs learned of
it when they conquered Persia about
650. In about 800 chess spread to China
(*see* Chinese chess) and via Korea to
Japan (*see* Shogi). It came to western
Europe via the Moors in Spain, and to
Russia via the Byzantine world. The
Vikings spread the game to Northern
Europe. By 1000, chess was known all
over Europe. After the renaissance, Italy
became the chess centre of the world.
About 1475 the slower pieces acquired
greater mobility, the queen became
powerful, queening a pawn became a
major objective, castling was evolved
and the modern game as we know it
came into existence.

In the 18th century Philidor and
France took over chess leadership. By
1840 Staunton and England became
dominant. Then, apart from Morphy's
brief dominance, central Europe and
Germany became the world chess centre
(Anderssen, Steinitz, Tarrasch and
Lasker). The 1920s and 1930s were the
age of Capablanca and Alekhine. The
1940s, 50s and 60s belonged to the
Russians (Botvinnik, Smyslov, Tal,
Petrosian and Spassky). Fischer's brief
dominance in the 1970s was followed
by the age of Karpov and Kasparov.

The first chess column in a newspaper
(*Liverpool Mercury*) appeared in 1813,
the first chess magazine (*Le Palamède*) in
1836, the *Handbuch* in 1843 and the first
international chess tournament (London) in 1851. Since then chess has
continued to flourish and to bring joy,
pleasure and amusement to millions.
See *A History of Chess* by H. J. R. Murray
(1913), *Geschichte und Literatur des
Schachspiels* by van der Linde (1874),
Chess: a History by H. Golombek (1976),
Chess: the History of a Game by R. Eales
(1985).

Hjartarson, Johann

[*February 8 1963–*]
Icelandic GM (1985) who was Icelandic
Champion in 1980 and 1984 and who
played on 4 Icelandic Olympiad teams
from 1980 to 1986. He won a few
Category VIII tournaments (Reykjavik
1984 and Gjovik 1985) and then in 1987
he became a Candidate by coming equal
1st at the interzonal at Szirak (XII).

He surprised everyone by winning
his first match +3=3−2 over Korchnoi. This put him in the quarter-finals,
but in early 1989 he lost +0=3−2 to
the mighty Karpov.

Hodgson, Julian Michael

[*July 25 1963–*]
English GM (1988) who was 2nd at the
London Lloyds Bank Open 1986, equal
1st at the Geneva Open 1988, equal 2nd
at Tel Aviv 1988(VIII) and scored a GM
norm at Kecskemet 1988.

Hoffer, Leopold

[*1842–August 28 1913*]
Hungarian-born English chess journalist
and organizer who helped run the Paris
1867 tournament and settled in London
in 1870. Steinitz helped Hoffer to get
established in England, but later they
became bitter enemies.

Hoffer founded and edited the *Chess Monthly* (1879–96). He was a close friend and supporter of Zukertort and Zukertort's contributions (1881–8) enriched the magazine. Hoffer wrote for the *Standard* and the *Westminster Gazette* and when Steinitz moved to America in 1882, Hoffer took over Steinitz's chess column in *The Field*.

He was extremely industrious. In spite of a quick, sharp temper and a serious case of snobbery, Hoffer appeared at all tournaments, knew every grand- and not-so-grand master, was friendly and humorous and was Mr Chess in England. He founded the British Chess Club in 1895, arranged all important English congresses and matches, edited match books on Janowski–Marshall and Lasker–Tarrasch and ran the 1907 Ostend tournament.

Throughout this busy and successful existence, Hoffer carried on a most bitter feud with Steinitz. They wrote unbelievably vicious articles about each other—Hoffer in the *Chess Monthly* and Steinitz in his *International Chess Magazine* (1885–91). These exchanges make fascinating reading even 100 years later.

Hole

The square in front of a backward pawn, i.e. a square in which an enemy piece cannot be attacked by pawns. Steinitz first used this term and warned that a hole on one's third rank, for instance at c3, d3, e3 or f3, can be a serious weakness.

Holmes, Oliver Wendell [*1809–1894*] US poet, novelist, essayist, physician and father of the famous supreme court justice, who often referred to chess in his writings and probably enjoyed playing chess.

Hoogoven

A Dutch iron works which has sponsored chess tournaments since 1938, first at Beverwijk and then (in 1968) at Wijk aan Zee, a seaside town near Beverwijk. The tournaments are held in January/February and are of category XII or XIII. Timman won in 1981 (equal 1st) and 1985. Karpov won in 1988.

Hooper, David Vincent

[*August 31 1915–*] British architect and author whose major works are *Steinitz* (1968), *Pocket Guide to Chess Endgames* (1970) and, with Kenneth Whyld, *The Oxford Companion to Chess* (1984).

Horowitz, Israel Albert (Al)

[*November 15 1907–January 18 1973*] American IM (1950) who owned and edited the leading US chess magazine *Chess Review* (founded by Kashdan) from 1933 to 1969, when Horowitz retired and sold it to *Chess Life*. He edited the *New York Times* chess column for 10 years and wrote quite a number of chess books.

He won or was equal 1st in three US Opens: 1936, 1938 and 1943 and played on four US Olympiad teams during 1931–50. In 1941 he lost a match to Reshevsky $+0 = 13 - 3$ for the US Championship.

Major works: *World Chessmasters in Battle Royal* (with Kmoch) (1949), *The Personality of Chess* (with Rothenberg) (1963).

Horse

A beginner's word for knight.

Hort, Vlastimil [*January 12 1944–*] Czech GM (1965) who was the leading Czech player of his day but who never quite made it into the world top ten. He was a Candidate in 1977 but lost his match to Spassky $+1 = 13 - 2$.

Hort won a great many tournaments including three Hastings (1967/8, 1974/5 and 1975/6), a US Open (1974) and a Category XII event at Amsterdam 1979.

One of his best achievements was equal 2nd at Reggio Emilia 1987(XIV).

He won 6 Czech Championships and played board 4 for the Rest of the World against the USSR in 1970 and scored $+1 = 3$ against Polugayevsky.

He has scored $+1 = 4 - 2$ vs Smyslov, $+0 = 7 - 1$ vs Keres, $+0 = 15 - 1$ vs Tal and $+0 = 3 - 1$ vs Fischer. He did less well against other top players: $+1 = 13 - 9$ vs Karpov, $+1 = 27 - 4$ vs Spassky, $+2 = 9 - 6$ vs Korchnoi and $+0 = 11 - 4$ vs Petrosian.

A rotund, friendly fellow, Hort settled in West Germany a few years ago.

Major work: *The Best Move* (with Jansa) (1975).

Horwitz, Bernard

[*May 10 1807–August 29 1885*] German-born painter and chess study composer who, with Kling, wrote the classic *Chess Studies* (1851)—an expanded version appeared in 1889. He and Kling also published a magazine: *The Chess Player* (1851–3).

Horwitz was one of the Berlin Pleiades and after settling in England in 1845, he worked as the chess professional at Kling's chess rooms (Oxford Street, London) in 1852 and in Manchester in 1857. He played in London 1851, beating Bird but being knocked out by Staunton. He was of approximately IM strength and lost matches to Harrwitz, Kolisch and Kieseritzky.

Horwitz's true love was problems, as one sees from his obituary in the 1885 *International Chess Magazine*: 'His knowledge in all matters of endgames and problems was simply marvellous.... To see Horwitz really in his glory, it was necessary to see him surrounded with about a dozen young problemists and solvers ... problem and endgame and study would be set up and solved whilst the old man's eye would gleam and his face broaden out into smiles.'

Horwitz did win the first study-composing tournament in 1862.

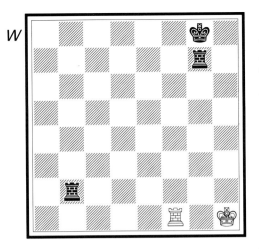

White to play and Black to win.
By Horwitz and Kling (1851)
1 ♖f8+ ♚h7 2 ♖h8+ ♚g6 3 ♖h6+ ♚f7 4 ♖f6+ ♚e7 5 ♖e6+ ♚d7 6 ♖d6+ ♚c7 7 ♖c6+ ♚b7 and Black wins.

Hübner, Robert [*November 6 1948– *] German GM (1971) and PhD who is a professional papyrologist (one who studies papyrus manuscripts) and a genuine intellectual. He was a Candidate 3 times (1971, 1980 and 1983) which puts him in rather rare company. In 1971 he faced Petrosian. After 6 draws and then a loss, Hübner resigned the match due to noisy playing conditions and stress. In 1980 he beat Adorjan +2 = 7 − 1, and then Portisch +2 = 9 − 0, and faced Korchnoi in the final. When his score stood +2 = 3 − 3 with two adjourned games he again resigned the match due to stress. Even with the loss he was marked as the third-ranked player in the world. In 1983 against Smyslov, with the score +1 = 12 − 1, a roulette wheel was used to break the tie and Hübner lost. Hübner then decided not to play in any more FIDE sponsored events.

He has played in the very strongest tournaments and apart from a few failures, has continually proved that he belongs to the world top ten. He was equal 2nd at the Palma interzonal 1970 (XII) and equal 3rd at Tilburg 1977 and 1978 (both Category XIV). At Turin 1982 (XVI) he had to withdraw halfway through because of illness. He was equal 2nd at Tilburg 1984 (XIV), equal 1st at Linares 1985 (XIV), equal 3rd at Brussels 1986 (XVI) and equal 2nd at Tilburg 1987 (XV).

In 1985 he lost an exhibition match +0 = 3 − 3 to Kasparov. Hübner has played on several West German Olympiad teams and in 1972 he won the gold medal for board 1 when he scored +12 = 6.

Hübner has both enormous chess talent and a delicate nature. He is probably the strongest German player since the days of Tarrasch and Lasker. His life scores are quite respectable: Smyslov (+3 = 19 − 4), Petrosian (+1 = 11 − 2), Korchnoi (+7 = 16 − 12), Tal (+1 = 4 − 3), Portisch (+4 = 25 − 5), Spassky (+2 = 12 − 3). He has not done as well against the two super Ks: Karpov (+0 = 12 − 5), Kasparov (+0 = 5 − 6).
See Dr Robert Hübner—60 Seiner Schönsten Partien by Fondern and Kleine (1981).

Hugo, Victor [*1802–1885*]
French poet, novelist, dramatist and lover of chess.

Hulak, Krunoslav [*May 25 1951– *]
Yugoslav GM (1976) who won the Yugoslav Championship in 1976 and played on several Yugoslav Olympiad teams. He was equal 1st at Varna 1974,

1st at Wijk aan Zee 1986 (VIII) and equal 1st at Banja Luka 1987 (VII). He had a good 2nd at Zagreb 1985 (XI), but has not shone in other tournaments of Category X to XII.

Hungarian Defence
1 e4 e5 2 ♘f3 ♘c6 3 ♗c4 ♗e7.
A passive defence used by Pest in their 1842 correspondence game versus Paris.

Hyde, Thomas [*1634–1701*]
English academic who was professor of Hebrew and Arabic at Oxford and librarian of Bodley's (1665–1701). He established the Indian origin of chess in his *Mandragorias seu Historia Shahiludii* (1694)—the first really scientific contribution to the history of chess.

Hypermodern
A school of thought developed in the 1920s, as a reaction to the established and dogmatic Steinitz/Tarrasch teachings. The leaders of this school were Nimzowitsch and Réti, ably seconded by Tartakower, Grünfeld and Breyer. Their major theorem was that one did not have to *occupy* the centre in order to control—one could put pressure on it or at least observe it carefully, to hold the balance in the position. To this end they developed the Grünfeld and Indian Defences to the queen's pawn openings, and the Réti Opening.

Tarrasch and his colleagues were not amused (*see* Teichmann for some of his views). Today much of hypermodern theory is valid. It has not replaced the Steinitz/Tarrasch school, but has become an addition or extension to Steinitz/Tarrasch.

I

Illegal Positions and the Laws
If during a game (but not after it is finished) it is found that an illegal move was made, the position shall be reinstated to what it was before the illegal move was made. The player who made the illegal move must then make a legal move with the piece he first touched. If no legal move with that piece is possible then he is free to make any legal move. If for some reason the position cannot be recreated, the game shall be annulled and a new game played. This applies to all sessions of play and to a game awaiting a decision by adjudication.

If, during a game, a piece was accidentally displaced and incorrectly replaced, or if, after an adjournment, the position was incorrectly set up, then all subsequent play is cancelled and the correct position shall be reinstated and the game shall continue. If for some reason the correct position cannot be recreated, the game shall be annulled and a new game played.

If during a game, it is found that the initial position of the pieces was incorrect, the game shall be annulled and a new game played.

Illescas Cordoba, Miguel
[*December 3 1965– *]
Spanish GM (1988) who was equal 1st at the Las Palmas Open 1987 and 4th at Montpellier 1988 (VII).

Ilyin–Genevsky, Alexander
[*1894–1941*]
USSR chess organizer and author who was of IM strength. He initiated the first USSR Championship in 1920 and played in most of these title events until 1937. He also played in Moscow 1925 and though he was only equal 9th, he did win his game against Capablanca.

He wrote pamphlets on the Alekhine–Capablanca match, *Notes of a Soviet Master* and Moscow 1925, and he edited *Shakhmaty* for 6 years. He was killed in the siege of Leningrad.

Immortal Game
See Anderssen.

Indian Defences
1 d4 ♘f6.

These hypermodern defences to the queen's pawn opening usually involve the fianchetto of a bishop:

A The King's Indian and Grünfeld: 1 d4 ♘f6 2 c4 g6.
B The Queen's Indian: 1 d4 ♘f6 2 c4 e6 3 ♘f3 b6.
   However the fianchetto may be postponed or in fact not used, as in:
C Bogo–Indian: 1 d4 ♘f6 2 c4 e6 3 ♘f3 ♗b4 + .
D Nimzo–Indian: 1 d4 ♘f6 2 c4 e6 3 ♘c3 ♗b4.
E Old Indian: 1 d4 ♘f6 2 c4 d6 3 ♘c3 e5.

The Indian name may have been used because slow development was characteristic of early versions of chess (where for example the pawn can only move one square, even on its initial move), and such early versions were played in India long after they disappeared from Europe.

Informator
See Chess Informant

Initiative
The ability to initiate action and thus to have the power to choose where and how to attack. This forces one's opponent onto the defensive. The successful player knows how to judge when he has the initiative, knows how to use it effectively and especially how to preserve or sustain it, until it can be transformed into a clear advantage in material, space, time or position.

By having the first move, White has the opening initiative and he tries to use it and sustain it. Black on the other hand tries to nullify it in order to equalize the position.

The initiative is important because it is accepted wisdom that to defend is more difficult than to attack. It is therefore sometimes worthwhile to give up material in order to seize the initiative.

Inkiov, Ventzislav Vladimirov

[May 19 1956–]
Bulgarian GM (1982) who won the Bulgarian Championship in 1982 and has played on Bulgarian Olympiad teams in 1982, 1984 and 1986. He was equal 2nd at Plovdiv 1984 (IX), the Bulgarian Championship 1986 (VIII) and Varna 1987 (VIII). His best result was a clear 2nd at Warsaw 1987 (X).

Inside Chess

A relatively new, but serious bi-weekly magazine that began in January 1988 under the editorship of GM Yasser Seirawan. It is published in Seattle USA.

International Chess Magazine

See Steinitz.

International Computer Chess Association (ICCA)

Founded in 1977, the ICCA organizes the triennial World Computer Chess Championship; and the annual World Microcomputer Chess Championship. Presidents have been: Benjamin Mittman, USA (1977–83); Monty Newborn, Canada (1983–6); David Levy, UK (1986–).

Winners of the World Computer Chess Championship have been:
- 1974 (Stockholm): KAISSA (USSR)
- 1977 (Toronto): CHESS 4.6 (USA)
- 1980 (Linz): BELLE (USA)
- 1983 (New York): CRAY BLITZ (USA)
- 1986 (Cologne): CRAY BLITZ (USA)
- 1989 (Edmonton): DEEP THOUGHT (USA)

Interposition

The placing of a piece in between an attacking piece and the attacked piece. The notion is straightforward but can be underestimated in complications:

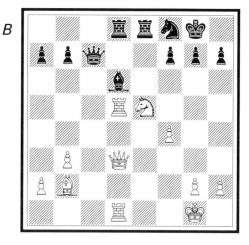

B

In Thomas–Euwe, Nottingham 1936, Euwe underestimated a White interposition and played 1 ... ♘e6? (better is 1 ... ♗c5+ 2 ♔h1 ♘e6) 2 g3?

Thomas could have won the bishop with 2 ♖xd6 ♖xd6 3 ♕xd6. He was concerned about 3 ... ♖d8 but the interposition 4 ♘d7 saves the day. If 4 ... ♕xd6 5 ♖xd6 ♘f8 then 6 ♘f6+ wins the rook.

Interzonals

The FIDE world is divided into 14 zones. Each zone has championships called zonals, and the winners of the zonals go forward to so-called interzonals. The top few from the interzonals go forward to the Candidates matches (or tournaments) to pick a challenger for the World Championship. This entire process is arranged in 3-year cycles. It began with zonals in 1947 and the first interzonal was held in 1948 in Saltsjobaden, Sweden.

Zonals took place in 1989 and early 1990, and the plan for 1990 is to hold the interzonal as a Swiss tournament with 64 entries. The top 11 finishers will join 3 seeded players from the 1989/90 Candidates matches to go forward to the 1991/92 Candidate matches (these 14 will play matches and the 7 winners will be joined by the loser of the 1990 world title match, to play more Candidates matches to select a challenger for the 1993 world title match).

Ioseliani, Nana Mikhailovna

[February 12 1961–]
USSR Woman GM (1980) who was equal 1st in the 1988 Candidates and won the play-off +1=4−0 over Akhmilovskaya, but lost the world title match +2=11−3 to Chiburdanidze. Ioseliani was USSR Women's Champion in 1981 and 82.

Isle of Lewis Chessmen

See Lewis Chessmen.

Isolated Pawn

See Pawn Structure.

Ivan IV (the Terrible), Vasilevitch

[1530–1584]
Tsar of Russia (1547–84) who did much to advance the arts and commerce, conquered Siberia, and made a commercial treaty with Queen Elizabeth of England. In 1581, in a fit of rage, he killed his oldest surviving son. He was, like most of the Tsars, an avid chess player, and owned sets of crystal, amber, stone and ivory.

He died just as he was about to play a game of chess. A contemporary diary describes the scene: 'The Tsar wore a loose gown, a shirt, and linen hose. He sat down on his bed and asked Boerken (one of his favourites) to bring the chess board. Ivan set the men up except he was having trouble getting the king to stand. His favourites, including Boris Godunov, stood near him, when he suddenly fainted, fell backwards and was "strangled and stark dead".'

Ivanchuk, Vasily

[March 18 1969–]
USSR GM (1988) who was 1st at Tallinn 1986 (VIII) and 2nd in the 1987 World Junior Championship. Then his strength took a leap upward and he was 1st at Lvov 1987 (X), equal 2nd at the 1988 Flohr Memorial (X) and 1st (ahead of Karpov) at Linares 1989. He played 6th board on the 1988 USSR Olympiad team and scored 6½–2½. He is a clear

2600+ player and some experts believe he has World Championship potential.

Ivanovic, Bozidar [*August 24 1949–*] Yugoslav GM (1978) who won the Yugoslav Championship in 1973, 1981 and was equal 1st in 1983. He played on Yugoslav Olympiad teams in 1982 and 1984. He beat Matulovic +2=5-1 in 1985, has won several Swiss Opens and had a respectable equal 4th at Titograd 1984 (XII).

Ivkov, Borislav [*November 12 1933–*] Yugoslav GM (1955) who achieved early prominence by winning the first World Junior Championship (1951). From 1955 to 1965 he played in many tournaments, with mixed success; a period in which his style underwent a radical change from an attacking player to that of a sober positional player, perhaps under the influence of Trifunovic.

In 1965 a new Ivkov emerged, instantly commanding world attention: equal 1st at Zagreb 1965 ahead of Petrosian, Portisch and Larsen, equal 2nd at the strong Havana 1965 tournament, and a Candidate for 1965. However, he lost his Candidates match +1=3−4 to Larsen and though Ivkov was equal 1st at Sarajevo 1967, equal 1st at Belgrade 1969, equal 2nd at Wijk aan Zee 1971 and equal 1st at Amsterdam 1974, there was a clear decline in form. Ivkov is an extremely handsome and imposing gentleman and the adulation of his fans and of the ladies may have contributed to his loss of form.

He was 1st or equal 1st in the Yugoslav Championships of 1958, 1963 and 1972, and he played on many Yugoslav Olympiad teams between 1956 and 1980. He was board 10 in the 1970 USSR vs Rest of the World match and lost +0=2−2 to Keres. In recent years Ivkov was 1st at Havana 1985 (IX) and equal 2nd at Cannes 1986 (X).

Ivkov–Portisch

Bled 1961

1 e4 e6 2 d4 d5 3 ♘c3 ♗b4 4 e5 c5 5 a3 ♗xc3+ 6 bc ♕c7 7 ♕g4 f5 8 ♕g3 ♘e7 9 ♕xg7 ♖g8 10 ♕xh7 cd 11 ♔d1 ♗d7 12 ♕h5+ ♔d8 13 ♘e2 ♖a4 14 ♘f4 ♕xe5 15 ♕f7 ♗d7 16 ♗d3 ♕d6 17 ♖e1

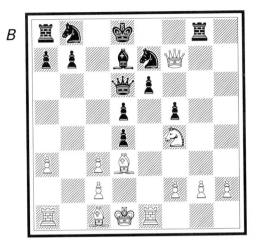

17 ... e5 18 a4 ♗e8 19 ♕e6 ♕xe6 20 ♘xe6+ ♔d7 21 ♘c5+ ♔c8 22 ♖xe5 ♘bc6 23 ♖e2 ♖xg2 24 ♗xf5+ ♔d8 25 ♘xb7+ ♔c7 26 ♗f4+ ♘e5 27 ♖xe5 ♘xf5 28 ♖e7+ ♔c6 29 ♖c7+ ♔b6 30 ♖b1+ ♔a6 31 ♖c6+ Resigns

J

J'Adoube
See Adjust.

Jaenisch, Carl Friedrich Andreyevich
[*August 11 1813–March 17 1872*] Russian theorist who was a major in the Russian army and gave it up (1840) to devote himself to chess. His main work was *Analyse nouvelle des ouvertures du jeu des échecs* (1842/43). He also wrote *Traité des applications de l'analyse mathématique au jeu des echecs* (1862/63).

Jaffe, Charles
[*March 1874–July 12 1941*] Russian-born US author and player of IM strength. He came to America in 1896, worked as a silk-mill merchant and in 1910 became a chess professional. He won 2 tournament games from Capablanca and a match with Mieses. In 1906 he edited the *Jewish Chess Magazine* and in 1937 wrote *Jaffe's Chess Primer*.

Janosevic, Dragoljub [*July 8 1923– *]
Yugoslav GM (1965) who is a well known chess columnist and blindfold simultaneous expert. He is famous for having beaten Fischer at Skopje 1967. His form is uneven and his best result was 1st at Vrsac 1969, ahead of Benko and Ivkov. Janosevic is a passionate poker player.

Janowski, David Markelovich
[*June 7 1868–January 15 1927*] Polish-born player of GM strength who settled in France in his early 20s. He had a fine 3rd at Vienna 1898 and an excellent equal 2nd at London 1899 but his best period was 1901–5 when he was 1st at Monte Carlo 1901, 1st at Hannover 1902, 3rd at Monte Carlo 1902, equal 1st at Vienna 1902, equal 2nd at Cambridge Springs 1904, equal 2nd at Ostend 1905 and equal 1st at Barmen 1905. During this time Janowski was

David Janowski: an attacking master who hated playing endgames.

among the best 5 or 6 players in the world.

Janowski was a very fast and brilliant player. His strength lay in the middlegame where he was famous as a master of attack. He especially loved the pair of bishops and used them with artistry and effect. His weakness was the endgame and he once said: 'I detest the endgame. A well-played game should be practically decided in the middlegame.' His other failing was his abhorrence of accepting a draw—he only drew about 20% of his tournament and match games. He lost many half points in equal positions by entering unnecessary complications. As Marshall put it: '... he could be tremendously stubborn. Janowski could follow the wrong path with more determination than any man I met! He was also something of a dandy and quite vain about his appearance'.

Janowski played many matches and had mixed results. His most frequent match opponent was Frank Marshall. They first met in 1899 and Janowski won +3−1, but in their first serious match, 1905, Janowski lost +5=4−8. A few days after this match ended, Janowski wrote to Marshall:

Dear Sir:
    I consider the result of our match far from proving our respective abilities. On the contrary,

as in the great majority of games, I allowed the 'win or draw' to escape me, I am persuaded that, normally, I should have won very easily.

I therefore challenge you to a return match on the following conditions: the first winner of ten games to be declared the winner, draws not to count. I offer you the advantage of four points, that is to say, my first four wins are not to count. Stakes are not to exceed 5000f ($1000). Janowski.

Their next match was in 1908 and Janowski did win, +5=3−2, but he lost in 1912, +2=2−6 and again in 1916, +1=3−4.

During the pre-World War One years, Janowski had a patron—the wealthy Pierre Nardus (1860−1935)—who financed three Janowski–Lasker matches. In early 1909, an exhibition match of 4 games ended +2−2, but in late 1909, Janowski was badly beaten +1=2−7. In 1910 Janowski was crushed +0=3−8 by the mighty Lasker. During this period Janowski said 'Lasker does not play chess, he plays dominoes'. As to the last match, Janowski is reputed to have said: 'I don't think I will win a game in this match. Lasker plays too stupidly for me to look at the board with any interest'.

Janowski's connection with the wealthy Nardus came to an end and in 1916 Janowski moved to America. He lived there until 1925 but his results, his income and his health were all low. He returned to Paris and soon died of tuberculosis. He was completely penniless and money had to be raised to pay for his funeral.

Janowski was a serious gambler with a special passion for roulette. After winning 1st prize (8000 francs) at Monte Carlo 1901, he sent most of it to his friends in Paris and urged them not to send any money to him, even if he asked. Soon he did ask, they refused and he became furious. With dire threats, he

forced his friends to send him his money, lost it all at the casino and left Monte Carlo poorer than when he arrived.

In terms of life scores, Janowski did quite well against the older masters: +5−2 vs Steinitz, +17=4−4 vs Chigorin and +6=4−2 vs Blackburne, but not so well against the other masters: +5=3−9 vs Tarrasch, +4=7−25 vs Lasker, +4=2−6 vs Pillsbury, +28=18−34 vs Marshall, +3−5 vs Rubinstein, +5=5−10 vs Maroczy, +13=13−20 vs Schlechter, +1=1−9 vs Capablanca and +2=2−3 vs Alekhine.

Voronkov and Plisetsky wrote a book about Janowski in 1987.

Janowski–Alapin

Barmen 1905

1 d4 d5 2 c4 e6 3 ♘c3 ♗e7 4 ♘f3 ♘f6 5 ♗g5 h6 6 ♗h4 dc 7 e3 a6 8 ♗xc4 b5 9 ♗b3 ♘bd7 10 ♕e2 c6 11 0-0 0-0 12 ♖ac1 ♗b7 13 ♖fd1 ♖c8 14 ♘e5 ♘xe5 15 de ♘d5 16 ♗xe7 ♘xc3 17 ♖xc3 ♕xe7 18 ♖3d3 ♖fd8 19 ♖d6 ♖xd6 20 ed ♕d7 21 e4 c5 22 e5 c4 23 ♗c2 ♕c6 24 f3 ♕c5+ 25 ♔h1 ♖d8 26 ♕e1 ♖d7 27 h3 ♗c6 28 f4 ♖a7 29 f5 ♗d7 30 f6 g6 31 ♕g3 ♔h7 32 h4 ♕c8 33 h5 ♕g8 34 ♖d4 ♗e8 35 ♖h4 ♕f8 36 ♖g4 ♕g8 37 ♕e3 ♖d7 38 ♖h4 ♕f8 39 g4 ♔h8 40 hg fg 41 ♖xh6+ ♖h7 42 ♖xh7+ ♔xh7 43 ♕g5 ♕f7

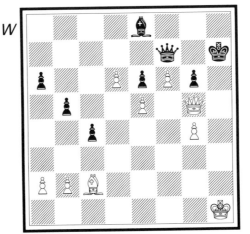

44 ♕h5+ ♔g8 45 ♗xg6 ♕xg6 46 ♕xg6+ ♗xg6 47 d7 Resigns

Jansa, Vlastimil

[*November 27 1942–*]
Czech GM (1974) who was Czech champion in 1974 and equal 1st in 1964 and 1984. He has played on a number of Czech Olympiad teams during 1964–6. He was equal 1st at Amsterdam 1974, 1st at Trnava 1982 and equal 1st at Prague 1985 (X) and at Borgarnes 1985 (VIII).

Japanese Chess
See Shogi.

John (Lackland) [*1167–1216*]
King of England (1199–1216), younger brother of Richard the Lionheart, who signed the Magna Carta, lost most of England's possessions in France and played chess. He was in the middle of a game (in 1213) when deputies from Rouen came to ask his help to lift the siege of their city (by King Philip Augustus of France).

Junge, Klaus
[*January 1 1924–April 17 1945*]
German player of GM strength and great promise. He was equal 1st in the 1941 German Championship, losing the play-off to Paul Schmidt. In 1942 he was equal 3rd at Salzburg, 2nd behind Alekhine in Poland, and equal 1st with Alekhine at Prague. This was Junge's last tournament because he was an officer in the German army and was killed in action just a few weeks before the war ended.

Junge was especially gifted in the endgame.

See Das War Klaus Junge by Budrich and Schulte (1956).

K

K

Symbol for the king.

Kagan, Bernhard

[*August 13 1866–November 27 1932*] Polish born German amateur who published *Kagans Neueste Schachnachrichten* from 1917 until his death in 1932. It started as a quarterly, became a monthly (1921) and was full of wonderful games, fine notes by GMs and entire tournaments (as supplements). It was a genuine labour of love.

Kahn, Victor   [*1889–October 6 1971*] Russian born French Jewish player and author who was champion of France in 1934. Major works: *L'Ouest Indienne* (1935), revised as *La Défense du fianchette de la dame*; *The Art of Checkmate* (with Renaud) (1947); *La Conuite de la Partie d'échecs* (1951).

Kaidanov, Grigory S

USSR GM (1988) who was 1st at Moscow 1987 (IX), 1st at Lvov 1988 (X), and 1st = at Hastings 1990.

Karlsson, Lars Carl-Gustaf

[*July 11 1955– *] Swedish GM (1982) who was 1st at Malmo 1979, 1st at Helsinki 1983, equal 1st at Hastings 1983/84 (XI), equal 2nd at Esbjerg 1984 (X) and equal 2nd at Cannes 1986 (X). He played on the Swed-

ish Olympiad teams during the 1980s.

Karnamak

A Persian epic about the life of Artaxerxes written around 600 AD which contains a reference to chess. This is very likely the first reference in all literature.

See an article by Theodor Nöldehe in *Beitrage zur Kunde der Indogermanischen Sprachen* IV, 21–69.

Karpov, Anatoly Evgenyevich

[*May 23 1951– *] World Champion 1975–85. USSR GM (1970) who is one of the very greatest players the world has ever seen. The recent study by Keene and Divinsky shows that Karpov is the second greatest of all time—a little behind Kasparov, but clearly ahead of Fischer, Botvinnik, Capablanca, and Lasker.

Karpov became World Champion in 1975 when Fischer refused to defend his title, and the general opinion then was that Fischer would have torn him to pieces. Karpov dispelled this opinion during the next ten years by playing in and winning almost every major tournament. He had well over twenty victories in tournaments of Category XIV and XV. No one was avoided, everyone was soundly beaten, and in terms of achievement and duration, Karpov's tournament record is phenomenal and unique.

Whether he would have beaten Fischer in 1975 is a moot point, but certainly by 1980 he was an overwhelming irresistible force. His rating was essentially 2700 or better from 1974 to 1988 (peaking in July 1989 at 2755) and he achieved this without having had a chance to beat Fischer and gain rating points—the usual way a new champion climbs the rating ladder.

Karpov was World Junior Champion in 1969, equal 1st at Moscow 1971

Anatoly Karpov, World Champion 1975–85.

93

(XIV) and in the 1974 Candidates matches he beat Polugayevsky $+3=5$, Spassky $+4=6-1$ and Korchnoi $+3=19-2$. He was 1st at Tilburg 1977 (XIV), equal 1st at Bugojno 1978 (XIV) and retained his title by beating Korchnoi $+6=21-5$ in 1978. During 1979–81 he won 7 Category XV tournaments and in 1981 he again retained his title by beating Korchnoi $+6=10-2$. He was 1st at London 1984 (XIV).

On September 10, 1984, Karpov began his title defence against the new challenger, Kasparov. The match was to go to the winner of six games. After nine games Karpov led $+4=5$ and it seemed that Karpov would win easily. However, Kasparov's resistance stiffened and after 26 games Karpov led $+4=22$ and after 46 games Karpov led $+5=40-1$. Karpov lost the next two games, and on February 15, with the score $+5=40-3$, FIDE president

Karpov, deep in thought. Few players have ever matched his ability to turn a small advantage into a win.

Campomanes simply stopped the match—an unprecedented and much criticized decision. In any case, a new match limited to 24 games was scheduled for November 1985.

In the summer Karpov was 1st at Amsterdam (XIV) and then met Kasparov in match number 2. Karpov lost $+3=16-5$. In 1986 Karpov was 1st at Brussels (XIII) and at Bugojno (XVI) and then faced Kasparov in match number 3 (the champion's right to a revenge match). Karpov lost again, this time $+4=15-5$.

In 1987 Karpov crushed Sokolov $+4=7$ to become the official challenger. After an equal 1st in Amsterdam (XVI) and a 1st at Bilbao (XII) Karpov met Kasparov in match number 4 and drew $+4=16-4$. Kasparov, as champion, retained the world crown. In these four matches the two super Ks met 120 times and Karpov scored $+16=87-17$. What is clear is that these two are clearly ahead of all other players—in fact, Kasparov is the only top player to have a plus score against Karpov.

In 1988 Karpov won the Active (now Rapid) Chess (30 minute games) world title—Kasparov did not compete.

In terms of life scores (to early 1987) Karpov has beaten Smyslov ($+3=10-1$), Korchnoi ($+23=57-13$), Tal ($+1=16$), Portisch ($+8=21-2$), Spassky ($+11=20-2$), Ljubojevich ($+10=13-2$), Timman ($+10=23-3$), Hübner ($+5=12$), Andersson ($+6=16-1$), Yusupov ($+2=2$), and Sokolov ($+4=8-1$). He drew ($+1=13-1$) with Petrosian and is behind Kasparov ($+17=95-19$) as of January 1 1990.

Karpov is extremely hard to beat—in almost 600 games against the very best opposition, he lost only 9% of his games. Only Capablanca at 8% was more difficult to beat. Kasparov has lost 10% and Spassky 13%.

Karpov played in six USSR Championships between 1970 and 1988 scoring 63%. He won the title in 1976 and 1983 and was equal 1st (with Kasparov) in 1988.

Besides being a great defender, Karpov is a superb strategist. His play resembles Capablanca's. He plays the board rather than the man, not overly ambitious with Black, but remorseless with White. Players say that when playing Karpov you do not feel threatened, in the beginning. Slowly some slight pressure appears and it keeps growing until you suddenly find you are lost.

Karpov was born in Zlatoust in the southern Urals. He is small and slender—almost fragile. He is 5'7½" with brown hair and slightly protruding greenish eyes. He studied with Botvinnik and Furman. He is calm, determined, and unusually courteous. Some think him cold and isolated, but he can be quite friendly. He collects stamps and art books and has an economics degree from Leningrad University.

He is a true Soviet man. He was brought up in the Soviet system, learned how to deal with it and is a 'winner'.

Some westerners do not like what he represents and he sometimes finds it difficult to understand why these westerners dislike him as a person.

See *The Best of Karpov* by P. R. Markland (1975), *The Complete Games of World Champion Anatoly Karpov* by O'-Connell, Levy and Adams (1976), *Anatoly Karpov's Games as World Champion 1975–77* by O'Connell and Levy (1978).

Karpov has written several books, including *Chess is My Life* (with A. Roshal) (1980), and a four-volume survey of opening trends in the late 1980s.

Kasparov–Karpov

Match 1987

1 c4 e5 2 ♘c3 ♘f6 3 ♘f3 ♘c6 4 g3 ♗b4 5 ♗g2 0-0 6 0-0 e4 7 ♘g5 ♗xc3 8 bc ♖e8 9 f3 e3 10 d3 d5 11 ♕b3 ♘a5 12 ♕a3 c6 13 cd cd 14 f4 ♘c6 15 ♖b1 ♕c7 16 ♗b2 ♗g4 17 c4 dc 18 ♗xf6 gf 19 ♘e4 ♔g7 20 dc ♖ad8 21 ♖b3 ♘d4 22 ♖xe3 ♕xc4 23 ♔h1

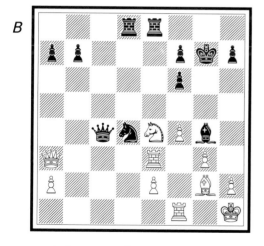

23 ... ♘f5 24 ♖d3 ♗xe2 25 ♖xd8 ♖xd8 26 ♖e1 ♖e8 27 ♕a5 b5 28 ♘d2 ♕d3 29 ♘b3 ♗f3 30 ♗xf3 ♕xf3+ 31 ♔g1 ♖xe1+ 32 ♕xe1 ♘e3 33 Resigns

Kashdan, Isaac

[*November 19 1905–February 20 1985*] US GM (1954) who showed promise in the early 1930s, but had to take a non-chess job to earn a living. He played in five US Olympiad teams between 1928 and 1937. He never won the US Championship—his best was equal 1st in 1942, but he lost the play-off +2=3−6 to Reshevsky. Kashdan was 2nd in the championships of 1946 and 1948. He was equal 1st in the 1938 US Open and clear 1st in the 1947 Open.

Internationally, apart from the Olympiads, he won small tournaments at Berlin 1930, Stockholm 1930 and Gyor 1930. He was 2nd at Frankfurt 1930, New York 1931, Hastings 1931/32 and Pasadena 1932. He beat L. Steiner +5=2−3 in 1930.

Kashdan founded *Chess Review* in 1933, but turned it over to Horowitz. He edited the chess column in the *Los Angeles Times*, directed the two Piatigorsky tournaments (1963 and 1966), edited the Piatigorsky tournament books and played a role in the US Chess Federation.

Kasparian, Henrikh Moiseyevich

[*February 27 1910–*] USSR IM (1950) and superb endgames composer who is a civil engineer. He was Armenian champion ten times and played in four USSR Championships between 1931 and 1952. He wrote many books on endgames, including: *2500 Finales* (1963), *Domination in 2545 Endgames* (1980), *Remarkable Studies* (1982).

See *Chess Magician* by Akopyan (1981).

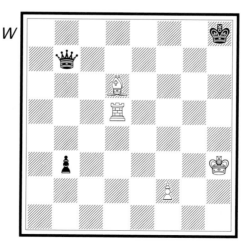

White to play and draw
Kasparian 1949

Solution: White would be happy to give up his bishop for the b-pawn if he could get his rook safely to e3, for then Black cannot break through. To do this White must prepare (e.g. if 1 ♖d3, ♕h7+ wins).

1 ♗e5+ ♔g8 2 ♖d8+ ♔f7 3 ♖d3 ♔e6 4 ♖e3 ♕h1+ 5 ♗h2+ ♔f5 6 ♖xb3 ♕f1+ 7 ♔g3 ♕c4 8 ♖f3+ ♔g5 9 ♗g1 (not 9 ♔g2 ♕e4 10 ♗g1 ♔g4 11 ♔h2 ♔xf3) 9 ... ♕g4+ 10 ♔h2 ♕xf3 stalemate.

Kasparov, Gary Kimovich

[*April 13 1963–*] World Champion 1985– . USSR GM (1980) who is probably the greatest chess player that ever lived. Since 1982 he has swept through the chess world like a raging torrent and Keene and Divinsky rank him as number one on the list of all-time greats. Kasparov dethroned the mighty Karpov in four

Gary Kasparov, who became the youngest World Champion when he defeated Karpov in 1985. He also holds the record for the highest Elo rating ever achieved.

grindingly difficult matches and these two super Ks stand clearly above both the active GMs as well as the giants of the past.

Kasparov won the World Junior Championship in 1980, was equal 2nd behind Karpov in Moscow 1981 (XV), but only equal 6th at Tilburg 1981 (XV). After this relative setback (at 18 years of age) he had a remarkable string of victories. He was equal 1st (with Psakhis) in the 1981 USSR Championship (XII) and then took seven clear first prizes in tournaments of Category XII–XVII (Brussels 1986) and another equal 1st (with Karpov) in the 1988 USSR championship. He topped this off with a clear 1st at Reykjavik 1988 (XV).

During this time Kasparov played eleven major matches, scoring $+42 = 116 - 19$ against the elite: Belyavsky, Korchnoi, Smyslov, Hübner, Andersson, Timman, Miles and Karpov (four times).

As a candidate he beat Belyavsky $+4 = 4 - 1$ and Korchnoi $+4 = 16 - 1$ in 1983 and Smyslov $+4 = 9$ in 1984 to become the official challenger. The title match against Karpov began September 10, 1984 and was to go to the first winner of six games. After nine games Kasparov was $+0 = 5 - 4$ and he realized that Karpov was stronger than everyone else and that he had much to learn from Karpov. Kasparov's strength grew under the pressure and he hung on, making the score $+0 = 22 - 4$ and $+1 = 40 - 5$. Kasparov won the next two games and on February 15, 1985, with the score $+3 = 40 - 5$, FIDE president Campomanes stopped the match—an unprecedented and much criticized decision. A new match, limited to 24 games, was scheduled for November 1985.

The second match stood at $+2 = 11 - 2$ when Kasparov won game 16—he calls it his supreme creative achievement—in a spectacular display of chess at the highest level. Kasparov went on to win the match $+5 = 16 - 3$.

In 1986 Karpov exercised his right to a revenge match, but Kasparov won again, this time $+5 = 15 - 4$. In 1987 Karpov was the official challenger and again Kasparov retained the world title, but only by drawing the match $+4 = 16 - 4$.

In terms of life scores (up to about the middle of 1987) Kasparov has beaten Karpov ($+19 = 95 - 17$ (January 1 1990)), Belyavsky ($+7 = 8 - 2$), Smyslov ($+6 = 10$), Korchnoi ($+5 = 9 - 1$), Timman ($+5 = 8 - 2$), Andersson ($+3 = 10$), Hübner ($+6 = 5$), Tal ($+1 = 5$), Portisch ($+2 = 4$), Geller ($+1 = 3$), Polugayevsky ($+2 = 2$), Larsen ($+3 = 1$), Ljubojevic ($+1 = 3$) and Short ($+2 = 1 - 1$). He drew with Petrosian ($+2 = 1 - 2$) and Seirawan ($+1 - 1$) and has lost to Spassky ($+0 - 2 = 2$) and Kholmov (-1).

He has played in four USSR Championships (1978, 1979, 1981 and 1988) being equal 1st in 1981 and 1988, and scoring over 60%. He played on four USSR Olympiad teams (1980, 1982, 1986, and 1988) scoring $+28 = 14 - 2$ for 79%.

Gary Kasparov—his real name is Weinstein—was born in Baku (the capital of Azerbaijan) to a Jewish father and an Armenian mother. After his father died, Gary's name was Russified, for public relations reasons—his mother's maiden name was Kasparyan.

Kasparov is a cocky genius. He plays with a fire and a brilliance that matches Tal, together with a solidity and superb defence that rivals Karpov. The combination is devastating for any opponent. His loss percentage against the elite is only 10% and only Capablanca at 8% and Karpov at 9% surpass him in this department.

His Elo ratings have increased steadily: 2595 (1980), 2625, 2640, 2690, 2710, 2715, 2720, 2735, 2750 (January 1 1988), 2760 (July 1 1988) and 2775 (January 1 1989), 2800 (January 1990), this last mark surpassing Fischer's previous all-time high of 2785.

Kasparov helped found the GMA (Grandmasters' Association) to service the needs of top players, somewhat in competition with FIDE. He is involved in many things and has a business manager in London. In January 1990, civil disturbances in his home town of Baku caused him to evacuate his family by airlifting them to safety.

Major Works: *My Games* (1983), *Fighting Chess* (1983), *The Test of Time* (1986), *Gary Kasparov: New World Chess Champion* (1986), *Batsford Chess Openings 2* (with Keene) (1989).

Karpov–Kasparov
Match 1985

1 e4 c5 2 ♘f3 e6 3 d4 cd 4 ♘xd4 ♘c6 5 ♘b5 d6 6 c4 ♘f6 7 ♘1c3 a6 8 ♘a3 d5 9 cd ed 10 ed ♗b4 11 ♗e2 ♗c5 12 0-0 0-0 13 ♗f3 ♗f5 14 ♗g5 ♖e8 15 ♕d2 b5 16 ♖ad1 ♘d3 17 ♘ab1 h6 18 ♗h4 b4 19 ♘a4 ♗d6 20 ♗g3 ♖c8 21 b3 g5 22 ♗xd6 ♕xd6 23 g3 ♘d7 24 ♗g2 ♕f6 25 a3 a5 26 ab ab 27 ♕a2 ♗g6 28 d6 g4 29 ♕d2 ♔g7 30 f3 ♕xd6 31 fg ♕d4+ 32 ♔h1 ♘f6 33 ♖f4 ♘e4

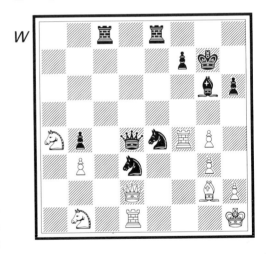

34 ♕xd3 ♘f2+ 35 ♖xf2 ♗xd3 36 ♖fd2 ♕e3 37 ♖xd3 ♖c1 38 ♘b2 ♕f2 39 ♘d2 ♖xd1+ 40 ♘xd1 ♖e1+ 42 Resigns

Korchnoi–Kasparov
Olympiad 1982

1 d4 ♘f6 2 c4 g6 3 g3 ♗g7 4 ♗g2 c5

5 d5 d6 6 ♘c3 0-0 7 ♘f3 e6 8 0-0 ed 9 cd a6 10 a4 ♖e8 11 ♘d2 ♘bd7 12 h3 ♖b8 13 ♘c4 ♘e5 14 ♘a3 ♘h5 15 e4 ♖f8 16 ♔h2 f5 17 f4 b5 18 ab ab 19 ♘axb5 fe 20 ♗xe4 ♗d7 21 ♕e2 ♕b6 22 ♘a3 ♖be8 23 ♗d2 ♕xb2 24 fe ♗xe5 25 ♘c4 ♘xg3 26 ♖xf8 ♖xf8 27 ♕e1 ♘xe4+ 28 ♔g2 ♕c2 29 ♘xe5 ♖f2+? (correct is 29 ... ♘xd2 30 ♘xd7 ♘f3+ 31 ♕e2 ♘h4+ 32 ♔g1 ♕xc3 33 ♕e6+ ♔h8 34 ♘xf8 ♕g3+ 35 ♔f1 ♕g2+ 36 ♔e1 ♘f3+ 37 ♔d1 ♕d2 mate) 30 ♕xf2 ♘xf2 31 ♖a2 ♕f5 32 ♘xd7 ♘d3

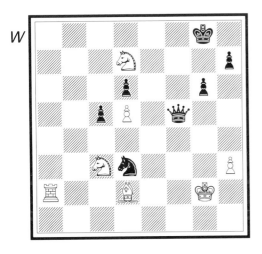

33 ♗h6? (correct is 33 ♖a8+ ♔g7 34 ♖a7 ♕f2+ 35 ♔h1 ♕xd2 36 ♘e5+ ♔f8 37 ♖a8+ ♔e7 38 ♖a7+ ♔d8 29 ♖a8+ with a draw—if 39 ... ♔c7 40 ♘b5+ ♔b7 41 ♖a7+, and mate to follow) 33 ... ♕xd7 34 ♖a8+ ♔f7 35 ♖h8 ♔f6 36 ♔f3 ♕xh3+ 37 Resigns

Kaufmann, Arthur Dr [1872–1940] Viennese player of GM strength who played only in Vienna. He drew +5−5 with Marco in 1893 and during 1893–8 held his own in tournaments with Schlechter and Marco. He stopped playing (because of delicate health) in 1898 and did not appear again until 1913, although Marco thanks him for his help with the great tournament book of Barmen 1905.

From 1913–16 Kaufmann again held his own in tournaments that included Vidmar, Spielmann, Tartakower, Réti and Schlechter. He beat Réti +4=1−1 in 1915 and Tartakower +2=2 in 1916 and on these successes he retired from the chess scene.

Kavalek, Lubomir [August 9 1943–] Czech GM (1965) who moved to Germany in 1968 and finally settled in the US in 1970. Trained in journalism and Russian literature, he has become an excellent organizer of top class tournaments. He now organizes for the GMA, (the Grandmasters Association), and continues to play at a high level.

Kavelek won the Czech Championship in 1962 and 1968. He was 1st at Varna, 1965, Amsterdam 1968, Caracas 1970, Bauang 1973, and Natanya 1973. He was equal 1st at Solingen 1974 and at the US Championships of 1972 and 1973. He won the US Championship in 1978. Perhaps his best result was equal 3rd at Tilburg 1977 (XIV). He was 1st at Bochum 1981 and continues to be a major force in US chess, with an equal 3rd in the 1985 US Championship (X) and an equal 4th in the 1986 US Championship (X)—he lost the play-off for 4th, +0=2−2 to Christiansen.

Kavalek played on Czech Olympiad teams in 1964 and 1966 and on seven US Olympiad teams between 1972 and 1986.

He was never a Candidate, but he has come close.

Keeble, John Frederick [1855–1939] British problem composer who edited the chess column in the Norwich Mercury (1902–12).

Keene, Raymond Dennis
                          [January 29 1948–]
English multi-talented chess personality who was England's second GM (1976) after Tony Miles (also 1976). Keene has written over fifty chess books, is well known on TV and is a world class chess organizer/administrator, having suc-

Grandmaster Raymond Keene, the second Englishman to gain the GM title.

cessfully run the 1986 world title match in London.

He won the British Championship in 1971, was 1st at the Capablanca Memorial masters in Cuba 1974 and was 1st at Dortmund 1980 (VIII). He played on eight English Olympiad teams between 1966 and 1980.

He contributed much effort to FIDE and in 1986 led an unsuccessful campaign to oust FIDE President Campomanes. Keene graduated from Cambridge with a masters degree in German Literature. He has an OBE (1985) and edits chess columns in the London Times and the Spectator. He is a man bubbling over with ideas for promoting his beloved game, a *bon vivant*, and a loyal friend.

His major works include: *Flank Openings* (1968), *Aron Nimjowitsch: A Reappraisal* (1974), *Staunton: the English World Champion* (with Coles) (1975), and *Warriors of the Mind* (with Divinsky) (1989).

Kempelen, Baron Wolfgang von
                                 [1734–1804]
See The Turk.

Keres, Paul Petrovich

[January 7 1916–June 5 1975]
Estonian GM (1950) who was truly the crown prince of chess because he was in the world top three or four from 1937 to 1963, and yet never became World Champion. He was a Candidate seven times—only Korchnoi (9) and Portisch (8) have bettered this. In the recent mathematical study of Keene and Divinsky, Keres placed sixteenth in the all-time list of greats.

He learnt much from correspondence chess, won the Estonian Championship in 1934, and was on the Estonian Olympiad team in 1935, 1937, and 1939. He was equal 1st at Bad Nauheim 1936 and at Margate 1937, 1st at Semmering

Paul Keres, the brilliant Estonian who finished second in the Candidates competition four times, but never became the challenger.

Baden 1937 ahead of Capablanca and equal 1st at the great AVRO tournament of 1938, the strongest tournament ever held up to that time—Category XVII. He only drew +2=4−2 with Ståhlberg in 1938, but he was 1st at Margate 1939 and he beat Euwe +6=3−5 in 1939/40. His play in the early 1930s was absolutely brilliant, sharp and breathtaking. In the later 1930s he matured into a sophisticated solid GM.

The war played havoc with his career. He was 2nd in the 1941 USSR Absolute Championship. Then, under German control, he was 2nd at Salzburg 1942 and equal 1st at Salzburg 1943. After the war he was again under Russian control and there are many rumours and stories. His relationship with Botvinnik is a mystery—some say Botvinnik helped get Keres out of jail in 1940 or '41, and others say Botvinnik helped put Keres into jail. Certainly Keres was Botvinnik's chief rival and it is curious that after 1940 Keres played so weakly against Botvinnik.

Keres came 3rd in the 1948 Hague/Moscow tournament to select a new World Champion (XVII). In Candidates tournaments, he was 4th in 1950, equal 2nd in 1953, 2nd in 1956, 2nd in 1959, equal 2nd in 1962 and in 1965 he lost his match +2=4−4 to Spassky.

Keres was 1st at Budapest 1952, equal 1st at Hastings 1954/55, 1st at Zurich 1961, equal 1st at Los Angeles 1963 (XIV), 1st at Beverwijk 1964/65 and 1st at Tallinn 1975. He beat Unzicker +4=4 in 1956 and Geller +2=5−1 in 1962. He played in thirteen USSR Championships between 1940 and 1973, scoring 114½–99½ for 59.2%, and he won the title three times (1947, 1950 and 1951). He played on seven USSR Olympiad teams between 1952 and 1964, scoring +53=32−3 for 78.2%.

In life scores, he beat Capablanca (+1=5), Bogoljubow (+4=5), Euwe

(+11=9−7), Fine (+3=8−1), Boleslavsky (+5=11−1), Smyslov (+9=23−8), Geller (+7=22−6), Korchnoi (+4=11−1), and Tal (+8=15−5). He held his own with Petrosian (+3=25−3), Fischer (+3=4−3) and Karpov (=2). He lost out to Alekhine (+1=8−5), Botvinnik (+3=9−8), Reshevsky (+4=9−6), Bronstein (+4=18−5), Stein (+0=6−2), Portisch (+1=3−4) and Spassky (+3=18−5).

Botvinnik was asked (1984) why Keres never became World Champion and he replied: 'Keres had a lot of talent, but he played in an old style. He did not have a significantly modern game, and he was psychologically unstable; when he had to win, he played weakly. Chess is a game for strong people with strong character'.

Keres was a slim, handsome man with a modest and sweet-natured disposition. He had a natural, gentle charm. He enjoyed mathematical ideas and problems and played a good game of bridge (a rarity for chess masters—exceptions being Ståhlberg, Bisguier and Rossetto).

Keres wrote well and annotated in depth. His major works are: *Theory of Chess openings*, 3 volumes (1952, 1953, and 1958), *Art of the Middle Game* (with Kotov) (1964), *Grandmaster of Chess*, 3 volumes (1964, 1966, and 1969) (these contain eighty well annotated games by Keres), *Practical Chess Endings* (1974).

Fine–Keres

Avro 1938

1 e4 e5 2 ♘f3 ♘c6 3 ♗b5 a6 4 ♗a4 ♘f6 5 0-0 ♗e7 6 ♕e2 b5 7 ♗b3 d6 8 a4 ♗g4 9 c3 0-0 10 ab ab 11 ♖xa8 ♕xa8 12 ♕xb5 ♘a7 13 ♕e2 ♕xe2 14 ♕xe4 ♘xe4 15 d4 ♗xf3 16 gf ♘g5 17 ♔g2 ♖b8 18 ♗c4 ed 19 cd ♘e6 20 d5 ♘c5 21 ♘c3 ♘c8 22 ♖e1 ♔f8 23 ♖e2 f5 24 ♘b5 ♘b6 25 b3 ♘xd5 26 ♘d4 ♘b4 27 ♗d2 d5 28 ♗xb4 ♖xb4 29 ♘c6 dc 30 ♘xb4 cb 31 ♘d5

31 ... ♘d3 32 ♖d2 b2 33 ♖d1 c5 34 ♖b1 c4 35 ♔f1 ♗c5 36 ♔e2 ♗xf2 37 ♘e3 c3 38 ♘c2 ♘e1 39 ♘a3 ♗c5 40 ♔xe1 ♗xa3 41 ♔d1 ♗d6 42 ♔c2 ♗xh2 43 ♖h1 ♗e5 44 ♖xh7 ♔f7 45 ♖h1 g5 46 ♖e1 ♔f6 47 ♖g1 ♔g6 47 ♖e1 ♗f6 49 ♖g1 g4 50 fg f4 51 g5 ♗d4 52 ♖d1 ♗e3 53 ♔xc3 ♗c1 54 ♖d6+ ♔xg5 55 ♖b6 f3 56 ♔d3 ♔f4 57 ♖b8 ♔g3 58 Resigns

Kevitz–Trajkovic Defence
1 d4 ♘f6 2 c4 ♘c6.

An exaggeratedly hypermodern defence designed to tempt White's centre pawns into exposed positions. After 3 d5 ♘e5 4 e4, however, White's pawn centre is more likely to represent a source of strength than weakness.

Key
The first move of the solution to a chess problem.

Kholmov, Ratmir Dimitrievich
[*May 13 1925–*]
USSR GM (1960) who was one of the strongest players of his time. He played most of his chess in the USSR and is not as well known as he deserves. He played in sixteen USSR Championships between 1948 and 1972, and scored over 56%. He was equal 1st in 1963, but lost the play-off (with Spassky and Stein). He won or was equal 1st in ten Lithuanian championships between 1949 and 1961.

Internationally he was 1st or equal 1st at Moscow 1960 (XII), Kecskemet 1962, Belgrade 1967, Havana 1968, Dubna 1973, Budapest 1976, and Tbilisi 1977.

He was never a Candidate nor did he ever make the USSR Olympiad team (usually filled with World Champions current, ex- or future) but his life scores reveal his strength. He beat Geller (+3 =16 −1), Petrosian (+1 =7 −0), Kasparov (+1) and Vaganian (+2 =2). He held his own with Keres (+1 =6 −1), Bronstein (+2 =13 −2), Korchnoi (+2 =16 −2), Fischer (+1 −1) and Karpov (=1). He did lose to Botvinnik (+0 =1 −2), Tal (+0 =16 −2), Smyslov (+0 =7 −3), Spassky (+1 =8 −5), and Boleslavsky (+0 =1 −5).

In 1987 he won the Moscow Championship (VIII). In 1982 he wrote a book of his best games: *Ratmir Kholmov*.

Kibitzer
A casual spectator who may offer free, unwanted advice to the players.

Kieseritzky Gambit
See King's Gambit, Kieseritzky.

Kieseritzky, Lionel Adelberto Bagration Felix
[*January 1 1806–May 18 1853*]
Baltic-European mathematics teacher of IM strength who is most famous for his variation of the King's Gambit [1 e4 e5 2 f4 ef 3 ♘f3 g5 4 h4 g4 5 ♘e5] and for losing the so-called Immortal Game to Anderssen in 1851.

He became a regular at the Café de la Régence in Paris 1839 and was efficient at giving odds and beating weak players. His best achievement was a win +7 =1 −4 over Horwitz in 1846. He edited *La Régence* from 1849 to 1851.

He was unlikeable and when he died penniless, he was buried in a pauper's grave because no one would contribute to his burial.

Kindermann, Stefan
[*December 29 1959–*]
German GM (1988) who played on West German Olympiad teams in 1982, 1984, 1986, and 1988. His best results are equal 1st at Dortmund 1985 (IX), 1st at Biel 1986 (VII) and 1st at Stary Smokovec 1987 (VIII).

King
The most important and usually the tallest piece. It can only move one square, in any direction, and once in each game it can castle. The game is over when the king is checkmated.

During the opening and middlegame the king should be carefully protected, but in the endgame it can play an aggressive and decisive role.

King and Pawn Endings
Such endings arise frequently and it is useful to know how to defend them and how to press for a win.

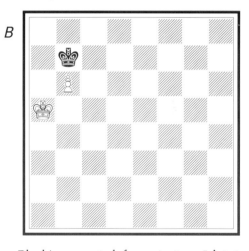

Black's correct defence is 1 ... ♔b8 2 ♔a6 ♔a8 3 b7+ ♔b8 and now White must either abandon his pawn or play 4 ♔b6, stalemate, and the game is drawn.

Black must not play 1 ... ♔a8? 2 ♔a6 ♔b8 3 b7 ♔c7 4 ♔a7 and White will queen his pawn and win.

The essence of this and other endings is zugzwang—timing things so your opponent must move when he does not want to move, because by moving he must give way.

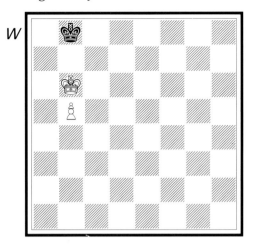

It is much easier for white when his king is in front of his pawn (unless it is a rook's pawn). Here 1 ♔a6 ♚a8 2 b6 ♚b8 3 b7 ♚c7 4 ♔a7 wins. Even if it is Black's move, he is lost: 1 ... ♚a8 2 ♔c7 ♚a7 3 b6+ and the pawn will queen.

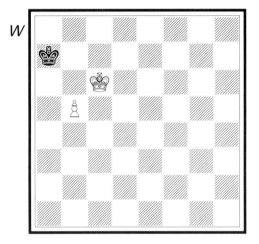

There are often hidden subtleties. It would be wrong to play 1 b6+ ♚a8 2 b7+ ♚b8 and Black draws. Even 1 b6+ ♚a8 2 ♔c7 is stalemate. The correct way to win is 1 ♔c7 ♚a8 2 ♔b6 ♚b8 3 ♔a6 ♚a8 4 b6 ♚b8 5 b7.

Another important aspect is the opposition—keeping your king directly opposite the enemy king, forcing him to move and give way.

With more pawns on the board the positions become more intricate.

See Endings and the references to Fine, Cheron, Averbakh and Hooper.

King, Daniel John   [*August 28 1963– *] English GM (1989) who was equal 4th at Bern 1987 (VII), equal 4th in the British Championship 1987 and equal 5th at London 1988 (category IX). In 1988 he was equal 2nd at Dortmund, and in 1989 he did well at the Lugano Open and was 2nd behind Larsen in London (X).

Kings's Field Sacrifice
A sacrifice on the castled king position, usually against the f-, g- or h-pawn.
See Double Bishop Sacrifice.

King Hunt
When a king finds himself out in the open and the enemy pieces swarm about, the chase is called a king hunt. A good example is this:

Ed. Lasker–Sir G. Thomas
1 d4 f5 2 ♘f3 e6 3 ♘c3 ♘f6 4 ♗g5 ♗e7 5 ♗xf6 ♗xf6 6 e4 fe 7 ♘xe4 b6 8 ♗d3 ♗b7 9 ♘e5 0-0 10 ♕h5 ♕e7

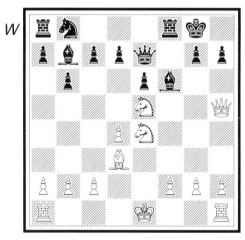

11 ♕xh7+ ♚xh7 12 ♘xf6+ ♚h6 13 ♘eg4+ ♚g5 14 h4+ ♚f4 15 g3+ ♚f3 16 ♗e2+ ♚g2 17 ♖h2+ ♚g1 18 ♚d2 mate.

King Pawn Opening
All openings commencing 1 e4.

Kingside
That half of the board consisting of the e-, f-, g- and h-files.

Kingside Castling
This is castling with the king's rook and is represented by 0-0.

King's Fianchetto (Benko's Opening)
1 g3.

This move was employed occasionally by Réti and Benko but it has little individual significance. It will normally transpose to Réti's Opening, the English Opening, or Barcza's Opening.

King's Gambit
1 e4 e5 2 f4.

A dashing sacrifice of a pawn for attacking chances and the hope that romance and reason can overcome crude material strength. White plans to get a strong centre, better development and a rapid attack on f7 using the open f-file. This gambit was extremely popular 100 years ago, but is not used very much today because there is a greater interest in positional play than in tactical play, and because players now defend well. Nevertheless Bronstein, Fischer and Spassky have used it because it does in fact have a positional aspect.

Black can decline the gambit (2 ... ♗c5), play the aggressive Falkbeer Counter-Gambit (2 ... d5) or accept the gambit (2 ... ef). When Black accepts the gambit pawn, White has several possibilities:

  A Breyer Gambit 3 ♕f3;
  B Keres Gambit 3 ♘c3;
  C King's Bishop's Gambit 3 ♗c4;
  D Lesser Bishop's Gambit 3 ♗e2;
  E King's Knight's Gambit 3 ♘f3 which can lead to:
      Allgaier Gambit 3 ... g5 4 h4 g4 5 ♘g5;
      Kieseritzky Gambit 3 ... g5 4 h4 g4 5 ♘e5;

Muzio Gambit 3 ... g5 4 ♗c4 g4 5 0-0;
Fischer Defence 3 ... d6;
Cunningham Defence
3 ... ♗e7.

The safest plan for Black is to take the pawn, but not to try to keep it. Black should give a pawn back at an appropriate moment e.g. 1 e4 e5 2 f4 ef 3 ♘f3 d5 4 ed ♘f6.

King's Indian Defence

1 d4 ♘f6 2 c4 g6.

Originally used by Paulsen and Chigorin, it is today one of the most popular defences to the queen's pawn opening. It was popular in the 1920s but poor results made it almost disappear in the 1930s. However Bronstein and Boleslavsky brought it back to life in the 1940s and proved that it was not only playable but gave Black chances.

The idea is to allow White to occupy the centre with e4 and then counterattack with ... f5. White's main options are:

A   Four Pawns Attack 3 ♘c3 ♗g7 4 e4 d6 5 f4 c5

B   Sämisch 3 ♘c3 ♗g7 4 e4 d6 5 f3

C   Classical 3 ♘c3 ♗g7 4 e4 d6 5 ♘f3 0-0 6 ♗e2 e5 7 0-0

D   Main Line 3 g3 ♗g7 4 ♗g2 0-0 5 ♘c3 d6 6 ♘f3.

See Grünfeld Defence.

Kipping, Cyril Stanley

[October 10 1891–February 17 1964] British problem composer who composed over 6000 problems and edited *The Problemist* (1931–64).

Kirov Ivanov, Nino

[February 8 1945–] Bulgarian GM (1975) who won the Bulgarian Championship in 1978 and played on the Bulgarian Olympiad team in 1974 and 1984. His best results are 1st at Coka 1973, equal 1st at Vrsac

1974 (VIII), equal 2nd at Potsdam 1985 (IX) and equal 3rd at Rome 1986 (X).

Klaric, Zlatko   [November 24 1956–]

Yugoslav GM (1983) who won a swiss Open in Thessaloniki 1984, and was equal 5th in Banja Luka 1985 (IX).

Klett, Philip   [1833–1910]

German problem composer who wrote *Klett's Schachprobleme* (1878).

Kling, Josef   [1811–1876]

German-born English musician, problem composer and author, who together with Horwitz, wrote *Chess Studies* (1851) and edited *The Chess Player* (1851–3).

Klinger, Josef   [June 6 1967–]

Austrian GM (1988) who was Austrian Champion (1985) and led the Austrian Olympiad team in 1986, scoring 9–3. He also led the Austrian team at the 1988 Olympiad.

Kmoch, Hans Joseph

[July 25 1894–February 14 1973] Austrian-born Czech IM (1950) who was a fine writer and annotator. He was 1st at Debrecen 1925 and played on the Austrian Olympiad team in 1927, 1930, and 1931. He wrote regularly for the US *Chess Review* and edited Carlsbad 1929.

Major works: *Die Kunst der Verteidigung* (1929), *Rubinstein's Chess Masterpieces* (1941), *Pawn Power in Chess* (1959).

Knaak, Rainer Fritz Albert

[March 16 1953–] East German GM (1975) who won the East German Championship many times from 1974 on and played on their 1972 Olympiad team. He was 1st or equal 1st at Olomouc 1972, Leipzig 1977, Halle 1978, Cienfuegos 1984 (IX) and equal 2nd at Potsdam 1985 (IX).

Knezevic, Milorad

[October 31 1936–] Yugoslav GM (1976) who came to his full chess strength in middle age. He was 1st or equal 1st in several category VII events: Lublin 1978, Sarajevo 1979, Timisoara 1979, and Bajmok 1980. Perhaps his best result was equal 3rd in the 1978 Yugoslav Championship (IX).

Knight

One of the most interesting pieces on the chessboard, whose move has not changed since chess was invented some 1500 years ago. The current laws describe it as:

> composed of two different steps; first it makes one step of one single square along the rank or file, and then, still moving away from the square of departure, one step of one single square on a diagonal. It does not matter if the square of the first step is occupied.

We use the symbol N for knight and the one that starts out at b1 (or b8 for Black) is called the queen's knight or QN, while the one starting on g1 (or g8 for Black) is called the king's knight or KN.

Knights have most influence when placed near the centre. A knight at h1 controls only 2 squares, while a knight at, say, e5 controls 8 squares.

Knights can be quite effective, as the following game illustrates:

Bogoljubow–Lothar Schmid
Bad Pyrmont 1949
1 e4 e5 2 ♘f3 ♘c6 3 ♘c3 ♘f6 4 d4 ed 5 ♘xd4 ♘xe4 6 ♘xc6 ♘xc3 7 ♘xd8 ♘xd1 8 ♘xf7 ♘xf2 9 ♘xh8 ♘xh1 10 ♗d3 ♗c5 11 ♗xh7 ♘f2 12 ♗f4 d6 13 ♗g6+ ♔f8 14 ♗g3 ♘g4 15 ♘f7 ♘e3 16 ♔d2 ♗f5 17 ♘g5 ♗xg6 18 ♘e6+ ♔e7 19 ♘xc5 ♘xc2 20 ♗h4+ ♔e8 21 ♘e6 ♔d7 22 ♘f4 ♘xa1 23 ♘xg6 ♖e8 24 ♗f2 ♘c2 25 ♘f4 ♘b4 26 Resigns.

Knight's Tour

One of the oldest known puzzles, the knight's tour problem is to find a sequence of 64 moves by which a knight can visit consecutively each square of the chessboard. A solution is called 're-entrant' if the knight finishes on a square which is a knight's move away from its starting square. The diagram shows a re-entrant knight's tour from an Arabian manuscript of the XIVth century.

32	35	30	25	8	5	50	55
29	24	33	36	51	56	7	4
34	31	26	9	6	49	54	57
23	28	37	12	1	52	3	48
38	13	22	27	10	47	58	53
19	16	11	64	61	2	43	46
14	39	18	21	44	41	62	59
17	20	15	40	63	60	45	42

The number of possible distinct solutions is immense—one estimate for the upper bound is:

$$\frac{168!}{105!\,63!}$$

where 168! is called factorial 168 and stands for the product of all the integers from 1 up to 168.

Even the more restricted re-entrant solutions number over 120 000 000.

See Puzzles.

Knockout Tournament

A tournament in which losers of a game or match are eliminated. Tennis tournaments are now played under such an arrangement. The opposite to a knockout tournament is a round robin tournament where each player meets every other player and no one is eliminated.

Kochiyev, Alexander Vasilyevich

[March 25 1956–] USSR GM (1977) who was European Junior Champion in 1975/76. He was equal 1st at Dortmund 1977 (VI), equal 6th at Leningrad 1977 (XIII), equal 2nd at Hastings 1978/79 (X), equal 3rd at Tallinn 1985 (IX) and equal 3rd at Dresden 1985 (IX). He played in the 1977 USSR Championship.

Kockelkorn, Carl   *[1843–1914]*

German problem composer who partnered Johannes Kohtz in composition.

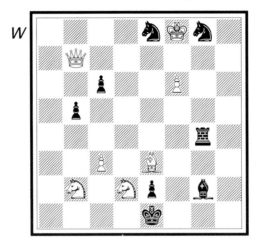

White to move and mate in 4 (1911).
1 ♕f7 (threatening 2 ♘d3+) 1 ... ♗d5 2 ♕a7 ♖a4 3 ♕h7 ♗e4 4 ♕h4++ or if 3... ♖e4 4 ♕h1++.

They wrote *101 Ausgewahlte Schachaufgaben* (1875) and *Das Indische Problem* (1903).

Kohtz, Johannes   *[1843–1918]*

See Kockelkorn.

Kolisch, Ignaz, Baron von

[April 6 1837–April 30 1879] Central European Jewish player of GM strength who was one of the top five or six players in the world during the 1860s. He studied in Italy and Vienna, became private secretary to the Russian (amateur) player Prince Urusoff and travelled about Europe in that capacity.

He beat Harrwitz in a few offhand games at the Café de la Régence, he beat Horwitz +3−1, crushed Barnes +10−1 and drew a match in 1860 with the mighty Anderssen +5=1−5. He won a small knockout tournament in Cambridge 1860, lost +3=2−4 to Anderssen in 1861 and embarked on a match with L. Paulsen—the winner to be the first who won ten games. After trailing +1=9−6, Kolisch showed his true strength by almost evening the score and when it stood +6=18−7 the match was abandoned as drawn.

In 1863 he challenged Morphy, but this was declined on the grounds that Morphy had beaten Anderssen decisively whereas Kolisch had not. Hoffer makes it clear that Kolisch was very angry about this. The climax of Kolisch's chess career was his clear 1st at Paris 1867, ahead of Winawer and Steinitz.

His play was original, brilliant and rich in combinations. He was one of the great attacking players of his time. Zukertort once asked Anderssen about Kolisch and about Steinitz, and Anderssen said: 'Kolisch is a tiger who jumps at your throat, whilst Steinitz is a pickpocket who steals a pawn and keeps it'.

In 1867, Kolisch abandoned chess as a profession and entered the world of finance. He had become friendly with Baron Albert Rothschild and opened a bank in Vienna in 1871. Soon he was wealthy and in 1881 was made a Baron of the Austro-Hungarian Empire. He bought a daily Viennese newspaper and wrote articles (under a pseudonym) for the arts and leisure section. He continued to support chess by financing many great tournaments: Baden-Baden 1870, Vienna 1873, Paris 1878, Vienna 1882, and London 1883.

See Ignaz von Kolisch, Schackmastare och Mecenat by S. Jonasson (1968).

Koltanowski, George

[September 17 1903–] Belgian-born US IM (1950), Honorary

GM (1988), and journalist who is best known for his simultaneous blindfold exhibitions—he set a world record in 1937 when he played 34 opponents and scored $+24=10$ in $13\frac{1}{2}$ hours. Najdorf broke this record in 1947 scoring $+39=4-2$ against 45 opponents.

Koltanowski was Belgium's leading player in the 1930s and played on the Belgian Olympiad team in 1927 and 1928. He was on the US Olympiad team in 1952, wrote a chess column in the *San Francisco Chronicle*, and was president of the US Chess Federation.

Major works: *Adventures of a Chess Master* (1955), *With the Chess Masters* (1972).

Konstantinopolsky, Alexander Markovich   [*February 19 1910– *]

USSR IM (1950) and honorary GM (1983) who played in six USSR Championships between 1937 and 1952. His best result was equal 2nd in the 1937 event. He won the first USSR Correspondence Championship and became a leading trainer. He worked with Bronstein in the middle 1940s, and with women players of the USSR.

Korchnoi, Viktor Lvovich

[*March 23 1931– *]

USSR GM (1956) who is one of the greatest players that ever lived. According to Keene and Divinsky, he ranks seventh in the all-time list of greats, just a step behind Lasker and Capablanca. Korchnoi is the only non-World Champion in the top ten of all time. He is also the busiest superstar in that he has played over 800 games against the elite of the chess world (players of ELO ratings above 2600) and he is one of the very few whose strength increased after he was forty years old.

Korchnoi was born in Leningrad, lived through the 1942 siege, graduated from Leningrad University with a history degree (1959) and left the Soviet Union (1976) to settle in Switzer-

Viktor Korchnoi (left) playing for his adopted country, Switzerland, against the USSR. His opponent is Kasparov, whilst behind him stand Belyavsky and Karpov.

land. He has been a Candidate nine times and his chess career follows closely the history of the Candidates matches.

He came fifth in the 1962 (last) round-robin Candidates. He led after the first (of four) cycles, but played too intensely and was burnt out before the last phase. He missed out in 1965, but appeared again in 1968, when he beat Reshevsky $+3=5$, beat Tal $+2=7-1$ and met Spassky in the finals. Spassky won $+4=5-1$, became the official challenger and went on to dethrone Petrosian. In 1971, Korchnoi beat Geller $+4=3-1$, but was then edged out by Petrosian $+0=9-1$. Petrosian went on to lose to Fischer in the final. In 1974 Korchnoi beat Mecking $+3=9-1$, beat Petrosian $+3=1-1$ and met Karpov in the final. Many believed that Korchnoi had missed his major opportunity in 1968 when he was 37. Now he was 43 and perhaps past his prime. However, the struggle with Karpov was heroic and Korchnoi lost with honour $+2=19-3$. In effect this match was

for the world title because Fischer refused to defend his title and Karpov became World Champion.

In 1977 Korchnoi beat Petrosian $+2=9-1$, beat Polugayevsky $+5=7-1$, and beat Spassky $+7=7-4$ in the final. At last Korchnoi was the official challenger. The title match was long and bitter. After being far behind, Korchnoi rallied and tied the score, but in the end he lost $+5=21-6$.

In 1980, Korchnoi beat Petrosian $+2=7$, beat Polugayevsky $+3=9-2$ and beat Hübner $+3=3-2$ in the final. Again Korchnoi was the official challenger. In 1981, age 50, Korchnoi again faced his 30-year-old opponent Karpov. This time Korchnoi lost $+2=10-6$. In 1983, Korchnoi beat Portisch $+4=4-1$ and then lost $+1=6-4$ to Kasparov, who went on to dethrone Karpov.

In 1985, Korchnoi was ill during the Montpellier Candidates and did not make the final play-offs. In 1988 he lost his first match, $+2=3-3$ to Hjartarson. His nineteen Candidates and world title matches form a remarkable achievement and it is clear that he was stronger in his mid-40s than he was in his mid-30s.

Korchnoi won many tournaments between 1948 and 1988. In particular, he was 1st in South Africa 1979 (XIV), equal 1st at Tilburg 1985 (XV) and 2nd at Brussels 1986 (XVI). He played in sixteen USSR Championships between 1952 and 1973, scoring 186–118 for 61.2%. He won the championship four times (1960, 1962, 1964/5 and 1970)— only Botvinnik and Tal have won it more often (6). Korchnoi played on six USSR Olympiad teams between 1960 and 1974, scoring $+50=31-3$ for 78%, and one of these losses occurred when he overslept!

His games are full of fantasy and imagination. He handles all phases of a game and all kinds of positions with great power but his speciality is the endgame. He is a genuine fighter and rarely has a short draw. To this end, he seeks to unbalance the game and, like his hero Lasker, will allow his opponent the initiative in order to launch one of his famous counter-attacks. He is resilient, has large reserves of determination and concentration, and though often in time trouble, can stand up to severe tension. He thus enjoys defending and is confident and successful with the black pieces.

Korchnoi is articulate, has an impish sense of humour and is a cheerful companion. He has an affinity for miracles and the occult and is said to be playing a game with Maroczy (1870–1951) through a medium.

In terms of life scores up to early 1987, he beat Reshevsky ($+3=8$), Geller ($+12=15-6$), Petrosian ($+16=49-9$), Tal ($+13=25-3$), Spassky ($+15=26-12$), Hübner ($+12=16-7$) and Timman ($+10=20-5$). He is even with Fischer ($+2=4-2$) and he lost to Keres ($+1=11-4$), Boleslavsky ($+1=5-4$), Smyslov ($+3=8-6$), Bronstein ($+5=8-6$), Portisch ($+7=12-9$), Karpov ($+13=57-23$), and Kasparov ($+1=9-5$).

Major works: *Chess is My Life* (1977), *Korchnoi's 400 Best Games* (with Wade and Blackstock) (1978).

See *Korchnoi's Chess Games* by Levy and O'Connell (1979).

Korchnoi–Spassky

Match 1968

1 d4 d5 2 c4 e6 3 ♘c3 ♗e7 4 cd ed 5 ♗f4 c6 6 ♕c2 g6 7 0-0-0 ♘f6 8 f3 ♘a6 9 e4 ♘b4 10 ♕b3 ♗e6 11 e5 ♘d7 12 a3 a5! 13 ab ab 14 ♘b1 c5 15 g4 c4 16 ♕e3 ♖a2 17 h4 ♕a5 18 ♖h2 ♖a1 19 ♗d3 b3? 20 ♘e2 ♗b4 21 h5 0-0 22 hg fg 23 ♖dh1 cd 24 ♕xd3 ♕c7+ 25 ♘c3

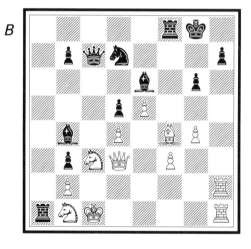

Spassky wrote: 'I sat for about twenty minutes … all I could see was the threat of a queen sacrifice and still Korchnoi managed to play (it)'.

25 … ♘b6? ♕xg6+ hg 27 ♖h8+ ♔f7 28 ♖1h7+ ♔e8 29 ♖xf8+ ♔xf8? 30 ♖xc7 ♘c4 31 ♖xb7 ♗xc3 32 bc b2+ 33 ♔c2 ♔e8 34 ♗g5 ♖a6 35 ♘d2 ♗c8 36 ♖e7+ ♔f8 37 ♘xc4 dc 38 ♔xb2 ♖b6+ 39 ♔c2 ♗b7 40

♖xb7 ♖xb7 41 f4 ♖h7 42 ♔b2 Resigns

Korolkov, Vladimir Alexandrovich

[1907–]

Soviet problem and endgame study composer who wrote *Izbrannie Etyudi* (1958).

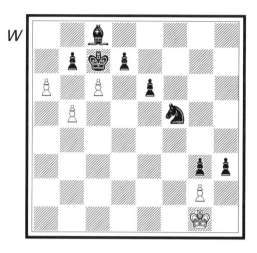

White to play and draw (1930).
1 a7 h2+ 2 ♔h1 ♘d6! 3 a8(♘)+ (Not 3 a8(♕) ♘e4 and 4 … ♘f2+ wins for Black) 3 … ♔d8 4 c7+ ♔e7 5 b6 and stalemate to follow.

Kostich, Boris

[*February 24 1887–November 3 1963*]
Yugoslav GM (1950) who is best known for his severe loss ($+0-5$) to Capablanca in 1919. In fact, he had a reasonable chess career. He was equal 1st in the 1935 Yugoslav Championship and 1st in 1938. He played on four Yugoslav Olympiad teams between 1927 and 1937.

He was 2nd at New York 1918, 2nd at Hastings 1919, equal 3rd at Budapest 1921, 1st at Trencianske Teplice 1928 and 1st at Ljubljana 1938. He beat Showalter $+7=5-2$ in 1916 and in 1962 he was equal 1st at a veterans tournament in Zurich.

His speciality was simultaneous blindfold exhibitions and in 1916 he temporarily set a record by playing thirty such games.

Kotov, Alexander Alexandrovich

[*August 12 1913–January 8 1981*] USSR GM (1950) who was a Candidate in both 1950 and 1953 and during the late 1940s and early 1950s was one of the ten best players in the world. He played in nine USSR Championships between 1939 and 1958, scoring close to 53%. He was 2nd in the 1939 Championship and equal 1st (with Bronstein) in the 1948 event.

Internationally, he was 2nd at Parnu 1947, 4th at Saltsjobaden 1948 (XIV) and 1st at Saltsjobaden 1952, Stockholm 1959/60 and Hastings 1962/63. In the Candidates tournaments he was 6th at Budapest 1950 and equal 8th at Zurich 1953—but these were both Category XVI events and even equal 8th put him in the world top ten. Kotov had a powerful attacking style and he was a dangerous opponent. In life scores he beat Flohr (+3=7−1), Bronstein (+4=6−3), Korchnoi (+1=2) and Spassky (+2=1); he held his own with Petrosian (+1=5−1), Smyslov (+3=9−3), Euwe (+1=1−1) and Reshevsky (+1=0−1); and he lost to Keres (+3=6−4), Botvinnik (+1=4−3), Najdorf (+0=5−2), Tal (+0=2−1) and Boleslavsky (+1=5−7).

He was an engineer during the war and became a serious chess author.

Major Works: *Alexander Alekhine* (1958), *The Soviet School of Chess*, with Yudovich (1958), *Kotov's Games* (1962), *Think Like a Grandmaster* (1971), *Play Like a Grandmaster* (1978).

Kouatly, Bachar

[*March 3 1958– *] French GM (1989) who was equal 2nd at Marseille 1988 (X) and equal 2nd at Geneva 1988 (IX). He is the first native Frenchman to be awarded the GM title.

Kovacevic, Vladimir (Vlado)

[*March 26 1942– *]

Yugoslav GM (1976) and mathematics teacher who surprised many by beating Fischer in their game at Zagreb 1970. Since then Kovacevic has been 1st or equal 1st at Sombor 1976, Virovitica 1976, Zagreb 1979, Maribor 1980 (VIII), Tuzla 1981, Vinkovci 1982, and Zabreb 1986 (VIII). He was 2nd at Hastings 1982/3 and equal 2nd at Zenica 1986 (VIII).

He played on the Yugoslav Olympiad team in 1982 and 1984.

Kozul, Zdenko   [*May 21 1966– *]

Yugoslav GM (1989) who was equal 1st at the Sibenik Open 1988.

Kraidman, Yair   [*November 1 1932– *]

Israeli GM (1976) who works in the Ministry of Finance as an accountant. He was equal 2nd at Natanya 1975 and equal 1st at Beer-Sheva 1976, and he played on ten Israeli Olympiad teams between 1958 and 1976.

Krasenkov, Mikhail

USSR GM (1989) who was equal 2nd at Balatonbereny 1988.

Krejcik, Josef Emil

[*January 22 1885–January 4 1957*] Viennese chess author, player and journalist whose major (mainly humorous) works are: *Dreizehn Kinder Caissens* (1924), *Artige and Unartige Kinder der Schachmuse* (1925), *Mein Abschied von Schach* (1955).

Kricheli, Josef Mikhailovich

[*May 10 1931– *] Soviet problem composer who specialized in helpmates. Here is a brilliant example of his art.

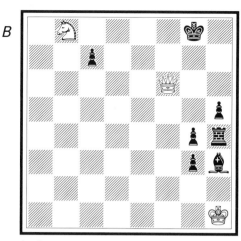

B

Black to make 25 moves so that White can then mate in 1 move (1966).

Advance the c pawn to c1 and make a bishop (5 moves)
Bring this bishop to h2 (3 moves)
Bring the light-coloured bishop to f7 (3 moves)
Bring king to e8 (2 moves).
Return the light-coloured bishop to h3 (3 moves)
Bring the dark-coloured bishop to e7 (3 moves)
Bring the king to c7 (2 moves)
Play ... ♗d6 and bring the king to a5 (3 moves)
Finally, play 25 ... ♗b4. At this point White can play ♕a6 mate.

Kriegspiel
See Varieties of Chess

Krogius, Nikolai Vladimirovich

[*July 22 1930– *] USSR GM (1964) and psychologist who played in seven USSR Championships between 1958 and 1971. In other events he was 1st at Varna 1960 and Sochi 1964, equal 1st at Sochi 1967, 1st at Varna 1969 and equal 3rd at Sochi 1973.

He was on Spassky's team in the 1972 World Championship match and in 1976 published a book on chess psychology. Then he became an organizer in the USSR Chess Federation and was president for some time. Kasparov claims that Krogius is a pro-

Karpov person and that Krogius made things difficult for Kasparov in Kasparov's early days. As Kasparov put it: 'Mr Gavrilin and Mr Krogius ... are my dedicated enemies. They hate Kasparov ... I don't speak to Krogius at all, not at all'.

Krylenko, Nikolai Vasilyevich

[1885–1938]
Russian Commissar for Justice who persuaded the USSR government to sponsor chess, and who organized the great Moscow tournaments of 1925, 1935 and 1936. He was involved with Stalin's purges of the 1930s but he himself was purged and executed.

Kubbel, Leonid I. (K.A.L.)

[December 25 1891–April 18 1942]
Soviet composer of endgame studies.

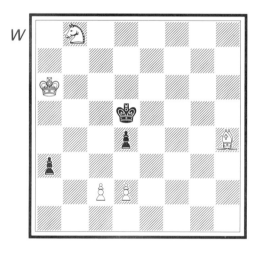

White to move and win (1922)
1 ♘c6 ♚xc6 2 ♗f6 ♚d5 (not ... ♚c5 3

♗e7 + wins) 3 d3 a2 4 c4 + ♚c5 (if ... dc 5 ♗xc3 wins) 5 ♚b7 a1(♛) 6 ♗e7 mate.

Kudrin, Sergey *[September 7 1959–]*
Russian-born US GM (1984) who was equal 1st at Copenhagen 1983 (IX), Beer-Sheva 1984 (IX), and Torremolinos 1985 (VII) and was equal 2nd at Marseille 1987 (X).

He is a strong player and has won several swiss Opens, but has yet to make his mark in the US Championships.

Kuligowski, Adam

[December 24 1955–]
Polish GM (1980) who was equal 1st at Nis 1979 (VII) and 1st at Warsaw 1980 (VII). He played on the Polish Olympiad team in 1980 and 1982.

Kupreichik, Viktor Davidovich

[July 3 1949–]
USSR GM (1980) who has played in eight USSR Championships between 1969 and 1987, but has scored much less than 50%. His critics say he is talented, but undisciplined.

Internationally he was 1st or equal 1st at Kirovakan 1978, Reykjavik 1980, Plovdiv 1980, Medina del Campo 1980 (IX), Hastings 1981/82, Sverdlovsk 1984 (IX), Zenica 1985 (VII), and a few swiss Opens in 1986.

Kurajica, Bojan *[November 15 1947–]*
Yugoslav GM (1974) who was World Junior Champion in 1965. He never lived up to his early promise due to lack of dedication. He was equal 1st at Sombor 1968, equal 3rd at Solingen 1974 and at Wijk aan Zee 1976. He was equal 2nd in the 1984 Yugoslav championship (IX) and equal 4th at Reggio Emilia 1985 (XII).

He played on the Yugoslav Olympiad team in 1980 and 1984. In 1969 he beat Kholmov 2½–1½ in the USSR–Yugoslavia match. Kurajica is a graduate in English and Italian from Zagreb University.

Kushnir, Alla Shulimovna

[August 11 1941–]
Russian born Israeli woman GM (1976) who was the number 2 woman player in the world during 1965–72. She lost 3 title matches to Gaprindashvili: +3=3−7 in 1965, +2=5−6 in 1969 and +4=7−5 in 1972. She was USSR Women's Champion in 1970 and moved to Israel in 1973.

Kuzmin, Gennadi Pavlovich

[January 19 1946–]
USSR GM (1973) who played in eight USSR Championships between 1965 and 1981, coming equal 3rd in 1972. In other events he was 1st or equal 1st at Hastings 1973/74, Baku 1977, Tallinn 1979, Kladovo 1980, Dortmund 1981 (IX) and Bangalore 1981 (VII) and he was 2nd at Tallinn 1985 (IX).

L

La Bourdonnais, Louis Charles Mahé de [*1797–December 13 1840*]

French player of GM strength who was the strongest player in the world from 1821 (when Deschapelles retired) to 1840. He was born in Réunion Island where his grandfather was Governor. By 1819 he was a star at the Café de la Régence and studied with Deschapelles. He beat Cochrane +7−0 in 1821 and Lewis +5−2 in 1823. In 1834 he played a celebrated series of 6 matches, a total of 85 games, against McDonnell—Ireland's best player—and won +45 =13−27. William Walker copied down all the moves and thus preserved the details of this first serious struggle for chess supremacy.

In 1836 La Bourdonnais, giving odds of pawn and 2 moves, was unable to beat Szen but he held his own giving Saint-Amant odds of pawn and move. He edited *Le Palamède* in 1836. He lost his money in land speculation and his health began to deteriorate. In 1840 he accepted the post of chess professional at Simpson's Divan but died soon after arriving in London. He is buried—near McDonnell—in Kensal Green cemetery, London.

La Bourdonnais had a boisterous and temperamental nature. George Walker, writing about the matches with McDonnell, says that La Bourdonnais 'talked and laughed a good deal at intervals, when winning, and swore tolerably round oaths in a pretty audible voice, when fate ran counter to his schemes'.

The entire set of 85 match games between La Bourdonnais and McDonnell can be found in the *Oxford Encyclopedia of Chess Games* by Levy and O'Connell (1981).

La Bourdonnais–McDonnell
Match 1834

1 d4 d5 2 c4 dc 3 e3 e5 4 ♗xc4 ed 5 ed ♘f6 6 ♘c3 ♗e7 7 ♘f3 0-0 8 ♗e3 c6 9 h3 ♘bd7 10 ♗b3 ♘b6 11 0-0 ♘fd5 12 a4 a5 13 ♘e5 ♗e6 14 ♗c2 f5 15 ♕e2 f4 16 ♗d2 ♕e8 17 ♖ae1 ♗f7 18 ♕e4 g6 19 ♗xf4 ♘xf4 20 ♕xf4 ♗c4 21 ♕h6 ♗xf1

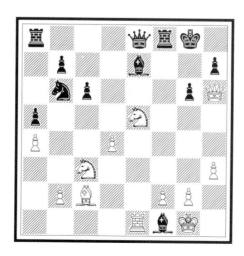

22 ♗xg6 hg 23 ♘xg6 ♘c8 24 ♕h8+ ♔f7 25 ♕h7+ ♔f6 26 ♘f4 ♗d3 27 ♖e6+ ♔g5 28 ♕h6+ ♔f5 29 g4 mate

Ladder

Many chess clubs have a ranking list of their members, often displayed on the club wall. Members may challenge anyone above them by one place, or sometimes two places. If the lower ranked player wins, he moves up the ladder and his defeated opponent moves down. This creates interest and avoids large discrepancies between opponents.

Lalic, Bogdan [*March 8 1964– *]

Yugoslav GM (1988) who was equal 1st at Pleven 1987 (VIII) and at Sarajevo 1988 (X).

Lange, Max

[*August 7 1832–December 8 1899*] German player (of IM strength), theoretician and problemist who was 1st at Dusseldorf 1862, 1863 and 1864, Hamburg 1868 and Aachen 1868. His *Handbuch der Schachaufgaben* (1862), was the first systematization of problems. His work included a book on Morphy (1859), a primer (1856), opening monographs and endgame collections. He edited the *Deutsche Schachzeitung* from 1858 to 1864.

He organized Leipzig 1894, invented the helpmate problem and is well remembered for the Max Lange Attack. He was a true all-round chess lover.

Larobok

See Collijn.

Larsen, Bent Jorgen

[*March 4 1935–*]
Danish GM (1956) who was a Candidate 4 times and between 1964 and 1972 was in the world top ten. He was one of the first post-war Western GMs to challenge Russian domination of international tournaments. He has won the Danish Championship many times and played on the Danish Olympiad team. At the 1956 Olympiad he had the best score (14–4) on 1st board and he decided to abandon his civil engineering studies to become a chess professional.

His style is highly aggressive—he will choose a risky continuation rather than tamely accept a draw—and thus more suited to tournament- than match-play. Larsen is renowned as a particularly ferocious competitor.

He began his serious winning at Mar del Plata 1958, and Wijk aan Zee 1960 and 1961. From Havana 1967 to Lugano 1970 he won or was equal 1st at 9 major tournaments. In his first Candidates (1965) he beat Ivkov +4=3−1 but was eliminated by Tal +2=5−3. In 1968 he beat Portisch +3=5−2 but lost to Spassky +1=3−4. In 1971 he beat Uhlmann +4=3−2 but was crushed by Fischer +0−6. In 1977 he lost to Portisch +2=3−5.

In 1970 he was chosen as 1st board in the USSR vs Rest of World match, scoring +1=1−1 against Spassky and +1 against Stein. He continued to win during the 1970s but not quite as well as in 1967–70—his peak period. He won at Buenos Aires 1980 (XIII), was 2nd at Bugojno 1980 (XV), 2nd at Niksic 1983 (XIV), equal 1st at Naestved 1985 (XIII), 1st at Reykjavik 1985 (XI), equal 1st at Hastings 1986/87 (X), and 1st at London 1989 (X).

In life scores he beat Najdorf (+8=2−2), Reshevsky (+3=5−1), Bronstein (+3=4−1) and Geller (+5=9−3), drew with Smyslov (+2=12−2), Polugayevsky (+3=7−3) and Andersson (+10=10−10), and lost to Botvinnik (+2=3−3), Keres (+0=4−2), Petrosian (+4=9−9), Korchnoi (+3=2−5), Tal (+7=17−12), Portisch (+14=15−25), Spassky (+6=16−19), Fischer (+2=1−10), Karpov (+2=9−7) and Kasparov (+0=1−3) (up to mid-1987).

In the openings, Larsen is noted for his 'anti-theoretical' bias: he tends to avoid heavily analysed variations if possible. He is known for his attempts to revive certain 19th century openings (e.g. Philidor's Defence) and for his successful experiments with opening systems involving an early queenside fianchetto for White.

Larsen is a well-read, intellectually alert, charming and attractive person. He writes regularly for several chess magazines and is a respected author.

Major works: *Larsen's Selected Games 1948–69* (1970), *Larsen's Good Move Guide* (1982).

See *Bent Larsen—the Fighter* by E. Brondum (1978).

Larsen–Petrosian

Santa Monica 1966

1 e4 c5 2 ♘f3 ♘c6 3 d4 cd 4 ♘xd4 g6 5 ♗e3 ♗g7 6 c4 ♘f6 7 ♘c3 ♘g4 8 ♕xg4 ♘xd4 9 ♕d1 ♘e6 10 ♕d2 d6 11 ♗e2 ♗d7 12 0-0 0-0 13 ♖ad1 ♗c6 14 ♘d5 ♖e8 15 f4 ♘c7 16 f5 ♘a6 17 ♗g4 ♘c5 18 fg hg 19 ♕f2 ♖f8 20 e5! ♗xe5 21 ♕h4 ♗xd5 22 ♖xd5 ♘e6 23 ♖f3 ♗f6 24 ♕h6 ♗g7

The great competitor, Bent Larsen, flanked by Kasparov (left) and Karpov.

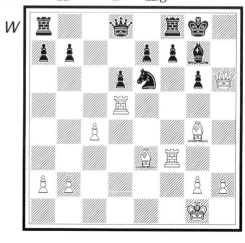

25 ♕xg6 ♘f4 26 ♖xf4 fg 27 ♗e6+
♖f7 28 ♖xf7 ♔h8 29 ♖g5 b5 30
♖g3 Resigns

Lasa, Baron Tassilo von Heydebrand und der

[*October 17 1818–July 27 1899*]
German diplomat, author, historian and
player of GM strength who was in the
top 2 or 3 in the world from 1845–55
and who was probably the very first
player ever to achieve a 2600 Elo rating.
He never played in a tournament or in a
formal match but in series of offhand
games he beat Staunton (1844 and
1853), Anderssen (1845, 1846 and perhaps 1850 or '51) and Löwenthal (1846).

He began as a member of the Berlin
Pleiades under Bledow, brought out the
first *Handbuch* in 1843 (it was his friend
Bilguer's idea but Bilguer died in
1840)—the first complete review of the
openings published in any language—
and he supervised the editions of 1852,
1858, 1864 and 1874. He wrote a great
deal—some 97 separate articles and
books (see October 1898, *Schachfreund*,
for the complete list). His major work
was *Zur Geschichte und Literatur des
Schachspiels* (1897). His works were
done with such extreme care that his
conclusions are accepted as final.

He was a successful Prussian diplomat, being posted to Vienna (1845), Rio
de Janeiro (1858), Weimar (1860) and in
1865 he became Prussian Ambassador
at Copenhagen. During this time he
collected a wonderful chess library of
over 2000 items (one report lists 3358
pieces) which was still intact in Poland
in 1957.

This Baron was one of the most
versatile and talented chess lovers of all
time.

See 'The Mighty Baron', *British Chess
Magazine*, June 1985, pages 226–32.

Lasker, Edward

[*December 3 1885–March 25 1981*]
German-born American IM (1963),
author, engineer and a distant relative of
Emanuel Lasker. He won the Berlin
Championship in 1909 and the US
Western Open five times. In 1923 he
lost narrowly (+4 = 9 − 5) to Marshall
in a US title match. His major works
include: *Chess Strategy* (1911), *Chess and
Checkers* (1918), *Chess for Fun and Chess
for Blood* (1942), *Adventure of Chess*
(1950), and *Chess Secrets* (1951).

Lasker, Emanuel

[*December 24 1868–January 11 1941*]
German-Jewish mathematician and World
Champion 1894–1921, who was one of
the greatest players that ever lived. The
recent mathematical study by Keene and
Divinsky places Lasker as the 6th greatest player of all time—behind Kasparov,
Karpov, Fischer and Botvinnik and just a
hair behind Capablanca. He stood clearly
above the chess world of his day and
even after losing the world title, he won
major tournaments and was a world
force until the age of 67—almost a
unique achievement.

His successes have been thoroughly
analysed and he has been accused

*Emanuel Lasker, the longest-reigning World
Champion in history.*

of hypnotizing his opponents, casting
spells, using psychological methods,
playing badly on purpose and of having
phenomenal luck. In fact he was the ideal
fighter: eager for battle, totally unafraid,
unbelievably subtle and profound, with
marvellous manoeuvring ability and
enormous, sustained power. He was the
first player to achieve a 2700 Elo rating.

Lasker was born in Berlinchen, Prussia.
He made his mark in 1889 in Germany, 1891 in England and 1893 in the
USA. In 1894 he won the world title by
defeating the ageing Steinitz +10
= 4 − 5. There followed a series of
outstanding tournament successes: firsts
at St Petersburg 1895/6, Nuremberg
1896, London 1899 and Paris 1900.

He then returned to his mathematical
studies and received his doctorate (1902)
for research on abstract algebraic systems, material used to this day.

In 1904 he began *Lasker's Chess Magazine* (1904–8) and was equal 2nd at
Cambridge Springs. In 1909 he was equal
1st with Rubinstein at St Petersburg. In
between, Lasker crushed several rivals in
matches: +8 = 7 − 0 vs Marshall (1907),
+8 = 5 − 3 vs Tarrasch (1908), +7
= 2 − 1 vs Janowski (1909). In 1910
Lasker had a close call against Schlechter
+1 = 8 − 1.

Towards the end of 1910, Lasker's star
shone even brighter, and for 8 years he
seemed almost god-like. In November
1910 he played a second match against
Janowski, winning +8 = 3 − 0. In
December 1912 he won an exhibition
game from Janowski. In April/May 1914
he played in the super-strong St Petersburg tournament. In the preliminary
rounds he only scored +4 = 5 − 1 (the
loss to Bernstein), but in the finals, his
incredible fighting spirit overcame a $1\frac{1}{2}$
point deficit and he edged out the seemingly unbeatable Capablanca, demolish-
ing the young Cuban in their critical
game. Lasker scored +6 = 2 − 0 in the
finals, creating masterpieces against the
cream of the world's GMs: Alekhine,

Capablanca, Tarrasch and Marshall. In 1916 he crushed Tarrasch +5 =1−0 and in Berlin 1918 he scored +3=3−0 against Rubinstein, Schlechter and Tarrasch. During this 8-year period Lasker scored +27=14−1 for 81% against 11 of the best GMs. Such a run has never been surpassed.

Capablanca, however, was not to be denied, and in 1921 Lasker lost his world title +0=10−4.

Lasker was the first master who seriously attempted, by demanding large fees, to improve the chess master's financial position. Even his enemies conceded that Lasker was worth every penny. Inflation in the 1920s wiped his resources away and Lasker returned to the chess wars. He came 1st at Mahrisch-Ostrau 1923, 1st at New York 1924 ahead of Capablanca and Alekhine, and 2nd at Moscow 1925, again ahead of World Champion Capablanca. In New York, Lasker created new endgame theory, over the board, when he drew with a lone knight against rook and pawn.

Lasker now devoted himself to philosophy, writing and teaching. In 1934 at the age of 66, Lasker returned to tournament play, coming 5th at Zurich, 3rd at Moscow 1935 where he was undefeated and only a point behind Botvinnik and Flohr, 6th at Moscow 1936 and equal 7th at Nottingham 1935. Lasker died in New York.

Some of Lasker's life scores are: +28=12−8 vs Steinitz, +11=4−2 vs Blackburne, +8=4−1 vs Chigorin, +18=8−4 vs Tarrasch, +5=4−5 vs Pillsbury, +5=12−2 vs Schlechter, +12=11−2 vs Marshall, +2=4−1 vs Rubinstein, +2=16−6 vs Capablanca, +3=4−1 vs Alekhine, +3=0−0 vs Euwe, and +0=3−1 vs Botvinnik.

Major works: *Common Sense in Chess* (1896), *St Petersburg 1909* (1909), *Mein Wettkampf mit Capablanca* (1922), *Lasker's Chess Manual* (1932), Alekhine–

Boguljubow Return Match (1935).

See *Lasker's Chess Career* by Reinfeld and Fine (1935), *Emanuel Lasker* by Dr J. Hannak (1952), *Lasker I* by Gilchrist and Whyld (1955), *Lasker II* by Gilchrist and Whyld (1957), *Lasker III* by Gilchrist and Whyld (1976).

Lasker's complex play has inpired all students of chess, and the following example of his play has been described as one of the most beautiful, most profound, most exciting and most difficult in the whole literature of the game.

Lasker–Napier
Cambridge Springs 1904
1 e4 c5 2 ♘c3 ♘c6 3 ♘f3 g6 4 d4 ed 5 ♘xd4 ♗g7 6 ♗e3 d6 7 h3 ♘f6 8 g4 0-0 9 g5 ♘e8 10 h4 ♘c7 11 f4 e5 12 ♘4e2 d5 13 ed ♘d4 14 ♘xd4 ♘xd5 15 ♘f5 ♘xc3 16 ♕xd8 ♖xd8 17 ♘e7+ ♔h8 18 h5 ♖e8 19 ♗c5 gh 20 ♗c4 ef 21 ♗xf7 ♘e4 22 ♗xe8 ♗xb2 23 ♖b1 ♗c3+ 24 ♔f1 ♗g4 25 ♖xh5 ♗xh5 26 ♖xh5 ♘g3+ 27 ♔g2 ♘xh5 28 ♖xb7 a5 29 ♖b3 ♗g7 30 ♖h3 ♘g3 31 ♔f3 ♗a6 32 ♔xf4 ♘e2+ 33 ♔f5 ♘c3 34 a3 ♘a4 35 ♗e3 resigns.

Lau, Rolf   [*October 19 1959−*]
West German GM (1986) who was equal 1st at Budapest 1985(VII), equal 2nd at New York 1985 (X), equal 2nd at Solingen 1986(X) and 1st at Budapest 1986 (VII). He played board 2 on the 1986 German Olympiad team.

Laws of Chess
In the 1850s many people, led by Lasa and Staunton, made serious efforts to create a unified code of laws for chess. FIDE finally established such a code (1929), and makes minor improvements and clarifications from time to time. The latest set (January 1989) includes the 1988 amendments. These laws deal with the basic rules and moves of the pieces, touch and move, illegal positions, wins, draws and losses, time controls and

clocks, adjournments and even the conduct of players: no private notes, no advice from others, no analysis on another board during play or during adjourned sessions are permitted and:

It is forbidden to distract or annoy the opponent in any manner whatsoever.

Lechtynsky, Jiri
[*November 25 1947−*]
Czech GM (1982) who was equal 1st at Halle 1981(VIII) and equal 2nd at the 1985 Budapest Open.

Legall, M. de Kermur, Sire de
[*1702−1792*]
French champion and king of the Café de la Régence— until Philidor reached maturity. Legall specialized in combination and he originated Legall's mate, illustrated in the only game of his that has been preserved:

Legall–Saint Brie   [*about 1755*]
1 e4 e5 2 ♗c4 d6 3 ♘f3 ♗g4 4 ♘c3 g6 5 ♘xe5 ♗xd1 6 ♗xf7+ ♔e7 7 ♘d5 mate

Legall took an interest in young Philidor, taught him for 3 years and by 1743 they played on equal terms. In 1755, however, Legall lost a match to Philidor but he continued to be France's second-best player until his 80s. It was said that Philidor was the only man who ever beat him. He was addicted to snuff and was said to be a brilliant conversationalist.

Lein, Anatoly Yakovlevich
[*October 28 1931−*]
USSR GM (1968) and mathematician who was equal 1st at Moscow 1970, 1st at Cienfuegos 1972, 1st at Novi Sad 1972 and 1973. He played in 6 USSR Championships.

In 1976 he moved to the USA. He was equal 1st in the 1976 US Open, played on the 1978 US Olympiad team and was equal 1st at Grand Manan 1984 (VIII).

Lengyel, Levente [*June 13 1933–*]
Hungarian GM (1964) who was 1st at Solingen 1968 and 1st at Reggio Emilia 1972/73. He was equal 1st in the 1962 Hungarian Championship but lost the play-off to Portisch. He played on the Hungarian Olympiad teams during the 1960s.

Leningrad
The glories of its days as St Petersburg were not fully carried over after it became Leningrad in 1917. Leningrad did have half of the 1941 USSR Absolute Championship (*see* Moscow) and the second half of the 1986 world title match Kasparov–Karpov (*see* London). In 1987 it held a Category XIV event won by Vaganian.

Leonardo da Cutri [*1542–1587*]
Giovanni Leonardo, nicknamed *il Puttino* (The Boy), one of the leading 16th century Italian players, was born in Cutri in Calabria. Details of his life are recounted in Salvio's chess romance *Il Puttino*, but Salvio's chronology is suspect and some incidents are embellished to show his hero in a favourable light.

As a youth, Leonardo moved to Rome to study law, and soon became known as a young player of great talent. In 1560 he played against and was defeated by the visiting Spanish cleric, Ruy Lopez. Over the next fourteen years Leonardo established a reputation as one of the two greatest Italian masters, his only rival being the Sicilian Paolo Boi. In 1574, Leonardo decided to try his skill abroad and together with Polerio and Rosces, he embarked on a tour of the Iberian Peninsula. While in Spain he gained his revenge against Ruy Lopez and defeated another Spanish expert, Ceron, in matches played in the presence of Philip II, who rewarded him liberally. (Salvio tells us that when asked by Philip to name a favour, Leonardo requested that his native town of Cutri be exempt from taxation for twenty years.) He also visited Portugal, where King Sebastian bestowed on him the name of *il Cavaliero 'errante'*.

Returning to Italy, Leonardo moved to Naples and took up a position as agent for the Prince of Bisignano. Under the patronage of the viceroy, the Duke d'Ossuna, he is said to have contested many games against Boi, proving of roughly equal strength. Leonardo died in 1587, probably poisoned by a jealous rival.

Leonhardt, Paul Saladin
[*November 13 1877–December 14 1934*]
Polish-born German journalist and player of almost GM strength. He was quite active during 1905–12. Most of his results were mediocre but he did achieve a few fine ones: 1st at Copenhagen 1907 ahead of Maroczy and Schlechter, 3rd at Carlsbad 1907 and equal 8th (out of 26) at Carlsbad 1911. In match play he lost + 4 = 5 − 6 to Spielmann in 1906 but beat Nimzowitsch + 4 = 1 − 0 in 1911. He was one of the top chess analysts of his day, with a deep insight into positions. During active play he perhaps saw too much, got into time trouble and then blundered. He gave up international competition in 1912 but played in German events up to 1929. In 1913 he wrote a monograph *Zur Spanischen Partie*.

Lerner, Konstantin Zaivelyevich
[*February 28 1950–*]
USSR GM (1986) who played in 5 USSR Championships between 1979 and 1986, coming 2nd in 1984 and equal 2nd in 1986. He scored 45–40 for 52.9% in these championships.

In other events he was 1st or equal 1st at Polanica Zdroj 1985 (IX) and 1986 (IX), Tallinn 1986 (VIII) and Moscow 1986 (XI).

Lesser Bishop's Gambit
See King's Gambit.

Levenfish, Grigory Yakovlevich
[*March 9 1889–February 9 1961*]
USSR GM (1950) who was one of the stars of Soviet chess in the 1920s and 1930s. He played in 12 USSR Championships between 1920 and 1949, scoring 118–94 for 55.7%. He was equal 1st with Rabinovich in the 1934 Championship and clear 1st in 1937.

Perhaps his best result was a drawn match + 5 = 3-5 with Botvinnik in 1937. He was equal 3rd behind Flohr and Reshevsky in Leningrad–Moscow 1939.

Major works: *Rook Endings* (with Smyslov) (1971), *Izbrannye partii i vospominanya* (autobiography) (1967).

Levitina, Irina Solomonovna
[*June 8 1954–*]
USSR Woman GM (1976) who was the 1984 challenger and lost the world title match + 2 = 7 − 5 to Chiburdanidze. Levitina was equal 3rd in the 1988 Candidates and was USSR Woman Champion four times during 1971–81.

Levy, David Neil Laurence
[*March 14 1945–*]
Scottish IM (1969) computer chess expert and author. Major works: *Gligoric's Chess Career* (1972), *Sicilian Dragon* (1972), *Staunton* (1975), *Games of Anatoly Karpov* (with O'Connell and Adams (1976), *Anatoly Karpov's Games as World Champion* with O'Connell) (1978), *Oxford Encyclopedia of Chess Games* (with O'Connell) (1981).

Lewis Chessmen
Some 78 chess pieces made from walrus tusk, in the 11th or 12th century, were discovered in 1831 on the Isle of Lewis in the Outer Hebrides. They are brilliant examples of 12th century design, full of vitality, charm and even humour. They are of Nordic origin—Scandinavian or Icelandic—and probably belonged to a merchant who accidentally lost part of his stock. Most of the pieces now live in the British Museum.

See *The Lewis Chessmen* by Michael Taylor (British Museum Publications) (1978).

Lewis, William

[*October 9 1787–October 22 1870*] English author who wrote *Chessboard Companion* (1838), *Treatise on the Game of Chess* (1844) and several other popular works on chess—including translations of Greco (1819) and Stamma (1822). Lewis was a leading chess teacher—his most famous pupil was Alexander McDonnell—and for a time ran chess rooms in St Martin's Lane (1825–7). In 1819 he operated the chess automaton The Turk when it was exhibited in London.

He was a player of IM strength. He lost a match +2 −5 to La Bourdonnais in 1825. Lewis is also remembered for his counter-gambit, 1 e4 e5 2 ♗c4 ♗c5 3 c3 d5.

Liberzon, Vladimir Mikhailovich

[*March 23 1937–*] USSR GM (1965) who played in 5 USSR Championships between 1960 and 1970. In other events he was 1st at Zinnowitz 1967 and Debrecen 1968. In 1973 he moved to Israel, won the 1974 Israeli Championship and played on several Israeli Olympiad teams between 1974 and 1980.

He was 1st at Venice 1974, Lone Pine 1975 and equal 1st at Beer-Sheva 1976, Natanya 1977 and Lone Pine 1979. More recently he was equal 4th at Beer-Sheva 1984 (IX).

Libraries

Of all board games, chess undoubtedly possesses the greatest literature. The largest public store of chess books, manuscripts and periodicals is the J. G. White Collection which is part of the Cleveland Public Library, Cleveland, Ohio, USA. It was founded in 1928 and probably now contains about 25 000 items relating to chess and draughts (checkers). A two volume catalogue is available and the library staff operate an excellent photocopying and question-answering service.

The best public European chess library is the van der Linde–Niemeijer collection at the Royal Library in The Hague, with some 15 000 items. The librarians there, Christiaan Bijl and Robert Verhoeven are extremely helpful and cherish chess books and chess players.

In Australia, the Victoria State Library in Melbourne has a substantial chess section, bequeathed by Magnus Victor Anderson (1884–1966).

Lothar Schmid's library is the best and largest private collection in the world. Not only does he have some 15 000 items, but he owns many unique and wonderful chess treasures. For example, van der Linde claimed there were only two copies of Hirsch's *Schach-Tractat* (Berlin 1747) extant. Schmid found a (third) copy in an obscure bookshop!

Liburkin, Mark Savelyevich

[*1910–1953*] Soviet composer of extremely elegant endgame studies.

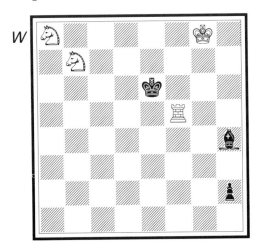

White to play and win (1932)
1 ♖f1 ♗f2 2 ♖h1 ♗g1 3 ♘b6 ♔e5 4 ♘d6 ♔f4 (if 4 ... ♔xd6 5 ♘c4+ and 6 ♘d2) 5 ♘d5+ ♔f3 6 ♘f5 ♔g2 7 ♘f4+ ♔f3 (if 7 ... ♔xh1 8 ♘g3 mate) 8 ♘g6 ♔g2 9 ♘gh4+ ♔h3 10 ♔f7 ♗f2 11 ♔g6 and wins.

Light Bishop

A bishop that moves on the light-coloured squares, i.e. one that starts out at f1 (White) or c8 (Black).

Lightning Chess

See Blitz

Lilienthal, Andrei Arnoldovich

[*May 5 1911–*] Hungarian GM (1950) who played on 3 Hungarian Olympiad teams (1933, 1935, 1937) and had a promising career with a 1st at Bad Stuben 1930, equal 2nd with Alekhine at Hastings 1933/34, and 1sts at Budapest, Ujgest and Barcelona in 1934.

In 1935 he went to live in the USSR and played in 8 USSR Championships between 1937 and 1954. He was equal 1st with Bondarevsky in the 1939/40 Championship ahead of Keres and Botvinnik. He was 1st at Baku 1944 and became a Candidate in 1950. He did not succeed in this Candidates tournament but he continued to play, coming equal 3rd at Moscow 1962. In 1976 he retired and returned to Hungary.

Linares

A small city in south central Spain which has staged a number of strong tournaments. In 1983 Spassky (6½) edged Karpov (6) and Andersson (6). In 1985 Ljubojevic (7) and Hübner (7) beat out Portisch (6½), Korchnoi (6½) and Spassky (6). In 1988 Timman (8½) won ahead of Belyavsky (7) and Yusupov (6½).

The strongest Linares tournament was held in 1989. Korchnoi was expected, but he walked out when he discovered that his enemy KGB colonel Baturinsky was to be the chief arbiter. On the other hand, Spanish GM Illescas was invited but not allowed to play

Linares 1989   Category XVI

	1	2	3	4	5	6	7	8	9	10	11	
1 Ivanchuk	–	½	½	1	1	½	1	½	½	1	1	7½
2 Karpov	½	–	1	0	½	1	1	1	½	½	1	7
3 Ljubojevic	½	0	–	0	½	½	1	1	1	½	1	6
4 Short	0	1	1	–	½	0	½	½	½	½	1	5½
Timman	0	½	½	½	–	½	½	½	1	½	1	5½
6 Yusupov	½	0	½	1	½	–	0	½	½	1	½	5
7 Belyavsky	0	0	0	½	½	1	–	1	1	½	0	4½
8 Portisch	½	0	0	½	½	½	0	–	½	½	1	4
9 Gulko	½	½	0	½	0	½	0	½	–	½	½	3½
Sokolov	0	½	½	½	½	0	½	½	½	–	0	3½
11 Hjartarson	0	0	0	0	0	½	1	0	½	1	–	3

because the sponsor, la Junta de Andalucia, insisted the tournament be Category XVI, and Illescas' relatively low rating would have pulled the average Elo below 2626. He received a consolation payment of $3500.

The star of the tournament was young Ivanchuk, who seems destined for the very top.

Belyavsky–Ivanchuk

1 e4 e5 2 ♘f3 ♘c6 3 ♗b5 ♗c5 4 c3 ♘f6 5 d4 ♗b6 6 ♘xe5 ♘xe5 7 de ♘xe4 8 ♕g4 ♗xf2+ 9 ♔e2 ♕h4 10 ♕xg7 ♖f8 11 ♘d2 ♗c5 12 ♘f3 ♕f2+ 13 ♔d1

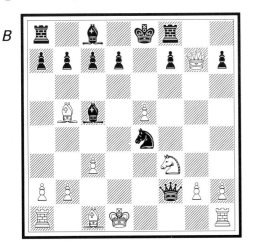

13 ... ♗e7! 14 ♖e1 ♕b6! 15 ♖xe4 ♕xb5 16 c4 ♕c6 17 ♕xh7 d5 18 ed ♕xd6+ 19 ♖d4 ♕b6 20 ♕e4 ♖g8 21 ♗e3 ♕xb2 22 ♖b1 ♕xg2 23 ♖b5 ♗g4 24 ♖f5 ♕f1+ 25 ♔c2 ♕e2+ 26 Resigns (after 26 ♔b3 ♗xf5 27 ♕xf5 ♕xe3+)

Lincoln, Abraham   [1809–1865]

16th President of the USA (1861–5) who was a skilful chess player and played regularly with Judge S. H. Treat, Chief Justice of the Illinois Supreme Court.

Linde, Antonius van der

[November 14 1833–August 12 1897] Dutch chess historian and philosopher who clarified the early history of chess. The Royal Dutch Library in The Hague bought his chess library and from it grew the present excellent chess library in The Hague.

Major works: *De Schaakpartijen van Gioachino Greco* (1865), *Das Schachspiel des XVI Jahrhunderts* (1874), *Geschichte und Literatur des Schachspiels* (1874), *Quellenstudien zur Geschichte des Schachspiels* (1881), *Das Erste Jahrtausend des Schachlitteratur* (1881).

Lipke, Paul

[June 30 1870–March 8 1955] German lawyer and player of GM strength who was 3rd at Kiel 1893, 2nd behind Tarrasch at Leipzig 1894, drew a match +1 =5 −1 with Berger in 1896 and was equal 8th at the great Vienna tournament of 1898. After that he simply gave up competitive chess.

He was considered the foremost blindfold player of his day, having no difficulty playing 10 games simultaneously.

Lipschutz, Samuel

[July 4 1863–November 30 1905] Hungarian-born US player of GM strength who won the US Championship in 1892 by beating Showalter +7 =7 −1. He was 6th in the strong London 1886 tournament and 6th (out of 20) in the large New York 1889 tournament. He was a top contender in US events. In 1886 he lost honourably to the extremely strong G. H. Mackenzie +3 =5 −5.

He contributed to Gossip's *Chess Player's Manual* (1888).

Literature and Chess

Chess has often played an important role in literature. From Boccaccio and Chaucer in the 14th century, a long list of famous authors have used it, including: S. Butler, L. Carroll, Dostoyevsky, George Eliot, Ian Fleming, Goethe, Hazlitt, Lamb, Nabokov, Poe, Rabelais, Ruskin, R. L. Stevenson, Tolstoy, and Zweig.

Professor Kester Svendsen wrote a bibliography of over 500 items on Chess Fiction (see the *Southwestern Journal*, Volume V, number 4). It only goes to 1945 and the world is waiting for someone to continue this to 1990 or to 2001.

Some especially interesting items are:
The Bishop Murder Case
S.S. Van Dine (1929)
The Defence
V. Nabokov (1930)
The Royal Game
S. Zweig (1944)
(certainly the best chess story ever written)
The Chess Players
F. P. Keyes (1960)

Master Prim
J. W. Ellison (1968)
The Dragon Variation
A. Glynn (1969)
The Eight
K. Neville (1988)

Litinskaya, (*née* Shul) Marta Ivanovna   [*March 25 1949– *]

USSR Woman GM (1976) who was 3rd in the 1986 Candidates and equal 3rd in the 1988 Candidates. She was USSR Woman Champion in 1972.

Living chess

A performance of a chess game with living pieces, usually done as a spectacle or pageant, with actors as pieces. The earliest known such display was held in Granada in 1408, given by Sultan Mohammed. Rabelais described one in Pantagruel (1564). In 1934 Botvinnik drew such a game with Riumin, with athletes as the pieces, and in 1962 Botvinnik drew with Smyslov at the Moscow Sports Palace, with ballet dancers for pieces.

The most famous living chess display occurs bi-annually (since 1954) at Morostica, a small Italian town near Vicenza, to commemorate a game played in 1454 between Rinaldo de Angarano and Vieri de Vallonara for the hand of Madonna Lionara.

Ljubojevic, Ljubomir   [*November 2 1950– *]

Yugoslav GM (1971) who is a spectacular tactician, an experimenter in the openings and an achiever of uneven results. He was never a Candidate but is generally considered in the world top dozen because he is capable of great achievement.

He was equal 1st or 1st at Palma 1971, Las Palmas 1975, Manila 1975, Wijk aan Zee 1976, Titovo Uzice 1978, Sao Paulo 1979, Buenos Aires 1979 and Brasilia 1981. More recently, his good results in high category tournaments are

impressive: equal 2nd at Bugojno 1982 (XIV), equal 2nd at Tilburg 1983 (XV), equal 1st at Linares 1985 (XIV), 1st at Amsterdam 1986 (XIII), equal 2nd at Bugojno 1986 (XVI), equal 1st at Reggio Emilia 1986 (XIII), 2nd at Tilburg 1986 (XV), equal 1st at Brussels 1987 (XIV), 1st at Belgrade 1987 (XIV) and 1st at Barcelona 1989 (XV).

In life scores (to mid-1987) he beat Spassky (+3 = 15 − 2), Polugayevsky (+4 = 11 − 3), Larsen (+8 = 13 − 3), Hübner (+5 = 10 − 3), Timman (+12 = 18 − 7), Andersson (+5 = 31 − 2) and Yusupov (+1 = 2). He drew with Korchnoi (+4 = 6 − 4). He lost to Smyslov (+1 = 4 − 3), Petrosian (+1 = 9 − 3), Tal (+1 = 10 − 2), Gligoric (+5 = 14 − 6), Portisch (+5 = 24 − 8), Karpov (+2 = 13 − 10), Kasparov (+0 = 3 − 1) and Beljavsky (+0 = 3 − 4).

He won the Yugoslav Championship in 1977 and 1982, and has played on the Yugoslav Olympiad team since 1972.

Polugayevsky–Ljubojevic
Linares 1985

1 d4 ♘f6 2 c4 e6 3 ♘f3 b6 4 ♘c3 ♗b4 5 ♕b3 a5 6 g3 ♘c6 7 ♗g2 a4 8 ♕c2 ♗a6 9 a3 ♗xc3+ 10 ♕xc3 ♘a5 11 ♘e5 d5 12 cd ♘xd5 13 ♕c2 ♘b3 14 ♕c6+ ♔f8 15 ♗g5 ♕e8 16 ♘d7+ ♔g8 17 e4

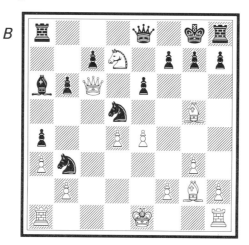

17 ... ♘xd4 18 ♕xa4 c5 19 ed ♗b5 20 ♕d1 ♕xd7 21 ♗e3 ♗e2 22 de ♕xe6

23 ♕xe2 ♘xe2 24 ♗xa8 ♕c4 25 ♖d1 ♘d4 26 ♗xd4 cd 27 ♗e4 g6 28 ♗d3 ♕a2 29 ♖b1 ♕b3 30 ♔d2 ♔g7 31 ♖hc1 ♖e8 32 ♖c7 ♖e6 33 ♖d7 ♕a4 34 ♖d5 ♖f6 35 f4 ♖e6 36 ♖c1 ♖e3 37 ♖c4 ♖xd3+ 38 ♔xd3 ♕d1+ 39 ♔e4 f5+ 40 ♔e5 ♕e2+ 41 ♔xd4 ♕e4+ 42 ♔c3 ♕xd5 43 Resigns

Lobron, Eric   [*May 7 1960– *]

US-born West German GM (1982) who won the German Championship in 1980 and played on the German Olympiad team in 1980, 1982 and 1984. He has had uneven results. His successes are equal 1st at Biel 1981, 1st at Ramat Hasharon 1982, equal 1st at Manila 1982, 1st at New York 1983 (X), 1st at New York 1985 (X), equal 1st at Biel 1986 (XII), Brussels 1987 (XI) and Ter Apel 1987 (XI)

Lolli, Giambattista   [*1698–June 4 1769*]

Italian player and author who, together with Ercole del Rio and Ponziani, formed the strength of the so-called Modenese School. In 1763 he published *Osservazioni Teoretico-Pratiche sopra il giuoco degli scacchi*, an extension (over 600 pages) of Ercole del Rio's 1750 book. Lolli covered all that was known at that time about openings and endgames.

Lombardy, William James   [*December 4 1937– *]

US GM (1960) who was World Junior Champion in 1957 and came 2nd in the 1960 US Championship. He led the US team to victory in the 1960 Student Olympiad, beating Spassky on board 1. In 1962 he lost a close match to Evans +2 = 5 − 3 and in 1963 he won the US Open. Then he became a Roman Catholic priest and devoted only part of his time to chess.

He played on 7 US Olympiad teams between 1958 and 1978, earning 2 draws with Botvinnik. He won the US Open in 1965 and was Fischer's second in the 1972 match with Spassky. He was equal 3rd at Monte Carlo 1969 (XI), equal 3rd at Reykjavik 1978 (XI), 2nd at Neskaupsstadur 1984 (VIII) and 3rd at Husavik 1985 (VIII).

Major works: *Modern Chess Opening Traps* (1972), *US Championship Chess* (co-author) (1974).

Lommer, Harold Maurice

[*1904–1980*]

British-born German endgame composer.

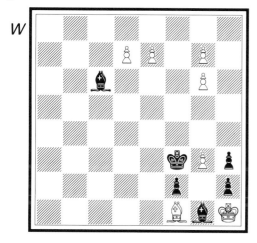

White to play and win (1933)

Black threatens 1 ... ♔xg3+ 2 ♗g2 ♗xg2 mate.

1 d8(♘), ♗d5 (if 1 ... ♗a8 e8(♕)) 2 g8(♗) ♗e4 3 e8(♖) (not 3 e8(♕) ♔xg3+ 4 ♕xe4 stalemate) and wins.

Major works: *1234 Modern Endgame Studies* (with M.A. Sutherland) (1938), *1357 Endgame Studies* (1975).

London

England's great metropolis, which has had a vigorous chess life for some 200 years. Chess was popularly played in coffee houses, for example the Philidor–Stamma match in 1747 took place at Slaughter's coffee house in St Martin's Lane. There was Purssell's in Cornhill, Salopian's in Charing Cross, Parsloe's (from 1774) in St James St and from 1828, the famous Simpson's in the Strand (it was first called Ries'). Simpson's still exists although chess has not been played there since 1903. These so-called Divans separated themselves into those for the upper classes and those for the middle or lower classes.

The very first chess tournament was played in 1849 at Ries' Divan (or Simpson's). It was played as a knockout and Buckle won. In 1851, London hosted the first international tournament, with 16 players, also played on a knockout basis. Anderssen won ahead of Wyvill, Williams and Staunton.

In 1862 London held the first international round robin tournament. It was the first to have a time limit — 20 moves in 2 hours. Draws did not count and drawn games were replayed until a definite result was arrived at. Anderssen (12) won the £100 first prize ahead of Paulsen (11), Owen (10), Macdonell (9), Dubois (9) and Steinitz (8). Blackburne, in his first major event, came near the bottom. Several top players did not play: Kolisch, Neumann, Staunton, Mackenzie and of course Morphy and Lasa.

In 1883 London held a top level tournament, with Steinitz, the world's leading player, and most of his nearest rivals: Zukertort, Blackburne and Chigorin. Only Paulsen and Weiss were missing. Zukertort was absolutely brilliant and this led to his famous match (1886) with Steinitz for the World Championship.

Time limit: 15 moves per hour.

Prizes: £250, 150, 120, 90, 70, 50, 25

Brilliancy prizes: Zukertort for his first win over Blackburne (*see* Zukertort); Rosenthal for his second win over Steinitz

Tournament Book: edited by Minchin, with good annotations by Zukertort, Steinitz, Mason and Bird.

London 1883

	1	2	3	4	5	6	7	8	9	10	11	12	13	14	
1 Zukertort	– –	0 1	d1 1	1 d1	dd1 1	1 d0	1 1	1 1	d1 d1	1 1	1 1	1 0	1 0	1 1	22
2 Steinitz	1 0	– –	1 0	0 0	0 dd1	1 1	1 d1	d0 d0	1 1	1 1	1 d1	1 1	1 d1	1 1	19
3 Blackburne	d0 0	0 1	– –	0 1	1 dd0	d0 0	1 d1	d1 d–	dd½ dd1	0 d1	1 d1	d1 1	1 1	1 1	16½
4 Chigorin	0 d0	1 1	1 0	– –	0 d1	1 1	d0 1	0 dd1	1 0	1 0	d1 0	1 d1	1 0	1 1	16
5 English	dd0 0	1 dd0	0 dd1	1 d0	– –	dd½ dd½	dd0 0	dd½ dd1	0 1	d0 1	1 1	d1 1	1 1	1 1	15½
MacKenzie	0 d1	0 0	d1 1	0 0	dd½ dd½	– –	0 d1	d0 d1	0 1	0 d1	1 d1	dd½ d1	d1 1	1 1	15½
Mason	0 0	dd0 0	d0 d1	dd1 1	dd0 0	d1 0	– –	d1 0	d1 0	1 1	dd½ 1	1 dd½	d1 1	1 1	15½
8 Rosenthal	0 0	d1 d1	d0 d–	1 dd0	dd½ dd0	d1 d0	d0 1	– –	dd½ dd1	d1 0	0 1	d0 1	1 1	d1 1	14
9 Winawer	d0 d0	0 0	dd½ dd0	0 1	1 0	1 0	d0 1	dd½ dd0	– –	d0 1	dd1 0	1 d1	1 1	d1 1	13
10 Bird	0 0	0 0	1 d0	0 1	d1 0	1 d0	0 0	d0 1	d1 0	– –	0 0	1 1	d1 1	d1 1	12
11 Noa	0 0	0 0	0 d0	d0 1	0 0	0 d0	dd½ 0	1 0	dd0 1	1 1	– –	0 1	1 1	1 0	9½
12 Sellman	0 1	0 0	dd0 0	0 dd0	dd0 0	dd½ d0	0 dd0	d1 0	0 d0	0 0	1 0	– –	1 1	0 1	6½
13 Mortimer	0 1	0 0	d0 0	0 0	0 0	1 0	0 d0	0 d0	0 0	0 0	d0 0	0 0	– –	0 1	3
Skipworth	0 0	0 0	0 0	0 0	0 0	0 0	d0 0	0 0	d0 0	1 0	1 0	1 0	1 0	– –	3

d = 1st or 2nd draw, which did not count and had to be replayed.

Blackburne and Rosenthal drew the first game of their second meeting, but did not replay as the prize list was not affected by the result.

Skipworth withdrew after playing Blackburne and Mortimer in the second round robin. His score therefore includes 11 losses by default.

Steinitz–Rosenthal

1 e4 e5 2 ♘f3 ♘c6 3 ♗b5 ♘f6 4 d3 ♗c5 5 c3 ♕e7 6 0-0 0-0 7 d4 ♗b6 8 ♗xc6 bc 9 ♘xe5 d6 10 ♘xc6 ♕xe4 11 ♘b4 c5 12 ♘c2 ♗a6 13 ♖e1 ♕h4 14 f3 d5 15 ♖e5 cd 16 cd ♘d7 17 g3 ♕h3 18 ♖e1 ♖ae8 19 ♗e3 ♖e6 20 ♘c3 ♘f6 21 ♘b4 ♖fe8 22 ♕d2 ♗c4 23 b3 ♗a5 24 ♘c2 ♗a6 25 b4 ♗c7 26 b5 ♗b7 27 ♘a4 ♘h5 28 ♘c5

B

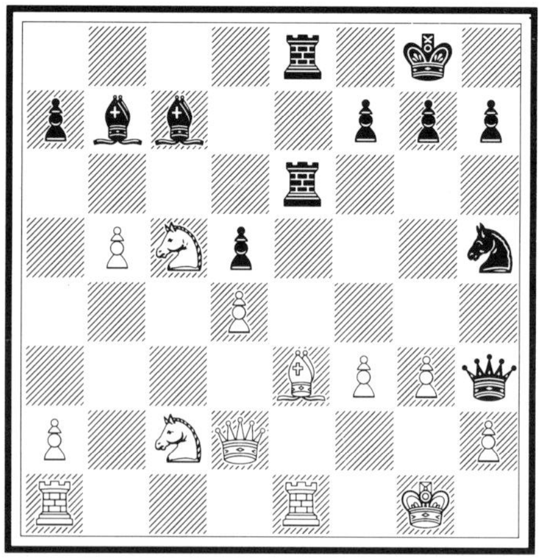

28 ... ♘xg3 29 ♘xe6 ♖xe6 30 ♗f4 (30 hg is correct) ♘e4! 31 ♖xe4 de 32 ♗xc7 ef 33 ♖e1 ♖g6+ 34 ♗g3 ♖xg3+ 35 hg f2+ 36 ♔xf2 ♕g2+ 37 ♔e3 ♕f3 mate

In 1899 London staged perhaps its strongest tournament ever. Most of the leading players were there: World Champion Lasker, his primary rivals Pillsbury and Maroczy, his ageing rivals Chigorin and Steinitz, the veterans Bird, Blackburne and Tinsley, and young Schlechter. There were two notable absentees: Charousek, who was seriously ill and in fact died in April 1900, and Tarrasch who announced he was giving up tournament chess!

With one round to go, Lasker (21½) had 1 more game, Janowski (18) had 1 more, Pillsbury (18) was all done and Maroczy (17) had 1 more. In the last round Lasker beat Schlechter, Maroczy beat Lee while Janowski got a good game against Steinitz. Janowski needed only a draw to win second prize but he made a silly exchange sacrifice and lost, ending up in a triple tie for second.

Time Limit: 15 moves per hour.

Prizes: Gold medal (value £13) and £250, £165, £100, £80, £65, £50, £40, £30, £20.

Brilliancy Prizes: Gold medal (value £11) to Lasker for his win over Steinitz. Lewis prize £10.10s to Blackburne for his win over Lasker.

Tournament Book: edited by Lord and Ward-Higgs, with light and unsatisfying comments by L. Hoffer.

The tournament proved that Lasker was in a class by himself and that the veterans Steinitz and Chigorin were past their prime. Teichmann was having serious eye problems and had to withdraw after 4 rounds. In fact he subsequently lost one of his eyes and ended up wearing a large eye patch.

Steinitz–Lasker

1 e4 e5 2 ♘c3 ♘f6 3 f4 d5 4 d3 ♘c6 5 fe ♘xe5 6 d4 ♘g6 7 ed ♘xd5 8 ♘xd5 ♕xd5 9 ♘f3 ♗g4 10 ♗e2 0-0-0 11 c3 ♗d6 12 0-0 ♖he8 13 h3 ♗d7 14 ♘e5 ♘h4 15 ♘f3 ♘xg2! 16 ♔xg2 ♗xh3+ 17 ♔f2 f6 18 ♖g1 g5 19 ♗xg5 fg 20 ♖xg5 ♕e6 21 ♕d3 ♗f4 22 ♖h1 ♗xg5 23 ♘xg5 ♕f6+ 24 ♗f3 ♗f5 25 ♘xh7 ♕g6 26 ♕b5 c6 27 ♕a5 ♖e7 28 ♖h5 ♗g4 29 ♖g5 ♕c2+ 30 ♔g3 ♗xf3 31 Resigns

Lasker–Blackburne

1 e4 e5 2 ♘f3 ♘c6 3 ♗b5 d6 4 d4 ♗d7 5 d5 ♘b8 6 ♗d3 ♗e7 7 ♘c3 ♘f6 8 ♘e2 c6 9 c4 ♘a6 10 ♘g3 ♘c5

London 1899

		1	2	3	4	5	6	7	8	9	10	11	12	13	14	15	
1	Lasker	–	1½	½1	½1	½1	01	11	11	1½	1½	½1	11	11	11	1	22½
2	Janowski	0½	–	01	10	11	1½	11	½1	00	11	10	11	01	1½	1	18
	Maroczy	½0	10	–	½½	½½	½1	01	1½	10	11	½1	½1	1½	11	1	18
	Pillsbury	½0	01	½½	–	½1	00	10	½½	11	11	11	11	1½	11	½	18
5	Schlechter	½0	00	½½	½0	–	1½	10	½1	½1	0½	11	11	11	11	1	17
6	Blackburne	10	0½	½0	11	0½	–	½0	01	1½	01	10	1½	11	11	½	15½
7	Chigorin	00	00	10	01	01	½1	–	1½	1½	01	½1	10	11	10	1	15
8	Showalter	00	½0	0½	½½	½0	10	0½	–	0½	0½	1½	11	11	01	1	12½
9	Mason	0½	11	01	00	½0	0½	0½	1½	–	00	01	00	11	½1	1	12
10	Cohn W.	0½	00	00	00	1½	10	10	1½	11	–	0½	1½	10	00	1	11½
	Steinitz	½0	01	½0	00	00	01	½0	0½	10	1½	–	½0	½1	11	1	11½
12	Lee	00	00	½0	00	00	0½	01	00	11	0½	½1	–	½1	½½	1	9½
13	Bird	0	10	0½	0½	00	00	00	00	00	01	½0	½0	–	11	1	7
14	Tinsley	00	0½	00	00	00	00	01	10	½0	11	00	½½	00	–	0	6
15	Teichmann	–	–	–	½	–	½	0	–	–	–	–	–	–	1	–	2

Teichmann withdrew after 4 rounds.

11 Bc2 b5 12 b4 Nb7 13 dc Bxc6 14 cb Bxb5 15 a4 Bd7 16 0-0 g6 17 h3 h5 18 Be3 a5 19 b5 Rc8 20 Rc1 Nc5 21 Nd2 h4 22 Ne2 g5 23 Bxg5 Rg8 24 Bxh4 Bxh3 25 Bg3 Be6 26 Re1 Ng4 27 Nf1 Bg5 28 Rb1 Rh8 19 Nc3 Bf4 30 Nd5 Qg5 31 f3

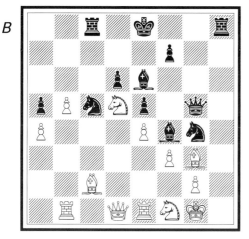

31 ... Rh1+ 32 Kxh1 Bxg3 33 Nxg3 Nf2+ 34 Kg1 Nxd1 35 Nf5 Bxf5 36 ef Qd2 37 Rexd1 Qxc2 38 Rbc1 Qxf5 39 Nb6 Rd8 40 Nc4 Nb7 41 Ne3 Qf4 42 Kf2 Qxa4 43 Rc7 Nc5 44 Rh1 Rd7 45 Rc8+ Ke7 46 R1h8 Qd4 47 Resigns

London staged the first real Olympiad in 1927. In terms of world title matches, London had McDonnell–La Bourdonnais in 1834, Steinitz–Anderssen in 1866 (both *de facto*, rather than official) and the first half of Karpov–Kasparov 1986.

In 1984 London was the scene of the second USSR vs the Rest of the World match. The first such match was held in 1970 (*see* Belgrade). The hero was Belyavsky who scored 3½–½ for the USSR.

The USSR team at the 1984 match against the Rest of the World. Back row (from left): Razuvayev, Romanishin, Vaganian, Karpov, Kasparov, Belyavsky, Tukmakov, Sokolov. Front row: Yusupov, Polugayevsky, Krogius (team captain), Smyslov, Tal.

London 1984					USSR vs Rest of the World				
1	½	½	½	Karpov	Andersson	0	½	½	½
½	½	½	1	Kasparov	Timman	½	½	½	0
½	0	½		Polugayevsky	Korchnoi	½	1	½	½
			½	Tukmakov					
0			½	Smyslov	Ljubojevic	1	0	½	½
	1	½		Tukmakov					
½	½	½	0	Vaganian	Ribli	½	½	½	1
1	1	½	1	Belyavsky	Seirawan	0	0		
					Larsen			½	0
½		1	½	Tal	Nunn	½	½	0	
	½			Romanishin	Chandler				½
½	½	½	½	Razuvayev	Hübner	½	½	½	½
½	½	½		Yusupov	Miles	½	½	½	1
			0	Romanishin					
0	1		0	Sokolov	Torre	1	0		1
		½		Romanishin	Chandler			½	
5	6	5½	4½ = 21			5	4	4½	5½ = 19

The USSR's opponents in 1984: Back row (from left): Hübner, Miles, Seirawan, Chandler, Ljubojevic, Ribli, Andersson, Nunn. Front row: Korchnoi, Larsen, Hasan (team captain), Timman, Torre.

Lone Pine

A small US town (pop. less than 2000) in eastern California where Louis Statham, a wealthy engineer, financed annual swiss tournaments from 1971 to 1981. By paying travel plus living expenses he was able to attract GMs from all over the world. In 1981 there were 61 players, 27 of whom were GMs, in a 9-round swiss. Korchnoi (7) won about $15 000, ahead of Gligoric (6½), Seirawan (6½) and Sosonko (6½). Previous winners included Larsen (1978), Petrosian (1976), Liberzon (1975) and Gligoric (1972). The series stopped in 1981 when Statham took ill in 1982 and died in 1983.

Long Games

Most games last between 25 and 60 moves. Very few go for more than 100 moves. Some incredibly long marathons are: Mar del Plata 1953, Pilnik drew with Czerniak in 191 moves (23 hours); Carlsbad 1907, Wolf beat Duras in 168 moves (22½ hours); Israel 1980, Stepak beat Mashian in 193 moves; Latvia 1989, Meiers–Ravsis drawn in 200 moves. At the Riga Championship 1988, Chekhov–Stavrinov lasted 209 moves, but the record now stands at 269 moves: I. Nikolic–Arsovic, Belgrade 1989.

Lopez, Ruy

1 e4 e5 2 ♘f3 ♘c6 3 ♗b5.

This so-called Spanish Opening maintains White's opening initiative a long time and is perhaps the strongest opening in White's armoury. Its major defect is that Black can avoid it by playing the Sicilian Defence (1 ... c5).

It was first mentioned in the Göttingen manuscript (1490) and carefully analysed by Ruy Lopez in 1561 (*Libro del Ajedrez*). White puts pressure on the centre by attacking the defender of Black's e-pawn. Though there is no immediate threat to the e-pawn, the strategic idea is profound and Black must play well to keep the balance. Black has two main choices.

(1) Defences without 3 ... a6 are not only old-fashioned, but (generally) passive:

Alapin	3 ..., ♗b4. White usually plays 4 c3;
Berlin	3 ..., ♘f6. After 4 0-0 ♘xe4 5 d4 Black gets a cramped game;
Bird	3 ..., ♘d4. After 4 ♘xd4 ed 5 0-0 White stands well;
Classical	3 ..., ♗c5. White usually plays 4 c3 followed by d4;
Cozio	3 ..., ♘ge7. White usually plays 4 d4;
Fianchetto	3 ..., g6;
Schliemann	3 ..., f5;
Steinitz	3 ..., d6;

(2) Defences with 3 ..., a6 (Morphy):

Exchange	4 ♗xc6;
Steinitz Deferred	4 ♗a4 d6;
Open (Tarrasch)	4 ♗a4 ♘f6 5 0-0 ♘xe4;
Marshall	4 ♗a4 ♘f6 5 0-0 ♗e7 6 ♖e1 b5 7 ♗b3 0-0 8 c3 d5;
Chigorin	4 ♗a4 ♘f6 5 0-0 ♗e7 6 ♖e1 b5 7 ♗b3 d6 8 c3 0-0 9 h3 ♘a5 10 ♗c2 c5 11 d4 ♕c7.

Many other variations of this vast opening are also possible.

Lopez de Segura, Ruy

[*about 1530–about 1580*]

Spanish priest from Zafra in Estremadura who was the leading Spanish player of his age. His skill at chess made him internationally famous and he was a favourite at the court of Philip II. In 1560 Lopez visited Rome on ecclesiastical business and defeated without difficulty the strongest Italian players, including the young Leonardo da Cutri. He also discovered Damiano's book, which he disliked, and decided to improve upon it. The result was the *Libro de la invencion liberal y arte del juego del Axedrez*, which Lopez published soon after his return to Spain in 1561. It contains general advice and a collection of recommended openings as well as copious criticisms of Damiano's games and analysis.

In 1574–5 the two best Italian players, Leonardo da Cutri and Paolo Boi, visited Madrid. Matches with Lopez were arranged under the patronage of Philip II, and Lopez, bowing to age, was defeated by each of them.

Los Angeles
America's west coast metropolis which staged two major tournaments sponsored by the Piatigorskys. In 1963 a Category XV tournament was won by Keres (8½) and Petrosian (8½) ahead of Najdorf (7½) and Olafsson (7½). This was the strongest tournament held in the US since New York 1927.

In 1966 it was again Category XV but this time it had the World Champion Petrosian—who had just successfully defended his title—and his two chief rivals Spassky and Fischer. Notable absentees were Tal, Botvinnik, Stein and Geller. First prize was $5000 with a total prize fund of $20 000.

After the first round robin Spassky (6) and Larsen (6) led, ahead of Reshevsky (5), while Fischer (3½) was back in 9th place. Fischer then had a remarkable run of 6 wins and a draw, and with 2 rounds to go, it was Spassky (10) and Fischer (10) far ahead of the others. Fischer had to face Spassky and Petrosian in the last 2 rounds while Spassky had Fischer and tail-ender Donner. Fischer got 2 draws but Spassky crushed Donner and won the tournament.

The tournament book is by Kashdan, with good annotations by the players.

Loshinsky, Lev Ilyich
[*January 17 1913–February 19 1976*]
Superb USSR problem composer who specialized in 2 and 3 movers. See *Grossmeister Shakhmatnoi* (1980) by Vladimirov, Kofman and Umnov for over 500 of his problems.

W

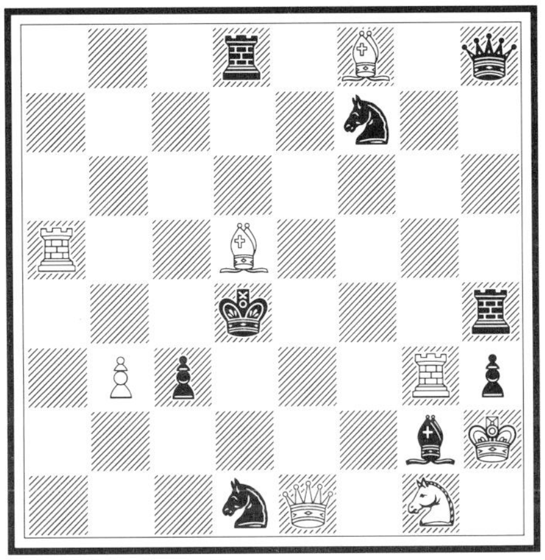

Mate in 2 (1949/50)
Solution: 1 ♗e4

Losing on Time
If a player oversteps the time limit (has not completed the prescribed number of moves in the allotted time), he loses the game, unless his opponent has only the king remaining, in which case the game is drawn.

Louis XIII [*1601–1643*]
King of France (1610–43) who had a chess board made of wood with spiked pieces, for travelling.

Loveday, Henry Augustus
[*1815–1848*]
Indian-born English problem composer who invented the Indian theme (self interference, to avoid stalemate, followed by a discovered checkmate).

Löwenthal, Johann Jacob (Janos Jakab) [*July 15 1810–July 20 1876*]
Hungarian of GM strength who came to live in England (1851) and played a major role in English chess. During the 1850s he was in the world top 7 or 8 and was probably the best opening theorist of his day.

He was born in Budapest, studied chess under Szen, but had to flee Hungary after the unsuccessful revolution of 1848. He first went to the US and while visiting New Orleans in 1850, lost +0=1−1 to the 13-year-old Morphy.

Löwenthal came to London for the

Los Angeles 1966 — 2nd Piatigorsky Cup

		1		2		3		4		5		6		7		8		9		10		
1	Spassky	–	–	1	½	½	1	½	½	1	½	½	½	½	½	½	½	1	½	½	1	11½
2	Fischer	0	½	–	–	0	1	½	1	½	½	½	½	½	1	0	1	1	1	½	1	11
3	Larsen	½	0	1	0	–	–	1	½	½	0	1	1	½	1	1	½	0	1	½	0	10
4	Portisch	½	½	½	0	0	½	–	–	½	½	1	½	½	½	½	½	½	1	½	1	9½
	Unzicker	0	½	½	½	½	1	½	½	–	–	½	½	½	½	½	½	1	½	½	½	9½
6	Petrosian	½	½	½	½	0	0	0	½	½	½	–	–	½	½	1	1	½	½	½	1	9
	Reshevsky	½	½	½	0	½	0	½	½	½	½	½	½	–	–	½	1	½	½	1	½	9
8	Najdorf	½	½	1	0	0	½	½	½	½	½	0	0	½	0	–	–	1	½	½	1	8
9	Ivkov	0	½	0	0	1	0	½	0	0	½	½	½	½	½	0	½	–	–	½	1	6½
10	Donner	½	0	½	0	½	1	½	0	½	½	½	0	0	½	½	0	½	0	–	–	6

1851 tournament but, in poor health, was eliminated by Williams in the first round. Shortly afterwards he gained his revenge by defeating Williams +7 =4 −5 in a match. In series of offhand games he lost to Lasa in 1846 and to Anderssen in 1851. In 1853 he lost a close match to Harrwitz +10 =12 −11 after having led by 7 games. In 1857 Löwenthal won at Manchester, ahead of Anderssen and in 1858 he won the strong BCA congress at Birmingham ahead of Falkbeer, Staunton and Saint-Amant—his finest tournament success. In 1858 he lost a match to Morphy +3 =2 −9, though he outplayed his opponent in the openings.

After 1860 he devoted less time to play and more to chess administration and journalism. He was at various times Secretary of the St George's Club and Manager of the BCA. With Medley he organized the London 1862 tournament. His literary work included chess columns in the *Era* and the *Illustrated London News*, and during 1863–7 he edited the *Chess Player's Magazine*. He wrote *Morphy's Games of Chess* (1860) and *The Chess Congress of 1862* (1863).

He died in Hastings and left his estate to promote chess. The solid silver trophy used for the English counties championship is called the Löwenthal cup in his memory.

See the *British Chess Magazine* (1926), pp. 345–8 and (1976), pp. 308–14 for more details.

Loyd, Sam

[*January 30 1841–April 11 1911*] US problem composer and puzzle inventor who dazzled the chess world with his brilliant problems (usually 3 movers).

See Sam Loyd and his Chess Problems by A. C. White (1913), *Cyclopedia of Puzzles* by S. Loyd Jr. (1914), *Mathematical Puzzles of Sam Loyd* by M. Gardner (1958).

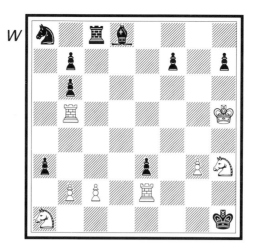

Mate in 5 (1858)
Solution: 1 b4 ♖c5 + (to prevent 2 ♖d5) 2 bc a2 3 c6 ♗c7 4 cb any 5 bxa8(♕) mate

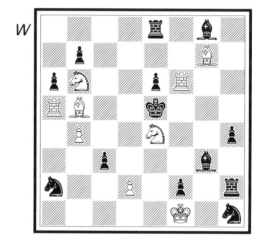

Mate in 3 (1903)
Solution: 1 ♔e2 f1(♕) + 2 ♔e3 or 1 ♔e2 f1(♘) 2 ♖f2 +

Lputian, Smbat Gariginovich

[*February 14 1958–*] USSR GM (1984) who played in 5 USSR Championships between 1980 and 1987, scoring 41–46. He has had mixed results—his best achievements are: 1st Berlin 1982 (IX), equal 1st Athens 1983 (VIII) and Irkutsk 1983 (IX), 1st Sarajevo 1985 (XI), 1st Irkutsk 1986 (X), equal 1st Hastings 1986/87 (X) and 1st Dortmund 1988 (XII).

Lucena, Luis Ramirez de

[*15th/16th Century*] Author of the earliest surviving printed work on chess, *Repeticion de amores y arte de Axedres* which was published in Spain in 1497. The book is divided into two sections: one on chess and one on love (another form of mock warfare). The chess material includes rudimentary analysis of ten opening variations, 150 problems and studies, and helpful psychological advice (such as 'Try to play soon after your opponent has eaten or drunk freely').

Lucena is also generally credited with the authorship of the Göttingen manuscript, a 33-page Latin tract which contains a similar mixture of opening analysis and problems, probably composed circa 1500.

Lukacs, Peter

[*July 9 1950–*] Hungarian GM (1986) who was Hungarian Champion in 1980 and does well in tournaments of Category VIII: 1st Helsinki 1983 (VIII), 1st Bucharest 1983 (VIII), equal 1st Vrnjacka Banja 1985 (VIII), equal 1st Polanica Zdroj 1986 (IX), equal 1st Havana 1986 (VIII), 1st Budapest 1987 (VIII).

Lukov, Valentin

[*December 11 1955–*] Bulgarian GM (1988) who was equal 1st at Halle 1987 (X).

Lundin, Erik Ruben

[*July 2 1904–*] Swedish IM (1950) and honorary GM (1983) who was Swedish Champion 10 times between 1932 and 1964, and who played on 9 Swedish Olympiad teams between 1930 and 1960.

He was equal 1st at Göteborg 1931, 2nd behind Alekhine at Orebro 1935, 1st at Ostend 1936, equal 2nd with Alekhine at Munich 1941, 1st at Bad Gasten 1948 and 1st at Zurich 1952. In 1933 he beat Spielmann +1 =5.

See Erik Lundin spelar upp sina schackminnen 1924–1979 (1979).

Lutikov, Anatoly Stepanovich
[*February 5 1933–October 1989*]
USSR GM (1974) who played in 6 USSR Championships between 1959 and 1969, coming 3rd in the 36th Championship 1968/69. In other events he was 2nd behind Spassky at Wijk aan Zee 1967, 1st at Dubna 1971, equal 1st at Leipzig 1973 and 1st at Albena 1976.

MacCutcheon Variation

See French Defence.

McDonnell, Alexander

[*May 22 1798–September 14 1835*] Irish player of GM strength who was Britain's leading player during the early 1830s. He was secretary to the committee of West India Merchants in London. He studied chess under William Lewis in the 1820s.

In 1834 he engaged in a marathon series of matches with the visiting French champion La Bourdonnais. Five complete matches of varying lengths were played and a sixth was left unfinished, comprising a probable total of 85 games (there is some dispute among chess historians over the details of the final two matches) with the victory going to La Bourdonnais + 45 = 13 − 27. The standard of play was high and these contests did much to kindle interest in chess in both France and England.

McDonnell's quiet reserved manner was in sharp contrast to La Bourdonnais' boisterous personality but on the board he played imaginative and sometimes brilliant chess. He died of Bright's disease and is buried in Kensal Green cemetery, London, near his great rival La Bourdonnais.

La Bourdonnais–McDonnell

Match 1834

1 d4 d5 2 c4 dc 3 e4 e5 4 d5 f5 5 ♘c3 ♘f6 6 ♗xc4 ♗c5 7 ♘f3 ♕e7 8 ♗g5 ♗xf2+ 9 ♔f1 ♗b6 10 ♕e2 f4 11 ♖d1 ♗g4 12 d6 cd 13 ♘d5 ♘xd5 14 ♗xe7 ♘e3+ 15 ♔e1 ♔xe7 16 ♕d3 ♖d8 17 ♖d2 ♘c6 18 b3 ♗a5 19 a3 ♖ac8 20 ♖g1 b5 21 ♗xb5 ♗xf3 22 gf ♘d4 23 ♗c4 ♘xf3+ 24 ♔f2 ♘xd2 25 ♖xg7+ ♔f6 26 ♖f7+ ♔g6 27 ♖b7 ♘dxc4 28 bc ♖xc4 29 ♕b1 ♗b6 30 ♔f3 ♖c3 31 ♕a2 ♘c4+ 32 ♔g4 ♖g8 33 ♖xb6 ab 34 ♔h4 ♔f6 35 ♕e2 ♖g6 36 ♕h5 ♘e3 37 Resigns

McDonnell, Rev. George Alcock

[*August 16 1830–June 3 1899*] Irish author and player of IM strength who was equal 3rd at Dundee 1867 and equal 3rd at London 1872. He wrote lively, entertaining material but it suffered from being inaccurate—even inventive. He was 'Mars' of the chess column in the *Ilustrated Sporting and Dramatic News* and he wrote *Chess Life and Pictures* (1883) as well as *The Knights and Kings of Chess* (1894).

MacKenzie, George Henry (Captain)

[*March 24 1837–April 14 1891*] Scottish-born US player of GM strength who was the recognized American chess champion from 1865 to about 1890, and during the 1880s was in the world's top 10. He played in many local and national US tournaments and matches and won them all. In America he was the link between Morphy and Pillsbury.

In international tournaments his peak results were 1st at Frankfurt 1887 and 2nd at Bradford 1888. In top level matches he drew + 4 = 2 − 4 with Burn in 1886, lost + 1 = 2 − 3 to Steinitz in 1883, edged Blackburne + 2 − 1 in 1883 and lost = 1 − 2 in 1888.

He was a Lieutenant in the British army, stationed in India, then a Captain in the US Army (North) in the civil war. From 1865 on he devoted himself to chess. He was from the older school and kingside attacks were his speciality. Steinitz says 'he combined uprightness with good temper and suavity of disposition and manners, which made him a great favourite wherever he was known'.

Magazines

Chess magazines give news, problems, annotated games, pictures and much pleasure to their subscribers, but the vast majority of such magazines go bankrupt in a short time. There are some notable exceptions, like the *Deutsche Schachzeitung* which has been running since 1846 (with a post-war break during 1945–1949).

The very first magazine was *Le Palamède*, Paris, 1836–40, edited by La Bourdonnais. He claimed to have 236 subscribers. The first English magazine was *The Philidorian*, London, 1837/38, edited by G. Walker.

The most important magazines are (were):

British Chess Magazine UK 1881– (longest continuous publication)
Chess UK 1935–
Chess Life and Review USA 1969–
Chess Monthly London 1879–96 Hoffer and Zukertort
Chess Monthly USA 1857–61 Fiske and Morphy
Chess Player's Chronicle London 1841–54 and off and on to 1902.
                                        Staunton
Chess Review New York 1933–1969 Horowitz
Deutsche Schachzeitung Berlin 1846–1945, 1950–
Deutsche Wochenshach (1889–1927)
International Chess Magazine New York 1885–1891 Steinitz
New in Chess Holland 1984– Timman
Schakend Nederland Holland 1893–
Shakhmatny Bulletin USSR 1955–64 USSR 1968–
La Strategy France 1867–1940
Wiener Schachzeitung Vienna 1898–1916, 1923–38, 1948–9.

Major Pieces
The queen and rook, in contrast to the bishop and knight, the minor pieces.

Makarichev, Sergey Yuryevich
[*November 17 1953–*]
USSR GM (1976) who won the European Junior Championship 1973/74, was equal 2nd at Amsterdam 1975 (XI), equal 1st at Novi Sad 1983 (VII), equal 2nd at Oslo 1984 (XIII) and 1st at Frunze 1985 (IX). He played in three USSR Championships during 1978–80 but scored only 25–26 in them. Somehow he never quite achieved as much as his early promise indicated.

Makogonov, Vladimir Andreyevich
[*August 27 1904–*]
USSR mathematics teacher, IM (1950) and honorary GM (1987) who played in 8 USSR Championships during 1927–47. He was equal 5th (with Botvinnik) in 1927, 4th in 1937, equal 4th in 1939 and equal 5th in 1944. In other tournaments he was equal 3rd at Leningrad/Moscow 1939 and 2nd at Sverdlovsk 1943. He was many times champion of Azerbaijan.

He contributed to the theory of the King's Indian Defence and the Queen's Gambit.

Malaniuk, Vladimir P.
[*July 21 1957–*]
USSR GM (1987) who was 1st at Minsk 1985 (IX), equal 1st at Lvov 1986 (IX), 1st at Frunze 1987 (VIII), equal 2nd at Tallinn 1987 (XI) and equal 2nd at Lvov 1988 (X). He played in four USSR Championships during 1983–8. He was equal 2nd in the 1986 tournament (X) but last in 1988.

Malich, Burkhard Georg Josef
[*November 29 1936–*]
East German GM (1975) who was East German Champion in 1957 and 1973 and who played regularly on East German Olympiad teams during 1958–72. Perhaps his best result was 3rd at Leipzig 1973.

Manchester Chess Club
The oldest chess club in Britain, which began on September 3 1817 in the Albion Hotel, Manchester. It organized several major tournaments in Manchester.

Manhattan Chess Club
The oldest chess club in America, which began in a café on the Bowery in lower Manhattan in 1877. Its members organized the great tournaments of New York 1924 and 1927. It was while watching a casual game at the Mahattan

club that Capablanca fell ill and died in 1942.

Mansfield, Comins
[*June 14 1896–March 27 1984*]
England's leading problem composer who was president of FIDE's problem commission 1963–71.

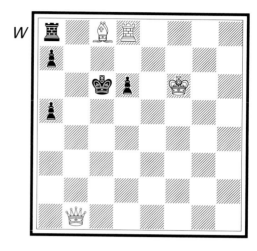

White to play and mate in 3 (1924)
1 ♗a6 ♚c5 2 ♕b5+ ♚d4 3 ♕e5++
1 ... ♚d5 2 ♕d3+ ♚c5 3 ♕xd6++
1 ... ♚c7 2 ♕b7+ ♚xd8 3 ♕e7++
1 ... ♜xd8 2 ♕b5+ ♚c7 3 ♕b7++

Major work: *Adventures in Composition* (1943). See: *A Genius of the two Mover* by A. C. White (1936), *Chess Problems of a Grandmaster* by B. P. Barnes (1976).

Mansuba
The Arabic word for an endgame position, usually posed as a problem. The Arabian ones deal of course with Shatranj and they run from about 1140 to 1795.

Marco, Georg
[*November 29 1863–August 29 1923*]
Romanian-born Austrian of GM strength, whose main claims to fame are his wonderful annotations and his excellent editorship of the *Wiener Schachzeitung* from 1898 to 1916. He played in

123

many tournaments (see the *Neue Wiener Schachzeitung* (1923), December pages 328–31) from 1890 to 1922 and his best results were equal 4th at Dresden 1892, 1st at Vienna 1895, 3rd at the Vienna Gambit tournament 1903, 4th at Cambridge Springs 1904 and equal 5th at Ostend 1905. He drew two matches with the young Schlechter: =10 in 1893 and +4=3−4 in 1894. He also drew +5−5 with Kaufmann in 1893, and he lost +1=1−5 to Weiss in 1895.

Marco played a solid classical game, but had a tendency to draw too often by being over-cautious. He began as a medical student but gave it up for chess. He served as secretary of the Viennese Chess Association. He was a very large powerful man and was often referred to as the strongest chess player in the world!

He was a deep analyst and his annotations had a charming mixture of satire and humour. He was a happy philosopher and taught an entire generation of Viennese masters. His major books were: *Vienna Gambit Tournament (1903), Barmen 1905, Ostend 1906, Carlsbad 1907* (with Schlechter), *Lasker–Tarrasch match 1908* and *Baden auf Wien Gambit Tournament 1914.*

Here is a typical example of his writings from the Carlsbad 1907 tournament book:

Vidmar–Teichmann

'26 ... ♖g6.

'Dr Tarrasch (in the *Berlin Lokalanzeiger* of Nov. 15, 1907) says: "Clearly this rook move is totally misguided. Black must simply take the e-pawn to achieve the better game e.g. 26 ... ♕xe5 27 ♕xc4 ♖d6 (this is much stronger than 27 ... e2 when white would have drawing chances with 28 ♖e1 ♕e3+ 29 ♔g2 ♘e6 30 ♖xe2 ♘f4+ 31 ♕xf4) 28 ♖e1 (or 28 ♖xd6 e2) 28 ... ♖d2 threatening ... ♗xf3 with a strong attack. One possible continuation is 29 ♗e4 ♖d4 30 ♕e2 ♖xe4 31 fe ♕xe4 32 ♖xe3 ♕h1+ 33 ♔f2 ♕g2 mate."

Oh deep and profound knowledge— are you not truly magnificent? Tarrasch's note was reprinted without comment in the *Deutsche Schachzeitung* and in various other chess publications.

The problem composer Teichmann saw however, probably with half a glance at the board (since he has only one eye), that he would achieve immortal fame (negatively!) with 26 ... ♕xe5 27 ♕xh7+ ♘xh7 28 ♖d8+ ♘f8 29 ♖h8+ ♔xh8 30 ♖xf8 mate.

How deplorable the imperfection of human nature is, when a great Grandmaster with unlimited time for analyses, shoots himself in the foot. *Errare humanum est.* Of course critics must themselves be careful and polite. In any case, we now understand why Teichmann avoided the e-pawn like the plague. Life is serious, art is cheerful.'

Mar Del Plata

Seaside resort in Argentina, a few hundred miles south of Buenos Aires, that held chess tournaments since 1928, the strongest of them from 1957–71.

Mariotti, Sergio   [*August 10 1946–*]
Italian GM (1974)—the first and only Italian GM of modern times. He was 2nd at Venice 1971 and played on the Italian Olympiad team in 1972, 1974, 1986 and 1988.

Marjanovic, Slavoljub

[*January 6 1955–*]
Yugoslav GM (1978) who was 1st at Belgrade 1979 (VII), Bor 1983 (VIII) and equal 1st at Vrnjacka Banja 1983 (VIII). He played 6th board on the 1984 Yugoslav Olympiad team and won the 1985 Yugoslav Championship. His best results were equal 2nd at Marseille 1986 (X), equal 2nd at Clichy 1987 (IX) and equal 1st at Rome 1988 (IX).

Maroczy Bind
See Sicilian Defence.

Maroczy, Geza

[*March 3 1870–May 28 1951*]
Hungarian GM (1950) who was in the world top 2 or 3 during 1896 to 1908. Apart from Lasker, Maroczy was the star player of this period, coming 1st or 2nd in 10 top level tournaments. He was 2nd behind Lasker at the powerful Nuremberg tournament 1896, equal 2nd behind Lasker at London 1899, 1st at Monte Carlo 1902, 2nd behind Tarrasch at Monte Carlo 1903, 1st at Monte Carlo 1904, 1st at Ostend 1905, equal 1st with Janowski at Barmen 1905, 2nd behind Schlechter at Ostend 1906, 2nd behind Rubinstein at Carlsbad 1907 and equal 1st with Schlechter and Duras at Vienna 1908. In 1896 he beat Charousek +6=6−2.

A title match with Lasker almost took place in 1906, but the finances fell through and after 1908 Maroczy played infrequently. He suffered privation during the Great War and in 1918 he went to Holland and England (where he gave lessons to Vera Menchik). He returned to active tournament play in 1920 coming 1st at Utrecht, drawing a match with young Euwe +2=5−2 in 1921 and coming equal 1st with Alekhine and Bogoljubow at Carlsbad 1923. Maroczy played on the Hungarian Olympiad team in 1927, 1930, 1933, and 1936. He was chief referee at the Alekhine–Euwe matches of 1935 and 1937.

In life scores Maroczy beat Black-burne (+5=3−0), Chigorin (+6=7 −4) Tarrasch (+3=12−2), Marshall (+11=10−4), Janowski (+10=5 −5), Bogoljubow (+7 =4−4), Vidmar (+3=10−0) and Euwe (+4 =15−3). He was edged out by Steinitz (+1=2−2), Schlechter (+1=29−2), Pillsbury (+3=7−4) and Rubinstein (+2=1−4). He lost decisively only to Lasker (+0=2−4), Capablanca (+0 =5−3) and Alekhine (+0 =5−6).

Maroczy was a positional player, an expert in the opening and an artist in the endgame. He was especially famous for his queen and pawn endings.

He was tall and modest, always courteous, polite and gentle. He taught mathematics as a profession.

In 1986 some mediums approached Korchnoi and asked if he would play against the spirit of some departed GM. Korchnoi asked for Capablanca but accepted Maroczy when they explained they could not get through to Capablanca, but that they had made contact with Maroczy. The game (as of December 1988) is still unfinished. Korchnoi explains that he got a clear advantage in the opening because 'Maroczy' was not aware of the latest theory, but once the middlegame began Korchnoi felt a great power and force in his opponent's play.

Major work: *Paul Morphy* (1909).

See: *Geza Maroczy* by J. Szely (1957) *Geza Maroczy: Leben und Lehren* by A. Foldeak (1971).

Marostica
See Living Chess.

Marovic, Drazen [*January 14 1938−]
Yugoslav GM (1975) and author who was 1st or equal 1st at Malaga 1968, Zabreb 1971, Virovitica 1978 and Ste Maxime 1982, and equal 2nd at Zabreb

1972. He edited the magazine *Sahovski Glasnik* and wrote an opening book *Teorija Otvorenja* (1971 and 1973). In English, he has written *An Opening Repertoire for Black* (with Parma) (1978, 1987).

Marshall Chess Club
The traditional rival of the Manhattan club. It began in the backroom of a mid-Manhattan restaurant in 1915.

Marshall Counter-Gambit
See Lopez, Ruy

Marshall, Frank James
[*August 10 1877–November 9 1944]
US player of GM strength who was in the world top ten from 1904 to 1925 and US Champion from 1909 to 1936. He was a sparkling and successful tournament player with wins at Cambridge Springs 1904 (ahead of Lasker), Nuremberg 1906 and Havana 1913 (ahead of Capablanca). He was also 3rd at Paris 1900, 3rd at Monte Carlo 1904, 4th at San Sebastian 1911, 5th at the great St Petersburg tournament of 1914, 4th at New York 1924 and 4th at Moscow 1925.

He won matches from Teichmann, Janowski, Mieses, Showalter, Leonhardt, Kostic, Duras and Edward Lasker. However at the very top level his match play was significantly below his tournament play. In 1905 he was crushed +1 =8−8 by Tarrasch; in 1907 he was routed by Lasker +0=7−8 in their world title match; and in 1909 he was badly beaten by Capablanca +1=14−8. Marshall tried to explain this:

'From the very first, I was an attacking player forever on the offensive ... I have always liked a wide open game and tried to knock out my opponent with a checkmate as quickly as possible

... I have always done better in tournaments than in match play, and no wonder: I've always had a passion for new faces, new places, novelties in opening play, slashing attack and counterattack. The grim business of wearing down your opponent has never appealed to me ...'

In terms of life scores, Marshall beat Pillsbury (+5=1−4), Chigorin (+7=8−4), Vidmar (+4=6−3), Schlechter (+8=20−5) and Janowski (+34=18−26). He was edged out by Rubinstein (+9=16−11) and Nimzowitsch (+5=8−6), and was beaten by Tarrasch (+7=18−13), Maroczy (+4=10−11), Lasker (+2=11−12), Capablanca (+2=28−20), and Alekine (+0=7−6).

Marshall played on 5 US Olympiad teams during 1930−7 and in some 55 major tournaments during 1900−41. This was more than any other GM up to the time of Keres, Gligoric and Smyslov (90 tournaments!).

In 1915 he founded the Marshall Chess Club and ran it until his death. He was a devoted family man, enjoyed cigars and alcohol, and was Mr Chess, USA, from the time of Pillsbury to the emergence of Kashdan and Reshevsky.

Major works: *Marshall's Chess 'Swindles* (1914), *My Fifty years of Chess* (1942).
See *Marshall's Best Games* by P. Wenman (1948).

Marshall's most famous *move* occurred in Breslau 1912:

Lewitsky − Marshall

1 d4 e6 2 e4 d5 3 ♘c3 c5 4 ♘f3 ♘c6 5 ed ed 6 ♗e2 ♘f6 7 0-0 ♗e7 8 ♗g5 0-0 9 dc ♗e6 10 ♘d4 ♗xc5 11 ♘xe6 fe 12 ♗g4 ♕d6 13 ♗h3 ♖ae8 14 ♕d2 ♗b4 15 ♗xf6 ♖xf6 16 ♖ad1 ♕c5 17 ♕e2 ♗xc3 18 bc ♕xc3 19 ♖xd5 ♘d4 20 ♕h5 ♖ef8 21 ♖e5 ♖h6 22 ♕g5 ♖xh3 23 ♖c5

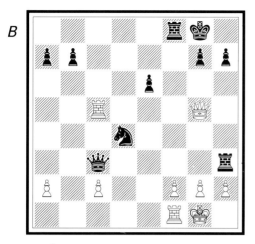

B

23 ... ♛g3 24 Resigns

Perhaps Marshall's finest game is:

Chigorin–Marshall

Vienna Gambit Tournament 1903

1 e4 e5 2 f4 ef 3 ♗c4 d5 4 ♗xd5
♛h4+ 5 ♚f1 g5 6 g3 ♛h6 7 ♘c3
♘f6 8 d4 ♘c6 9 ♚g2 ♗d7 10 h4
♖g8 11 ♘f3 gh 12 ♘e2 h3+ 13 ♚f1
fg 14 ♗xh6 g2+ 15 ♚g1 ♗xh6 16
♛d3 ♘g4 17 ♖xh3 ♗e3+ 18 ♚xg2
♘f2+ 19 ♖g3 ♖xg3+ 20 ♚xg3
♘xd3 21 cd ♘b4 22 ♖f1 ♘xd5 23 ed
♚e7

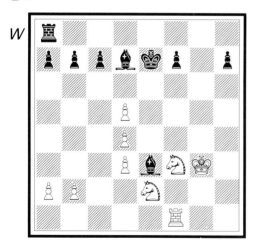

W

24 ♘e5 ♖g8+ 25 ♚f3 ♗h6 26 ♖d1
♗g5 27 ♖h1 ♗f5 28 ♘g3 ♗g6 29
♘e4 h6 30 ♘c5 b6 31 ♘e4 f6 32
♘xg6+ ♖xg6 33 ♚g4 ♗e3+ 34
♚f5 ♖g1 35 ♖xg1 ♗xg1 36 d6+ cd
37 ♘xf6 ♗xd4 38 ♘g8+ ♚d7 39
♘xh6 ♗xb2 40 ♚e4 ♚c6 41 d4 b5 42

♘f5 b4 43 ♘e7+ ♚d7 44 ♘d5 a5 45
♚d3 ♚c6 46 ♚c4 ♗c1 47 ♘e7+
♚d7 48 ♘d5 ♚e6 49 ♘b6 ♗d2 50
♚d3 ♗c3 51 ♚c4 ♗e1 52 ♘d5 ♚f5
53 ♘b6 ♚e4 54 ♘c8 d5+ 55 ♚c5 a4
56 ♘d6+ ♚d3 57 ♘b5 a3 58 Resigns

Martinovic, Slobodan

[*July 25 1945– *]
Yugoslav GM (1979) who was 1st at
Zrenjanin 1980 (VIII), 1st at Bor 1984
(VIII) and 1st at Lille 1986 (VI).

Mason, James

[*November 19 1849–January 15 1905*]
Irish player of GM strength who lived
in the US during 1861–78 and then in
England (1878–1905). During the 1880s
he was quite active and belonged to the
world top ten. His finest hour was 3rd
prize at Vienna 1882. Though successful
on the tournament trail (3rd at Nuremberg 1883, equal 5th at London 1883,
equal 2nd at Hamburg 1885, equal 3rd
at Bradford 1888, 3rd at Amsterdam
1889, 7th at New York 1889 and equal
5th at Manchester 1890), he never fulfilled his early promise.

In matches he beat Bird +11=4−4
in 1876 and Capt. Mackenzie +1
=2−0 in 1882.

Perhaps he is best remembered for his
successful books: *The Principles of Chess*
(1894), *The Art of Chess* (1895), *St Petersburg 1895/6* (with Pollock), *Chess Openings* (1897) and *Social Chess* (1900).

Master

An imprecise term for a strong player.
FIDE titles like International Grandmaster, International Master and FIDE Master give more precise descriptions.

Matanovic, Aleksandar

[*May 23 1930- *]
Yugoslav GM (1955) who is inextricably linked with the development of
chess in post-war Yugoslavia. He com-

peted in some 16 Yugoslav Championships winning in 1962 (with Minic), in
1969 and in 1978. He played in 4
interzonals but never made it to the
Candidates. He was on 11 Yugoslav
Olympiad teams during 1954–78, scoring 72% on 2nd board in 1956. His best
results are equal 1st at Titovo Uzice
1966 and equal 1st at Vratsa 1975.
More recently he was equal 1st in the
1983 London swiss and 4th at Graz
1984 (IX).

Matanovic is a fine positional player,
but he lacks the will necessary for world
class results. Recently he has concentrated his effort on *The Encyclopaedia of
Chess Openings* (5 volumes, 1974–79)
and on the popular and useful *Informators* (1966–). He is also co-chairman of
FIDE's commission on publications
(CHIPS).

Match

A contest between two players as
distinct from a tournament where there
are more than two. The first significant
match was the set of games between
La Bourdonnais and McDonnell in
1834.

There was some debate about tournament winners versus match champions.
Lasker won the world title in a match
(1894). Tarrasch won the tournament at
Ostend (1907) and claimed to be the
world tournament champion. When
Lasker beat Tarrasch in their 1908 match
it became accepted wisdom that the true
measure of strength is a head to head
match.

Kasparov, World Champion by
match victories over Karpov, won the
1989 World Cup, which is in effect the
tournament world championship.

Match Tournament

A tournament where players play individual matches with all of the other
players (e.g. Moscow/The Hague
1948 or St Petersburg 1895/96). These

matches are usually of 4 or more games. When they are of only 2 games, it is just called a double round tournament (e.g. AVRO 1938 or London 1899).

Mathematics and Chess

There is a clear connection between the kind of minds that are attracted to chess and those drawn to mathematics. There is the obvious ability to calculate in one's head, plus the less clear geometric harmony and intuition. Creativity using mental processes is a deeply satisfying pleasure. Nevertheless not every mathematician is a chess player and certainly not every chess player is a mathematician.

To create at chess requires only knowledge of the rules plus a little experience. To create new mathematics requires years of study and thus it often happens that students of mathematics transfer over to chess because they can start creating immediately, instead of learning about topology, group theory and Lebesque integration before they even arrive at the frontiers of mathematical knowledge. These transfer students abandon their mathematical studies and devote themselves to chess. Réti did exactly that, and learnt how financially insecure a chessmaster's lot can be. Their pension plans are especially minuscule.

On the other hand many mathematicians turn away from their initial interest in chess because of its struggle and the need to mentally vanquish and crush a human opponent. They are prepared to struggle with the unknown in order to wrest a new theorem from the darkness of ignorance, but they retreat in horror from intellectually beating up some other human being.

In addition to Réti, many other mathematical minds did turn to chess. Adolf Anderssen taught mathematics at the junior college level and Euwe taught mathematics at the university level. Keres was well trained in mathematics.

Nunn was a professional mathematician before turning full-time to chess. The greatest multi-talent was Lasker. Not only was he the greatest chess player of his day, but he produced some significant, new mathematical ideas—ideas that are used to this day in abstract algebra.

Creative mathematicians do not have much time for chess, but another reason for playing infrequently is that chess is too much like mathematics and thus they get no recreational relief from this beloved hobby.

Mating Net

A configuration where the king is in the midst of the battle and there are mating threats in the air.

Mating Sacrifice

The sacrifice of material to achieve mate. For example:

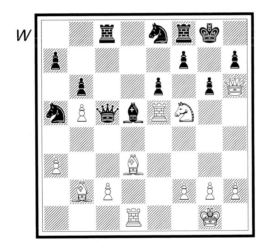

Spielmann–Honlinger, Vienna 1929
1 ♘e7+ ♕xe7 2 ♕xh7+ ♔xh7 3 ♖h5+ ♔g8 4 ♖h8 mate.

Matthews, Robin C.O.

[June 16 1927–]
British leader in mate in 3 problems who wrote *Chess Problems: Introduction to an Art* (with M. Lipton and J. Rice) 1963.

White to move and mate in 3 (1957)
1 b4 threatening 2 ♗xb1 and 3 ♖a3++ 1 ... ♗b6 2 ♖d5 ♗xd5 3 ♘b5 or 2 ... ♖xd5 3 ♘e4 1 ... ♗c5 2 ♖b7 1 ... ♖bxb5 2 ♕d5 1 ... ♗b7 2 ♖c5 ♗xc5 3 ♘b5 or 2 ... ♖xc5 3 ♗xd4 1 ... ♗d5 2 ♖bb6 1 ... ♖hxb5 2 ♖b6.

Mattison, Herman Karlovich

[*December 27 1894–November 16 1932*]
Latvian endgame study composer and player of IM strength who composed over sixty excellent studies. He led the Latvian team at the 1931 Olympiad and there he beat World Champion Alekhine in a rook and pawn endgame.

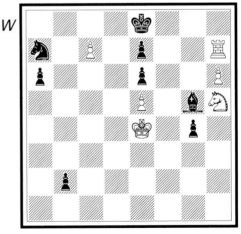

White to play and draw
1 ♖h8+ ♔f7 2 ♖b8 ♘b5 3 ♖f8+ ♔g6 4 ♘f4+ ♔h7 5 ♖h8+ ♔xh8 6 c8(♕)+ ♔h7 7 ♕c2 b1(♕) 8 ♔e3+ ♕xc2 stalemate.

Matulovic, Milan [June 10 1935–]

Yugoslav GM (1965) who had wins or equal 1sts at Belgrade 1963, Belgrade 1965, Skopje 1969, Belgrade 1969, Sarajevo 1971, Birmingham 1975, Vrbas 1976, Helsinki 1981, Vrnjacka Banja 1985 and 1986. He won the Yugoslav Championship in 1965 and 1967, played on 5 Yugoslav Olympiad teams during 1964–72, and played in the 1970 USSR vs Rest of the World match, losing $1\frac{1}{2}$–$2\frac{1}{2}$ to Botvinnik.

He was never a Candidate, but he will be remembered for his work on opening theory, for his extravagant and sometimes antisocial behaviour and for the famous incident at the 1967 interzonal when he made a blunder against Bilek, said J'adoube (I adjust) and took his move back, eventually drawing the game. He is sometimes referred to as J'adoubovic.

Matulovic has a clear, forceful style but it leaves little room for imagination.

Max Lange Attack

1e4 e5 2♘f3 ♘c6 3♗c4 ♘f6 4d4 ed 5 0-0 ♗c5 6e5

This dangerous attack was analysed by Max Lange in the 1854 *Deutsche Schachzeitung*. Black has many resources, but must tread carefully to avoid the pitfalls.

Mecking, Henrique da Costa

[February 2 1952–]
Brazilian GM (1972) who made his mark at an early age, winning the Brazilian Championship in 1965 and 1967. He was 1st at Vrsac 1971 and 1st at the 1973 interzonal (Petropolis). This qualified him for the 1974 Candidates, where he lost his first match $+1=9-3$ to Korchnoi.

He was equal 2nd at Las Palmas 1975, equal 2nd at Manila 1975 and 1st at the 1976 interzonal (Manila). Thus he again became a Candidate, where in 1977, he lost his first match $+0=11-1$ to Polugayevsky. In spite of these setbacks Mecking was now in the world top ten

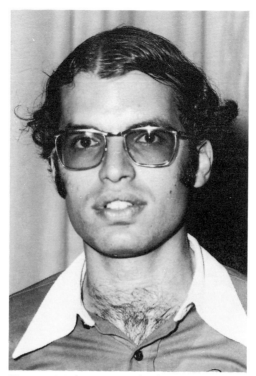

Henrique Mecking, of Brazil, whose career was sadly cut short by a debilitating illness.

and great things were expected of this 25 year old star.

In 1979 Mecking took ill with Myasthenia—a weakness of the muscles—and he had to give up playing competitively.

Mednis, Edmar John

[March 22 1937–]
Latvian-born US GM (1980) and author who wrote *How to beat Bobby Fischer* (1974) and *Practical Endgame Lessons* (1979). He was on the 1962 US Olympiad team, was equal 3rd in the 1961/62 US Championship, 3rd at Houston 1974, equal 4th at New York 1980 (IX) and equal 1st at Puerto Rico 1984 (v).

Meduna Eduard [September 11 1950–]

Czech GM (1987) who was equal 1st at Prague 1984 (VII), equal 1st at Trnava 1986 (VIII) and 1st at Debrecen 1987 (VIII).

Menchik, Vera Francevna

[February 16 1906–June 27 1944]

Women's World Champion 1927–1944. Russian-born Czech/English player who won the women's world title in 1927, 1930, 1931, 1933, 1935, 1937 and 1939 and beat her main rival Sonja Graf of Germany in 1934 ($+3-1$) and again in 1937 ($+9=5-2$). In the seven title tournaments Menchik scored $+78=4-1$ and proved her immense superiority over all other women players.

She did play in men's tournaments and had some fine wins (over Euwe, Reshevsky, and Sultan Khan for example, all members of the so-called Vera Menchik club), but she achieved only modest overall results. Perhaps her best result was 3rd at Maribor 1934, ahead of Spielmann. She beat Mieses $+4=5-1$ in 1942 (although he was 77 by then)

Vera Menchik, the first Women's World Champion, who utterly dominated women's chess before the Second World War.

She was killed by a V1 bomb in London, together with her mother and sister.

Mephisto

Chess automaton created by Charles Godfrey Gumpel. It took Gumpel some 6 or 7 years to complete and was first exhibited at his Leicester Square home in 1878.

The figure was dressed in red velvet trimmed with black. The face was that of a conventional stage Mephistopheles, with a shrewd, but not malevolent appearance. The head was close shaven and surmounted by a pink hat with a black border and decorated with two large feathers. The hands, the left of which wore a black kid glove, were slim and well shaped, as was the torso. The feet were crossed, one a neatly proportioned human foot, the other a cloven hoof. The figure sat behind an ordinary chess table and, since there was no cabinet and viewers were allowed to examine Mephisto even during play, it was evident that, for the first time, here was a chess automaton that could not possible conceal within itself a human player. Almost certainly, the mechanism was operated electrically.

Mephisto had but one operator, Isidor Gunsberg, and with his help it became the first automaton in history to win a tournament—the Counties Chess Association Handicap, played in London in 1878. Gunsberg also acted as editor of a chess column in the London periodical *Knowledge*, from 1881 until 1890, under the guise of Mephisto.

Mephisto's playing career ended at the Paris Exposition of 1889 and its subsequent whereabouts are unknown. The name, however, lives on as a modern brand of chess computer.

See Automatons, Ajeeb, The Turk.

See The English Devil by K. Whyld in the *British Chess Magazine*, July 1977.

Meran

See Slav Defence.

Mestel, Andrew Jonathan

[*March 13 1957– *]
English GM (1982) who won the World Cadet (under 18) Championship in 1974 and the British Championship in 1976, 1983 and 1988. He has played on several English Olympiad teams during 1976–88. His best international results were equal 2nd at Esbjerg 1984 (X) and 3rd at Hastings 1983/84 (XI).

Middlegame

The part of the game that follows the opening phase. It is the most difficult and the most beautiful part, where a lively imagination has great opportunity to create wonderful combinations.

Mieses, Jacques (Jakob)

[*February 27 1865–February 23 1954*]
German–Jewish GM (1950) who played sharp and brilliant but uneven chess, who chose risky openings (Vienna Gambit, Centre Counter and Danish Gambit), won 12 brilliancy prizes, but never made it into the top ten. His best results were 1st at Vienna 1907 and equal 3rd at Ostend 1907. He lost matches to most of the best players of his day: Lasker, Tarrasch, Rubinstein, Marshall and Teichmann. He did draw +6=2−6 with Janowski in 1895.

Mieses wrote a supplement to Bilguer's *Handbuch* in 1921, revised the 'little' Dufresne, published several primers and wrote *Instructive Positions from Master Chess* in 1938. He organized and reported on chess events. In particular, he ran San Sebastian 1911 and introduced the idea that players should receive travelling and living expenses—something accepted as normal in the 1980s.

He came to live in England in 1938 to escape the Nazis. At his death he was planning a major work to be called *More than 70 years in International Chess*. He was from a well-to-do family and acquired the manners, polish and education of a gentleman. He was a *bon-vivant*, a gourmet, a debonair and witty conversationalist with a fine sense of humour.

When someone addressed him as Mister Myseas he identified himself as Meister Mieses. When, at about 80, he beat an opponent who was 82 or 83, he stood up (shakily) and shouted 'Youth Will Triumph'.

Mikenas, Vladas Ivanovich

[*April 17 1910– *]
Estonian-born Lithuanian IM (1950) and honorary GM (1987) who was 4th at Kemeri 1939 and equal 1st at Lublin 1971. He played in 9 USSR Championships during 1940–70 and was on 5 Lithuanian Olympiad teams during 1931–9. His dashing and sharp style makes his games exciting to study.

Mikhalchishin, Adrian Bogdanovich

[*November 18 1954– *]
USSR GM (1978) who was equal 1st at Nikolaev 1983 (VII) and 2nd at Hastings 1985/86 (IX). He played in 4 USSR Championships during 1978–85 but scored only $31\frac{1}{2}$–$38\frac{1}{2}$.

Milan

Italy's industrial centre and home of the La Scala opera, which staged a strong (Category XIV) tournament with 6 of the world top 9 in 1975 (missing Korchnoi, Polugayevsky and Spassky). There was a preliminary round robin (won by Portisch) followed by playoffs among the top 4 finishers. Young Karpov beat Portisch in the final to carry off first prize.

Miles, Anthony John [*April 23 1955– *]

English GM (1976) who was the World Junior Champion in 1974 and the first Englishman to earn the GM title since FIDE titles were introduced in 1950. Miles began studying mathematics at Sheffield University, became a chess

		1	2	3	4	5	6	7	8	9	10	11	12	
1	Portisch	–	½	½	½	½	½	1	½	0	1	1	1	7
2	Karpov	½	–	½	1	½	½	½	1	0	1	½	½	6½
	Petrosian	½	½	–	½	½	½	½	½	½	1	1	½	6½
	Ljubojevic	½	0	½	–	½	1	½	0	1	½	1	1	6½
5	Smejkal	½	½	½	½	–	½	1	½	½	0	1	½	6
6	Tal	½	½	½	0	½	–	0	0	1	½	1	1	5½
	Browne	0	½	½	½	0	1	–	½	½	½	½	1	5½
8	Unzicker	½	0	½	1	½	1	½	–	½	0	0	½	5
	Andersson	1	1	½	0	½	0	½	½	–	0	0	1	5
	Gligoric	0	0	0	½	1	½	½	1	1	–	0	½	5
	Larsen	0	½	0	0	0	0	½	1	1	1	–	1	5
12	Mariotti	0	½	½	0	½	0	0	½	0	½	0	–	2½

Semi-finals:

Karpov	½	½	½	½ = 2
Petrosian	½	½	½	½ = 2
Portisch	½	½	1	½ = 2½
Ljubojevic	½	½	0	½ = 1½

3rd/4th:

Petrosian	1	½	½	½	0	½ = 3
Ljubojevic	0	½	½	½	1	½ = 3

Final:

Karpov	½	1	½	½	½	½ = 3½
Portisch	½	0	½	½	½	½ = 2½

The first British Grandmaster, Tony Miles. His success paved the way for the dramatic rise of English strength in the 1980s.

professional and Sheffield awarded him an honorary MA (1975) for his chess achievements.

He was 2nd at Tilburg 1977 (XIV) and equal 3rd at Tilburg 1978 (XIV) and he won or was equal 1st at Amsterdam 1976 and 1977, Biel 1977, London 1980, Las Palmas 1980, Vrbas 1980 and Baden Baden 1981. He won the British Championship in 1982 and drew a match +4=2−4 vs Hort in 1983.

Then came a series of superb victories: 1st at Tilburg 1984 (XIV), equal 1st at Portoroz 1985 (XII) and equal 1st with Hübner and Korchnoi at the double-round Tilburg 1985 (XV). In May 1986 Miles played a short match with Kasparov and was crushed +0=1−5. Since then his achievement level went

down: 5th at Wijk aan Zee 87 (XIII), 4th at Ter Apel 1987 (XI) and 11th at San Francisco 1987 (X).

Miles is a tough competitor with an aggressive and dangerous style. He led the English team at the 1984 Olympiad and played 9th board in the 1984 USSR vs Rest of the World match. He has represented the USA since 1987.

Milic, Borislav

[October 20 1925–May 28 1986] Yugoslav GM (1977) who was one of the Yugoslav stars immediately after the war. He played in some 15 Yugoslav Championships and was on the Yugoslav Olympiad team in 1952 and 1956. His best result was 1st at Vienna 1951. From 1977 on, he was General Secretary of the Yugoslav Chess Federation.

Milner-Barry, Sir Philip Stuart

[September 20 1906–] English player of IM strength who is known for his variation in the Nimzo-Indian Defence: 1 d4 ♘f6 2 c4 e6 3 ♘c3 ♗b4 4 ♕c2 ♘c6. He played on four English Olympiad teams during 1937–56, was chess correspondent for *The Times* and came 2nd at Hastings 1953.

He was the true chess amateur in that he pursued a full-time career in the British Civil Service. He broke codes during the Second World War and later, became Under-Secretary of the Treasury.

Milos, Gilberto

[October 30 1963–] Brazilian GM (1988) who was 1st at Santiago 1987 (VI) and equal 1st at Buenos Aires 1988 (VIII). He played on the Brazilian Olympiad teams of 1984, 1986, and 1988.

Minckwitz, Johannes

[April 11 1843–May 20 1901] German author and player of IM strength who was involved in all things connected with chess. He edited the *Deutsche Schachzeitung* (1865–76 and 1897–86), the chess column in the *Leipziger Illustriertien Zeitung* (1881–99), several tournament books, and wrote *Das ABC des Schachspiels* (1879), *Humor en Schachspiel* (1885) and *Der Kleine Schachkönig* (1888). In play, he was 2nd at Barmen 1869, equal 1st at Krefeld 1871 and 2nd at Graz 1880.

On May 15, in a fit of despondency, he threw himself under an electric train, lost both of his arms and died five days later.

Miniature
See Brevity

Minor Exchange
See Exchange

Minor Pieces
The bishop and knight, in contrast to the queen and rook, the major pieces.

Minority Attack
An attack by 2 or 3 pawns against 3 or 4 pawns respectively with the idea of breaking up the enemy pawn structure and leaving him with weak isolated or backward pawns. It occurs most frequently in the Exchange Variation of the Queen's Gambit. It was pioneered by Pillsbury and used by Steinitz, and is now a standard plan. A good example is the following position, reached after 23 moves in Najdorf–Eliskases, Mar del Plata 1947:

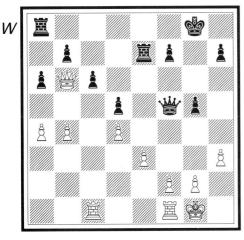

1 b5 ab 2 ab cb (not 2 ... ♖c8 3 bc ♕e6 4 cb) 3 ♖c5 ♔g7 4 ♕xb5 and Black's queenside has been torn up and he has two weak isolated pawns. White in fact went on to win.

Mobility
The ability to move one's pieces to any important part of the chessboard, easily and quickly. Mobility is often obtained by controlling more space and/or controlling the centre. With mobility one can launch successful attacks or at least focus more power on some critical square or battlefield.

Modena School
Ercole del Rio, Lolli and Ponziani were the leaders of 18th century chess life in Modena—an Italian town near Bologna. They stressed quick development but practised free castling and underestimated the importance of a strong pawn centre.

Modern Chess Openings (MCO)
An opening manual that first appeared in 1911 with clear and well organized columns of opening variations. It was co-authored by R. C. Griffith (1872–1955) and J. H. White (1880–1920). There were new editions in 1913, 1916, 1925 and 1932. It gradually replaced Bilguer's *Handbuch* and by 1939 Fine's 6th edition was the leading opening authority. There were post-war editions in 1946, 1952, 1957 and the 10th edition by 1965 by Larry Evans was its high water mark. Then it became supplanted (for professional players) by Euwe's *Archives*, the *Informators* and Matanovic's *Encyclopedia of Chess Openings* because a single volume could no longer hold the large amount of opening knowledge. The 11th edition was in 1972, the 12th in 1982.

See also *Batsford Chess Openings*.

Mohr, Stefan [*October 22 1967– *]
West German GM (1989) who was equal 3rd at Budapest 1988 (X).

Mokry, Karel [*February 7 1959– *]
Czech GM (1984) who was 1st at Reggio Emilia 1984 (IX), equal 1st at Trnava 1984 (VIII) and 1st at Trnava 1988 (VIII). He played on the 1984 (board 5) and 1986 (board 4) Czech Olympiad teams.

Moltke, Helmuth Karl Bernhard, Count von [*1800–1891*]
Prussian field marshal and commander in chief in the Franco Prussian war of 1870–1, who was a brilliant strategist and a chess player. He believed that a clever chess player would make an equally capable strategist in the field.

Montaigne, Michael-Eyguem de [*February 28 1533–September 13 1592*]
Great French essayist, lawyer, mayor of Bordeaux and chess player.

Monte Carlo
Beautiful playground of the rich and famous, and gambling centre for the elite, which staged 4 tournaments at the beginning of the century. In 1901 (February), Janowski ($10\frac{1}{4}$) won ahead of Schlechter ($9\frac{1}{2}$). Draws were replayed once—if both games were drawn each player received $\frac{1}{2}$, but if the second game was decisive, the winner got $\frac{3}{4}$ and the loser $\frac{1}{4}$.

In 1902 (February March) Maroczy ($14\frac{3}{4}$) edged out Pillsbury (14).

In 1903 the draw replayment was dropped. Tarrasch (20) won ahead of Maroczy (19) and Pillsbury ($18\frac{1}{2}$). In 1904 Maroczy ($7\frac{1}{2}$) beat out Schlechter (7) and Marshall ($6\frac{1}{2}$) and at the end of the Masters tournament, a Rice Gambit tournament was won by Marshall (6) and Swiderski (6).

Some 63 years later major tournaments returned to Monte Carlo. In 1967 Fischer (7) won ahead of Smyslov ($6\frac{1}{2}$), Geller (6) and Larsen (6). In 1968 Larsen completed his famous series of 5 consecutive major victories during 1967/68, when he (9½) came ahead of Botvinnik (9), Smyslov (8½) and Hort (8½).

Monticelli, Mario [*March 16 1902– *] Italian IM (1950) and honorary GM (1985) who was on five Italian Olympiad teams during 1927 to 1935. He won the Italian Championship three times (1929, 1934 and 1939) and was equal 1st at Budapest 1926 and equal 1st at Milan 1938. He is a journalist by profession.

Montpellier
Charming city in the south of France, which staged the 1985 Candidates tournament (XIV). Kasparov and Karpov were busy playing a match for the world title but everyone else was at Montpellier (except Hübner and Ljubojevic). The arrangement was for the top 4 finishers to hold play-off matches with the winner to meet the loser of Kasparov–Karpov.

With 2 rounds to go Tal (8) and Yusupov (8) led Sokolov (7½) Timman (7½) Vaganian (7) and Spassky (7). Tal met tail-enders Seirawan and Spraggett but he lost to Seirawan and only drew with Spraggett. Vaganian closed with 2 wins (over Spraggett and Nogueiras) while Sokolov beat Ribli and drew with Timman. Yusupov, Timman and Spassky each scored 2 draws. Thus Yusupov, Vaganian and Sokolov went into the matches and Tal played Timman for the fourth spot. This match was drawn +1 =4−1 but Timman won on tie break. Sokolov beat Vaganian (+4=4−0) and in the final beat Yusupov (+4=7−3) but lost +0=7−4 to Karpov.

Prizes: Swiss Francs: 30 000, 22 000, 16 000, 10 000, 7000, 6000, 5000, 4000.

Montreal
Canada's cosmopolitan centre which staged the last 8 games of the Lasker–Steinitz match during May 3–26, 1894 (the first 8 were in New York and the middle 3 in Philadelphia). Then in 1979 Montreal held a super-tournament with 7 of the world top ten. Only Korchnoi (2695), Polugayevsky (2625) and Petrosian (2610) were absent—and of course Fischer (2780) who had not played for 7 years.

At halftime it was Karpov (6½) Tal (6) Portisch (6) and Ljubojevic (5½). With 2 rounds to go it was Tal (11) Karpov (10½) and Portisch (9½). Tal drew his last 2 games while Karpov beat Ljubojevic and drew with Kavalek to share first. Kavalek was involved with the organization and at half-time was dead last with 1½–7½. He had a remarkable recovery and actually won 6½–2½ the second round robin to end a respectable equal 7th.

Brilliancy prizes: 1st Tal 1, Spassky 0, round 10; 2nd Larsen 1, Karpov 0, round 12.

Tournament book by Tal, Chepizhny and Roshal with fine annotations to about half of the games.

Spassky–Tal
1 d4 ♘f6 2 c4 e6 3 ♘f3 b6 4 e3 ♗b7 5 ♗d3 d5 6 b3 ♗d6 7 0-0 0-0 8 ♗b2 ♘bd7 9 ♘bd2 ♕e7 10 ♖c1 ♖ad8 11 ♕c2 c5 12 cd ed 13 dc? bc 14 ♕c3 ♖fe8 15 ♖fd1 d4 16 ed cd 17 ♕a5 ♘e5 18 ♘xe5 ♗xe5 19 ♘c4 ♖d5 20 ♕d2 (see diagram over page) 20 ... ♗xh2+ 21 ♔xh2 ♖h5+! 22 ♔g1 ♘g4 23 Resigns

	Montpellier 1985	1	2	3	4	5	6	7	8	9	10	11	12	13	14	15	16	
1	Yusupov	–	0	1	½	½	1	½	½	½	½	½	½	1	½	1	½	9
	Vaganian	1	–	½	0	½	0	½	½	½	½	½	1	½	1	1	1	9
	Sokolov	0	½	–	½	½	0	½	1	½	½	½	1	1	1	½	1	9
4	Timman	½	1	½	–	½	1	½	½	½	1	1	0	½	½	½	0	8½
	Tal	½	½	½	½	–	½	½	½	1	0	½	½	1	1	½	½	8½
6	Spassky	0	1	1	0	½	–	½	½	½	1	½	½	½	½	1	0	8
	Belyavsky	½	½	½	½	½	½	–	0	½	½	1	½	½	½	½	1	8
8	Smyslov	½	½	0	½	½	½	1	–	½	½	½	½	½	½	0	1	7½
	Chernin	½	½	½	½	0	½	½	½	–	½	½	½	½	½	½	1	7½
10	Seirawan	½	½	½	0	1	0	½	½	½	–	1	½	½	0	½	½	7
	Short	½	½	½	0	½	½	0	½	½	0	–	1	1	½	½	½	7
	Portisch	½	0	0	1	½	½	½	½	½	½	0	–	0	1	½	1	7
13	Ribli	0	½	0	½	0	½	½	½	½	½	0	1	–	½	1	½	6½
	Korchnoi	½	0	0	½	0	½	½	½	½	1	½	0	½	–	1	½	6½
15	Nogueiras	0	0	½	½	½	0	½	1	½	½	½	½	0	0	–	1	6
16	Spraggett	½	0	0	1	½	1	0	0	0	½	½	0	½	½	0	–	5

	1		2		3		4		5		6		7		8		9		10		
1 Tal	—	—	½	½	½	1	½	½	½	½	1	1	½	1	1	½	½	½	1	½	12
2 Karpov	½	½	—	—	½	½	1	1	1	1	1	1	½	½	1	½	½	½	½	0	12
3 Portisch	½	0	½	½	—	—	½	½	½	½	½	½	1	½	½	½	1	½	1	1	10½
4 Ljubojevic	½	½	0	0	½	½	—	—	½	½	½	0	½	½	1	0	1	1	1	½	9
5 Timman	½	½	0	0	½	½	½	½	—	—	½	½	½	½	½	0	½	1	1	½	8½
6 Spassky	0	0	0	0	½	½	½	1	½	½	—	—	½	1	1	½	½	½	0	1	8½
7 Hübner	½	0	½	½	0	½	½	½	½	½	½	0	—	—	1	0	½	½	1	½	8
8 Kavalek	0	½	0	½	½	½	0	1	½	1	0	½	0	1	—	—	½	½	0	1	8
9 Hort	½	½	½	½	0	½	0	0	½	0	½	½	½	½	½	½	—	—	1	1	8
10 Larsen	0	½	½	1	0	0	0	½	0	½	1	0	0	½	1	0	0	0	—	—	5½

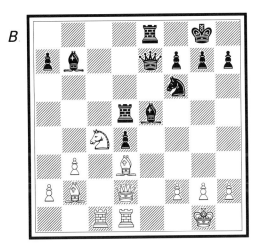

B

Moralities

See Cessolis.

Morovic Fernandez, Ivan

[*March 24 1963–*] Chilean GM (1986) who is the first and only Chilean GM. He was equal 2nd at Vrsac 1985 (X) and equal 1st at Las Palmas 1987 (IX). He won the Chilean Championship in 1981 and has played on the Chilean Olympiad teams in 1984, 1986 and 1988. In 1988 he lost a match +0 = 4 − 2 to Korchnoi.

Morphy, Paul Charles

[*June 22 1837–July 10 1884*] US Champion who was one of the greatest players that ever lived. He was further ahead of his contemporaries than any other player in history. By 1858 he was clearly the best player in the world. Morphy's chess career was extremely short. He learnt the game at about age 10, beat the visiting GM Löwenthal +1 = 1 in 1850, won the American Chess Congress title in 1857, ahead of Paulsen, went to Europe in 1858 and beat Löwenthal +9 = 2 − 3, Harrwitz +5 = 1 − 2 and Anderssen +7 = 2 − 2. He tried to arrange a match with Staunton but the English champion claimed he was too busy to play. In less serious matches Morphy beat Mongredien +7 = 1 − 0 and John Owen (alias Alter) +5 = 2 − 0 while spotting Owen pawn and move.

In 1859 Morphy issued an open challenge to any player in the world, offering pawn and move odds, for serious stakes. No one accepted the challenge though Baron von der Lasa seriously considered it. Lasa felt that at age 41, he was too old. Thus by 1860, Paul Morphy decided to give up competitive chess. This amazing decision not only deprived the world of wonderful games that might have been (against Steinitz, Zukertort and Kolisch for example), but set a tone for future American stars like Fischer and, to a lesser degree. Fine. Morphy became a legend in his own time, similar to Fischer 115 years later.

In the recent Keene and Divinsky book, Morphy places 11th on the all-time list of greats, but this conclusion is somewhat unclear because Morphy played too few games to allow anyone to get a solid mathematical grip on his strength.

Morphy had a prodigious memory, knew the openings thoroughly and was an excellent tactician. He sensed that he must not start an attack until he had completed his development and this set him above his contemporaries. As

Paul Morphy, who swept all before him and then, suddenly, retired. Over a century later, his fellow countryman Bobby Fischer similarly bowed out whilst at the very top.

Lasker put it, his attacks were a natural development of forces which crushed his opponent with cumulative effect.

While playing, Morphy stared constantly at the board, and only when he felt certain of victory did he look up.

Morphy was born in New Orleans to a Spanish–Irish father and a French–Creole mother. He was slim, five feet four inches in height and had hands and feet that were unusually small. His face was like that of a teenage girl. He took a law degree from the University of Louisiana in 1857, spoke four languages and was quite musical.

His last 25 years were a sad conclusion to the flowering prospects that surrounded him in 1859. He inherited a large estate (some $140 000), he never practised law, he never married, his mental state began to deteriorate, he felt persecuted, he believed people were trying to poison him, he sued his brother-in-law (the executor of his father's estate) and lost, he was almost put into an asylum and he was cared for by his mother and sister until he died (of a brain haemorrhage). He did go regularly to the opera but shunned all social intercourse.

See *Paul Morphy*, by Max Lange, translated by Ernest Falkbeer (1859), *Paul Morphy*, by J. J. Löwenthal (1860), *Paul Morphy, his later life* by C. A. Buck (1902), *Paul Morphy* by Geza Maroczy (1909), *Morphy's Games of Chess* by Philip W. Sergeant (1915), *The Chess Players* by Frances Parkinson Keyes (1960), *Paul Morphy* by D. Lawson (1976).

Morphy–Harrwitz
Match 1858
1 e4 e5 2 ♘f3 d6 3 d4 ed 4 ♕xd4 ♘c6 5 ♗b5 ♗d7 6 ♗xc6 ♗xc6 7 ♗g5 f6 8 ♗h6 ♘h6 9 ♘c3 ♕d7 10 0-0 ♗e7 11 ♖ad1 0-0 12 ♕c4+ ♖f7 13 ♘d4 ♘g4 14 h3 ♘e5 15 ♕e2 g5 16 ♗g3 ♖g7 17 ♘f5 ♗g6 18 f4 gf 19 ♖xf4 ♔h8 20 ♖h4 ♗f8 21 ♗xe5 fe 22 ♖f1

♕e6 23 ♘b5 ♕g8 24 ♖f2 a6 25 ♘xc7 ♖c8 26 ♘d5 ♗xd5 27 ed ♖c7 28 c4 ♗e7 29 ♖h5 ♕e8

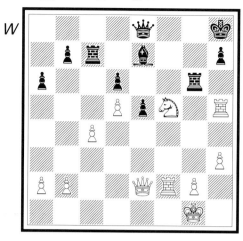

30 c5 ♖xc5 31 ♖xh7+ ♔xh7 32 ♕h5+ ♔g8 33 ♘xe7+ ♔g7 34 ♘f5+ ♔g8 35 ♘xd6 Resigns

Morry, William Ritson
[*September 5 1910– *]
English chess organizer who conceived the idea of a World Junior Championship (for under 20 year olds) and held the first World Junior in Birmingham 1951.

Mortimer, James
[*April 2 1833–February 24 1911*]
American player, journalist and dramatist who was, for a time, in the US diplomatic service. In 1855 he was in Paris and was later decorated by Napoleon III. By 1864 he was secretary to the *Cercle des Échecs* and editor of *La Palamède*. He came to England in 1870, had his plays produced and played in tournaments. His dramas fared better than his tournament play. He came last at Ostend 1907 but he did beat Tartakower and Blackburne. While reporting on San Sebastian 1911, he died in Spain.

Moscow
The heart of the Russian empire had held championships for both Tsarist Russia (1899 and 1901) and the USSR (1920 and 1924) but it did not hold an

international tournament until 1925 when the Soviet Union decided to give their young players the chance to meet the world chess elite. Capablanca, Lasker, Rubinstein, Réti and Marshall came but Alekhine, Vidmar, Bernstein and Euwe were not there. The tournament turned out to be Bogoljubow's great triumph. He (15½) came ahead of Lasker (14) Capablanca (13½) and Marshall (12½). The veteran Lasker had again come out ahead of World Champion Capablanca, and though 56, Lasker seemed indestructible. The USSR players (Romanovsky (11½), Ilyin-Genevsky (10½) and Bohatirchuk (10)) acquitted themselves honourably, coming ahead of Rubinstein (9½) and Spielmann (9½).

In 1935 Lasker and Capablanca again came to Moscow to meet the best of the Russians, this time led by their young champion Botvinnik. Flohr (13) and Botvinnik (13) were equal 1st but the star of the tournament was 66 year old Lasker (12½) who was undefeated, came 3rd, tied for the brilliancy prize for his win over Capablanca and once again came ahead of his great rival Capablanca (12). It is curious that Capablanca had given a simultaneous exhibition in Moscow, back in 1925, and lost a game to the 14 year old Botvinnik.

In 1936 another strong tournament found Capablanca (13) ahead of Botvinnik (12) with Flohr (9½) a distant 3rd. Lasker (8) at 67½ was equal 2nd at the halfway mark but his age finally began to tell and he ended up 6th—the first time he ever came behind Capablanca in a tournament.

In the XIIth USSR Championship (1940), Bondarevsky (13½) and Lilienthal (13½) were equal 1st, ahead of Smyslov (13), Keres (12), Boleslavsky (11½) and Botvinnik (11½). Since Botvinnik had won the title in 1931, 1933 and 1939, since he had such fine results at Nottingham 1936 and AVRO 1938, and since he was negotiating for a world title match with Alekhine, he was able to impose his will and force a so-called Absolute Championship with the top 6 finishers from the XIIth Championship. This took place in 1941 in Leningrad (March 23–April 6) and Moscow (April 11–April 29). Though this was not an international tournament, it was the strongest (Category XV) tournament held in Moscow up to that time. It was certainly a young man's tournament—no one was over 29.

One of the most exciting games was:

Smyslov–Botvinnik

1 e4 e5 2 ♘f3 ♘c6 3 ♗b5 a6 4 ♗a4 ♘f6 5 d3 d6 6 c3 ♗e7 7 0-0 0-0 8 ♖e1 b5 9 ♗c2 d5 10 ♘bd2 de 11 de♗e6 12 h3 h6 13 ♘h2 ♘h7 14 ♘g4 ♗g5 15 ♕e2 ♕d6 16 ♘e3 ♖fd8 17 ♘f3 ♗xe3 18 ♕xe3 ♕e7 19 ♘h2 ♘f8 20 ♕f3 ♖d7 21 ♘f1 ♘h7 22 ♘g3 ♖ae8 23 ♘f5 ♕f6 24 g4 ♘e7 25 ♕g3 ♗c4 26 f3 ♗d3 27 ♗b3 c5 28 ♗e3 c4 29 ♗d1 ♘g5 30 h4 ♘e6 31 a4 b4 32 cb ♘f4 33 ♔h1 g5 34 b5 a5 35 ♗c5 ♘xf5 36 gf ♔h7 37 ♕g4 gh 38 ♖g1 h5 39 ♕g5 ♕xg5 40 ♖xg5 f6 41 ♖g1 ♘h3 42 ♖e1 ♖g8 43 ♖a2! ♗b1 44 ♖a1 ♗d3 45 ♖a2 ♘f4 46 b4 ♖c8 47 b6 ♖b7 48 ♗e3 ab 49 a5 b3 50 ♖a3? (50 ♖b2 holds the game) b2 51 ♗a4 c3 52 ♖b3 ♘e2 53 ♗b5 ♗xb5 54 ♖xb5 ♘d4 55 ♗xd4 ed 56 a6 (see diagram) 56 ... ♖xb6! 57 ♖xb6 d3 58 ♖g1 d2 59 ♖xf6 ♖c7 60 ♖fg6 d1(♕) 61 Resigns ('One of the most original endings in my chess career'—Botvinnik)

B

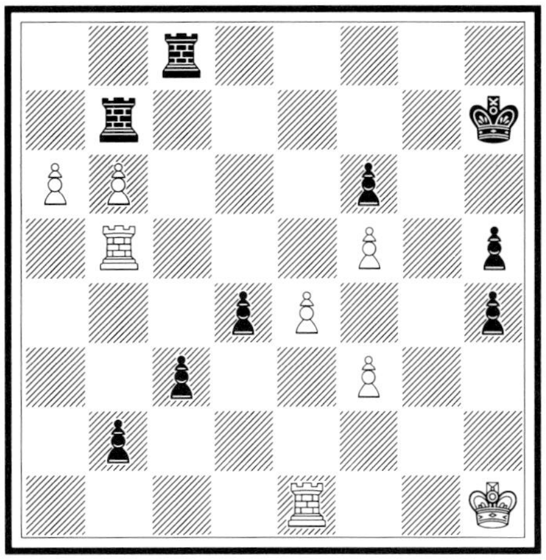

When Alekhine died in 1946 he left the World Championship vacant. Fide organized a world championship tournament and invited the 6 greatest players of the day: Keres, Botvinnik, Reshevsky, Smyslov, Euwe and Fine. Fine declined the invitation—it is said that his final exams for the PhD in psychology unfortunately coincided with the tournament dates. FIDE went ahead with the 5 who accepted, though it might well have added Najdorf. In any case, in 1948 the strongest chess tournament (XVII) of all time (up to 1990) took place, first at the Hague and then at Moscow.

Euwe was sadly below his best. Keres played well except against Botvinnik. Smyslov justified his inclusion but Reshevsky disappointed his fans. Botvinnik played like a World Champion and ran away with the tournament. He would have preferred to have beaten Alekhine in a match, but this was the next best thing.

Time Limit: 40 moves in 2½ hours and than 16 moves per hour.

Prizes: $5000, $3000, $2000, $1500, $1000.

Tournament books: by Golombek with in-depth annotations; by Horowitz and Kmoch with fine annotations.

From 1948–72 Soviet players dominated the chess world and Moscow became the chess centre of the world. There were many wonderful tournaments and a few were of top strength:

1956 Alekhine Memorial.
The world top two appropriately tied for 1st.

1964 Zonal.
This was an all-Russian affair and did not have Petrosian or Botvinnik but it was almost a Category XVI event, and launched Spassky on his road to the world title.

1967 50th Jubilee of the Russian revolution.
Stein showed star quality and Bobotsov played above his strength but World Champion Petrosian had to settle for equal 9th and challenger Spassky was only equal 6th.

1971 Alekhine Memorial.
Karpov made his mark, veteran Smyslov had an excellent 3rd while World Champion Spassky was again equal 6th.

Leningrad/Moscow 1941 USSR Absolute Championship

		1				2				3				4				5				6				
1	Botvinnik	–	–	–	–	1	½	½	½	1	½	1	½	1	½	1	½	1	½	0	1	0	1	½	1	13½
2	Keres	0	½	½	½	–	–	–	–	1	1	0	½	½	0	½	½	0	1	½	1	1	½	1	½	11
3	Smyslov	0	½	0	½	0	0	1	½	–	–	–	–	½	1	½	1	½	1	½	½	½	½	½	½	10
4	Boleslavsky	0	½	0	½	½	1	½	½	½	0	½	0	–	–	–	–	1	1	½	1	½	0	0	½	9
5	Lilienthal	0	½	1	0	1	0	½	0	½	0	½	½	0	0	½	0	–	–	–	–	1	½	1	1	8½
6	Boundarevsky	1	0	½	0	0	½	0	½	½	½	½	½	½	1	1	½	0	½	0	0	–	–	–	–	8

The Hague/Moscow 1948 — World Championship

		1					2					3					4					5					
1	Botvinnik	—	—	—	—	—	½	½	1	½	½	1	1	1	1	0	1	½	0	1	1	1	½	1	½	½	14
2	Smyslov	½	½	0	½	½	—	—	—	—	—	0	0	½	1	½	½	½	1	½	½	1	1	0	1	1	11
3	Keres	0	0	0	0	1	1	1	½	0	½	—	—	—	—	—	0	½	1	0	½	1	½	1	1	1	10½
	Reshevsky	0	½	1	0	0	½	½	0	½	½	1	½	0	1	½	—	—	—	—	—	1	½	½	1	1	10½
5	Euwe	0	½	0	½	½	0	0	1	0	0	0	½	0	0	0	0	½	½	0	0	—	—	—	—	—	4

Moscow 1956 — Alekhine Memorial

		1	2	3	4	5	6	7	8	9	10	11	12	13	14	15	16	
1	Botvinnik	—	½	½	½	½	1	0	½	½	1	1	1	1	1	1	1	11
	Smyslov	½	—	½	½	½	½	½	½	½	1	1	1	1	1	1	1	11
3	Taimanov	½	½	—	½	1	1	½	½	½	½	½	1	½	1	1	1	10½
4	Gligoric	½	½	½	—	0	½	½	½	1	½	½	1	1	1	1	1	10
5	Bronstein	½	½	0	1	—	½	½	½	½	½	1	½	1	½	1	1	9½
6	Najdorf	0	½	0	½	½	—	½	½	1	½	½	½	1	1	1	1	9
7	Keres	1	½	½	½	½	½	—	1	0	½	0	½	½	½	1	1	8½
	Pachman	½	½	½	½	½	½	0	—	½	½	½	½	½	1	1	1	8½
9	Unzicker	½	½	½	0	½	0	1	½	—	1	½	½	½	1	0	1	8
	Stahlberg	0	0	½	½	½	½	½	½	0	—	½	½	1	1	1	1	8
11	Szabo	0	0	½	½	0	½	1	½	½	½	—	½	½	½	0	½	6
12	Padevsky	0	0	0	0	½	½	½	½	½	½	½	—	0	½	1	½	5½
	Uhlmann	0	0	½	0	0	0	½	½	½	0	½	1	—	1	½	½	5½
14	Ciocaltea	0	0	0	0	½	0	½	0	0	0	½	½	0	—	1	½	3½
15	Sliwa	0	0	0	0	0	0	0	0	1	0	1	0	½	0	—	½	3
16	Golombek	0	0	0	0	0	0	0	0	0	0	½	½	½	½	½	—	2½

Moscow 1964 — Zonal Tournament

		1	2	3	4	5	6	7	8	9	10	11	12	13	14	
1	Spassky	—	—	½	½	½	½	0	1	½	1	1	½	0	1	7
2	Bronstein	½	½	—	—	½	½	½	½	1	0	1	½	½	½	6½
	Stein	½	½	½	½	—	—	½	½	½	1	½	1	0	½	6½
4	Kholmov	1	0	½	½	½	½	—	—	1	½	0	½	½	½	6
5	Korchnoi	½	0	0	1	½	0	0	½	—	—	½	½	1	1	5½
	Suetin	0	½	0	½	½	0	1	½	½	½	—	—	1	½	5½
7	Geller	1	0	½	½	1	½	½	½	0	0	0	½	—	—	5

Moscow 1967 — 50th Jubilee Tournament

		1	2	3	4	5	6	7	8	9	10	11	12	13	14	15	16	17	18	
1	Stein	–	½	½	½	½	1	½	½	½	1	½	½	0	1	1	1	½	1	11
2	Gipslis	½	–	½	½	½	½	½	½	½	½	½	½	1	1	½	½	½	1	10
	Bobotsov	½	½	–	½	½	½	½	½	½	½	½	½	1	1	½	½	½	1	10
	Smyslov	½	½	½	–	½	1	½	½	½	½	½	½	1	½	1	½	0	1	10
	Tal	½	½	½	½	–	0	1	½	½	0	1	½	½	½	1	1	½	1	10
6	Portisch	0	½	½	0	1	–	½	1	0	1	1	½	0	½	1	½	1	½	9½
	Bronstein	½	½	½	½	0	½	–	½	½	½	½	½	½	1	½	1	1	½	9½
	Spassky	½	½	½	½	½	0	½	–	0	½	½	1	½	½	1	½	1	1	9½
9	Geller	½	½	½	½	½	1	½	1	–	½	½	0	0	½	½	½	½	½	8½
	Keres	0	½	½	½	1	0	½	½	½	–	½	½	½	½	½	½	1	½	8½
	Petrosian	½	½	½	½	0	0	½	½	½	½	–	1	1	0	½	½	1	½	8½
	Najdorf	½	½	½	½	½	½	½	0	1	½	0	–	½	½	½	½	1	½	8½
13	Gheorghiu	1	0	0	0	½	1	½	½	1	½	0	½	–	½	½	½	½	½	8
14	Gligoric	0	0	0	½	½	½	0	½	½	½	1	½	½	–	½	1	½	½	7½
15	Bilek	0	½	½	0	0	0	½	0	½	½	½	½	½	½	–	½	½	½	6
	Filip	0	½	½	½	0	½	0	½	½	½	½	½	½	0	½	–	½	0	6
	Pachman	½	½	½	1	½	0	0	0	½	0	0	0	½	½	½	½	–	½	6
	Uhlmann	0	0	0	0	0	½	½	0	½	½	½	½	½	½	½	1	½	–	6

Moscow 1971 — Alekhine Memorial

		1	2	3	4	5	6	7	8	9	10	11	12	13	14	15	16	17	18	
1	Karpov	–	½	½	½	½	½	½	½	1	1	1	1	½	½	½	½	½	1	11
	Stein	½	–	½	½	½	½	½	½	½	1	½	½	1	½	1	½	1	1	11
3	Smyslov	½	½	–	½	1	½	½	½	½	½	½	½	½	1	1	½	1	½	10½
4	Tukmakov	½	½	½	–	½	½	½	½	½	½	1	½	½	½	½	1	1	½	10
	Petrosian	½	½	0	½	–	½	1	½	½	½	1	½	½	½	½	1	1	½	10
6	Tal	½	½	½	½	½	–	½	1	½	½	0	½	½	0	1	½	1	1	9½
	Spassky	½	½	½	½	0	½	–	½	½	½	0	1	1	1	½	½	½	1	9½
8	Byrne R	½	½	½	½	½	0	½	–	1	½	0	1	½	½	½	1	½	½	9
	Hort	0	½	½	½	½	½	½	0	–	½	1	½	½	1	½	½	½	1	9
	Bronstein	0	0	½	½	½	½	½	½	½	–	0	½	½	½	1	1	1	1	9
11	Korchnoi	0	½	½	0	0	1	1	1	0	1	–	0	1	½	0	1	½	½	8½
12	Savon	0	½	½	½	½	½	0	0	½	½	1	–	½	0	½	½	½	1	7½
	Gheorghiu	½	0	½	½	½	½	0	½	½	½	0	½	–	1	½	½	½	½	7½
	Olafsson	½	½	0	½	½	1	0	½	0	½	½	1	0	–	½	0	½	1	7½
15	Uhlmann	½	0	0	½	½	0	½	½	½	0	1	½	½	½	–	0	½	½	6½
	Balashov	½	½	½	0	0	½	½	0	½	0	0	½	½	1	1	–	0	½	6½
17	Parma	½	0	0	0	0	0	½	½	½	0	½	½	½	½	½	1	–	½	6
18	Lengyel	0	0	½	½	½	0	0	½	0	0	½	0	½	0	½	½	½	–	4½

1981 A training tournament to bring Karpov to fighting trim for his upcoming title defence against Korchnoi. Spassky, Tal, Hübner, Larsen and of course Korchnoi were not there but a fine cross section of top non-Soviet GMs were mixed with top Soviets, including young Kasparov, to make this Category XV tournament memorable. Karpov was impressive, Smyslov's equal 2nd at age 60 was a fine achievement and Kasparov gave notice of his future greatness.

One of the more interesting games was:

Polugayevsky–Torre

1 d4 d5 2 c4 c6 3 ♘f3 ♘f6 4 ♘c3 e6 5 ♗g5 dc 6 e4 b5 7 e5 h6 8 ♗h4 g5 9 ♘xg5 hg 10 ♗xg5 ♘bd7 11 ef ♗b7 12 g3 c5 13 d5 ♘b6 14 de ♕xd1+ 15 ♖xd1 ♗xh1 16 e7 a6

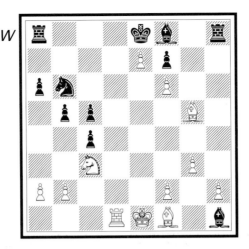

17 h4! ♗h6 18 f4 b4 19 ♖d6 ♗b8 20 ♘d1 ♗xg5 21 fg ♘d5 22 ♗xc4 ♘xe7 23 fe ♔xe7 24 ♖f6 ♖hf8 25 ♘e3 ♗e4 26 ♖xa6 ♖bd8 27 ♖f6 ♖d6 28 ♖f4 ♖d4 29 h5 ♗d3 30 ♘d5+ ♔d6 31 ♖xd4 cd 32 ♗b3 ♗c2 33 ♗xc2 ♔xd5 34 ♗b3+ ♔e5 35 g4 ♔f4 36 g6 ♔e3 37 g7 ♖c8 38 ♔f1 d3 39 ♔g2 ♔f4 40 h6 Black lost on time

Moscow staged the 12th Olympiad in 1956 and has enjoyed a dozen World Championship matches: Lasker–Steinitz 1897, nine matches in a row from 1951 to 1969, and the Karpov-Kasparov matches of 1984 and 1985.

Mouret, Jacques-François
[? 1787–1837]
French player who was chess tutor to Louis Philippe (1773–1850), king of France during 1830–48. Mouret was one of the hidden operators of the automaton The Turk, and he sold the Turk's secret—the only operator to do so.

Move
A single turn by either White or Black. In counting the length of a chess game however, a single White move plus the next single Black move (if played) constitutes one move in the game. Thus a 50 move game means 50 white moves and 50 (or perhaps only 49) Black moves.

Movies
See Cinema

Murey, Yaacov [*August 2 1941–*]
Israeli GM (1987) who was equal 3rd at Hastings 1982/83 (XI), equal 2nd at Marseille 1987 (X) and 1st at the Seville Open 1987. He played board 5 on the 1984 Israeli Olympiad team.

Moscow 1981

		1	2	3	4	5	6	7	8	9	10	11	12	13	14	
1	Karpov	–	½	1	½	½	½	1	1	½	½	½	½	1	1	9
2	Polugayevsky	½	–	½	½	½	½	½	½	1	½	½	1	½	½	7½
	Smyslov	0	½	–	½	½	½	½	1	½	½	½	1	1	½	7½
	Kasparov	½	½	½	–	½	½	½	1	0	½	½	1	½	1	7½
5	Gheorghiu	½	½	½	½	–	½	½	½	½	½	½	½	1	½	7
	Portisch	½	½	½	½	½	–	½	0	½	1	1	1	0	½	7
7	Balashov	0	½	½	½	½	½	–	½	½	½	1	½	0	1	6½
	Belyavsky	0	½	0	0	½	1	½	–	1	1	½	½	½	½	6½
9	Petrosian	½	0	½	1	½	½	½	0	–	½	½	½	½	½	6
	Andersson	½	½	½	½	½	0	½	0	½	–	½	½	½	1	6
11	Smejkal	½	½	½	½	½	0	0	½	½	½	–	0	1	½	5½
	Torre	½	0	0	0	½	0	½	½	½	½	1	–	1	½	5½
	Timman	0	½	0	½	0	1	1	½	½	½	0	0	–	1	5½
14	Geller	0	½	½	0	½	½	0	½	½	0	½	½	0	–	4

Murray, Harold James Ruthven
[*June 24 1868–May 16 1955*]
Chess historian and school inspector who wrote the definitive *A History of Chess* (1913), a 900 page piece of first class scholarship. In it he traced the development of chess from seventh century *chaturanga* to the present game and the end of the nineteenth century. He studied von der Lasa, van der Linde and learnt Arabic to prepare himself for this task.

The book is very detailed and it is not altogether easy to read. Casual chess lovers might find his *A Short History of Chess* (1963) more readable. This short version was unfinished at his death and brought to press by Goulding-Brown and Golombek.

Murray also wrote *A History of Board Games other than Chess* (1952). He was the son of Sir James A. H. Murray, the first editor of the *Oxford English Dictionary*.

Murshed, Niaz   [*May 13 1966–*]
Bangladesh GM (1986/87) who was 2nd at Calcutta 1986 (VIII) and 1st at Calcutta 1988 (VII). Murshed is the first and only GM from Bangladesh.

Music
Though music, like chess and mathematics, produces child prodigies, there is little overlap between music and chess. There have been chess ballets and musicals, and Philidor was a world class figure in both fields. Nevertheless, apart from Taimanov's piano playing and Smyslov's singing, few Grandmasters were or are musicians.

Muzio Gambit
See King's Gambit.

Mysterious Rook Move
Moving a rook to a closed file which discourages the opponent from making a freeing move because it would open up the action of the rook.

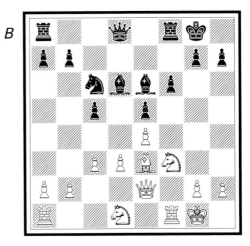

B

In the diagram (reached in Blackburne-Nimzowitsch) white is anxious to open up his game with d4. Black makes a mysterious rook move 1 ... ♖e8 and now if 2 d4 ed and the black rook comes to life on the open e-file.

Nimzowitsch coined the term and stressed the usefulness of this manoeuvre.

N

N

Symbol for a knight.

Najdorf, Miguel (Mendel)

[*April 15 1910– *]
Jewish, Polish-born, Argentine GM (1950) who was in the world top ten during the late 1940s and the 1950s, and was a Candidate in 1950 (coming 5th) and again in 1953 (coming equal 6th).

Najdorf was a pupil of Tartakower and by 1935 he defeated his mentor in a short match +2=1−1. He was equal 2nd in the 1935 Polish Championship and represented Poland in the Olympiads of 1935, 1937 and 1939. War broke out during the Buenos Aires Olympiad of 1939 and Najdorf, along with most of the Polish team, sought asylum in Argentina. He became an Argentine citizen in 1944 and changed his first name to Miguel.

After the war Najdorf emerged as a leading tournament competitor, a position he maintained for some 25 years. He was 1st at Prague 1946, Barcelona 1946, Venice 1948, Bled 1950, Amsterdam 1950 and Havana 1962 (ahead of Spassky, Smyslov etc.). He especially shone at Mar del Plata where he was 2nd in 1953, 1955 and 1957, equal 1st in 1959 (with Pachman, ahead of Fischer), 1st in 1961, 1965 and 1968, and equal 1st in 1969. He played 11 times on the

Argentine Olympiad team during 1950–76, and won the prize for the best score on first board in 1950 and 52.

Najdorf's aspirations toward the World Championship were less successful. He was, curiously, not selected for the 1948 world match tournament, even after Fine declined to play. This was a great disappointment for Najdorf. He continues to play to this day (December 1989), coming equal 2nd at Buenos Aires 1979 (XI) and 4th at Buenos Aires 1988 (VIII), and he continues to be a powerful blitz player at the age of 78.

Miguel Najdorf, an active Grandmaster even in his 70s and 80s.

In matches he drew +2=4−2 with Fine in 1949 but lost to Reshevsky +4=6−8 in 1952 and +4=9−5 in 1953. In terms of life scores Najdorf beat Boleslavsky (+2=4−0) and held his own with Keres (+2=11−2), Euwe (+2=9−2), Fine (+3=7−3), Spassky (+1=8−1) and Portisch (+1=7−1). He was edged out by Botvinnik (+1=1−2), Smyslov (+0=11−1), Tal (+1=5−3) and Karpov (+0=2−1), and he lost decisively to Reshevsky (+10=22−19), Petrosian (+1=9−6), Larsen (+2=2−8) and Fischer (+1=4−4).

Najdorf is an exuberant, colourful character who is full of self-confidence. His deep strength is in the middlegame and he himself admitted that he was weaker in theory than his rivals. Fine says Najdorf lacks the patience to build up a solid positional game. Najdorf held records for simultaneous play (202 games: +182=12−8 in 1943) and blindfold simultaneous play (45 games: +39=4−2 in 1947).

Major work: *Zurich 1953* (2 volumes)
See *Najdorf Luego y gano* by R. Castelli (1968).

Najdorf–Botvinnik
Groningen 1946
1 d4 e6 2 c4 ♘f6 3 ♘c3 ♗b4 4 ♕c2 d5 5 cd ed 6 a3 ♗xc3+ 7 bc c5 8 ♘f3 ♕a5 9 ♘d2 ♗d7 10 ♘b3 ♕a4 11

♛b2 ♞a6 12 e3 c4 13 ♞d2 0-0 14
♝e2 b5 15 ♝d1 ♛a5 16 ♝c2 ♜fe8
17 0-0 ♜ab8 18 ♞f3 ♛c7 19 ♞e5
♝e6 20 f3 ♞c5 21 ♝d2 ♞a4 22 ♛b1
♜b6 23 ♛e1 ♞d7 24 ♛h4 ♞f8 25 e4
f6 26 ♞g4 ♞g6 27 ♛h5 ♛f7 28
♜ae1 ♜6b8 29 ♞e3 ♞e7 30 ♛h4 f5

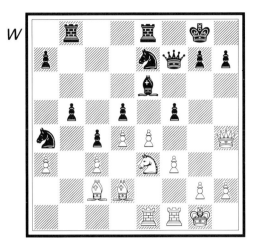

31 g4 f4 32 ed ♞g6 33 de ♜xe6 34
♝xg6 hg 35 ♞g2 ♝be8 36 ♜xe6
♜xe6 37 ♞xf4 ♜f6 38 ♛g5 ♞xc3 39
♝xc3 ♜xf4 40 ♔g2 Resigns

Napier, William Ewart

[*January 17 1881–September 7 1952*]
English-born US player of GM strength
who is most famous for his sensational
loss to Lasker at Cambridge Springs
1904 (*see* Lasker). Napier himself
believed that the best game he ever
played was this very loss. He only
played in a few international events,
his best result being equal 5th at
Hanover 1902. He did win the brilliancy
prize there for his game against
Bardeleben.

Napier won the British Championship in 1904 after winning a play-off
match +1=3−0 with Atkins. In 1905
he drew a match +4=2−4 with
Mieses but lost +1=4−5 to Teichmann and +1=1−3 to Marshall. He
married Pillsbury's niece and successfully settled down to his (insurance)
business.

Napoleon

[*August 15 1769–May 5 1821*]
French Emperor who was a keen but
inexpert player. He began to play during his student days and enjoyed the
game during his exile at St Helena.
Several game scores have been attri-
buted to him but in fact, they were
composed after his death. *See* the 1925/
26 volume of *Cahiers de L'Échiquier
Français.*

National Master

A rank below Fide Master, but given by
national federations. It corresponds to
about a 2200 Elo rating and varies from
country to country.

Nemet, Ivan   [*April 14 1943– *]

Yugoslav GM (1978) who was Yugoslav Champion in 1979, and equal 2nd at
Malmo 1979 (VIII).

Neumann, Gustav Richard Ludwig

[*December 15 1838–February 16 1881*]
Polish-born German player of GM
strength who was in the world top 5
during the late 1860s. He was 1st ahead
of Steinitz at Dundee 1867 and 3rd at
Baden-Baden 1870. He founded and
edited the *Neue Berliner Schachzeitung*
with Anderssen from 1864 to 1867. In
1865 he won a local Berlin tournament
scoring 34–0. In matches he beat
Winawer +3=0−0 in 1867 but lost to
Paulsen +3=3−5 in 1864.

He suffered severe mental illness,
possibly as a result of a head injury in
childhood, and stopped playing after
1872.

One of the greatest fighting games in
chess history is his 96 move struggle
with Steinitz from Baden-Baden 1870. It
has flaws but still leaves the reader with
a thrilling sense of excitement:

Neumann–Steinitz

1 d4 f5 2 e4 fe 3 ♞c3 ♞f6 4 ♝g5 c6 5
♝xf6 ef 6 ♞xe4 d5 7 ♞g3 ♛b6 8
♛e2+ ♔f7 9 0-0-0 ♞a6 10 ♛f3 g6

11 ♝d3 ♞b4 12 ♔b1 h5 13 h3 h4 14
♞3e2 ♞xd3 15 ♜xd3 ♝f5 16 ♜b3
♛c7 17 ♞f4 ♝e4 18 ♛g4 ♝f5 19
♛f3 ♝d6 20 ♞1e2 a5 21 ♜hg1 a4 22
♜e3 ♜ae8 23 g3 ♝e4 24 ♛g4 ♝f5
25 ♜xe8 ♜xe8 26 ♛f3 ♛a5 27 ♔c1
♛a6 28 ♞c3 b5 29 g4 ♝c8 30 ♞d1 b4
31 ♞e3 b3 32 a3 bc 33 g5 f5 34 ♞xc2
♛c4 35 ♞g2 ♜e2 36 ♞ge1 f4 37
♔d1 ♜e4 38 ♞g2 ♛b3 39 ♛c3
♛xc3 40 bc ♝xh3 41 f3 ♜e8 42
♞xh4 h8 43 ♞g2 ♜h5 44 ♞ge1
♝f5 45 ♞b4 ♝d7 46 ♜g2 ♔e6 47
♞1d3 ♔f5 48 ♞b2 ♜h1+ 49 ♔c2
♜a1 50 ♞xa4 ♜xa3 51 ♞c5 ♝xc5 52
dc d4 53 cd ♜xf3 54 d5 ♝g3 55 ♜f2
f3 56 dc ♝e6 57 ♔d2 ♔e4 58 ♜f1
♜g2+ 59 ♔c3 ♜e2 60 c7 ♜e3+ 61
♔d2 ♜e2+ 62 ♔d1 ♝b3+ ♔c1
♝e6 64 ♞c2 ♝c8 65 ♔d1 ♝g4 66 c6
♔f4 67 ♞d4 ♜e8 68 ♔d2 ♜c8 69
♔d3 ♔g3 70 ♜g1+ ♔f4 71 ♜f1
♔g3 72 ♜g1+ ♔f4 73 ♜f1 ♜e8 74
♔c4 ♔g3.

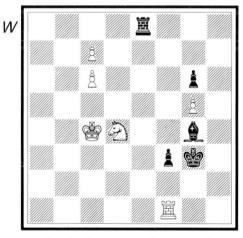

75 ♞xf3 ♝xf3 76 ♜xf3+ ♔xf3 77
♔d5 ♜a8 78 ♔e5 ♔e3 79 ♔f6 ♜c8
80 ♔xg6 ♔f4 81 ♔f6 ♜xc7 82 g6
♜xc6+ 83 ♔f7 ♔f5 84 g7 ♜c7+ 85
♔f8 ♔f6 86 g8(♞)+ ♔e6 87 ♞h6
♜h7 88 ♞g4 ♜h4 89 ♞e3 ♜e4 90
♞d1 ♜f4+ 91 ♔g7 ♜f3 92 ♔g6
♔e5 93 ♔g5 ♔d4 94 ♔g4 ♜f1 95
♞b2 ♜b1 96 ♞a4 ♜b4 97 Resigns

Neustadtl score

See Tie Breaking systems.

New in Chess

A Dutch publication package that started in 1984. It includes an excellent monthly magazine edited by Grandmaster Timman, available in an English edition, and a series of quarterly volumes (yearbooks) edited by Grandmaster Sosonko.

The magazine has penetrating articles, excellent pictures and deep analysis. The yearbooks have large numbers of games plus articles on opening theory.

Newspaper Chess Columns

These are usually weekly items containing news, a game and a problem. The first column was in the *Liverpool Mercury* (1813). Today there are chess columns in newspapers all over the world. Some of the most distinguished are those written by Robert Byrne (*New York Times*), Raymond Keene (*The Times*), Leonard Barden (*Guardian*) and Larry Evans in a syndicated network of columns throughout the USA.

The longest running column was the one from the *Illustrated London News*. It was founded by Staunton in 1845, but was discontinued in 1986.

New York

The mighty city of the USA whose first tournament was in 1857 when Morphy beat Paulsen in the final knockout and went on to conquer the entire chessworld. The next major event in 1889, saw 20 players in a double round robin. Chigorin (29) and Weiss (29) edged out Gunsberg (28½) and Blackburne (27), and then played a 4 game play-off but all 4 games were drawn. Steinitz did not play but he wrote a fine tournament book which is now a rare collector's item.

In 1924 New York staged a great tournament by having the 3 giants of the age: Capablanca, Lasker, and Alekhine. It was something like a rematch of the 1914 St Petersburg tournament, with all of them 10 years older. There was a good mixture of veterans (Janowski, Maroczy and Marshall) with younger hypermoderns (Réti, Tartakower and Bogoljubow), though some top challengers (Vidmar, Nimzowitsch and Rubinstein) were absent. Everyone expected World Champion Capablanca to win and wondered how Lasker, the 55 year old dethroned lion would perform. Lasker ran away with the tourament, scoring a phenomenal 80% against the elite of the chess world. Capablanca started slowly (4 draws), had a shock when he lost to Réti—his first tournament loss in 8 years—and then made a fine run of 8 points in the last 9 rounds. But Lasker scored 7½ in the last 9 and ended up a full 1½ points ahead of the World Champion. As Helms put it: 'History as made in St Petersburg had repeated itself. Lasker again was King! Once more the chess world, expressed in terms of tournament play, lay at his feet.'

Time limit: 30 moves in 2 hours and then 15 moves per hour.

Prizes: $1500, $1000, $750, $500, $250.

Brilliancy Prizes: Silver cup + $75 in gold to Réti for his win over Bogoljubow, $50 to Marshall for his win over Bogoljubow, $25 to Capablanca for his win over Lasker.

Tournament book: edited by Helms with quite magnificent annotations by Alekhine. There are some mistakes, but this is probably the best tournament book ever written, rivalled only by Bronstein's *Zurich 1953*.

Réti–Bogoljubow

1 ♘f3 ♘f6 2 c4 e6 3 g3 d5 4 ♗g2 ♗d6 5 0-0 0-0 6 b3 ♖e8 7 ♗b2 ♘bd7 8 d4 c6 9 ♘bd2 ♘e4 10 ♘xe4 de 11 ♘e5 f5 12 f3 ef 13 ♗xf3 ♕c7 14 ♘xd7 ♗xd7 15 e4 e5 16 c5 ♗f8 17 ♕c2 ed 18 ef ♖ad8

New York 1924

		1		2		3		4		5		6		7		8		9		10		11		
1	Lasker	–	–	½	0	1	½	½	1	1	1	1	1	1	1	½	1	½	1	½	1	1			16
2	Capablanca	½	1	–	–	½	½	½	½	0	1	½	1	1	1	1	1	1	½	½	1	½	1		14½
3	Alekhine	0	½	½	½	–	–	½	½	1	0	1	½	½	½	½	½	1	1	½	½	1	1		12
4	Marshall	½	0	½	½	½	½	–	–	½	1	0	½	0	1	½	0	½	1	1	½	1	1		11
5	Réti	0	0	1	0	0	1	½	0	–	–	½	½	0	1	1	1	0	1	0	1	1			10½
6	Maroczy	0	0	½	0	0	½	1	½	½	½	–	–	0	1	½	½	1	1	½	1	1	0		10
7	Bogoljubow	0	0	0	0	½	½	1	0	1	0	1	0	–	–	0	1	1	1	½	1	0	1		9½
8	Tartakower	½	0	0	0	½	½	½	1	0	0	½	½	1	0	–	–	1	0	½	0	½	1		8
9	Yates	½	0	0	½	0	0	½	0	0	1	0	0	0	0	0	1	–	–	1	1	½	1		7
10	Lasker, Edward	½	0	½	0	½	½	0	½	0	1	½	0	½	0	½	1	0	0	–	–	0	½		6½
11	Janowski	0	0	½	0	0	0	0	0	0	0	0	1	1	0	½	0	½	0	1	½	–	–		5

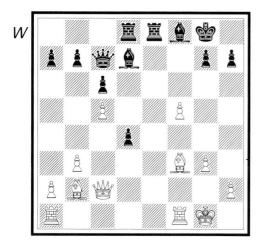

19 ♗h5 ♖e5 20 ♗xd4 ♖xf5 21 ♖xf5
♗xf5 22 ♕xf5 ♖xd4 23 ♖f1 ♖d8 24
♗f7+ ♔h8 25 ♗e8! Resigns (after 25
... ♗xc5+ 26 ♕xc5 ♖xe8 27 ♕f8+
♖xf8 28 ♖xf8 mate)

In 1927 New York held a six-man
quadruple round tournament with
Capablanca and his main challengers
Alekhine and Nimzowitsch. Lasker was
invited, but had some dispute with the
organizers. Other notable absentees
were Réti, Euwe, Rubinstein and Bogoljubow. Nevertheless, the tournament
was about Category XV.

Capablanca was an easy victor. With 3
rounds to go he was already assured of
1st prize. He declared that he would
draw his last 3 games (against Alekhine,
Vidmar and Nimzowitsch) in order not
to affect the struggle for 2nd place. It
seems that Nimzowitsch played some
bizarre moves and got into a bad position. Capablanca complained to the tournament director that unless Nimzowitsch
played better, he (Capablanca) would be

forced to win the game! Finally Capablanca actually dictated the last 4 or 5
moves, which Nimzowitsch played
rather apprehensively, and the game was
drawn. Alekhine ended up 2nd and
became the official challenger, though
Capablanca had agreed, before this tournament began, to play a match with him!

Prizes: $2000, $1500, $1000.

Brilliancy Prizes: $125 to Capablanca
for his win over Spielmann (see Capablanca), $100 to Alekhine for his win
over Marshall, $75 to Nimzowitsch for
his second win over Marshall, $50 to
Vidmar for his second win over Nimzowitsch.

Tournament book by Alekhine with
in-depth annotation.

Alekhine–Marshall

1 d4 ♞f6 2 c4 e6 3 ♞f3 ♞e4 4 ♞fd2
♗b4 5 ♕c2 d5 6 ♞c3 f5 7 ♞dxe4 fe 8
♗f4 0-0 9 e3 c6 10 ♗e2 ♞d7 11 a3
♗e7 12 0-0 ♗g5 13 f3 ♗xf4 14 ef
♖xf4 15 fe ♖xf1+ 16 ♖xf1 e5 17
♕d2 c5

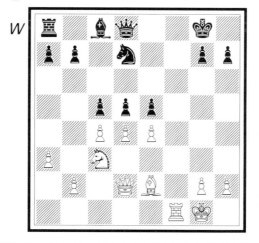

18 de d4 19 ♕f4 dc 20 ♕f7+ ♔h8 21
bc! ♕g8 22 ♕e7 h6 23 ♗h5 a5 24 e6
g6 25 ed ♗xd7 26 ♖f7 Resigns

New York enjoyed some World
Championship match games: part of
the Steinitz–Zukertort match 1886, all
of Steinitz–Gunsberg 1890/91, part of
Lasker–Steinitz 1894 and part of
Lasker–Marshall 1907.

Niemeijer, Meindert

[February 18 1902–October 5 1987]
Dutch bibliophile and lawyer who in
1948, donated his library of some 7000
chess books to the Royal Dutch Library
at The Hague. He wrote many books on
chess problems and several on bibliography.

Nikolac, Juraj   [April 22 1932–]

Yugoslav GM (1979) who was equal 1st
at Vrnjacka Banja 1978 (VIII) and 1st at
Maribor 1987 (VII).

Nikolic, Predrag   [September 11 1960–]

Yugoslav GM (1983) who showed real
promise with a 1st at Novi Sad 1984
(XII) and an equal 1st at Bor 1986 (XI).
He had an especially fine 1987 with
wins at Sarjevo (XII) and Havana (XIII)
and a fine equal 2nd at Tilburg (XV). In
1988 he tried three Category XV events
(Reggio Emilia, Linares and Brussels),
but only placed 7th, 11th and equal
10th.

He was Yugoslav Champion in 1980
and 1984, and played board 2 for
Yugoslavia in the Olympiads of 1984,
1986 and 1988.

New York 1927

		1				2				3				4				5				6				
1	Capablanca	–	–	–	–	1	½	½	½	1	½	1	½	½	½	1	½	½	½	1	½	1	1	½	1	14
2	Alekhine	0	½	½	½	–	–	–	–	½	0	1	½	½	½	½	½	1	½	½	1	½	1	½	1	11½
3	Nimzowitsch	0	½	0	½	½	1	0	½	–	–	–	–	1	0	0	½	1	1	½	½	1	½	½	1	10½
4	Vidmar	½	½	0	½	½	½	½	½	0	1	1	½	–	–	–	–	½	½	½	½	½	0	1	½	10
5	Spielmann	½	½	0	½	0	½	½	0	0	0	½	½	½	½	½	½	–	–	–	–	½	½	1	½	8
6	Marshall	0	0	½	0	½	0	½	0	0	½	½	0	½	1	0	½	½	½	0	½	–	–	–	–	6

Nikolic, Stanimir [*January 26 1935–*] Yugoslav GM (1978) who was 1st at Smederevska Palanka 1978 (VII).

Nimzowitsch, Aron Isaewitsch
[*November 7 1886–March 16 1935*] Latvian-born Jewish player of GM strength who was perhaps the most colourful personality in the chess world of the 1920s and 30s. He made his impressive mark not only with his successful play but also with his profound writings and his eccentric behaviour away from the chessboard.

He learnt the moves at an early age from his father (an accomplished master in his own right), but it was not until 1904 while in Germany (ostensibly to study mathematics) that Nimzowitsch began to concentrate on chess. At first his talent lay in the purely tactical and combinational field but several failures led him to undertake a complete revision of his chess ideas, laying more stress on positional play, restrictive strategy and consolidation. With his changed outlook Nimzowitsch achieved significant successes, including equal 2nd behind Rubinstein at San Sebastian 1912 and equal 1st with Alekhine at the All-Russian Championship St Petersburg 1913.

The war of 1914–18 combined with the Russian Revolution brought an abrupt halt to Nimzowitsch's activities. About 1920 he left Latvia for Scandinavia, changing his name in the process from Niemzowitsch to Nimzowitsch. He stopped in Sweden but eventually settled in Denmark. His return to tournament competition in the early 1920s was disastrous but gradually he played himself into form, securing a number of successes, including equal 1st with Rubinstein at Marienbad 1925, 1st at Dresden 1926 (scoring 8½ out of 9 ahead of Alekhine 7 and Rubinstein 6½) and 1st at Hanover 1926. It was during this productive period that Nimzowitsch's most influential work appeared: *Mein System* (1925). It underwent several revisions until 1928 and is still a bestseller in many translations over the entire chess-playing world.

Nimzowitsch was 3rd at the Candidates tournament in New York 1927, where Alekhine became the challenger. When Nimzowitsch came 1st at Carlsbad 1929, ahead of Capablanca, he was perhaps justified in calling himself the Crown Prince of the Chess World. After 1929, Nimzowitsch's best results (2nd at San Remo 1930, 3rd at Bled 1931) were achieved in the shadow of Alekhine. Heart trouble caused Nimzowitsch's sudden decline and by 1934 it was clear that his old force was gone.

In playing style, Nimzowitsch belonged to the so-called hypermodern school, which held (*inter alia*) that control of the centre did not necessarily imply occupation by pawns. Adherence to these views, combined with a decided mutual incompatibility, brought him into frequent opposition with the great German master of the classical school, Dr Siegbert Tarrasch. Neither master was averse to self-adulation and the bitterness emanating from their first meeting in 1904 was never entirely eradicated. In fact hostility towards Tarrasch and his works was a recurring theme of Nimzowitsch's literary endeavours.

Nimzowitsch's contribution to chess literature was more than just witty ridicule of Tarrasch or the discovery of a novel method of play. It was the elaboration of a new chess vocabulary which made intelligible the hitherto vaguely articulated strategy of masterplayers. He possessed an unrivalled facility for capturing the essence of an already known operation or structure with a memorable and meaningful word or phase, which thereby increased speed of comprehension and assisted clarity of thought. Nimzowitsch introduced into chess terminology such phrases as 'the passed pawn's lust to expand', 'mysterious rook move', 'prophylaxis', '7th rank absolute' and 'hanging pawns'. It is an established phenomenon that rapid advances in performance are often immediately preceded by advances in modes of expression, and we may indeed detect an upsurge in the general level of chess after the publication of *My System*. Nimzowitsch's writings were penned with such enthusiastic and allusive wit that only the most hardened could resist the appeal of his message. Consider the following on the subject of the isolated pawn ' ... We no longer consider it necessary to render the enemy isolani absolutely immobile; on the contrary, we like to give him the illusion of freedom, rather than shut him up in a cage (the principle of the large zoo applied to the small beast of prey)'.

Nimzowitsch also made a major contribution to opening theory—in fact it is difficult to think of anyone who in our time has exerted a comparable influence. Apart from his most famous brainchild, the Nimzo-Indian Defence, which he introduced into international practice at St Petersburg 1914, he also pioneered the Winawer Variation of the French Defence, known in Europe as the Nimzowitsch Variation. In addition he carried out important investigations into Philidor's Defence, 3 e5 in the French Defence, the Queen's Indian Defence and English Opening. He was also responsible for the invention of the defence 1 e4 ♘c6, the Nimzowitsch Variation of the Sicilian Defence (1 e4 c5 2 ♘f3 ♘f6) and he was the first great master to employ 1 b3 as White's opening move.

In life scores Nimzowitsch beat Tarrasch (+5=4−2), Marshall (+6=8−5) and Maroczy (+1=8−0). He lost to Rubinstein (+6=11−7), Vidmar (+2=9−4), Alekhine (+3=9−9), Capablanca (+0=6−5) and Schlechter (+1=4−3).

Major works: *Die Blockade* (1925),

144

Mein System (1925), Die Praxis Meines Systems (1929).

See Aron Nimzowitsch: A Re-appraisal by R. D. Keene (1974).

Johner–Nimzowitsch
Dresden 1926

1 d4 ♘f6 2 c4 e6 3 ♘c3 ♗b4 4 e3 0-0 5 ♗d3 c5 6 ♘f3 ♘c6 7 0-0 ♗xc3 8 bc d6 9 ♘d2 b6 10 ♘b3 e5 11 f4 e4 12 ♗e2 ♕d7 13 h3 ♘e7 14 ♕e1 h5 15 ♗d2 ♕f5 16 ♔h2 ♕h7 17 a4 ♘f5 18 g3 a5 19 ♖g1 ♘h6 20 ♗f1 ♗d7 21 ♗c1 ♖ac8 22 d5 ♔h8 23 ♘d2 ♖g8 24 ♗g2 g5 25 ♘f1 ♖g7 26 ♖a2 ♘f5 27 ♗h1 ♖cg8 28 ♕d1 gf 29 ef ♗c8 30 ♕b3 ♗a6 31 ♖e2 ♘h4 32 ♖e3 ♗c8 33 ♕c2 ♗xh3

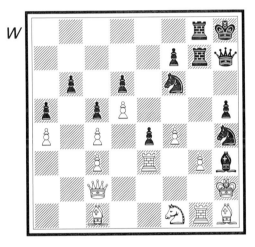

34 ♗xe4 ♗f5 35 ♗xf5 ♘xf5 36 ♖e2 h4 37 ♖1g2 hg+ 38 ♔g1 ♕h3 39 ♘e3 ♘h4 40 ♔f1 ♖e8 41 Resigns

Nimzowitsch Defence

1 e4 ♘c6.

After 2 d4 Nimzowitsch himself preferred 2 ... d5 or 2 ... e6 with French Defence type of positions. Another possibility is 2 d4 e5. This defence is now considered rather eccentric and is seldom used.

Nimzo-Indian Defence

1 d4 ♘f6 2 c4 e6 3 ♘c3 ♗b4.

The idea of this defence, pressure on e4, stems from Nimzowitsch, who introduced it to master chess in the 1920s. The sequence of moves had been played before him, in particular by Blackburne in the 1880s, but it was without any strategic idea and always transposed to some form of Queen's Gambit.

There are four main lines for White: 4 ♕c2, 4 ♕b3, 4 e3 (the Rubinstein Variation) and 4 a3 (the Sämisch Variation).

Nimzowitsch–Larsen Attack

1 b3.

This was first introduced into master chess by Nimzowitsch in the 1920s and has since become a recognized alternative to the more deeply analysed regular openings after its adoption by Larsen. It is hardly a vigorous attempt to gain an early advantage. For example 1 b3 e5 2 ♗b2 ♘c6 3 c4 ♘f6 4 e3 d6 5 ♘c3 g6 6 ♘f3 ♗g7. Theoretically the chances are even but a complex middlegame lies ahead.

Noah's Ark Trap

1 e4 e5 2 ♘f3 ♘c6 3 ♗b5 a6 4 ♗a4 d6 5 d4 b5 6 ♗b3 ♘xd4 7 ♘xd4 ed 8 ♕xd4? (better is 8 c3) c5 9 ♕d5 ♗e6 10 ♕c6+ ♗d7 11 ♕d5 c4 winning, as in Dworzynsky–Keres, 1956 Olympiad.

Nogueiras, José de Jésus

[July 17 1959–]

Cuban GM (1979) who was Cuban Champion in 1978 and 1984 (joint) and played on all 5 Cuban Olympiad teams in the 1980s. He was 2nd at the Taxco interzonal 1985 (X) and became a Candidate but did not do well at Montpellier 1985. Perhaps his best recent result was 3rd at Havana 1987 (XIII).

Notation

It is a happy miracle that a method of recording chess games was invented long ago, so that today, anyone can play over—just as they happened—chess games played 1000 years ago, or games by Philidor, Morphy, Steinitz, Lasker, Capablanca or Fischer. It is like having a built-in three dimensional colour movie of the chessboard during these real life happenings.

Today there is only one universally accepted notation—the one invented by the Arabs in the 9th century and called Algebraic notation.

Algebraic

8	a8	b8	c8	d8	e8	f8	g8	h8
7	a7	b7	c7	d7	e7	f7	g7	h7
6	a6	b6	c6	d6	e6	f6	g6	h6
5	a5	b5	c5	d5	e5	f5	g5	h5
4	a4	b4	c4	d4	e4	f4	g4	h4
3	a3	b3	c3	d3	e3	f3	g3	h3
2	a2	b2	c2	d2	e2	f2	g2	h2
1	a1	b1	c1	d1	e1	f1	g1	h1
	a	b	c	d	e	f	g	h

The 64 squares are each indicated by a letter from a to h and a number from 1 to 8. The letter indicates the column, the number indicates the rank or row from the white side of the board. The squares thus have coordinates.

In the initial position of the pieces, the white pieces are placed on ranks 1 and 2, while the black pieces are placed on ranks 7 and 8.

Each piece is usually indicated by the first letter, a capital letter, of its name. In English, K = king, Q = queen, R = rook, B = bishop, but N = knight. In other languages we get F for fou = bishop in French, or L for läufer or loper = bishop in German or Dutch. Pawns are recognized by their location; 'e2' is the pawn on the square e2. Thus the absence of any capital letter indicates a pawn.

Each move of a piece is represented by the capital letter representing the piece and the name of the square of arrival. Thus Be5 means the bishop moves to the square e5. If there is any ambiguity, the square of departure is also given. So N(e3)f5 means the knight that is now on e3 moves to the square f5. It is enough just to give the file of departure, as in Nef5, or alternatively the rank of departure: N3f5.

Each move of a pawn is represented by the name of the square of arrival. Thus c5 means the pawn moves to the square c5.

When a piece makes a capture, an 'x' is inserted between the capital letter representing the piece and the square of arrival. Thus Bxe5 means the bishop captures whatever enemy piece or pawn is on e5. Again, if there is any ambiguity the square of rank or file of departure is given. Thus Nexf7 means the knight on the e-file takes whatever enemy piece or pawn is on f7.

When a pawn makes a capture, the file of departure is given. Thus ef means the pawn on the e-file takes something on the f-file. This may also be written as exf, or the arrival square may be specified: exf5, for instance. For an *en passant* capture, the letters e.p. are sometimes added, and it is useful to include the square of arrival. Thus ef3 e.p. or exf3 e.p. means the pawn on the e-file captures the black pawn on the f-file, en passant, and the white pawn ends up on f3.

If there is any ambiguity about a pawn capture, the square of arrival is included. Thus ef4 means the pawn on the e-file takes something at f4.

When a pawn reaches the 8th rank and is promoted, the move is given by, say, d8(R) or b1(Q).

Other symbols used are:

0-0   means castling on the kingside;
0-0-0 means castling on the queenside;
+   means check;

+ +   means mate *or* double check (some users);
?   means a bad move;
??   means a terrible move;
!   means a good and surprising move;
!!   means a sensationally good move;
!?   means a surprising but not necessarily sound move;
?!   means a (probably) dubious move

Figurine algebraic
This is algebraic that uses figure representation for the pieces instead of capital letters:
King = ♚
Queen = ♛
Bishop = ♝
Knight = ♞
Rook = ♜

Thus Be5 becomes ♝e5.

Descriptive
A system used in the English-speaking chess world until the 1980s. The 8 files were called QR (for queen's rook), QN, QB, Q, K, KB, KN and KR. The rows or ranks were numbered 1 to 8, but from each side of the board. Thus every square had two different names. For example the square f3 in algebraic was, in descriptive, called KB3 from White's point of view and KB6 from Black's point of view. Here are the same moves given in both notations.

Algebraic	Descriptive
1 e4 c5	1 P-K4 P-QB4
2 Nf3 d6	2 N-KB3 P-Q3
3 d4 cd	3 P-Q4 PxP
4 Nxd4 Nf6	4 NxP N-KB3

A Spanish descriptive notation also exists.

Forsythe Notation
A simple and effective method of describing a chess position, invented about 1883 by David Forsyth of Glasgow and New Zealand (1854–1909).

Starting with the top row of the board, the pieces and the number of vacant squares are given in order, with capital letters for White and lower case for Black. Thus the following position is given by:

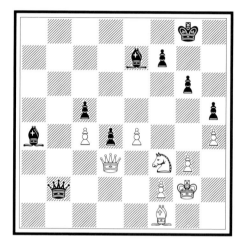

6k1/4bp2/6p1/2p4p/b1PpP2p/
3Q1NP1/1q3PK1/5b2

Nottingham
English city famous for its sheriffs and the great tournament of 1936. Every top GM was there including 5 World Champions from Lasker 1894 to Botvinnik 1963. The four best English players were there and this pulled down the average strength, but not the excitement. It was the first time Capablanca had played Alekhine since their 1927 match; it was Lasker's last tournament; it was the first time Alekhine had come 6th for over 24 years (in Vilna 1912).

With 3 rounds to go Euwe (8) Capablanca (8) and Botvinnik (8) were tied. Capablanca beat Alexander, Botvinnik beat Vidmar, but Euwe lost to Lasker. With 2 rounds to go Capablanca (9) drew with Fine while Botvinnik (9) was losing to Euwe (8):

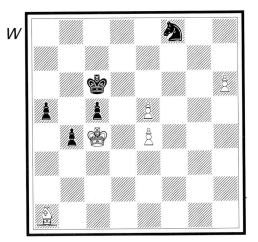

Euwe now missed the win (56 e6?) which Alekhine gives: 56 ♔b3! ♔b5 57 e6 a4+ 58 ♔a2 ♘g6 59 h7 ♔c6 60 e7 ♔d7 61 ♗f6 c4 62 ♔b1 ♔e8 63 e5 ♔f7 64 e6+ ♔e8 65 ♗g5 ♘h8 66 ♗h4 ♘g6 67 ♗f6 winning.

After the text 56 e6? ♔d6 57 ♗g7 ♘h7 58 e7 ♔xe7 59 ♔xc5 ♔f7 60 ♔b5 ♔g6 61 ♔xa5 b3 62 ♔b4 b2 63 ♗xb2 ♔xh6 with a draw.

Thus going into the last round it was Capablanca (9½) and Botvinnik (9½), and they both displayed nervousness. Botvinnik got into a bad position against Winter and was lucky when Winter decided to take a safe draw. Capablanca got a winning position against Bogoljubow but blundered and was lucky to find a draw.

Time limit: 36 moves in 2 hours and then 18 moves per hour.

Prizes: £200, £150, £100, £75.

Brilliancy prize: Botvinnik for his win over Tartakower.

Tournament Book: by Watts with good annotations by Alekhine.

Botvinnik wrote about an interesting moral/legal point: 'During the Nottingham Tournament my game with Lasker remained unfinished after 4 hours play. During the 2 hour break I analysed the adjourned position and came to the conclusion that a draw was inevitable, if Lasker had sealed the correct and, as it seemed to me, the only possible move. Some 20 minutes before play was to be resumed I sought out Lasker and offered him a draw . . . if he had sealed the move which I considered the only one possible. Lasker was embarrassed; he said he had sealed another move, which in his opinion was also adequate to ensure a draw. Now it was my turn to be embarrassed. He tried to reassure me, but agreed with me that I ought not to take my analysis any further (for the secrecy of the sealed move had been violated). He refused to take my pocket chess-set which I offered to him (as guarantee that I should not go on with the analysis) declaring that he trusted me completely. Our game ended in a draw.'

Nunn, John Denis Martin (Dr)

[April 25 1955–]
English GM (1978) who took his PhD (mathematics) from Oxford (1978) and set out on an academic career, but turned chess professional in 1981. He was British Champion in 1980, equal 1st at Wijk aan Zee 1982 (XII), equal 3rd in the super-strong tournament at Brussels 1986 (XVI), equal 3rd at Brussels 1988 (XV) and 1st at Wijk aan Zee 1990 (XIII). In spite of these excellent results he has never made it to the Candidates and is number 3 in England behind Short and Speelman. In 1987 Nunn lost +0=4−2 to Portisch.

He has played on the England Olympiad team continuously from 1976 to 1988 and was a gold medal winner in 1984. He is also a remarkably quick chess problem solver. It would seem that he is still one step away from belonging to the world top 10.

Nottingham 1936

		1	2	3	4	5	6	7	8	9	10	11	12	13	14	15	
1	Botvinnik	–	½	½	½	½	½	½	½	1	1	1	1	1	1	½	10
	Capablanca	½	–	½	½	1	1	0	½	1	½	½	1	1	1	1	10
3	Euwe	½	½	–	½	1	0	½	0	1	½	1	1	1	1	1	9½
	Fine	½	½	½	–	½	½	½	1	½	1	½	1	1	½	1	9½
	Reshevsky	½	0	0	½	–	1	½	1	1	1	½	1	1	1	½	9½
6	Alekhine	½	0	1	½	0	–	1	½	½	1	1	½	1	½	1	9
7	Flohr	½	1	½	½	½	0	–	1	1	1	½	0	0	1	1	8½
	Lasker	½	½	1	0	0	½	0	–	½	1	½	1	1	1	1	8½
9	Vidmar	0	0	0	½	0	½	0	½	–	1	½	½	1	½	1	6
10	Bogoljubow	0	½	½	0	0	0	0	0	0	–	½	1	1	1	1	5½
	Tartakower	0	½	0	½	½	0	½	½	½	½	–	0	0	1	1	5½
12	Tylor	0	0	0	0	0	½	1	0	½	0	1	–	½	½	½	4½
13	Alexander	0	0	0	0	0	0	1	0	0	0	1	½	–	½	½	3½
14	Thomas	0	0	0	½	0	½	0	0	½	0	0	½	½	–	½	3
15	Winter	½	0	0	0	½	0	0	0	0	0	0	½	½	½	–	2½

John Nunn: not only a top-flight Grandmaster, but also one of the game's most respected writers.

Major works: *The Complete Pirc* (1989), *The Benoni for the Tournament Player* (1982), *Secrets of Grandmaster Play* (with Peter Griffiths) (1987), *Beating the Sicilian* (1984).

Nuremberg

German city (Tarrasch's birthplace) which staged a super-strong tournament in the summer of 1896. All the leading players of the time were there, including World Champion Lasker and his four main rivals: Pillsbury, Tarrasch, Steinitz and Chigorin. There were the veterans Blackburne, Schallopp and Winawer, as well as the young tigers: Schlechter, Maroczy, Janowski, Walbrodt and Charousek.

With 3 rounds to go, Lasker (11½) led Maroczy (10), Pillsbury (10) and Tarrasch (10). With 2 rounds to go, Lasker (12½) led Pillsbury (11) and Tarrasch (11). With 1 round to go Lasker (13½) had clinched first prize and firmly established himself as the world's leading player in both match play and tournaments. Maroczy (11½) was second followed closely by Pillsbury (11), Tarrasch (11) and Steinitz (11).

In the last round Pillsbury won a long struggle with the ageing Steinitz, while Tarrasch had an even longer cliff-hanger with Albin—who played 'as if his life depended on the result' (Tarrasch). Maroczy however, worked out a hard win over Showalter, took the second prize and gave notice that he now belonged to the world top 5. Lasker relaxed somewhat ('he was bored with winning'—Tarrasch) and lost to young Charousek.

The Baron Albert V. Rothschild Brilliancy Prize went to Pillsbury for his wonderful win over Lasker.

The tournament book, by Tarrasch, has excellent, deep and witty annotations.

Pillsbury–Lasker

1 e4 e6 2 d4 d5 3 ♘c3 ♘f6 4 e5 ♘fd7 5 f4 c5 6 dc ♘c6 7 a3 ♘xc5 8 b4 ♘d7 9 ♗d3 a5 10 b5 ♘6b8 11 ♘f3 ♘c5 12

Nuremberg 1896

		1	2	3	4	5	6	7	8	9	10	11	12	13	14	15	16	17	18	19	
1	Lasker	–	½	0	1	0	1	½	½	1	1	1	0	1	1	1	1	1	1	1	13½
2	Maroczy	½	–	1	½	1	0	½	½	½	½	½	1	½	1	1	1	1	1	½	12½
3	Pillsbury	1	0	–	1	½	1	½	0	0	1	0	½	1	1	1	½	1	1	1	12
	Tarrasch	0	½	0	–	1	1	½	½	1	1	0	1	1	1	1	½	½	½	1	12
5	Janowski	1	0	½	0	–	1	1	1	1	0	½	0	1	½	1	1	0	1	1	11½
6	Steinitz	0	1	0	0	0	–	1	½	½	1	1	1	1	0	0	1	1	1	1	11
7	Schlechter	½	½	½	½	0	0	–	½	½	1	½	½	½	1	1	½	½	1	1	10½
	Walbrodt	½	½	1	½	0	½	½	–	½	1	0	0	½	1	1	1	1	1	0	10½
9	Schiffers	0	½	1	0	0	½	½	½	–	½	0	½	½	1	½	½	1	1	1	9½
	Chigorin	0	½	0	0	1	0	0	0	½	–	1	1	½	1	1	1	0	1	1	9½
11	Blackburne	0	½	1	1	½	0	½	1	1	0	–	0	0	0	1	0	1	1	½	9
12	Charousek	1	0	½	0	1	0	½	1	½	0	1	–	½	0	½	1	1	0	0	8½
13	Marco	0	½	0	0	0	0	½	½	½	½	1	½	–	½	1	½	½	1	½	8
14	Albin	0	0	0	0	½	1	0	0	0	0	1	1	½	–	0	½	½	1	1	7
15	Winawer	0	0	0	0	0	1	0	0	½	0	0	½	0	1	–	1	1	1	½	6½
16	Porges	0	0	½	½	0	0	½	0	½	0	1	0	½	½	0	–	½	0	1	5½
	Showalter	0	0	0	½	1	0	½	0	0	1	0	0	½	½	0	½	–	0	1	5½
18	Schallopp	0	0	0	½	0	0	0	0	0	0	0	1	0	0	0	1	1	–	1	4½
19	Teichmann	0	½	0	0	0	0	0	0	1	0	0	½	1	½	0	½	0	0	–	4

♗e3 ♘bd7 13 0-0 g6 14 ♘e2 ♗e7 15 ♕e1 ♘b6 16 ♘fd4 ♗d7 17 ♕f2 ♘6a4 18 ♖ab1 h5 19 b6 ♘xd3 20 cd ♗xa3

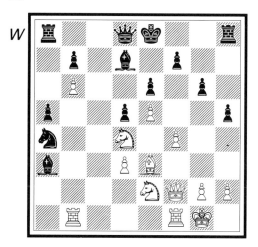

21 f5 gf 22 ♘f4 h4 23 ♖a1 ♗e7 24 ♖xa4! ♗xa4 25 ♘dxe6 fe 26 ♘xe6 ♗d7 27 ♘xd8 ♖xd8 28 ♗c5 ♖c8 29 ♗xe7 ♔xe7 30 ♕e3 ♖c6 31 ♕g5+ ♔f7 32 ♖c1 ♖xc1+ 33 ♕xc1 ♖c8 34 ♕e1 h3 35 gh ♖g8+ 36 ♔f2 a4 37 ♕b4 ♖g6 38 ♔f3 a3 39 ♕xa3 ♖xb6 40 ♕c5 ♖e6 41 ♕c7 ♔e7 42 ♔f4 b6 43 h4 ♖c6 44 ♕b8 ♗e8 45 ♔xf5 ♖h6 46 ♕c7+ ♔f8 47 ♕d8 b5 48 e6 ♖h7 49 ♔e5 b4 50 ♕d6+ Resigns

Ten years later, in 1906, Nuremberg staged a strong (but not superstrong) tournament. Marshall (12½) won ahead of Duras (11), Forgacs (10½), Schlechter (10½) and Chigorin (10). Poor Tarrasch (7½) was only equal 9th and Janowski (4) was equal 16th or last.

Nuremberg also enjoyed a few World Championship games, Alekhine–Bogoljubow, in 1934.

Obstructive Sacrifice

A sacrifice of material to obstruct the opponent's development. For example, in Alekhine's Defence: 1 e4 ♘f6 2 ♘c3 d5 3 e5 ♘6d7 4 e6 fe 5 d4 when Black's development has been obstructed.

Odds

See Handicap.

O'Kelly de Galway, Count Alberic

[*May 17 1911–October 3 1980*] Belgian GM (1956) who won the third World Correspondence Championship (1959–62). He was many times Belgian Champion and played on 8 Belgian Olympiad teams during 1937–68. He was a fine linguist (6 languages), an author and the chief arbiter at the World Championship matches of 1966 and 1969.

Major works: *34 Mal Schachlogik* (1965), *The Sicilian Flank Game* (1969).

Olafsson, Fridrik

[*January 26 1935–*] Icelandic lawyer and GM (1958) who was president of the world chess federation (FIDE) 1978–82. He was equal 1st at Hastings 1955/56, 2nd at the Wageningen zonal 1958 and equal 5th with Fischer at the Portoroz interzonal 1958. This made Olafsson a Candidate and though he did not do well at the 1959 Candidates tournament, he did score wins over Fischer, Keres and Petrosian. After his victory over Petrosian, he was carried round the main square of Zagreb in triumph on the shoulders of his ardent supporters.

Olafsson was equal 3rd at the 1963 Piatigorsky, 2nd at Lugano 1970, equal 2nd at Wijk aan Zee 1971, equal 1st at Reykjavik 1972, equal 2nd at Las Palmas 1974, equal 1st at Wijk aan Zee 1976 and equal 1st at Reykjavik 1976.

He was many times champion of Iceland, played on a number of Icelandic Olympiad teams—scoring +10 = 8 at Varna 1962 to win the first board prize—and beat Pilnik twice in matches: +4 = 2 − 0 in 1955 and +4 = 1 − 3 in 1957.

Major work: *Spassky–Fischer Match* (with F. Johannsson) (1973).

Olafsson, Helgi

[*August 15 1956–*] Icelandic GM (1985) who was Icelandic Champion in 1978 and 1981 and played on the Icelandic Olympiad team throughout the 1980s. His best results are equal 2nd at Copenhagen 1985 (XI) and equal 4th at Dortmund 1988 (XII).

Old Indian Defence

1 d4 ♘f6 2 c4 d6 3 ♘c3 e5.
First employed by Chigorin and hence also known as the Chigorin Indian Defence. While not unsound, this defence is rarely encountered in modern master practice, being regarded as inflexible and strategically limited.
See Indian Defences.

Olympiads

Team championships organized by FIDE that began in London 1927, and now are staged regularly every 2 years. National teams compete for the Hamilton–Russell Cup. The 28th Olympiad was held at Thessaloniki, Greece, in 1988 when 108 men's teams and 56 women's teams participated. The men's teams meet on 4 boards, though they may have up to 6 players; women play over 3 boards, with one reserve. In the past, preliminary groups and then finals were played, but now the entire event is played on the swiss system.

Hungary had excellent results in the early years. Then the US teams came to the fore in the 1930s. Since the Second World War, the USSR has dominated the event.

The most lavish Olympiads were held in Havana (1966) and in Dubai (1986). The 29th Olympiad is at Novi Sad, Yugoslavia, 1990.

The women's competitions began in 1957.

See *Chess Olympiads 1927–1968* by Arpad Foldeak (1979).

Open Defence

See Lopez, Ruy.

Olympiad Winners

Year	Venue	Men	Women
1927	London	Hungary	—
1928	The Hague	Hungary	—
1930	Hamburg	Poland	—
1931	Prague	USA	—
1933	Folkestone	USA	—
1935	Warsaw	USA	—
1937	Stockholm	USA	—
1939	Buenos Aires	Germany	—
1950	Dubrovnik	Yugoslavia	—
1952	Helsinki	USSR	—
1954	Amsterdam	USSR	—
1956	Moscow	USSR	—
1957	Emmen	—	USSR
1958	Munich	USSR	—
1960	Leipzig	USSR	—
1962	Varna	USSR	—
1963	Split	—	USSR
1964	Tel Aviv	USSR	—
1966	Havana	USSR	USSR (in Oberhausen)
1968	Lugano	USSR	—
1969	Lublin	—	USSR
1970	Siegen	USSR	—
1972	Skopje	USSR	USSR
1974	Nice	USSR	USSR (in Medellin)
1976	Haifa	USA	Israel
1978	Buenos Aires	Hungary	USSR
1980	Malta	USSR	USSR
1982	Lucerne	USSR	USSR
1984	Thessaloniki	USSR	USSR
1986	Dubai	USSR	USSR
1988	Thessaloniki	USSR	Hungary

Open File

A file on which there are no pawns. Rooks operate wonderfully well on open files because they can use them to get to all parts of the board or to penetrate the enemy position, especially the seventh rank. It is an advantage to be able to control an open file (especially when there is only one).

Open Game

A game where there is free movement of the pieces. Also a general term for openings commencing 1 e4 e5.

Open Tournament

A tournament open to any player.

Opening

The beginning part of the game from the initial set up of the pieces to the point where both sides have most of their pieces developed. The opening is then over and the middlegame begins.

During the opening phase, master players struggle for control of the centre, for greater mobility for their pieces and for the optimal placing of their pieces. They try to avoid creating permanent weaknesses in their own positions and to provoke permanent weaknesses in the enemy position. In the early 19th century the main objective in the opening was to attack the enemy king, but Steinitz's theories and better defensive play established that such premature attacks are doomed to failure and more modest goals are best.

Fashion plays a large role in the selection of openings. Most games in the 19th century began with 1 e4 e5. By the 1930s 1 d4 was the big favourite. Today, 1 e4 and 1 d4 are most popular, but the flank openings (1 c4 1 ♘f3 1 g3) are also common.

Some important opening treatises are (were):
1837 — Alexandre — *Encyclopédie*
1843–1916 — Bilguer (Lasa) — *Handbuch*
1889 — Freeborough and Ranken — *Chess Openings*
1911 — Griffiths and White — *Modern Chess Openings*
1921 — Collijn — *Larobok*
1939 — Euwe — *Schaakopeningen*
1974 — Matanovic — *Encyclopedia of Chess Openings*
1982 — Kasparov and Keene — *Batsford Chess Openings*

Opposition

When kings face each other with one square between them they are said to be in opposition. Whoever must move first must give way and allow the other king to advance. A player is said to have the opposition if the kings are in opposition and if his opponent must move first.

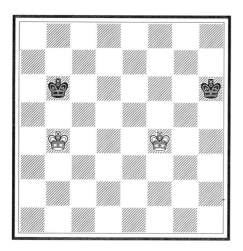

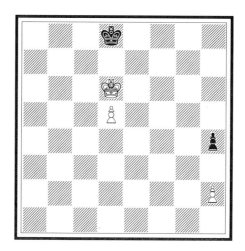

In the diagram, the kings on the left are in square (or frontal) position. Those on the right are in diagonal opposition.

Having the opposition is generally an advantage because one can then advance one's king or at the very least prevent the opponent from advancing his king.

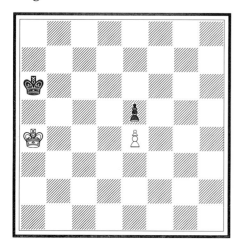

Here White wants to get to the fifth rank to attack the black e-pawn. If White has the opposition then Black must move first: 1 ... ♔b6 2 ♔b4 ♔c6 3 ♔c4 ♔d6 4 ♔b5 (giving up the opposition but getting to the fifth rank and winning) 4 ... ♔d7 5 ♔c5 ♔e6 6 ♔c6 ♔e7 7 ♔d5 ♔f6 8 ♔d6.

One can gain a tempo and thus capture the opposition if one has an 'extra' pawn move.

If it is Black's move, then White has the opposition, and if Black moves his

king then White will advance his king and be able to queen his c-pawn. However Black can play 1 ... h3, and now he has the opposition. Black can then keep the opposition and draw the game.

Calculating who has the so-called distant opposition, when the kings are far apart, takes some experience.

See King and Pawn Endings.

Orang Utan Opening

A name given by Tartakower to 1 b4, also called Sokolsky's Opening.

See *The Debut 1 b4* by Sokolsky (1963).

Orthodox Defence

See Queen's Gambit.

Oscar

An award given by AIPE, the organization of chess reporters to the male and female players of the year.

Ostend

A fashionable seaside resort in Belgium which staged three major tournaments. In 1905 every top level player was there except for the World Champion, Lasker. Maroczy achieved the greatest victory of his career. There were 12 brilliancy prizes awarded, the first going to Janowski for his win over Tarrasch.

Janowski–Tarrasch

Ostend 1905

1 d4 d5 2 ♘f3 c5 3 c3 e6 4 ♗f4 ♕b6 5 ♕b3 ♘f6 6 e3 ♘c6 7 h3 ♗e7 8 ♘bd2 ♗d7 9 ♗e2 0-0 10 0-0 ♖fc8 11 ♘e5 ♗e8 12 ♗g3 ♘d7 13 ♘df3 ♘f8 14 ♖fd1 ♘a5 15 ♕c2 c4 16 ♘d2 f6 17 ♘ef3 ♗g6 18 ♕c1 h6 19 ♘h2 ♕d8 20 ♗f3 b5 21 e4 ♘c6 22 ed ed 23 ♖e1 b4 24 ♘df1 bc 25 bc ♕a5 26 ♘e3 ♗f7 27 ♕d2 ♗a3 28 ♖ab1 ♘d7

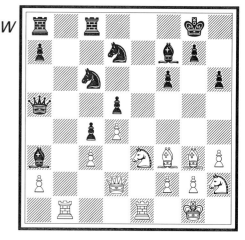

29 ♖b7 ♘b6 30 ♘f5 ♕a6 31 ♘xh6+ gh 32 ♖xf7 ♔xf7 33 ♕xh6 ♔g8 34 ♕g6+ ♔h8 35 ♕xf6+ ♔g8 36 ♕g6+ ♔h8 37 ♖e5 Resigns

In 1906 both Lasker and Tarrasch were absent, but everyone else was there. The arrangement was a complete five-stage affair for 36 players where Schlechter (21) scored a great victory ahead of Maroczy (20), Rubinstein (19), Bernstein (18), Burn (18), Teichmann (18), Marshall (16½), Janowski (16) and Perlis (14).

In 1907 there was a regular masters tournament of 29 players, won by Rubinstein (19½) and Bernstein (19½), and a so-called Grandmaster tournament. For this the organizers hoped to get the 6 greatest: Lasker, Maroczy, Tarrasch, Schlechter, Marshall and Janowski. Unfortunately Lasker and Maroczy declined, so Chigorin and Burn were substituted.

With 3 rounds to go, Janowski (11) led Tarrasch (10½) and Schlechter (10).

Ostend 1905

		1	2	3	4	5	6	7	8	9	10	11	12	13	14	
1	Maroczy	–	10	01	½½	½0	1½	½½	11	11	11	11	11	½1	11	19½
2	Janowski	01	–	10	01	01	½0	11	11	½1	1½	1½	11	1½	½1	18
	Tarrasch	10	01	–	½½	1½	01	11	01	½1	1½	1½	½1	1½	11	18
4	Schlechter	½½	10	½½	–	½½	½½	½½	½1	½½	½1	½1	½0	1½	½½	15½
5	Marco	½1	10	0½	½½	–	½½	½0	1½	½0	½1	½1	½½	01	½1	14
	Teichmann	0½	½1	10	½½	½½	–	½0	01	½1	10	0½	½½	11	1½	14
7	Burn	½½	00	00	½½	½1	½1	–	10	0½	01	0½	½1	11	½½	12½
	Leonhardt	00	00	10	½0	0½	10	01	–	10	01	11	10	11	½1	12½
	Marshall	00	½0	½0	½½	½1	½0	1½	01	–	½½	10	00	11	11	12½
10	Wolf	00	0½	0½	½0	½0	01	10	10	½½	–	½½	½1	11	1½	12
11	Alapin	00	0½	0½	½0	½0	1½	1½	00	01	½½	–	½½	1½	11	11½
12	Blackburne	00	00	½0	½1	½½	½½	½0	01	11	½0	½½	–	0½	10	10½
13	Chigorin	½0	0½	0½	0½	10	00	00	00	00	00	0½	1½	–	1½	6½
14	Taubenhaus	00	½0	00	00	½0	0½	½½	½0	00	0½	00	01	0½	–	5

The decisive game between Tarrasch and Janowski was a magnificent struggle, which Tarrasch won. Schlechter only drew with Burn. With 2 rounds to go, Tarrasch (11½) led Janowski (11) and Schlechter (10½). Tarrasch beat Chigorin while Janowski drew with Schlechter. With one round to go, Tarrasch (12½) led Janowski (11½) and Schlechter (11). In the last round Schlechter beat Tarrasch, but Janowski lost to Marshall.

Tarrasch was given the title of World Tournament Champion but this soon evaporated when he lost decisively to Lasker in 1908.

Time Limit: 30 moves in 2 hours, then 15 moves per hour.

Prizes: Tarrasch—Gold medal and 2603.50 francs, Schlechter 2277.50 francs, Janowski 1950.50 francs, Marshall 1950.50 francs, Burn 779.50 francs, Chigorin 438.50 francs.

Tournament book by Tarrasch with wonderful and deep annotations.

Tarrasch–Janowski

1 e4 e5 2 ♘f3 ♘c6 3 ♘c3 ♘f6 4 ♗b5 ♗e7 5 0-0 d6 6 d4 ♘d7 7 ♘e2 0-0 8 ♘g3 ♘xd4 9 ♘xd4 ed 10 ♕xd4 ♗f6 11 ♕d1 ♖e8 12 c3 a6 13 ♗a4 b5 14 ♗b3 ♗b7 15 ♗d5 c6 16 ♗b3 ♘c5 17 ♗c2 d5 18 ed ♕xd5 19 ♕xd5 cd 20 ♗e3 ♘e6 21 ♘f5 ♖ad8 22 ♖ad1 g6 23 ♘d4 ♘xd4 24 cd ♖c8 25 ♗d3 ♖e6 26 ♖c1 ♖ec6 27 ♖xc6 ♖xc6 28 ♖a1 ♗c8 29 ♔f1 ♗f5 30 ♔e2 ♗xd3+ 31 ♔xd3 ♖c4 32 b3 ♖c6 33 a4 b4 34 ♗d2 a5 35 ♖e1 ♖c8 36 g4 h6 37 h4 ♗xh4 38 ♖e5 ♖d8 39 ♗xh6 ♔h7 40 ♗d2 ♗f6 41 ♖e1 ♖d7 42 ♖c1 ♔g7 43 ♗f4 ♗d8 44 ♖c6 f6 45 ♗d6 ♔f7 46 ♗c5 g5 47 ♔d2 ♗c7 48 ♔c2 ♗d8 49 ♔d3 ♗c7 50 ♔e2 ♗f4 51 ♖a6 ♗c7 52 ♔d3 ♗d8 53 ♖c6 ♗c7 54 ♔c2 ♗d8 55 ♔d2 ♗c7 56 ♗b6 ♗xb6 57 ♖xb6 ♖c7 58 ♖d6

W

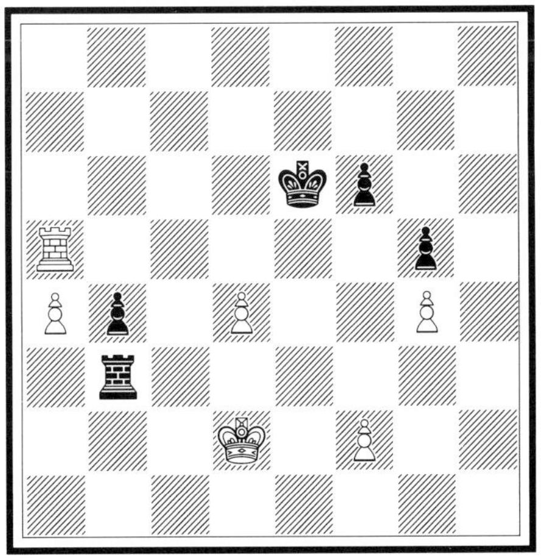

Ostend 1907

		1				2				3				4				5				6				
1	Tarrasch	–	–	–	–	½	½	1	0	½	1	½	1	½	1	½	½	1	½	1	0	1	½	0	1	12½
2	Schlechter	½	½	0	1	–	–	–	–	1	1	½	½	½	0	1	0	½	1	½	½	½	½	1	1	12
3	Janowski	½	0	½	0	0	0	½	½	–	–	–	–	1	0	1	0	1	1	1	1	1	1	½	1	11½
	Marshall	½	0	½	½	½	1	0	1	0	1	0	1	–	–	–	–	0	½	1	1	½	½	1	1	11½
5	Burn	0	½	0	1	½	0	½	½	0	0	0	0	1	½	0	0	–	–	–	–	½	1	1	1	8
6	Chigorin	0	½	1	0	½	½	0	0	0	0	½	0	½	½	0	0	½	0	0	0	–	–	–	–	4½

Rc3 59 Rxd5 Rxb3 60 Rxa5 Ke6
(see diagram) on previous page 61 Rf5
Ra3 62 a5 Ke7 63 Kc2 Ke6 64 Rb5
Kd6 65 Kb2 Ke6 66 Rb6+ Kd5 67
Rxf6 Kc4 68 Rf5 Rb3+ 69 Kc2
Rc3+ 70 Kd2 Rd3+ 71 Ke2
Rxd4 72 a6 Rd8 73 Rxg5 b3 74 Rg7
b2 75 Rb7 Kc3 76 f4 Ra8 77 f5
Rxa6 78 Ke3 Ra4? [78 ... Ra1 would
hold the draw] 79 Rxb2 Rxb2 80 f6!
Ra1 81 g5 Rf1 82 Kd4 Kb3 83 Ke5
Kc4 84 g6 Re1+ 85 Kd6 Rd1+ 86
Ke6 Re1+ 87 Kf7 resigns

Ostojic, Predrag [*February 22 1938– *]
Yugoslav GM (1975) who was joint
Yugoslav Champion in 1968 and 1971.
His best international results were 1st at
San Juan 1971, 1st at Sao Paulo 1973,
equal 1st at Vrnjacka Banja 1975 and 1st
at Sandefjord 1976.

Outpost

A well protected piece on the enemy
side of the board, on a square that
cannot be attacked by an enemy pawn,
which makes life so uncomfortable for
the enemy that he must soon exchange
the outpost piece and thus pay some
price for this removal.

Nimzowitsch coined the phrase and
gave this example:

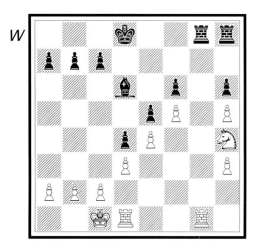

Black has a hole at g6. If 1 Ng6,
Black could just leave the knight there.
However 1 Rg6 makes this rook a real

outpost. Not only does it attack the f-
pawn, but White threatens 2 Rdg1 to
control the g-file. Then if 1 ... Rxg6 2
fg, White gets a strong passed pawn
and the knight becomes an outpost with
3 Nf5.

Outside Passed Pawn

A passed pawn, away from the bulk of
the other pawns. It is usually an asset
because it can be used as a decoy.

In the diagram the a-pawn is an
outside passed pawn and White can win
by 1 a4 Ke6 2 a5 Kd6 3 a6 Kc6 4 a7
Kb7 5 Kxd5 Kxa7 6 Kxe4 and wins.

Overload

A situation where a piece or pawn has
too many defensive tasks to perform.

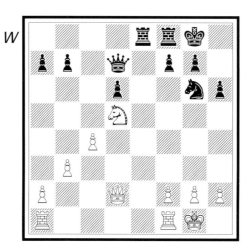

In the diagram, the black g-pawn
protects the h-pawn and also prevents

Nf6+ forking the king and queen. It is
overloaded, because after 1 Qxh6
Black dare not play 1 ... gh because of 2
Nf6+. Thus White wins an important
pawn.

Overprotection

A principle of Nimzowitsch which
states that concentrating as many pieces
as possible, even more than seemingly
necessary, on a strategically important
square, is good for maintaining control
and good for the overprotectors
because they can draw strength from
the energy of the critical square. This
may be somewhat obscure, but it is
eloquent.

P

Pachman, Ludek [*May 11 1924–*]
Czech author and GM (1954) who was
Czech Champion 7 times during 1946–
66, and played on the Czech Olympiad
team from 1952 to 1966. He played in 4
interzonals but never became a Candidate. His best results were equal 1st at
Mar del Plata 1959 and equal 2nd at
Havana 1963.

After the unsuccessful 1968 Czech
uprising, Pachman opposed the communist regime and was sent to prison.
There he intentionally caused injuries to
his head and spine. He was freed in 1972
and allowed to go to West Germany.
There he played on the West German
Olympiad team in 1976 and won the
West German Championship in 1978.

He edited the FIDE magazine for
several years from the late 1950s to the
mid 1960s.

Major works: *Modern Chess Theory*
(1948), *Modern Chess Strategy* (1955),
Modern Chess Tactics (1962), *Czechmate
in Prague* (1975), *Meine 100 beste Partien
und meine Probleme* (1978).

Padevsky, Nikola Bochev
[*May 29 1933–*]
Bulgarian lawyer and GM (1964) who
was Bulgarian Champion in 1954, 1955,
1962, and 1964. He played on Bulgarian
Olympiad teams almost continuously
during 1956 to 1978. His best results
were equal 1st at Varna 1960 and at

Varna 1975 (VII).

Pairings
The arrangement of who plays who in a
given round of a tournament. For round
robins, there are established tables (see
Deutsche Schachzeitung (1886), pages
134–7) for any number of competitors
up to 24. The players draw lots before
the tournament begins and then the
entire schedule is established and everyone knows exactly who they play on
each day (unless the rounds are drawn
by lot, each day).

Swiss tournaments are more complex.
The idea is to have players with the
same score meet each other, and to try
to balance the number of whites and
blacks each player gets. Of course two
players must not meet more than once.
There is no unique solution, especially
since some games from the previous
round may be unfinished.

See: The Chess Competitor's Handbook
by B. Kazic (1980), *The Official Laws of
Chess*, by FIDE (1989).

Palamède, Le
See Magazines.

Palatnik, Semyon [*March 26 1950–*]
USSR GM (1978) whose best result was
equal 2nd at Kiev 1978 (X). He was 3rd
at Hradec Kralove 1981 (IX), equal 2nd
at Trnava 1987 (IX), 1st at Hradec Kra-

love 1988 (VII) and equal 1st at Calicut
1988 (VII). He is a middle-level GM
who had never reached the finals of a
USSR Championship.

Panchenko, Alexander N.
[*October 5 1953–*]
USSR GM (1980) who peaked with a
win at Sochi 1980 (XI) but has not been
able to reach that level again. He did
win at Bayamo 1988 (VII), but has not
yet played in a USSR Championship
final.

Panno, Oscar Roberto
[*March 17 1935–*]
Argentine civil engineer and GM (1955)
who was World Junior Champion in
1953 and Argentine Champion in 1953
and in 1985. He became a Candidate in
1956 but did not succeed against the
top guns (Smyslov, Keres, Bronstein,
Geller, Petrosian and Spassky). Panno
pursued his engineering career seriously
and was basically out of chess competition from 1958 to 1968. On his return
he had a fine string of successes: 1st at
Buenos Aires 1968, equal 2nd at Caracas
1970, equal 1st at Palma 1971 and
Palma 1972, 2nd at Buenos Aires 1977
and equal 3rd at Termas de Rio Hondo
1987 (X).

Panno played on some 10 Argentine
Olympiad teams during 1954–88 and
won the top 2nd board prize in 1966.

He is a talented and strong GM who perhaps wisely never devoted himself entirely to chess.

Panov, Vasily Nikolayevich

[*November 1 1906–January 1973*] USSR author and IM (1950) who contributed to the theory of the Caro–Kann and the Ruy Lopez. He was chess correspondent for *Izvestia* and played in 5 USSR Championship finals during 1934–48.

Major works: *Moscow 1956, Comprehensive Chess Openings* (3 vols.) (with Estrin) (1980).

Panov–Botvinnik Attack

See Caro–Kann.

Paoli, Enrico

[*January 13 1908–*] Italian author and IM (1951) who was Italian Champion in 1951, 1957 and 1968, and played on 4 Italian Olympiad teams during 1954–76. He now organizes the strong tournament at Reggio Emilia each year.

Major work: *Strategia e tattica sulla scacchiera* (1953).

Paris

France's magnificent capital that ruled the chess world from 1740 via Legall, Philidor, Deschappelles and La Bourdonnais, to 1840. (*See* Café de la Régence) It staged 3 major international tournaments.

In 1867 Kolisch (21) scored his great triumph ahead of Steinitz (19½), Winawer (19½) and Neumann (19). Unfortunately Anderssen and Blackburne were both absent.

In 1878 Steinitz did not participate. Zukertort (16½) and Winawer (16½) tied for 1st and Zukertort won the playoff +2=2−0. Other scores were Blackburne (14½), Bird (13), Mackenzie (13) and Anderssen (12½)—this turned out to be Anderssen's last tournament.

In 1900 Lasker (14½) was a clear winner ahead of Pillsbury (12½), Maroczy (12) and Marshall (12). Tarrasch and Teichmann did not play.

In 1924 Paris was the scene for the birth of FIDE and the idea of Olympiads. It was also the site of the 1843 Staunton–Saint–Amant match.

Parma, Bruno

[*December 30 1941–*] Yugoslav GM (1963) who was World Junior Champion in 1961 and who played on several Yugoslav Olympiad teams from 1962 onwards. His best results were 1st at Bucharest 1968, equal 1st at Sarajevo 1970, at Natanya 1971 and at Vrsac 1973.

Parma is a fine positional player in the mould of Petrosian, but his early promise came to nothing though lack of ambition. His later tournament performances have lacked incisiveness.

Passed Pawn

See Pawn Structure

Patzer

A weak player who is not entirely aware of his failings and may even on occasion boast of his skill. There may be more patzers than many people think.

Paulsen, Louis

[*January 15 1833–August 18 1891*] German player of GM strength who had a distinguished tournament career during the 1860s and 70s, was in the world top 5 or 6 and had an unblemished match record. He is best known for his contributions to opening theory and his profound modern insights—ideas that became accepted long after his death.

Paulsen was 2nd at New York 1857 (losing +1=2−5 to Morphy), 1st at Bristol 1861, 2nd to Anderssen at London 1862, 2nd at Baden-Baden 1870, 1st at Krefeld 1871, 1st at Leipzig 1877 ahead of Anderssen and Zukertort, 2nd at Leipzig 1879 and equal 4th at Breslau 1889. In matches he scored +7=18 −6 vs Kolisch in 1861, +3=2−3 vs Anderssen in 1862, +5=0−2 vs Dr Lange in 1864, +5=3−2 vs Neumann in 1864, +5=1−4 vs Anderssen in 1876, +5=1−3 vs Anderssen in 1877 and +5=0−2 vs Schwarz in 1879.

Paulsen was an excellent blindfold player, his top effort was 14 games simultaneously in 1858. He was also a deep strategist and an eminent theorist and analyst. He invented the Dragon Variation in the Sicilian and his system is used frequently in the 1980s. He experimented with an early e5 for Black in the Sicilian and it has only recently been accepted as playable. He was perhaps the first great master of defence and was far ahead of his time.

Steinitz wrote: ' . . . in the early part of my career and when I just met Kolisch and Anderssen I expressed myself in very derogatory terms about Paulsen's system of play. But both warmly defended Paulsen . . . and this set me thinking. I began to recognize that Chess genius is not (just) deep and brilliant finishing strokes after the original balance of power and position has been overthrown, but that it also requires . . . still more extraordinary powers, though perhaps of a different kind, to maintain that balance or respectively to disturb it at the proper time in one's own favour. Paulsen struck at the root of the game . . . he paved the way to the development of principles in the middle part and in the ending which generated position judgement and helped to dispense with mere combination tactics . . . Paulsen (is) a genius of the highest order.'

Though Paulsen was a modest, unassuming, straightforward and honest gentleman, and had no enemies, he was overshadowed by Morphy, Anderssen and Steinitz, and he suffered public derision for being a pioneer of modern chess thought. He lived simply, drank only water—no spirits, coffee or tea, and did not smoke. As his brother put it: 'Strict rectitude, conscientiousness, punctuality and love of truth were his special distinctions.' Paulsen died of diabetes.

Pawn

The smallest piece on the chessboard, which moves straight ahead and captures diagonally. In the pre-renaissance period it could only move 1 square at a time, even on its initial move; there was no *en passant* rule, and when it reached the 8th rank it had to be promoted to a minister (the old form of our queen), but this was no great achievement because the minister was a weak piece.

Since the renaissance, the basic pawn move is the same, but on its initial move it has the option of moving 2 squares, the *en passant* rule exists, and when a pawn reaches the 8th rank it has the option of being promoted to a powerful queen or underpromoted to a rook or a bishop or a knight.

Pawn and Move
See Handicap

Pawn and Two Moves
See Handicap

Pawn Chain

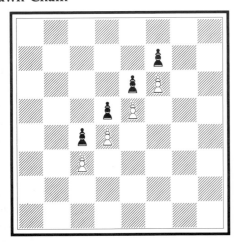

A diagonal set of pawns that protect each other and are opposed by an enemy pawn chain. In the diagram the white chain runs from c3 to f6 and the

pawn at c3 is called the base of the chain. The black pawn chain runs from f7 to c4, with base at f7.

Pawn Snatching

Spending time winning pawns instead of completing the development of one's pieces and countering the opponent's preparations for attack.

Pawn Structure

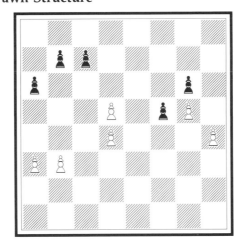

The white h-pawn is said to be *backward*: it cannot be protected by another pawn, it cannot advance unless supported by pieces or as a sacrifice. It is on a half-open file, with a 'hole' in front of it in which an enemy piece can live securely because it cannot be attacked by a white pawn.

A backward pawn has problems but the seriousness depends on how easy it is for the enemy to attack it. In some openings a player may accept the liability of a backward pawn for some other compensation and such a trade-off is desirable if the backward pawn cannot be easily attacked.

The white g-pawn is said to be *blocked*.

The two white d-pawns are very sick and are said to be *doubled* and *isolated* (there are no white pawns on the adjacent c- and e-files.

The white a- and b-pawns are the healthiest—such a side by side structure is said to be a *phalanx*.

The black f-pawn is said to be a *passed* pawn because it can move forward to f1 without interference from white pawns.

Penrose, Jonathan Dr

[*October 7 1933–*]
English IM (1961) who won the British championship 10 times (a record) during 1958 to 1969, and played on 9 English Olympiad teams during 1952–74. Tournament stress forced Penrose to withdraw from over the board competition in the early 1970s. His doctorate is in psychology. He is currently (1990) the top-rated correspondence player in the world.

Perlis, Julius

[*January 19 1880–September 11 1913*]
Polish-born Austrian lawyer and player of GM strength who was active from 1906 to 1912. His best result was 5th at San Sebastian 1912. He combined a good positional sense with a sharp combinational style. Perlis died of exposure in an Alpine mountaineering accident.

Perpetual Check

A situation where one player continues to give various checks and the other player (though not threatened with mate) cannot escape from these checks. The game is then a draw by agreement or by threefold repetition of the position.

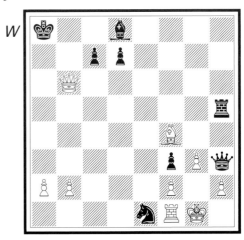

In the diagram White is threatened with mate and has no way to prevent it. He therefore plays 1 ♕a6+ ♚b8 2 ♕b6+ ♚c8 (the c-pawn is pinned by the white bishop); 3 ♕a6+ ♚b8 and the checks can go on forever. Thus the game is drawn by 'perpetual check'.

Petroff, Alexander Dmitrievich

[*February 12 1794–April 22 1867*] Russia's first player of GM strength who in 1824 wrote the first thorough Russian chess book (in 2 volumes): *The Game of Chess Systematized, with a Supplement containing Philidor's Games and Annotations to Same*. Petroff's play was deep and rich in combination. He was especially good in the endgame. He won matches against Jaenisch, Urusov and Shumov. He was invited to play in London 1851, but declined and thus never competed against western masters.

Petroff was called the Russian La Bourdonnais and the Northern Philidor although he disagreed with Philidor's view that with best play, White should win. Petroff established (with Jaenisch) that 1. e4 e5 2 ♘f3 ♘f6 was sound and this is now called Petroff's Defence. He wrote a manual on draughts and a book of reminiscences: *Scenes from the Life of Chess Players* (1844).

Petroff was socially well connected and in 1840 went to Warsaw as undersecretary of state, where he played many interesting games with Hoffman.

Hoffman–Petroff

Warsaw 1844

1 e4 e5 2 ♘f3 ♘c6 3 ♗c4 ♗c5 4 c3 ♘f6 5 d4 ed 6 e5 ♘e4 7 ♗d5 ♘xf2 8 ♚xf2 dc+ 9 ♚g3 cb 10 ♗xb2 ♘e7 11 ♘g5? ♘xd5 12 ♘xf7

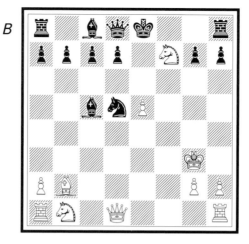

12 ... 0-0! 13 ♘xd8 ♗f2+ 14 ♚h3 d6+ 15 e6 ♘f4+ 16 ♚g4 ♘xe6 17 ♘xe6 ♗xe6+ 18 ♚g5 ♖f5+ 19 ♚g4 h5+ 20 ♚h3 ♖f3 mate

Petrosian, Arshak B.

[*December 16 1953– *] USSR GM (1984) who was equal 1st at Erevan 1980 (X) and clear 1st at Erevan 1984 (IX). He played in the 1985 USSR Championship, but without success, and has some way to go to carry on the successes of his great namesake Tigran.

Petrosian, Tigran Vartanovich

[*June 17 1929–August 13 1984*] World Champion 1963–9. USSR (Armenian) GM (1952) who was one of the all-time stars—Keene and Divinsky rate him as the 10th greatest player of all time. His formative years were dogged by personal misfortune. Both his parents died during the second world war and at one time the young Petrosian was forced to work as a caretaker in an officers' club to maintain what was left of his family. His main consolation was chess, and although his progress was comparatively rapid it was achieved by stages and exhibited no prodigious or meteoric quality. At this early stage his most influential chess mentor was A. S. Ebralidze, who instilled in him a deep and lasting regard for the play and principles of Capablanca and Nimzowitsch.

In later years Petrosian was, in fact, to raise the Nimzowitschian theory of prophylaxis to an almost fanatical level, developing from this his own highly individualistic, pragmatic and flexible style with a penchant for deep strategic manoeuvres which often baffled his opponents.

He played in four Candidates tournaments where he was 5th at Zurich 1953, equal 3rd at Amsterdam 1956, clear 3rd at Bled 1959 and finally 1st at Curaçao 1962. This victory made him the challenger and in 1963 he beat Botvinnik +5=15−2 to become World Champion. Critics found his play colourless, with too many short draws, and accused him of lacking fighting spirit. Even his victory over Botvinnik was considered convincing rather than spectacular, and the overriding impression was that Botvinnik succumbed not by any innate inferiority in his play but as a result of the age difference (18 years). In many games Petrosian hovered perilously on the brink of defeat and only Botvinnik's fatigue combined with his own eel-like defensive ability continued to salvage

Tigran Petrosian, World Champion 1963–9.

the half points. Nevertheless, Petrosian did win one memorable game, the 5th, which demonstrated that the application of pure technique in a simplified position can create a deeply aesthetic effect.

Petrosian defended his title against Spassky in 1966 and won + 4 = 17 − 3, thus becoming the first World Champion to win a title match outright since 1934 (Alekhine over Bogoljubow). In 1969, however, Petrosian lost + 4 = 13 − 6 to Spassky.

In the Candidates matches of 1971, Petrosian beat Hübner + 1 = 6 − 0, and beat Korchnoi + 1 = 9 − 0 but lost to Fischer + 1 = 3 − 5. In 1974, Petrosian beat Portisch + 3 = 8 − 2 and then lost + 1 = 1 − 3 to Korchnoi. In 1977 he lost + 1 = 9 − 2 to Korchnoi and in 1980 he again lost to Korchnoi + 0 = 7 − 2. Petrosian thus played an important role in Candidates competition from 1953 to 1980 — a remarkable achievement.

Petrosian played in 16 USSR Championships during 1949 to 1983, winning the title 4 times and scoring an overall 177–111 for 61.5%. He also played on all ten USSR Olympiad teams during 1958 to 1978, scoring an amazing + 79 = 50 − 1 (to Hübner in 1972, on time in a drawn position). In other tournaments he did very well, but people expected even more. He was equal 1st at the 1963 Piatigorsky, Buenos Aires 1964, San Antonio 1972, Amsterdam 1973, Rio de Janeiro 1979, and Las Palmas 1980. He was clear 1st at Lone Pine 1976 and Tallinn 1979. He was equal 2nd at Milan 1975 (XIV) and 2nd at Tilburg 1981 (XV).

In life scores he beat Botvinnik (+ 6 = 18 − 3), Najdorf (+ 6 = 9 − 1), Tal (+ 5 = 36 − 4), Polugayevsky (+ 6 = 13 − 2) and Reshevsky (+ 2 = 8 − 0). He held his own with Keres (+ 3 = 25 − 3), Karpov (+ 1 = 13 − 1) and Kasparov (+ 2 = 1 − 2). He lost to Korchnoi (+ 9 = 49 − 16), Spassky (+ 10 = 53 − 11), Portisch (+ 6 = 26 − 7),

Geller (+ 2 = 33 − 6), Smyslov (+ 2 = 28 − 6) and Fischer (+ 4 = 15 − 8). He certainly faced the very best players of his time.

In spite of his outstanding record, Petrosian has continually had an unimpressive public image. What can explain this apparent paradox? Perhaps the answer is to be sought in his leaning towards a negative, defensive style, aimed more at avoiding loss rather than at playing, come what may, for victory. Indeed in his best years, Petrosian achieved a reputation for almost total invincibility, not a trait to endear a player automatically to his public. In addition to stylistic factors Petrosian exhibited a distressing lack of ambition during his tenure of the world title, being content to aim for high prizes in tournaments rather than go all-out for first place. Many believe that his talent was capable of further development had it been supported by less indolence, more determination to succeed and ambition to exploit his untapped reservoirs of power.

Petrosian was the editor of the weekly magazine 64 from 1968 to 1977. He wrote *Chess Logic, Some Problems of Logic of Chess Thought* (Erevan 1968), which earned him a Master of Philosophical Science degree.

See *Petrosian, His Life and Games* by V. L. Vasiliev (1969), *Petrosian's Best Games 1946–63* by P. Clarke (1964), Petrosian, World Champion by A. O'Kelly (1965)

Petrosian–Botvinnik

Match 1963

1 c4 g6 2 d4 ♘f6 3 ♘c3 d5 4 ♘f3 ♗g7 5 e3 0-0 6 ♗e2 dc 7 ♗xc4 c5 8 d5 e6 9 de ♕xd1+ 10 ♔xd1 ♗xe6 11 ♗xe6 fe 12 ♔e2 ♘c6 13 ♖d1 ♖ad8 14 ♖xd8 ♖xd8 15 ♘g5 ♖e8 16 ♘ge4 ♘xe4 17 ♘xe4 b6 18 ♖b1 ♘b4 19 ♗d2 ♘d5 20 a4 ♖c8 21 b3 ♗f8 22 ♖c1 ♗e7 23 b4 c4 24 b5 ♔f7 25 ♗c3 ♗a3 26 ♖c2 ♘xc3+ 27

♖xc3 ♗b4 28 ♖c2 ♔e7 29 ♘d2 c3 30 ♘e4 ♗a5 31 ♔d3 ♖d8+ 32 ♔c4 ♖d1 33 ♘xc3 ♖h1 34 ♘e4 ♖xh2 35 ♔d4 ♔d7 36 g3 ♗b4 37 ♔e5 ♖h5+ 38 ♔f6 ♗e7+ 39 ♔g7 e5 40 ♖c6 ♖h1

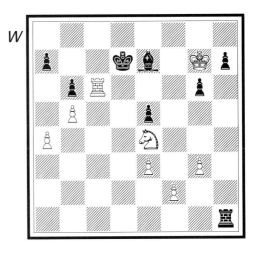

41 ♔f7 ♖a1 42 ♖e6 ♗d8 43 ♖d6+ ♔c8 44 ♔e8 ♗c7 45 ♖c6 ♖d1 46 ♘g5 ♖d8+ 47 ♔f7 ♖d7+ 48 ♔g8 Resigns

Petrov, Vladimir

[*September 27 1907–March 15 1945*] Latvian player of GM strength who was equal 1st with Flohr and Reshevsky, ahead of Alekhine, Keres and Fine, at Kemeri 1937. During the 1930s Petrov was Latvian Champion 4 times and played on all 7 Latvian Olympiad teams (1928–39) winning the top prize for board 3 in 1931. He was only 10th (out of 20) in the 1940 USSR Championship but he came 2nd at Sverdlosvsk 1942. Sadly, he died in a prison camp during the war.

Petursson, Margeir

[*February 15 1960–*] Icelandic GM (1986) who was champion of Iceland in 1986 and played on all the Icelandic Olympiad teams during the 1980s. He was equal 1st at Gausdal 1985 (IX), equal 2nd at Reykjavik 1985 (XI), 1st at Hastings 1985/86 (IX) and 1st at Torshavn 1987 (VIII).

Pfleger, Helmut [*August 6 1943– *]
German medical doctor and GM (1975)
who was German Champion (joint) in
1964 and has represented Germany
in some 6 Olympiads during 1964–82.
He won the top prize for board 4 in
the 1964 Olympiad. His best results
were equal 1st at Polanica Zdroj 1971,
1st at Lorenco Marques 1973, equal 1st
at Montilla Moriles 1973 and 2nd at
Manila 1975.

Phalanx
See Pawn Structure

Philately
See Stamps

Philidor, François-André Danican

[*September 7 1726–August 31 1795*]
French opera composer and chess player
of GM strength who dominated the
chess world during the entire second
half of the 18th century, both as a player
and as an author.

Philidor began to be a regular at the
Café de la Régence about 1740 and the
best player in France, Legall, took an

*Philidor: the leading player throughout the second
half of the 18th century.*

interest in him. At first Legall spotted
him a rook but in 3 years Legall could
only beat him on equal terms. By the
late 1740s Philidor surpassed his
mentor. Philidor visited England in
1747 and crushed Stamma +8 =1 –1.
By then it was generally accepted that
Philidor was the best player in the
world.

In 1749 Philidor published his celebrated *Analyse du jeu des Échecs* and this
swept the world with some 100 editions
in many languages. It was the first book
that dealt clearly with the middlegame,
the endgame and the overall strategy of
the game. His most famous notion was
that 'pawns are the soul of chess' by
which he meant that the pawn structure
often determines the nature of the position. This was quite new and in fact the
entire book was far ahead of its time.

Philidor also amazed the 18th century
world by playing 2 and even 3 games
simultaneously blindfold (he was the
first to do so).

Between 1750 and 1770, Philidor was
the leading opera composer in France.
When Gretry began to surpass him in
this field, Philidor concentrated more on
chess. He visited London annually and
played at Slaughter's Coffee House, the
Salopian Coffee House and Parsloe's
Club. On his visit in 1793 he found he
could not return to France because the
revolutionary government had put him
on the banned list—Philidor had many
connections with powerful and even
royal personages. He died in London
and is buried in St James, Piccadilly. A
few days after his death, his name was
finally removed from the banned list,
but it came too late.

Philidor's ancient family name was
Danican (of Scottish origin). A musical
ancestor played the hautboy at Ver-
sailles and Louis XIII enjoyed this so
much that he called this ancestor Philidor after the previous expert woodwind
player Filidori. Thus Danican became
Philidor.

Philidor almost always gave odds
because he had no equals. We thus have
no games of Philidor in his prime. What
has survived are his games at odds, from
his late years.

See *The Life of Philidor* by G. Allen
(1863, reprinted 1971).

Atwood–Philidor (Playing 3 games simultaneously blindfolded)
London 1794

1 e4 c5 2 f4 e6 3 ♘f3 ♘c6 4 c3 d5 5 e5
f5 6 d4 ♘h6 7 a3 ♘f7 8 ♗e3 ♕b6 9
♕d2 ♗d7 10 ♕f2 c4 11 ♗xc4 dc 12
d5 ♕c7 13 dc ♗xc6 14 ♗xa7 ♗xf3 15
gf g5 16 ♗e3 gf 17 ♗xf4 ♘xe5 18
♗xe5 5 ♕xe5+ 19 ♕e2 ♕xe2+ 20
♔xe2 h5 21 ♘d2 ♖c8 22 ♖hg1 ♔f7
23 ♖g2 ♗e7 24 ♖ag1 ♗f6 25 ♘f1 e5
26 ♘e3 ♔e6 27 ♖d1 ♖hg8 28 ♖xg8
♖xg8

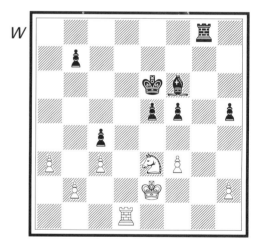

29 ♘xc4 ♖g2+ 30 ♔d3 ♖xh2 31
♖d2 ♖h3 32 ♔e2 b5 33 ♘e3 ♖h2+
34 ♔e1 ♖xd2 35 ♔xd2 ♗g5 36
♔e2 ♗xe3 37 ♔xe3 h4 38 ♔f2 e4 39
♔g2 e3 and Black queens a pawn and
wins.

Philidor's Legacy
A most beautiful smothered mate that
does in fact occur from time to time, in
actual play.

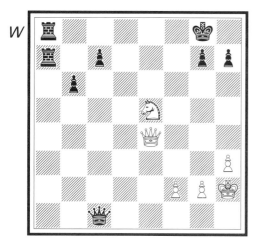

White wins with 1 ♕d5+ ♚h8 2 ♘f7+ ♚g8 3 ♘h6+ ♚h8 4 ♕g8+ ♖xg8 5 ♘f7++

Philidor's Defence
1 e4 e5 2 ♘f3 d6

Philidor preferred 2 ... d6 to the more usual 2 ... ♘c6 because he wanted to keep his c-pawn mobile. His idea was to answer 3 d4 with 3 ... f5 but that is considered too risky today. The usual line is 3 d4 ♘f6 4 ♘c3 ♘bd7 5 ♗c4 ♗e7 6 0-0 0-0 with a solid but cramped position.

Another possibility is 3 d4 ♘d7 (the Hanham Variation).

Philidorian, The
See Magazines

Philip II   [1527–1598]
King of Spain (1556–98) who set the armada against England, and patronized chess players. Ruy Lopez played before him and was presented by Philip himself, with a gold neck chain plus a rook suspended from it.

Philip III   [1578–1621]
King of Spain (1598–1621) who enjoyed chess and gave a pension of 200 crowns per year to Domenico di Leonardis for his chess prowess.

Piatigorsky
See Los Angeles

Pietzsch, Wolfgang
[*December 21 1930– *]
East German GM (1965) who was East German Champion 4 times during 1949–67. He played on 6 East German Olympiad teams during 1952–68. His best result was 1st at Leipzig 1965.

Pigusov, Evgeny   [*March 31 1961– *]
USSR GM (1987) who was equal 1st at Havana 1986 (VIII) and at Sochi 1987) (XI). He was equal 2nd at Moscow 1987 (IX) Dordrecht 1988 (IX).

Piket, Jeroen   [*January 27 1969– *]
Dutch GM (1989) who was equal 3rd at the Lugano Open 1989 and equal 1st at Munich 1989 (X)

Pillsbury, Harry Nelson
[*December 5 1872–June 17 1906*]
US player of GM strength who was in the world top four during 1895 to 1903. He burst upon the scene at Hastings

Pillsbury, who stunned the chess world by winning his first international tournament (Hastings 1895), the strongest tournament held until then.

1895 when he came 1st ahead of all the greats: Lasker, Steinitz, Tarrasch, Chigorin etc. The chess world was impressed not only with his victory but with the quality of his games. His moves flowed smoothly and logically, his ideas were crystal clear and there was a fresh, open honesty, almost an innocence, about him and his play. Besides being probably the strongest tournament ever held (up to that time), this was Pillsbury's very first international tournament and no one had ever won a major tournament on their first attempt. It was as if Morphy had been reborn.

Pillsbury played in 13 international tournaments and was almost always near the top. After Hastings he was 3rd at St Petersburg 1895/96, equal 3rd at Nuremberg 1896, 3rd at Budapest 1896, equal 1st at Vienna 1898 where he lost the play-off +1=1−2 to Tarrasch, equal 2nd at London 1899, 2nd at Paris 1900, equal 1st at Munich 1900, 2nd at Hanover 1902, 2nd at Monte Carlo 1902, 3rd at Monte Carlo 1903, 4th at Vienna 1903 and equal 8th at Cambridge Springs 1904. It is curious that in the midst of all this success, Pillsbury never won an outright international 1st prize after Hastings.

The tragedy was that Pillsbury contracted syphilis in St Petersburg 1895/96, was not well during 1896, recovered, but began to succumb to the disease in 1903 and was seriously ill in 1904.

Lasker came ahead of Pillsbury at St Petersburg, Nuremberg, London and Paris, and though their individual score was level, Lasker proved the better tournament player.

In life scores Pillsbury beat Schlechter (+8=9−2), Janowski (+6=2−4), and Maroczy (+4=7−3). He was level with Lasker (+5=4−5), Steinitz (+5=3−5), and Tarrasch (+5=2−5). He lost to Chigorin (+7=6−8) and Blackburne (+3=4−5).

Pillsbury was a superb blindfold player. His maximum was 22 simultaneous blindfold games (Moscow 1902). But his most remarkable performance was on his rest day at Hanover 1902. There he played 21 such games against players from the Hauptturnier—one level below master. His opponents included Bernstein, Cohn, Dyckhoff, Kagan, Exner, Englund, Fleischmann (Forgacs) and Fahrni, all of whom became well known. Pillsbury scored +3=11−7 against this formidable company.

Some said Pillsbury was ruining his health with such strenuous displays, but it was syphilis not simultaneousness that was to kill him in a short time.

Pillsbury worked inside the famous automaton Ajeeb, placed 7th at New York 1893 (where Lasker scored 13–0), reported on the 1894 Lasker–Steinitz match, beat Showalter +10=3−8 in 1897 and +7=2−3 in 1898, and was 1st at Buffalo 1901.

Pillsbury had a superb combinatorial talent and was most formidable in middlegames where clear direct plans were needed. His weaknesses, according to Fine, were an impatience in inferior positions and a difficulty in dealing with unclear middlegames where subtle manoeuvering was required. Pillsbury specialized in and popularized the Ruy Lopez and the Queen's Gambit.

Pillsbury was a heavy smoker of cigars. His main rival, Lasker—also a cigar smoker—called Pillsbury: '... a pathfinder ... a source of pleasure and joy'.

See *Pillsbury's Chess Career* by Sergeant and Watts (1923), *Pillsbury's Best Games* by P. Wenman (1948)

Pillsbury–Tarrasch
Hastings 1895

1 d4 d5 2 c4 e6 3 ♘c3 ♘f6 4 ♗g5 ♗e7 5 ♘f3 ♘bd7 6 ♖c1 0-0 7 e3 b6 8 cd ed 9 ♗d3 ♗b7 10 0-0 c5 11 ♖e1 c4 12 ♗b1 a6 13 ♘e5 b5 14 f4 ♖e8 15 ♕f3 ♘f8 16 ♘e2 ♘e4 17 ♗xe7 ♖xe7 18 ♗xe4 de 19 ♕g3 f6 20 ♘g4 ♔h8 21 f5 ♕d7 22 ♖f1 ♖d8 23 ♖f4 ♕d6 24 ♕h4 ♖de8 25 ♘c3 ♗d5 26 ♘f2 ♕c6 27 ♖f1 b4 28 ♘e2 ♕a4 29 ♘g4 ♘d7 30 ♖4f2 ♔g8 31 ♘c1 c3 32 b3 ♕c6 33 h3 a5 34 ♘h2 a4 35 g4 ab 36 ab ♖a8 37 g5 ♖a3 38 ♘g4 ♗xb3 39 ♖g2 ♔h8 40 gf gf 41 ♘xb3 ♖xb3

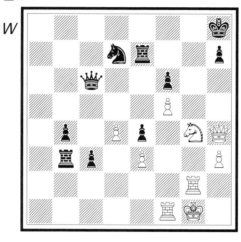

42 ♘h6 ♖g7 43 ♖xg7 ♔xg7 44 ♕g3+ ♔xh6 45 ♔h1 ♕d5 46 ♖g1 ♕xf5 47 ♕h4+ ♕h5 48 ♕f4+ ♕g5 49 ♖xg5 fg 50 ♕d6+ ♔h5 51 ♕xd7 c2 52 ♕xh7 mate

Pilnik, Herman

[*January 8 1914–November 12 1981*] German-born Jewish–Argentine GM (1952) who was Argentine Champion in 1942, 1945, and 1958, and played on 5 Argentine Olympiad teams during the 1950s. He first drew attention when he came 3rd (behind Alekhine and Najdorf) in a speed tournament in Buenos Aires 1939. He was equal 2nd at Mar del Plata 1942, equal 1st at Mar del Plata 1944 and equal 2nd at Mar del Plata 1945. He was equal 3rd at New York 1948/49, 2nd at Bled 1950, equal 1st at Lucerne 1951, 1st at Beverwijk 1951, 1st at Vienna 1951/52, 1st at Stuttgart 1954 and in 1956 he became a Candidate. He was outclassed in this top level but he did have a 3rd at Santiago 1959 ahead of Fischer.

Pilnik moved and travelled a great deal. He finally settled in Venezuela where he taught chess at the Caracas Military Academy.

Pin

A piece or pawn is said to be pinned if it obstructs an attack on its king or other valuable unit. It is thus immobilized—absolutely when it shields the king and for all practical purposes when it shields a valuable unit.

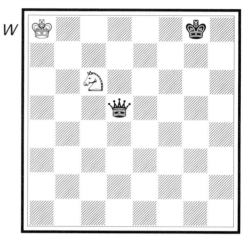

Here White has a great urge to play 1 ♘e7+ forking the king and queen. However the knight is pinned and it would be actually illegal to move the knight and expose the white king to capture.

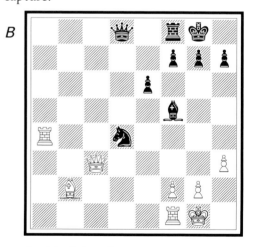

The black knight is pinned on the g-pawn, for if the knight moves then White mates with ♕xg7++. However the knight can legally move and in

fact 1 ... ♘e2+ wins the queen and the game.

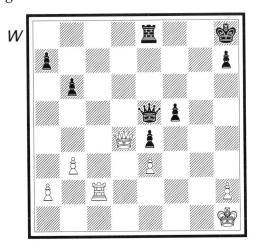

This position from Dunkelblum–Canal, Venice 1953 shows a fine partial pin: 1 ♖c8 threatening both 2 ♕xe5+ and 2 ♖xe8+ After 1 ... ♕xd4 2 ♖xe8+ ♔g7 3 ed White is a rook up.

Pinter, Jozef   [November 9 1953–]
Hungarian GM (1982) who was Hungarian Champion in 1978 and 1979. He showed much promise and began to come into his own in 1985 when he was equal 1st at Szirak (XI), 1st at Copenhagen (XI) and equal 1st at Prague (X). Then he came 2nd at Szirak 1986 (XII), 1st at Warsaw 1987 (X) and equal 2nd at Dortmund 1988 (XII). He has never been a Candidate but he is a strong effective GM. He played on all 5 Hungarian Olympiad teams during the 1980s.

Pion Coiffé
See Handicap

Pirc, Vasja
        [December 19 1907–June 2 1980]
Yugoslav author, historian and GM (1953) who was the third Yugoslav (after Vidmar and Kostic) to become a GM. He was Yugoslav Champion in 1935 (joint), 1936 and 1937 (also in 1948 and 1953) and thus established himself as the leading Yugoslav player.

He was on 6 Yugoslav Olympiad teams during 1931–54.

In international tournaments his best results were 1st at Novi Sad 1936, at Lodz 1938 and at Bad Haezburg 1938. He was 3rd at Noordwyk 1938 and equal 1st at Marianske Lazne 1948. In 1949 he drew a match with Euwe +2=6−2.

Pirc was an inventive player and is perhaps best remembered as a prolific author whose originality greatly contributed to opening theory, e.g. with the Pirc–(Robatsch) Defence 1 e4 d6 2 d4 ♘f6 3 ♘c3 g6.

Pirc–Robatsch Defence (Pirc Defence)

1 e4 d6 2 d4 ♘f6 3 ♘c3 g6
First played by Paulsen at Nuremberg 1883, but popularized by Pirc and Ufimtsev in the 1940s. The Robatsch version has a different sequence but is basically ... d6 ... g6 ... ♗g7 and ... ♘f6. It is a fluid kind of defence which tries to keep the game closed until Black is ready to break out.

White has quite a few promising lines: 4 f4, 4 ♘f3, 4 ♗c4, 4 ♗g5 and 4 f3

See *The Complete Pirc* by John Nunn (1989).

Plachetka, Jan   [February 18 1945–]
Czech GM (1978) who was equal 1st at Polanica Zdroj 1975, 1st at Sofia 1979 (VII), 1st at Trnava 1979 (VIII) and equal 1st at Strasbourg 1985 (VII). He played on the Czech Olympiad team from 1980 to 1986.

Planinc, Albin   [April 18 1944–]
Yugoslav GM (1972) who was 1st at Ljubljana 1969 and equal 1st with Petrosian at the IBM Amsterdam 1973 tournament, ahead of Spassky, Szabo etc. He specializes in apparently outdated openings into which his imaginative play infuses new life.

Plaskett, Harold James
        [March 18 1960–]
Cyprus-born English GM (1985) who was 1st at Plovdiv 1984 (IX) and equal 2nd at Hastings 1984/85 (IX).

Platov, Vasily Nikolayevich
        [1881–1952]
and

Platov, Mikhail N.   [1883–1938]
Latvian brothers who composed endgame studies together.

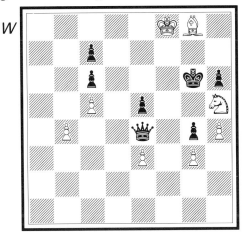

White to play and win (1904)
1 ♗h7+ ♔xh5 2 ♔g7 ♕xh7+ 3 ♔xh7 e4 4 ♔g8 ♔g6 5 ♔f8 winning or 1 ♗h7+ ♔xh5 2 ♔g7 ♕d3 3 ♗xd3 e4 4 ♗b5 cb 5 ♔f6 winning.

They wrote: *Sammlung der Endspielstudien* (1914) and *Sbornik Shakhmatnykh Etyudov* (1928).

Play-Off
If two (or more) players end up in a tie, then a short match (or round robin) between them is the ideal way to break the tie. Such a tie-breaking match is called a play-off.
See Tie Breaking Systems.

Pleiades
See Berlin Pleiades

Pocket Chess Set
A small (often folding) chess board with flat pieces, which can be carried in a pocket.

163

Poetry

Chess has been used quite frequently in poetry—see our epigraph (p 00) for example. Browning, Byron, Dante, T. S. Eliot, Keats, Pound, Spenser and Tennyson are some of the famous poets who have referred to chess in their work.

See *The Poetry of Chess* by Andre Waterman (1981).

Poisoned Pawn

A pawn left undefended in the opening (usually the white b-pawn) which if taken gives the opponent time to launch a dangerous attack.

Polerio, Giulio Cesare   [1548–1612]

Italian player and author who travelled with Leonardo to Spain in 1574 where they beat Ruy Lopez. He wrote (1594): *Trattato de scacchi di Giulio Cesare Polerio* which carefully recorded the openings played in his time.

He is also believed to have written: *L' elegantia sottilita verita della virtuosissima professione de' scacchi*, a free translation of Ruy Lopez—see the National Library at Florence

Polgar, Judit   [23 July 1976–]

Hungarian IM (1988) and Woman GM-

Judit Polgar, the youngest of the three phenomenal sisters and the strongest 12 year-old in history.

(1988) who was 3rd at the female under 16 World Championship in 1986, 1st at the World Mixed in London, October 1988, gold medallist on board 2 at the women's Olympiad November 1988 and who won the Hastings Challengers in December 1988. She is the youngest of the three Polgar sisters and many say she is not only the best of them but has the potential to become World Champion by beating Kasparov (or Karpov) in 10 to 20 years.

Judit Polgar ranked 1st on the January 1 1990 FIDE ranking list for women, with 2550, ahead of her sister Zsuzsa (2500). The Woman World Champion, Chiburdanidze was rated 2470 on that list. She ranked equal 55th on the men's list in 1989 and, this is probably a record for a 12-year old.

Polgar Zsofia   [November 2 1974–]

Hungarian Woman GM (1989) and who played on board 4 for the successful Hungarian women's Olympiad team in 1988. She scored a record 2900 + rating performance for her win at an Open in Rome (1989).

Polgar, Zsusza   [April 19 1969–]

Hungarian IM (1984) who won the female under-16 World Championship in 1981. She was equal 2nd in the Hungarian (men's) Championship 1986 (VIII) and equal 5th at Bilbao 1987 (XII). She led the Hungarian women's Olympiad team to victory in 1988 and won the bronze medal for board 1. She ranked second (2500) on the January 1 1989 FIDE rating list for women, behind her sister Judit, but ahead of World Champion Chiburdanidze.

Zsusza Polgar is the oldest of the three remarkably talented Polgar sisters.

Polish Defence

1 d4 ♘f6 2 ♘f3 b5

Black seems to neglect the centre, but his position is not without resources and both Spassky and Larsen have occasionally experimented with this line.

Polish Immortal

A brilliant game won by Najdorf which Tartakower called the Polish Immortal.

Glucksberg–Najdorf

Warsaw 1935

1 d4 f5 2 c4 ♘f6 3 ♘c3 e6 4 ♘f3 d5 5 e3 c6 6 ♗d3 ♗d6 7 0-0 0-0 8 ♘e2 ♘bd7 9 ♘g5 ♗xh2+ 10 ♔h1 ♘g4 11 f4 ♕e8 12 g3 ♕h5 13 ♔g2 ♗g1 14 ♘xg1 ♕h2+ 15 ♔f3 e5 16 de

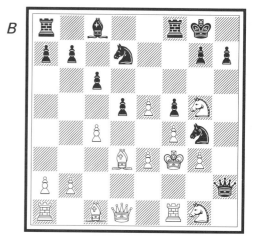

16 ... ♘dxe5+ 17 fe ♘xe5+ 18 ♔f4 ♘g6+ 19 ♔f3 f4 20 ef ♗g4+ 21 ♔xg4 ♘e5+ 22 fe h5 mate

Pollock, William Henry Krause   [February 21 1859–October 5 1896]

Irish author and player of IM strength, who was 1st at Belfast 1886 and wrote the tournament booklet on St Petersburg 1895/6 with Mason.

See *Pollock Memories* by Mrs Rowland (1899)

Polugayevsky, Lev Abramovich   [November 29 1934–]

USSR GM (1962) who did not reach his peak until his mid-30s but then reached almost the very highest level. He played in 20 USSR Championships during 1956 to 1983, scoring an overall 207–136 for 60.4%. He was equal 1st in three consecutive championships (1967, 1968 and 1969) and even in 1983 he was equal 3rd (XIV).

Lev Polugayevsky (left), seen here with Petrosian advising a thoughtful Fidel Castro at the 1966 Olympiad in Havana.

Polugayevsky was a Candidate three times. In 1974 he lost +0=5−3 to Karpov. In 1977 he beat Meching +1=11−0 but then lost +1=7−5 to Korchnoi. In 1980 he beat Tal +3=5−0 but again lost to Korchnoi +2=9−3.

He has had a long string of fine tournament victories from Mar del Plata 1962 to Haninge 1988 (XIII). He was equal 2nd at Moscow 1981 (XV), at Bugojno 1982 (XIV) and at London 1984 (XIV). Not only was Polugayevsky among the top 6 players during the 1970s and early 1980s but the Keene and Divinsky study places him 12th on the list of all-time great players.

In life scores he beat Tal (+8=19−1), Geller (+9=19−4) and Najdorf (+2=3−0). He held his own with Smyslov (+3=16−3) and Spassky (+2=15−2). He lost to Korchnoi (+7=29−19), Petrosian (+2=13−6), Karpov (+0=14−4) and Kasparov (+0=2−2).

Polugayevsky played on the USSR Olympiad team from 1978 to 1984.

He has great talent, but his excitable disposition probably interfered with his climb to the very top.

Major work: *Grandmaster Preparation* (1981).

See *Grandmaster Polugayevsky* by Y. V. Damsky (1982).

Polugayevsky–Petrosian

27th USSR Championship 1960
1 d4 ♘f6 2 c4 e6 3 ♘c3 ♗b4 4 e3 0-0 5 ♗d3 d5 6 ♘f3 c5 7 0-0 dc 8 ♗xc4 b6 9 ♕e2 ♗b7 10 ♖d1 ♘bd7? 11 d5 ♗xc3 12 de ♗a5 13 ed ♕c7 14 e4 ♘xd7 15 ♘g5 ♖ad8 16 ♗xf7+ ♖xf7 17 ♘e6 ♕c8 18 ♘xd8 ♗a6 19 ♕e3 ♖e7 20 ♕b3+ c4 21 ♕a3 ♘c5 22 ♗e3 ♖xe4 23 ♗xc5 ♕xc5 24 ♕f3 Resigns (if 24 ... ♖e7 25 ♘e6)

Pomar, Arturo [*September 1 1931– *] Spanish GM (1962) who was a child prodigy that caught the imagination of the press and became quite famous. Though he won some 7 Spanish Championships during 1946–66 and played on many Spanish Olympiad teams during 1958–76, he never fulfilled his early promise.

His best results were equal 1st at Madrid 1960 and Torremolinos 1961, 1st at Malaga 1964, 2nd at Palma 1966 and 1st at Malaga 1971. He had nervous breakdowns in 1965 and 1966, which interfered with his participation in competition.

Alekhine took an interest in young Pomar and devoted a section of his last book (Legado 1946) to him.

Ponziani, Domenico Lorenzo

[*November 9 1719–July 15 1796*] Italian law professor, player and author who, together with Erocle del Rio and Lolli, formed the strength of the so-called Modenese School. In 1769 he wrote *Il giuoco incomparabile degli scacchi*, which covered a wider range of openings (including the Allgaier Variation of the King's Gambit, the Vienna Game and Ponziani's Opening   1 e4 e5 2 ♘f3 ♘c6 3 c3) than his colleagues Lolli and Ercole del Rio.

Ponziani's Opening

1 e4 e5 2 ♘f3 ♘c6 3 c3
White plans to strike at the centre with d4 and to recapture there with a pawn. However, Black has several ways to equalize because he is under no direct threat. The best is the natural 3 ... ♘f6.

Popovic, Petar [*February 14 1959– *] Yugoslav GM (1981) who was equal 1st at Pecs (1980 (VI), Novi Sad 1981 (VIII), Bor 1985 (X) and Pucarevo 1987 (IX). He was equal 2nd at Novi Sad 1984 (VII) and at Cannes 1986 (X) but perhaps his best result was equal 4th at Belgrade 1987 (XIV).

He played a drawn match (+1=6−1) with Chiburdanidze in 1986 and played on the Yugoslav Olympiad team in 1986 and in 1988.

Portisch, Lajos [*April 4 1937– *] Hungarian GM (1961) who was one of the most successful players of the last 25 years. He is extremely hard-working, modest, talented and a first class sportsman. He ranks 21st on the all-time list of great players, according to Keene and Divinsky, and is probably the best player Hungary has ever produced.

Portisch was Hungarian Champion 9 times during 1958–81 and a member of about a dozen Hungarian Olympiad teams. He was a Candidate 8 times (only Korchnoi at 9, has appeared more frequently) though has never become the official challenger. In 1965 he lost +1=3−4 to Tal. In 1968 he lost +2=5−3 to Larsen. In 1974 he lost +2=8−3 to Petrosian. In 1977 he beat Larsen +5=3−2 but then lost +2=9−4 to Spassky. In 1980 he tied +1=12−1 with Spassky and went through on tie break only to lose +0=9−2 to Hübner. In 1983 he lost +1=4−4 to Korchnoi. In 1985 he did not make the final play-offs at Montpellier. In 1988 he beat Vaganian +1=5−0 but lost +1=3−2 to Timman in early 1989.

Portisch has played in over 80 serious tournaments and over a dozen have been Category XIV, XV or XVI. In recent years he was equal 3rd at Niksic 1983 (XIV), equal 2nd at Tilburg 1983 (XV), equal 3rd at Linares 1985 (XIV), equal 1st at Portoroz 1985 (XII), equal 1st at Sarajevo 1986 (XII), equal 4th at Bugojno 1986 (XVI) and equal 4th at Reggio Emilia 1988 (XV). In other non-Candidate matches he lost +1=3−2 to Timman in 1984 but beat Nunn +2=4−0 in 1987.

In life scores up to about mid-1988, Portisch beat Larsen (+25=15−14), Reshevsky (+4=9−0), Keres (+4 =3−1), Korchnoi (+9=12−7) and Petrosian (+7=26−6). He lost to seven World Champions: +4=15−7 to Tal, +6=50−12 to Spassky, +4=24−7 to Smyslov, +2=21−8 to Karpov, +0=5−4 to Fischer, +0=4−2 to Kasparov and +0 =3−1 to Botvinnik.

Portisch's style is positional, full of subtle ideas and deep manoeuvring.

See *Selected Games of Lajos Portisch* by E. Varnusz (1979).

Portisch–Gheorghiu

Manila 1974 (Brilliancy Prize)

1 d4 ♘f6 2 c4 g6 3 ♘c3 d5 4 ♘f3 ♗g7 5 ♕b3 dc 6 ♕xc4 0-0 7 e4 ♗g4 8 ♗e3 ♘fd7 9 ♕b3 ♘b6 10 ♖d1 ♘c6 11 d5 ♘e5 12 ♗e2 ♘xf3+ 13 gf ♗h5 14 ♖g1 ♕d7 15 ♖g3 c6 16 dc ♕xc6 17 ♘b5 ♘c8 18 ♖d5 ♔h8 19 ♖c5 ♕f6 20 ♗d4 ♕h4 21 ♗xg7+ ♔xg7 22 ♕c3+ ♔g8 23 ♘c7 ♖b8 24 ♖cg5 f6 25 ♘e6 ♖e8 26 f4 ♗xe2 27 ♖h3 ♕xg5 28 ♘xg5 fg 29 ♔xe2 gf 30 ♕c4+ ♔g7 31 ♖xh7+ ♔xh7 32 ♕f7+ ♔h6 33 ♕xe8 Resigns

Positional Judgment

The ability to evaluate a position in terms of strengths and weaknesses, as distinct from calculating tactical sequences of moves. This involves weighing isolated pawns, doubled pawns, open files, holes, mobility and the initiative.

This kind of judgment plays a major role when there are no clear tactical road signs. Then a player must choose between several reasonable-looking moves where deep calculation is not possible. To make these difficult choices he must look for the road that maximizes his position's positional strengths like space, mobility and initiative. In other words, he must learn how to improve his position quietly.

Karpov is the great master in this area and studying his games will be useful to any student who wishes to gain a deep understanding of positional play and positional judgment.

Positional Sacrifice

A sacrifice of material for a positional advantage and not for winning material or increasing the power of one's attack. A good example is Bronstein's opening play in Spassky–Bronstein, Amsterdam 1956: 1 d4 ♘f6 2 c4 g6 3 ♘c3 ♗g7 4 e4 d6 5 f3 e5 6 d5 ♘h5 7 ♗e3 ♘a6 8 ♕d2 ♕h4+ 9 g3 ♘xg3 10 ♕f2 ♘xf1 11 ♕xh4 ♘xe3 12 ♔f2 ♘xc4

Black has sacrificed his queen for 2 bishops and 2 pawns and the hope that his army will have a good positional future in order to balance the material deficit.

Postage Stamps

See Stamps

Post Mortem

At the end of a game the players often go to an analysis room to discuss their game, and to find out where the mis-takes were made. Such 'post mortem' sessions can be extremely illuminating. They often produce beautiful variations that didn't occur in the game and reveal how GMs think (assuming the players *are* GMs).

Potter, William Norwood

[*August 17 1840–March 13 1895*] English author and player of IM strength who edited the *City of London Chess Magazine* (1874–6), wrote the chess section for the *Encyclopaedia Brittannica*, and contributed well-written chess articles to the *Westminster Papers* during 1868–79.

He lost +2=8−4 to Zukertort in 1875 and drew +5=11−5 with Mason in 1879. He and Steinitz led the London end of a correspondence match with Vienna (led by Kolisch) in 1872–4 and London won +1=1−0.

Prepared Variation

An opening innovation prepared at home and kept secret until an important opportunity arises where it can be used. See for example Marshall's Counter-gambit in the Ruy Lopez, which Marshall held back for some years before unleashing it against Capablanca.

Preti, Jean-Louis

[*1798–January 27 1881*] Italian born flautist and chess author who settled in France in 1826, specialized in endgames and founded the monthly magazine *La Strategy* in 1867. He edited this magazine almost until his death.

Major Works: *Traité complet théorique et pratique sur les fins de parties au jeu des échecs* (1858), *Stratégie raisonnée des fins de partie* (with Durand) (1871).

Prins, Lodewijk   [*January 27 1913– *]

Dutch IM (1950), International Arbiter (1960) and Honorary GM (1982) who was Dutch Champion in 1965 and played on the Dutch team in all 12 Olympiads from 1937 to 1968. His best tournament result was 1st at Madrid 1951. Prins is a tall, charming gentleman and a serious author.

Major Works: *Master Chess* (1940), *Maastricht* (1946), *Hastings 1945/4* and *1946/47*, *Het Schaakphenomeen Capablanca* (with Euwe) (1949), *Amsterdam 1950* (with Euwe)

Problems

Composed positions, often quite different from those that occur in real life, given as problems to the reader to mate in a certain number of moves (or to selfmate or helpmate, where both sides cooperate). There is an unwritten convention that the positions should be 'real' in the sense that they can actually be reached from the initial set up of the pieces. The 'games' that are needed to prove a position can be reached need not be well played!

Problems (called *Mansuba*) first appeared in 9th century Arabian manuscripts. Since then there has been much growth and development and today there is a large body of problems including fairy problems with new, weird pieces (*see* Grasshopper) and retrograde analysis.

The problem world is filled with people who enjoy composing and solving problems. It has its own history, theory, conventions, themes and beloved composers. A large part of this world has little to do with actually playing chess.

See *The Chess Problem*, by H. Weenink (1926), *Chess Problems: Introduction to an Art* by Lipton, *Matthews and Rice* (1963), *An ABC of Chess Problems*, by J. M. Rice (1970).

Prokes, Ladislav [1884–1966]

Czech player and endgame composer who played on the Czech Olympiad team (1927, 1928 and 1931).

Major Work: *Kniha Sahovych Studii* (1951).

Promotion

When a pawn reaches the 8th rank it must become a piece of its own colour i.e. a queen, rook, bishop or knight. It cannot remain a pawn, it cannot become a king and it cannot change its colour. If it becomes a rook, bishop or knight the transformation is called an underpromotion.

Theoretically it is possible for a player to have 9 queens—though such a harem-like situation has never occurred in real life.

See Pawn

Protect

A piece 'A' is said to protect a piece 'B' if 'A' can capture any enemy piece that captures 'B'. If the attacking piece is less valuable than the attacked piece, then this protection is inadequate.

Prophylaxis

A Nimzowitschian word used to describe the essence of position play, including strategems to prevent one's opponent from freeing his position.

Protected Passed Pawn

A passed pawn that is protected by another pawn.

Psakhis, Lev Borisovich [November 29 1958–]

USSR (Siberia) GM (1982) who started out superbly by being equal 1st at the 1980 USSR Championship and again in 1981. Since then his achievements have been less spectacular. He played in 6 USSR Championships during 1980–7, scoring 56% overall.

Psakhis has never been a Candidate, but recently he has crept closer to that elite group with an equal 1st at Sarajevo 1986 (XII), clear 1st at Szirak 1986 (XII) and equal 2nd at Trnava 1988 (XII).

Psychology and Chess

Psychologists have been intrigued with chess masters since Binet examined them with his IQ test in 1894. Their studies have as yet not produced any profound insights.

See *Thought and Choice in Chess*, by A. De Groot (1966), *The Psychology of the Chessplayer*, by R. Fine (1967), *Psychologie des Schachspiels*, by Djakov, Petrowski and Rudik (1927).

Puc, Stojan [April 9 1921–]

Yugoslav IM (1950) and honorary GM (1984) who was successful in numerous Yugoslav tournaments, but never achieved the same status abroad. For many years he was the leading Slovenian player after Pirc. Puc's best result was equal 1st at Dortmund 1951. He played on the 1950 Yugoslav Olympiad. team.

Purdy, Cecil John Seddon [March 27 1906–November 5 1979]

Australian author and IM (1951) who won the first World Correspondence Chess Championship 1950–3 and was Australia's Mr Chess. He founded and edited *The Australian Chess Review* 1929–67 (it was called *Check* in 1945 and *Chess World* from 1946 on). He was New Zealand Champion in 1924 and Australian Champion in 1935, 1937, 1949 and 1951. He was non-playing team captain of the 1974 Australian Olympiad team.

Major Works: *World Title Match of 1935* (1936), *World Title Match of 1937*, (1938), *Among These Mates* (1939) (under the pseudonym of Chielamangus).

Puzzles

Chess contributes a good deal to the world of puzzles. The knight's tour, the 8 queens puzzle (place 8 queens on the board so no one can capture another) and the 8 rooks puzzle (place 8 rooks on the board so no one can capture another, and compute how many ways this can be done) are good examples.

See *Mathematical Recreations*, by Rouse Ball.

Q
Symbol for the queen

Queen

The queen is the second largest piece in a chess set, but by far the strongest one. She combines the moves of the rook and bishop moving along ranks and files (like the rook) or along diagonals (like the bishop) and in each case, as far as there are unobstructed lines.

This was not always the case. In *Chaturanga* (late 6th century) our queen was then called a *mantri* (a minister or counsellor) and could only move to one adjacent diagonal square. It was not until chess came to Europe (10th century) that the queen began to have increased powers—it could then leap three squares. Only by 1475 did the queen obtain its present power.

Queen's Gambit
1 d4 d5 2 c4.

One of the most popular of all openings, especially since the start of the 20th century. The plan is to put pressure on the black d-pawn with the object of luring it away from the centre. Black has many possible defences.

Albin Counter Gambit
2 ... e5 3 de d4

Named after the Austrian master Albin, this line is held to be unsound. White can maintain the upper hand with ♘f3 and g3.

Catalan System—*see* Catalan

Chigorin's Defence
2 ... ♘c6.

A rarity in contemporary international chess, since White keeps an edge with 3 ♘c3 dc 4 ♘f3.

Marshall's Defence
2 ... ♘f6.

White gains the advantage after 3 cd ♘xd5 4 ♘f3 followed by e4, since Black has no counter to White's central preponderance.

Orthodox Defence

The main line of this defence is: 1 d4 d5 2 c4 e6 3 ♘c3 ♘f6 4 ♗g5 ♗e7 5 e3 0-0 6 ♘f3 ♘bd7 7 ♖c1 c6 8 ♗d3 dc 9 ♗xc4 ♘d5 10 ♗xe7 ♕xe7 11 0-0 ♘xc3 12 ♖xc3 e5 13 de, the Rubinstein variation. Then 13 ... ♘xe5 14 ♘xe5 ♕xe5 15 f4 ♕f6 16 f5 b5 17 ♗d3 b4 18 ♖c2 ♖d8 19 ♕e2 a5 with equality.

Semi-Slav Defence

A sub-variation of the Slav Defence where Black temporarily locks in his queen's bishop whilst simultaneously preparing queenside counterplay with c5. The theoretically important Meran System (deriving its name from Rubinstein's games played at Meran 1924) runs as follows: 1 d4 d5 2 c4 c6 3 ♘f3 ♘f6 4 ♘c3 e6 5 e3 ♘bd7 6 ♗d3 dc 7 ♗xc4 b5 8 ♗d3 when extreme com-

plications can arise from 8 ... a6 9 e4 c5 and now 10 e5 or 10 d5.

Slav Defence
2 ... c6.

This supports the d-pawn without locking in the queen's bishop. In many lines it also helps prepare a possible ... b5 after ... dc. One of the most popular lines of the Slav is the Dutch Variation, 1 d4 d5 2 c4 c6 3 ♘f3 ♘f6 4 ♘c3 dc 5 a4 ♗f5 6 e3 e6 7 ♗xc4 ♗b4 8 0-0 0-0 which has been extensively analysed since its debut in the 1937 Alekhine–Euwe world title match.

Symmetrical Defence
2 ... c5.

An idea of Rubinstein which was definitely refuted in Portisch–Bronstein, Monaco 1969: 3 cd ♘f6 4 e4! ♘xe4 5 dc ♘xc5 6 ♘f3 e6 7 ♘c3 ed 8 ♕xd5. After this game the defence vanished from master chess.

Tarrasch Defence
2 ... e6 3 ♘c3 c5.

Black accepts an isolated pawn (after 4 cd ed) in exchange for active piece play.

Westphalia Defence
1 d4 d5 2 c4 e6 3 ♘f3 ♘f6 4 ♘c3 ♘bd7 5 ♗g5 ♗b4 6 cd ed 7 e3 c5.

This was analysed by Spielmann and other GMs aboard the liner Westphalia while crossing the Atlantic on their way to New York 1927. It was with this defence that Spielmann lost to Capablanca (who won the 1st brilliancy prize for it); *see* Capablanca.

Queen's Gambit Accepted

1 d4 d5 2 c4 dc.

Ninety years ago it was considered obligatory for Black to defend his d-pawn with all the resources at his command. However, during the 1930s a new method was devised whereby Black temporarily surrenders the centre, to avoid the cramped Orthodox Defence and to avoid the locking in of the queen's bishop. The main line here is 3 ♘f3 ♘f6 4 e3 e6 (4 ... ♗g4 is a modern Russian idea) 5 ♗xc4 c5 (striking back at the centre to free his game) 6 0-0 a6 7 ♕e2

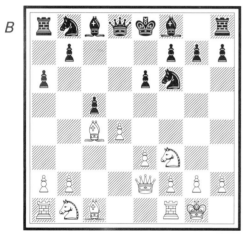

B

Now 7 ... ♘c6 or 7 ... b5 are Black's main alternatives. In this line, White normally maintains a slightly freer position.

Queen's Indian Defence

1 d4 ♘f6 2 c4 e6 3 ♘f3 b6
This was popularized by Nimzowitsch and the hypermoderns. Its idea is to control the square e4. White has difficulty maintaining any opening advantage. The main line is 4 g3 ♗b7 5 ♗g2 ♗e7 (or 5 ... ♗b4+ or 5 ... c5) 6 0-0 0-0 7 ♘c3 ♘e4 or 7 ... d5.

Black can also try 4 ... ♗a6 the exaggerated fianchetto.

Queen's Pawn Counter-Gambit

1 e4 e5 2 ♘f3 d5

A violent and incorrect attempt by Black to seize the initiative. White gains an edge with either 3 ed or 3 ♘xe5.

Queen Pawn Opening

1 d4

Queenside

That half of the board consisting of the a-, b-, c- and d-files.

Queenside Castling

This is castling with the queen's rook and is represented by 0-0-0.

Queenside Pawn Majority

The advantage of a majority of pawns on the queenside is a frequent strategic aim in modern master games. Such a majority must be capable of producing a passed pawn—an outside passed pawn, to be a clear advantage. The term queenside must not be taken too literally since the important characteristic is not the original presence of queens but the absence of kings from the majority wing. The accurate description is really: a majority of pawns on the side from which the kings are absent.

Such a majority will produce a passed pawn far from the enemy king. On the other hand a passed pawn produced from a kingside majority would necessarily remove protection from the king.

A good example is the following game:

Eliskases–Flohr

Semmering Baden 1937

1 d4 ♘f6 2 c4 g6 3 ♘c3 d5 4 ♗f4 ♗g7 5 e3 0-0 6 ♘f3 c5 7 cd ♘xd5 8 ♗e5 ♘xc3 9 bc cd 10 ♗xg7 ♔xg7 11 cd ♕a5+ 12 ♕d2 ♘c6 13 ♗e2 ♖d8 14 ♕xa5 ♘xa5 15 0-0 ♗e6 16 e4 ♗g4 17 ♖fd1 e6 18 ♔f1 ♗xf3 19 ♗xf3 ♖ac8 20 ♖d2 e5 21 d5 ♘c4 22 ♖e2 ♘d6 23 ♖b1 ♖c4 24 g3 ♖dc8

25 ♗g2 ♖c1+ 26 ♖xc1 ♖xc1+ 27 ♖e1 ♖xe1+ 28 ♔xe1 f5 29 f3 fe 30 fe b5

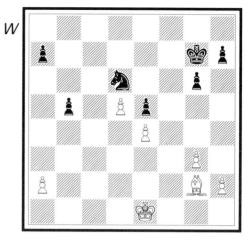

W

Black has two advantages: A good knight versus a bad bishop and a queen-side pawn majority. They are perhaps not sufficient to force a win but White's defence is difficult.

31 ♔d2 a5 32 ♔d3 ♔f6 33 ♗f3 ♔e7 34 h4 h6 35 ♗d1 ♔d8 36 a4 ba 37 ♗xa4 ♔c7 38 ♗c2 ♔b6 39 ♔c3 ♔b5 40 ♔b3 ♔c5 41 ♗a4 ♘c4 42 ♗b3 ♘d2 43 ♗c2 ♘f1 44 ♔xa5 ♘xg3 45 ♔a4 ♘h5 46 ♔b3 ♔d4 47 ♔b4 ♘f6 48 d6 g5 49 hg hg 50 ♔b5 g4 51 ♗d1 g3 52 ♗f3 ♔e3 53 ♗h1 ♔f2 54 ♔c6 g2 55 ♗xg2 ♔xg2 56 d7 ♘xd7 57 ♔xd7 ♔f3 58 Resigns

Queening Square

The square in the 8th rank on which a pawn is promoted (usually to a queen).

Quinteros, Miguel Angel

[*December 28 1947– *]
Argentine GM (1973) who won the Argentine Championship in 1966 and 1980, and played on many Argentine Olympiad teams during 1970 to 1984.

He was equal 2nd at Portoroz 1973, equal 1st at Torremolinos 1973, 1st at Lanzarote 1974, 2nd at Lone Pine 1976, equal 2nd at London 1977, 1st at Moron 1982, 2nd at New York 1983 (X), 1st at Netanya 1983 (IX) and equal 3rd at Baden-Baden 1985 (IX).

In 1987 FIDE, in its wisdom, barred Quinteros from playing in FIDE events for 3 years because he went to play in South Africa, thus breaking a FIDE rule. There is now a move to attempt to bar him for a much longer period because he has continued to play in South Africa.

R
Symbol for rook.

Rabar, Braslav
[September 27 1919–December 6 1973]
Yugoslav IM (1950) who was Yugoslav Champion (1951) played on 3 Yugoslav Olympiad teams in the early 1950s, coedited the monthly magazine *Sahovski Glasnik* and designed an opening classification system used in the *Chess Informant*.

Rabelais, François   *[1490–1553]*
French satirist whose romances contained references to chess (see his *Fifth Book of Pantagruel*).

Rabinovich, Ilya Leontyevich (or Elias)   *[1891–1942]*
USSR teacher and player of GM strength who played in 8 USSR championships during 1920–39, scoring 79–58 for 57.7%. He was co-champion with Levenfish in 1934. He had a respectable 7th at Baden-Baden 1925 but his international results were not as good as his successes in USSR Championships.

Rabinovich was Leningrad Champion 4 times during 1920–40. He wrote books on the endgame and the openings, was primarily a positional player and perished in the siege of Leningrad.

Radio Matches
See Cable and Radio Matches

Radulov, Ivan   *[January 7 1939–]*
Bulgarian engineer and GM (1972) who was Bulgarian Champion in 1971, 1974, 1977 and 1980, and was a regular on the Bulgarian Olympiad team from 1968 to 1986. He was equal 1st at Torremolinos 1971, 1st at Helsinki 1972, 1st at Montilla 1974 (XII), equal 1st at Montilla and Bajmok 1975, and 2nd at Silkeborg 1983 (VII).

Ragozin, Vyacheslav Vasilievich
        [October 8 1908–March 11 1962]
USSR GM (1950) who played in 11 USSR Championships during 1934 to 1956, his best result being equal 2nd in 1937. In other events, he was equal 3rd Leningrad–Moscow 1947 (XII). He won the 2nd World Correspondence Championship 1956–8.

He was Botvinnik's trainer, editor of the monthly *Shakhmaty*, author and an active worker in FIDE.

Major works: *Botvinnik–Tal 1960 match*, *Ragozin's Best Games*, edited by Beilin (1964).

Raicevic, Vladimir   *[May 2 1949–]*
Yugoslav GM (1976) who was equal 1st at Vrnjacka Banja 1976, 1st at Valjevo 1984 (VII) and 1st or equal 1st at some recent open tournaments: Baymok 1984, Novi Becey 1985 and Bled 1986.

Rajkovic, Dusan   *[June 17 1942–]*
Yugoslav GM (1977) who was equal 1st at Vrnjacka Banja 1976, equal 1st at Smederevska Palanka 1977, clear 1st at S. Palanka 1979, equal 1st in the 1983 Yugoslav Championship (VIII) and equal 2nd at Novi Sad 1986 (VII).

Rank
A horizontal row running from left to right. The white pieces are initially set up on the 1st rank and the white pawns on the 2nd rank.

Ranken, Charles Edward, Reverend
        [January 5 1828–April 12 1905]
English player and author who, in collaboration with Lord Randolph Churchill (Winston's father), founded the Oxford University Chess Club, who edited the *Chess Player's Chronicle* (1877) and who wrote for the *British Chess Magazine*.

Major Work: *Chess Openings Ancient and Modern* (with E. Freeborough) (1889).

Rantanen, Yrjo Aukusti
        [April 23 1950–]
Finnish GM (1981) who was 3rd at Helsinki 1981 (VIII) and 1st at Jarvenpaa 1982 (VII). He was champion of Finland in 1976 and 1978, and played on several Finnish Olympiad teams.

Rapid Chess

Chess played at a rate of 30 minutes for each player for the entire game. This is much faster than normal tournament play of 40 moves in 2 hours and then 20 moves per hour, but not as fast as blitz, where each player has only 5 minutes (usually) for the entire game.

Rapid chess allows reasonably well thought-out plans to be made and quite good games to be produced. No game lasts more than an hour and this allows 4, 5 or sometimes 6 rounds to be played in one day.

Rapid chess is becoming extremely popular. The first rapid chess world championship was held in Mexico in December 1988. After a 13-round Swiss for 61 players, there were knock-out matches for the top 8. In the semifinals Karpov beat Ehlvest $2\frac{1}{2}$–$1\frac{1}{2}$ and Gavrikov beat Tukmakov $2\frac{1}{2}$–$1\frac{1}{2}$. In the final it was 4–4 and Karpov won on tiebreak.

FIDE has (August 1989) authorized Rapid chess ratings to be calculated. (Rapid chess was previously known as 'Active' chess by FIDE. In the USA, 'action chess' is the favoured term; in the UK 'quickplay' is used.)
See Time Limit.

Rapid Transit Chess
A US term for blitz or speed chess.

Rashkovsky, Nukhim Nikolayevich
[April 18 1946–]
USSR GM (1980) who played in 7 USSR Championships during 1972–87 but scored less than 50%. He was 1st at Sochi 1979, equal 3rd at Kuibyshev 1986 (IX) and equal 2nd at Vrnjacka Banja 1987 (VIII).

Rating Systems
The desire to estimate the playing strengths of chess players both past and present seems to be widespread. Rating systems are attempts to do this. The

first try was done by Brumfitt in 1891 (in the *British Chess Magazine*). Then came the Ingo System (1948 by Anton Hosslinger), the Harkness System (1951) and an English system based on Ingo–Harkness (1953) by Sir Richard Clarke.

The first statistically sound method was done by Arpad Elo (1960). This was adopted by FIDE in 1970 and rating lists are produced twice a year.

Keene and Divinsky recently (1989) published another statistically sound method for estimating lifetime strengths.
See Elo.

See also *Warriors of the Mind* by Keene and Divinsky (1989).

Razuvaev, Yuri Sergeyevich
[October 10 1945–]
USSR GM (1976) who was equal 2nd at Cienfuegos 1976, equal 1st at Dubna 1976, 1st at Polanica Zdroj 1979, equal 1st at Keszthely 1981, equal 1st at Dortmund 1985 (IX) and equal 1st at Jurmala 1987 (X).

He played in 5 USSR Championships during 1972–85 but overall he scored less than 50%.

Soviet Grandmaster Yuri Rasvvayev.

Ree, Hans
[September 15 1944–]
Dutch GM (1980) who studied mathematics and philosophy at Amsterdam University and gave them up to become a chess professional. He was 1st at Ter Apel 1966, equal 1st at Vancouver 1971, 1st at Graz 1979, equal 1st at Amsterdam 1980 (IX) and equal 1st at Ter Apel (XI). He was Dutch champion in 1967, 1969, 1971 and 1982, and he played on many Dutch Olympiad teams during 1966 to 1984.

He beat Donner $+2=5-1$ in 1971.

Reggio Emilia
City in northern Italy about 100 miles inland from Genoa, which stages a strong (usually XIV or XV) tournament over New Years. Tukmakov won in 1987/88 (XV), Gurevich won in 1988/89 (XIV), and the 1989/90 (XVI) winner was Ehlvest.

Reinfeld, Fred
[January 27 1910–May 29 1964]
US author who wrote over 100 books. Most of them have little real content but a few are worthwhile.

Major works: *Dr Lasker's Chess Career* (with Reuben Fine) (1935), *Practical End-Game Play* (1940).

Remis
German word for a draw.

Repetition of Position
A threefold repetition of a position may lead to a draw upon a claim by the player having the move if:
  (a) the same position has just appeared for the third time, with the same player having the move each time; or if
  (b) he declares to the arbiter his intention of making a move, and writes this move on his scoresheet, and this move will produce the same position, for the third time, with the same player having the move each time.

The position is considered the same if pieces of the same kind and colour occupy the same squares (even though two white rooks for example, might have changed places); and if the possible moves of all the pieces are the same, including the right to castle or to take a pawn *en passant*. Thus the diagram position, where we assume the Black king and rook to be this far unmoved, is not considered the same as the position reached after 1 ... ♖h4+ 2 ♔a3 ♖h8 3 ♔a4 because Black can no longer castle.

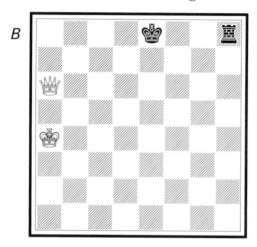

When a claim for a draw is made, the arbiter stops the clocks and examines the claim. If it is valid, the game is drawn. If the claim is found to be incorrect then the arbiter adds 5 minutes to the claimant's used time. If this means that the claimant has overstepped the time limit then he forfeits the game on time. Otherwise the game continues.

Reshevsky, Samuel Herman

[*November 26 1911– *]
Polish-born US GM (1950) who was a famous child prodigy, giving simultaneous exhibitions at the age of 8, and who matured into one of the world top 5 during 1935 to 1960. He played in The Hague/Moscow 1948 World title tournament, coming equal 3rd behind Botvinnik and Smyslov, and he was a Candidate twice after that. He was equal 2nd in the 1953 Candidates and in 1968

Samuel Reshevsky in 1935.

he was eliminated +0=5−3 by Korchnoi. He ranks 22nd on the Keene and Divinsky all-time list of great players.

Reshevsky came to the US in 1920, took a degree in accounting at the University of Chicago 1934 and then went to Europe to meet the great players of his day. He was 1st at Margate 1935 (ahead of Capablanca), equal 3rd at Nottingham 1936 (XIV), equal 3rd at Semmering 1937 (XIV), equal 1st at Kemeri 1937, 1st at Hastings 1937/38 and equal 4th at the super-strong AVRO 1938 (XVII).

He won the US Championship in 1936, 1938, 1940, 1942 and 1946 and was 1st at Los Angeles 1945. After his equal 3rd at The Hague/Moscow 1948, he wanted to play in the 1950 Candidates but world politics interfered when the US would not give him a visa to Budapest. He was 2nd at Amsterdam 1950, 1st at New York 1951, equal 1st at Dallas 1957, equal 1st at Buenos Aires 1960 and 1st at Natanya 1969.

In matches Reshevsky beat Horowitz +3=13−0 in 1941, Kashdan +6 =3−2 in 1942, Najdorf +8=6−4 in 1952, Gligoric +2=7−1 in 1952, Najdorf +5=9−4 in 1953 and Benko +3=5-2 in 1960. In 1961 he played an exciting drawn match +2=7−2 with the young Fischer and was given the

winner's share when Fischer withdrew. In the 1964 interzonal play-off Reshevsky lost +0=1−2 to Portisch and in the 1968 Candidate he lost to Korchnoi.

Reshevsky has continued to play well into his 70s. He won the US Championship for a 6th time in 1969, he was equal 1st at the 1984 Reykjavik Open and lost +1=5−2 to Christiansen in 1984.

Reshevsky played on 8 US Olympiad teams during 1937 to 1974.

In life scores he beat Najdorf (+19 =22−10), Gligoric (+4=24−2), Keres (+6=9−4), Fine (+4=13 −1), Euwe (+6=6−2) and Flohr (+1=8-0). He held Capablanca (+1 =4−1) and lost to Spassky (+0 =2−1), Alekhine (+1=2−2), Petrosian (+0=8−2), Korchnoi (+0=8 −3), Portisch (+0=9−4), Botvinnik (+2=7−5), Fischer (+4=13−9) and Smyslov (+2=15−5).

Reshevsky is a short, grim and determined man with little charm or graciousness. He uses most of his allotted time for the first half of the game and has severe time pressure to complete his 40 moves. At AVRO 1938 he was in time trouble in 12 of his 14 games. However, he is a superb time pressure player. Euwe described Reshevsky as liking boring positions and as having inexhaustible patience, tenacity and endurance.

Major work: *Reshevsky on Chess* (1948) *How Chess Games are Won* (1962).

Resign

To give up the game before being checkmated.

Réti, Richard

[*May 28 1889–June 6 1929*]
Jewish-Czech (Austro-Hungarian) player of GM strength who studied mathematics in Vienna and, after much internal debate, gave it up for chess. He became the leading representative of the so-

called hypermodern school, which believed that controlling the centre is just as good as occupying it. Réti popularized 1 ♘f3 d5 2 c4, now called Réti's Opening, and beat Capablanca with it at New York 1924—Capablanca's first defeat in 8 years.

His best results were 1st at Kashau 1918, 1st at Göteborg 1920, equal 1st at Teplitz-Schonau 1922, 2nd at Carlsbad 1923, 2nd at Mahrisch Ostrau 1923, 1st at Vienna 1928 and equal 1st at Brno 1928.

Réti won the Czech Championship in 1925 and played on the 1927 Czech Olympiad team, achieving the best score on board 1. He set a record for simultaneous blindfold at Sao Paulo 1925, when he scored + 20 = 7 − 2 against 29 opponents.

He was genial, friendly, witty and had no poison in his soul. He was well educated, cultured and had an artistic temperament. He wrote two excellent books and composed beautiful endgame studies.

Réti died suddenly (and unexpectedly) of scarlet fever.

Major works: *Modern Ideas in Chess* (1922, German; 1923, English), *Masters of the Chessboard* (1930, German; 1933, English)

See *Réti's Best Games of Chess* by Golombek (1954).

White to play and draw (1921)

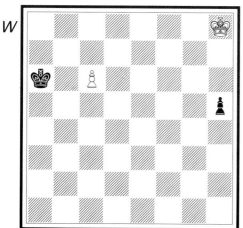

1 ♔g7 ♔b6 2 ♔f6 h4 3 ♔e5 h3 4 ♔d6 h2 5 c7 h1(♛) 6 c8(♛) Draw

Réti Opening

1 ♘f3

Popularized by Réti as part of his new hypermodern style of play. It offers flexible development combined with numerous transpositional possibilities. After 1 ♘f3 d5 2 c4 the opening often takes on an independent character, one important variation being the Lasker System: 2 ... c6 3 b3 ♘f6 4 g3 ♗f5 5 ♗g2 e6 6 ♗b2 ♘bd7 7 0-0 h6 8 d3 ♗e7, with even chances.

Retrograde Analysis

In some problems it is important to know whether castling is still legal or whether an *en passant* capture is available. To this end one must figure out what the last few moves were or how the given position came into being. This kind of analysis is called retrograde. For example:

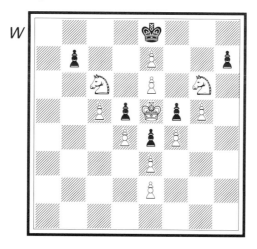

White to move and mate in two moves (Dawson 1914)

What was Black's last move? It must have been either ... d5 or ... f5 but which one? To reach the given position, the white pawns must have made 10 captures. Since there are 6 black men on the board, all 10 missing black men must have been captured by the white pawns. In particular the black bishop that started out at c8 must have been taken by a white pawn. No white pawn could have captured this bishop

on the square c8 so the capture must have taken place elsewhere. Therefore the bishop must have left c8. To do so the black d-pawn must have been moved some time ago. Therefore Black's last move must have been ... f5. So the solution is 1 gf *en passant* followed by 2 f7 mate.

See Retrograde Analysis, by Dawson and Hundsdorfer (1915), *Introduction to Retrograde Analysis*, by Fabel (1973), *The Chess Mysteries of Sherlock Holmes*, by Raymond Smullyan (1979), *The Chess Mysteries of the Arabian Knights*, by Raymond Smullyan (1981).

Reykjavik

The capital of Iceland, where there are more and better chess players *per capita* than anywhere else in the world. It first rose to prominence when it staged the spectacular Fischer–Spassky match of 1972. In 1987 it held a Category XIV tournament won by Short (8) ahead of Tal (7), Timman (7), Korchnoi (6½) and Portisch (6½). Unfortunately neither Kasparov nor Karpov participated.

In October 1988 it held World Cup III (XV) where Kasparov led the way while the 50 year olds (Portisch, Spassky, Korchnoi) found themselves near the bottom. Only Tal (at 51) showed to advantage, with a fine 3rd prize. (See table next page)

Ribli, Zoltan [*September 6 1951– *] Hungarian GM (1973) who was a Candidate twice. He almost made it into the candidates in 1980, but missed out on tie break. He became a Candidate in 1983 where he beat Torre + 3 = 6 − 1 but then lost to Smyslov + 1 = 7 − 3. He was also a Candidate at Montpellier 1985, but he did not make the final play-offs.

In tournaments, he began winning at Kecskemet 1972 and more recently he was 2nd at Bugojno 1984 (XIV), equal

Reykjavik 1988 World Cup III Category XV

		1	2	3	4	5	6	7	8	9	10	11	12	13	14	15	16	17	18	
1	Kasparov	–	½	½	1	1	½	1	1	½	½	1	0	½	½	½	½	1	½	11
2	Belyavsky	½	–	1	½	1	0	½	½	1	½	½	½	1	½	1	0	½	1	10½
3	Tal	½	0	–	½	½	½	½	1	½	1	½	½	½	1	1	½	½	½	10
4	Hjartarson	0	½	½	–	½	½	½	1	½	½	½	0	1	½	0	1	1	1	9½
	Ehlvest	0	0	½	½	–	½	0	1	½	1	½	½	1	½	½	1	½	1	9½
6	Yusupov	½	1	½	½	½	–	½	½	½	½	½	½	0	½	½	1	½	½	9
	Sax	0	½	½	½	1	½	–	½	½	½	½	1	½	½	0	½	1	½	9
	Timman	0	½	0	0	0	½	½	–	½	½	1	1	1	½	½	½	1	1	9
9	Nunn	½	0	½	½	½	½	½	½	–	½	½	½	½	½	1	½	1	0	8½
	Speelman	½	½	0	½	0	½	½	½	½	–	½	½	½	1	½	½	1	½	8½
	Andersson	0	½	½	½	½	½	½	0	½	½	–	1	½	½	½	½	½	1	8½
12	Sokolov	1	½	½	1	½	½	0	0	½	½	0	–	0	½	½	½	½	1	8
	Nikolic	½	0	½	0	0	1	½	0	½	½	½	1	–	½	½	½	1	½	8
14	Ribli	½	½	0	½	½	½	½	½	½	0	½	½	½	–	½	½	0	1	7½
15	Portisch	½	0	0	1	½	½	1	½	0	½	½	½	½	½	–	½	0	0	7
	Spassky	½	1	½	0	0	0	½	½	½	½	½	½	½	½	½	–	½	0	7
17	Korchnoi	0	½	½	0	½	½	0	0	0	0	½	½	0	1	1	½	–	1	6½
18	Petursson	½	0	½	0	0	½	½	0	1	½	0	0	½	0	1	1	0	–	6

2nd at Tilburg 1984 (XIV), equal 1st at Portoroz 1985 (XIII), 1st at Reggio Emilia 1987 (XIV) and equal 4th at Belfort 1988 (XV).

He was Hungarian Champion in 1973, 1974 and 1977, and has been a regular on the Hungarian Olympiad team from 1970 to 1988.

He played board 5 for the Rest of the World against USSR in 1984, where he beat Vaganian +1=3−0.

Rice, Isaac Leopold
[February 22 1850–November 2 1915–]
Bavarian-born US lawyer, law professor and industrialist who donated large sums to promote chess and in particular to analyse his gambit invention 1 e5 e5 2 f4 ef 3 ♘f3 g5 4 h4 g4 5 ♘e5 ♘f6 6 ♗c4 d5 7 ed ♗d6 8 0-0. At Brighton, in August 1903, Lasker played 6 Rice Gambits against Chigorin and Chigorin won +2=3−1.

Rice's daughter Dorothy married P. Hal Sims, the bridge star of the early 1930's. She is alleged to have invented psychic bridge bidding.

Rice, John Michael *[July 19 1937–]*
British IM (1969) and problem composer who edited the problem section of the *British Chess Magazine* (1961–74).

Major works: *An ABC of Chess Problems* (1970), *The Serieshelpmate* (1971), *Chess Problems: Introduction to an Art* (with Lipton and Matthews) (1963). *The Two Move Chess Problem: Tradition and Development* (with Lipton) (1966).

Richter, Kurt
[November 24 1900–December 29 1969]
German author and IM (1950) who won the German Championship in 1935 and played on the German 1936 Olympiad team. He was a sharp attacking player.

Major works: *Kurzgeschichten um Schachfiguren* (1947), *Die Hohe Schule der Schachfiguren* (1952), *Einfalle-Reinfalle* (1960).

See *Kurt Richters Beste Partien*, by Brinckmann (1961).

Richter–Rauzer Attack
See Sicilian Defence

Rinck, Henri *[1870–1952]*
Prolific French endgame composer.

W

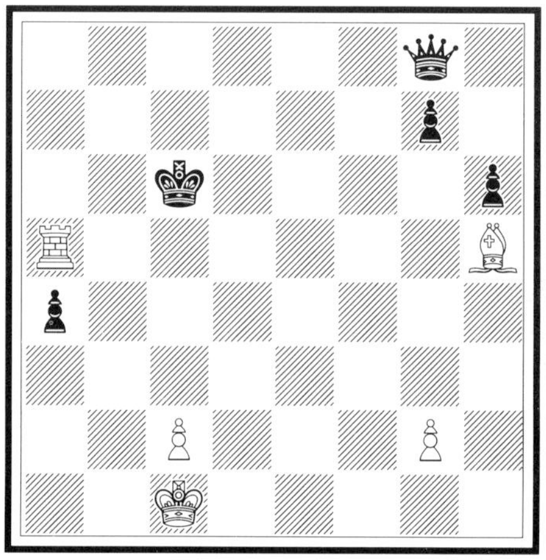

White to play and win (1903)
1 ♖a8 ♕a2 (not ... ♕xa8 3 ♗f3+) 2 ♖xa4 ♕g8 (not ... ♕xa4 3 ♗e8+) 3 ♖a8 ♕h7 4 ♗g6 ♕xg6 5 ♖a6+ ♔ moves 6 ♖xg6

Rittner, Horst Robert [*July 16 1930–*]
East German player who won the 6th World Correspondence Championship 1968–71.

Riumin, Nikolai Nikolayevich
[*1908–1942*]
USSR player of GM strength who was champion of Moscow from 1931 to 1936. He played in 3 USSR Championships in the early 1930s, coming 2nd in 1931 and equal 3rd in 1934. His best international result was equal 2nd at Leningrad 1934. His playing career ended when he took seriously ill in 1936.

Rivas Pastor, Manuel
[*July 13 1960–*]
Spanish GM (1987) who was 1st at Havana 1983 (VII). Torremolinos 1983 (VII) and Salamanca 1987 (VII), and equal 1st at Las Palmas 1987 (IX). He was Spanish champion in 1978, 1979 and 1981 and played on three Spanish Olympiad teams during the 1980s. His style is unstable and he has been known to withdraw from tournaments.

Rivière, Jules Arnous de
[*May 4, 1830–September 11, 1905*]
Leading French player of the 1850s and 60s, of almost GM strength, who played many offhand games with Morphy ($+6=2-18$) in 1858, 1859 and 1863. He beat Löwenthal $+2=0-0$ in 1867 and narrowly lost to Chigorin $+4=1-5$ in 1883.

Robatsch, Karl [*October 14 1928–*]
Austrian GM (1961) who is known for his defence 1 e4 g6 2 d4 ♝g7 (the Pirc–Robatsch Defence). He was Austrian Champion in 1960 and played on a number of Austrian Olympiad teams from 1954 to 1980—winning the gold medal on board 1 in the 1960 Olympiad. He was 2nd at Kapfenberg 1955, equal 2nd at Varna 1957, equal 1st at Madrid 1961, equal 2nd at Wijk aan Zee 1962 and equal 3rd at Halle 1963.

Rodriguez, Amador
[*October 18 1957–*]
Cuban GM (1977) who was 1st at Vrnjacka Banja 1977 (VIII), equal 1st at Cienfuegos 1984 (IX), equal 2nd at Havana 1985 (IX), 1st at Pancevo 1987 (IX) and 1st at Bayamo 1987 (VII). He was joint Cuban Champion in 1984 and has played on all the Cuban Olympiad teams during the 1980s.

Rodriguez, Orestes   [*July 4 1943–*]
Peruvian GM (1978) who was 1st at Alicante 1974, equal 1st at Reggio Emilia 1975, 1st at Orense 1977 (VII), equal 1st at Lanzarote 1977 (VIII) and equal 3rd at Malgrat de Mar 1978 (IX). He is a regular on Peruvian Olympiad teams.

Rogard, Folke
[*July 6 1899–June 11 1973*]
Swedish lawyer and chess organizer who was president of the Swedish Chess Federation in 1939 and president of FIDE from 1949 to 1970. He was charming, suave and effective. He led and strengthened FIDE through the difficult cold war years.

Rogers, Ian   [*June 24 1960–*]
Australian GM (1985) who was equal 1st at Nuroro 1984 (VII), equal 1st at Wijk aan Zee 1985 (VII), 1st at Kragujevac 1985 (VII) and 1st at Calcutta 1988 (VIII). Perhaps his best result was equal 3rd at Szirak 1986 (XII). He was Commonwealth Champion (equal) in 1983, and Australian Champion in 1979 and 1985. He has played on several Australian Olympiad teams during the 1980s.

Rogoff, Kenneth Saul
[*March 22 1953–*]
US GM (1978) who was 3rd in the World Junior Championship 1971, equal 1st at Norristown 1973, 2nd in the US Championship 1975 and equal 1st at Orense 1976 (VIII).

Rohde, Michael Arthur
[*August 26 1959–*]
US GM (1988) who was equal 1st at San Francisco 1987 (X) and equal 2nd at the St John 1988 Open.

Romanishin, Oleg Mikhailovich
[*January 10 1952–*]
USSR GM (1976) who has a distinguished tournament record with many victories, from Odessa 1974 to Erevan 1986. He is a talented player with an aggressive style, but he has never made it into the Candidates. Perhaps his best performances were 2nd at Tilburg 1979 (XV) and equal 3rd at Leningrad 1987 (XIV). He has played in 9 USSR Championships during 1974–83 and he scored $78\frac{1}{2}$–$66\frac{1}{2}$ for 54%, but he never won the title. He was equal 2nd in 1975, equal 3rd in 1980 and 3rd in 1981. He is a strong GM but not in the top rank.

Romanovsky, Peter Arsenyevich
[*July 30 1892–March 1 1964*]
USSR IM (1950) who was almost of GM strength and played in 8 USSR Championships during 1920–45. He won the championship in 1923, was equal 1st in 1927, was 2nd (to Alekhine) in 1920 and 2nd (to Boguljubow) in 1924. Overall he scored $78\frac{1}{2}$–$57\frac{1}{2}$ for 57.7%. Internationally he was equal 2nd at Leningrad 1934.

Major Work: *Mitelshpil* (1929).

Rook
A so-called major piece which moves on the ranks and files. It was the strongest piece on the board before the queen became powerful in the fifteenth century.

It was, originally, a chariot (*Ratha* in Sanskrit, then *Rukh* in Persian) but became a tower—*Rocco* (in Italian), *Tour* (French), *Turm* (Germany), *Torre* (Spanish), but a boat (*Ladia*) in Russian. It is often colloquially called a castle in English.

Its basic move has not changed at all since chess was invented but there was ambiguity about castling until about 1474.

Rook and Pawn Endings

These endings occur more often than any other type and they usually come down to ♚ + ♖ + ♙ versus ♚ + ♖. Having the extra pawn is an advantage, but not necessarily a decisive one. Since long difficult struggles often hinge on the outcome of such an ending, it is useful and satisfying to know the correct methods to convert the extra pawn into a win or to prove that the defence can hold the draw.

The experienced defender can generally hold the draw when his king is in front of the pawn: the Black rook stays on his 3rd rank to prevent the white king from advancing. Whenever White plays his pawn to the 6th rank to create a cover for his king the black rook must immediately go to its 8th rank to threaten infinitely many checks from behind the white king.

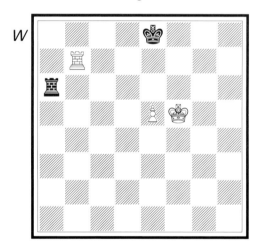

Thus 1 e6 ♖a1 2 ♚f6 ♖f1+ and White can make no progress. This method of defence was discovered by Philidor.

Black has good drawing chances even if the White ♚ gets to the 6th rank. On this diagram White threatens 1 ♖a8+ ♚d7 2 e6+ ♚d6 3 ♖d8+ ♚c7 4 e7.

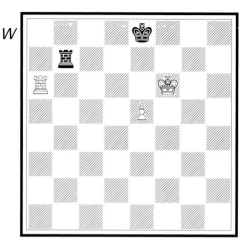

If Black plays passively 1 ... ♖b8 he will lose 2 e6 ♖c8 3 ♖h7. The correct way to defend is 1 ... ♖b1. Then neither 2 ♖a8+ ♚d7 nor 2 ♚e6 ♚f8 (to the short side) 3 ♖a8+ ♚g7 4 ♖e8 ♖a1 or 4 ♚d6 ♚f7 leads to anything for White.

The critical winning position is the so-called Lucena position. It was in fact first analysed by Salvio (1634) and he gave credit for it to Scipione Genovino.

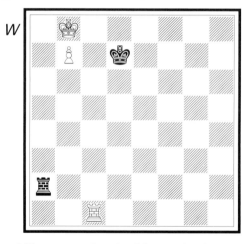

White wins by 'building a bridge': 1 ♖c4 ♖a1 2 ♖d4+ ♚e7 3 ♚c7 ♖c1+ 4 ♚b6 ♖b1+ 5 ♚c6 ♖c1+ 6 ♚b5 ♖b1+ 7 ♖b4.

There are many subtleties involved in these endings and the student is referred to the major treatises: Fine's *Basic Chess Endings* (1941), Cheron's *Handbuch der Endspiele* (1952), Hooper's *Pocket Guide to Chess Endgames* (1970), Smyslov and Levenfish's *Rook Endings* (1971, 1989)

and Averbakh's *Lehrbuch der Endspiele* (1972).

Rossetto, Hector Decio

[September 8 1922–] Argentine GM (1960) who was Argentine Champion 5 times during 1942–72 and played on 6 Argentine Olympiad teams during 1950–72, winning the top prize for board 5 at the 1952 Olympiad. He was a regular at the annual Mar del Plata events: 1st in 1949, equal 2nd in 1950, 1st in 1952 and equal 2nd in 1961. Perhaps his best result was equal 4th at Buenos Aires 1960 (X).

Rossetto captained the Argentine women's team at the 1988 Olympiad. He is a cultured gentleman who is a talented bridge player with an eye for beautiful things.

Rossolimo, Nicholas

[February 28 1910–July 24 1975] Russian born GM(1953) of Greek/Russian parents, who moved to Paris in 1929 and to New York in 1953. In France he was 2nd at Paris 1938 behind Capablanca, won the French Championship in 1948, the Paris Championship 5 times, played on 2 French Olympiad teams (1950, 1972) and drew two matches with Tartakower (in 1948 and 1949).

He was 1st at Hastings 1948/49, 1st at Gijon 1950, equal 1st at Southsea 1951 and 1st at Beverwijk 1953. In the US he won the US Open in 1955 and played on 3 US Olympiad teams (1958, 1960 and 1966).

Rossolimo worked as a bellhop, a taxi driver and a singer. He ran a chess studio in New York, played the accordion, spoke 5 languages and was a brown belt at judo. He died by accidentally falling down 2 flights of stairs.

Rothschild, Baron Albert Freiherr von

[October 29 1844–February 11 1911] Viennese banker and chess patron who helped finance Vienna 1873, 1882, 1898

Rotterdam 1989   World Cup V   Category XV

		1	2	3	4	5	6	7	8	9	10	11	12	13	14	15	16	
1	Timman	–	0	½	1	½	1	1	½	1	1	1	½	½	½	½	1	10½
2	Karpov	1	–	½	0	½	0	½	½	½	1	1	1	1	0	1	1	9½
3	Vaganian	½	½	–	½	½	½	½	1	½	1	1	0	1	½	½	½	9
4	Nunn	0	1	½	–	½	½	½	½	½	½	½	½	½	1	½	1	8½
5	Ehlvest	½	½	½	½	–	1	½	0	0	½	0	1	½	1	½	1	8
	Salov	0	1	½	½	0	–	½	1	1	0	½	1	0	½	½	1	8
	Sokolov	0	½	½	½	½	½	–	½	0	½	½	½	1	½	1	1	8
	Van der Wiel	½	½	0	½	1	0	½	–	1	½	½	½	½	½	1	½	8
9	Short	0	½	½	½	1	0	1	0	–	1	0	½	1	½	½	½	7½
10	Seirawan	0	0	0	½	½	1	½	½	0	–	½	½	½	1	1	½	7
11	Nogueiras	0	0	0	½	1	½	½	½	1	½	–	½	½	½	0	½	6½
	Sax	½	0	1	½	0	0	½	½	½	½	½	–	½	½	½	½	6½
	Yusupov	½	0	0	½	½	1	0	½	0	½	½	½	–	1	½	½	6½
14	Ljubojevic	½	1	½	0	0	½	½	½	½	0	½	½	0	–	½	½	6
	Portisch	½	0	½	½	½	½	0	0	½	0	1	½	½	½	–	½	6
16	Hjartarson	0	0	½	0	0	0	0	½	½	½	½	½	½	½	½	–	4½

Hübner was scheduled to play, but withdrew ill following a draw (his only game) against Nogueiras.

and 1908, as well as the gambit tournament of 1903. He also gave money for many brilliancy prizes. He was president of the Vienna Chess Association 1872–83 and honorary president of the Vienna Chess Club 1885–1911.

He was a strong amateur player and spent several hours every day at the club playing over master games and working on problems and endgame studies.

Rotlevi, G. A.   [1889–1920]
Polish player of almost GM strength who showed great promise. He was equal 1st at Lodz 1909, 2nd to Alekhine at St Petersburg All Russian 1909, 1st at the Hauptturnier at Hamburg 1910, 2nd at Munich 1911 and 4th at the powerful Carlsbad tournament of 1911.

He lost +5 =5 −8 to Salwe in 1909 but beat him +3 =6 −1 in 1911. At this point a serious nervous illness forced him to abandon competitive chess.

Rotterdam
Busy port city of Holland which staged the 5th leg of the World Cup in June 1989. With 3 rounds to go, Karpov (9½) had a commanding lead over Timman (8½). Timman closed with wins over Nogueiras and Seirawan to score 10½. Karpov, perhaps in a desperate attempt to catch Kasparov in the overall World Cup standings, lost his last 3 games—an unprecedented event. He got excellent games against Salov, Ljubojevic and Nunn and in each case seemed to lose his bearings and allow his position to disintegrate. A great victory for Timman, but a sad and perhaps ominous second prize for Karpov.

Round Robin Tournament
A tournament where every player plays against every other player. Such a tournament is quite different than a knock-out tournament or a swiss tournament.

Rousseau, Jean Jacques
    [June 28 1712–July 2 1778]
Celebrated French author and philosopher who had a passion but little talent for chess. He often played at the Café de la Régence. In his 'confessions' he writes:

(1736) 'There was a Genevese named Bagueret ... one of the most worthless, senseless fellows I ever met ... proposed teaching me to play at chess, of which game he understood something ... behold me fascinated with chess! ... pass whole days and nights in studying. After incredible efforts, during 2 or 3 months ... I go to the coffee-house ... so many combinations were fermenting in my head, and my imagination was so stupefied, that all appeared confusion. I tried to exercise myself with Philidor's or Stamma's book ... but I was still equally perplexed ... I could never advance one step beyond the improvement of the first sitting ...'
(1742) '... chess to which I regularly dedicated ... the evenings when I did not go to the theatre. I became acquainted with M. de Legall, ... Philidor and all the great chess players of the day, without making the least improvement. However, I had not doubt but, in the end, I should become superior to them all ...'

Royal Game

A common description of chess, because kings play the central role. Though many kings played chess, the sport of kings still seems to be horse racing.

Roycroft, Arthur John [1929–]

British endgame composer who founded (1965) and edited *EG*, a quarterly devoted to endgame studies. See his *The Chess Endgame* (1981).

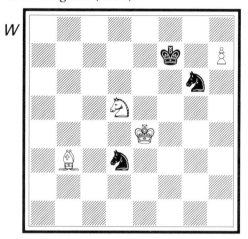

White to move and win (1954)

1 ♘f4+ ♚g7 2 ♘xg6 ♘c5+ 3 ♚d5 ♚xh7 4 ♗c2 ♘b7 5 ♘e5+ ♚g7 6 ♘c6 ♚f7 7 ♗a4 ♚f8 8 ♗b5 ♚e8 9 ♘a5+ and 10 ♘xb7. If 4 ... ♘a6 5 ♚d6 ♘b4 6 ♗b1 ♚g7 7 ♘e5 ♚f8 8 ♘d7+ ♚e8 9 ♘c5 ♚d8 10 ♗f5 ♚e8 11 ♘e6 ♚f7 12 ♗b1 ♚f6 13 ♘c7 and 14 ♚c5

Rubinstein, Akiba Kiwelowicz

[*October 12 1882–March 14 1961*] Polish GM (1950) who belonged to the world top 4 during 1909 to 1923 and who produced games of profound, almost magical beauty. Rubinstein was born in Stawiski, Poland (then part of Russia), the youngest of twelve children. His father died shortly before his birth and Akiba was raised by his grandparents, who gave him an orthodox Jewish religious education in keeping with the family traditions of Talmudic scholarship.

He had no contact with chess until the age of 16. Once he learned the game, he abandoned his religious studies, devoted himself entirely to chess and in about 1901, moved to the city of Lodz because it had a thriving chess club and a prominent master, George Salwe. Rubinstein improved rapidly as a player and in 1903 he first drew +5=0−5 with Salwe and then beat him +5=2−3. By 1907 Rubinstein came equal 1st at Ostend, 1st at Carlsbad and 1st at the Russian national in Lodz. In 1908 he beat Teichman +3=1−2, Marshall +3=3-2 and Mieses +5=2−3. He crowned it all by coming equal 1st with World Champion Lasker at St Petersburg 1909, beating Lasker in their individual game.

In 1911 Rubinstein was equal 2nd at San Sebastian, behind the new star Capablanca, though he beat the Cuban in their individual game. He was equal 2nd behind Teichmann at Carlsbad 1911. In 1912 Rubinstein was 1st at San Sebastian, 1st at Pistyan, equal 1st at Breslau, 1st at Warsaw and 1st at the Russian national in Vilna, where he beat young Alekhine twice.

Between 1907 and 1913, Rubinstein's record was superb and unsurpassed. Many believed he was the strongest player in the world and could even dethrone the mighty Lasker. However, raising the $2500 for a world title match seemed difficult.

Asked in 1913 about challengers, Lasker said: '... Rubinstein is the man who has the most reasonable hope of success. His style is of extraordinary fineness, and his knowledge of the game can hardly be surpassed by any living player. I am convinced that the battle between us will be hard and heavy, and neither will win his laurels easily'.

Ståhlberg wrote: 'Rubinstein's games from this period (1909–12) are remarkable for their clarity and power. He had a deep positional understanding, brilliant combinatorial abilities and an outstanding endgame technique'.

Réti wrote: '... he is the greatest artist among chessplayers ... all is refined tranquility; for with him in building his game the position given to every piece is the necessary one. It is not a matter of a fight for him, but the working out of a victory, and so his games create the impression of a great structure from which not one stone dare be shifted'.

Fine wrote: 'In the endgame he is supreme. And it is here, above all, that he provides us with an inexhaustible galaxy of masterpieces. In the rook and pawn endings especially he is beyond compare, ... black magic ... Better chess cannot by played by mortal man'.

Then something went wrong. Rubinstein began to feel persecuted. He believed that a fly was always settling on his head and disturbing him during play. He believed that at night, there was knocking on the door and walls of his room. He thought it was Réti, then he decided it was some princess. He believed people were trying to infect him with germs. He would no longer shake hands and he could only eat alone, in the privacy of his room.

The first collapse came at St Petersburg 1914, when he did not even make the finals. In spite of his illness, he came 2nd at Berlin 1918 and beat Schlechter +2=3−1 in 1918. In 1920 he was 2nd at Göteborg and beat Bogoljubow +5=3−4. In 1922 he was 1st at Triberg and 1st at Vienna, ahead of Alekhine.

His results became erratic and were sometimes marred by elementary blunders. It is remarkable that he could still be a top level GM while carrying his enormous persecution complex. He was 2nd at Baden-Baden 1925, equal 1st at Marienbad 1925, 2nd at Hanover 1926, Berlin 1926 and Budapest 1929, 1st at Rogaska Slatina 1929 and 3rd at San Remo 1930.

Rubinstein led the Polish Olympiad team in 1930 (scoring +13=4−0 for

88.2%) and in 1931 (+6=7−3). He stopped playing serious chess in 1932 and after spending some time in a sanatorium, lived in reduced circumstances in Belgium. During the war (1939−45) the Nazis, miraculously, left him alone.

Rubinstein made deep and lasting contributions to opening theory (in the Ruy Lopez, the Four Knights and the Queen's Gambit against the Tarrasch Defence).

In life scores he beat Marshall (+11=16−9), Bogoljubow (+13 =10−12), Nimzowitsch (+7=11−6), Teichmann (+6=11-5), Schlechter (+6=14−2), Maroczy (+4=11−2), Vidmar (+4=6-3), Janowski (+5 =0−3), Chigorin (+3=0−2) and he crushed Tarrasch (+8=12−0). He held Capablanca (+1=7−1), Euwe (+2=1−2) and Bernstein (+1=7 −1). He lost only to Lasker (+1 =4−2) and Alekhine (+5=2−8). Keene and Divinsky rank him as the 44th greatest player of all-time, but among GMs born before 1900 he ranks 5th (behind Capablanca, Lasker, Morphy and Alekhine).

In 1921 Rubinstein edited Collijns *Larobok* but otherwise left no literary legacy. His masterpieces are his games.

See Rubinstein's Chess Masterpieces by H. Kmoch (1933, German: 1941, English), *Akiba Rubinstein*, by Razuvaev and Murakhveri (1980).

Rubinstein–Lasker
St Petersburg 1909
1 d4 d5 2 ♘f3 ♘f6 3 c4 e6 4 ♗g5 c5 5 cd ed 6 ♘c3 cd 7 ♘xd4 ♘c6 8 e3 ♗e7 9 ♗b5 ♗d7 10 ♗xf6 ♗xf6 11 ♘xd5 ♗xd4 12 ed ♕g5 13 ♗xc6 ♗xc6 14 ♘e3 0-0-0 15 0-0 ♖he8 16 ♖c1 ♖xe3 17 ♖xc6+ bc 18 ♕c1! ♖xd4 19 fe ♖d7 20 ♕xc6+ ♔d8 21 ♖f4 f5 22 ♕c5 ♕e7 23 ♕xe7+ ♔xe7 24 ♖xf5 ♖d1+ 25 ♔f2 ♖d2+ 26 ♔f3 ♖xb2 27 ♖a5 ♖b7 28 ♖a6 ♔f8 29 e4 ♖c7 30 h4 ♔f7 31 g4 ♔f8 32 ♔f4 ♔e7 33

h5 h6 34 ♔f5 ♔f7 35 e5 ♖b7 36 ♖d6 ♔e7 37 ♖a6 ♔f7 38 ♖d6 ♔f8 39 ♖c6 ♔f7 40 a3 Resigns

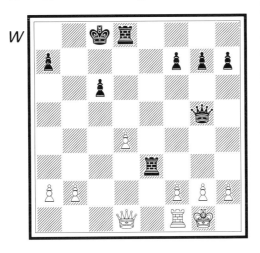

Rotlevi–Rubinstein
Lodz 1907 (The Rubinstein Immortal)
1 d4 d5 2 ♘f3 e6 3 e3 c5 4 c4 ♘c6 5 ♘c3 ♘f6 6 dc ♗xc5 7 a3 a6 8 b4 ♗d6 9 ♗b2 0-0 10 ♕d2 ♕e7 11 ♗d3 dc 12 ♗xc4 b5 13 ♗d3 ♖d8 14 ♕e2 ♗b7 15 0-0 ♘e5 16 ♘xe5 ♗xe5 17 f4 ♗c7 18 e4 ♖ac8 19 e5 ♗b6+ 20 ♔h1 ♘g4 21 ♗e4 ♕h4 22 g3

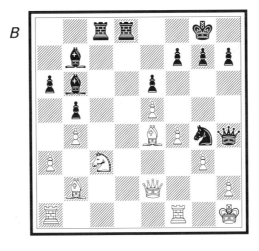

22 ... ♖xc3 23 gh ♖d2 24 ♕xd2 ♗xe4+ 25 ♕g2 ♖h3 26 Resigns

Rubtsova, Olga Nikolayevna
[*August 20 1909–]*
USSR Woman GM (1976) who was Woman World Champion (1956–8). She

was USSR Woman Champion in 1927, 1931 and 1937 and 1949.

Rudenko, Ludmila Vladimirovna
[*July 27 1904–March 1986*]
USSR Woman GM (1976) who was Women's World Champion (1950–3). She was USSR Women's Champion in 1952.

Rueb, Alexander
[*December 27 1882–February 2 1959*]
Dutch lawyer, author and chess organizer who was one of the founders of FIDE (Paris 1924) and its first president (1924 to 1949). He had a vast knowledge of endgame studies, on which he wrote a standard work (5 volumes): *Bronnen van Schaakstudie* 1949–55.

Rueb owned a large and famous chess library which was destroyed by bombs in 1945. He rebuilt it after the war and it is now in the Amsterdam University Library.

Rules, History Of
In its modern form, chess has existed essentially since the fifteenth century, when the queen and bishop were altered to their present status. National differences, however, remained for centuries afterwards on such points as castling, the *en passant* rule, pawn promotion, and stalemate. For example Philidor in his *Analyse* of 1749 complains bitterly of his countrymen who allow a new queen to appear on the board before the old one has been exchanged—a practice of which he clearly disapproved! In England, the set of rules which eventually became the norm was that of the London Chess Club, written by Sarratt in 1808. Sarratt was instrumental in introducing to Britain the continental practice of scoring a stalemate as a draw. At the first international tournament, London 1851, the code of rules was written by Staunton, and later published by him in *Chess Praxis* (1860).

The laws of chess now in universal use are those of FIDE which date in substance from 1929. A FIDE commission exists to clarify any ambiguities or doubtful points which may arise.

Rusinek, Jan [1950–]
Brilliant Polish endgame composer.
White to play and draw
1 a7 (not 1 g8(♕) ♖xg8 2 a7 ♘e4 3 ♔b7 ♗d5+ 4 ♔a6 ♘d6 and wins) 1 ... ♗a6+ 2 b7 ♘e4 3 g8(♘)+ ♔e8 4 ♘f6+ ♘(4)xf6 5 a8(♗) (not 5 a8(♕)

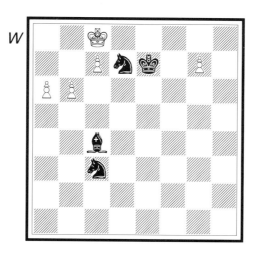

W

♘d5 and 6 ... ♘e7 mate) 5 ... ♘e5 6 ♔b8 ♘c6+ 7 ♔c8 ♗f1 8 b8(♖) (if 8 b8(♕) ♗a6+ 9 ♕b7 ♘e4 and 10 ... ♘d6 mate, or 8 b8(♘) ♘e7+ 9 ♔b7 ♗g2+ 10 ♘c6 [if 10 ♔a7 ♘c8+ and 11 ... ♗xa8 wins] 10 ... ♗xc6+ 11 ♔a7 ♗d7 [not 11 ... ♘c8+ 12 ♔b8 ♘d7+ 13 ♔xc8 ♗xa8 stalemate] and black will eventually win.) 8 ... ♗a6+ 9 ♖b7 ♘e4 stalemate.

Ruy Lopez

See Lopez, Ruy

S

Sacrifice

A move that voluntarily gives up material in the hope of gaining some other (potentially more valuable) advantage. This can be tactical, like speeding up one's development, or increasing the force of one's attack, or positional, like creating an outpost or gaining control of a critical square.

A sacrifice, even if not entirely sound or correct, has the advantage of surprising one's opponent and may cause him to overlook the best defence.

Sahovic, Dragutin   [August 8 1940–]

Yugoslav GM (1978) who was equal 1st at Lone Pine 1977, 1st at Sombor 1978 (VII), equal 1st at Dubna 1979 (IX), 1st at Vrnjacka Banja 1984 (VIII) and equal 1st at Montpellier 1988 (VII).

Saint-Amant, Pierre Charles Fournier de

[September 12 1800–October 29 1872] French diplomat and player of IM strength who was a regular at the Café de la Régence. He studied under Deschapelles and Schlumberger and led the Paris team to their + 2 − 0 correspondence victory over the Westminster club in 1836. When La Bourdonnais died in 1840, Saint-Amant became the leading player of France —

Deschapelles was still alive, but deep in retirement.

As a wine merchant, Saint-Amant visited England in 1843 and there he lost a casual match + 4 = 1 − 6 to Cochrane but beat Staunton + 3 = 1 − 2. This led to a serious challenge and the so-called Grand Chess Match between England and France. In fact this match could be considered the first world championship match. Staunton came to Paris (November 1843) and the stakes of £100 (or 2500 French francs) were to go to the first player to score 11 wins. Saint-Amant lost + 6 = 4 − 11 and the French chess supremacy of 100 years (Legall, Philidor, Deschapelles and La Bourdonnais) came to an end.

Saint-Amant drank coffee and took snuff. He was a much slower player than Staunton, who wrote about Saint-Amant: 'Decidedly slow, I never knew a man with such powers of endurance; after 14 hours he appears to be as fresh as when he first sat down'.

Saint-Amant edited *Le Palamède* from 1842 to 1847. He tried to arrange a return match with Staunton but Staunton took ill with pneumonia on his way to Paris in 1844. Saint-Amant went on to a distinguished career: Governor of the Tuileries (1849), French Consul in California (1851). He played in Birmingham 1857, losing + 1 − 2 to Falkbeer. He retired to Algeria in 1861.

Saint-Amant–Staunton

Match 1843

1 d4 e6 2 c4 d5 3 ♘c3 ♘f6 4 ♘f3 c5 5 e3 ♘c6 6 a3 b6 7 ♗d3 ♗d6 8 cd ed 9 ♗b5 ♗b7 10 dc ♗xc5 11 b4 ♗d6 12 ♗b2 0-0 13 ♘e2 ♕e7 14 0-0 ♖ad8 15 ♖c1 ♘e5 16 ♘ed4 ♘xf3+ 17 ♕xf3 ♕e5 18 g3 ♘e4 19 ♕e2 ♕g5 20 f4 ♕g6 21 ♖c2 ♗c8 22 f5 ♕h6 23 ♗d3 ♖fe8 24 ♗c1 ♗d7 25 ♕f3 ♗a4 26 ♖g2 ♖c8 27 ♖e1 ♘g5 28 ♕xd5 ♘h3+ 29 ♔f1 ♗e5 30 ♖ge2 ♗xd4 31 ♕xd4 ♖ed8

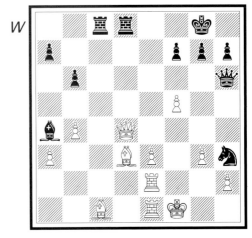

32 b5 ♕h5? (32... ♖xd4 33 ed g5 34 fxg6 ep ♖xc1 35 gf+ ♔xf7 36 ♖e7+ ♔f6 37 ♖e6+ ♔g5 38 ♖e5+ ♔f6 with equality) 33 g4 ♖xd4 34 ed f6 35 gh Resigns.

Saint George Chessmen

See Chess pieces and Sets.

Saint John

City in maritime Canada (New Brunswick) that staged a chess festival in early 1988. This included 7 Candidates matches as well as the World Blitz Championship (in the form of knockout matches). The favourites for the latter were Kasparov and Karpov, but Kasparov lost to Georgiev while Karpov lost to Chernin. The two finalists were Tal and Vaganian, with Tal sweeping the final 4–0 to win the $50 000 first prize.

St Petersburg

The cultural capital of Russia that staged several super-strong tournaments. Chigorin invited the first 5 prizewinners of Hastings 1895 to a multiround tournament in St Petersburg. These 5 prizewinners were in fact the 5 strongest players in the world, but Dr Tarrasch declined Chigorin's invitation because of his medical responsibilities. Tarrasch's participation would certainly have made it the *crème de la crème*, rivalled only by AVRO 1938 and The Hague/Moscow 1948.

The wise money thought it would be a fight between Pillsbury and Chigorin, because Steinitz was close to 60 and past his prime and because World Champion Lasker was considered too frail for a severe contest. During Hastings 1895, Lasker was convalescing from a severe bout of typhoid fever and many erroneously assumed that he was permanently frail.

After 9 rounds, Pillsbury ($6\frac{1}{2}$) led Lasker ($5\frac{1}{2}$), Steinitz ($4\frac{1}{2}$) and Chigorin ($1\frac{1}{2}$). The 10th round, January 4, 1896, saw Lasker win a most brilliant, truly noble, game from Pillsbury. From then on Pillsbury's game collapsed and he scored 3 draws and 5 losses in the last 8 rounds. The obvious explanation is that the round 10 loss deeply upset him. However W. Korn put forth another explanation: Pillsbury visited a brothel between December 6 and December 12 where he contracted syphilis; symptoms appeared between December 27 and January 2, and a doctor told Pillsbury he had the fatal disease on January 4, just before round 10. Pillsbury did in fact die of syphilis 10 years later (age $33\frac{1}{2}$) and the Korn theory would certainly explain Pillsbury's collapse.

Time limit: 30 moves in 2 hours and then 15 moves per hour.

Prizes: Lasker £99, Steinitz £74, Pillsbury £59, Chigorin £47.

Tournament Book by Mason and Pollock with quite good annotations.

In 1909 St Petersburg held a Chigorin memorial tournament where Lasker faced a new crop of young stars. Tarrasch, Janowski and Maroczy were not there but Lasker had his work cut out to keep step with Rubinstein. Lasker lost a beautiful game to Rubinstein in round 3 and by round 5 he was $1\frac{1}{2}$ points behind Rubinstein. Lasker then had a splendid run of $9\frac{1}{2}/10$. Before the last round, Rubinstein (14) led Lasker ($13\frac{1}{2}$), but Lasker beat Teichmann while Tartakower held Rubinstein to a draw. Thus the two leaders shared the honours, a full $3\frac{1}{2}$ points ahead of their closest pursuers.

Time limit: 37 moves in $2\frac{1}{2}$ hours, then 23 moves in $1\frac{1}{2}$ hours, then 15 moves per hour.

Prizes (Roubles): 1000, 750, 550, 400, 280, 190, 120, 80, 50, 30.

Brilliancy Prizes: 120 roubles to Schlechter for his win over Salwe, 80 roubles to Forgacs for his win over Tartakower.

Tournament Book by Lasker with sparse but excellent annotations.

In 1914 St Petersburg invited only winners of at least one major tournament plus the winners (Alekhine and Nimzowitsch) of the recent All Russian championship. Unfortunately the Hapsburg Empire stars (Schlechter, Maroczy, Duras and Spielmann) did not come, but Lasker met Capablanca and Alekhine for the first time. There were the veterans Blackburne and Gunsberg, plus the front rank of Tarrasch, Rubinstein, Bernstein, Janowski and Marshall. When Alekhine played Blackburne there was an age difference of over 50 years.

The arrangement was a preliminary round robin among the 11 competitors followed by a double round final among the top 5 finishers, with the preliminary scores to be carried forward.

Everyone expected a great struggle between Lasker, Rubinstein and Capablanca, and there was surprise and disappointment when Rubinstein failed to make the final five. In the finals, Lasker began $1\frac{1}{2}$ points behind but he scored 7/8 against this elite group, playing masterpieces day after day. Lasker won this Category XVI final by a mere $\frac{1}{2}$ a point but he played the greatest set of games ever seen in the history of chess.

St Petersburg 1895/6

		1						2						3						4						
1	Lasker	–	–	–	–	–	–	1	1	½	0	1	½	0	0	½	1	½	½	1	½	1	1	½	1	11½
2	Steinitz	0	0	½	1	0	½	–	–	–	–	–	–	1	½	½	1	1	1	0	1	1	0	0	½	9½
3	Pillsbury	1	1	½	0	½	½	0	½	½	0	0	0	–	–	–	–	–	–	1	1	1	0	0	½	8
4	Chigorin	0	½	0	0	½	0	1	0	0	1	1	½	0	0	0	1	1	½	–	–	–	–	–	–	7

		1	2	3	4	5	6	7	8	9	10	11	12	13	14	15	16	17	18	19	
1	Lasker	–	0	1	½	½	1	1	1	1	½	1	1	0	1	1	1	1	1	1	14½
	Rubinstein	1	–	1	1	½	½	½	1	1	1	1	½	0	1	½	1	1	1	1	14½
3	Duras	0	0	–	0	0	1	½	0	1	½	1	0	1	1	1	1	1	1	1	11
	Spielmann	½	0	1	–	0	1	1	½	½	1	½	½	1	0	½	1	½	½	1	11
5	Bernstein	½	½	1	1	–	0	1	0	1	1	1	1	½	0	0	0	½	½	1	10½
6	Teichmann	0	½	0	0	1	–	0	½	½	½	1	½	1	½	1	½	1	1	½	10
7	Perlis	0	½	½	0	0	1	–	½	1	½	1	½	1	½	1	½	0	0	1	9½
8	Cohn, E.	0	0	1	½	1	½	½	–	0	0	½	1	½	0	½	½	½	1	1	9
	Salwe	0	0	0	½	0	½	0	1	–	0	1	½	1	1	½	0	1	1	1	9
	Schlechter	½	0	½	0	0	½	½	1	1	–	0	0	1	1	½	0	1	½	1	9
11	Mieses	0	0	0	½	0	0	0	½	0	1	–	1	½	1	1	1	0	1	1	8½
	Tartakower	0	½	1	½	0	½	½	0	½	1	0	–	0	0	½	1	1	1	½	8½
13	Duz Khotmirsky	1	1	0	0	½	0	0	½	0	0	½	1	–	½	½	½	1	0	1	8
14	Forgacs	0	0	0	1	1	½	½	1	0	0	0	1	½	–	½	½	½	0	½	7½
15	Burn	0	½	0	½	1	0	0	½	½	½	0	½	½	½	–	1	½	½	0	7
	Vidmar	0	0	0	0	1	½	½	½	1	1	0	0	½	½	0	–	½	1	0	7
17	Speijer	0	0	0	½	½	0	1	½	0	0	1	0	0	½	½	½	–	½	½	6
18	V. Freymann	0	0	0	½	½	0	1	0	0	½	0	0	1	1	½	0	½	–	0	5½
19	Znosko-Borovsky	0	0	0	0	0	½	0	0	0	0	0	½	0	½	1	1	½	1	–	5

Nenarokow withdrew after four rounds and his score was cancelled. He beat Perlis, drew with Burn, and lost to Mieses and Duras.

Prizes (Roubles): 1200, 800, 500, 300, 200.

Brilliancy prizes: 1st to Capablanca for his win over Bernstein, 2nd to Tarrasch for his win over Nimzowitsch

Tournament Book by Dr Tarrasch with his usual deep and excellent annotations.

The Tarrasch win over Nimzowitsch was similar to Lasker's famous win over Bauer in 1889 and therefore the judges (Burn, Pollner and Znozko–Borovsky) downgraded it and awarded the 1st prize to a much less brilliant game. Tarrasch was not pleased with the decision.

Nimzowitsch–Tarrasch

1 d4 d5 2 ♘f3 c5 3 c4 e6 4 e3 ♘f6 5 ♗d3 ♘c6 6 0-0 ♗d6 7 b3 0-0 8 ♗b2 b6 9 ♘bd2 ♗b7 10 ♖c1 ♕e7 11 cd ed 12 ♘h4 g6 13 ♘hf3 ♖ad8 14 dc bc 15 ♗b5 ♘e4 16 ♗xc6 ♗xc6 17 ♕c2 ♘xd2 18 ♘xd2 d4 19 ed ♗xh2+ 20 ♔xh2 ♕h4+ 21 ♔g1

B

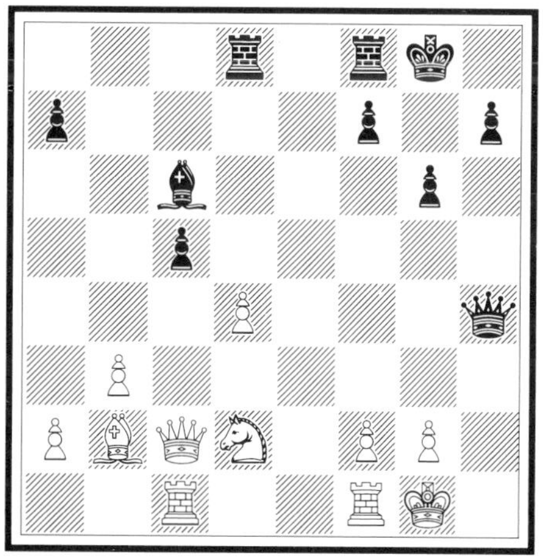

21 ... ♗xg2 22 f3 ♖fe8 23 ♘e4 ♕h1+ 24 ♔f2 ♗xf1 25 d5 f5 26 ♕c3 ♕g2+ 27 ♔e3 ♖xe4+ 28 fe f4+ 29 ♔xf4 ♖f8+ 30 ♔e5 ♕h2+ 31 ♔e6 ♖e8+ 32 ♔d7 ♗b5 mate

Lasker–Capablanca

1 e4 e5 2 ♘f3 ♘c6 3 ♗b5 a6 4 ♗xc6 dc 5 d4 ed 6 ♕xd4 ♕xd4 7 ♘xd4 ♗d6 8 ♘c3 ♘e7 9 0-0 0-0 10 f4 ♖e8 11 ♘b3 f6 12 f5 b6 13 ♗f4 ♗b7 14 ♗xd6 cd 15 ♘d4 ♖ad8 16 ♘e6 ♖d7 17 ♖ad1 ♘c8 18 ♖f2 b5 19 ♖fd2 ♖de7 20 b4 ♔f7 21 a3 ♗a8 22 ♔f2 ♖a7 23 g4 h6 24 ♖d3 a5 25 h4 ab 26 ab ♖ae7 27 ♔f3 ♖g8 28 ♔f4 g6 29 ♖g3 g5+ 30 ♔f3 ♘b6 31 hg hg 32 ♖h3 ♖d7 33 ♔g3 ♔e8 34 ♖dh1 ♗b7

W

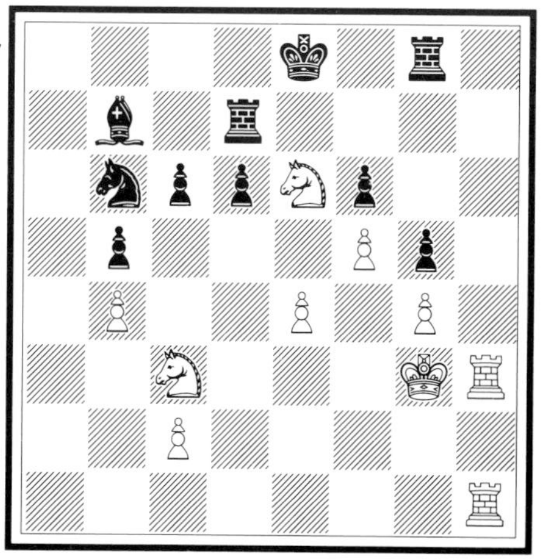

35 e5! de 36 ♘e4 ♘d5 37 ♘6c5 ♗c8 38 ♘xd7 ♗xd7 39 ♖h7 ♖f8 40 ♖a1 ♔d8 41 ♖a8+ ♗c8 42 ♘c5 Resigns

St Petersburg 1914

		1	2	3	4	5	6	7	8	9	10	11	
1	Capablanca	–	½	½	1	½	1	½	1	1	1	1	8
2	Lasker	½	–	½	½	½	0	1	½	1	1	1	6½
	Tarrasch	½	½	–	½	½	1	½	1	1	0	1	6½
4	Alekhine	0	½	½	–	1	½	1	½	½	½	1	6
	Marshall	½	½	½	0	–	1	½	½	1	1	½	6
6	Bernstein	0	1	0	½	0	–	½	½	½	1	1	5
	Rubinstein	½	0	½	0	½	½	–	½	½	1	1	5
8	Nimzowitsch	0	½	0	½	½	½	½	–	0	½	1	4
9	Blackburne	0	0	0	½	0	½	½	1	–	0	1	3½
	Janowski	0	0	1	½	0	0	0	½	1	–	½	3½
11	Gunsberg	0	0	0	0	½	0	0	0	0	½	–	1

Final

		1		2		3		4		5		
1	Lasker	6½	–	–	½	1	1	1	1	½	1	1	13½
2	Capablanca	8	½	0	–	–	½	1	1	0	1	1	13
3	Alekhine	6	0	0	½	0	–	–	1	1	1	½	10
4	Tarrasch	6½	0	½	0	1	0	0	–	–	0	½	8½
5	Marshall	6	0	0	0	0	0	0	½	1	½	–	8

This was the decisive game of the tournament.

Capablanca–Bernstein

1 d4 d5 2 ♘f3 ♘f6 3 c4 e6 4 ♘c3 ♘bd7 5 ♗g5 ♗e7 6 e3 c6 7 ♗d3 dc 8 ♗xc4 b5 9 ♗d3 a6 10 e4 e5 11 de ♘g4 12 ♗f4 ♗c5 13 0-0 ♕c7 14 ♖c1 f6 15 ♗g3 fe 16 b4 ♗a7 17 ♖xb5 ab 18 ♘xb5 ♕d8 19 ♘d6+ ♔f8 20 ♖xc6 ♘b6 21 ♗h4 ♕d7 22 ♘xc8 ♕xc6 23 ♕d8+ (better is 23 ♗e7+) ♕e8 24 ♗e7+ ♔f7 25 ♘d6+ ♔g6 26 ♘h4+ ♔h5 27 ♘xe8 ♖xd8 28 ♘xg7+ ♔h6 29 ♘gf5+ ♔h5 30 h3 ♘c8 31 hg+ ♔xg4 32 ♗xd8 ♖xd8 33 g3 ♖d2 34 ♔g2 ♖e2 35 a4 ♘b6 36 ♘e3+ ♔h5 37 a5 ♘d7 38 ♘hf5 ♘f6 39 b5 ♗d4 40 ♔f3 ♖a2 41 a6 ♗a7 42 ♖c1 ♖b2 43 g4+ ♔g6 44 ♖c7 ♖xf2+ 45 ♔xf2 ♘xg4+ 46 ♔f3 Resigns

Sajtar, Jaroslav [December 3 1921–] Czech IM (1950) and honorary GM (1985) who played on the Czech Olympiad team in 1952 and 54. His best result was equal 2nd at Warsaw 1947. From 1956 on he devoted himself to chess organization and FIDE.

Saladin [1138–1193] Kurdish sultan of Egypt who fought the Christians during the Crusades. He was a highly cultured and civilized man, famous for his victories, his valour and his magnanimity. He was, naturally, a fine chess player, and legend has it that he taught Richard Coeur de Lion how to play.

Salov, Valery [May 26 1964–] USSR GM (1986) who won the World Cadet Championship in 1980 and the European Junior Championship in 1985.

He was equal 1st in the 1987 USSR Championship (XII), losing the play-off +0=2−2 to Belyavsky, equal 3rd at Leningrad 1987 (XIV) and equal 1st at Szirak 1987 (XII). Salov became a Candidate in 1988, but lost +0=5−1 to Timman. He was 2nd at Brussels 1988 (XV) and equal 3rd with Yusupov behind Karpov and Kasparov at the 1988 USSR Championship (XIV).

Salov is already in the world top 10 and although he lost matches to Timman and Belyavsky his impressive results and his youth mark him as a serious future force.

Salvio, Alessandro [1570–1640] Italian (Neopolitan) author who wrote *Trattato dell'inventione et arte liberale del gioco di scacchi* in 1604, stressing the Italian school of chess and dedicated to his patron Fulvio de Costanzo, Marquis of Corleto; *La Scaccaida* in 1612, a tragedy in verse, on chess; and *Il Puttino altramente detto il cavaliere errante* in 1634, a somewhat unreliable life of Leonardo da Cutri.

He created a chess 'academy' in Naples that met regularly at the home of Judge Rovito. He popularized 1 e4 e5 2 f4 ef 3 ♘f3 g5 4 ♗c4 g4 5 ♘e5 which is now known as the Salvio Gambit.

Salwe, Georg Henryk Salomonovich [October 24 1862–December 15 1920] Polish player of GM strength who was a middle-level player at the top tournaments during 1906 to 1912. His best results were 1st at the 4th Russian Championship at St Petersburg 1906 ahead of Chigorin and 2nd at Dusseldorf 1908. He lost a match to Chigorin +5=3−7 in 1906. Salwe was the star of Lodz until Rubinstein appeared. At first Salwe held his own against Rubinstein (+5=4−5 in 1903), but in 1904 Salwe lost +3=2−5 to the young genius.

Salwe was a large man with an even larger moustache who inspired many young Polish players.

Sämisch, Friedrich (Fritz)

[September 20 1896–August 16 1975] German GM (1950) and theoretician who contributed to the King's Indian and Nimzo-Indian openings. He won the Austrian Championship in 1921, beat Reti +4=3−1 in 1922, and was 3rd at Baden-Baden 1925. Then he was 2nd at Berlin 1928, 1st or equal 1st at Dortmund 1928, Brno 1928, Swinemunde 1930, and Berlin 1930, and he played on the 1930 German Olympiad team.

He had a serious problem with time pressure and spent his energy on building up his game. He used to say: 'If I could play the first twenty moves, I would not mind somebody else finishing the game for me'. He lost many games on time and in a 1969 tournament he is said to have lost all thirteen games that way.

San Sebastian

A Spanish seaside resort on the Atlantic side, near the French border, which held 2 major tournaments (1911 and 1912). They were organized by Mieses and were the first at which all competitors were given travel money and living expenses. However, only top players were invited, those who had won two 4th prizes or better, in major tournaments. An exception was made for Capablanca because he had recently crushed Marshall in a match. Capablanca justified this decision by repeating Pillsbury's 1895 feat of winning a major event at his first attempt.

All the top players were there except Lasker, and it was probably the strongest tournament since Nuremberg 1896. Capablanca led all the way, though Rubinstein made a great effort to catch him. Rubinstein won brilliantly over Capablanca in round 13 and had a clear win over Spielmann in round 14, but missed his way in time trouble and only drew.

Time limit: 15 moves per hour.

Prizes (Francs): 5000, 3000, 2000, 1500.

Baron Albert von Rothschild brilliancy prize: 500 to Capablanca for his win over Bernstein.

Tournament book by Mieses and Lewitt with fair annotations.

Capablanca–Bernstein

1 e4 e5 2 ♘f3 ♘c6 3 ♗b5 ♘f6 4 0-0 ♗e7 5 ♘c3 d6 6 ♗xc6+ bc 7 d4 ed 8 ♘xd4 ♗d7 9 ♗g5 0-0 10 ♖e1 h6 11 ♗h4 ♘h7 12 ♗xe7 ♕xe7 13 ♕d3 ♖ab8 14 b3 ♘g5 15 ♖ad1 ♕e5 16 ♕e3 ♘e6 17 ♘3e2 ♕a5 (better is ... ♘xd4 18 ♘xd4 ♖fe8) 18 ♘f5 ♘c5 19 ♘ed4 ♔h7 20 g4 (better is 20 c3) ♖be8 21 f3 ♘e6 22 ♘e2 ♕xa2 23 ♘eg3 ♕xc2 24 ♖c1 ♕b2 25 ♘h5

B

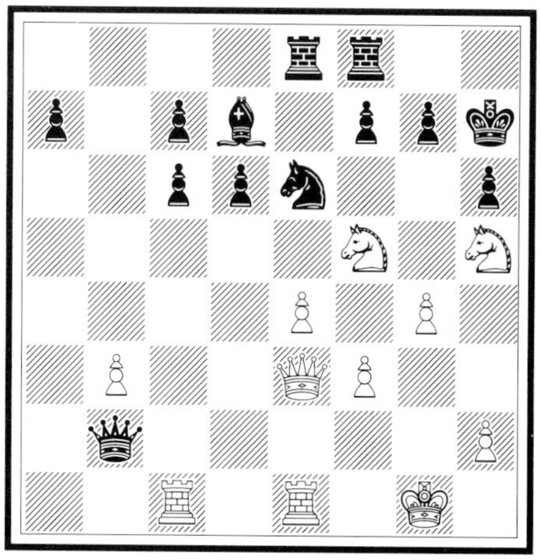

25 ... ♖h8? (correct is 25 ... g5 26 e5 ♘f4 27 ♘xf4 ♗xf5 28 ♘d3 ♗xd3 29 ♕xd3+ ♔g8 and Black stands better) 26 ♖e2 ♕e5 27 f4 ♕b5 28 ♘fxg7 ♘c5 29 ♘xe8 ♗xe8 30 ♕c3 f6 31

San Sebastian 1911

		1	2	3	4	5	6	7	8	9	10	11	12	13	14	15	
1	Capablanca	–	0	½	½	1	½	½	1	1	½	1	½	1	½	1	9½
2	Rubinstein	1	–	½	½	½	½	½	½	½	½	1	½	½	1	1	9
	Vidmar	½	½	–	0	½	½	½	1	½	½	1	½	1	1	1	9
4	Marshall	½	½	1	–	½	½	½	½	½	1	1	½	½	0	1	8½
5	Nimzowitsch	0	½	½	½	–	½	0	½	1	1	½	½	½	½	1	7½
	Schlechter	½	½	½	½	½	–	½	0	½	½	1	½	½	1	½	7½
	Tarrasch	½	½	½	½	1	½	–	1	½	0	½	½	1	0	½	7½
8	Bernstein	0	½	0	½	½	1	0	–	1	1	½	1	0	1	0	7
	Spielmann	0	½	½	½	0	½	½	0	–	½	½	1	½	1	1	7
10	Teichmann	½	½	½	0	0	½	1	0	½	–	0	½	½	1	1	6½
11	Janowski	0	0	0	0	½	0	½	½	½	1	–	½	1	1	1	6
	Maroczy	½	½	½	½	½	½	½	0	½	1	–	½	½	0	0	6
13	Burn	0	½	0	½	½	½	0	1	½	½	0	½	–	0	½	5
	Duras	½	0	0	1	½	0	1	0	0	0	0	½	1	–	½	5
15	Leonhardt	0	0	0	0	0	½	½	1	0	0	0	1	½	½	–	4

♘xf6+ ♔g6 32 ♘h5 ♖g8 33 f5+ ♔g5 34 ♕e3+ resigns

The 1912 (February 19–March 19) tournament was strong but did not have either Lasker or Capablanca. There were 11 players and they played a double round robin (Forgacs withdrew after the first round robin). Rubinstein (12½) won ahead of Spielmann (12), Nimzowitsch (12) and Tarrasch (11½).

Sanguinetti, Raul C.

[February 3 1933–]
Argentine IM (1957) and honorary GM (1982) who was Argentine champion 7 times and played on 6 Argentine Olympiad teams from 1956 to 1974.

Saragossa Opening

1 c3

A passive opening that was popular around 1920 at the Saragossa club in Spain. It offers to play a Caro–Kann Defence with White, but Black need not reply 1 ... e5. No one uses it in master chess today.

Sarratt, Jacob Henry   [1772–1819]

English schoolmaster, author and player who adopted the title 'Professor of Chess'. His writings include: *A Treatise on the Game of Chess* (1808), *The Works of Damiano, Ruy Lopez and Salvio* (1813), *The Works of Gianutio and Gustavus Selenus* (1817), and a *New Treatise on Chess* (1821) (published posthumously).

He is usually credited (1807) with introducing into England the continental practice of counting a game ending in stalemate as a draw.

Sassa

Legendary philosopher who is supposed to have invented chess to break an Indian King's addiction to backgammon (nard). As payment he is alleged to have asked for 1 grain of corn on the 1st square of the chessboard, to be continuously doubled on each of the other 63 squares. This sounds modest but adds up to $2^{64}-1$ or about 18 followed by 18 zeros—more grains than the entire world possesses.

Savon, Vladimir Andreyevich

[September 26 1940–]
USSR GM (1973) who played in 9 USSR Championships during 1961 to 1974. His best period was the early 1970s when he won the 1971 championship (XII) ahead of Smyslov, Tal and Karpov and was equal 3rd in 1972. He played 6th board on the 1972 USSR Olympiad team, scoring 86.7%.

In international tournaments his best results were equal 1st at Debrecen 1970, equal 1st at Vilnius 1975, equal 2nd at Portoroz 1977 (XII) and equal 2nd at Kiev 1978 (X).

Sax, Gyula   [June 18 1951–]

Hungarian GM (1974) who was European Junior Champion in 1972, Hungarian Champion in 1976 and 1977 (equal) and who played regularly on the Hungarian Olympiad team during 1972 to 1988.

He had many first prizes from Reggio Emilia 1973/74 to an equal 1st at Amsterdam 1979 (XII). However, he seemed unable to break into the higher levels. Things improved when he was equal 1st at Rome 1986 (X), 1st at Warsaw 1987 (X) and equal 1st at the Subotica interzonal 1987 (XI). This made him a Candidate in 1988 but he was eliminated $+0=3-2$ by Short.

Scacchia Ludus

See Vida

Schakend Nederland   [1983–]

Interesting monthly Dutch chess magazine which is a continuation of the Dutch *Tijdschrift*.

Scheveningen

See Sicilian Defence.

Schiffers, Emanuel Stepanovich

[May 4 1850–December 12 1904]
Russian player of almost GM strength who taught an entire generation of Russian players (including Chigorin) the finer points of chess. He was 2nd to Chigorin at both the 1st All Russian Championship (1899) and the 2nd (1900/1). In the 3rd (1903) he could only manage equal 11th. He played some 5 matches with Chigorin, doing well in the 1870s but losing decisively in the 80s and 90s. Internationally he lost $+4=1-6$ to Steinitz in 1896 and his best tournament result was a creditable 6th at Hastings 1895.

Schiffers was born in St Petersburg, studied science and taught law before devoting himself to chess. He was kind and genial, without a trace of arrogance. He successfully introduced the idea of public chess lectures (1889). In later life he suffered from depression. In the spring of 1904 he injured himself in a fall and never recovered.

Schlechter, Carl

[March 2 1874–December 27 1918]
Viennese player of GM strength who was in the world top five during 1900–18. He learned the game in 1890 and by 1892 was among the elite of Viennese chess, having drawn a match with Marco. From Leipzig 1894 until the war in 1914, Schlechter played in almost all the great tournaments and seldom came below 5th. He was equal 1st with Pillsbury at Munich 1900, 1st at Ostend 1906, and Hamburg 1910, equal 1st at Stockholm 1906, Vienna 1908 and Prague 1908. In matches he beat Janowski $+6=3-1$ in 1902, drew with the mighty Lasker $+1=8-1$ in 1910, held Tarrasch $+3=10-3$ in 1911 and only in 1918 did he lose a match ($+1=3-2$ to Rubinstein).

Schlechter was a total master of Steinitzian theory and, at a time when this theory was not universally understood, some of his success was due to that knowledge alone. He has been accused of drawing with other Steinitzian experts and coasting along on victories over the unknowledgeable. Certainly Schlechter drew an inordinate number of games; e.g. in 32 games all told against Maroczy, 29 were draws (Schlechter won 2 and lost 1). However, much of this peaceableness was due to Schlechter's unusually amiable character. He was small in stature, bright-eyed, shy, modest, and extremely friendly. His gentleness manifested itself in his talk and even in his relaxed walk. Schlechter was liked by all who knew him. He lacked the deep aggressiveness of an Alekhine or even the milder belligerence of a Pillsbury.

Schlechter was an expert in opening theory, with special knowledge of the Ruy Lopez. He edited the 8th edition of Bilguer's *Handbuch* and this work (1916) became the definitive book on openings. Schlechter was chess editor of the *Allge-*

Carl Schlechter, who came closest to toppling Lasker.

meine Sport-Zeitung, and was a fine problem solver and composer.

The climax of Schlechter's career was his dramatic ten-game match in 1910 with Lasker. Schlechter had won the fifth game (with some luck) and there had been eight draws. All he had to do was to draw game ten to win the match. There has been much debate about whether Schlechter would have become world champion if he had won the match. It seems fairly clear that he would have. In any case, he had enormous chivalry and he played for a win. This game, which lasted three days, has been described as the most exciting struggle in all chess history. At the last moment Schlechter missed his way, the match was drawn and Lasker retained his title.

Schlechter continued his chess activities during the war. After losing to Rubinstein in early 1918, he played in a quadrangular tournament with Mieses, Vidmar, and Rubinstein in April 1918 (coming 2nd) and in another with Lasker, Rubinstein and Tarrasch in October 1918 (coming 3rd). In between, in August, he was equal 3rd at Kaschau.

Schlechter died (in Budapest) of starvation, in the aftermath of the Great War.

In terms of life scores, he beat Steinitz (+ 3 = 2 − 2), Janowski (+ 20 = 13 − 13), Chigorin (+ 9 = 10 − 6), Vidmar (+ 6 = 16 − 3), Nimzowitsch (+ 3 = 4 − 1) and Alekhine (+ 2 = 0 − 0). He lost to Tarrasch (+ 6 = 27 − 7), Rubinstein (+ 2 = 14 − 6), Lasker (+ 2 = 12 − 5), Pillsbury (+ 2 = 9 − 8) and Blackburne (+ 2 = 6 − 3).

His victories could be as gentle as Schlechter himself.

Burn–Schlechter
Carlsbad 1911

1 d4 d5 2 c4 e6 3 ♘c3 c5 4 e3 ♘f6 5 ♘f3 a6 6 ♗d3 ♘c6 7 0-0 ♗d6 8 b3 0-0 9 ♗b2 cd 10 ed dc 11 ♗xc4 b5 12 ♗d3 ♘b4 13 ♗b1 ♗b7 14 a3 ♘bd5

15 ♘e4 ♘f4 16 ♖e1 ♖c8 17 g3 ♘xe4 18 ♗xe4 ♗xe4 19 ♖xe4 ♘d5 20 ♕d3 ♕e7 21 b4 ♖c6 22 ♘e5 ♗xe5 23 de ♖fc8 24 ♗d4 ♖c1+ 25 ♖e1 ♖xe1+ 26 ♖xe1 ♖c4 27 ♗b2 ♕c7 28 ♖e2 ♕c6 29 ♕d2 h6 30 ♕d3 ♕c8 31 ♖d2 ♕c7 32 ♔g2 a5 33 ba ♕xa5 34 ♗d4 ♕a8 35 f3 ♕a4 36 ♗b2 h5 37 ♖f2 g6 38 ♕d2 ♕b3 39 ♔h3 ♖c8 40 ♔h4 ♔g7 41 ♔h3 ♖c4

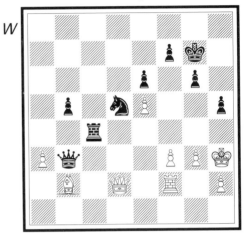

W

42 ♗c1 ♕b1 43 ♗b2 h4 44 ♔g2 ♕f5 45 ♖e2 ♕b1 46 ♖f2 ♖c8 47 ♗d4 ♖c1 48 ♔h3 ♕f5+ 49 g4 ♘f4+ 50 ♔xh4 g5+ 51 ♔g3 ♕h7 52 Resigns

Schliemann Defence
See Lopez, Ruy.

Schmid, Lothar Maximilian Lorenz
[*May 10 1928– *]
West German GM (1958) who has the largest and finest privately owned chess library in the world, rivalled only by the public collections at Cleveland and the Hague. In addition to books and magazines, Schmid's collection contains many unique and wonderful chess items. Schmid is also an art collector, a publisher and a *bon vivant*.

He was 1st at Travemunde 1951, 1st at Zurich 1954, equal 1st at Malaga 1963, equal 2nd at Bamberg 1968, 1st at Mar del Plata 1970 and 1973. He came equal 2nd in the World Correspondence Championship 1955–8 and played on 11 West German Olympiad teams during 1950–74. He won the Dyckhoff Memorial Correspondence Tournament in 1954–6.

His serious dedication to chess and his fairmindedness has made him popular as a chess judge and he has served as chief arbiter at world title matches: Fischer–Spassky 1972, Karpov–Korchnoi 1978 and Kasparov–Karpov 1986.

Schmidt, Paul Felix

[*August 20 1916–August 11 1984*] Estonian IM (1950) who was almost of GM strength and a rival to Keres. He was Estonian Champion in 1936 and 1937, German Champion in 1941 and played on the Estonian Olympiad team in 1937 and 1939.

He was 1st at Tallinn 1935, 1st at Parnu 1937, equal 1st with Alekhine at Krakow 1941, 2nd at the German Championship 1940, Vienna 1943, Kassel 1947, and Saarbrucken 1950.

He held Keres $+3=1-3$ in 1936 and beat Junge $+3=1-2$ in 1941. Schmidt earned a PhD (1951) in science, went to live in the USA and retired from competitive chess.

Schmidt, Wlodzimierz

[*April 10 1943– *] Polish GM (1976) who won the Polish Championship 5 times during 1971 to 1988, and was a regular on the Polish Olympiad team from 1962 to 1988. He won quite a number of Category VII and VIII tournaments from Polanica Zdroj 1973 to Vinkovici 1986. He was equal 2nd at Warsaw 1987 (X).

Curiously, Schmidt was the first Polish GM, because Najdorf, Tartakower and Rubinstein received their titles in 1950 when they represented Argentine, France and Belgium respectively.

Scholar's Mate

1 e4 e5 2 Qh5 Nc6 3 Bc4 d6? 4 Qxf7 mate. An elementary trap that novices may fall into. One good way to avoid it is to play 3 ... g6 and if 4 Qf3 Qf6.

Schools of Chess

The table below shows, in broad terms, how chess has developed under the influence of the leading players. In some cases, for example the era of von der Lasa and Anderssen, it is not sensible to talk of a 'school', but it is still interesting to see how these players fit into the table. Where a player was World Champion and/or clearly the leading player in the world, the dates are given in the third column. (Some overlaps have been permitted.)

Player	Born/Died	World Champion or world leading player	Schools and their philosophies
Ruy Lopez	1530–80	1560	
Boi	1528–98	1575	
Leonardo da Cutri	1542–87	1575	
Salvio	1570–1640	1600	
Greco	1600–34	1620	
Legall	1702–92	1730–47	
Philidor	1726–95	1747–95	Stressed mobility and structure of pawns
Lolli	1698–1769		*Modenese:* stressed quick development and attacks on the king. Underplayed the centre and pawn structure
Ercole del Rio	1718–1802		
Ponziani	1719–96		
Deschapelles	1780–1847	1800–20	
La Bourdonnais	1795–1840	1820–40	
Staunton	1810–74	1840–50	Stressed the centre and used flank openings
von der Lasa	1818–99	1850–1	
Anderssen	1818–79	1850–8	
Morphy	1837–84	1858–66	Stressed the centre and open positions
Steinitz	1836–1900	1866–94	Stressed defence, accumulation of small advantages. Only well prepared attacks from a better position will succeed and must be undertaken to preserve the advantage.
Tarrasch	1862–1934		
Lasker	1868–1941	1894–1921	
Capablanca	1888–1942	1921–27	

Nimzowitsch	1886–1935		*Hypermoderns:* can control centre with pieces since central pawns can be attacked. Réti opening, English, Fianchettoes and flank openings.
Réti	1889–1929		
Alekhine	1892–1946	1927–46	
Euwe	1901–81	1935–7	
Botvinnik	1911–	1948–63	Developed dynamic defensive systems: King's Indian, Boleslavsky Sicilian, based on accepting weaknesses if they cannot be easily attacked. Mostly Soviet inspired.
Smyslov	1921–	1957–8	
Tal	1936–	1960–1	
Petrosian	1929–84	1963–9	
Spassky	1937–	1969–72	
Fischer	1943–	1972–5	
Karpov	1951–	1975–85	
Kasparov	1963–	1985–	

Schussler, Harry [*June 24 1957–*]

Swedish GM (1988) who was 1st at the Gausdal 1983 Open, equal 3rd at Havana 1985 (VIII) and equal 1st at the Malmo 1986 Open. He played on all the Swedish Olympiad teams during the 1980s.

Score

The record of the moves of a game. In official tournament or match games each player is required to keep a score.

Scotch Game

1 e4 e5 2 ♘f3 ♘c6 3 d4.

This opening, known since 1750, got its name from the correspondence match between Edinburgh and London (1824). It was used by Blackburne and Chigorin, but is seldom used today because the central break comes too soon and Black equalizes easily with 3 ... ed 4 ♘xd4 ♗c5.

Sealed Move

See adjournment.

Second

One who aids a player in a match or tournament by preparing opening analysis, running errands and helping with adjournment analysis.

See-saw

A sequence of alternating direct and discovered checks. See Torre, Carlos, for his win over Lasker—the last 10 moves are a fine example.

Seirawan, Yasser [*March 24 1960–*]

Syrian-born US GM (1980) who was World Junior Champion in 1979 and a Candidate twice: at Montpellier 1985 he did not make the final play-offs and in 1988 he lost +0=2−3 to Speelman. Seirawan won the US Championship in 1981 (equal 1st) and 1986, and played on 4 US Olympiad teams during 1980–8.

He was equal 1st at Wijk aan Zee 1980 (XI), equal 2nd at Bad Kissingen 1981 (XII), 3rd at London 1982 (XIV), 2nd at Biel 1985 (XII) and equal 2nd at Zagreb 1987 (XII).

Seirawan's family (English mother and Syrian father) came to the US in 1967. He is a handsome and charming man who needs a bit more fire to get into the world top ten.

Yasser Seirawan of the USA.

Selenus, Gustavus (Augustus, Duke of Brunswick)

[*April 10 1579–September 17 1666*]

Selenus was the pseudonym of the Duke of Brunswick-Luneberg-Danneburg. He wrote *Das Schach oder König-Spiel* in 1616, the first printed German chess book on openings. He ran universities (Rostock and Tubingen) in his teens and travelled extensively. He translated Ruy Lopez's work and included it in his book. He gave the first account of the village of Strobeck's involvement with chess. He founded the Bibliotheca Augusta in Wolfenbuttel. Sarratt published an English translation of Selenus (1817).

Selfmate

A problem where White moves first and forces Black to mate him (White). It used to be called sui-mate.

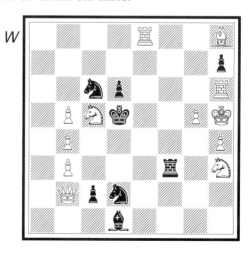

E. Holladay 1960
White to selfmate in 2 moves.

Key: 1 ♘e4
If 1 ... ♘e7 2 ♘c3+ ♖xc3 mate
If 1 ... ♘e5 2 ♘f6+ ♖xf6 mate
If 1 ... ♘xb3 2 ♛xb3+ ♖xb3 mate
If 1 ... any other move 2 ♘f4+
♖xf4 mate.

Semi-Slav Defence
See Queen's Gambit.

Sergeant, Philip Walsingham
[1871–1952]
English author who wrote a number of useful and lucid books. He collaborated with Griffith on 3 editions of *Modern Chess Openings*.

Major works: *Morphy's Games of Chess* (1916), *Charousek's Games of Chess* (1919), *Pillsbury's Chess Career* (1923) (with Watts), *A Century of British Chess* (1934), *Championship Chess* (1938).

Seventh Rank
A most important location for a rook because many enemy pawns live there and are vulnerable when attacked from the side. Getting both rooks on to the seventh rank is usually a decisive advantage.

Shakespeare, Chess in
Chess is referred to in *The Taming of the Shrew*, *King John* and *King Lear*, but in *The Tempest* a stage direction says: 'The entrance of the cell opens and discovers Ferdinand and Miranda playing chess'.

Shamkovich, Leonid Alexandrovich
[June 1 1923–]
Russian-born US GM (1965) who moved from the USSR to the US (via Israel and Canada) in 1975. He played in 6 USSR Championships during 1954 to 1972, coming equal 5th in the 32nd Championship 1964/65. He was equal 1st at Sochi 1967 and at Timisoara 1972.

In the US, Shamkovich was equal 1st at New York 1976, equal 1st at the US Open 1976 and equal 1st at New York 1977 (VIII).

Shatranj
See Early Versions of Chess.

Shinkman, William Anthony
[December 25 1847–May 25 1933]
Bohemian-born US problem composer who rivalled Sam Loyd as America's number one problemist. He composed over 3000 problems and developed self-mate themes.
See *The Golden Argosy* by A. C. White (1929).

Shipley, Walter Penn
[June 20 1860–February 17 1942]
US chess patron and organizer who was treasurer of the Lasker–Marshall world title match and referee for both the Marshall–Capablanca match and the Lasker–Capablanca match. He was a key organizer of Cambridge Springs 1904 and New York 1924.

Shipley was a prominent Philadelphia lawyer, but had time to edit a chess column (in the *Inquirer*) for over 30 years. He was president of the strong Franklin Chess Club. He was a strong amateur and won casual games from Pillsbury, Weiss, Zukertort and Dr Lasker.

Short, Nigel David   [June 1 1965–]
English GM (1984) who together with Speelman, has brought English chess glory back to the time when Staunton played a major role in world chess events. Short was 2nd to Kasparov at the 1980 World Junior Championship and since 1985 has taken a firm seat in the world top ten. He was a Candidate twice: at Montpellier 1985 he did not make the final play-offs; in 1988 he easily beat Sax +2=3−0 but then was eliminated by Speelman +0=3−2.

England's strongest player, Nigel Short. The former child prodigy has survived the pressures of early success to reach the highest level.

Short was 1st at Esbjerg 1984 (X), 1st at Wijk aan Zee 1986 (XII), equal 1st at Wijk aan Zee 1987 (XIII), 1st at Reykjavik 1987 (XIV), 1st at Hastings 1987/88 (XIII), 1st at the 4-player Amsterdam 1988 (XVII), 2nd at Tilburg 1988 (XVI) and 1st at Hastings 1988/89 (XIV).

He won the British Championship in 1984 and 1987 and played on the English Olympiad teams in 1984, 1986 and 1988.

In spite of this brilliant record, there are a few surprising blemishes. Short could only manage 11th at Brussels 1987 (XIV) and 8th at Belfort 1988 (XV) and his loss to Speelman was a disappointment to his supporters. He is a charming, smiling young man and may not have enough killer instinct to climb to the very top.

Showalter, Jackson Whipps
[February 4 1860–February 6 1935]
US player of IM strength who was US Champion in 1888, 1890, 1891, 1895 and 1906. His best results were two close losses to Pillsbury (+8=3−10 in 1897 and +3=2−7 in 1898) and 5th at Cambridge Springs 1904.

Sicilian Defence

1 e4 c5.

This goes back to the 16th century and was given its name by Greco. It came to prominence in 1834 when La Bourdonnais used it in his match with Macdonell. It really came into its own by 1950 and today it is Black's main weapon against 1 e4, because it not only avoids the Ruy Lopez but is sound and aggressive.

Black creates an unbalanced position and the usual development is for White to keep the centre under control and attack on the kingside—often with a pawn storm. Black on the other hand counterattacks on the queenside using the half-open c-file. If Black survives the kingside attack he usually has better prospects in the ending because his pawn structure is sounder.

White can develop with ♘c3 and g3 (closed) or with ♘f3 and ♗b5 (Rossolimo), but his most common method is 2 ♘f3 and 3 d4 cd 4 ♘xd4. Then Black can select from:

Dragon	... g6 and ... d6
Najdorf	... a6 and ... d6
Scheveningen	... e6 and ... d6
Paulsen	... e6 and ... ♘c6
Boleslavsky	... e5.

White's choices are c4 (Maroczy Bind), ♗g5 (Richter–Rauzer attack) and 0-0-0 (Yugoslav).

White can also try the off-beat Wing Gambit: 2 b4.

See *How to play the Sicilian Defence*, by Levy and O'Connell (1978, 1987).

Sigurjonsson, Gudmundur

[*September 25 1947– *] Icelandic lawyer and GM (1975) who was Icelandic champion in 1965, 1968 and 1972, and was a regular on the Iceland Olympiad team during 1966 to 1986. He was 1st at Reykjavik 1970, equal 1st at San Feliu de Guixols 1974 and Orense 1976, equal 2nd at Hastings 1974/75 and at Cienfuegos 1976, and equal 1st at Brighton 1982 (VIII).

Simagin, Vladimir Pavlovich

[*June 21 1919–September 25 1968*] USSR GM (1962) who played in 7 USSR Championships during 1951–65 with modest results. He did however win the Moscow Championship in 1947 and 1959. His best international results were equal 2nd at Sarajevo 1963 and equal 1st at Sochi 1967. Simagin made contributions to the Sicilian and Grünfeld Defences.

See Simagin, by Voronkov (1981).

Simic, Radoslav   [*June 9 1948– *]

Yugoslav GM (1984) who was equal 1st at Stara Pazova 1983 (VIII), equal 1st at the Bad Worishofen Open 1987 and equal 1st at Montpellier 1988 (VII).

Simpson's Divan

Famous London café-restaurant located at 100 The Strand. Founded in the 1820s, the Divan remained a centre of London chess until 1903, when a renovation of the building enlarged the dining facilities at the expense of the chess rooms. Nearly all the great 19th century masters visited and played there and the first English tournament, won by Buckle, was staged there in 1849. In 1852 Elijah Williams published a collection of 150 games played at the Divan under the title *Horae Divaniani*. The modern visitor finds only a restaurant, but an antique set and board—said to have been used by Staunton, Morphy, Steinitz and Lasker among others—are still displayed in the foyer.

See London.

Simultaneous Display

An exhibition where a 'master' takes on a number of weaker opponents all at the same time i.e. simultaneously. The usual arrangement is for 20 or 30 players to be seated on the outside of a rectangle while the master walks about the inside of the rectangle. The master usually plays White on all the boards. He goes from board to board and an opponent is expected to make his move immediately after the master comes to his board. It is

Gary Kasparov gives a clock simultaneous display on ten boards. The use of clocks make life much harder for the Grandmaster.

permissible to make a move immediately after the master moves so a sequence of 2 or more quick moves may be made by both sides.

Capablanca scored +120=1−0 at a 7 hour display in Cleveland 1922. Najdorf scored +226=14−10 at an 11 hour session in Sao Paulo 1950. Stahlberg played 40 boards in Buenos Aires 1941, but allowed defeated opponents to be replaced by fresh, new players. After 36 hours he had scored +364=14−22.

It is also possible for the master to play blindfold (*see* Pillsbury), or to play with clocks. Here all the master's clocks might be going at the same time and thus 10 games is the usual maximum number attempted. A difficult display is a tandem simultaneous, where two masters go about the inside rectangle, moving alternately at each board.

Giving such displays is the traditional way for a master to earn some income e.g. 40 boards at £15 per player yields the master £600 less expenses, for the long evening's work.

Sitzfleisch

In German this means rear end or 'sitting flesh'. It has come to mean the ability to sit and concentrate for long periods of time.

64 *[1935–41; 1946–]*

A weekly Soviet chess paper filled with well annotated games, cartoons and comments by top Soviet GMs.

Skelleftea

A small town in Sweden that staged the last of the six World Cup tournaments for 1988/89. Karpov tried hard to catch Kasparov, but Kasparov rationed his energies carefully to win the World Cup. Kasparov in fact let slip five favourable positions, which he could have won. But rationing is important (*see* Chess in our Time). For example, in Kasparov–Ribli, the following position was reached after 25 ... ♗d4 and a draw was agreed. Vaganian immediately pointed out that 26 ♖xb5 would have won.

W

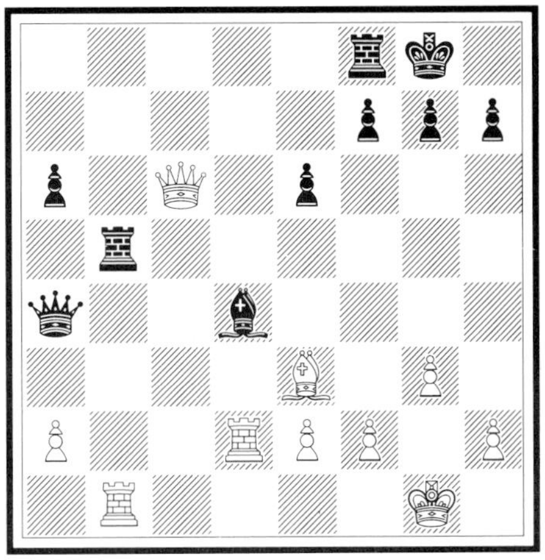

After 26 ♖xb5 ♗xe3 27 ♖d8! ♕xb5 (if 27 ... ♖xd8 28 ♖d5 wins) 28 ♕d6 ♗xf2+ (not 28 ... ♖e8 29 ♕e7) 29 ♔xf2 ♕f5+ and White can escape from the seemingly endless checks: 30 ♔g1 ♕b1+ 31 ♔g2 ♕e4+ 32 ♔h3 ♕f5+ 33 g4 ♕f1+ 34 ♔g3 ♕e1+ 35 ♔f3 ♕f1+ 36 ♔e3 ♕h3+ 37 ♔d4 ♕xg4+ 38 ♔c5 ♕f5+ 39 ♔b6 ♕b1+ 40 ♔a7 ♕g1+ 41 ♔xa6 and it is curious how the White a- and e-pawns prevent any further checks.

Skelleftea 1989 World Cup VI Category XVI

		1	2	3	4	5	6	7	8	9	10	11	12	13	14	15	16	
1	Karpov	–	½	½	1	½	½	½	1	½	½	½	½	1	½	1	½	9½
	Kasparov	½	–	1	½	1	½	½	½	½	½	½	½	½	1	½	1	9½
3	Portisch	½	0	–	½	½	1	1	½	0	½	1	½	1	1	0	½	8½
	Seirawan	0	½	½	–	½	½	½	1	½	1	½	½	½	1	½	½	8½
	Short	½	0	½	½	–	1	½	½	½	0	½	1	½	½	1	1	8½
6	Salov	½	½	0	½	0	–	1	½	½	½	½	½	1	1	1	0	8
	Sax	½	½	0	½	½	0	–	½	1	½	½	½	1	1	½	½	8
8	Andersson	0	½	½	0	½	½	½	–	1	½	½	½	½	½	½	1	7½
	Nunn	½	½	1	½	½	½	0	0	–	0	½	½	1	½	½	1	7½
10	Hübner	½	½	½	0	1	½	½	½	1	–	½	½	0	0	½	½	7
	Ribli	½	½	0	½	½	½	½	½	½	½	–	½	½	½	½	½	7
	Tal	½	½	½	½	0	½	½	½	½	½	½	–	½	½	½	½	7
13	Ehlvest	0	½	0	½	½	0	0	½	0	1	½	½	–	1	½	1	6½
14	Korchnoi	½	0	0	0	½	0	0	½	½	1	½	½	0	–	1	1	6
	Nikolic	0	½	1	½	0	0	½	½	½	½	½	½	½	0	–	½	6
16	Vaganian	½	0	½	½	0	1	½	0	0	½	½	½	0	0	½	–	5

Skittles

Friendly fast games of chess, often played without a clock.

Slater, James Derrick

[*March 13 1929–*]
English financier, chess patron and benefactor who added £50 000 to the prize fund and thus possibly convinced Fischer to start his 1972 match with Spassky. Slater also established a charitable trust in 1973, to help young English players with coaching and travel money. In a dozen years England became the 2nd strongest chess nation.

Slaughter's Coffee-House

London café, also known as Old Slaughter's, founded on a site in St Martin's Lane by John Slaughter in 1692, closed in 1843. A private room was set aside for chess, and from 1700 to 1770 many leading English players congregated there. Among the more famous were Cunningham, Stamma, and the mathematician De Moivre who, according to Murray, 'lived for nearly thirty years on the petty sums he made at Slaughter's by chess'.
See London.

Slav Defence

See Queen's Gambit.

Sliwa, Bogdan

[*February 4 1922–*]
Polish IM (1953) and honorary GM (1987) who won the Polish Championship 6 times during 1946 to 1960 and played on 7 Polish Olympiad teams during 1952 to 1966.

Smagin, Sergey

USSR GM (1987) who was equal 1st at Tashkent 1984 (X) and Dresden 1985 (IX), clear 1st at Trnava 1987 (IX) and Zenica 1987 (IX), equal 1st at Sochi 1987 (XI) and 1st at Berlin 1988 (XI).

Smagin played in two USSR Championships, 1985 and 1986. He came equal 4th in 1985.

Smejkal, Jan

[*March 22 1946–*]
Czech GM (1972) who won the Czech Championship in 1973, 1979 and 1986, and has been on most of the Czech Olympiad teams during 1968 to 1988. He just missed getting into the 1974 Candidates.

For some 20 years he has been a consistent GM with victories at Polanica Zdroj 1970 and 1972, Smederevska Palanka 1971, Palma 1972, Novi Sad 1976, Vrsac 1977 (IX), Leipzig 1977 (IX), Warsaw 1979 (X), Trencianske-Teplice 1979 (IX) and Baden-Baden 1985 (IX). Most recently he was equal 4th at Munich 1988 (XII).

Smothered Mate

A mating position in which the king is smothered by his own men. *See* Philidor's Legacy as a fine example.

Smyslov, Vasily Vasilievich

[*March 24 1921–*]
World Champion 1957–8. USSR GM (1950) who is one of the ten greatest players that ever lived. According to Keene and Divinsky, Smyslov ranks as the 9th greatest player of all time. After coming 3rd at Groningen 1946, Smyslov was invited to play in the 1948 Moscow/The Hague tournament to crown a new World Champion. He came 2nd to Botvinnik, but ahead of Keres, Reshevsky and Euwe. After this Smyslov was a Candidate seven times.

At Budapest 1950 Smyslov came 3rd, but at Zurich 1953 (XVI) he came 1st and became the official challenger. In 1954 he held Botvinnik $+7 = 10 - 7$, but this left the world crown on Botvinnik's head. Smyslov, however, was not to be denied. He won the 1956 Candidates and again became the official challenger. This time (1957) Smyslov won $+6 = 13 - 3$ and became World Cham-

Vasily Smyslov, World Champion 1957–8. Smyslov fought three title matches with Botvinnik, emerging with a slight overall superiority. He also finished runner-up to Botvinnik in the World Championship Match-Tournament of 1948.

pion. However, he lost the return match $+5 = 11 - 7$ in 1958 to the powerful Botvinnik and had to return to the Candidates tournament of 1959.

Botvinnik wrote: 'For five years, between 1953 and 1958, he (Smyslov) was unbeatable ... (he) scored wins thanks to his admirable skill in positional play and his excellence in the endgame ...'

Smyslov came 4th at the 1959 Candidates behind Tal, Keres, and Petrosian. He appeared again in the 1965 Candidates—now in match form. He lost $+0 = 5 - 3$ to Geller. Everyone was pleasantly surprised when Smyslov again became a Candidate in 1983. He held Hübner $+1 = 7 - 1$ (winning on the spin of a roulette wheel!) beat Ribli $+3 = 7 - 1$, and faced young Kasparov (over forty years his junior) in the final. Smyslov (age 62) felt the angels were looking after him and was confident about the outcome. The angels, however, departed and Smyslov lost +0=9−4. Finally, at Montpellier 1985, Smyslov did not make the final play-offs.

In between all of this world title activity, Smyslov played in nineteen USSR Championships, plus the so-called Absolute Championship of 1941, during 1940–88. In the nineteen regular championships he scored 200½–148½ for 57.4% and was equal 1st in 1949 and 1955. He was 2nd in 1944 and equal 2nd in 1971. He played on nine USSR Olympiad teams during 1952–72, scoring +69=42−2.

Smyslov played in almost 100 tournaments. His major successes were: 1st at Zagreb 1955, 1st at the Alekhine Memorial, Moscow 1956, 1st at Moscow 1960 and 1963, 1st at Havana 1965, equal 1st at Monte Carlo 1969, 1st at Graz 1984, and equal 1st at Rome 1988. He was also equal 2nd at Reggio Emilia 1987 (XIV).

In terms of life scores (to mid-1987) he beat Petrosian (+6=28−2), Portisch (+7=24−4), Bronstein (+7=22−4), Reshevsky (+5=15−2), Korchnoi (+6=8−3) and Euwe (+7=0−1). He held Tal (+5=19−5) and lost to Botvinnik (+21=48−26), Geller (+7=31−11), Keres (+8=23−9), Spassky (+2=15−4), Kasparov (+0 =10−6), Fischer (+1=5−3) and Karpov (+1=10−3).

Smyslov's chess outlook is similar to that of Capablanca. He sees deeply and quickly and is not overly impressed with opening theory. He has continued to play at the highest level, well into his sixties and his successes at age 66 rival those of Lasker. Smyslov is a tall gentle soul with a deep interest in music and a fine baritone voice.

Major Work: *My Best Games* (1952) Russian, 1958 English).

See *Smyslov World Champion* by Liepnieks and Spence (1958).

Smyslov–Geller
USSR Championship 1951

1 e4 c5 2 ♘c3 ♘c6 3 g3 g6 4 ♗g2 ♗g7 5 d3 d6 6 ♗e3 ♖b8 7 ♕d2 b5 8 ♘d1 b4 9 h3 e6 10 ♘e2 ♘d4 11 0-0 ♘e7 12 ♘xd4 cd 13 ♗h6 0-0 14 ♗xg7 ♔xg7 15 f4 e5 16 b3 ♕c7 17 a3 ♘c6 18 ♘b2 f6 19 f5 a5 20 h4 ba 21 ♖xa3 ♘b4 22 ♘c4 gf 23 ♖xa5 fe 24 de ♗e6 25 ♖fa1 ♗xc4 26 ♖a7 ♖b7 27 ♖xb7 ♕xb7 28 bc ♘c6 29 ♔h2 ♖a8

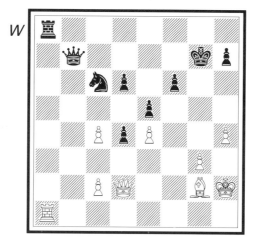

30 ♖f1 ♖a2? 31 ♖xf6 ♕e7 32 ♕h6+ ♔g8 33 c5 ♖xc2 34 cd ♕g7 35 d7 ♕xh6 36 ♖xh6 ♘d8 37 ♖d6 ♔f7 38 g4 ♔e7 39 ♖d5 ♘f7 40 g5 ♖c6 41 ♗h3 ♖d6 42 ♔g2 ♖xd5 43 ed ♘d6 44 h5 ♘e4 45 g6 hg 46 hg ♘f6 47 d6+ ♔d8 48 g7 Resigns. After 48 ... e4 49 ♗e6 d3 50 ♔f2 d2 51 ♔e2 e3 52 ♔d1 Black is in zugzwang and must give everything up.

Keres–Smyslov
Zurich 1953

1 c4 ♘f6 2 ♘c3 e6 3 ♘f3 c5 4 e3 ♗e7 5 b3 0-0 6 ♗b2 b6 7 d4 cd 8 ed d5 9 ♗d3 ♘c6 10 0-0 ♗b7 11 ♖c1 ♖c8 12 ♖e1 ♘b4 13 ♗f1 ♘e4 14 a3 ♘xc3 15 ♖xc3 ♘c6 16 ♘e5 ♘xe5 17 ♖xe5 ♗f6 18 ♖h5 g6 19 ♖ch3 (see diagram) 19 ... dc 20 ♖xh7 c3 21 ♕c1 ♕xd4 22 ♕h6 ♖fd8 23 ♗c1 ♗g7 24 ♕g5 ♕f6 25 ♕g4 c2 26 ♗e2 ♖d4 27 f4 ♖d1+ 28 ♗xd1 ♕d4+ 29 Resigns.

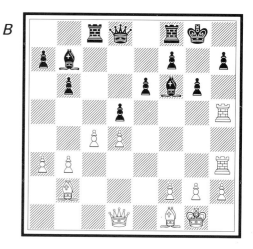

Sokolov, Andrei Y. [*March 20 1963–*]
USSR GM (1984) who burst upon the chess scene like a rocket. He was World Junior Champion in 1982 and he won the 1984 USSR Championship (X). He was equal 2nd at Novi Sad 1984 (XII) and equal 1st at the 1985 Montpellier Candidates (XIV). In the ensuing matches he crushed Vaganian +4=4−0 and edged out Yusupov +4=7−3 in 1986, and in 1987 he faced the mighty Karpov in the final.

Sokolov lost +0=7−4 to Karpov and this put a stop to his amazing sweep. He was equal 2nd at Bugojno 1986 (XVI) and was seeded into the 1988 Candidates. Here he surprisingly lost +1=9−2 to Spraggett. Sokolov was equal 4th at Belfort 1988 (XV) and equal 1st at Biel 1988 (XIII). He did not do well in the 1985 and 1988 USSR Championships, though his overall score in 3 USSR championships is 31–22 for 63.9%.

Sokolov played on the 1984 and 1986 USSR Olympiad teams. Now at age 26, it may be that he has already passed his peak. However he is young enough to catch a second wind and go to the top.

Sokolov, Ivan [*June 13 1968–*]
Yugoslav GM (1987) who was equal 1st at Portoroz 1987 (IX), equal 1st at opens in Belgrade 1987 and Saltsjobaden 1988, and who won the Yugoslav Championship in 1988 (VIII). He played on the 1988 Yugoslav Olympiad team.

Sokolsky, Alexei Pavlovich

[1908–1969/70]
USSR author and player of IM strength who was in four USSR Championships during 1944–54. He specialized in 1 b4, known as Sokolsky's opening, a move used by Tartakower (which he called Orang-Utan) in 1919, but dating back to 1888.

Major Works: *The Modern Openings in Theory and Practice* (1962), *Debyut 1 b4* (1963).

Solkoff Score

See Tie-Breaking Systems.

Soltis, Andrew Eden [*May 28 1947– *]

US author and GM (1980) who was 1st at Reggio Emilia 1971/2 and equal 1st at New York 1977.

Major works: *The Best Games of Boris Spassky* (1973), *The Great Chess Tournaments and their Stories* (1975), *The Book of Chess Lists* (1984).

Sonneborn–Berger Score

See Tie-Breaking Systems.

Sosonko, Gennady [*May 18 1943– *]

Siberian-born Dutch GM (1976) who moved via Israel to Holland in 1972. He won the Dutch Championship in 1973 and 1978 (equal) and has played on all the Dutch Olympiad teams from 1974 to 1988.

He was equal 1st at Wijk aan Zee 1977 (XI), Nijmegen 1978 (IX) and Wijk aan Zee 1981 (XII). In even stronger tournaments, he was 3rd at Amsterdam 1980 (XIV), equal 3rd at Tilburg 1982 (XIV) and more recently equal 4th at Haninge 1988 (XIII). In 1984 he held Timman +1=0-1.

Sosonko is a sensitive and well educated GM, having studied economic geography at the university of Leningrad. He is popular as a discussion leader of ongoing games at tournaments.

Soviet Union

See Moscow, Saint Petersburg, USSR/ Russian Championships and Leningrad.

Space Advantage

The ability to use more of the chessboard than your opponent, resulting in greater mobility for your pieces.

Spanish Opening

See Lopez, Ruy.

Spassky, Boris Vasilievich

[*January 30 1937– *]
World Champion 1969–72. USSR GM (1955) who is one of the ten greatest players that ever lived. According to Keene and Divinsky, Spassky ranks as the 8th greatest player of all time. He won the World Junior Championship in 1955 and was a Candidate seven times. In 1956 he came equal 3rd in the powerful Amsterdam candidates—a

Boris Spassky, World Champion 1969–72, pictured here at the Alekhine Memorial tournament, Moscow 1971.

remarkable achievement for a nineteen year old. He appeared again in 1965 when he beat Keres +4=4−2, Geller +3=5−0 and Tal +4=6−1 to become the official challenger. In 1966 he lost narrowly +3=17−4 to Petrosian. But Spassky was not to be denied. In 1968 he beat Geller +3=5−0, Larsen +4=3−1 and Korchnoi +4=5−1 to again become the official challenger. In 1969 he became champion of the world by beating Petrosian +6=13−4.

Spassky's challenger in 1972 was the US star Fischer—an opponent to whom he had never lost. Spassky prepared himself with care and depth—his opening repertoire bristled with theoretical novelties. Fischer created a circus-like atmosphere and it was not clear from hour to hour whether he would play or not. Finally, amid much ballyhoo, the match got under way. Spassky won the first game and was awarded game 2 by default. Then, Fischer came to life and Spassky began to blunder. After an heroic, but uneven resistance, Spassky watched helplessly as he lost his crown +3=11−7 to the disconcerting and eccentric genius from New York.

In 1974 Spassky beat Byrne +3 =3−0, but lost +1=6−4 to young Karpov. In 1977, Spassky beat Hort +2=13−1 and Portisch +4=9−2, but lost the final to Korchnoi +4=7−7. In 1980 Spassky held his own +1=12−1 against Portisch, but lost on tie break, and at Montpellier 1985 Spassky missed out on the final play-offs (he was equal 6th).

In between all of this world title activity, Spassky played in eleven USSR Championships during 1955 to 1973, scoring $130\frac{1}{2}$ to $76\frac{1}{2}$ for 63%. He won the championship in November 1961 and in 1973, and was equal 1st in 1956 and 1963 (losing the playoffs). He played on seven USSR Olympiad teams during 1962 to 1978.

Spassky won many tournaments, in particular: Moscow 1964 (XV), Piatigorsky 1966 (XV), Leiden 1970 (XV), Bugojno 1978 (XIV) (equal) and Linares 1983 (XIV). He was equal 2nd at Reggio Emilia 1987 (XIV), but only equal 4th at Belfort 1988 (XV).

In life scores to about mid-1987, he beat Portisch (+12=50−6), Tal (+10=23−6), Timman (+7=24−3), Bronstein (+4=19−0), Petrosian (+11=53−10), Keres (+5=18−3), Smyslov (+4=15−2) and Kasparov (+2=2−0). He lost to Korchnoi (+12=26−15), Fischer (+5=13−7) and Botvinnik (+0=6−1). He did very badly against Karpov (+2=20−11).

In his best years (the 1960s) Spassky was under the good influence and steadying hand of his friend and trainer Bondarevsky. Spassky was then the universal player—he seemed to have no weaknesses and he could play all kinds of positions. His talent flowed in a large even wave filled with force and beauty. Spassky is handsome, modest and has a deep Russian soul, a soul filled with restlessness and melancholy. He was not entirely comfortable as World Champion. In addition, he (the 8th greatest) had the misfortune to be confronted by Fischer (3rd greatest), Karpov (2nd greatest), and Korchnoi (7th greatest) during the 1970s.

Spassky's third wife, Marina, is a charming French woman. He moved to Paris in 1975 and kept his USSR connection. In time this connection unravelled and since 1984 Spassky has played on the French Olympiad team. During the 1980s his play has become passive, he produces many short draws and he concentrates on tennis.

Spassky has kept in touch with Fischer over the years and they meet from time to time. Spassky's chess force was diminished after his 1972 loss, but he is still a serious chess power. Some believe Spassky was destroyed by Fischer, but the converse may even be

more true: Fischer was completely wiped out of chess by Spassky. Like a good friend and parent, Spassky is concerned and feels responsible for Fischer's welfare and Fischer's disappearance.

See *Spassky's 100 Best Games*, by B. Cafferty (1972), *Fischer vs. Spassky*, by S. Gligoric (1972), *Bobby Fischer's Conquest of the World Chess Championship*, by R. Fine (1973).

Spassky–Fischer
Siegen Olympiad 1970

1 d4 ♘f6 2 c4 g6 3 ♘c3 d5 4 cd ♘xd5 5 e4 ♘xc3 6 bc ♗g7 7 ♗c4 c5 8 ♘e2 ♘c6 9 ♗e3 0-0 10 0-0 ♕c7 11 ♖c1 ♖d8 12 h3 b6 13 f4 e6 14 ♕e1 ♘a5 15 ♗d3 f5 16 g4 fe 17 ♗xe4 ♗b7 18 ♘g3 ♘c4 19 ♗xb7 ♕xb7 20 ♗f2 ♕c6 21 ♕e2 cd 22 cd b5 23 ♘e4 ♗xd4 24 ♘g5 ♗xf2+ 25 ♖xf2 ♖d6 26 ♖e1 ♕b6 27 ♘e4 ♖d4 28 ♘f6+ ♔h8 29 ♕xe6

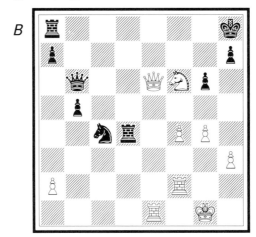

29 ... ♖d6 30 ♕e4 ♖f8 31 g5 ♖d2 32 ♖(1)f1 ♕c7 22 ♖xd2 ♘xd2 34 ♕d4 ♖d8 35 ♘d5+ ♔g8 36 ♖f2 ♘c4 37 ♖e2 ♖d6 38 ♖e8+ ♔f7 39 ♖f8+ Resigns (after 30 ... ♔xf8 40 ♕h8+ ♔f7 41 ♘xc7).

Spassky–Petrosian
Match 1969

1 e4 c5 2 ♘f3 d6 3 d4 cd 4 ♘xd4 ♘f6 5 ♘c3 a6 6 ♗g5 ♘bd7 7 ♗c4 ♕a5 8 ♕d2 h6 9 ♗xf6 ♘xf6 10 0-0-0 e6 11 ♖he1 ♗e7 12 f4 0-0 13 ♗b3 ♖e8 14

♔b1 ♗f8 15 g4 ♘xg4 16 ♕g2 ♘f6 17 ♖g1 ♗d7 18 f5 ♔h8 19 ♖df1 ♕d8 20 fe fe

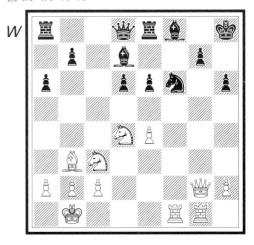

21 e5 de 22 ♘e4 ♘h5 23 ♕g6 ed 24 ♘g5 Resigns. After 24 ... hg 25 ♕xh5+ ♔g8 26 ♕f7+ ♔h8 27 ♖f3.

Spassov, Luben Dimitrov
[*March 22 1943– *]
Bulgarian GM (1976) who won a number of minor tournaments in the mid-1970s. He was equal 1st at Pamporova 1981 (VIII) and 2nd at Warsaw 1983 (IX). He played on the Bulgarian Olympiad team in 1978 and 1980.

Speelman, Jonathan Simon
[*October 2 1956– *]
English GM (1980) who was a middle-level GM in the early 1980s. He had problems with his eyes, and when these were finally solved his strength as a player increased dramatically about 1986. He was equal 1st at Hastings 1983/84 (XI), Hastings 1986/87 (X), Beer Sheba 1987 (XI) and the Subotica interzonal 1987 (XI). He was 2nd at Hastings 1987/88 (XII). He was a Candidate in 1988 and beat Seirawan +3=2−0. Then he beat Short +2 =3−0, but in 1989 he lost +1=5−2 to Timman in the semi-final.

Speelman belongs to the world top ten, though he was unsuccessful in three 1988 Category XV events (Brussels, Belfort and Reykjavik). Though he is past

Jon Speelman: once thought too cautious to succeed, he has gone further in the World Championship than any other British player.

the first blush of youth, he has room and talent for more growth.

He won the British Championship in 1978, 1985 and 1986, and played on all the English Olympiad teams during the 1980s. He is a superb analyst and a fine author. Speelman is tall and gentle, with a passion for difficult crossword puzzles.

See *Best Chess Games 1970–80, Developments in the Caro–Kann 1984/85, Analysing the Endgame* (1988).

Spielmann, Rudolf

[*May 5 1883–August 22 1942*] Austrian-Jewish player of GM strength who played frequently (more than 120 tournaments and 50 individual matches) and had many disappointments mixed in with his successes. His best results were equal 3rd at St Petersburg 1909, equal 2nd at San Sebastian 1912, 1st at Baden bei Wien 1914, 1st at Stockholm 1919, equal 1st at Teplice Schonau 1922, 1st at Semmering 1926 and equal 2nd at Carlsbad 1929. However, he was equal 17th at Carlsbad 1923 and equal 12th at Moscow 1925.

In matches he beat Nimzowitsch +4=1−1 in 1908, Reti +4=1 in 1910 and +3=3 in 1921, Tartakower +3=1−2 in 1910 and again +3 =1−2 in 1921, Ståhlberg +4=1−1 in 1930 and Bogoljubow +4=2−3 in 1932. Spielmann played on the Austrian Olympiad team in 1931 and 1935.

Spielmann loved combinations and complex positions where he could use his rich imagination. He had no trouble winning the King's Gambit Accepted tournament at Abbazia 1912. His generation was absorbed in and fascinated with hypermodernism, but he was a lone artistic romantic voice in this hypermodern landscape.

He was friendly, pleasant, sensitive, extremely modest and moody. If he lost to someone he considered weaker than him, he lost interest in the tournament and ended up near the bottom. Though he had served in the Austrian army during the first world war, he had to flee the Nazis and went to Sweden in 1939.

Major works: *Ein Rundflug durch die Schachwelt* (1929), *Bad Sliac* (1932), *The Art of Sacrifice in Chess* (1935).

See *The Career of R. Spielmann*, by J. L. Spence (3 vols.) (1969–74).

Alekhine–Spielmann

Carlsbad 1923
After 15 rounds, Alekhine led with 11 while Spielmann was dead last with 4. The night before round 16, Spielmann was drinking away his sorrows when Réti asked him about sportsmanship and preserving the rights of other players. Spielmann agreed and the following conversation took place:

S I'll win tomorrow.
R Do you realize who you are to play?
S It doesn't matter.
R But it does—you're paired with Alekhine.
S So much the better.
R And you are to play Black.
S So much the better.

1 d4 ♘f6 2 c4 e6 3 ♘f3 d5 4 ♘c3 ♘bd7 5 ♗f4 dc 6 e3 ♘b6 7 ♗xc4 ♘xc4 8 ♕a4+ c6 9 ♕xc4 ♘d5 10 ♗e5 f6 11 ♗g3 ♕b6 12 ♕e2 ♗b4 13 ♖c1 ♘xc3 14 bc ♗a3 15 ♖d1 ♕b5 16 c4 ♕a5+ 17 ♘d2 0-0 18 0-0 b6 19 f4 ♗a6 20 ♗e1 ♕a4 21 ♖f2 ♖ad8 22 ♖b1 c5 23 dc ♗xc5 24 ♘b3 ♗a3 25 ♘d4 ♗xc4 26 ♕g4 f5 27 ♕g3 ♖f7 28 h3 ♗c5 29 ♖d2 ♖c7 30 ♔h2 ♗xd4 31 ed ♗d5 32 ♕e3 ♖dc8 33 ♕e5 h6 34 ♖bb2 ♖c3 35 ♕e2 ♕a3 36 ♖d1

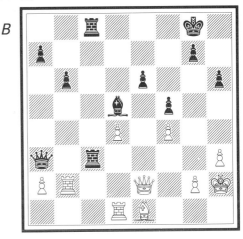

36 ... ♕xb2 37 ♕xb2 ♖c2 38 ♖d2 ♖xb2 39 ♖xb2 ♖c4 40 ♗b4 a5 41 ♗d6 ♔f7 42 a3 ♖c6 43 ♗b8 ♔e8 44 ♗a7 ♖c7 45 ♗b8 ♖c8 46 ♗e5 g6 47 g4 ♖c3 48 gf gf 49 ♖xb6 ♖xa3 50 ♗d6 ♖c3 51 ♗c5 h5 52 h4 a4 53 ♖a6 ♖c2+ 54 ♔g1 ♖g2+ 55 ♔f1 ♖g4 56 ♖xa4 ♖xh4 57 ♗d6 ♖h1+ 58 ♔f2 h4 59 ♗a7 ♖h2+ 60 ♔f1 h3 61 ♖e7+ ♔d8 62 ♖h7 a2 63 Resigns

It is said that Alekhine returned to his hotel room and smashed every bit of furniture.

Spiridonov, Nikolai

[*February 28 1938– *] Bulgarian GM (1979) who was Bulgarian Champion in 1969 and equal 1st at Polanica Zdroj 1971 and Varna 1974.

Spite Check

A player in a lost position who is about to resign may, if it is possible and if the spirit moves him, give a final check just before he resigns. It is a mild act of defiance and is called a spite check.

Spraggett, Kevin Berry

[*November 10 1954–*] Canadian GM (1985) who is probably the strongest player Canada has ever had. He was a Candidate twice: at Montpellier 1985 he did not make the final play-offs; in 1988 he beat A. Sokolov $+2=9-1$ but was eliminated in 1989 by Yusupov $+1=6-2$.

Spraggett won the Canadian Championship in 1984 and played on the 1986 Canadian Olympiad team. He was equal 1st in the 1985 Commonwealth Championship, 1st at Montreal 1986 (VIII), and equal 2nd at Hastings 1989/90 (XIV).

Ståhlberg, Anders Gideon Tom

[*January 26 1908–May 26 1967*] Swedish GM (1950) who was a Candidate twice (1950 and 1953) and during the early 1950s was just on the edge of the world top ten. He was Swedish Champion 4 times during 1927–39 and played on 13 Swedish Olympiad teams during 1928–64. His best results were equal 3rd at Dresden 1936, 2nd at Stockholm 1937, 1st at Mar del Plata 1941, equal 1st at Buenos Aires 1941, 1st at Buenos Aires 1947, 1st at Trencianske Teplice 1949, 3rd at Amsterdam 1950 and equal 3rd at Budapest 1952.

In matches he beat Spielmann $+3=4-1$ in 1933 and Nimzowitsch $+4=2-2$ in 1934. He held Keres $+2=4-2$ in 1938 and lost to Fine $+2=2-4$ in 1937 and Gligoric $+1=9-2$ in 1949.

Ståhlberg was an excellent card player (especially bridge), liked good living, was a linguist and a connoisseur of wine and alcohol. He was cultivated, witty and charming. He acted as arbiter at 5 World Championship matches during 1957–63.

Major works: *Chess and Chessmasters*

(1937) Swedish, 1955 (English), *I Kamp med Varldseliten* (1958).

Stalemate

When a king is not in check and when his side cannot make any legal move, the position is called a stalemate and the game is a draw.

The rules regarding stalemate have varied throughout the history of chess. Assuming that White makes a move and Black is stalemated, then at various times and places the following different rules were in force: (1) Black wins; (2) White wins; (3) it is illegal to stalemate your opponent—you must give him room to move; (4) if there is a stalemate, Black can remove the White piece that confines him, or any White piece he chooses. And today we all universally accept (5) the game is a draw.

It is curious that from 1600–1800, in England, option (1) was used, and it wasn't until Sarratt's laws of 1808 that (5) was accepted.

See Stalemate, by Murray, *British Chess Magazine*, pages 281–9 (1903).

Stalin, Josef Vissarionovich

[*December 21 1879–March 5 1953*] Soviet dictator who enjoyed chess.

Stamma, Philip
[*18th century*]
Author from Aleppo (Syria) who wrote *Essai sur le Jeu des Échecs*, in Paris 1737, a book with 100 endgame/problems, and *The Noble Game of Chess*, in London 1745, a book with some 74 opening lines, plus the 100 problems from 1737. He introduced the algebraic notation to Europe.

Stamma was soundly defeated $(+1=1-8)$ by young Philidor in 1747 at Slaughter's Coffee House in St Martin's Lane, London.

Stamps
The first stamp with a chess motif was issued by Bulgaria on September 29 1947. It was a 9 leva stamp with a

picture of a knight. Since then hundreds of stamps dealing with chess have been issued by over 40 countries. They commemorate Olympiads, Candidates tournaments, World Championships and great masters. For example in 1976 Cuba issued stamps showing Ruy Lopez (1 centavo), Philidor (2 centavo), Steinitz (3 centavo), Lasker (13 centavo) and Capablanca (30 centavo). Former World Champion Karpov is an avid collector.

See Chess on Stamps, by P. C. Burnett (1972), *Checkmate*, by Sutcliffe and Ulfstromer 1980 (5 volumes).

Stanley, Charles Henry
[*1819–?*]
English-born US player and author who started the first chess column in the USA in 1845 (in the *Spirit of the Times*), founded the *American Chess Magazine* (1846/47) and in general played a busy and important role in US chess. In matches he beat Rousseau $+15=8-8$ in 1845 for the large stake of $1000. He drew $+3=0-3$ with Löwenthal in 1850 and $+4=0-4$ with Saint-Amant in 1852.

Major works: *Morphy's Match Games* (1859), *The Chess Player's Instructor* (1859).

Staunton, Howard
[*? 1810–June 22 1874*]
English Shakespearian scholar and player of GM strength who was, during the 1840s, the leading player in the world—the only Englishman to achieve that distinction. He devoted his considerable energy and talent to chess in all of its dimensions—player, organizer, author, columnist, law maker and piece design selector.

Staunton learnt chess relatively late in life (about 1830), lost to Alexandre and W. D. Evans (1838) and only came to his full strength in 1840. He beat Popert in 1840 and during 1841/42 played over 600 games with John Cochrane, with Staunton winning about 400 of them. Fate took a hand when Saint-

Howard Staunton. By defeating Saint-Amant in 1843, Staunton showed himself to be the world's strongest player, thus ending one hundred years of French supremacy.

Amant, the leading French player, visited London in April 1843. Staunton lost a hard fought match $+2=1-3$ to the visiting Frenchman (played at the St George's Club) and issued a formal challenge for a more serious encounter. This Grand Chess Match between England and France was played for £100 to the first player to win 11 games, at the Paris Chess Club during November–December 1843. Staunton won convincingly $+11=4-6$ and broke the 100-year French domination of world chess (Legall, Philidor, Deschapelles and La Bourdonnais).

The match created quite a stir and Staunton enjoyed relating: 'Why sir! Couriers were waiting at the close of each game, to dispatch the news to all the crowned heads of Europe'.

In 1844 Staunton went to Paris for a return match with Saint-Amant, but caught pneumonia which damaged his heart, and no return match was ever played. In 1846 Staunton beat Horwitz $+14=3-7$ and Harrwitz $+7=0-0$. He also held his own spotting Harrwitz pawn and two moves ($+4=0-3$) and pawn and one move ($+1=1-6$).

In 1851 Staunton was the moving spirit in holding the first international tournament: London 1851. He lost $+1=0-4$ to Anderssen and ended up 4th when he lost $+3=1-4$ to Williams.

Staunton went on to beat Williams $+6=1-4$ and Jaenisch $+7=1-2$ later in 1851. In 1853 when Staunton met von der Lasa, they played a dozen games and Staunton lost $+4=3-5$. He also played at Birmingham 1858 but lost $+0=0-2$ to Löwenthal, the ultimate winner.

In 1858 Morphy came to Europe, swept all before him and actively sought a match with the renowned British chess lion Howard Staunton. No match ever took place and much has been written about Staunton avoiding inevitable defeat. Certainly Staunton could have been more direct in refusing to play, instead of continually postponing and claiming he was deep into his edition of Shakespeare. This did leave a slight blot on an otherwise distinguished and honourable career. In fact two consultation games were played in London, July 1858, between Morphy and Barnes versus Staunton and Owen, and the Morphy side won both.

During the 1840s and 50s, Staunton did an enormous amount for chess. He founded and edited the first English chess magazine *The Chess Player's Chronicle* (1841–54); he was chess editor (1841–74) of the *Illustrated London News*; he visited clubs throughout England and stimulated both players and organizers; he established the first international tournament—London 1851; and he made efforts to unify the laws of chess and consulted Lasa on this important topic. He rounded this all off with a series of successful books: *The Chess Player's Handbook* (1847), *The Chess Player's Companion* (1849), The *Chess Tournament 1852*, *The Chess Player's Text Book* (1852) and *Chess Praxis* (1860). And perhaps most important of all, he sponsored Nathaniel Cook's pleasing and harmonious chess piece design of 1835, and this design is now known as the Staunton pattern and is used universally as the accepted norm.

Staunton did some acting in his youth and ended up editing an edition of Shakespeare. Acting also gave him a dominating presence which was not always appreciated. He was widely admired but widely disliked.

His play had a fresh aggressiveness that was original and powerful. He had excellent analytic powers and deep strategic insight. Fischer (1964) ranked him as one of the ten greatest players of all time:

> Staunton was the most profound opening analyst of all time. He was more theorist than player, but nonetheless he was the strongest player of his day. Playing over his games, I discover that they are completely modern; where Morphy and Steinitz rejected the fianchetto, Staunton embraced it. In addition, he understood all of the positional concepts which modern players hold so dear, and thus—with Steinitz—must be considered the first modern player.

In the March 1890 issue of the *Chess Monthly*, the editor writes:

> During our time he (Staunton) led the life of a recluse and we never had the good fortune of meeting him. Shortly before his death Kolisch paid a flying visit on his way to Vienna, and a select few dined together at the old Hummums, Covent Garden, a favourite resort of Staunton's. We were unfortunately otherwise engaged that day, and so missed the rare opportunity of seeing him. We were told afterwards by Kolisch that he was the old Staunton again, and behind a 'churchwarden', his

favourite canaster, and his grog he was brim full of anecdotes of Auld Lang Syne. If we recollect right, a week later he was dead.

Major works: *The Chess Player's Handbook* (1847), *Edition of Shakespeare* (1857–60), *Memorials of Shakespeare, Facsimile of the First Folio* (1864), *The Great Schools of England*.

See *Howard Staunton: the English World Chess Champion*, by Keene and Coles (1975), *Howard Staunton*, by Levy (1975).

Saint-Amant–Staunton

Match 1843

1 e4 c5 2 c4 e6 3 ♘c3 ♘e7 4 d3 ♘bc6 5 ♗e3 ♘g6 6 f4 d6 7 ♘f3 ♗e7 8 a3 ♗f6 9 ♗e2 0-0 10 0-0 ♗d4 11 ♕d2 ♘xf4 12 ♘xd4 cd 13 ♗xf4 e5 14 ♘d5 ef 15 ♕xf4 ♗e6 16 ♕g3 ♗xd5 17 cd ♘e5 18 ♖f2 ♖c8 19 ♗g4 ♖c5 20 ♖af1 ♕g5 21 h3 ♖c1 22 ♔h2 ♖xf1 23 ♖xf1 ♕d2 24 ♖f2 ♕e1 25 ♖c2 ♕b1 26 ♖d2 g6 27 ♕f2 h5 28 ♗d1 ♕c1 29 g4 hg 30 hg

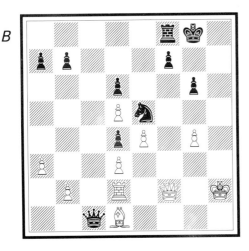

B

30 ... ♕xd1 31 ♖xd1 ♘xg4+ 32 ♔g3 ♘xf2 33 ♔xf2 ♖c8 34 ♖d2 ♔g7 35 ♔f3 ♖c1 36 ♖h2 ♔f6 37 ♖h8 ♖d1 38 ♔e2 ♖b1 39 ♔f3 ♖xb2 40 ♖e8 ♖b6 41 e5+ de 42 ♔e4 ♖d6 43 ♖xe5 ♖d7 44 ♔xd4 g5 45 ♖e1 g4 46 ♔c5 ♔g5 47 d6 f5 48 ♖e7 ♖d8 49 ♔d5 ♔f4 50 d7 g3 51 ♖g7 ♔f3 52 ♔e5 g2 53 ♔e6 f4 54 d4

♔f2 55 d5 g1(♕) 56 ♖xg1 ♔xg1 57 ♔e7 ♖xd7+ 58 ♔xd7 f3 59 ♔c7 f2 60 d6 f1(♕) 61 d7 ♕d3 62 d8(♕) ♕xd8+ 63 ♔xd8 b5 64 ♔c7 a5 65 ♔b6 b4 66 a4 b3 67 ♔xa5 b2 68 ♔a6 b1(♕) 69 a5 ♕b4 70 Resigns.

Stean, Michael Francis

[*September 4 1953– *] English GM (1977) who played on 5 English Olympiad teams during 1974 to 1983. His best results were 1st at Vrsac 1979 (IX), 1st at Smederevska Palanka 1980 (IX) and 1st at Beer Sheba 1982 (VIII).

Stean specializes in opening theory and was one of Korchnoi's seconds during 1977–81.

Major works: *Sicilian: Najdorf* (1976), *Simple Chess* (1978).

Stein, Leonid Zakharovich

[*November 12 1934–July 4 1973*] USSR (Ukraine) GM (1962) who was one of the great players of all time, on a par with Tal and Keres, and yet fate decreed that he should never become a Candidate.

He played in 9 USSR Championships during 1961–71 and won the title 3 times (1963, 65 (XII) and late 1966 (XIII)), scoring 113½–65½ for 63.4%. He played on the USSR Olympiad team in 1964 and 1966. He had a wonderful tournament record: equal 2nd at Moscow 1964 (XV), 1st at Moscow 1967 (XIV), equal 1st at Hastings 1967/68, 1st at Kecskemet 1968, 1st at Tallinn 1969, equal 1st at Moscow 1971 (XIV), 1st at Zagreb 1972 and equal 1st at Las Palmas 1973.

In terms of life scores he beat Tal (+4 =13 −0), Korchnoi (+2 =13 −1), Bronstein (+4 =9 −1), Spassky (+3 = 9 −1), Keres (+2 =6 −0) and Gligoric (+6 =0 −0). He held Botvinnik (+1 =2 −1), Smyslov (+1 =11 −1) and Reshevsky (+0 =7 −0). He only

lost to Geller (+1 =10 −7), Petrosian (+1 =8 −3), Fischer (+0 =1 −1) and Karpov (+0 =3 −2).

How could anyone with such a record not have been a Candidate? Fide used to have a rule that the number of players from any one country in the Candidates was limited or restricted—the so-called Nationality Rule. Stein placed equal 6th in the 1962 Interzonal, but was excluded because he was from the USSR, and Benko went through. Stein placed 5th in the 1964 interzonal, but was again excluded and Ivkov and Portisch went through. In 1967 Stein was equal 6th, the nationality rule had been abolished, he had to play off, and did not make it. In 1973 he died shortly before the interzonal in Rio.

Stein was an intuitive, romantic, original, and ingenious player. He was good natured and generous. However, nothing came easily to him. He was an uneducated factory worker, a late starter, a chain smoker with bad teeth. As Kotov said: 'The gods have tried him'. Stein wanted desperately to become a Candidate and said: 'When I get there [the Candidates] my whole life will take another course. You won't recognize me. Then, I'll really start to play!'

See *Leonid Stein, Master of Attack*, by R. Keene (1976).

Lutikov–Stein

USSR Championship 1965

1 e4 e5 2 ♘f3 ♘c6 3 ♗b5 a6 4 ♗a4 ♘f6 5 0-0 ♗e7 6 ♖e1 b5 7 ♗b3 0-0 8 c3 d6 9 h3 ♘d7 10 d4 ♗b7 11 ♘bd2 ♘a5 12 ♗c2 c5 13 ♘f1 cd 14 cd ♖c8 15 ♘e3 g6 16 ♘g4 h5 17 ♘e3 ed 18 ♘xd4 ♗f6 19 ♘b3 ♘c4 20 ♘xc4 bc 21 ♘d4 ♖e8 22 b4 d5 23 ♖b1 de 24 ♗a4 ♖e7 25 ♗e3 ♘e5 26 b5 ab 27 ♘xb5 ♘d3 28 ♖e2 ♖a8 29 ♘a7 ♕c7 30 ♖b6 ♖e6 31 ♘b5

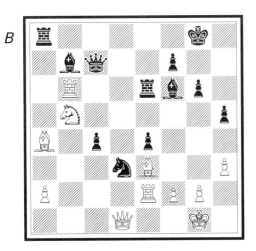

31 ... ♕xb6 32 ♗xb6 ♖xb6 33 ♘c7
♖xa4 34 ♕xa4 ♖b1+ 35 ♔h2
♗e5+ 36 g3 e3 37 f3 ♗xf3 38 ♕e8+
♔g7 39 ♘e6+ ♔f6 40 ♖g2 ♘f2 41
Resigns

If 41 ♖g1 ♘g4+ 42 hg ♖b2+ 43
♔h3 hg+ 44 ♔h4 ♖h2 mate. Or if 41
♕d8+ ♔xe6 42 ♕e8+ ♔f6 43
♕h8+ ♔f5 44 ♕c8+ ♔g5 45
♕d8+ ♔h6.

Steiner, Endre (Andreas)

[June 27 1901–December 29 1944]
Hungarian player of almost GM
strength who played on 6 Hungarian
Olympiad teams during 1924–37. He
was 3rd at Portsmouth 1923 (beating
Alekhine), 2nd at Trencianske Teplice
1928 and 1st at Kecskemet 1933. His
younger brother Lajos was also a master
player.

Steiner, Herman

[April 15 1905–November 25 1955]
Hungarian born US IM (1950) who
played on 4 US Olympiad teams (1928,
1930, 1931 and 1950), was US Champion in 1948 and was the leading chess
organizer on the west coast of the US.
He opened a Hollywood Chess Club
whose regulars included Humphrey
Bogart and Jose Ferrer.

Steiner, Lajos

[June 14 1903–April 22 1975]
Hungarian author and IM (1950) who
played on 3 Hungarian Olympiad teams
(1931–5) and was Hungarian Champion
in 1931 and 1936. He was equal 2nd at
Kecskemet 1927, 2nd at Hastings 1927/
28, and equal 1st at Vienna 1935. He
beat Lilienthal +3 = 2 − 1 in 1935. In
1939 he settled in Australia and won the
Australian Championship 5 times during 1945–59. His older brother Endre
was also a master player.

Major Work: *Kings of the Chess Board*
(1948).

Steinitz Defence

See Lopez, Ruy.

Steinitz, Wilhelm

[*May 17 1836–August 12 1900*]
World Champion 1886–94. Steinitz was
the first official chess champion of the
world and perhaps the most profound
thinker the game has ever seen. Though
not as great in sensing complex combinations as his rivals Zukertort and
Chigorin, his deep insights into defensive play and into the accumulation of
small but enduring advantages changed
the outlook of an entire generation of

Wilhelm Steinitz, the first official World Champion.

chess-masters and baffled his more
talented opponents. Before Steinitz,
everyone believed that winning
depended on inventiveness and luck,
and that rapid kingside attacks were
desirable. After Steinitz, everyone realized that a successful winning attack
could not exist unless one side had a
clear positional advantage; that relatively minor items like doubled, isolated
or backward pawns, a queenside pawn
majority, or two bishops versus bishop
and knight, were often significant con-
tributing factors; and that the best
defence consisted in avoiding permanent positional weaknesses. Morphy
had shown the way in open positions,
but Steinitz illuminated the more complex domain of closed positions. Steinitz
himself played in the pre-Steinitz way
until the early 1870s. Then he changed
his ways and began to play in the post-
Steinitz fashion.

In effecting this major transformation, Steinitz suffered much abuse, but
he displayed enormous confidence, even
stubbornness, and participated in controversy with obstinate and often bitter
relish.

Born in Prague, of Jewish parents,
Steinitz went to study in Vienna in 1858
and represented Austria in his first international tournament, London 1862 (he
came 6th out of 14). He took up resid-
ence in London and in 1866 defeated
Anderssen (recognized as the best active player in the world) +8 = 0 − 6.
Steinitz's reign as World Champion is
sometimes taken from this date though
he did not coin the phrase until 1886
(after Morphy died). Steinitz won tournaments in London 1872, Vienna 1873
and New York 1894, and tied for first or
came second in Dundee 1867, Baden-
Baden 1870, Vienna 1882, London
1883, St. Petersburg 1895/96 and New
York 1897. Even in 1898 at the age
of 62, Steinitz came 4th out of 19 in
the gruelling 36 round tournament at
Vienna.

Steinitz dominated British chess, winning matches against Bird (1866) and Blackburne (1876). He became chess editor of *The Field*. Zukertort rivalled Steinitz's dominance and the clash of their personalities led to fierce rivalry. In 1886 these two chess colossi played the first match billed as the World Championship. Steinitz had won an earlier match $+7=4-1$ in 1872, over the young Zukertort, and he succeeded in this great match $+10=5-5$. Zukertort could not understand why he lost, took ill and died two years later.

In 1882 Steinitz left England and went to live in New York. There he founded and edited the *International Chess Magazine* (January 1885–December 1891). For English readers these 7 volumes are wonderful to read—full of deep annotations and controversy. The editorials are so intense that battles that raged over 100 years ago come vividly to life. These (expensive) volumes are available in the Olms edition of 1985.

In 1889 Steinitz defeated his next great rival, Chigorin, $+10=1-6$ and again in 1892, $+10=5-8$. He also beat Gunsberg $+6=9-4$ in 1890. In 1894 Steinitz was dethroned by the young Lasker $+5=4-10$ and in their return match 1896/97, Steinitz could do no better than $+2=5-10$. He took ill (in Moscow) and was put into a mental home. He recovered and continued to play, but in 1900 he again had mental problems and died a pauper in New York. Steinitz is buried in the Evergreen Cemetery, Brooklyn.

Steinitz had a deep will to win. Young Frank Marshall played in a simultaneous exhibition against Steinitz in 1893 and wrote: '. . . a short, heavy-set bearded man with a large head . . . he limped. Near sighted, he leaned over each board and peered at the pieces . . . he gave me an encouraging smile. One of the greatest waiting players of all

time, he had such a fierce desire to win, that even in simultaneous exhibitions he hated to draw'.

Steinitz's results would have been even better if he had not experimented with inferior opening variations and had not stubbornly continued to use them after everyone else realized they were unsound.

He was a striking but short figure, with a massive head, a prominent forehead and powerful shoulders and arms. He was a good swimmer. Below his chest, however, he was much smaller, having unusually short legs. He also walked with a limp.

In life scores he beat Chigorin ($+27 =8-24$), Blackburn ($+25=7-8$), Zukertort ($+19=11-9$), Anderssen ($+10=0-9$), and Maroczy ($+2=2 -1$). He held his own with Pillsbury ($+5=3-5$) and lost to Tarrasch ($+0=1-3$) and Lasker ($+8=12 -26$).

Steinitz produced many famous games (*see* Bardeleben; Neumann). Many authors wrote in praise of Steinitz and his contributions to chess. See especially, *Lasker's Manual of Chess* (1927).

Major Works: *Modern Chess Instructor* (1889, 1895), *Sixth American Chess Congress* (1891), *International Chess Magazine* (1885–91).

See *A Memorial to Steinitz*, by Devide (1901), *Schachmeister Steinitz*, by Bachmann (4 vols) (1910–21), *Steinitz*, by Gilchrist and Hooper (1968).

Steinitz–Dr Simonson

New York 1883 (simultaneous display)
1 e4 e5 2 f4 ef 3 ♘f3 g5 4 h4 g4 5 ♘e5 h5 6 ♗c4 ♘h6 7 d4 d6 8 ♘d3 f3 9 gf ♗e7 10 ♗e3 ♗xh4+ 11 ♔d2 gf 12 ♕xf3 ♗g4 13 ♕f4 ♘c6 14 ♘c3 ♘e7 15 ♖af1 ♖h7 16 ♖xh4 ♘g6 17 ♖xg4 ♘xf4 18 ♖gxf4 c6 19 ♖f6 ♘g4 20 ♗xf7+ ♔d7 21 ♗e6+ ♔c7 22 ♖f7+ ♖xf7 23 ♖xf7+ ♔b6 24

♗xg4 hg 25 d5+ c5

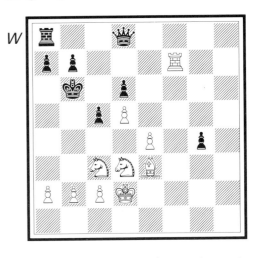

26 e5 ♔a6 27 ♗xc5 dc 28 ♘xc5+ ♔b6 29 ♖xb7+ ♔xc5 30 ♔d3 ♕a5 31 b4+ ♕xb4 32 ♘e4+ and White wins.

Stoltz, Gosta

[May 9 1904–July 25 1963] Swedish GM (1954) who played on 9 Swedish Olympiad teams and won the Swedish Championship 5 times, during 1927–54. His best international results were equal 4th at Bled 1931, 1st at Munich 1941 ahead of Alekhine and Bogoljubow, and equal 2nd at Prague 1946. During the early 1930s he held his own in short matches against Kashdan, Flohr, Spielmann and Nimzowitsch.

Stoltz was a hard drinking automobile mechanic with a genuine talent for combinative play, and some believe that his alcohol problem prevented him from achieving much more.

Spielmann–Stoltz

Match 1930
1 e4 e6 2 d4 d5 3 ♘d2 ♘f6 4 e5 ♘fd7 5 ♗d3 c5 6 c3 ♘c6 7 ♘e2 ♕b6 8 ♘f3 cd 9 cd ♗b4+ 10 ♔f1 f6 11 ♘f4 fe 12 ♘xe6 e4 13 ♗f4 ef 14 ♗c7 ♘f6 15 ♘xg7+ ♔f7 16 ♗xb6 ♗g4

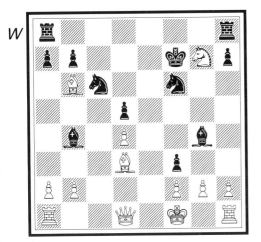

W

17 g3 ♗h3+ 18 ♔g1 ♔xg7 19 ♗c7
♖he8 20 ♗e5 ♘xe5 21 de ♖xe5 22
♕b3 ♗c5 23 ♗f5 ♗xf5 24 ♕xb7+
♔g6 25 ♕xa8 ♖e2 26 h4 ♗xf2+ 27
♔f1 ♗d3 28 h5+ ♔g5 29 Resigns

There is no answer to the threat of
29 ... ♖d2 mate.

Stonewall System

1 d4 d5 2 e3 c5 3 c3 ♘f6 4 ♗d3 g6 5
f4.

A cumbersome opening, in which
White tries to engineer a kingside attack
by adopting a reversed Dutch Defence,
while maintaining a firm grip on the
e5 square. Black's position is preferable because White has gratuitously
weakened his central light coloured
squares.

Strategy

Long-range planning as distinct from
tactical short range combinations.

Strategie, La   [1867–1940]

A French chess magazine founded by
J. L. Preti. It had a good run of 73 years.

Strobeck

A village in East Germany where chess
and Courier (a variation of chess) were
popular. Selenus mentioned it in his
1616 book.

Strong square

An important square from which a piece
can be especially effective and not easily
driven away.

Suba, Mihai   [June 1 1947–]

Romanian GM (1978) who was Romanian champion in 1980, 1981 and 1986,
and who played on the Romanian
Olympiad team during 1980 to 1986.
He was equal 2nd at Baile Herculane
1982 (X), 1st at Dortmund 1983 (X),
equal 1st at Prague 1985 (X) and equal
1st at Timisoara 1987 (IX).

In August 1988 Suba applied for
political asylum in Britain. He played for
England in the 1989 European Team
Championship.

Subandhu

Author of *Vasavadatta* (a Sanskrit romance) which refers to chess and provides evidence of the origin of chess in
the sixth century.

Suetin, Alexei Stepanovich

[November 16 1926–]
USSR author and GM (1965) who
played in 10 USSR Championships during 1950 and 1966, coming equal 4th in
1963 and again in 1965. He was 1st or
equal 1st in some ten moderate strength
tournaments from Sarajevo 1965 to
Dubna 1979 (IX).

Major works: *Modern Chess Opening
Theory* (1962), *A Contemporary Approach
to the Middle Game* (1971).

Sultan Khan, Mir

[1905–April 25 1966]
India's most famous player (of GM
strength) and the only Indian to become
British Champion. He was born in Mit-
tha (Punjab). His skill at the Indian
variety of chess brought him to the
attention of a local notable, Colonel
Nawab Sir Umar Hayat Khan, who
employed him as a servant and encouraged his chess-playing activities, teaching him the standard European game. In
1928 Sultan won the All-India Championship (+ 8 = 1 − 0).

He spent most of the years 1929–33
in Britain on the staff of Sir Umar. His
exceptional natural talent, especially in
the middlegame and endgame, was
quickly noticed by the English masters
Winter and Yates and training sessions
with these players helped to overcome
his lack of theoretical knowledge and
tournament experience. Even though he
was unable to read European (chess)
books, and was uncomfortable and often
ill in the British climate, he won the
British Championship in 1929, 1932 and
1933, and played on three British Empire Olympiad teams in 1930, 1931 and
1933. In other events he was 2nd at
Liege 1930, 3rd at Hastings 1930/31
where he beat Capablanca in their individual game, and equal 3rd at London
1932. In match play he beat Tartakower
(+ 4 = 5 − 3) in 1931 and lost to Flohr
(+ 1 = 3 − 2) in 1932.

Sultan returned to India with his
master Sir Umar in December 1933 and
played little serious chess afterwards.
He died in Sargodha, Pakistan.

See *Mir Sultan Khan*, by R. N. Coles
(1965).

Sultan Khan–Capablanca

Hastings 1930/31

1 ♘f3 ♘f6 2 d4 b6 3 c4 ♗b7 4 ♘c3 e6
5 a3 d5 6 cd ed 7 ♗g5 ♗e7 8 e3 0-0 9
♗d3 ♘e4 10 ♗f4 ♘d7 11 ♕c2 f5 12
♘b5 ♗d6 13 ♘xd6 cd 14 h4 ♖c8 15
♕b3 ♕e7 16 ♘d2 ♘df6 17 ♘xe4 fe
18 ♗e2 ♖c6 19 g4 ♖fc8 20 g5 ♘e8
21 ♗g4 ♖c1+ 22 ♔d2 ♖8c2+ 23
♕xc2 ♖xc2+ 24 ♔xc2 ♕c7+ 25
♔d2 ♕c4 26 ♗e2 ♕b3 27 ♖ab1 ♔f7
28 ♖hc1 ♔e7 29 ♖c3 ♕a4 30 b4
♕d7 31 ♖bc1 a6 32 ♖g1 ♕h3 33
♖gc1 ♕d7 34 h5 ♔d8 35 ♖1c2 ♕h3
36 ♔c1 ♕h4 37 ♔b2 ♕h3 38 ♖c1
♕h4 39 ♖3c2 ♕h3 40 a4 ♕h4 41
♔a3 ♕h3 42 ♗g3 ♕f5 43 ♗h4 g6 44
h6 ♕d7 45 b5 a5 46 ♗g3 ♕f5 47 ♗f4
♕h3 48 ♔b2 ♕g2 49 ♔b1 ♕h3 if (...
♕xf2 50 ♗h5 ♕h4 51 ♖h2 wins) 50
♔a1 ♕g2 51 ♔b2 ♕h3

205

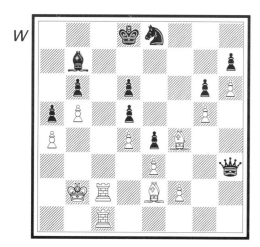

52 ♖g1 ♗c8 53 ♖c6 ♕h4 54 ♖gc1 ♗g4 55 ♗f1 ♕h5 56 ♖e1 ♕h1 57 ♖ec1 ♕h5 58 ♔c3 ♕h4 59 ♗g3 ♕xg5 60 ♔d2 ♕f5 61 ♖xb6 ♔e7 62 ♖b7+ ♔e6 63 b6 ♘f6 64 ♗b5 ♕f3 65 ♖b8 Resigns.

Sunye Neto, Jaime [May 2 1959–] Brazilian GM (1986) who was Brazilian Champion 6 times during 1976 to 1982 and played on the Brazilian Olympiad teams during 1978 to 1986. He was equal 2nd at Havana 1985 (IX) and 1st at Zenica 1986 (VIII).

Suradiradja, Herman [October 14 1947–] Indonesian GM (1978) who was 1st at Primorsko 1977 (VI) and equal 1st at Plovdiv 1978 (VII).

Suttles, Duncan [December 21 1945–] US born Canadian GM (1973) who was Canadian champion in 1969 and played on 8 Canadian Olympiad teams during 1964 and 1984. He was equal 1st at the 1973 US Open.

Suttles' style is unusual and he specializes in irregular openings. His positions look awkward, but his play is sound and he is remarkably good in finding ingenious defences in what seem to be hopeless positions. He studied mathematics and now applies computer technology to stock-market analysis.

Sveshnikov, Evgeny Ellinovich

[February 11 1950–] USSR GM (1977) who played in 7 USSR Championships during 1973 to 1985, but without great success. His best results were equal 1st at Sochi 1976 (X), 1st at Le Havre 1977 (VIII), 1st at Cienfuegos 1979 (VIII), equal 2nd at Novi Sad 1979 (XI), 1st at Sochi 1985 (XI) and 1st at Hastings 1984/85 (IX).

Swiderski, Rudolf

[July 28 1878–August 12 1909] German player of almost GM strength who was equal 1st at Coburg 1904 and equal 1st at the Monte Carlo 1904 Rice Gambit tournament. He was a dangerous opponent, having wins over Schlechter and Rubinstein. He committed suicide shortly after his 31st birthday.

Swindle

A lucky victory where a player in a lost position sets a last trap and his opponent snatches defeat from the jaws of victory by falling into the trap.

Swiss System

An effective method for running tournaments with large numbers of players (say 500). It was invented by Dr Julius Muller of Switzerland and first used in Zurich 1895. The idea is to have, in each round, players paired with opponents who have the same scores or scores as closely similar as possible. No player can meet the same opponent twice, and at the end of each round, players should have had as close to an equal number of whites and blacks as possible. There is no unique way to achieve these objectives and making up the pairings is quite difficult.

A Swiss is similar to a knock-out except that all competitors play through to the end of the event. Thus they can recover from poor starts or be knocked downwards from good starts. When players win a game they meet stronger opposition (other winners). When they lose they meet weaker opposition (other losers) and thus for most players their standings rollercoaster. Thus the number of rounds plays an important role in the accuracy of the final placings. Some scores were on the rise, others on

	Swiss	Knock-out	Round Robin = All-Play-All
Accuracy of final results	First place accurate Other place accuracy depends on number of rounds	Only first place accurate	All placings accurate
Number of players possible in N rounds	2^N but might handle even more	2^N	$N+1$
Importance of each game	Later ones are more valuable	Each one is crucial	All are equally important
Remarks	Complicated pairings and no easy way to avoid complaints	Frustrating for those knocked out early	Fairest but very limited in number of players

the fall, and one more round might well reverse the direction of many of these.

A Swiss accurately picks an overall winner (and loser) but all other placings are not accurate. With say 128 ($=2^7$) players, one needs at least 7 rounds to get a winner (otherwise there could be two players each with 6–0). Accepted wisdom says that two extra rounds are required to get one more accurate placing. Thus to get accuracy for the top 4 places one needs $7+2+2+2=13$ rounds when there are 128 starters.

Weekend Swisses of 6 rounds (1 on Friday, 3 on Saturday and 2 on Sunday) are quite popular. There are also 11 round Swisses taking up to two weeks. The 1990 interzonal is planned as a 13 round Swiss for 64 players.

See Lone Pine; Pairings.

Symmetrical Defence
See Queen's Gambit.

Szabo, Laszlo   [*March 19 1917– *] Hungarian GM (1950) who was the leading Hungarian player from 1945 until the advent of Portisch (1960). Szabo was a Candidate three times: 1950, 1953 and 1956. He was unsuccessful in the first two but at Amsterdam 1956 (XV) he placed equal 3rd and this was the peak of his career.

He played on 11 Hungarian Olympiad teams during 1935 to 1968, and won the Hungarian Championship 8 times during 1935 to 1967. Szabo was 1st or equal 1st at Hastings 1938/39, Vienna 1947, Hastings 1947/48, Budapest 1948, Venice 1949, Hastings 1949/50, Wageningen 1957, Zagreb 1964, Budapest 1965, Sarajevo 1972, Hilversum 1973, Hastings 1973/74, Dortmund 1974 and Kapfenburg 1976. He was also equal 4th at Groningen 1946 and 2nd at Saltsjobaden 1948 (XIV).

Szabo had a fine attacking style and was able to beat anyone, but he never quite made it into the world top ten.

In life scores he beat Boleslavsky ($+2=3-1$), Euwe ($+5=5-2$), Timman ($+3=4-0$), and held Spassky ($+3=13-3$), but he lost to Portisch ($+6=13-8$), Keres ($+3=12-5$), Najdorf ($+3=14-5$), Bronstein ($+2=9-7$), Smyslov ($+1=10-6$), Petrosian ($+1=8-6$), Korchnoi ($+0=6-6$), Botvinnik ($+1=6-3$), Reshevsky ($+0=7-2$), Tal ($+0=5-3$) and Fischer ($+0=2-3$).

Major works: *100 000 moves in 50 years* (1981), *My Best Games* (1986).

Szen, Joseph
       [*c. 1800–January 13 1857*] Hungarian player of IM strength who was particularly good at endgames. He led Budapest to a correspondence victory (1842–6) over Paris. He became a regular at the Café de la Régence and could hold his own against La Bourdonnais if given odds of pawn and 1 or 2 moves. He was 5th at London 1851 and lost $+1=1-3$ to Harrwitz in 1853.

T

TN

A theoretical novelty (a new move in an opening variation).

Tactics

Short range combinatorial-type moves that can and should be carefully calculated. They are different from long-range or strategic plans which cannot be calculated out.

Taimanov, Mark Yevgenyevich

[February 7 1926–]
USSR pianist, TV chess professor and GM (1952) who was a Candidate twice (1953 and 1971) and who played in 23 USSR Championships during 1948–76, a record tied only by Geller.

Taimanov was equal 8th in the strong 1953 Candidates. In 1971 he was crushed +0=0−6 by Fischer. In the USSR Championships he scored an overall $233\frac{1}{2}$–$179\frac{1}{2}$ for 56.6% and he was equal 1st twice—1952 when he lost the play-off +1=3−2 to Botvinnik, and in 1956 when he beat Spassky and Averbakh for the title. He was equal 2nd in 1954 and 1962. Taimanov's best period was 1946–56, when he belonged to the world top 10. He played on the USSR Olympiad team in 1956.

Taimanov won many tournaments and had a good run when he was equal 1st at Reykjavik 1968, 1st at Zalaegerszeg 1969, 1st at Wijk aan Zee 1970 and equal 1st at Skopje 1970.

The Russian chess bureaucracy was not entirely pleased with Taimanov's humiliating loss to Fischer in 1971 and his career became beset with difficulties. Nevertheless he continues to play and was equal 2nd at Sesimbra 1987 (VII). He is also the most prominent chess professor on Soviet TV. Taimanov has written important opening works on the Nimzo-Indian, Réti and the Dutch defence.

Taimanov–Korchnoi

USSR Championship 1952
1 d4 ♘f6 2 c4 g6 3 ♘c3 d5 4 cd ♘xd5 5 g3 ♗g7 6 ♗g2 ♘b6 7 e3 a5 8 ♘ge2 a4 9 0-0 0-0 10 ♘e4 ♘8d7 11 ♗d2 c6 12 ♖c1 ♘d5 13 ♘2c3 a3 14 ba ♖xa3 15 ♘xd5 cd 16 ♗b4 ♖a6 17 ♘c3 ♘f6 18 ♕b3 ♗e6 19 ♘b5 ♘e8 20 ♖c5 b6 21 ♖c3 ♗d7 22 a4 ♘f6 23 ♖fc1 h5 24 ♗f1 ♔h7 25 ♖a1 ♗xb5 26 ♗xb5 ♖a7 27 ♖c6 ♖h8 28 ♖ac1 h4 29 ♕c2 e5 30 de ♘g4 31 ♕e2 ♘xe5 32 ♖d6 ♕a8 33 f4 ♘c4 34 ♗c6 ♕f8 (see diagram) 35 ♖d7 ♕xb4 36 ♖xa7 ♘xe3 37 ♖xf7 ♕d4 38 ♕f2

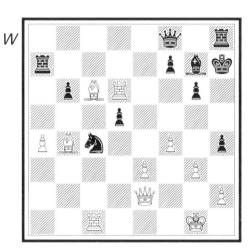

♖c8 39 ♖e1 ♔g8 40 ♗d7 hg? (better was 40... ♖c3) 41 ♖xg7+ ♕xg7 42 ♗e6+ ♔f8 43 ♕xe3 gh+ 44 ♔h1 d4 45 ♕a3+ ♖c5 46 ♕f3 ♕a7 47 ♗b3 ♕d7 48 ♕a8+ ♖c8 49 ♕e4 ♖c3 50 ♕e5 ♖e3 51 ♕f6+ Resigns

Tal, Mikhail Nekhemyevich

[November 9 1936–]
World Champion 1960–1. Latvian–Jewish GM (1957) who burst upon the chess world like a tornado, sweeping everything and everyone before him. He won the USSR Championship in 1957 and won it again in 1958. He won the 1958 interzonal, scored the highest percentage (+12=3−0) at the 1958 Olympiad, came equal 2nd in the 1959 USSR Championship, was 1st at Zurich

Attacking genius Mikhail Tal, World Champion 1960–1.

1959 and won the 1959 Candidates (where he beat Fischer +4=0−0 in their individual games). In 1960 he crushed Botvinnik +6=13−2 and on May 7, 1960, Tal, aged 23½ was chess champion of the world—the youngest ever (Kasparov was to break this record 25 years later).

Tal has a wild combinative instinct and a hair-raising style. He is quick, confident, aggressive and delights in sacrifices that may not be altogether sound but are full of fathomless complexities. He himself treads his way through the maze with brilliance, imagination and absolutely no nervous anxiety. He revels in the complex struggle and with his penetrating stare, he truly plays the role of a magician.

As his successes increased, experts pronounced his sacrifices unsound and assured the chess world that the big three—Keres, Smyslov and Botvinnik—would destroy him. They were astonished to see the big three fall before his furious onslaught, crumbling under the depth of the complexities combined with the time pressure of a real game.

Tal was born with a badly deformed hand and a frail constitution. He abused his body by smoking and drinking to excess, and in failing health he lost the 1961 return match +5=6−10 to the mighty Botvinnik. Botvinnik wrote:

I was surprised by his ability to figure out complex variations. Then the way he sets out the game; he was not interested in the objectivity of the position, whether it's better or worse, he only needed room for his pieces. All you do then is figure out variations which are extremely difficult. He was tactically outplaying me; I made mistakes. Well, in the first match I got to know him very well. In the second match I realized that you cannot tackle him if the pieces are mobile and active. I played closed positions in which Tal could gain no advantage. Tal had no positional understanding for closed games and that is how I won the return match with a big difference in points.

If Tal would learn to program himself properly then it would become impossible to play him.

Tal played in the 1962 Candidates at Curaçao but had to withdraw when he went to hospital with kidney failure. This kidney was finally removed in 1969 and he has struggled on since then with his remaining non-healthy kidney.

In the 1965 Candidates matches, Tal beat Portisch +4=3−1 and then Larsen +3=5−2, but was eliminated by Spassky +1=6−4. In the 1968 Candidates matches Tal beat Gligoric +3=5−1 but was put out by Korchnoi +1=7−2. Tal's next Candidates appearance was in 1980 when he lost +0=5−3 to Polugayevsky. At Montpellier 1985 Tal almost made the final play-offs when he held Timman +1=4−1, but lost on tie break.

In other matches Tal beat Bronstein +1=3−0 in 1966, lost +1=3−4 to Larsen in 1969, held Andersson +1=4−1 in 1983 and beat Timman +2=3−1 at the end of 1988.

Tal played in 19 USSR Championships during 1956–79 and scored an overall 199½–129½ for 60.6%. He was 1st six times (only Botvinnik was 1st as often): 1957, 1958, 1967, 1972, 1974 and 1978. He played on 7 USSR Olympiad teams during 1958–80 and scored +59=31−2.

In the two great world blitz championships, Tal was 2nd to Fischer in 1970 and was 1st in 1988, ahead of Kasparov, Karpov, etc.

Tal won dozens of tournaments; in particular he was 1st or equal 1st at Bled 1961, Tallinn 1971 and Montreal 1979 (XV). More recently he was equal 2nd at Reykjavik 1987 (XIV) and 3rd at Reykjavik 1988 (XV).

In life scores (to mid-1987) Tal is up on Larsen, Gligoric, Bronstein, Portisch, Najdorf, Hübner and Fischer (+4 =5−2). He is even with Geller, Smyslov, Timman and Botvinnik (+12 =20−12). He is a bit behind Petrosian (+4=36−5), Karpov (0 =16−1) and Kasparov (+0=5−1) and is behind Keres, Spassky, Stein, Seirawan, Polugayevsky and Korchnoi (+3=25−13).

Tal has been in the world top 10 for over 30 years. Keene and Divinsky rank him, kidney trouble and all, as the 14th greatest player of all time. In good health he would have ranked with the gods.

Major work: *Tal–Botvinnik 1960—Match for the World Championship* (1970).

See *Tal's Best Games* by P. H. Clarke (1961), *Complete Games of Mikhail Tal, 1936–59*, by H. Thomas (1980), *Complete Games of Mikhail Tal, 1960–66*, by H. Thomas (1979), *Complete Games of Mikhail Tal, 1967–73*, by H. Thomas

(1979), *Tal's 100 Best Games*, by B. Cafferty (1975), *Michael Tal*, by Bouwmeester and Withuis (1961).

Tal–Botvinnik
Match 1960

1 e4 e6 2 d4 d5 3 ♘c3 ♗b4 4 e5 c5 5 a3 ♗xc3+ 6 bc ♕c7 7 ♕g4 f5 8 ♕g3 ♘e7 9 ♕xg7 ♖g8 10 ♕xh7 cd 11 ♔d1 ♗d7 12 ♕h5+ ♘g6 13 ♘e2 d3 14 cd ♗a4+ 15 ♔e1 ♕xe5 16 ♗g5 ♘c6 17 d4 ♕c7 18 h4 e5 19 ♖h3 ♕f7 20 de ♘cxe5 21 ♖e3 ♔d7 22 ♖b1 b6 23 ♘f4 ♖ae8

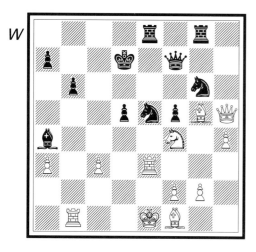

24 ♖b4 ♗c6 25 ♕d1 ♘xf4 26 ♖xf4 ♘g6 27 ♖d4 ♖xe3+ 28 fe ♔c7 29 c4 dc 30 ♗xc4 ♕g7 31 ♗xg8 ♕xg8 32 h5 Resigns

Tal–Fischer
Zagreb 1959

1 d4 ♘f6 2 c4 g6 3 ♘c3 ♗g7 4 e4 d6 5 ♗e2 0-0 6 ♘f3 e5 7 d5 ♘bd7 8 ♗g5 h6 9 ♗h4 a6 10 0-0 ♕e8 11 ♘d2 ♘h7 12 b4 ♗f6 13 ♗xf6 ♘hxf6 14 ♘b3 ♕e7 15 ♕d2 ♔h7 16 ♕e3 ♘g8 17 c5 f5 18 ef gf 19 f4 ef 20 ♕xf4 dc (see diagram) 21 ♗d3 cb 22 ♖ae1 ♕f6 23 ♖e6 ♕xc3 24 ♗xf5+ ♖xf5 25 ♕xf5+ ♔h8 26 ♖f3 ♕b2 27 ♖e8 ♘f6 28 ♕xf6+ ♕xf6 29 ♖xf6 ♔g7 30 ♖ff8 ♘e7 31 ♘a5 h5 32 h4 ♖b8 33 ♘c4 b5 34 ♘e5 Resigns

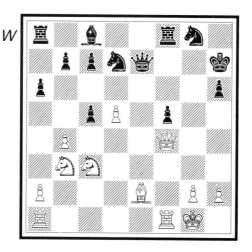

Tarjan, James Edward

[February 22 1952–] US GM (1976) who was 1st at Subotica 1975, 1st at Vancouver 1976, 2nd in the 1978 US Championship, equal 1st at Vrsac 1983 (X) and equal 3rd in the 1984 US Championship (XI).

Tarjan played on 5 US Olympiad teams during 1974–82.

Tarrasch, Siegbert

[March 5 1862–February 17 1934] German–Jewish medical doctor and player of GM strength who was in the world top 5 during 1890–1914. He was also the leading chess author of his day and taught an entire generation the finer points of both Steinitzian theory in closed positions, and Morphy's mobility in open positions.

Tarrasch won 4 major tournaments in a row: Breslau 1889, Manchester 1890, Dresden 1892 and Leipzig 1894; and in 1893 he drew +9=4−9 a thrilling match with Chigorin (who was then at the very height of his powers) Havana tried to arrange a world title match with Steinitz in 1890/91, but Tarrasch took his medical obligations seriously and did not accept. He also turned down a challenge from a young upstart called Lasker. Had Tarrasch accepted these challenges he might well have become World Champion, but it was Lasker who took the world title away from the ageing Steinitz (1894) and from 1895 on, Tarrasch was never able to come ahead of the phenomenal Lasker.

Tarrasch was 4th at Hastings 1895 (Lasker was 3rd) and equal 3rd at Nuremberg 1896 (Lasker was 1st). With Lasker absent, Tarrasch won the great Vienna 1898 Jubilee tournament, beating Pillsbury +2=1−1 in the play-off. Tarrasch won at Monte Carlo 1903, crushed Marshall +8=8−1 in 1905 and won at Ostend 1907. The clash between Tarrasch and Lasker came in 1908. They were not on speaking terms and when asked how he would deal with this, Tarrasch said he would say only two words to Lasker: Check Mate! But it was not to be. Tarrasch lost +3=5−8.

Tarrasch held Schlechter +3=10 −3 in 1911, came a respectable 4th at St Petersburg 1914, but lost +0=1−5 to Lasker in 1916. After the war, in

Dr Siegbert Tarrasch, the great champion of the classical school.

which his son was killed (1915) in the fighting, Tarrasch's playing strength took a marked fall. Of course, he was in his late 50s and might well have retired. He played regularly during 1920–28, and it was sad to see him coming near the bottom. His life score figures, particularly against the younger masters, in no way reflect his great strength of the 1890s.

In life scores he beat Schlechter (+7 =27 −6), Marshall (+13 =18 −7), Janowski (+9 =3 −5), Teichmann (+7 =2 −5) and Steinitz (+3 =1 −0). He held Pillsbury (+5 =2 −5) and lost to Chigorin (+13 =8 −14), Maroczy (+2 =13 −3), Capablanca (+1 =3 −2), Lasker (+4 =8 −18), Alekhine (+1 =2 −9) and Rubinstein (+0 =12 −8).

In 1927, he led the German Olympiad team, scoring +4 =9 −2.

Tarrasch's writings are dogmatic, but magnificent. They are full of wit and charm and they come to grips with the essential matter of each game in an exciting and deep way. His major work was *Dreihundert Schachpartien* (1895) which contains 300 of his own games up to 1894, and includes his wonderful match with Chigorin. Then came: *Nuremberg 1896* (1897), *Marshall–Tarrasch* (1905), *Marshall–Lasker* (1907), *Ostend* (1907), *Lasker–Tarrasch* (1908), *Schlechter–Tarrasch 1911* (1912), *St Petersburg* (1914), *Tarrasch–Mieses* (1916), *Baden Baden* (1925), *The Game of Chess* (1931), *Die Moderne Schachpartie* (1912).

Tarrasch was the leading chess authority, called Praeceptor Germaniae and later Praeceptor Mundi. He was born with a club foot, though he pointed out that it did not prevent him from making rapid progress. He seemed to take himself quite seriously and was vain about his appearance and his clothes. He was committed to Germany's cause in the First World War and must have been shocked with the rise of Hitler and anti-semitism in his beloved Germany.

Tarrasch's games were razor sharp and were excellent examples of his writings, in particular, his belief in mobility for his pieces, even at the expense of an isolated pawn. He believed that chess was not an idle waste of time, but a significant pursuit, and he wrote: 'Chess, like music, like love, has the power to make men happy'.

See *Tarrasch's Best Games*, by Reinfeld (1947), *Siegbert Tarrasch*, by Neistadt (1983).

Chigorin–Tarrasch

Match 1893

1 e4 e6 2 ♕e2 c5 3 g3 ♘c6 4 ♘f3 ♗e7 5 ♗g2 d5 6 d3 ♘f6 7 0-0 0-0 8 ♘c3 a6 9 ♗g5 h6 10 ♗f4 b5 11 ♖fe1 d4 12 ♘d1 ♘d7 13 ♔h1 ♖e8 14 ♖g1 e5 15 ♗d2 ♘f8 16 ♘e1 ♘e6 17 f4 ♗b7 18 f5 ♘g5 19 ♘f2 ♖c8 20 ♕h5 ♘h7 21 ♘f3 c4 22 ♗f1 cd 23 cd ♘g5 24 ♗xg5 ♗xg5 25 ♘g4 ♔f8! 26 ♗e2 ♗f6 27 h4 ♕d6 28 ♘fh2 ♘e7 29 ♖af1 ♘g8 30 ♗d1 ♖c7 31 ♗b3 ♖ec8 32 ♘f2 ♗d8 33 ♕e2 a5 34 ♘f3 a4 35 ♗d1 ♗c6 36 g4 f6 37 ♘h3 ♗e8 38 ♕h2 ♗f7 39 a3 ♗b3 40 ♘f2 ♗xd1 41 ♘xd1 ♖c2 42 ♕g3 b4 43 ab ♕a6! 44 ♘f2 ♖xb2 45 g5 hg 46 hg ♖cc2 47 ♘g4 ♕d6

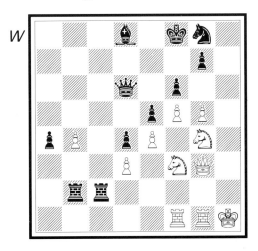

48 gf ♗xf6 49 ♕h3 a3 50 ♘xf6 ♕xf6 51 ♖g6 a2! 52 ♖xf6+? (52 ♘g5!) gf

53 ♖d1 ♖b1 54 ♕f1 ♖cb2 55 ♘d2 ♖xd1 56 ♕xd1 ♖xd2 57 ♕c1 ♖xd3 58 ♔g2 ♖c3 59 ♕a1 ♖c2+ 60 ♔f3 d3 61 ♕d1 ♖b2 62 ♕a4 d2 63 Resigns

Tarrasch Defence
See Queen's Gambit.

Tarrasch Open Defence
See Lopez, Ruy.

Tarrasch Trap
A famous but natural pitfall that occurred in Tarrasch–Marco, Dresden 1892. 1 e4 e5 2 ♘f3 ♘c6 3 ♗b5 d6 4 d4 ♗d7 5 ♘c3 ♘f6 6 0-0 ♗e7 7 ♖e1 0-0? 8 ♗xc6 ♗xc6 9 de de 10 ♕xd8 ♖axd8 11 ♘xe5 ♗e4 12 ♘xe4 ♘xe4 13 ♘d3 f5 14 f3 ♗c5+ 15 ♘xc5 ♘xc5 16 ♗g5 ♖d5 17 ♗e7 Resigns (if 17 ... ♖f7 18 c4 wins the exchange)

Tartakower, Savielly Gregorievich

[February 21 1887–February 5 1956] Russian-born Jewish lawyer (1909) and GM (1950) who studied law in Vienna and settled in Paris in 1924. He played often during 1906 to 1950, but achieved only modest results, partly because he enjoyed experimenting with bizarre openings. His best results were 2nd at Budapest 1913, 2nd at Vienna 1913, 2nd at The Hague 1921, equal 3rd at Teplice Schonau 1922, 2nd at Vienna 1922 and his peak was equal 1st at London 1927 and 1st at Liege 1930.

He played on 6 Polish Olympiad teams during 1930–9 and was Polish Champion in 1935 and 1937. He played on the 1950 French Olympiad team and was French Champion in 1953. In matches, he beat Spielmann in 1913, but lost in 1921. He beat Réti in 1919 and in 1920, and drew +1 =4 −1 with Grünfeld in 1922.

Tartakower was a fine raconteur who enjoyed paradoxes, witty epigrams and translating poetry. He loved gambling and lost all of his income to this vice. He served in the Austrian army during the First World War and served under De Gaulle in the Second World War.

He was an excellent and witty author. Major works: *Die Hypermoderne Schachpartie* (1925), *Breviary of Chess* (1937), *500 Master Games* (with DuMont) (1952), *My Best Games, 1905–1930* (1953), *My Best Games, 1931–1954* (1956).

Maroczy–Tartakower
Teplice–Schonau 1922
1 d4 e6 2 c4 f5 3 ♘c3 ♘f6 4 a3 ♗e7 5 e3 0-0 6 ♗d3 d5 7 ♘f3 c6 8 0-0 ♘e4 9 ♕c2 ♗d6 10 b3 ♘d7 11 ♗b2 ♖f6 12 ♖fe1 ♖h6 13 g3 ♕f6 14 ♗f1 g5 15 ♖ad1 g4 16 ♘xe4 fe 17 ♘d2

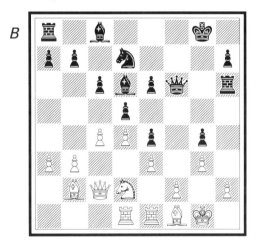

B

17 ... ♖xh2 18 ♔xh2 ♕xf2+ 19 ♔h1 ♘f6 20 ♖e2 ♕xg3 21 ♘b1 ♘h5 22 ♕d2 ♗d7 23 ♖f2 ♕h4+ 24 ♔g1 ♗g3 25 ♗c3 ♗xf2+ 26 ♕xf2 g3 27 ♕g2 ♖f8 28 ♗e1 ♖xf1+ 29 ♔xf1 e5 30 ♔g1 ♗g4 31 ♗xg3 ♘xg3 32 ♖e1 ♘f5 33 ♕f2 ♕g5 34 cd ♗f3+ 35 ♔f1 ♘g3+ 36 Resigns

Tattersall C. E. C. *[1877–1957]*
English composer and compiler of the first major anthology of endgames: *A Thousand End-Games* (1910–11) (2 volumes).

Technique
The manner and ability with which a chessplayer employs the technical skills of his art.

Teichmann, Richard
[December 24 1868–June 15 1925] German student of modern languages and player of GM strength who was in the world top 10 from 1902 to 1921. He began with a good 3rd at Leipzig 1894, but had serious eye trouble. At London 1899 he had to withdraw after 4 rounds and, in fact, lost the use of his right eye and wore an eye patch.

He returned to major tournament competition in 1902 and until 1910, had a long series of 4th and 5th prizes, mostly 5th. He had so many (about 8 of them) that he was dubbed Richard V.

Teichmann understood positional play well, he saw deeply into the game (he often joked that he could see more with one eye than most others with two), he was a tenacious defender and in an individual encounter he could beat anybody. His weakness was laziness. He was friendly, non-belligerent, and was quite comfortable always coming 5th. He took many draws and was careless, especially against weaker opponents. At the great Carlsbad tournament of 1911, a new fire appeared in him and he played in his best form. He was 1st ahead of a large (25 others) powerful field.

Teichmann won matches against Mieses, Spielmann, and von Bardeleben, and in 1921 drew +2=2−2 with the mighty Alekhine.

He was a fine analyst and a brilliant problemist. Teichmann was not impressed with the new style and denounced Réti's opening (1 ♘f3 followed by g3 and b3) as 'that stupid double-hole opening'. He also said: 'In the first place, there is no such thing as a hypermodern school; in the second place, Nimzowitsch is its founder'.

In life scores, he beat Schlechter (+4=21−2) and Alekhine (+3

=3−2); was level with Marshall (+7=17−7) and Nimzowitsch (+1=5−1); was a touch behind Rubinstein (+5=11−6), Maroczy (+1=12−2), Tarrasch (+5=2−7), and Janowski (+4=4−5); and lost to Chigorin (+3=1−8), Pillsbury (+1=5−4), Lasker (+0=0-4), and Capablanca (+0=1−2).

Rotlewi–Teichmann
Carlsbad 1911
1 d4 d5 2 ♘f3 ♘f6 3 c4 e6 4 ♘c3 ♗e7 5 ♗g5 ♘bd7 6 e3 0-0 7 ♕c2 c5 8 0-0-0 ♕a5 9 cd ed 10 dc ♘xc5 11 ♘d4 ♗e6 12 ♔b1 ♖ac8 13 ♗d3 h6 14 ♗xf6 ♗xf6 15 ♗f5 ♖fd8 16 ♗xe6 fe 17 ♕g6 d6 18 ♖c1 a6 19 f3 ♖d8 20 ♖c2 ♖xd4 21 ed e5 22 ♕g4 ed 23 ♖xd4 ♘e6 24 ♕e5 b5 25 b3 d4 26 ♘e4 d3 27 ♖d2 ♘d4 28 ♖c1 ♘c2 29 ♕b2 ♘a3+ 30 ♔a1 ♘c2+ 31 ♔b1 ♘a3+ 32 ♔a1 ♘c2+ 33 ♔b1 ♖c6 34 ♖cd1 ♖dc8 35 ♖xd3 ♘a3+ 36 ♔a1 b4 37 ♖d7

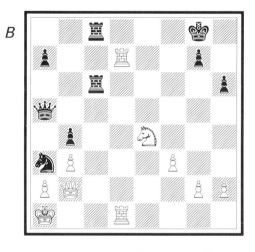

B

37 ... ♕e5! 38 ♖d8+ ♖xd8 39 ♖xd8+ ♔h7 40 ♖d1 ♕xb2+ 41 ♔xb2 ♖c2+ 42 ♔a1 ♖xg2 43 ♖h1 g5 44 ♘f6+ ♔g7 45 ♘e4 ♔g6 46 ♘d6 a5 47 ♖c1 ♖xh2 48 ♘c4 ♘b5 47 ♘e5+ ♔g7 50 ♘g4 ♖e2 51 ♖c5 ♖e1+ 52 ♔b2 ♘a3 53 ♖c7+ ♔f8 54 ♖c1 ♖e2+ 55 ♔a1 ♘c2+ 56 ♔b1 ♘a3+ 57 ♔a1 ♘b5 58 ♖c5 ♖e1+ 59 ♔b2 ♘a3 60 ♖c1 ♖e2+ 61 ♔a1 ♖e6 62 ♖h1 ♔g7 63 ♖c1

♔g6 64 ♖c6 ♖xc6 65 ♘e5+ ♔f5 66 ♘xc6 h5 67 ♘d4+ ♔e5 68 ♘e2 ♘c2+ 69 ♔b2 ♘d4 70 Resigns

Tempo
A unit of time which can be crucial in a closely balanced ending. Sometimes, to avoid zugzwang, it is necessary to actually lose a tempo, but most of the time losing tempi is disadvantageous. Three lost tempi are often equivalent to one lost pawn.

Teschner, Rudolf
[February 16 1922–]
German IM (1957) who edited the *Deutsche Schachzeitung* for over 30 years from 1950 on. He was East German Champion in 1948 and West German Champion in 1951, and he played on the West German Olympiad team in 1952 and 1956.

Major work: *Der Kleine Bilguer* (with K. Richter) (1953).

Theatre
Chess often appears on the stage. Dramatists including Shakespeare, Fletcher (The Spanish Curate 1622), Middletown (Game at Chess 1624), Goldoni, Yeats and Shellan (The Chessmaster 1974) have made interesting use of it.

See Art and Chess, Ballet; Chess and the Arts; Music

Theory
The accumulated body of chess knowledge. Some of it is definitive, like how to mate with bishop and knight. Some of it is fashion mixed with experience, like opening variations.

Thomas, Sir George Alan
[June 14 1881–July 23 1972]
Turkish-born British IM (1950) who won the British Championship in 1923 and 1934 and played on 7 English Olympiad teams during 1927–39. His best result was equal 1st with Euwe and Flohr at Hastings 1934/35 ahead of Capablanca and Botvinnik. He also excelled at tennis, hockey and badminton—he was All-England badminton singles champion from 1920 to 1923.

He inspired younger players and was games editor of the *British Chess Magazine*.

Threat
A move that attacks a valuable unit either immediately or by a combinatorial sequence of moves, or one that plans to create a positional weakness in the enemy camp e.g. by occupying and controlling an open file, penetrating to the 7th rank, doubling the enemy's pawns, etc. The ultimate threat is, of course, checkmate.

Three-Dimensional Chess
The idea is intriguing but, so far, there are no universally accepted versions of how to play it. Ferdinand Maack (1861–1930) suggested 8 regular chess boards stacked on top of each other, with normal pieces and pawns. The white pieces are set up on the bottom board and the white pawns just above them; the black army is set up on the top two boards, and the moves extended into 3 dimensions.

Charles Beatty suggested only 4 normal boards (in 1945) and Dawson used 5 smaller 5 × 5 boards for some fairy problems (in 1926).

Three Knights Game
1 e4 e5 2 ♘f3 ♘c6 3 ♘c3.

When Black wishes to avoid the quiet Four Knights Game (3 … ♘f6) he can try 3 … ♗b4 when the natural 4 ♘d5 gives White an edge; or he can try 3 … g6 when 4 d4 ed 5 ♘d5 keeps the opening initiative.

Tie-Breaking Systems
Round Robin or Swiss
The best way to break a tie is to (1) have a play-off. When there is no time for a play-off one can see (2) who had the most wins, or (3) who won the individual game between the tied players, or if that was a draw (4) who drew with Black.

More sophisticated methods compute:

(5) Sonneborn–Berger (Neustadtl, Svensson) Score = (Sum of scores of players you beat) + $\frac{1}{2}$ (Sum of scores of players you drew with)

(6) Coons Score = Sonneborn–Berger Score + $\frac{1}{5}$ (Sum of scores of players you lost to)
For unfinished round robins:

(7) Your Sonneborn–Berger Score + (your point score)^2
For tournaments where not everyone plays the same number of games:

(8) Gelbfuhs Score = (Sum of scores, divided by number of games played, of players you beat). + $\frac{1}{2}$ (Sum of scores, divided by number of games played, of players you drew with).

This is equivalent to (5) when everyone plays the same number of games.

For Swiss Tournaments Only
(9) Solkoff Score = Sum of scores of *all* your opponents

(10) Buchholtz Score = (Your Solkoff Score) × (Your point score)

(11) Harkness or Median Score = Sum of the scores of all your opponents, leaving off the highest and lowest scores. In tournaments with more than 8 rounds one can leave off the two highest and two lowest scores. In tournaments with more than 12 rounds one can leave off the three highest and three lowest scores.

(12) Best early score = Sum of your round by round totals.

For example, if players A's round by round totals were 1, 2, 3, $3\frac{1}{2}$, 4, his sum is $13\frac{1}{2}$. If player B's totals were 0, 1, 2, 3, 4 his sum is only 10. The point is that A probably met stronger opponents by winning early.

For Prize Distribution

Tietz System: To spread out the prize fund in a round robin with n players, Tietz divided the players into prizewinners (those who scored more than 50%) and the others. He computed M, the maximum number of points the prizewinners can score above the average. This turns out to be $n^2/8$ when n is even and $(n^2-1)/8$ when n is odd.

Then he computes Q, the actual number of points above average that the prizewinners scored. Then Q/M of the total prize fund is divided among the prizewinners according to each

score above average. The remaining portion of the money is divided among all the players according to their score.

To illustrate, we take the preliminary round robin of St Petersburg 1914 and assume that there were 1500 roubles to be distributed.

Now: $n = 11$; $M = ((11)^2-1)/8$
$$= 120/8 = 15;$$
$$Q = 3 + 1\frac{1}{2} + 1\frac{1}{2} + 1 + 1 = 8.$$
Thus $8/15(1500) = 800$ roubles goes to the prizewinners and the remaining 700 to all the players. (see table, below)

Tietz System

See Tie-Breaking Systems.

Tilburg

City in south-eastern Holland which began staging major tournaments (Interpolis) in 1977. There have now been 13 'Tilburgs'. The first eight were single round robins with 12 players. The format was changed in 1985 to double round robins with 8 players.

	Score	Above Average	From the General 700 Roubles	From the prize fund of 800 Roubles	TOTAL
Capablanca	8	3	$8/55 \times 700 = 101\frac{9}{11}$	$\frac{3}{8} \times 800 = 300$	$401\frac{9}{11}$
Lasker	$6\frac{1}{2}$	$1\frac{1}{2}$	$6\frac{1}{2}/55 \times 700 = 82\frac{8}{11}$	$1\frac{1}{2}/8 \times 800 = 150$	$232\frac{8}{11}$
Tarrasch	$6\frac{1}{2}$	$1\frac{1}{2}$	$82\frac{8}{11}$	150	$232\frac{8}{11}$
Alekhine	6	1	$76\frac{4}{11}$	150	$176\frac{4}{11}$
Marshall	6	1	$76\frac{4}{11}$	100	$176\frac{4}{11}$
Bernstein	5		$63\frac{7}{11}$	100	$63\frac{7}{11}$
Rubinstein	5		$63\frac{7}{11}$		$63\frac{7}{11}$
Nimzowitsch	4		$50\frac{10}{11}$		$50\frac{10}{11}$
Blackburne	$3\frac{1}{2}$		$44\frac{6}{11}$		$44\frac{6}{11}$
Janowski	$3\frac{1}{2}$		$44\frac{6}{11}$		$44\frac{6}{11}$
Gunsberg	1		$12\frac{8}{11}$		$12\frac{8}{11}$
TOTAL	55	8	700	800	1500

gayevsky) including young Kasparov.

1982 (XIV) Karpov (7½) won ahead of Timman (7). Missing were Kasparov, Korchnoi, Belyavsky, Ljubojevic, Spassky and Tal.

1983 (XV) This Tilburg had 10 of the world top 15. Missing were Kasparov, Korchnoi and Tal.

1984 (XIV) Miles (8) won ahead of Hübner (6½) Tukmakov (6½) Ribli (6½) and Belyavsky (6½) but the big guns (Kasparov, Karpov, Korchnoi and Vaganian) were absent.

1985 (XV) Miles (8½) Hübner (8½) and Korchnoi (8½) tied for 1st but 6 top players were absent.

1987 (XV) Belyavsky (8½) won ahead of Ljubojevic (8) and Karpov (7½), but many top players were absent.

1987 (XV) Timman (8½) won ahead of Hübner (8) and Nikolic (8) but Tal, Short, Belyavsky and the super Ks were absent.

1988 (XVI) The first category XVI Tilburg and a wonderful Karpov victory. Kasparov, Belyavsky and Speelman were absent.

1989 (XVI) Won by Kasparov (12) ahead of Korchnoi (8½).

Time Limits

All serious chess games today are subject to a time limit e.g. 40 moves in 2 hours. Failure to complete the moves in the allowed time results in the loss of the game (unless the opponent has only a bare king, in which case it is a draw).

Time limits were first introduced in 1861 for the Anderssen–Kolisch match. Unregulated thinking time had pre-

Tilburg 1979 — Category XV

		1	2	3	4	5	6	7	8	9	10	11	12	
1	Karpov	—	½	½	½	1	1	½	½	½	1	½	1	7½
2	Romanishin	½	—	½	½	0	½	1	1	½	1	½	1	7
3	Portisch	½	½	—	½	½	1	½	0	½	½	1	1	6½
4	Sax	½	½	½	—	½	0	½	1	½	½	½	1	6
5	Sosonko	0	1	½	½	—	1	½	0	1	0	½	½	5½
	Larsen	0	½	0	1	0	—	½	1	½	1	1	0	5½
	Spassky	½	0	½	½	½	½	—	½	1	½	½	½	5½
8	Timman	½	0	1	0	1	0	½	—	½	½	½	1	5½
9	Hübner	½	½	½	½	0	½	0	½	—	½	½	1	5
	Hort	0	0	½	½	1	0	½	½	½	—	½	1	5
11	Kavalek	½	½	0	½	½	0	½	½	½	½	—	½	4½
12	Smyslov	0	0	0	0	½	1	½	0	0	0	½	—	2½

Tilburg 1980 — Category XV

		1	2	3	4	5	6	7	8	9	10	11	12	
1	Karpov	—	½	1	½	1	½	½	0	1	1	1	½	7½
2	Portisch	½	—	½	½	½	1	½	1	½	½	½	1	7
3	Timman	0	½	—	½	½	½	½	1	½	½	1	1	6½
4	Sosonko	½	½	½	—	½	½	½	½	½	1	½	½	6
	Spassky	0	½	½	½	—	0	½	1	1	1	½	½	6
6	Tal	½	0	½	½	1	—	½	½	½	½	½	½	5½
7	Hort	½	½	½	½	½	½	—	0	½	½	½	½	5
	Larsen	1	0	0	½	0	½	1	—	½	0	1	½	5
9	Andersson	0	½	½	½	0	½	½	½	—	½	½	½	4½
	Ribli	0	½	½	0	0	½	½	1	½	—	½	½	4½
	Hübner	0	½	0	½	½	½	½	0	½	½	—	1	4½
12	Kavalek	½	0	0	½	½	½	½	½	½	½	0	—	4

Tilburg 1981 — Category XV

		1	2	3	4	5	6	7	8	9	10	11	12	
1	Belyavsky	—	½	0	1	½	½	½	½	1	1	1	1	7½
2	Petrosian	½	—	½	½	½	½	½	1	1	½	½	1	7
3	Portisch	1	½	—	½	1	0	½	½	0	1	1	½	6½
	Timman	0	½	½	—	½	½	1	1	0	1	½	1	6½
5	Ljubojevic	½	½	0	½	—	½	½	½	½	1	1	½	6
6	Andersson	½	½	1	½	½	—	½	0	½	0	½	1	5½
	Spassky	½	½	½	0	½	½	—	1	½	½	½	½	5½
	Kasparov	½	0	½	0	½	1	0	—	1	½	1	½	5½
9	Sosonko	0	0	1	1	½	½	½	0	—	0	½	½	4½
	Larsen	0	½	0	0	0	1	½	½	1	—	0	1	4½
11	Hübner	0	½	0	½	0	½	½	0	½	1	—	½	4
12	Miles	0	0	½	0	½	0	½	½	½	0	½	—	3

	1	2	3	4	5	6	7	8	9	10	11	12	
1 Karpov	–	½	½	½	½	1	½	½	½	½	1	1	7
2 Ljubojevic	½	–	½	½	½	1	½	½	½	1	1	0	6½
Portisch	½	½	–	½	½	½	½	1	½	½	½	1	6½
4 Vaganian	½	½	½	–	½	½	1	1	½	0	0	1	6
Sosonko	½	½	½	½	–	0	½	½	½	1	1	½	6
6 Polugayevsky	0	0	½	½	1	–	½	½	½	1	½	½	5½
Spassky	½	½	½	0	½	½	–	½	½	½	½	1	5½
Hübner	½	½	0	0	½	½	½	–	½	½	1	1	5½
9 Andersson	½	½	½	½	½	½	½	½	–	½	½	0	5
Timman	½	0	½	1	0	0	½	½	½	–	½	1	5
11 Seirawan	0	0	½	1	0	½	½	0	½	½	–	½	4
12 van der Wiel	0	1	0	0	½	½	0	0	1	0	½	–	3½

	1		2		3		4		5		6		7		8		
1 Karpov	–	–	½	½	½	1	½	1	1	1	½	½	1	1	½	1	10½
2 Short	½	½	–	–	½	0	½	½	½	½	1	1	½	1	1	½	8½
3 Hjartarson	½	0	½	1	–	–	½	½	½	0	½	½	½	1	0	1	7
Nikolic	½	0	½	½	½	½	–	–	½	0	½	1	½	½	½	1	7
Timman	0	0	½	½	½	1	½	1	–	–	0	1	½	0	1	½	7
6 Hübner	½	½	0	0	½	½	½	0	1	0	–	–	½	½	½	½	5½
van der Wiel	0	0	½	0	½	0	½	½	½	1	½	½	–	–	0	1	5½
8 Portisch	½	0	0	½	1	0	½	0	0	½	½	½	1	0	–	–	5

viously given rise to widely-publicized abuses. Morphy is said to have been reduced to tears by the slowness of Paulsen's play, and Staunton's criticism of Williams provides another famous example: 'Consumes hours over moves where minutes might suffice and depends not upon outmanoeuvring but out-sitting his antagonist'.

Sandglasses were used at London 1862, tumbling clocks at London 1883 and a timepiece similar to our modern tournament clock was developed by Veenhoff of Groningen about 1900. The laws of chess state that in games where clocks are used, a move is not completed until the clock has been pressed.

Traditionally, groups of moves are timed rather than individual moves. Within the group a player is free to allocate his thinking time as he wishes: taking perhaps 20 minutes over 1 move and 10 seconds over another. Various time limits are used in club and local events. Forty moves in 2½ hours and then 16 moves per hour was quite common for international competitions, but recently there has been a trend to 40 moves in 2 hours and then 20 moves per hour, in order to have 6 hour sessions and very few adjourned games.

One popular recreation is 'blitz' or 5-minute chess, in which each player is given 5 minutes for the entire game. A relatively new variation is 'Rapid chess' (also called 'active', 'action' or 'quick-play') in which each player is given 30 minutes for the entire game.

See Rapid Chess; Blitz; Clocks; Time Trouble.

Time Trouble
In having to make 40 moves in say 2 hours, many players find that they have used most of their time for only 20 or 25 moves. They must then make a large number of moves (say 15) in a short time (say 1 minute). Such time trouble or time pressure often leads to frenzied play and blunders. When both players are in severe time trouble, the frenzy is more than doubled, the tension electric and exciting chaos reigns.

Some players (for example Reshevsky) seem to enjoy time pressure. Others (such as the young Capablanca) never get into time trouble.

Timman, Jan Hendrik

[December 14 1951–]
Dutch GM (1974) who was a Candidate twice and has a remarkable tournament record, having played in some 20 tournaments of Category XIV, XV, XVI and XVII during 1978–88. He has also played in some 10 short matches against the very best GMs and is a solid member of the world's top ten.

He was first a Candidate at Montpellier 1985 and made it into the final play-offs by holding Tal +1=4−1 and winning on tie break. He lost, however, to Yusupov +1=4−4 in 1986. Timman was again a Candidate in 1988. He beat Salov +1=5−0 in 1988, Portisch +2=3−1 in 1989, and Speelman +2=5−1 in 1989 to reach the Candidates final against Karpov, which he lost: +0=5−4.

Timman's best results are: 2nd at Tilburg 1982 (XIV), 1st at Bugojno 1984 (XIV), 2nd at Amsterdam 1985 (XIV), equal 1st with Karpov at the 4-man Amsterdam 1987 tournament (XVI), 1st at Tilburg 1987 (XV), 2nd at Belgrade 1987 (XIV) and 1st at Linares 1988 (XV). In non-Candidates matches, he beat Polugayevsky +2=5−1 (1979), Portisch +2=3−1 (1984) and Ljubojevic +3=3−0 (1987); he held his own with Spassky +1=4−1 (1983), Yusupov +0 =6 −0 (1987) and Short +2=2−2; and he lost to Kasparov +1=2−3 (1985) and Tal +1=3−2 (1988).

Timman has been an outstanding talent since his early teens and is adored by the Dutch. He is the strongest Dutch player and a worthy successor of Dr Euwe. He has played on the Dutch Olympiad team regularly from 1974 to 1986 and has been Dutch Champion many times since 1974. In fact, he has been the strongest non-Russian player for some time, but he has taken a long time reaching his maximum potential. There have been downs as well as ups— he was equal last at Belfort 1988 (XV) and in 4-man tournaments in Amster-

Jan Timman, the strongest-ever Dutch player and a more than worthy successor to Euwe.

dam, he was last in March 1988 (XVII) behind Short, Karpov and Ljubojevic, while in May 1988 (XVII) he was third (or second last) behind Kasparov and Karpov.

In life scores, Timman is behind Kasparov, Karpov, Korchnoi and Spassky. He is about even with Tal, is ahead of Portisch and had a big edge on Vaganian (+8=0−1) to mid-1987.

Timman is an attacking player, a fighter in the mould of Emanuel Lasker. He wrote *De Tweekamp Spasski–Fischer 1972*, with Euwe, and has edited *New in Chess* as well as the *Schaakbulletin*. He is currently active with Kasparov in the Grandmasters Association. Timman has outgrown his teenage rebelliousness and has matured into a charming contented Dutchman who looks as if he just stepped out of an oil painting by Hals or Rembrandt. In Holland he is well known and treated as if he were the Prince of Amsterdam.

Timman–Hübner

Tilburg 1988

1 e4 e6 2 d4 d5 3 ♘c3 ♗b4 4 e5 c5 5 a3 ♗xc3+ 6 bc ♘e7 7 ♘f3 ♕a5 8 ♗d2 ♘bc6 9 ♗e2 cd 10 cd ♕a4 11 ♖b1 ♘xd4 12 ♗d3 ♘ec6 13 ♖b4 ♘f5 14 ♕c1 b6 15 c4 ♘xb4 16 ♖xb4 ♕c6 17 0-0 0-0 18 ♕f4 ♗b7 19 ♗xf5 ef 20 ♘d4

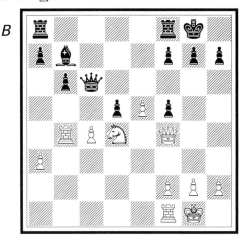

20 ... ♕c5? 21 ♘xf5 ♗c8 22 ♘xg7 ♔xg7 23 ♕g5+ ♔h8 24 ♕f6+ ♔g8 25 ♕g5+ ♔h8 26 ♕f6+ ♔g8 27 ♖b3 ♖e8 28 ♖g3+ ♔f8 29 ♖g7 ♖e7 30 e6 ♗xe6 31 ♖xh7 Resigns

Timoshchenko, Gennady Anatolyevich

[April 27 1949–]
Middle-level USSR GM (1980) who was 1st at Polanica Zdroj 1976 (IX), equal 1st at Helsinki 1986 (IX), but only equal 5th at Plovdiv 1988 (X). He played in 2 USSR Championships (1978, 1981), but scored under 50%.

Timur (Tamerlane)

[1336–1405]
Mongol emperor and conqueror who was interested in chess and whose court contained Ala'addin as Tabrizi, known as Aladdin—lawyer and chess expert. He preferred a 10 × 11 board with extra pieces (called Great Chess). He named his son Shah Rukh (check to the rook— then the most powerful piece).

Titles

See FIDE.

Todorcevic, Miodrag

[November 10 1940–]
Yugoslav GM (1989) who was 1st at

Budel 1987 (VIII), equal 2nd at Pancevo 1987 (IX) and 1st at Marseille 1988 (X).

Tolstoy, Count Leo

[*1828–November 20 1910*]
Brilliant Russian novelist who was a fanatic about chess.

Tolush, Alexander Kazimirovich

[*May 1 1910–March 3 1969*]
USSR GM (1953) who played in 10 USSR Championships during 1939–58. His best championship result was equal 2nd in 1950. Internationally, his best result was 1st at Bucharest 1953 ahead of Petrosian, Smyslov, Boleslavsky, and Spassky.

Toran, Roman   [*October 8 1931–*]

Spanish IM (1954) who is active in FIDE. He was Spanish Champion in 1951 and 1953 and played on the Spanish Olympiad team 5 times during 1958 to 1974.

Torre, Carlos

[*November 29 1904–1978*]
Mexican IM (1963) and honorary GM (1977) who played in 4 European tournaments in 1925, his best result being equal 5th at Moscow 1925 (where he beat Lasker in their individual game). In 1926, he won the Mexican Championship, had a nervous breakdown, and gave up competitive chess.

Reuben Fine visited him in 1934 and won +1=1−0 in two exhibition games.

Torre–Lasker

Moscow 1925

1 d4 ♘f6 2 ♘f3 e6 3 ♗g5 c5 4 e3 cd 5 ed ♗e7 6 ♘bd2 d6 7 c3 ♘bd7 8 ♗d3 b6 9 ♘c4 ♗b7 10 ♕e2 ♕c7 11 0-0 0-0 12 ♖fe1 ♖fe8 13 ♖ad1 ♘f8 14 ♗c1 ♘d5 15 ♘g5 b5 16 ♘a3 b4 17 cb ♘xb4 18 ♕h5 ♗xg5 19 ♗xg5 ♘xd3 20 ♖xd3 ♕a5 21 b4 ♕f5 (best is 21... ♕d5) 22 ♖g3 h6 23 ♘c4 ♕d5 24 ♘e3 ♕b5

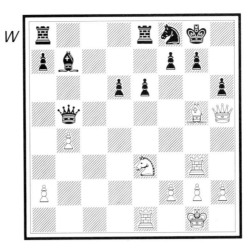

25 ♗f6 ♕xh5 26 ♖xg7+ ♔h8 27 ♖xf7+ ♔g8 28 ♖g7+ ♔h8 29 ♖xb7+ ♔g8 30 ♖g7+ ♔h8 31 ♖g5+ ♔h7 32 ♖xh5 ♔g6 33 ♖h3 ♔xf6 34 ♖xh6+ ♔g5 35 ♖h3 Resigns

Torre, Eugenio   [*November 4 1951–*]

Philippine GM (1974) who was Asia's first official GM. He was 1st at Torremolinos 1974, and 1st at the 4-man Manila 1976 tournament (XV) ahead of Karpov. Then he was 1st at Manila 1979, 2nd at Hastings 1980/81, 1st at Medina del Campo 1981, and equal 1st at the Toluca 1982 interzonal. This made Torre a Candidate, but in 1983 he lost +1=6−3 to Ribli.

He has not made it back into the Candidates, but he has had some good results: 3rd at Bugojno 1984 (XIV), equal 3rd at Brussels 1986 (XIII), equal 3rd at Biel 1988 (XIII) and a drawn match +1=4−1 with Short in 1988.

Torre has been a regular on the Philippine Olympiad team from 1970 to 1988 and has been Philippine Champion in 1974 and 1976.

Torre Attack

1 d4 ♘f6 2 ♘f3 e6 3 ♗g5.

This was evolved by the Mexican star Carlos Torre during the 1920s. Normally a transposition to the Queen's Gambit Orthodox Defence will occur, but Black can imbue this line with individual significance by continuing 3 ... h6 4 ♗h4 g5 5 ♗g3 ♘e4 6 ♘bd2 ♘xg3 7 hg ♗g7, with even chances.

Touch Move (Touch and Move)

A fundamental rule in tournament chess which says that if you touch a piece (without saying 'J'adoube' or 'I adjust'), you must move it. If you touch a piece that cannot make a legal move then there is no penalty—you are free to make any legal move you wish.

The rule is not always adhered to, as Bronstein relates concerning his game with 75 year old Duz-Khotimirsky in Moscow 1954:

> Duz-Khotimirsky played a hurried move and, whilst I was considering my reply decided ... to change his move. The spectators gasped, the judges wanted to stop the clocks, but Fedor Ivanovich suddenly shouted at everyone: 'What on earth is this? Look, I made a bad move and now I'm changing it for a good one. Rules, you say? To hell with your rules, this is chess. Besides, you don't object?' said my opponent, turning to me.
> 'Please, it's my pleasure!' And the game went on as if nothing had happened.

Bronstein won the game in 19 moves.

Tournament

A contest among players, arranged either as a knock-out, round robin or Swiss. Such events began in the late 1840s and have flourished. Today there are many fine tournaments each year.

See Chess in our Time.

See also *Chess Tournament Crosstables* (covering 1851–1930) in 4 volumes by J. Gaige (1969–74).

Trap

An attractive and natural continuation or move, that has a hidden, concealed danger. That is why Tarrasch said 'mistrust is the most necessary characteristic of the chess player'.

See Tarrasch Trap.

Travelling Chess Set

A small folding chess board, often with holes for small pieces to fit in, or magnetic pieces and board. Computerised versions are also available.

Trebitsch, Leopold

[1842–December 12 1906]
Austrian industrialist and chess patron after whom 20 memorial tournaments were held (Vienna 1907–38).

Trebuchet

An unusual double zugzwang position:

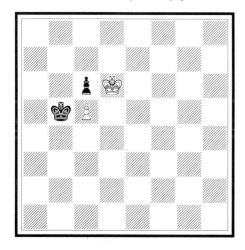

Whoever plays must lose.

Treybal, Karel

[February 2 1885–October 2 1941]
Czech player of almost GM strength who was champion of Czechoslovakia in 1907 and 1921 and who played on the Czech Olympiad team in 1930, 1933 and 1935. His best result was equal 6th at Carlsbad 1923. He was a victim of the Nazis.

Triangulation

A method of losing the move. In the diagram, if it is Black's move, he must lose:

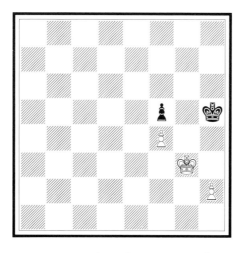

1 ... ♚g6 2 ♔f3 ♚h5 3 ♔e2 ♚h4 4 ♔d3 ♚g4 5 ♔e3 ♚h6 6 ♔d4.

However, if it is White's move, he can 'triangulate' with 1 ♔h3 ♚g6 2 ♔g2 ♚h5 (or 2 ... ♚h6 3 ♔f2 ♚g6 4 ♔e3 ♚h5 5 ♔d4 ♚g4 6 ♔e5) 3 ♔g3 and White has 'lost the move' and wins.

Trifunovic, Petar

[August 31 1910–December 8 1980]
Yugoslav lawyer and GM (1953) who came to prominence after the Second World War and won the Yugoslav Championship 5 times during 1945–61. He played on 7 Yugoslav Olympiad teams during 1935–62. His best results were 3rd at Belgrade 1954, 1st at Prague 1961 and 1st at Beverwijk 1962. He drew +1=10−1 with Najdorf in 1949.

In his best years Trifunovic enjoyed the reputation of being impossible to beat. He favoured strictly positional chess and relied heavily on his superb endgame technique. Excessive caution prevented him from achieving world class results.

Tringov, Georgi Petrov

[March 7 1937–]
Bulgarian GM (1963) who played on about a dozen Bulgarian Olympiad teams during 1956–82 and was Bulgarian Champion in 1963, 1981 and 1985. His best tournament result was equal 3rd at Vinkovci 1976.

Tripled Pawns

Three pawns of the same colour, all on one file. This rarely occurs, but when it does the pawns are usually extremely weak.

Troitzky, Alexei Alexeyevich

[1866–1942]
Generally regarded as the founder of the art of modern endgame study composition. He was a leader in retrograde analysis and wrote *500 Endspielstudien* (1924) as well as *Chess Studies* (1937). See also *Izbrannye Etyudii* by Korolkov and Chekhover (1959).

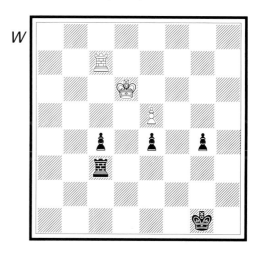

White to play and draw (1935).

1 e6 (not 1 ♖g7 e3 2 ♖xg4+ ♔f2 wins), 1 ... ♖d3+ (not 1 ... e3 2 e7 ♖d3+ 3 ♔c5) 2 ♔e5 (not 2 ♔c5 ♖d8 3 e7 ♖e8 4 ♔xc4 e3 5 ♔d3 ♔f2 6 ♖c2+ ♔f3 7 ♖c7 e2 8 ♔d2 ♔f2 wins). 2 ... e3 3 ♖xc4 e2 (not 3 ... g3 4 e7 e2 5 ♖e4) 4 ♖xg4+ ♔f2 5 ♖e4 ♖e3 6 ♖xe3 ♔xe3 7 e7 (not 7 ♔f6 e1=♕; 8 e7 ♔d4 wins) 7 ... e1=(♕), 8 ♔e6 and now both 8 ... ♔d4+ 9 ♔d7 and 8 ... ♔f4+ 9 ♔f7 draw.

Trompowsky Attack

1 d4 ♘f6 2 ♗g5.

Named after a Brazilian player who often used it in the 1930s.

219

Tsars

Murray's History tells us that chess was the favourite game of the Tsars of Russia in the 16th and 17th century. They kept special craftsmen (*shakhmatniks*) at the Oruzheni Palace, who made and repaired chess sets. The inhabitants of Kholmogory (50 miles south of Archangel) were famed for their skill in carving bone chess sets.

Tseitlin, Mikhail Semyenovich

[June 16 1947–]
USSR GM (1987) who was champion of Moscow (1976, 1977) and equal 1st at Naleczow 1979 and Pernik 1981.

Tseshkovsky, Vitaly Valerianovich

[September 25 1944–]
USSR GM (1975) who won many first prizes, but never made it to the Candidates level. He played in 9 USSR Championships during 1968–87, with erratic results. He was equal 1st with Tal in 1978 and he won outright in 1986 (Category X), but he came last in 1987. Overall he scored less than 50% in the 152 games he played in these 9 championships.

Internationally he won at Bucharest 1974, Leipzig 1975, Dubna 1976, Banja Luka 1981, Sochi 1981 and Minsk 1982. However, in the interzonal at Manila 1976 (Category XII) he was only 4th and in the Category XIII tournament at Lvov 1978 he was equal 3rd.

Tukmakov, Vladimar Borisovich

[March 15 1946–]
USSR GM (1972) who has a distinguished tournament record, but has never been a Candidate. During 1967–87 he played in 13 USSR Championships, scoring about 50%, and coming 2nd in 1970 and 2nd in 1983 (XIV). In 1984 he played on the USSR Olympiad team.

Internationally he was equal 4th at Moscow 1971 (XIV), 1st or equal 1st at Amsterdam 1974, Las Palmas 1978 and Vilnius 1978. He was equal 2nd at Erevan 1982 (XII), equal 2nd at Tilburg 1984 (XIV), equal 1st at Szirak 1985 (XI), equal 2nd at Dortmund 1987 (XII) and he had his best result coming 1st at Reggio Emilia 1987/88 (XV). He needs one slight step up to enter the Candidates level, but time is running out.

Turin

Northern Italian city which had a Category XVI tournament including World Champion Karpov, in 1982. However, 5 of the world top ten were absent: Korchnoi, Kasparov, Tal, Timman and Belyavsky. Almost complete gridlock was achieved with 75% of the games played drawn.

Turk, The   [1769–1854]

A chess-playing 'automaton', designed by the Hungarian engineer and inventor Baron Wolfgang von Kempelen in 1769 as an amusement for the court of the Empress Maria Theresa. The device consisted of a life-size figure, clad in Turkish robes, attached to a large cabinet or chest. The cabinet was divided into two compartments and a sliding drawer; it had a chessboard inlaid on its upper surface.

At the start of an exhibition the interior structure of the cabinet and the figure, containing a bewildering array of machinery, would be displayed to the spectators, who were invited to confirm that the machine operated without help from any human agency. After the doors and panels had been re-closed, members of the audience would play chess against the automaton, which usually won with ease. The Turk did lose to Philidor.

The Turk was a complicated hoax, with a strong human player concealed within the cabinet. A detailed account of the mechanics of the illusion can be found in a series of articles by K. Harkness and J. S. Battell, published in *Chess Review* (1947). (*See also*: *The Turkish Automaton* by Sheila Braine (1899), *The Great Chess Automaton* by Charles M. Carroll (1975), *Der Schachautomat des Baron von Kempelen* by M. Faber (1983).

Curiously, Edgar Allan Poe's famous 1836 article was wrong about several aspects of the Turk.

The Turk's first performance took place before the Hapsburg court in

Turin 1982																Category XVI
		1		2		3		4		5		6		7		
1	Karpov	—	—	½	½	0	1	1	½	½	½	½	½	½	1	7
	Andersson	½	½	—	—	½	½	½	½	½	½	1	½	½	1	7
3	Ljubojevic	1	0	½	½	—	—	0	½	½	1	½	½	½	1	6½
	Portisch	0	½	½	½	1	½	—	—	0	½	½	1	½	1	6½
5	Spassky	½	½	½	½	½	0	1	½	—	—	½	½	0	1	6
6	Kavalek	½	½	0	½	½	½	½	0	½	½	—	—	½	1	5½
7	Hübner	½	0	½	0	½	0	½	0	1	0	½	0	—	—	3½

Hübner withdrew after the first round robin and defaulted his remaining games.

Vienna in 1770. Public exhibitions continued intermittently for almost 85 years. In 1783/4 Kempelen and his device visited several European cities, including Dresden, Leipzig, Paris and London. After Kempelen's death in 1804, the Turk was purchased by a Bavarian showman and musician, Johann Nepomuk Maelzel, who had himself designed an automatic orchestra operated by foot pedals for which he had persuaded Beethoven to compose some music. In 1809, during the Wagram campaign, Napoleon played (unsuccessfully) against the Turk in Vienna.

For a time The Turk was in the private collection of Prince Eugene de Beauharnais, who bought its secret for 30 000 francs, but Maelzel acquired it again in 1817 and toured extensively with the machine: Paris 1818, London 1818–20, Amsterdam 1821–2 and in America 1826–36. In 1837 both Maelzel and The Turk's current operator, Schlumberger—the tutor of Saint-Amant—died of yellow fever while returning from Havana to the USA. The automaton ended its days at the Chinese Museum in Philadelphia, where it perished in a fire in 1854.

Some of the names of the players who inhabited The Turk's interior are known. These include: Allgaier (1809), Weyle, Alexander (1818), Boncourt (1818), Lewis (1818–19), Williams (1819), Mouret (1820) and Schlumberger (1826 onwards).

See Automatons.

Twiss, Richard   [*1747–1821*]
English author who wrote *Chess* in 1789 and *Miscellanies* in 1805, with many chess references and items.

Two Knights Defence
1 e4 e5 2 Nf3 Nc6 3 Bc4 Nf6.
First given by Polerio in 1560, this natural defence must be followed up with a pawn sacrifice after 4 Ng5 d5 5 ed Na5 6 Bb5+ c6 7 dc bc 8 Be2 h6 9 Nf3 e4 10 Ne5, when Black has counterplay for the pawn.

Black's options are:
5 ... Nxd5 when White maintains an edge with 6 d4 or can try 6 Nxf7 the 'Fried Liver Attack'.
5 ... Nd4 (Fritz Variation) 6 c3 b5 7 Bf1
5 ... b5 (Ulvestad's Variation) 6 Bf1 which is good for White.
An earlier Black option is 4 ... Bc5 (Wilkes–Barre or Traxler–Keres line).
White has a lively option: 4 d4 ed 5 0-0 Bc5 6 e5, the famous Max Lange Attack.
See *Two Knights Defence* by Estrin (1983).

U

Ubilava, Elizbar [*August 27 1950–*]
USSR GM (1988) who was 1st at Trencianske Teplice 1985 (IX), 1st at Eforie Noird 1988 (X) and equal 1st at Tbilisi 1988 (XI).

Udovcic, Mijo [*September 11 1920–*]
Yugoslav lawyer and GM (1962) who was equal 2nd with Smyslov, behind Taimanov, at Dortmund 1961. He was Yugoslav Champion in 1963, played on the 1964 Yugoslav Olympiad team and withdrew from tournament play in 1969.

Uhlmann, Wolfgang
                [*March 29 1935–*]
East German GM (1959) who was East German Champion 8 times during 1955–85 and a regular on the East German Olympiad teams since 1956. He was a Candidate in 1971 but lost $+2=3-4$ to Larsen. His best period was in the late 1960s when he scored many equal 1sts: Sarajevo 1964, Havana 1964, Zagreb 1965, Hastings 1965/6, Zinnowitz 1967 and Berlin 1968. He was clear 1st at the 1969 Raach zonal.

Uhlmann was also equal 1st at Hastings 1975/6, 1st at Vrbas 1977, 1st at Halle 1981 and 1982. More recently he was 1st at Potsdam 1985 (IX), equal 3rd at Dresden 1985 (IX) and equal 3rd at Leipzig 1986 (IX).

222

Underpromotion
See Promotion

Unpinning
To release a piece from being pinned. There are several effective ways to accomplish this: attack or deflect the pinner, remove the valuable piece against which the pin operates, or counterpin, as in the diagram.

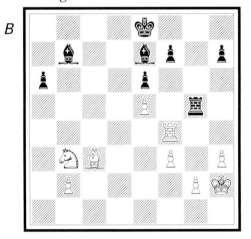

Becker–Marshall, Carlsbad 1929
    Marshall tried 1 ... f6 2 ef ♗d6 (a lovely pin) 3 f7 + ♔f8 4 ♗b4 (a lovely unpin or counter-pin, and White went on to win).

Unsound
A combination, strategic plan or composed problem that is faulty. In practice quite a few unsound combinations and unsound strategic plans are successful, because one's opponent does not find the best defence.

Unzicker, Wolfgang [*June 26 1925–*]
West German judge and GM (1954) who won 7 West German Championships during 1946–65 and played on 13 West German Olympiad teams during 1950–82. He was the leading Germany player from the late 1940s to the advent of Hübner in the early 1970s. He has a fine tournament record, though he never became a Candidate.

Unzicker was 1st at Augsburg 1946, 1st at Hastings 1950–51, 2nd at Leningrad 1960, equal 1st at Sochi 1965, 1st at Maribor 1967, equal 1st at Amsterdam 1980 and more recently 1st at Almada 1988. But his best performance was probably equal 4th at Santa Monica 1966 (XV).

In 1956 he lost $+0=4-4$ to Keres and all 8 games opened with the Ruy Lopez.

USSR/Russian Championships
There were some 9 Russian championships between 1899 and 1914. From 1920 to 1989 there were 56 USSR Championships plus the so-called Absolute Championship in 1941. These tournaments were not as high category ones as the Candidates or World Cup tournaments, but their games sparkled with original ideas and sheer excite-

ment—especially during the 1940s, 50s and 60s. For students of the game, these tournaments are perhaps the best textbooks one can find.

1899 Chigorin
1901 Chigorin
1903 Chigorin
1906 Salwe
1907/8 Rubinstein
1909 Alekhine
1911 Levitsky
1912 Rubinstein
1914 Nimzowitsch, Alekhine
1920 Alekhine
1923 Romanovsky
1924 Bogoljubow
1925 Bogoljubow
1927 Bohatirchuk, Romanovsky
1929 Verlinsky
1931 Botvinnik
1933 Botvinnik
1934 Levenfish, Rabinovich, I.
1937 Levenfish
1939 Botvinnik
1940 Bondarevsky, Lilienthal
1941 (Absolute), Botvinnik
1944 Botvinnik
1945 Botvinnik
1947 Keres
1948 Bronstein, Kotov
1949 Bronstein, Smyslov
1950 Keres
1951 Keres
1952 Botvinnik
1954 Averbakh
1955 Geller
1956 Taimanov
1957 Tal
1958 Tal
1959 Petrosian
1960 Korchnoi
1961 Petrosian
1961 Spassky
1962 Korchnoi
1963 Stein
1964/5 Korchnoi
1965 Stein
1966/7 Stein
1967 Polugayevsky, Tal
1968/9 Polugayevsky
1969 Petrosian
1970 Korchnoi
1971 Savon
1972 Tal
1973 Spassky
1974 Belyavsky, Tal
1975 Petrosian
1976 Karpov
1977 Gulko, Dorfman
1978 Tal, Tseshkovsky
1979 Geller
1980/1 Belyavsky, Psakhis
1981 Kasparov, Psakhis
1982/3 Karpov
1984/5 Sokolov
1985 Gurevich
1986 Tseshkovsky
1987 Belyavsky
1988 Kasparov, Karpov
1989 Vaganian

For the 56 regular USSR Championships, the most frequent participants (they had to qualify to play) were:

23 Championships: Geller and Taimanov
20 Championships: Bronstein and Polugayevsky
19 Championships: Tal and Smyslov
16 Championships: Korchnoi and Petrosian

The most frequent winners (1st or equal 1st) were:

Botvinnik	6 wins in 11 attempts
Tal	6 wins in 19 attempts
Spassky	4 wins in 11 attempts

Moscow 1988 — 55th USSR Championship — Category XIV

		1	2	3	4	5	6	7	8	9	10	11	12	13	14	15	16	17	18	
1	Kasparov	–	½	½	1	½	1	1	½	½	½	½	½	½	½	1	1	½	1	11½
	Karpov	½	–	1	½	½	½	½	½	½	1	½	½	½	½	1	1	1	1	11½
3	Yusupov	½	0	–	1	½	0	½	½	½	½	1	1	½	½	½	1	½	1	10
	Salov	0	½	0	–	½	½	0	1	½	½	1	½	1	1	½	1	1	½	10
5	Eingorn	½	½	½	½	–	½	½	1	½	½	0	½	1	½	½	½	1	½	9½
	Ivanchuk	0	½	1	½	½	–	½	1	0	½	0	½	½	1	½	½	1	1	9½
8	Belyavsky	½	½	½	0	0	0	½	–	½	0	½	½	1	1	1	½	½	1	8½
9	Ehlvest	½	½	½	½	½	1	½	½	–	½	0	½	0	0	1	½	½	½	8
	Gavrikov	½	0	½	½	½	½	½	1	½	–	½	½	½	½	½	½	0	½	8
	Smyslov	½	½	0	0	1	1	0	½	1	½	–	½	½	½	0	½	½	½	8
	Sokolov, A.	½	½	0	½	½	½	½	½	½	½	½	–	½	½	½	0	1	½	8
	Vaganian	½	½	½	0	0	½	½	0	1	½	½	½	–	½	½	1	½	½	8
14	Khalifman	½	½	½	0	½	0	½	0	1	½	½	½	½	–	½	½	½	½	7½
15	Shirin	0	0	½	½	½	½	½	0	0	½	1	½	½	½	–	0	1	½	7
	Gurevich	0	0	0	0	½	½	½	½	½	½	½	1	0	½	1	–	½	½	7
17	Malaniuk	½	0	½	0	0	0	½	½	½	1	½	0	½	½	0	½	–	½	6
	Kharitonov	0	0	0	½	½	0	½	0	½	½	½	½	½	½	½	½	½	–	6

Petrosian   4 wins in 16 attempts
Korchnoi   4 wins in 16 attempts
Karpov   3 wins in 6 attempts
Stein   3 wins in 9 attempts
Belyavsky   3 wins in 12 attempts
Keres   3 wins in 13 attempts
Polugayevsky 3 wins in 20 attempts

     The 1988 Championship had both super Ks and was a high Category XIV:

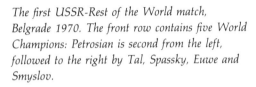

The first USSR-Rest of the World match, Belgrade 1970. The front row contains five World Champions: Petrosian is second from the left, followed to the right by Tal, Spassky, Euwe and Smyslov.

Vacating Sacrifice

A sacrifice the sole purpose of which is to get rid of one's own piece to make room for a more effective piece.

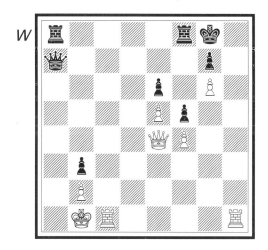

In this otherwise desperate situation, White has: 1 ♖h8+ ♚xh8 2 ♕h1+ ♚g8 3 ♕h7 mate.

Vadasz, Laszlo   [January 27 1948–]

Hungarian GM (1976) who was equal 1st at Vrnjacka Banja 1975, equal 1st at Budapest 1976 and equal 3rd in the 1976 Hungarian Championship.

Vaganian, Rafael Artemovich
[October 15 1951–]

USSR (Armenian) GM (1971) who is overflowing with talent (some GMs call him a genius), but is a touch undisciplined. He was a Candidate twice: in 1986 he lost +0=4−4 to Sokolov and in 1988 he lost +0=5−1 to Portisch. Vaganian played in 11 USSR Championships during 1967–1989, scoring about 50% overall, coming equal 2nd in 1975 and winning in 1989. He played on the 1984 and 1986 USSR Olympiad teams.

He has an excellent tournament record which includes 1st at Vrnjacka Banja 1971, 1st at Sao Paulo 1977, 1st at Las Palmas 1979, 1st at Manila 1981,

The talented but erratic Rafael Vaganian.

equal 1st to Moscow (1982 (X), 1st at Hastings 1982/83 (XI), equal 4th at Tilburg 1983 (XV), 1st at Biel 1985 (XII), equal 1st at Naestved 1985 (XIII), equal 1st at Montpellier 1985 (XIV), equal 1st at Sochi 1986 (XII) and a fine 1st at Leningrad 1987 (XIV). In 1988 he was equal 1st at Esbjerg (XI).

Vaganian–Forintos
Moscow 1975

1 d4 ♞f6 2 c4 e6 3 ♞f3 d5 4 ♞c3 ♝e7 5 ♝f4 0-0 6 e3 ♞bd7 7 ♕c2 c6 8 cd ♞xd5 9 ♞xd5 ed 10 ♝d3 ♝b4+ 11 ♚e2 ♞f6 12 ♞e5 ♜e8 13 g4 g6 14 ♜ag1 ♝d6 15 h4 c5 16 h5 cd 17 hg ♝xe5 18 g5 ♝g4+

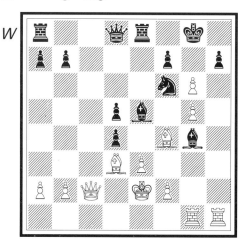

19 ♖xg4 ♜c8 20 gh+ ♚h8 21 ♝xe5 ♜xe5 22 gf ♜xc2+ 23 ♝xc2 d3+ 24 ♝xd3 ♜e8 24 ♜hg1 Resigns

Vaiser, Anatoly Volfovich

[March 5 1949–]
USSR GM (1985) who was equal 3rd at Sochi 1982 (XI) and equal 1st at Sochi 1983 (XI).

Value of Pieces and Pawns

Value depends on the overall position and on how well certain pieces work together. For example, 2 bishops are worth more than twice the value of a single bishop.

One rough estimate is: Pawn = 1; Bishop = Knight = 3; Rook = 4½; Queen = 9.

Dr Lasker gave the following table of values (based on his experience):

Queen	= 11
King's rook	= 7
Queen's rook	= 6
King's bishop	= 5
Queen's bishop	= 4½
Either knight	= 4½
d- or e-pawn	= 2
c- or f-pawn	= 1½
b- or g-pawn	= 1¼
a- or h-pawn	= ½

Van den Berg, Carel Benjamin

[February 12 1924–June 30 1971]
Dutch lawyer, author and IM (1963) who was an eminent chess theorist. He was editor of *Losbladige Schaakberichten*, collaborator with Euwe on the *Theorie der Schaakopeningen* series and a member of the 1958 Dutch Olympiad team.

Van der Wiel, John T. H.

[August 9 1959–]
Dutch GM (1982) who, next to Timman, is the strongest Dutch player. He was Dutch Champion in 1984 and has played on all the Dutch Olympiad teams of the 1980s. He was European Junior champion 1978/79, equal 3rd at Wijk aan zee 1982 (XIII), 1st at Novi Sad 1982 (XI), 2nd at Amsterdam 1986 (XIII), equal 2nd at Wijk aan Zee 1986 (XII), equal 1st at Ter Apel 1987 (XI) and 1st at Amsterdam 1987 (XIII).

He has not yet made it to the Candi-dates level, but he is growing in strength and taking advantage of the many opportunities to meet the greatest GMs of the day that are offered by the rich Dutch chess life. He came last in the 4 man Amsterdam tournament of 1987 (XVI) and 1988 (XVIII), but losing out to Kasparov, Karpov and Timman is no shame and can be a fine learning experience.

Van't Kruijs Opening

1 e3.

Rarely played invitation to an inverted French Defence, which was first mentioned by Lucena in 1497 and played by the Dutchman Van't Kruijs in the mid 19th century.

Variations

Different sequences of moves. Opening books are often filled with columns of moves—each one giving a different variation.

Varieties of Chess

Alice

Played with one extra board (empty to start with). When a man is moved, it is (at the end of the move) transferred over to the corresponding square on the other board. As men begin to appear on this second board, any legal move can be made on either board and then transferred. A move cannot be made if the transfer square is occupied. A man on one board cannot capture a man on the other board.

Here is a sample game: 1 d4 e5 2 de ♗e7 3 ♕xd7 ♕d4 4 f3 ♗h4 mate.

It is curious that one can never interpose a man from the same board to stop a check, because the interposer gets transferred to the other board.

Alice was invented in 1954 by V. Rylands and named after Alice in *Through the Looking Glass*.

Checkless

Neither player may give check unless it is mate. This introduces some curious consequences—the king becomes an attacking piece and an indirect protector because a piece cannot be taken if it results in a mateless check.

Circe

Each captured man must be put back on the board, on its original square except for colour. That is, for a rook, bishop or knight, on the square of the same colour as that of the square on which it was captured. Pawns are replaced on the second rank of the file on which they were captured.

If the replacement square is occupied, the man is permanently removed from the board. A man cannot be captured if replacing him puts the capturer's king in check.

This was invented in 1967 by P. Monreal and J. P. Boyer.

Courier

Chess played on a board 12 squares wide with the usual 8 ranks, with extra pieces (alfil, courier, Mann, fers and sneak) and 12 pawns. It was played primarily in Germany and particularly in Strobeck.

There is a famous painting, *The Chess Game*, by Lucas van Leyden (16th century) which has a 12 × 8 board. Leyden was probably not an idiot and had copied a Courier board.

Double move (Marseilles)

Each player makes two consecutive moves on his turn, but he cannot give check with the first move. If a player is put in check he must deal with it on the first of his two moves.

Four-handed

There have been quite a few suggestions for adjusting chess to accommodate four players. One reasonable way is to use a normal 8 × 8 board with an extra 24 squares (8 × 3) attached to each of the four sides. Four players sit one at each side and two clearly distinguished chess sets are needed. The pieces are set up on the 16 squares in front of each player, opposite players partnering one another. Play proceeds clockwise, the object being to mate both opponents. Pawns promote on an opponent's (not the partner's) back row, if they ever manage to capture often enough to get there.

See: Chess Eccentricities, by G. H. Verney (1885).

Great

Any variety of chess played on a board larger than 8 × 8. There have been many suggestions.

See: My One Contribution to Chess, by F. V. Morley (1947).

Hexagonal

Six sided figures (hexagons) can be used to fill a plane surface just as well as squares. This allows a possible variant for 3 players.

Hexagonal Chess was conceived specifically as a three-handed game by the Viennese engineer Sigmund Wellisch in 1912. His original board had 91 cells in three colours. Subsequent designs by H.D. Baskerville (1929) and, more recently, the Australian-based Englishman Alan Patton (1975) though varying in size and shape, maintained the preference for a three player variant.

However the modern, two-handed, version of the game was proposed by Wladislaw Glinski in 1949 and has become the standard version for International competition.

Kleptomania

The same as Pocket Knight Chess except the players may each pocket a bishop (or a rook, or a queen).

Kriegspiel

Each player sees only one board with only his own pieces on it. An umpire has a third board with a full chess set and he copies whatever moves are made (or attempted) by each player, telling them only if an attempted move is playable or not. A player may enquire whether any pawn captures are possible. If the answer is yes, the player must try at least once to make a pawn capture. The umpire announces any check by stating its direction (i.e. on rank, on the file, on the long or short diagonal, or from a knight). Captures are announced by the umpire's stating the square e.g. 'capture on e5'. No other information is made available and each player must guess or deduce his opponent's moves.

It was invented by W. H. Temple around 1890.

See: British Chess Magazine (1944).

Losing or Must-capture

Captures are compulsory. If more than one capture is possible, the player can choose which one to make. The winner is the one who loses all his men, including his king, or who is unable to make a move. Kings are not special. They can be offered for capture. Pawns may be promoted to kings.

No-capture

Neither side may capture unless a capture is the only way to prevent mate.

Pawns game

An unusual way to handicap. White removes one of his rooks and places 3 or 4 extra pawns on his 3rd rank. Or White removes his queen and places 7 or 8 or 9 extra pawns on his 3rd and 4th rank.

Pocket knight or Tombola

Each player starts the game with his queen knight in his pocket. Once during the game a player may place his 'pocket knight' anywhere on the board instead of making a move.

Progressive or Scotch or Blitzkrieg

White plays one move, Black replies with two successive moves, White then plays three moves in a row, Black four, White five, and so on. Check may be given only with the last move of a sequence and must be attended to with the first move of the next player's sequence. This was popularized by Znosko–Borovsky in 1947

Randomized

To do away with memorized opening variations, the 8 pieces are shuffled about on the first rank before the game begins. The bishops must end up on different coloured squares and Black's pieces are set up exactly the same as the White pieces.

One way to do this is to first set up all the pawns in the usual way. Then white places any piece he chooses at a1 and black must place a similar piece at a8. Then Black places any piece he chooses at b8 and White must place a similar piece at b1. This continues until all 8 pieces are placed. Some decision about castling must be agreed to in advance.

Refusal

On each move, a player has the right, if he wishes to exercise it, to refuse his opponent's last move and oblige him to play another, which must then be accepted.

Replacement

Each captured man must be put back on the board, but anywhere the capturer decides, except that pawns cannot be put on their own first rank.

Rifle

Captures are made by removing the captured man but not occupying the square. Thus when a man captures, the man does not move. When a bishop, rook or queen captures an enemy man giving check, it is illegal to interpose a man on the square of capture.

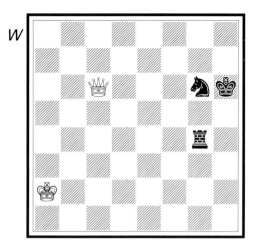

In the diagram, White can play 1 ♕xg6+. The Queen remains at c6 and the black knight is simply removed from the board. The black king is now in check. It is illegal for Black to play 1 ... ♖g6 because this is interposing a man on g6, the square of capture. This was invented in 1921 by W. J. Seabrook.

Round or Zatrikion
A version of chess played on a circular board and popular several hundred years ago.

Screen
The same as randomized except that each player can set his own pieces up in his own way on the back row. A screen can be used during the setting up process to prevent your opponent seeing how you set up your pieces.

Take me
Captures are compulsory only if demanded, otherwise identical to Losing Chess.

Three-handed
Accommodating three people for chess has not proved an easy task. There have been several suggestions. (*See* Hexagonal).
See Three-Dimensional Chess

Vasavadatta

A prose romance in Sanskrit by Subandhu, written at the beginning of the 7th century. It is the second earliest clear reference to the game of chess. (*See* Karnamak)

Vasyukov, Evgeny Andreevich

[*March 5 1933– *]
USSR GM (1961) who played in 11 USSR Championships during 1959–80, coming 3rd in 1967 and equal 4th in 1961. He was 1st or equal 1st at Moscow 1961, Belgrade 1961, Moscow 1962, Berlin 1962, Varna 1964, Reykjavik 1968, Skopje 1970 and Varna 1971. His best result was 1st at Manila 1974 (XII). More recently he was 1st at Zalaegerszeg 1977 and equal 2nd at Eforie Nord 1988 (X)

During 1955–78, Vasyukov won the Moscow Championship 6 times.

Veidt, Conrad

[*January 22 1893–April 3 1943*]
German monocled movie actor who was a keen chess fan.

Velikov, Petar   [*March 30 1951– *]

Bulgarian GM (1982) who won the Bulgarian Championship in 1987 and played on the Bulgarian Olympiad team in 1982, 1984 and 1986.

Velimirovic, Dragoljub

[*May 12 1942– *]
Yugoslav GM (1973) who was Yugoslav Champion in 1970 and 1975, and has played on about half a dozen Yugoslav Olympiad teams during 1974–88. He has a fine tournament record and a spectacular style that makes him popular and much admired.

He was 1st at Vrnjacka Banja 1973, 1st at Novi Sad 1975, equal 1st at Zemun 1980, equal 1st at Titograd 1984 (XII), 1st at Vrsac 1985 (X), equal 1st at Vrsac 1987 (XII) and he won the Metz Open in 1988.

Velimirovic–Ljubojevic

Yugoslav Championship 1972
1 e4 c5 2 ♘f3 d6 3 d4 cd 4 ♘xd4 ♘f6 5 ♘c3 a6 6 ♗g5 e6 7 f4 ♗e7 8 ♕f3

♕c7 9 0-0-0 ♘bd7 10 ♗d3 b5 11 ♖he1 ♗b7 12 ♘d5 ♘xd5 13 ed ♗xg5

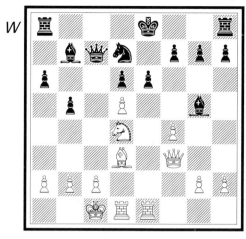

14 ♖xe6+ fe 15 ♘xe6 ♕a5 16 ♕h5+ g6 17 ♕xg5 ♖g8 18 ♖d2 ♘f8 19 ♘xf8 ♕d8 20 ♘xh7 ♕xg5 21 fg ♔f7 22 ♘f6 ♖h8 23 g3 ♗c8 24 h4 ♗f5 25 ♗xf5 gf 26 h5 ♖a7 27 ♖f2 resigns

Vera, Reynaldo G. [*January 7 1961– *]

Cuban GM (1988) who was equal 3rd at Cienfuegos 1984 (IX), equal 1st at Varna 1986 (VIII) and equal 4th at Portoroz 1987 (IX). He played on the Cuban Olympiad team in 1986 and 1988.

Vida, Marco Gerolamo (Marcus Hieronymus) [*1490–September 27 1566*]

Bishop of Alba (1532) who wrote a Latin poem: *Scacchia Ludus* in 1513, which was widely admired and translated. It deals with a chess game between Apollo and Hermes.

Vidmar, Milan

[*June 22 1885–October 9 1962*]
Yugoslav electrical engineer and GM (1950) who was Yugoslavia's first GM. He devoted his main energy to his engineering and academic career, becoming Dean at Ljubljana University. In spite of thus being an amateur chess player, Vidmar belonged to the world top 6 during 1911–30.

He began his chess career at Coburg 1904. He was equal 3rd at Vienna 1907,

3rd at Prague 1908, and equal 2nd with Rubinstein, just behind Capablanca, at San Sebastian 1911. At Mannheim 1914 he was 2nd when the outbreak of war stopped the tournament. He won two 4-man tournaments: Vienna 1917/18, and Berlin 1918, and he was 2nd at Kaschau 1918. He had a fine 3rd at London 1922 and was 3rd at Semmering 1926. He was 4th at London 1927 and 4th at New York 1927 (XV). At Carlsbad 1929 he was equal 5th but he was suffering a crisis of self confidence. Chess had become a means of livelihood to an ever-increasing number of leading players thus making it extremely difficult even for amateurs of Vidmar's calibre to compete without serious theoretical preparation. Disillusioned, Vidmar withdrew from the tournament arena after winning the 1939 Yugoslav Championship.

Vidmar played on the Yugoslav Olympiad teams of 1931 and 1935, and he was the chief referee at The Hague/Moscow 1948 to select a new World Champion.

He enjoyed bridge and tarock (a European card game), smoking and food, getting rather round as he aged. Nimzowitsch and Najdorf were special friends of his. Vidmar was respected in Imperial Austria and Royal Yugoslavia. During the Second World War, the invading Nazis as well as the Italian Fascists left him alone. The Tito regime pampered him and even communists had nothing against him. They all respected him for his engineering and his chess.

Major works:

Goldene Schachzeiten (1961), Carlsbad 1911 (1912).

Vidmar–Nimzowitsch
Semmering 1926
1 d4 ♘f6 2 c4 e6 3 ♘f3 ♗b4+ 4 ♗d2 ♕e7 5 e3 ♗xd2+ 6 ♘bxd2 d6 7 ♕c2 c5 8 g3 b6 9 ♗g2 ♗b7 10 0-0 ♘c6 11 a3 0-0 12 ♖ad1 ♖fd8 13 ♖fe1 ♖ac8

14 ♘b3 cd 15 ed ♘b8 16 ♘fd2 ♗xg2 17 ♔xg2 ♕b7+ 18 ♔g1 ♖c7 19 ♕d3 ♘bd7 20 f4 g6 21 ♖c1 ♖dc8 22 h3 h5 23 ♖c3 d5 24 cd ♖xc3 25 bc ♕xd5 26 c4 ♕d6 27 ♕f3 ♔g7 28 ♔g2 ♕xa3 29 ♖a1 ♕b2 30 ♖b1 ♕c2 31 ♖c1 ♕f5 32 ♖e1 ♖d8 33 ♕c3 h4

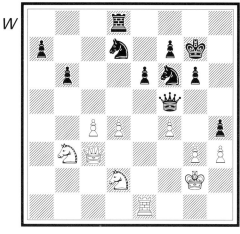

34 d5 hg 35 ♘d4 ♕xf4 36 ♖f1 ♕d6 37 ♘e4 ♕c7 38 ♘xf6 ♘xf6 39 ♘b5 ♕e7 40 d6 ♕f8 41 ♕xf6+ ♔g8 42 ♖f4 ♖d7 43 ♖h4 ♕g7 44 ♕xg7+ ♔xg7 45 ♖d4 a6 46 ♘c7 ♔f6 47 ♖d1 ♔e5 48 ♘e8 a5 49 ♔xg3 a4 50 ♔g4 a3 51 ♖a1 ♔d4 52 ♘f6 ♖xd6 53 ♖d1+ ♔xc4 54 ♖xd6 a2 55 ♖c6+ ♔b5 56 ♖c1 ♔a4 57 ♘d7 b5 58 ♘c5+ ♔a3 59 ♘d3 ♔b3 (if ... b4 60 ♖c8!) 60 ♘c5+ ♔b2 61 ♘d3+ ♔b3 62 ♘c5+ ♔a3 63 ♘d3 ♔b3 64 ♔f3 Resigns

Vienna
One of Europe's great cities, famous for desserts, opera and chess.

The Vienna chess club was founded in 1857 and had its first major tournament in 1873. Steinitz and Blackburne tied for 1st ahead of Anderssen, and Steinitz won the play-off + 2 = 0-0. For the next 50 years Vienna staged many wonderful tournaments, including 20 Trebitsch Memorials (1907–38). The Barons Rothschild and Kolisch provided financial and moral support. Some of the stronger Viennese tournaments were:

1903 Chigorin (13) won a King's Gambit Accepted tournament ahead of Marshall (11½), Marco (11) and Pillsbury (10).

1904/5 Schlechter (14½) edged out Maroczy (14).

1907 Mieses (10) won ahead of Duras (9), Maroczy (8½) and Vidmar (8½).

1908 Duras (14), Maroczy (14) and Schlechter (14) came ahead of Rubinstein (13), Teichmann (12) and Spielmann (11½).

1922 Rubinstein (11½) won ahead of Tartakower (10), Wolf (9½), Alekhine (9), Maroczy (9) and Tarrasch (9).

However the two jewels in Vienna's chess diadem occurred in 1882 and 1898. Every great player came to Vienna 1882, including Steinitz, the world's best, and his two main rivals, Blackburne, and Zukertort. The total prize fund was equivalent to £450, with 1st prize set at £210. Winawer had his best result and even held Steinitz +1−1 in a play-off.

In 1898 Vienna held the so called Kaiser Jubilee tournament, celebrating the 50th anniversary of Franz Josef's accession to the throne. All the great masters were there except for World Champion Lasker, Teichmann (who was having eye problems), and Charousek who was fatally ill.

With 3 rounds to go, Pillsbury (26½) led Tarrasch (26) Janowski (24) and Steinitz (23½). Tarrasch drew with Chigorin while Pillsbury lost a 91 move struggle with Burn. Thus Tarrasch and Pillsbury were neck and neck. They both won their last 2 games and finished in a tie for first. A 4-game play-off was held and Tarrasch achieved the greatest triumph of his career, winning +2 = 1 −1.

Time limit: 30 moves in 2 hours and then 15 moves per hour.

Prizes (Kronen): 6000, 4000, 2500,

Vienna 1882

		1	2	3	4	5	6	7	8	9	10	11	12	13	14	15	16	17	18	
1	Steinitz	–	1½	½½	½1	0½	10	½½	11	01	1½	01	11	10	11	11	01	11*	11*	24
	Winawer	0½	–	00	½0	1½	10	11	10	01	1½	11	11	11	11	11	11	11*	01*	24
3	Mason	½½	11	–	½1	0½	½½	½½	11	11	10	01	½1	11	1½	0½	11	01*	½1*	23
4	Mackenzie	½0	½1	½0	–	½½	10	½1	1½	½0	11	11	01	01	11	10	1½	11*	11*	22½
	Zukertort	1½	0½	1½	½½	–	0½	0½	11	11	00	11	01	01	11	11	11	11*	01*	22½
6	Blackburne	01	01	½½	01	1½	–	½½	0½	10	01	10	1½	11	11	10	11	01*	11*	21½
7	Englisch	½½	00	½½	½0	1½	½½	–	11	½0	½½	½½	½½	0½	01	11	11	11*	½	19½
8	Paulsen L.	00	01	00	0½	00	1½	00	–	½½	½1	½1	½1	11	½1	½1	11	½1*	½1*	18½
9	Wittek	10	10	00	½1	00	01	½1	½½	–	½0	01	½½	10	½½	½1	1½	½1*	11*	18
10	Weiss	0½	0½	01	00	11	10	½½	½0	½1	–	0½	0½	11	0½	01	00	11*	11*	16½
11	Hruby	10	00	10	00	00	01	½½	½0	10	1½	–	½½	10	11	01	10	01*	11*	16
12	Schwarz	00	00	½0	10	10	0½	½½	½0	½½	1½	½½	–	00	½0	11	½0	01*	11*	14
	Chigorin	01	00	00	10	10	00	1½	00	01	00	01	11	–	00	11	1½	01*	01	14
14	Meitner	00	00	0½	00	00	00	10	½0	½½	1½	00	½1	11	–	01	01	01*	11*	13
15	Bird	00	00	1½	01	00	01	00	½0	½0	10	10	00	00	10	–	11	½1*	01	12
16	Ware	10	00	00	0½	00	00	00	00	0½	11	01	½1	0½	10	00	–	01*	11*	11
17	Noa	00*	00*	10*	00*	00*	10*	00*	½0*	½0*	00*	10*	10*	10*	10*	½0*	10*	–	½0*	9
18	Fleissig	00*	10*	½0*	00*	10*	00*	½0	½0*	00*	00*	00*	00*	10	00*	10	00*	½1*	–	7

Noa withdrew from the second round robin and lost his remaining games by default.
Fleissig withdrew after 10 games, again defaulting the remainder
* Scored by forfeit

Vienna 1898

		1	2	3	4	5	6	7	8	9	10	11	12	13	14	15	16	17	18	19	
1	Tarrasch	–	01	10	1½	1½	1½	½1	½½	½1	½1	½½	11	11	11	1½	1½	11	11	1½	27½
	Pillsbury	10	–	10	½1	1½	10	½0	1½	01	½1	11	11	1½	½1	11	11	11	11	11	27½
3	Janowski	01	01	–	11	1½	11	1½	00	½½	11	½0	11	1½	11	11	00	½1	11	11	25½
4	Steinitz	0½	0½	00	–	½1	10	½½	11	1½	½1	½½	01	11	11	01	1½	1½	11	11	23½
5	Schlechter	0½	0½	0½	½0	–	½½	11	½½	½½	½1	0½	1½	½1	1½	11	0½	½1	11	11	21½
6	Chigorin	0½	10	00	01	½½	–	10	01	1½	1½	½0	10	01	11	10	11	10	01	11	20
	Burn	½0	½1	0½	½½	00	01	–	1½	0½	½½	½½	½0	½0	11	01	11	1½	11	11	20
8	Lipke	½½	0½	11	00	½½	10	0½	–	½½	½½	½0	1½	11	1½	0½	½1	½½	11	½½	19½
	Maroczy	½0	10	½½	0½	½½	0½	1½	½½	–	½½	1½	11	½½	01	0½	01	1½	½½	11	19½
10	Alapin	½0	½0	00	½0	½0	0½	½½	½½	½½	–	½1	1½	11	00	10	11	½1	10	11	18
11	Blackburne	½½	00	½1	½½	1½	½1	½½	½1	0½	½0	–	½½	½0	0½	½0	½½	00	11	½1	17
	Schiffers	00	00	00	10	0½	01	½1	0½	00	0½	½½	–	01	1½	11	½1	½1	11	½1	17
13	Marco	00	0½	0½	00	½0	10	½1	00	½½	00	½1	10	–	11	½1	1½	½1	½1	10	16½
14	Showalter	00	½0	00	00	0½	00	00	0½	10	11	1½	01	00	–	½1	11	11	01	11	15
15	Walbrodt	0½	00	00	10	00	01	10	1½	1½	01	½1	00	½0	½0	–	00	11	½0	11	14½
16	Halprin	0½	00	11	0½	1½	00	00	½0	10	00	½½	½0	0½	00	11	–	½½	1½	½1	14
17	Card	00	00	½0	0½	½0	01	0½	½½	0½	½0	11	½0	½0	00	00	½½	–	11	½1	12½
18	Baird, D. G.	00	00	00	00	00	10	00	00	½½	01	00	00	½0	10	½1	0½	00	–	½1	8
19	Trenchard	0½	00	00	00	00	00	00	½½	00	00	½0	½0	01	00	00	½0	½0	½0	–	5

Schwartz withdrew after eight rounds, and his score was cancelled.

1500, 1000, 800, 700, 600, 500, 400, 200.

Rothschild Brilliancy prizes: 400 Kronen to Pillsbury for his win over Halprin in round 4; 300 Kronen to Lipke for his win over Janowski in round 22; 200 Kronen to Marco for his win over Burn in round 32.

Tournament book by the editors of the *Wiener Schachzeitung*: Marco, Halprin and Fahndrich. It has light but good annotations.

Halprin–Pillsbury

1 d4 d5 2 ♘f3 ♘f6 3 e3 c5 4 b3 cd 5 ed ♘c6 6 c4 ♗g4 7 ♗e2 e6 8 0-0 dc 9 bc ♖c8 10 ♗b2 ♗e7 11 ♘bd2 0-0 12 ♕b3 ♕c7 13 ♖ac1 ♖fd8 14 ♕e3 ♗d6 15 g3 ♕a5 16 ♗d3 ♕h5 17 ♘g5 e5! 18 d5 ♘d4 19 h4 h6 20 ♘ge4 ♘xe4 21 ♘xe4 ♘f3+ 22 ♔g2 ♗b8 23 ♖h1 f5 24 ♘c3 e4 25 ♗e2 ♖e8 26 ♘b5

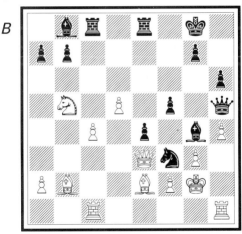

26 ... f4 27 ♕a3 e3 28 d6 ♘e5 29 ♗xe5 f3+ 30 ♔h2 ♖xe5 31 ♗d3 ♗d7 32 fe ♕g4 33 ♗f1 ♖h5 34 ♖c2 ♖xb5 35 ♖d2 ♖e5 36 ♕b2 ♖xe3 37 ♕xb7 ♗c6 38 ♕b2 f2 39 Resigns

In 1910 Vienna enjoyed half of the Lasker–Schlechter world title match. By 1923 Schlechter, Kolisch and Rothschild were gone, the Austro–Hungarian Empire was gone, and so was the golden age of Viennese chess. The desserts and the opera are still flourishing.

Vienna Game

1 e4 e5 2 ♘c3.

The idea is to prepare f4 while preventing ... d5. Tartakower joked that 'the strength of 2 ♘c3 is that it threatens nothing'. Weaver Adams believed it was the surest road to victory, but Black has an easy time obtaining equality.

After 2 ... ♘f6 3 f4 d5 4 fe ♘xe4 5 ♘f3 ♗e7 6 d4 0-0 7 ♗d3 f5 8 ef ♗xf6 9 0-0 ♘c6 there is equality.

Visserman, Eeltje

[*January 24 1922–1978*] Dutch problem composer who edited *Probleemblad* (1957–70) and the *Jaarboek* (1957–64).

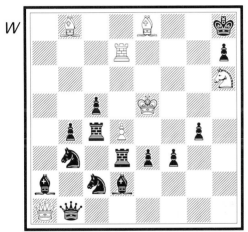

White to move and mate in 3 moves (1965).

1 ♗h5 (threatening 2 ♖d8+ ♔g7 3 ♘f5 mate)
If 1 ... ♖xcd4 2 ♔f5 and 3 ♗e5 mate
1 ... ♖dxd4 2 ♔e6
1 ... ♘bxd4 2 ♔e4
1 ... ♘cxd4 2 ♔d5

Vladimirov, Evgeny

[*January 20 1957–*] USSR GM (1989) who was 3rd at Havana 1986 (X), 1st at Tashkent 1987 (VII) and 1st at Frunze 1988 (IX).

Voellmy, Erwin

[*September 9 1886–January 15 1951*]

Swiss author and mathematics teacher who was Swiss Champion 3 times during 1911–22, who was the Swiss representative at the first FIDE meeting (1924) and who edited the chess column in the *Basler Nachrichten* for 40 years.

Major work: *Schachtaktik* (4 volumes) 1927–30.

Vogt, Lothar Helmut

[*January 17 1951–*] East German GM (1976) who was East German Champion in 1977 and 1979, and played on the East German Olympiad team in 1988. He was 1st at Kecskemet 1977 and equal 3rd at Leipzig 1983 (IX).

Volga Gambit

See Benko Gambit.

Voltaire, Jean Francois Marie Arouet

[*February 21 1694–May 30 1778*] French writer and cleric who enjoyed playing chess.

Vukic, Milan

[*August 19 1942–*] Yugoslav GM (1975) who won the Yugoslav Championship 3 times in the early 1970s and was 1st at Banja Luka 1974, equal 1st at Bajmok 1975, equal 1st at Varna 1975, 1st at Vukovar 1976 and equal 1st at Zemun 1980.

Vukovic, Vladimir

[*August 26 1898–November 18 1975*] Yugoslav author and IM (1951) who edited *Sahovski Glasnik* at a time when there was no organized chess life in Yugoslavia. He played on the Yugoslav Olympiad team in 1927 and 1936. He was a distinguished author whose major works were *The Art of Attack in Chess* (1965) and *The Chess Sacrifice* (1968).

Vyzmanavin, A.

[*January 1 1960–*] USSR GM (1989) who was equal 1st at Protvino 1988 (XII).

Wade, Robert Graham

[*April 10 1921– *]
New Zealand-born English author and IM (1950) who won the British Championship in 1952 and 1970 and played on the English Olympiad team 6 times during 1954–72. He played on the New Zealand Olympiad team in 1970.

Wade is active in British chess and in charge of the large Batsford chess library in London.

Major works: *Botvinnik–Bronstein* (with Winter) (1951), *Petrosian–Botvinnik* (1963), *Soviet Chess* (1967), *The Chess Player* (1968), *World Chess Championship, Botvinnik to Kasparov* (with Whiteley and Keene) (1986).

Wahls, Matthias [*January 26 1968– *] West German GM (1989) who was equal 1st at Dortmund 1989 and equal 4th at Munich 1989 (X).

Waiting Move

A move in an ending that tries to capture the opposition or tries to avoid zugswang by 'losing a move'.

See Triangulation.

Walbrodt, Karl August

[*November 28 1871–October 3 1902*]
Dutch-born German player of GM strength who had great talent but suffered from tuberculosis and lack of ambition. He was equal 4th at Dresden 1892, equal 1st at Kiel 1893 and 2nd at Berlin 1897, but did not do well at the major tournaments of Hastings 1895 and Vienna 1898.

In matches he beat von Bardeleben $+4=4-0$ in 1892, held Mieses $+5=3-5$ in 1894 and lost to Pillsbury $+0=1-2$ in 1893, Tarrasch $+0=1-7$ in 1894 and Janowski $+2=2-4$ in 1897.

It is said that he did not look after himself properly and that riotous living shortened his life.

Walker, George

[*March 13 1803–April 23 1879*]
English music publisher, author and chess organizer who founded clubs, columns and magazines in England. He started the Westminster Chess Club in 1831 and St Georges in 1843. He wrote a chess column in *The Lancet* in 1823–4 and in *Bell's Life* in London 1835–73. He edited *The Philidorian* in 1837–8. He arranged La Bourdonnais' visits to London and gave money to poverty stricken chess players. He wrote *Games at Chess by Philidor and his Contemporaries* (1835), *Chess Studies* (1844) containing 1000 games, including the La Bourdonnais–McDonnell match games, and *Chess and Chess Players* (1850), an entertaining but inaccurate book.

It was a different Walker (William Greenwood) who copied down the La Bourdonnais–McDonnell games in 1834.

Weak Square

An important square that cannot be well defended.

See Hole.

Weenink, Henri Gerard Marie

[*October 17 1892–December 2 1931*]
Dutch problem composer and player who composed over 400 problems. He was 1st at Amsterdam 1930 ahead of Euwe and Spielmann, and played on 4 Dutch Olympiad teams during 1927–31. He was probably the strongest playing problemist of all time. He died of tuberculosis.

Major work: *The Chess Problem* (1926). See: *H. G. M. Weenink*, by Euwe *et al.* (1932).

Weiss, Max

[*July 21 1857–March 14 1927*]
Hungarian-born Austrian player of GM strength who studied mathematics but gave it up for chess. He had a short but excellent chess career coming equal 2nd at Hamburg 1885, equal 2nd at Frankfurt 1887 and equal 1st with Chigorin at New York 1889. He drew the play-off match $+0=4-0$ and established himself as one of the world top 5. He now gave up tournaments and devoted himself to his banking career in Vienna at

Rothschild's bank. He did beat Marco +5 = 1 − 1 in 1895.

Weiss played a careful positional style and he himself was described as a man of kindly disposition, quiet, modest behaviour, and courteous manners.

Westerinen, Heikki Markku Julius

[*April 27 1944–*] Finnish GM (1975) who won the Finnish Championship 4 times during 1965–70 and who is a regular on the Finnish Olympiad team (since 1962). He was 1st at Sant Feliu de Guixols 1973 and Dortmund 1975. He has an original and combinative style of play that brooks no compromise.

Westphalia Defence

See Queen's Gambit.

White, Alain Campbell

[*March 3 1880–April 23 1951*] US problemist and benefactor who financed and produced annual problem books as Christmas presents for his friends, during 1905 and 1936. *Sam Loyd and his Chess Problems* was the 1913 book and Weenink's *The Chess Problem* was the 1926 volume. He collaborated with Frank Altschul on more problem books during the early 1940s.

White, John Griswold

[*1845–1928*] US lawyer and founder of perhaps the largest chess library in the world: the White Collection in the Cleveland Public Library, Ohio. He also left money to purchase new chess books and keep the collection up to date.

Wiener Schachzeitung

[*1898–1916, 1923–38, 1948–9*] Excellent Austrian chess magazine that was probably the best chess magazine in the world during the early 1900s when G. Marco was its editor.

Wijk aan Zee

See Hoogoven.

Wilder, Michael

[*August 17 1962–*] US GM (1988) who was equal 1st at the 1987 London Open, equal 3rd at the 1987 US Championship (XII) and who won the 1988 US Championship (XII).

Wilkes–Barre Variation

See Two Knights Defence.

Will to Win

When top players of approximately equal strength, talent, experience and knowledge, meet, the thing that often decides the winner is some indefinable quality related to strength of character. It is an extra spark of energy, clearly visible in players like Kasparov, Fischer, Steinitz, Botvinnik and Alekhine.

Williams, Elijah

[*1810–September 8 1854*] English player of almost GM strength who was famous for the slowness of his play (chess clocks were not yet in fashion). He was an apothecary in Bristol and in 1844 moved to London, where he could make a living from chess.

Williams played in London 1851 where he beat Löwenthal +2 = 0 − 1, lost to Wyvill +3 = 0 − 4 and beat Staunton +4 = 1 − 3 to gain the 3rd prize. In matches, he lost decisively to Harrwitz in three matches (1846, 1852 and 1853) +2 = 8 − 17 overall. In 1851 he lost +5 = 4 − 7 to Löwenthal and to Staunton +4 = 3 − 6, though he won the stakes with Staunton because Staunton had spotted him 3 games.

An analysis of his 1851 games reveals that Williams had developed a sophisticated style, employing positional devices which were not to become current for a further 60 years. In 1852 he published a collection of games (*Horae Divanianae*) being a selection of 150 games by leading masters, most of

which had been played at Simpson's Divan. He wrote the chess column for *The Field* from 1853 to September 1854.

He died of cholera at Charing Cross Hospital, London.

Winawer, Simon Abramowicz

[*March 5 1838–January 12 1920*] Polish businessman and player of GM strength who, as a virtual unknown, came equal 2nd with Steinitz at Paris 1867. He was equal 1st at Paris 1878, equal 3rd at Berlin 1881, equal 1st at Vienna 1882 and 1st at Nuremberg 1883, and belonged to the world top 10 during this time. He was only 9th at London 1883 and concentrated on his business affairs after that. He did return to the tournament trail during 1892–1901 but not with the same success.

In matches he lost +0 = 0 − 3 to Neumann in 1867 and +2 = 0 − 5 to Janowski in 1896.

One of the main variations in the French Defence is named after him: 1 e4 e6 2 d4 d5 3 ♘c3 ♝b4.

Winawer Variation

See French Defence; Winawer, Simon Abramowicz.

Wing Gambit

See Sicilian Defence.

Winter, William

[*September 11 1898–December 17 1955*] English author and IM (1950) who was British champion in 1935 and 1936, and who played on 4 English Olympiad teams during 1930–5. He had an artistic, revolutionary temperament, a bohemian life-style, an alcohol problem and he spent 6 months in jail (for sedition). Nevertheless, he wrote fine chess books.

Major works: *Modern Master Play* (with F. D. Yates) (1929), *Chess for Match Players* (1936), *Kings of Chess* (1954).

Wisker, John

[*May 30 1846–January 18 1884*] English editor of IM strength who won the British Championship in 1870 and 1872, and edited (with Skipworth) the *Chess Player's Chronicle* during 1872–6. He also wrote a chess column in the *Sporting Times*. In 1877 he moved to Australia, hoping to cure his tuberculosis.

Wolf, Heinrich

[*October 20 1875–1943*] Austrian player of GM strength whose best results were equal 1st at Vienna 1902, 2nd at Vienna 1905 and 3rd at Vienna 1922. He drew +1=6−1 with Bernstein in 1902 and retired from active play in 1923. He was killed during the war by the Nazis.

Woman's Grandmaster Title

WGM titles were introduced in 1977. Since Gaprindashvili and Chiburdanidze have the full GM title and one or more of the Polgar sisters will soon also have a full GM title, and since more and more top women players prefer to play in men's (mixed) events, interest in WGM titles may not grow.

Wood, Baruch Harold

[*July 13 1909–April 4 1989*] English editor and player who founded and edited *Chess* from 1935 to 1988, and conducted chess festivals in Whitby, Eastbourne and Southport. Wood played on the 1939 English Olympiad team, was a FIDE judge and was chess correspondent of the *Daily Telegraph* and *Illustrated London News*.

Wood Pusher

An unthinking chess player whose main accomplishment is pushing the wooden pieces about the board. Not a compliment.

World Championship

This title was first used during the 1886 match between Steinitz and Zukertort. Before that there were many players who were recognized as the best player of their day (*see* Schools of Chess and World Champions). *See also*: Steinitz, Lasker, Capablanca, Alekhine, Euwe, Botvinnik, Smyslov, Tal, Petrosian, Spassky, Fischer, Karpov and Kasparov.

Separate championships have been held for women since 1927. *See*: Menchik (1927–44), Rudenko (1950–3), Bykova (1953–6) and 1958–62, Rubtsova (1956–8), Gaprindashvili 1962–78, Chiburdanidze (1978–).

World Computer Championship

These events began in 1974 and are held every 3 years. In 1974 there were 13 entries and Kaissa (USSR) won. At the 6th Championship in 1989, there were 24 entries. First was Deep Thought (USA), second was BeBe (USA), and equal 3rd were Cray Blitz (USA), Hitech (USA) and Mephisto (Germany).

World Cup

A scheme devised by the GMA where

Final Place	Name	Brussels			Belfort			Reykjavik			Barcelona			Rotterdam			Skelleftea			Total
		Place	Score	Cup points	Place	Score	Cup points	Place	Score	Cup points	Place	Score	Cup points	Place	Score	Cup Points	Place	Score	Cup points	
1	Kasparov, G.	–	–	–	1	11.5	29	1	11	27.5	1–2	11	(26.5)	–	–	–	1–2	9.5	26.5	83
2	Karpov, A.	1	11	27.5	2	10.5	27	–	–	–	–	–	–	2	9.5	(26)	1–2	9.5	26.5	81
3	Salov, V.	2	10	25	–	–	–	–	–	–	3	10	23.5	5–8	8	(18)	6–7	8	20	68.5
4	Ehlvest, J.	–	–	–	3	9	24.5	4–5	9.5	20.5	–	–	–	5–8	8	23	13	6.5	(12)	68
5	Ljubojevic, L.	3–5	9.5	25	10–13	6.5	13.5	–	–	–	1–2	11	28	14–15	6	(10.5)	–	–	–	66.5
6	Nunn, J.	3–5	9.5	22	–	–	–	9–11	8.5	20.5	–	–	–	4	8.5	23	8–9	7.5	(17.5)	65.5
7–8	Belyavsky, A.	3–5	9.5	22	10–13	6.5	(13.5)	2	10.5	25	8–12	7.5	16.5	–	–	–	–	–	–	63.5
7–8	Short, N.	–	–	–	8	7.5	(18)	–	–	–	5–6	9	20.5	9	7.5	20	3–5	8.5	23	63.5
9–10	Hübner, R.	–	–	–	4–7	8	21	–	–	–	5–6	9	22	Withdrew			10–12	7	14.5	57.5
9–10	Timman, J.	10–13	7.5	13	14–16	5.5	(9)	6–8	9	16.5	–	–	–	1	10.5	28	–	–	–	57.5
11	Sokolov, A.	9	8	16	4–7	8	21	12–13	8	(11)	–	–	–	5–8	8	20	–	–	–	57
12	Portisch, L.	6–7	9	19.5	–	–	–	15–16	7	(11)	–	–	–	14–15	6	13.5	3–5	8.5	23	56
13	Tal, M.	10–13	7.5	16	–	–	–	3	10	25	Withdrew			–	–	–	10–12	7	14.5	55.5
14	Sax, G.	16	6	(10)	–	–	–	6–8	9	20.5	–	–	–	11–13	6.5	13.5	6–7	8	20	54
15	Andersson, U.	6–7	9	22	10–13	6.5	(13.5)	9–11	8.5	14	–	–	–	–	–	–	8–9	7.5	17.5	53.5
16	Seirawan, Y.	10–13	7.5	13	–	–	–	–	–	–	14–15	6.5	(10.5)	10	7	16.5	3–5	8.5	23	52.5
17	Ribli, Z.	–	–	–	4–7	8	21	14	7.5	(8.5)	8–12	7.5	16.5	–	–	–	10–12	7	14.5	52
18	Speelman, J.	8	8.5	18	9	7	16.5	9–11	8.5	16.5	13	7	(10.5)	–	–	–	–	–	–	51
19	Vaganian, R.	Withdrew			–	–	–	–	–	–	8–12	7.5	19	3	9	23	16	5	7.5	49.5
20	Yusupov, A.	–	–	–	14–16	5.5	(9)	6–8	9	20.5	8–12	7.5	13.5	11–13	6.5	13.5	–	–	–	47.5
21	Spassky, B.	–	–	–	4–7	8	21	15–16	7	11	8–12	7.5	13.5	Withdrew			–	–	–	45.5
22	Nikolic, P.	10–13	7.5	13	–	–	–	12–13	8	14	7	8	16.5	–	–	–	14–15	6	(10)	43.5
23	Korchnoi, V.	15	6.5	8	–	–	–	17	6.5	(6.5)	4	9.5	25	–	–	–	14–15	6	10	43
24	Hjartarson, J.	–	–	–	14–16	5.5	9	4–5	9.5	20.5	14–15	6.5	10.5	16	4.5	(8)	–	–	–	40
25	Nogueiras, J.	14	7	10	10–13	6.5	13.5	–	–	–	16–17	5.5	(7.5)	11–13	6.5	13.5	–	–	–	37

In the World Cup, only the top three finishes are counted. The lowest score is shown in parentheses. In tournaments where local players participated, only results against World Cup players are counted in calculating World Cup points.

25 of the world's best play in 4 out of 6 super-tournaments and count their 3 best results. The tournaments have 16 or 17 players plus a player from the host country. Each player earns points by adding his actual score to his placing (17 for coming 1st, 16 for coming 2nd and so on, down to 2 for coming 16th) plus $\frac{1}{2}$ a point for those tournaments with only 16 entries.

Qualifying tournaments were held in 1989 to select the elite 25 for the second World Cup in 1991–2. The 1988–89 World Cup had the 25 players shown on the table.

First prizes of $20 000 were offered during 1988/89, and $100 000 went to the winner of the World Cup.

World Junior Championship

The premier FIDE-sponsored tournament for young players—competitors must be under 20 on September 1 of the year of the event. The championships were started in 1951 on a biennial basis but became annual events in 1973. Some of the greatest players of our time have won this title on their way to greater glory.

1951 Ivkov
1953 Panno
1955 Spassky
1957 Lombardy
1959 Bielicki
1961 Parma
1963 Gheorghiu
1965 Kurajica
1967 Kaplan
1969 Karpov
1971 Hug

1973 Belyavsky
1974 Miles
1975 Chekhov
1976 Diesen
1977 Yusupov
1978 Dolmatov
1979 Seirawan
1980 Kasparov
1981 Cvitan
1982 Sokolov
1983 Georgiev
1984 Hansen
1985 Dlugy
1986 Arencibia and Agdestein
1987 Anand
1988 Lautier, Ivanchuk, Serper and Gelfand.
1989 V. Spasov

World Team Championship

Besides sponsoring the Olympiads, which now have more than 100 countries, FIDE has begun a World Team Championship for ten top teams: 5 top finishers in the last Olympiad; 4 teams representing Europe, Asia, Africa and the Americas; plus 1 team from the host country.

It is planned to be held every 4 years. The first event was in 1985 with 6 man teams. The USSR won and Hungary was second. The second championship was held in 1989 with 4 man teams, the USSR again winning.

World Youth Team Championships

This event began in 1954 as a team championship for students under 30 years old and evolved into one for youths under 25. It was held about every 2 years and was dominated by

teams from the USSR. It is no longer played.

Wurzburg, Otto

[*August 10 1875–October 1 1951*] American problem composer who was W. Shinkman's nephew.

White to play and mate in 4 (1937). 1 ♗f5 ♚f3 2 ♚g1 ♚e2 3 ♗c2 ♚f3 (or 3 ... ♚e1 4 ♖e4 mate) 4 ♗d1 mate. Or 1 ♗f5 ♚f1 2 ♗g4 ♚f2 3 ♗d2 ♚g3 (or 3 ... ♚f1 4 ♖f4 mate) 4 ♗e1 mate.

Wyvill, Marmaduke [1814–June 1896]
English Member of Parliament and player of almost GM strength who was 2nd at London 1851 and whom Staunton called 'one of the finest players in England'. Wyvill had a deep understanding of the English Opening and the Sicilian Defence. He was an MP (Richmond, Yorkshire) during most of 1847–68. He never lost his interest in chess and was a member of the General Committee for London 1883.

X

X

The lowercase 'x' is the symbol used to represent the taking of a piece, i.e. 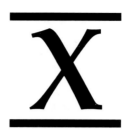xe3, the bishop removes the piece on square e3.

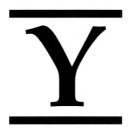

Y

Yanofsky, Daniel Abe

[*March 26 1925–*]
Polish born Canadian lawyer and GM (1964) who was the first GM in the British Commonwealth. He was Canadian Champion 8 times during 1941–65 and played on 11 Canadian Olympiad teams during 1939–80. He was 1st at Ventnor City 1942, 1st at the US Open 1942, equal 1st at Hastings 1953 and he won the British Championship in 1953. He is an expert in the Ruy Lopez and the French Defence, though his great strength is his endgame play.

Yanofsky edited *Canadian Chess Chat* for several years and is active in civic politics.

Major work: *Chess the Hard Way* (1953).

Yates, Frederick Dewhurst

[*January 16 1884–November 10 1932*]
English accountant and player of almost GM strength who won the British Championship 6 times during 1913–31, and who played on 3 English Olympiad teams during 1927–31. His other results were mediocre, but he could beat the strongest opposition on occasion (eg. Alekhine, Euwe, Rubinstein and Vidmar). Perhaps his best result was 5th at San Remo 1930.

Yates was for many years the chess correspondent of the *Manchester Guardian*. He died accidentally, in his rooms, by asphyxiation from a faulty gas connection.

Major works: *Modern Master Play* (with Winter) (1929), *101 of My Best Games* (1934).

Year Books
Useful annual summaries of chess events. Perhaps the earliest English one is *The Chess Player's Annual* for 1856 by Charles Tomlinson. An excellent English series ran from 1907 to 1917, edited by Michell, Stevens, Watts and Foster. Ludwig Bachmann ran excellent *German Schach Jahr Bucher* for 1897 to 1930.

There were USSR yearbooks for 1932–6 by Grekov and Maizelis, and for 1946–61 by Ragozin, Abramov and Bielin.

More recently Kevin O'Connell put out *Batsford Chess Yearbooks* for 1975 and 1976 and a *Batsford FIDE Chess Yearbook* for 1977.

Young, Franklin Knowles

[*1857–December 19 1931*]
US author who wrote six books during 1896–1923, in which he applied battlefield principles to the chessboard. The books were ridiculed by contemporary masters.

Major works: *The Grand Tactics of Chess* (1896), *Chess Strategies* (1900).

Yudovich, Mikhail Mikhailovich

[*June 8 1911–*]
USSR author and IM (1950) who played in 6 USSR Championships during 1931–47. His best result was equal 3rd in the 1931 Championship.

Major work: *The Soviet School of Chess* (with Kotov) (1951 Russian, 1958 English).

Yugoslav Variation
See Sicilian Defence.

Yusupov, Artur Mayakovich

[*February 13 1960–*]
USSR GM (1980) who won the World Junior Championship in 1977 and has been a Candidate twice. In 1986 he beat Timman +4=4−1, but lost +3=7−4 to Sokolov. In 1988 he beat Ehlvest +2=3−0 and in early 1989 he beat Spraggett +2=6−1. In late 1989, however, he was beaten by Karpov (+1=5−2) in the semifinals.

Yusupov has played on 3 USSR Olympiad teams (1984, 1986 and 1988) and in 6 USSR Championships during 1979–88. He scored an overall 54½–45½ in these championships and his best result was 2nd in 1979. In other tournaments he was 1st at Erevan 1982 (XII), equal 4th at Linares 1983 (XIV), 1st at Tunis 1985 (XI), equal 1st at Montpellier 1985 (XIV) and 3rd at Linares 1988

(XV). In a non-candidates match he held Timman $+0=6-0$ in 1986.

Yusupov is a large, handsome, bearded man who is a major force among the Candidates who are one step below the mighty pair of Kasparov and Karpov.

Artur Yusupov analyses with Gary Kasparov.

Z

Zagorovsky, Vladimir Pavlovich
[*June 29 1925– *]
USSR correspondence GM (1965) who won the 4th World Correspondence Championship 1962–5, came 4th in 1965–8, 2nd in 1968–71, equal 3rd in 1972–5 and equal 1st in 1975–9 but lost on tie-break.

Zaitsev, Alexander Nikolayevich
[*June 15 1935–October 31 1971*]
USSR GM (1967) who played in 4 USSR Championships during 1962–9 and was equal 1st in 1968/69, losing the play-off to Polugayevsky. His best international result was equal 1st at Sochi 1967.

In a seemingly straightforward operation to correct a limb, he unfortunately died of a blood clot.

Zaitsev, Igor Arkadyevich
[*May 27 1938– *]
USSR GM (1976) who played in 5 USSR Championships during 1962–70, with no great success. He was equal 1st at Moscow 1968, Moscow Champion in 1969 and equal 1st at Dubna 1979.

Zaitchik, Gennady
[*February 11 1957– *]
USSR GM (1984) who was 1st at Kecskemet 1983 (IX) and 1st at Polanica Zdroj 1984 (VIII).

Zapata Ramirez, Alonso
[*August 22 1958– *]
Colombian GM (1984) who played on the Colombian Olympiad team during the 1980s, and who was 2nd at Havana 1983 (VII), 1st at Bayamo 1984 (VIII), and equal 2nd at Dortmund 1984 (IX).

Zatrikion
See Round Chess under Varieties of Chess.

Zeitnot
The German word for time pressure or time trouble. Often used by English-speakers.

Znosko–Borovsky, Eugene Alexandrovich
[*August 16 1884–December 31 1954*]
Russian music critic, author and player of IM strength who was equal 3rd in the 1908 All-Russian Championship. He went to live in Paris around 1920 and was 3rd at Nice 1930 and 1st at Paris 1930.

His books have not stood the test of time but in their day were quite popular. He fought and was wounded in both the 1905 Russo–Japanese war and the First World War.

Major works: *The Middle Game in Chess* (1922), *How Not to Play Chess* (1931), *Art of Chess Combination* (1936).

Zonals
See Interzonals.

Zugzwang
A disagreeable obligation to move, where any move leads to a serious weakening of the position.

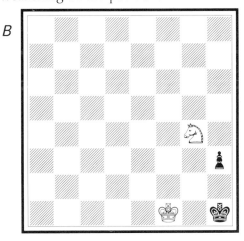

In the diagram, if it is Black's turn to move, he can only play 1 ... h2. Then 2 ♘f2 mate. Black is thus in zugzwang. He would much rather not move for if it were White's turn to move, the game would in fact be a draw.

Zukertort, Johann Hermann
[*September 27 1842–June 20 1888*]
Polish-born English–Jewish player of GM strength who was one of Steinitz's great rivals and who belonged to the world top 2 or 3 during 1872–86. He was 3rd at London 1872, 3rd at Leipzig

1877, equal 1st at Paris 1878, winning the play-off $+2=2-0$ over Winawer, 2nd at Berlin 1881, equal 4th at Vienna 1882 and clear 1st at the powerful London 1883, 3 points ahead of 2nd (Steinitz). This led to the great match of 1886, the first ever to be called a World Championship. This was appropriate because Morphy had died (1884) and Steinitz and Zukertort were unquestionably the two strongest players of the day.

The match was war to the death, because they had a profound feud going on, because they had different styles of play and because Steinitz sought truth at all cost while Zukertort seemed to be constantly making up fairy tales. After 5 games Zukertort led 4–1. After 10 it was all even. After 15 Steinitz led 8–7 and then Zukertort's resistance broke and he finally lost $+5=5-10$. The match actually broke Zukertort's spirit and health and he was soon dead—while playing a game at Simpson's Divan he had a cerebral stroke.

In other matches Zukertort lost $+3=1-8$ to Anderssen, his teacher, in 1868 but won $+5=0-2$ in 1871. He lost $+1=4-7$ to Steinitz in 1872 but beat Rosenthal $+7=11-1$ in 1880 and Blackburne $+7=5-2$ in 1881.

Zukertort claimed that he was of noble descent, had a photographic memory, spoke 9 languages, studied theology, social science, chemistry at Heidelberg, physiology at Berlin, took his MD at Breslau 1865, was a doctor in the Prussian army, decorated for bravery, was a consummate fencer, an excellent marksman, one of the best whist players in the world, a superb domino player and was a music critic during the early 1860s.

What we do know is that he edited (with Anderssen) the *Neue Berliner Schachzeitung*, he contributed excellent notes and analysis to the *Chess Monthly*, that he played 16 simultaneous blindfold games ($+11=4-1$) in London on

December 16, 1876, that he was emotional, highly strung and took opiates.

Zukertort could play like a god and even his enemy, Steinitz, described the following game as: 'One of the most noble combinations conceived over the chess board . . . one of the most brilliant games on record'.

Zukertort–Blackburne

London 1883

1 c4 e6 2 e3 ♘f6 3 ♘f3 b6 4 ♗e2 ♗b7 5 0-0 d5 6 d4 ♗d6 7 ♘c3 0-0 8 b3 ♘bd7 9 ♗b2 ♕e7 10 ♘b5 ♘e4 11 ♘xd6 cd 12 ♘d2 ♘df6 13 f3 ♘xd2 14 ♕xd2 dc 15 ♗xc4 d5 16 ♗d3 ♖fc8 17 ♖ae1 ♖c7 18 e4 ♖ac8 19 e5 ♘e8 20 f4 g6 21 ♖e3 f5 22 ef ♘xf6 23 f5 ♘e4 24 ♗xe4 de 25 fg! ♖c2 26 gh+ ♔h8 27 d5+ e5 28 ♕b4!

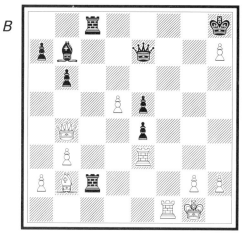

28 ... ♖8c5 (if 28 ... ♕xb4 White mates in six) 29 ♖f8+!! ♔xh7 30 ♕xe4+ ♔g7 31 ♗xe5+ ♔xf8 32 ♗g7+ Resigns

See *Johannes Zukertort: Artist of the Chessboard*, by Jimmy Adams (1989).

Zurich

Major city of Switzerland which held an interesting tournament in 1934 with 8 Swiss players and 8 top GMs. It was won by Alekhine (13) ahead of Euwe (12) Flohr (12) Bogoljubow ($11\frac{1}{2}$) and the 65 year old Lasker (10). But Zurich's major chess show was the 1953 Candidates tournament. Everybody was

there, except of course Botvinnik. Many of the games were hard fought and rich in drama and it was all made especially memorable by Bronstein's magnificent tournament book. Najdorf also published a tournament book (in Spanish–2 volumes) with accurate and penetrating annotations.

Smyslov was in superb form and he had to be to keep ahead of Bronstein, Keres and Reshevsky. Brilliancy prizes were awarded to Kotov for his win over Averbakh, and Euwe for his win over Geller but perhaps the most interesting game was the great draw Keres–Reshevsky from Round 11.

Time Limit: 40 moves in $2\frac{1}{2}$ hours and then 16 moves per hour.

Keres–Reshevsky

1 d4 ♘f6 2 c4 e6 3 ♘c3 ♗b4 4 e3 c5 5 ♗d3 0-0 6 a3 ♗xc3+ 7 bc b6 8 e4 ♗b7 9 ♗g5 h6 10 h4 d6 11 e5 de 12 de ♗e4! 13 ♖h3! ♗xd3 14 ♖xd3 ♕c7 15 ♗xf6 gf 16 ♕g4+ ♔h8 17 ♕f3 ♘d7 18 0-0-0 ♘xe5 19 ♕xf6+ ♔h7 20 ♖d6 ♘xc4 21 ♘f3 ♘xd6 22 ♘g5+ ♔g8 23 ♕xh6 f6 24 ♘xe6 ♕e7

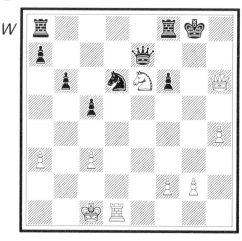

25 ♖xd6 (the winning line according to Bronstein, is 25 ♕g6+ ♔h8 26 ♕h5+ ♔g8 27 ♖d3! ♘e4 28 ♘xf8 ♖xf8 29 ♕g4+ ♘g5 30 ♖e3 ♕g7 31 ♖g3 ♔h8 32 hg) 25 ... ♖f7 26 ♕d2 ♖e8 27 f4 f5 28 ♕d5 ♔h8 29 ♕e5+ ♕f6 30 ♔c2 c4 31 ♕d2 ♔g8 32 ♕d5

♕xh4 33 ♕xc4 ♕f2+ 34 ♔c1 ♕g1+ 35 ♔c2 ♕xg2+ 36 ♔b3 b5 37 ♕d4 ♕f1 38 ♔b4 ♕c4+ 39 ♕xc4 bc 40 ♔xc4 ♖c8+ 41 ♔b5! Drawn

Averbakh–Kotov

1 d4 ♘f6 2 c4 d6 3 ♘f3 ♘bd7 4 ♘c3 e5 5 e4 ♗e7 6 ♗e2 0-0 7 0-0 c6 8 ♕c2 ♖e8 9 ♖d1 ♗f8 10 ♖b1 a5 11 d5 ♘c5 12 ♗e3 ♕c7 13 h3 ♗d7 14 ♖bc1 g6 15 ♘d2 ♖ab8 16 ♘b3 ♘xb3 17 ♕xb3 c5 18 ♔h2 ♔h8 19 ♕c2 ♘g8 20 ♗g4 ♘h6 21 ♗xd7 ♕xd7 22 ♕d2 ♘g8 23 g4 f5 24 f3

B

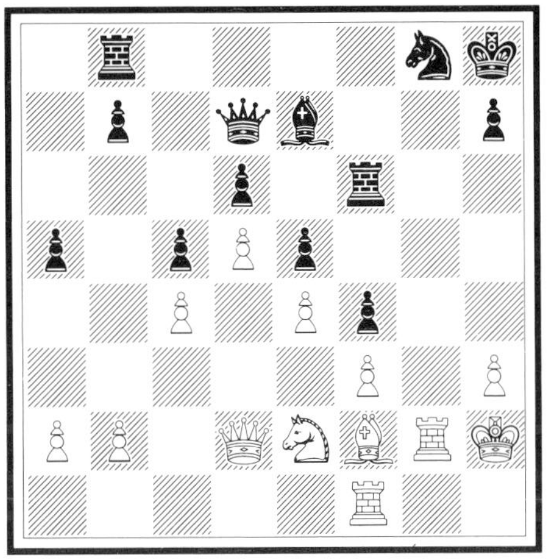

♗e7 25 ♖g1 ♖f8 26 ♖cf1 ♖f7 27 gf gf 28 ♖g2 f4 29 ♗f2 ♖f6 30 ♘e2 30 ... ♕xh3+!! 31 ♔xh3 ♖h6+ 32 ♔g4 ♘f6+ 33 ♔f5 ♘d7 34 ♖g5 ♖f8+ 35 ♔g4 ♘f6+ 36 ♔f5 ♘g8+ 37 ♔g4 ♘f6+ 38 ♔f5 ♘xd5+ 39 ♔g4 ♘f6+ 40 ♔f5 ♘g8+ 41 ♔g4 ♘f6+ 42 ♔f5 ♘g8+ 43 ♔g4 ♗xg5 44 ♔xg5 ♖f7 45 ♗h4 ♖g6+ 46 ♔h5 ♖fg7 47 ♗g5 ♖xg5+ 48 ♔h4 ♘f6 49 ♘g3 ♖xg3 50 ♕xd6 ♖3g6 51 ♕b8+ ♖g8 52 Resigns

Zvorikina, Kira Alekseeva

[*September 29 1919–*]

USSR engineer and woman GM (1977) who was USSR Woman Champion 3 times during 1951–6 and who won the 1959 Woman Candidates tournament to become the challenger. In the world title match 1959/60, Zvorikina lost +2=5−6 to Bykova.

Zwischenzug

A forcing, in-between move, that can surprisingly change an attractive line into a bad one.

W

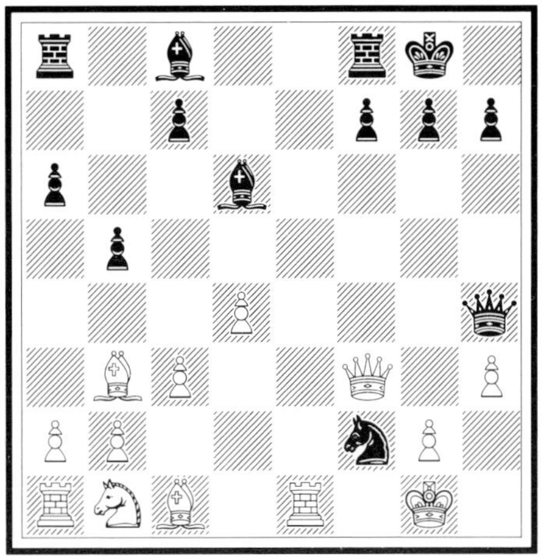

This position arises in the Ruy Lopez, Marshall attack after 15 ... ♘xf2. Now 16 ♕xf2 looks most attractive because after 16 ... ♗g3 17 ♕xf7+ ♖xf7 18 ♖e8 is mate. However this overlooks a fine *zwischenzug*. After 16 ♕xf2? ♗h2+! 17 ♔f1 ♗g3 and now if 18 ♕xf7+ ♖xf7 is check and White has no time for 19 ♖e8 mate. White should therefore play 16 ♗d2.

Zurich 1953 Candidates Tournament

		1	2	3	4	5	6	7	8	9	10	11	12	13	14	15	
1	Smyslov	– –	½ ½	1 1	½ 1	½ ½	1 1	½ ½	½ 0	½ ½	½ ½	½ ½	½ ½	1 ½	1 1	1 ½	18
2	Bronstein	½ ½	– –	1 ½	1 1	½ ½	½ 0	½ ½	½ ½	1 ½	½ ½	½ ½	0 1	1 ½	½ ½	½ ½	16
	Keres	0 0	0 ½	– –	½ ½	½ 1	½ 1	½ ½	½ ½	½ ½	0 ½	1 1	1 ½	½ 1	½ ½	1 1	16
	Reshevsky	½ 0	0 0	½ ½	– –	½ ½	½ ½	½ ½	1 0	½ ½	½ 1	½ 1	1 ½	½ 1	1 1	1 ½	16
5	Petrosian	½ ½	½ ½	½ 0	½ ½	– –	½ ½	0 ½	½ ½	0 0	½ ½	½ ½	1 1	½ 1	1 ½	1 1	15
6	Geller	0 0	½ 1	½ 0	½ ½	½ ½	– –	1 1	½ 0	0 1	½ ½	0 1	1 ½	½ 1	0 1	½ ½	14½
	Najdorf	½ ½	½ ½	½ ½	½ ½	1 ½	0 0	– –	1 ½	1 ½	½ 0	½ ½	½ ½	½ ½	0 ½	1 1	14½
8	Kotov	½ 1	½ ½	½ ½	0 1	½ ½	½ 1	0 ½	– –	1 0	1 ½	0 0	1 0	1 ½	0 ½	0 1	14
	Taimanov	½ ½	0 ½	½ ½	½ ½	1 1	1 0	0 ½	0 1	– –	1 0	½ ½	½ ½	½ 0	0 ½	1 1	14
10	Averbakh	½ ½	½ ½	1 ½	½ 0	½ ½	½ ½	½ 1	0 ½	0 1	– –	½ ½	½ ½	0 ½	1 1	0 0	13½
	Boleslavsky	½ ½	½ ½	0 0	½ 0	½ ½	1 0	½ ½	1 1	½ ½	½ ½	– –	½ 0	½ ½	½ 1	½ ½	13½
12	Szabo	½ ½	1 0	0 ½	0 ½	0 0	0 ½	½ ½	0 1	½ ½	½ ½	½ 1	– –	1 ½	½ ½	1 ½	13
13	Gligoric	0 ½	0 ½	½ 0	½ 0	½ 0	½ 0	½ ½	0 ½	½ 1	1 ½	½ ½	0 ½	– –	½ 1	1 1	12½
14	Euwe	0 0	½ ½	½ ½	0 0	0 ½	1 0	1 ½	1 ½	1 ½	0 0	½ 0	½ ½	½ 0	– –	1 ½	11½
15	Ståhlberg	0 ½	½ ½	0 0	0 ½	0 0	½ ½	0 0	1 0	0 0	1 1	½ ½	0 ½	0 0	0 ½	– –	8

Index

Numerals in *italics* indicate a main entry.
Tables are indicated (T).

244